P9-BXZ-234

Ambassador's
Journal

A Personal Account of the Kennedy Years

BOOKS BY
JOHN KENNETH GALBRAITH

American Capitalism: The Concept
of Countervailing Power
A Theory of Price Control
Economics and the Art of Controversy
The Great Crash, 1929
The Affluent Society
The Liberal Hour
Economic Development
The Scotch
The New Industrial State
The Triumph
Indian Painting: The Scene, Themes and Legends
(*with Mohinder Singh Randhawa*)
Ambassador's Journal: A Personal Account
of the Kennedy Years

Ambassador's Journal

A Personal Account of the Kennedy Years

John Kenneth Galbraith

Illustrated with photographs
and maps drawn by Samuel H. Bryant

HOUGHTON MIFFLIN COMPANY BOSTON

1969

First Printing R

Copyright © 1969 by John Kenneth Galbraith
All rights reserved. No part of this work may be repro- ·
duced or transmitted in any form by any means, electronic
or mechanical, including photocopying and recording, or by
any information storage or retrieval system, without
permission in writing from the publisher.

Selections from this book have appeared in the October,
1969, issue of *American Heritage*.

Library of Congress Catalog Card Number: 69-15012
Printed in the United States of America

*In memory of the President and Prime Minister
who graced these years — and my life.*

Acknowledgments

WHATEVER the response to these adventures, no one will think them deficient in guidance to persons, events, places, general geography, even history. And most will have some sense of the prodigious job of checking that was involved. (Nothing is more remarkable than one's ability to misspell names or misplace initials of people he knows well and meets often.) Many of the footnotes and all of the checking was accomplished — diligently, doggedly, intelligently, good-humoredly and with uncompromising firmness when I suggested that something be slighted — by Hazel Denton. Were she not my friend there might have been no book. Certainly there would have been none now.

In India, as I tell elsewhere, Helen Eisenman transcribed my original notes in moments that rightfully, I am sure, were her own. She is still in the State Department and any well-motivated ambassador would do well to seek her out. Later in Cambridge and at various times, Mrs. Marjorie Javan, Mrs. Joanne Casper, Mrs. Grace Johnson and Mrs. Mary Anne Reynolds took these notes and typed them into a semblance of a book. There is no feature of the American economy so sound as that which causes attractive young women to work, far below their talent, for deserving older men, in order to put their husbands through graduate school.

Over the years I have established a wonderful reputation for hard work, high productivity or possibly both. It is a fraud. I merely have Andrea Williams, as a devoted friend and collaborator, to do everything I do not wish to do myself. Never was there so much as in the scheduling, producing and proofing of this book and otherwise guiding it through the press. I have lived while Andrea has labored. Greater love hath no woman.

Catherine Galbraith served as always as my general conscience and censor and eliminated many of the more flagrant breaches of fact and taste, and all that remain are mine. One error so remedied was an impossible love affair of Rama; another was the death of a man still vital; another was my description of a Maharajah's palace as flea-bitten. The latter she persuaded me would be resented; and anyhow the fleas, so far as one could judge, had been adequately occupied with people. My wife's eye for Indian life and culture is better than mine. It has greatly improved this book, as it greatly did our years in India. It will be evident a year or so hence in a small volume on this endlessly fascinating country which she is now completing.

J.K.G.

Contents

Illustrations

Introduction

IN THE AUTUMN of 1960, after John F. Kennedy had called to tell me that I was to be his Ambassador to India, I decided it would be an interesting time and that I would keep a full account of what happened. It was a taxing decision. At the end of a long day, the temptation to say to hell with it and go to bed can be overwhelming. Even worse is the temptation to take care of one's high resolve with a few perfunctory words. The more important the events, the wearier you are and the better the seeming excuse for dismissing it all.

Nevertheless, I persisted and this is the result. Sometimes I wrote in the evening, more often when I got up next morning. If I had a journey in prospect, I saved up and wrote on the plane. And I also wrote more faithfully of travels than of sedentary days at the Embassy so the journal gives an exaggerated impression of movement. However, I did travel a lot. The date and place of the entry refer, in each instance, to the date and place of writing and not necessarily of the events described.

When the border conflict broke out between China and India in the autumn of 1962 (simultaneously with the Cuban missile crisis), my responsibilities increased at least twentyfold. Communication with Washington also came more or less to an end as it does in emergencies and I discovered that there are many worse things than being the man on the spot. I had then to resort to dictation which for me, as I suspect for others, is a vague and wordy substitute for writing things down. These dictated notes, like the previous hand-written ones, were transcribed and put away. I never read them until after my return from India.

A writer who does any systematic writing is pretty certain to have some use in mind. According to legend, Churchill sent a copy of his wartime minutes to the printer for future use in his memoirs at the same time as he dispatched the original to a cabinet colleague or general. Increasingly, it became evident that the Kennedy years were to be a gay and rewarding interlude in our history. Increasingly, and sadly, it became evident to anyone in India at the time that the Nehru era was drawing to a close. I soon came to see these notes as a possibly interesting and useful document on both. In other respects, I had picked a good time to go to India — the Goa crisis, the Chinese conflict, the problem of Kashmir and the most determined attack so far on India's backwardness all favored me. But I thought it would be most instructive of all to tell in a day-to-day fashion just what an ambassador does and does not do — how he runs his embassy, reaches or postpones decisions, persuades the government to which he is accredited, wishes he might persuade Washington, sees visiting potentates, suffers boredom and has an occasional sense of achievement which runs as wine in his bloodstream.

Soon, too soon, it all was history. At noon in Dallas on November 22, 1963, the Kennedy Administration came to an end. Six months later, the other great figure in these pages, Jawaharlal Nehru, was also dead. Perhaps I would have been tempted within the next year or so to publish this account had I not been deeply involved in another book. Those who argue against too early exposure of the historical record are usually associated with something that is not wholly to their credit. But in any case I decided for postponement.

Before I left Washington for India in 1961, President Kennedy asked me to write him occasionally and tell him what an ambassador does. Quite possibly I took this request more seriously than he intended; in any case, at frequent though irregular intervals, I told him of what I was doing in India and of my anxieties and instinct for reform on Vietnam, Laos, Berlin, and also domestic tax reduction which I opposed. I tried to avoid tedium in these letters; there is a certain competition for the President's eye.

In this I evidently succeeded. He liked the letters and shortly before his death suggested to Edward K. Thompson, then Managing Editor of *Life*, that they be published. When, after his death, I was asked by *Life*, I concluded that this would indeed be premature and that the President, on reflection, would have agreed. This is no longer so, and I have put them in the journal at the appropriate places. I have not, of course, included the President's responses which were few and sparse.

These letters are here in their original form. Only a few paragraphs, amiable enough but candid about the personalities, purposes and ambitions of particular Indian statesmen, including Mr. Krishna Menon, have been deleted. Also, reluctantly, I deleted a paragraph from one of the letters, responding I believe to a request from the President, listing with reasons the members of the State Department who, in the interests of a more effective foreign policy, should forthwith be fired. One or two other untasteful references were slightly edited.

The journal has undergone more editing. I have not deleted many secret matters for these I did not put in. And for an ambassador they are much less numerous and much less exciting and wicked than is commonly imagined.

My principal problem was the derelictions of individuals, and on this I followed a double standard: anything I wrote that might reflect adversely on an American (including, on rare occasions, myself) I left. Anything embarrassing to an Indian I was more disposed to delete.

The distinction is a sound one. A certain number of President Kennedy's appointees, resembling in this respect the appointees of other Presidents since Washington, devoted their principal effort to avoiding any thought or action that might interfere with their

enjoyment of high office. Criticism from conservatives was especially to be avoided, more often than not by adopting their policy.
To a considerable extent, they succeeded in their effort; their life
was tranquil, their enjoyment undiluted. But for posterity to grant
these men a similar exemption from adversity would be too kind.
The price of an easy time in the present must, surely, be a low score
in the history books. Anything else is unfair to those who are willing to risk attack in order to get things done.

But, on the other side, diplomats are paid to get along with the
people of the country to whom they are accredited, and they do not
have the right to revert to normal after they leave. So I have been
cautious in criticizing Indian officials and politicians. This involved
few changes. On rereading the journal, I discovered that my
instinct was to be much less severe on Indian than on American
officialdom. My Indian friends will find, here and there, a sentence
or word that will strike them as pejorative or, at a minimum, unduly candid. I beg of them not to be angry. These are the comments of a friend. They are also the price of saying anything
interesting. I think, when I was in India, I was welcomed because
I was not blandly flattering and hence hopelessly dull.

I would also ask Indian scholars to be forgiving of my decisions
on how to render Indian words — Benares, Banaras, Baranasi or
Varanasi — into English. As they know, there is no absolute standard and hence no way of satisfying all preferences.

I have made many cosmetic changes in the original — tightening
sentences, rectifying number and tense, eliminating redundant
words, improving syntax. In the dictated sections, these faults were
especially numerous. No historical merit attaches to bad English.
Were an addition really important, I put it in the footnotes. On
matters of major historical interest, the Vietnam record for example,
I have avoided changes and certainly any which reflect either hind-
sight or a desire to improve on my own performance. Elsewhere a
certain number of utterly uninteresting or repetitious passages have
been excised. Perhaps the reader will think there should have been

more. In the interest of a full record of how things looked at the time, I leaned to letting things stay. But everyone has a ready recourse, one indeed that I urge. He can read selectively, and he can always skip.

Now I must give the reader some information on our personal ménage and economy and some other details which will help in understanding the pages that follow.

Our family at the time of our departure for India numbered six. In addition to my wife, Catherine Atwater, usually called Kitty, we had our three sons, Alan, twenty, at Harvard, Peter, ten, and James, nine, who were in school in Cambridge and who continued at the American International School in New Delhi, and Emily G. Wilson who for twenty years, with authority backed by competence and love, had managed our children, household, cooking and any number of other matters associated with our existence. In New Delhi when we arrived, the Ambassador's house on Ratendone Road, a modest-size bungalow from the days of the British Raj, was much too small to hold all this family. Accordingly, Emily and the two younger boys lived in half of another house down the street. Alan, after an initial summer in India, returned to Harvard. A year and a half later we were all able to house ourselves in the new Residence designed by Edward Durell Stone immediately adjacent to the Chancery, also and even more famously of his design.

Our houses required a remarkably ample staff for their operation — bearer, which in India roughly is a butler, assistant bearers, cook and assistant cooks, sweepers, gardeners, guards, drivers, laundrymen and more. Some were on the payroll of the Embassy, some were charged to the Ambassador, and the basis for this financially interesting distinction was never clear. Except where food was involved, all were tolerably efficient. The Indian-style food which was usually, although not exclusively, served at receptions was not bad. Food prepared in European style was uniquely inedible. Our principal predecessors in office had been, in order, Chester Bowles, John Sherman Cooper and Ellsworth Bunker. Between these civilized men and their even more remarkable wives and the household staff, there had been a deep bond of respect and affection. Few inheritances could have been more important in easing our life in our new and exotic land and occupation.

New Delhi has, roughly speaking, three seasons. From October to March, the days are sunny and warm, the nights cool. Around Christmastime, a fire is welcome and even necessary. From April through June, it is hot beyond belief — a dry searing heat that led Kipling to speak of a pile of sand under a burning glass. From June to September, it rains — not steadily but recurrently and often for two or three days at a time. While it is raining, it is moderately cool; when the rain stops, it is hot and humid. This disquisition is necessary for, although American and Indian officials live and work in air conditioning, it is impossible to write about India without mentioning the weather. In this journal, it compels comment as it did in Scott's account of his journey to the South Pole and for the same reason.

An embassy is rather like a state government — it is organized to function with good leadership, in the absence of leadership and in spite of it. The New Delhi Mission staff was very good. It had been selected with discrimination by my predecessors, and India is not the type of place where the time-serving, socially ambitious or John O'Hara type of officer aims to be. To go there he must have something in mind. The Ambassador in New Delhi operates from a large, light, pleasant office in the new Stone Chancery. Most business was done not at the desk but around a low coffee table on which there was always a bowl of flowers selected and arranged with great chromatic and geometric precision. There is no view from the windows because Edward Stone's screen surrounds the building. Could one look out, it would be to the Chinese Embassy on one side, the British across and the Soviet Embassy on the other side. Office work is conducted with only the rarest recourse to the telephone. Washington does not call because when it is noon in Washington it is midnight in New Delhi, give or take an hour or so, and the line is not secure. And the local system, though good, is not extensive. Also for the reason that few people in Washington ring up the President, so in New Delhi there is a certain reluctance in ringing up the American Ambassador. Rank or anyhow formal grandeur has its advantages.

The most important man in an Embassy, not excluding the Ambassador, is often the Deputy Chief of Mission, as these pages suggest. He deputizes for the Ambassador, provides professional continuity, directs subordinate officers and, with suitable tact, tells his superior what he should do. Benson E. L. (Lane) Timmons, my D.C.M. during nearly all of my tour, had an office interconnecting with mine through a lavatory. The Political Counselor of the Embassy supervises and keeps track of all relations with the government to which the Ambassador is accredited. In New Delhi, an Economic Minister combined general supervision of economic questions with administration of the AID program. Other counselors and attachés and their staffs — commercial, consular, press, agricultural, scientific and military — deal with their special subjects and, on occasion, have trouble keeping busy. In New Delhi, the Air and Naval Attachés, out of the infinitely greater wealth of the Pentagon, possessed planes and provided transportation for the Ambassador. Two secretaries of extraordinary competence, Aloha Baguley and Helen Eisenman, presided over the Ambassador's outer office, and I think of them with affection. One of Helen Eisenman's extracurricular assignments was to type this journal. She always said she enjoyed it and even if she didn't, it was good of her to say so. A young Foreign Service Officer is always assigned to the Ambassador as his personal assistant on everything from planning travel to purchasing newspapers. It is a job that must cause a great many young men to think again about their choice of career. The United States Marine Corps, as most must know, provides a guard detachment for our Missions abroad. Its members also with ferocious enthusiasm inspect offices to make sure that no one has left any classified papers on top of his desk.

In Washington, Indian matters were handled or otherwise by a hierarchy of officials. At the top, below the Secretary, was the Chief of the Bureau of Middle East and South Asian Affairs, in my time the unstalwart Talbot whose frightened retreat from liberalism to the Cold War is adequately chronicled in the pages that follow. An officer embracing the South Asian countries of India, Pakistan, Ceylon and Nepal was next below, and one or two further rungs down was a harried man who was called the India Desk Officer. With exceptions, these lesser officers were hard-working, informed and capable. That their resulting performance left something to be desired they would, with suitable discretion, concede. The State Department, to a remarkable degree, is the sum of less than its parts.

I have identified nearly everyone whose name appears in this journal. Americans need to be reminded as to who even quite famous Indians are and what they do. I've assumed the converse even as regards Robert McNamara.

Bachelors can be ambassadors. Perhaps once it was an advantage, given the diverse forms of persuasion that were held to be used. In New Delhi, it would have been inconceivable. The household, entertainment, a wide range of protocol activities, concern for the problems of the American community, association with wives and families of my Indian and diplomatic associates, cultivation of the arts and representation of the Ambassador at a succession of functions during my absence were all accomplished by my wife. She even found time to learn Hindi to the point of making a quite acceptable speech in the language. There is little about this in the present diary for, in truth, I knew little about it — I was rather astonished at the scope of her activities when she recounted them in an article in *The Atlantic Monthly* of May 1963.[1] It would be wrong, therefore, for anyone to assume that, as regards all an Ambassador and his family do, this journal is complete.

JOHN KENNETH GALBRAITH
Newfane, Vermont
Summer 1968

[1] See Appendix I, page 603.

Ambassador's
Journal

A Personal Account of the Kennedy Years

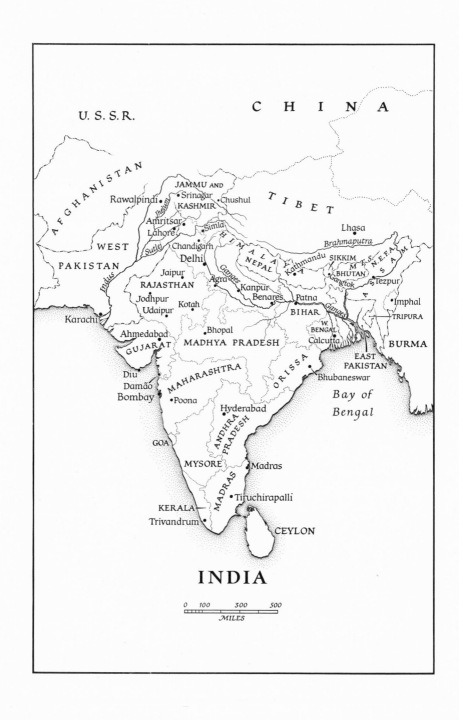

U. S. S. R.

C H I N A

AFGHANISTAN

JAMMU AND
•Srinagar
KASHMIR   •Chushul

T I B E T

Rawalpindi•
Amritsar•
Lahore•   •Simla
WEST   Chandigarh•
PAKISTAN   Delhi•

Lhasa•

Brahmaputra

Jaipur•
RAJASTHAN
Jodhpur•   Kotah•
Udaipur•

HIMALAYA
NEPAL   Kathmandu•   SIKKIM
Agra•   •Kanpur   MTS.   NEFA
Ganges   Benares•   Patna•   BHUTAN   ASSAM
Gangtok•   •Tezpur
BIHAR   Ganges

Karachi•

Ahmedabad•
GUJARAT
•Bhopal
MADHYA PRADESH

•Imphal
TRIPURA

W.
BENGAL
Calcutta•

Diu•
Damão•
Bombay•   •Poona
MAHARASHTRA

Hyderabad•

ORISSA

EAST
PAKISTAN

BURMA

•Bhubaneswar

Bay of
Bengal

GOA•

ANDHRA
PRADESH

MYSORE   •Madras
MADRAS
•Tiruchirapalli

KERALA
Trivandrum•

CEYLON

INDIA

0   100   300   500
MILES

I

Before the Curtain

December 7, 1960 — Cambridge

For the last several days, there have been agreeable rumors that I am to be the Ambassador to India. And slightly more than rumors. J.F.K. asked Arthur Schlesinger[1] in strict confidence how I would like it. These queries do not forever remain a secret though I did not learn about it for an hour or two. This post has been my prime aspiration, although in the last weeks I have been slightly diverted by the newspaper speculation of going to the Senate.

This morning J.F.K. called and in characteristic rapid-fire fashion, asked me my views on about a dozen candidates for various posts.[2] The most interesting were Bundy[3] for State and Mc-Namara[4] for Treasury. Then he told me he wanted me to go to India. I expressed my pleasure and then said I wanted to put a plain question to him: "Would that be more useful than the Senate with the prospect of bringing some decency back to Massachusetts

[1] Arthur M. Schlesinger, Jr. Close personal friend; Special Assistant to President Kennedy.

[2] Prior to the beginning of the diary, I had served with Arthur Schlesinger, Jr., and Sargent Shriver on a highly informal committee on personnel. I had suggested McNamara for Treasury as an alternative to Douglas Dillon whom we had opposed, mistakenly, as an obdurate Republican. The original suggestion came (to me at least) from W. H. (Ping) Ferry of the Center for Democratic Institutions in Santa Barbara, California. I have always supposed that McNamara declined the Treasury — in modern times, a much less important post — and while doing so, sufficiently impressed the President-elect to be offered Defense.

[3] McGeorge Bundy. He became Special Assistant to the President for National Security Affairs, and later head of the Ford Foundation.

[4] Robert S. McNamara. Eventually Secretary of Defense and later head of the International Bank for Reconstruction and Development.

Democratic politics?" He said yes, "by a factor of five to one." Freshman Senators are not very useful; did I really want to spend my time with Massachusetts politicians whom he described amiably as "that gang of thieves." I told him I would not raise the matter again.

I told Emily[5] who was much pleased and later my wife who is pleased but slightly appalled at the prospect. I wonder if I can take Mrs. Williams,[6] without whom I would be harassed and desolate. The appointment of the Secretary of State has become of more than normal interest to me.

December 8 — Cambridge

Walter Lippmann called to congratulate me in a highly unofficial manner. He and J.F.K. had a long talk a day or so ago during which Kennedy told him that I was going to India. Walter had expressed approval.

I imagine that not everyone in the State Department will be so happy. I will be thought too outspoken. A good diplomat, I assume, is an articulate man who articulates only what he is told. There will be a little fuss in the Senate, I imagine. But Goldwater[7] will lead the opposition which should be enough to ensure a favorable vote.

December 10 — Poughkeepsie, New York

Elizabeth Farmer[8] called last night to ask about Jesse Tapp[9] for Treasury. I said it would be a disaster (much too conservative) and she later called back to say that this genial estimate had been

---

[5] Emily G. Wilson. She has been the Galbraith housekeeper since 1940.

[6] Andrea D. Williams. Then and still my secretary, assistant and beloved friend. Regrettably, she did not accompany me to India but returned to Harvard with me in the summer of 1963.

[7] At that time, Senator from Arizona. He paid no attention.

[8] Personal friend and for a number of years an assistant to Walter Lippmann. Her husband, Thomas Farmer, a distinguished lawyer, was acting as a talent scout for Kennedy. He later became Counsel for the Agency for International Development, AID.

[9] Then Chairman of the Board of the Bank of America. He held various agricultural posts under Roosevelt.

accepted. In the process, she told me that Chalmers Roberts[10] had a story about my going to India. So briefly has the *Boston Globe*. It is a trifle difficult to know what one should say to people in these circumstances. It is the privilege of the President-elect to announce appointments. But to say that there is nothing to it or that you don't know anything about it is to be less than truthful.

December 13 — Cambridge

Yesterday Dean Rusk was made Secretary of State with Chester Bowles as Undersecretary. I know Rusk only slightly; Bowles, of course, is an old friend.[11] The papers this morning carry the news that I am to go to India, and the *New York Post* called for confirmation about seven this morning. I told them I thought any word should come from the President-elect.

Adlai Stevenson has accepted the United Nations post, although rather reluctantly. He wanted the Department but failed in urging his case. He has the same difficulty in advancing his personal aims that I do but has an even more difficult combination of diffidence and vanity. In politics you don't need to be intelligent, but you must be able to argue for what you want with the proper unction and force.

December 14 — Cambridge

The *New York Times* and *Boston Herald* have minor headlines on my prospective appointment. They are under a Washington dateline and seem to come from J.F.K. No one can complain that Kennedy's staffing is conducted with unnecessary secrecy. The motto is public positions publicly arrived at.

Last night at a Department (of Economics) dinner there was vast curiosity about my prospect. But very restrained. It was a little like your daughter's illegitimate child — much interest but a

[10] Chief of the National News Bureau of the *Washington Post*.
[11] From price control days in World War II. He was Ambassador to India from 1951 to 1953, became Undersecretary of State in 1961 and then returned to India in 1963 to take my place.

marked reluctance to come out and ask about it. I began to have doubts and slept badly as the result of wondering whether I should abandon — or postpone — my writing at this stage. A talk with James Perkins[12] this morning somewhat reassured me. He thinks I can use an embassy post for a new kind of reporting on Asia and the Far East. He asked why not make the post J.F.K.'s quiet source of literate intelligence on the region. Why not?

December 16 — Cambridge

Yesterday Mrs. Lincoln[13] called to suggest a trip to Palm Beach on Friday, December 23. I agreed with indecent haste and then faced the problem of getting reservations at the very peak of the Christmas rush to Florida. With Mrs. Williams, I decided that, in the emergency, name-dropping was in order. It worked. In a democracy, one should scrupulously avoid using influence except when it is needed. I have noticed that people who are called upon rather like it. The head of the Pullman Company once got me a bedroom to Los Angeles at the end of the war. (I was then at *Fortune*.) When I thanked him, he said with some feeling: "Doctor, I hope I never live to see the day when special privilege is abolished from our democracy."

Last night, the weather being bad, I went to New York to be on hand for a meeting at Prudential[14] in Newark today. A friend came over to the Dorset and we chatted for an hour or so. When she left, I tossed off my shirt and trousers to have a shower — I was very tired — and noticed that she had left behind some filigree earrings I had brought her from Pakistan early last year and which I had only now remembered to bring to New York. There followed an accident which should not happen to an aspiring diplomat.

---

12 Then Vice-President of the Carnegie Corporation which had been sponsoring the book on which I had been engaged for some two years and which became *The New Industrial State*. It was finally published in 1967.
13 Evelyn Lincoln, J.F.K.'s personal secretary. See her book, *My Twelve Years with John F. Kennedy* (New York: D. McKay & Co., 1965).
14 Of which I was briefly an adviser.

I opened the door to see if the excessively slow elevator had departed. My door was recessed behind a corner of the wall, and I stepped out to peer around that. The door slammed shut behind me and locked. I was inelegantly and utterly naked in the hall of a sizable hotel. Only my friend was in sight; the elevator was still to come. I signaled and got her coat; she went down to the lobby. Then modestly clad in the coat, and trying to look unconcerned, I rang for the elevator and asked for the porter to come with a passkey. He came and let me in. I quickly dressed and sauntered down to the lobby with the coat. She put it on, and we went for a stroll around the block. By then, it seemed amusing. Before, it was terrifying. To maintain one's dignity and aplomb without clothes in an empty hall, lined with doors that could open at any moment, is a test which all putative ambassadors should be required to pass.

December 17 — Cambridge

A letter dated December 10 from J.F.K. arrived and proposed that I come to Florida. It had taken eight days from Washington to Cambridge. An earlier letter also took eight days and led me to suggest to J.F.K. that the Post Office was a key spot in his administration. (He later cited this time lag in appointing Ed Day the new Postmaster General.)

December 24 — Cambridge

Yesterday I went to Palm Beach. I went to New York the night before, on to Florida on the ten o'clock jet and arrived (slightly late) about one o'clock. I taxied over to the Kennedy house and on the way heard a call on the cab radio for a cab to go to that address to pick up "a Mr. Heller." That told me Walter Heller's appointment to the Council of Economic Advisers must have gone through. I am much pleased for, with others, I have urged him for the post.

The house, a long, white, vaguely Spanish and not unhandsome structure designed by Mizner, fronts directly on the ocean. One enters from the street. After being duly checked by the Secret Service, I found the President-elect with Mr. Joseph P. Kennedy and J.B.K. in the living room. We had a drink together and then Jackie disappeared. She was not feeling well but was much pleased by some books that I had brought her — a couple of volumes of about-to-be-published verse from Houghton Mifflin. I had also collected some history volumes and novels for J.F.K. He was attracted by a volume by J. H. Plumb on Walpole, but I don't suppose he will have time to do much aimless reading in the near future.[15] We had lunch on the terrace, talked, and then I had a nap while the President-elect and his father played golf. Then I went for a walk on the ocean side and talked with a Secret Service man who was studying marine biology. He was examining beach crabs with the field glasses he had with him to spot approaching assassins. Then I met Caroline and the baby and talked further with J.F.K. We were joined by Bob and Ethel for a family dinner. Thereafter I talked again with the President-elect and at midnight was driven back to the airport. I was somewhat tired and more so when I got to Boston at breakfast time.

We refought the election — J.F.K. is not persuaded that being a Catholic was an advantage. Nixon was less alert, less effective than he had expected. And he was also less willing to take risks; thus he sat out the jailing of Martin Luther King while J.F.K. called Mrs. King to express sympathy, and Bob called the judge. Incidentally, the brothers acted individually; neither knew what the other was doing. J.F.K.: "The finest strategies are usually the result of accidents." Bob shares my view that Henry Cabot Lodge's[16] faux pas — the offer of a cabinet position to a Negro in Harlem, its withdrawal the next day in Virginia — was one of the classic errors of politics. If one is wrong on some vital questions

---

[15] J.B.K., writing to thank me for the poetry a few days later, said that her husband had finished it the same night.

[16] Nixon's Vice-Presidential running mate.

of foreign policy, the opposition must still explain why it is an error. But no citizen is so benighted that he could not see that this was stupid. And it was equally damaging in both the North and the South which takes skill. Bob Kennedy thought that Nixon was saved from serious trouble over his brother's involvement with Howard Hughes — a big loan on a not very valuable corner covered by a service station — only because he had a generally sympathetic and hence not very penetrating press. I received credit for raising the alarm signals over New Jersey a few days before the election.[17] J.F.K. thought his only serious mistake was in not spending more time in California and less in New York when it became clear that New York was certain. I urged my final view — that he was the only Democrat who could have won and Nixon the only Republican who could have lost.

Our talks during the day ranged over a great number of matters. The problem of filling the subordinate positions in the Federal Executive is appalling. Several hundred important and fairly influential jobs must be filled within the next few weeks if the Government is to function effectively. J.F.K. thinks there must be some better way. "I must make the appointments now; a year hence I will know who I really want to appoint."

He obviously devoted a great amount of time to thought and discussion of cabinetmaking, and this is reflected in his choices. Bill Fulbright,[18] incidentally, was his primary choice for State although he is well pleased by Rusk.[19] Bob talked him out of appointing Fulbright — the objection of Negroes and the use that the Russians might make of the appointment being, in his view, decisive. One of the leading candidates for Agriculture — Fred Heinkel of Missouri — destroyed himself by his interview. He slumped down in a chair, and when J.F.K. asked him what he would do

[17] As the result of campaigning in northern New Jersey, I concluded that the state, contrary to assumption, was far from safe. Kennedy thereupon scheduled a further visit.
[18] Then, as at this writing, Chairman of the Senate Foreign Relations Committee.
[19] See page 3.

about overproduction, he replied, "That is a terrible problem. I suppose we shall just have to give it away abroad." I had predicted this general reaction to Heinkel, who is a very good farm leader, to Sargent Shriver.[20] Orville Freeman[21] is much more Kennedy's type. He asked especially that I work with Freeman during the next few weeks.

On the issue of economic recession and a tax cut, I urged that needed public expenditures be pressed first as an anti-recession measure. Thereafter, if unemployment was still high, taxes could be reduced. I believe J.F.K. agrees. He faces trouble with William McChesney Martin, Jr., Chairman of the Federal Reserve, and dislikes the prospect of a fight with him — which he thinks may be inevitable. Martin has been in office for a long time and, in his chosen sphere, obviously regards himself as superior to the President. It is the old notion that money gives a man position above politics and that banking, like the judiciary, is a separate power. I doubt, however, that in a showdown the President would be without resources. I would rather welcome this row were I in the White House.

In the last eight years, the Eisenhower Administration has swept problems under the rug. Now they must have attention. But, one senses, our liberal friends have not got down to hard cases — to what should be done about wage-price stabilization, foreign aid, disarmament, Far Eastern policy and a dozen other matters. The various New Frontier papers being prepared for the Administration are vague and unspecific. Not much is in tight, programmatic form that can be submitted to Congress. J.F.K. says at the moment his only major new idea is the Peace Corps. "If Scotty Reston[22] finds out that this is all there is on the New Frontier, he will write

[20] Brother-in-law of the President, the first Director of the Peace Corps and then, concurrently, Director of the Office of Economic Opportunity. At the time of writing, he is Ambassador to France.

[21] Then Secretary-designate of Agriculture, after being defeated by a narrow margin for reelection as Governor of Minnesota.

[22] James Reston, then chief Washington correspondent for the *New York Times*.

quite a story." Some hard work must obviously be done in these next few weeks.

On India, he asked me if I were happy. I told him entirely so. He then proposed letting it stand for a while — certainly until after the Inauguration — while I pitched in on more current matters. I agreed and told him before leaving in the evening that if these continued to be pressing, he could count on me for as long as I was needed. "I can give help on a new AID program from Cambridge but not from New Delhi." I did tell him that I was averse to a desk job in Washington.

J.F.K. is functioning as President-elect from a small library off the living room of the Palm Beach house — a chintz and bookish office about fifteen feet square. He was putting in his own long distance calls and giving a credit card number. Once he looked for a letter from Harold Macmillan to show me; he was struck by its elegance, information and style. It could not be found, and I suggested that after he became President, he might want to have a special filing cabinet for communications from other heads of state. He said the idea was constructive and hazarded the guess that Caroline had walked off with this one.

Eisenhower was pleasant at the time of J.F.K.'s visit early this month. There were no papers on his desk, and J.F.K. asked him what he did with them after he had read them. He was sorry he asked for Ike seemed embarrassed. Eisenhower said that Adenauer was an oriental figure, and he had some similar characterization for de Gaulle. He told Kennedy he would refrain from criticizing him except in the event of fiscal irresponsibility or the recognition of Red China.

December 30 — St. Paul

This morning I pulled myself out of bed after only a few hours sleep — a dreary meeting of the Executive Committee of the American Economic Association had lasted until after midnight — and caught a plane to St. Paul–Minneapolis. After hedge-hopping stops at Des Moines, Waterloo and Rochester, I arrived a little before noon and was picked up by Governor Freeman's car and taken to the Capitol. Freeman's office was full of the disorder and confusion of last-minute packing. Some of the files, I noticed, were going into empty whiskey cartons.

I had been asked by J.F.K. at Palm Beach to go out and have a talk with Freeman — he was uncertain of Freeman's ideas on agriculture but knew something of mine. Freeman and I talked for several hours — the general farm program, the organization of the USDA,[23] the people and who would be loyal to the Secretary and who primarily to themselves, the possibility of hanky-panky in the commodity stabilization operations and a dozen other matters.

Freeman is enormously able, very enthusiastic about the job and still unaware of what he had ahead of him. The misfortune of a defeated politician is that his field of choice narrows so drastically. So, poor bastard, he may have to be a Secretary of Agriculture.

The trouble with this post is not that the problem is beyond solution. With strong action — firm controls, cross-compliance so that controls on one crop do not shove farmers into another, production payments as the basic technique of support and a few other steps — the farm problem would disappear. But there is well-dug-in opposition to every one of these steps. If one takes account of this opposition, he will end up doing nothing. Freeman sees this clearly enough.[24]

Toward the end of the afternoon, we drove out to a beautiful house of some friends — the Jacobsons — overlooking a lake. The latter is called Lake Farquar which Freeman explained was an Indian name. I told him I assumed that he had lost the Scottish vote. There we discussed a few novelties. I think better nutrition should be a part of Robert Kennedy's fitness program (something on which he had dwelt at Palm Beach.) Surely no youngster

---

[23] United States Department of Agriculture.
[24] And to a remarkable extent he overcame the opposition and solved the farm surplus problem as for thirty years it had been known.

should play touch football on a diet of beans and prunes. Why shouldn't a food allotment be a standard supplement to unemployment compensation?

In the late afternoon, a State highway patrolman drove me back to the airport. He has been driving the Governor for years. Now, he told me, he faces a return to the force or the risks of a new post in Washington. We always reflect on how the fortunes of politics affect the life of the first man. The change and uncertainty is much greater for those below.

The trip back was shortened by fewer stops and total weariness. On the way up, I had concentrated on the adventures of Arabella Trefoil and Senator Gotobed. On the way back, even this mental effort was far too great.

January 9, 1961 — Cambridge

The President-elect was here today, and I am reported as having been closeted with him. In .fact, I did not see him. However, I learned from one of his aides that the Indian Government has given its *agrément* to my appointment with much enthusiasm. (This could not have been true unless by most informal query.) This is very amusing. A fortnight ago, I dropped a pleasant note to Dean Rusk congratulating him on his appointment and saying, anent the rumors of my going to India, that perhaps a word might go to Ellsworth Bunker.[25] He has been a good and loyal servant; I had heard that Rusk wanted to keep him in the Department; he might be told what was pending but that the rumors portended no immediate change. I got back a very stiffly worded letter from Rusk saying that he had asked the people around Kennedy to talk less about the ambassadorial posts, that only a president and not a president-elect could ask for the *agrément* of the government to which the ambassador would be accredited, and that none of this had any reflection on my abilities. I dictated a rather nasty retort, saying I did not need instruction on these matters, especially from one

[25] See page xi.

who had not shared perceptibly in the effort that elected Kennedy, and that I was not seeking the place. Eventually I was persuaded not to send it. Or rather I compromised on a less tart version. But now, evidently, the Indian Government has been sounded out — if not formally asked. Anyhow, Reuters has carried the story from New Delhi, and I have been receiving cables of congratulation.

One of the few people in the United States who can think about foreign policy — and not merely reflect what isn't necessarily so — is Walt Rostow.[26] He had been promised, more or less, that he would be Assistant Secretary of State for Policy Planning. Now Rusk wishes to put George McGhee[27] in the job. George is an old friend of mine and was in the Truman State Department as Ambassador to Turkey. His qualifications as a planner are somewhat exiguous. Walt is upset. However, he had a very good breakfast with the President-elect today and has been promised a useful role.[28]

January 10 — Cambridge

The *Globe* yesterday ran my picture as the next Ambassador to India. Theodore Sorensen[29] asked me to give him a hand on domestic matters "until your appointment is confirmed." I have decided to stop being enigmatic, inscrutable or coy and admit it all.

I have been wondering what to do about Harvard. It is a trifle disconcerting to give up a lifetime post, and we all like life in Cambridge. My first thought was to ask for a leave of absence. But that is limited to two years, and I couldn't promise absolutely to be back in that time. And there is something cowardly in trying to protect oneself against every eventuality. The university professor who thinks deeply of how to secure his own future regularly ends up thinking of nothing else. So I have decided to resign and

[26] Not, in later times on Vietnam, a man whose views enlisted my sympathy.
[27] He became head of the Policy Planning Staff, subsequently Undersecretary of State, then Ambassador to the Federal Republic of Germany.
[28] He was taken into the White House on Bundy's staff, went later to State as Chief of the Policy Planning Council where he made peace with Rusk, and was brought back to the White House by President Johnson as an adviser on National Security Affairs.
[29] Special Counsel to President Kennedy.

tell President Pusey that if I am not worth rehiring, I shouldn't have been kept in the absence of an ambassadorship. The courage required is not so enormous. If not Harvard, there is M.I.T., Tufts, Fletcher, Brandeis, Wellesley and possibly Shady Hill. If I do not teach, I could write more. And we probably have enough money so I would not be reduced to trade. Having made the decision to resign, I feel rather good about it.[30]

January 11 — Cambridge

This morning at 9:30 A.M., I visited Mr. Pusey to tell him that, in the event of being offered the post in India — which I said I deemed likely — I planned to resign. He received the news with great equanimity and said that he hoped it might be early in the term so there would be a minimum of academic disturbance. (The interview, the only one I have ever had with him, took about five minutes.) I am a little comforted by the greater regret of my colleagues. Alex Gerschenkron[31] called me this evening much distressed and tried to persuade me to ask for a leave of absence. I stood fast.

A university, in our society, acts as a prop to the individual. As a member of the university community, he is much; divorced from it, he is on his own and maybe much less. So resignation seems a remarkably formidable step. But if one has strength in his own right, he does not need the crutch. I hope that is my situation. I am susceptible to doubts, however. On occasion in these last days, I have wondered if I have been reckless.

January 18 — Washington

There was a long and interesting meeting last evening at David Bell's[32] office in the Old State Building — Douglas Dillon,[33] Joe

[30] Later, after all this, I did find myself much more reluctant to resign and obtained a leave of absence.
[31] Professor of Economics at Harvard and longtime friend.
[32] The newly designated Director of the Bureau of the Budget.
[33] Secretary-designate of the Treasury.

Fowler,[34] Ted Sorensen,[35] George Ball,[36] Walter Heller,[37] James Tobin[38] — to consider the Economic Report of the President. This must go up to the Congress early in February. The notion is to use it to spell out rather specifically the legislative program of the new session.

The discussion was dominated — too much I thought — by the problem of gold outflow. It is a symptom rather than a cause. If we can remedy the present shortcomings in the balance of payments, we will, of course, have no gold problem. Otherwise gold outflows will continue. Elementary since Adam Smith. Jim Tobin and Douglas Dillon pressed the case for legislation to reduce the reserve requirement — the gold coverage of the currency. I argued strongly against. The new administration would be thought to be tampering with the currency in a most alarming way. No one could explain otherwise. The gold outflow would increase. And the reform itself was not fundamental. I was joined by George Ball and others, and in the end the proposal was more or less shelved.

I am undertaking to second Ted Sorensen on the problem and will help with the drafting. Immediately I am going to pursue the agricultural, labor and defense aspects of the message.

[34] Henry H. Fowler, Undersecretary-designate of the Treasury.
[35] See page 12.
[36] Undersecretary-designate of State for Economic Affairs and close personal friend. He later very briefly became Ambassador to the United Nations.
[37] See page 5.
[38] Professor of Economics at Yale and a newly designated member of the Council of Economic Advisers.

II

The Beginning

January 22 — Washington

The Inaugural, the equivalent of a four-day carnival, is now over. Kitty came down and we housed ourselves with the George Balls.[1] At first, I struggled against increasingly hopeless odds to get Commerce, Agriculture and Labor to work on their proposals for the economic message. The new cabinet members, with the singular exception of Arthur Goldberg,[2] were highly unclear about what they wanted to do. So were their next men. One could not bypass them to deal with the permanent civil service for the latter wished guidance from their new bosses or thought it polite to ask. In the end I decided that more time would simply be required for the message and concentrated instead on the festivities. One minor problem was that everyone was moving, hard to reach on the telephone and impossible to find at home.

On Wednesday night (January 18), at J.F.K.'s request, I went to the Hill to see the final draft of the Inaugural Address. (I had written a draft which I had taken to Palm Beach and turned in a revision when J.F.K. visited Cambridge.) I was late and dashed through the Kennedy office to Ted Sorensen's, shouldering a pleasant, rather chubby man somewhat perfunctorily aside. He intro-

[1] See page 14.
[2] Secretary of Labor — later, of course, Supreme Court Justice and Ambassador to the United Nations.

duced himself, rather apologetically, as the new Senator from Massachusetts.

The address bore little resemblance to my contributions although some of the language and tone survived. It was short, economical of words and said something. My phrases about aid to the underdeveloped lands being given "not to defeat communism, not to win votes, but because it is right" survived as did my suggestion that we should never negotiate out of fear but never fear to negotiate. In going over it, I added the sentence, "Let us begin" at one point to give proper cadence, and a day or two later it was mildly historic. A low score but not completely negligible. A ghost-writer is like an unloved dog in a poor family. He must be content with scraps. The Kennedy-Sorensen draft, though less daring, was probably a lot wiser than mine. I made a number of suggestions, mostly cosmetic, though I urged the elimination of a mildly hectoring tone toward the allies and the poor countries. These were accepted with the exception of a line about those who mount the tiger ending up inside. I thought it out of tune. Others differed.

There must have been a party that night, but I forget where. The next day I worked, against the handicap of a frightful headache, until early afternoon and then went home and to bed. Before going, I responded to the depression of the scene and my head by writing out a draft letter withdrawing my name from consideration as Ambassador. I couldn't believe I wanted it; during the day, the new Secretary of State was cited as resenting all the political appointments.

On the night before the Inaugural came a thick snowstorm. In 1933 when Roosevelt was inaugurated, all the banks were inoperative. In 1961, it was the automobiles. The New Frontier began, most appropriately, with the greatest traffic jam in human history. We made our way around Georgetown on foot and were among the few to arrive at parties on time. The Kennedys were snowbound and failed entirely to arrive at a party at Philip Graham's.[3]

[3] Philip L. Graham, publisher of the *Washington Post*.

We were there for a while, then went on to dinner with Chester Bowles.[4] Chet was much upset at the newspaper reporting on Senate questioning on where he stood on recognizing Red China. The *Star* had him opposing; the *Post* advocating. I told him I thought it showed considerable skill.

Inauguration Day was bright, clear and very cold. My wife and I were covered from dawn to dark by a television team. They were doing a documentary on the events as seen through our eyes. Nothing could have added more to our status than the cameras. The television people also provided us with a car and chauffeur so they could record our observations.

Our seats were just close enough to the podium so that we could not see the proceedings. The prayers were of exceptional length, especially that of the Cardinal[5] who began by exhorting God and ended by instructing Him. John Steinbeck, who accompanied us, claimed afterward that he had a conversation with the Almighty who said, "I hadn't realized there was anything much going on in the United States until around noon, and then I received one hell of a blast." The Inaugural speech was well received.

It took a couple of hours to get uptown, and we missed the early part of the parade. The rest was tedious. Each state had a governor, a stereotyped football band with drum majorettes, a hideous float and a National Guard, police or other marching unit. All looked alike; none took my mind off the bitter cold. We had fine seats in front of the White House. But we were still cold. About four we went to the Bowleses' for drinks and on to a number of other parties ending up around eleven at the Inaugural Ball in the Armory. To reach the latter, we walked the last half dozen blocks; those who didn't were confined to their cars for upwards of two hours.

The ball was a vast conclave of seeming strangers whom, it turned out, one mostly knew. Most of the men were in tails; the

[4] See page 3.
[5] Richard Cardinal Cushing of Boston.

women were mostly overdressed. No one did much dancing. However, our television team attracted the attention of other cameras, and we were challenged to perform. I felt, and I think looked, fairly muscle-bound. In a singularly uninspiring ceremony, the members of the Cabinet and their wives walked across the dance floor in the direction of the Kennedy box. It proved that all could walk. Stevenson received the most applause. By a combination of walking and riding, we arrived home about 4 A.M. At the ball, Mac Bundy urged me to go to India — and swallow my pride re Rusk.

Saturday, I was briefed formally on India in the morning and then went to a fine luncheon party at Phil Stern's[6] in Alexandria. There I learned that Bowles had taken literally my withdrawal and had removed my name from the ambassadorial list. Thomas Farmer had then intervened to have it restored. More afternoon parties and then an all-night costume party by Marie Ridder and Scotty Lanahan[7] in McLean, Virginia, near the CIA. All the liberal establishment was present without exception. (I wore my kilt. Dining in Georgetown beforehand we heard someone say, "It's what you can expect from now on.") Sunday, we talked more about ambassadorial life with the Penfields[8] and came home to a dinner party in Cambridge.

My principal impression of the week was the gaiety of the crowds. Everyone seems to be intensely pleased with both the Kennedys and themselves.

[6] Philip M. Stern, economist and author, was on Stevenson's staff in 1952 and was about to join the State Department as Deputy Assistant Secretary for Public Affairs. He did not long remain on companionable terms with Dean Rusk.

[7] Washington writers and newspaperwomen. Mrs. Lanahan, now Mrs. Clinton Grove Smith, an accomplished writer, is the daughter of F. Scott Fitzgerald.

[8] James K. Penfield, a Foreign Service Officer, was one of the few old China hands to survive the mistake of predicting that the Communists would defeat Chiang Kai-shek. A distinguished and liberal man, I asked for him as my Deputy Chief of Mission. Possibly to prevent having two like-minded men in one place, the Department promptly made him Ambassador to Iceland.

January 24 — Washington

I am back working on the messages. Washington is becoming more organized, and one begins to gain a clear view of what must be done. At noon, I had a conference with Sorensen at the White House. It was bustling with activity, but I managed to get in and out of the West Wing offices unseen. I was struck by how shabby it all is. The halls and anterooms are not more elegant or inspiring than those of a smallish Latin American republic. I was endowed with rights to a White House car. This is a considerable status symbol but also a major convenience. As cars go, they are exceptionally clean and exceedingly well driven.

My tasks include stimulating expressions of policy on the balance-of-payments problem from the Departments of Agriculture and Commerce. They promise not to be stimulating. I would like to see agricultural support prices shifted to production payments at least for cotton. Then cotton would move at world prices — and perhaps we could sell quite a bit more.[9] (Cotton remains one of our largest sources of foreign earnings. Far more than most people realize, the United States owes its eminence in world markets not to its industry but to its incomparably efficient agriculture.) The effect of the change on the Latin American and Egyptian producers might not be welcome for our support prices now prop up their market too. I am going to see if I can get the Pentagon to take a more comprehensive view of the dollar problem in relation to troop deployment. It is a touchy matter, but external dollars are now a scarce resource. More than internal ones we must conserve them. At present, everyone strikes for military savings on the things he has seen — dependents, officers' cars and what not. Much such remedy is window dressing.

January 25 — Washington

At noon, I went to a meeting on the State of the Union message in the White House. There is to be a State of the Union message,

9 This change was effected in ensuing years by Secretary Freeman.

and several subsequent ones covering the economy, the balance of payments, the budget, health, education and the rest. I am drafting parts of the Union message and one or two of the subsequent ones including that on the payments balance. Once such responsibility would have worried me. Now I realize that I can do it better than anyone else who is available. Modesty is a vastly overrated virtue.

After the meeting, Mac Bundy told me "The Boss" (a new term) had been asking for me. I went into Ken O'Donnell's[10] office and presently the President came through, grabbed me by the arm, and we had an hour-and-a-half chat which included a tour of the upstairs of the White House. We saw where Ike's golf shoes had poked innumerable holes in his office floor. When we left the office in the West Wing for the house proper, we went headlong into a closet. The President turned over furniture to see where it was made, dismissed some as Sears, Roebuck and expressed shock that so little — the Lincoln bed apart — consisted of good pieces. Only expensive reproductions. The effect is indeed undistinguished although today the house was flooded with sunlight and quite filled with flowers.

We chatted about the best and fastest remedy for recession — stronger unemployment compensation is by far the fastest; what should you read to stay abreast on agriculture? — I do not know; the Inaugural address — he liked my lines and thought I should be pleased; the State Department — Dean Rusk is going to be too busy and Chet Bowles too preoccupied with the revolution of rising expectations and four or five other revolutions; my ambassadorship — it is set; other related embassies — he is willing to consider Bill Blair for Pakistan.[11] It was great fun. I was an hour late for lunch with Ed Rhetts[12] but was forgiven since I had mentioned his name for a job.

[10] Assistant to President Kennedy. Directed the White House staff.

[11] William McCormack Blair, Jr., later Ambassador to Denmark and to the Philippines. I was anxious to have a congenial and cooperative neighbor in Karachi.

[12] C. Edward Rhetts, later Ambassador to Liberia.

After lunch, I installed myself in Cordell Hull's old office in Old State. (The President had offered me Sherman Adams' former office in the White House. I was afraid that as an economist inside the White House I would seem to be undercutting Walter Heller and would also be too much in the newspapers' eye.) The rest of the day I spent putting people to work on drafts for the State of the Union message and reading those that had come in. The latter, except for some pointed and factual documents from Goldberg, were very thin. They said nothing and with a minimum of style and intelligence.

January 27 — Washington

We had a long meeting at the White House to consider the State of the Union message — economic aspects. Dillon, Fowler,[13] Leddy,[14] from Treasury; Goldberg[15] from Labor; Heller, Gordon,[16] Tobin from the Council of Economic Advisers and several others. There was a further long discussion of repealing the 25 percent gold cover clause which Dillon supported but not with fervor. I opposed it with fervor. It would, as I have said, set off a hideous debate; everyone would be persuaded in the process that something horrible was happening to the dollar; the gold outflow would be worse than ever. Better wait. The need for action may not arise; if necessary, it can be done at the last minute; in any case, there are powers to suspend the clause requiring a minimum cover which could be used. In the end, I had the better of it; there is a great advantage in being certain. Since the opposing arguments did not impress me, I have naturally forgotten them!

Goldberg introduced a proposal for wage-price stabilization which was highly inadequate — nothing but a high-level debating

---

[13] See page 14.
[14] John Leddy, Assistant Secretary for International Affairs, Department of the Treasury.
[15] See page 15.
[16] Kermit Gordon, formerly Professor of Economics at Williams College. He became a member of the Council of Economic Advisers and later Director of the Budget, and then President of the Brookings Institution.

society in my view. I also intervened vigorously on that. It was a very long meeting, and since I had spent the morning drafting parts of the S. of U. message, I ended up very tired.

The problem of drafts of the message presents an interesting question of clearance. Obviously the members of the Cabinet should know what goes to the President. But it is less clear that they should pass on them, and thus on what the President says. Nor does time allow. So I read the drafts as they went to Sorensen, to Freeman, Goldberg, et al., and then told them that, thereafter, it was in the President's hands. I should imagine he would wish to check important matters of substance bearing on a particular department. But surely there is no right to review what the President is to say.

Tonight another deep snow. Had it not been for a White House car with chains, I would not have got home.

January 28 — Washington

For the last two days, I have been deep in the State of the Union message, and tonight it is finished. The President has put in several hours on it, and Sorensen has worked day and night for the last four days. From any point of view, I don't think it could be better. The economic sections are excellent and do not spare the Eisenhower Administration in their review of unemployment, declining product, business failures, farm income and continuing price advance. The affirmative part portends good legislation, even if some is yet to be devised or thought out. The tone of the foreign policy section is good, and there is an excellent section designed to encourage government workers and re-endow them with pride of profession. My views on foreign aid and development, perhaps not unnaturally, are strongly articulated.[17]

[17] There is always exaggeration, the effect of personal vanity aside, in accounts of what one contributed. One is aware of what one urged and not of others who urged the same. In the case of this message, a far larger burden was carried by Ted Sorensen and, of course, the President than by all others combined.

The Kennedy top command is highly confident. I do detect already one weakness. Apart from the President, it is going to be too professional — too aware of criticism, too sensitive to what cannot be done. There are no political buccaneers with a fine enthusiasm for action — in the manner of Harold Ickes or Hugh Johnson. The message — or a late draft — has a passage calling for some spirit of adventure in the public servant. It could be addressed to the Cabinet.

January 29 — Washington

I worked all morning — Sunday — on drafts for the balance-of-payments message. What prose! Meaning was everywhere elaborately but not deliberately concealed. I finally got a new and more tolerable version.

This afternoon there was a big party at the White House. I was invited verbally and arrived without a ticket — since I had a White House car, I was waved into the grounds. After some telephoning, it was concluded that I belonged. The mood was gay and agreeable; I found I knew almost everyone; Jackie looked tall and soignée. For the first time in the White House at a public function, hard liquor was served. There was also smoking but, I believe, no smutty stories. The Republic may be in decline, but more likely it is only becoming less stuffy. Afterward there was an agreeable party at the Lippmanns' and thereafter dinner with the Harrimans[18] and the Murrows. I doubt that Ed is going to be a success at USIA to which he has just been appointed.[19] He is too inclined to act when he should think — and plays for effect. But after dinner he settled down and talked quite rationally.

[18] W. Averell Harriman, Ambassador-at-Large under Presidents Kennedy and Johnson, is a longtime personal friend.
[19] Ed Murrow had been a news analyst and commentator with CBS for some twenty-six years before heading up the United States Information Agency. In my initial reaction, I could scarcely have been more mistaken. I soon came to think of him as the most effective of the New Frontier appointments.

January 30 — Washington

This morning I struggled again with the balance-of-payments message. Robert Roosa, the new Treasury Undersecretary,[20] came over to the White House. He is not entirely in agreement with the rest of the Treasury. I gave him my latest draft to read. Reconciliation is not my forte; I find it much easier to decide. Were I to stay here, I would, without question, soon be the most unpopular man in town.

I lunched with George Ball in his new offices at State. It conveys the impression of hideousness at no great expense. George McGovern[21] was there, and we talked about Food for Peace — and food for surplus disposal. He, at least, has the enthusiasm of the amateur.

This afternoon Walter Heller and I had a long talk with the President — an interruption in an even larger meeting on the economic message. The President's office has been painted; it has some new orange-colored sofas by the fireplace and looks altogether better.

We talked of ways of getting the interest rates down. The Federal Reserve had submitted through Roosa some language which made no sense except that it seemed to urge that nothing be done. It had been billed as a great concession. The President telephoned Roosa, read it to him over the phone and asked him to explain. I think Bob had trouble; it sounded as though static was coming back over the line. We discussed other parts of the message and several proposals of mine for strengthening it — such as giving every unemployed family $20 worth of food a week. Evidently, however, we would have to buy the food from the CCC,[22] and though the government already owns the food and would receive the money, we would still have to pay for it which

[20] Later a New York banker.

[21] George S. McGovern. Former Congressman and later Senator from South Dakota. Then the newly designated head of the Food for Peace program attached to the White House.

[22] Commodity Credit Corporation.

would cost money. That is finance. Back at the meeting everyone enthusiastically explained why nothing could be done.

I also talked a little with the President about India. The President thinks I should be off in about three weeks.

He seemed set to continue with meetings for several more hours. This must be the most energy that has been brought to the office since T.R.

January 31 — Washington

This morning I had a long visit with Robert Roosa. I asked him why the banks and the Federal Reserve could never bring themselves to express any warmth and compassion for the unemployed and needed always to warn of the dangers of action. I had as text a draft on internal interest rate policy agreed upon by Federal Reserve and Treasury. It used one line to suggest lowering rates and twenty to tell of the dangers. I pointed out that this attitude had made every central bank in the world an immediate arm of the government — I personally think a good thing, too. Bob agreed. The President had said (jokingly) that having the Federal Reserve independent is like having the unions exempt from law.

After lunch with Dillon and Roosa, there was a long and interesting meeting in the Cabinet Room of the President's Committee on Management and Labor Policy. This is the culmination of years of sales effort on my part. Public machinery for restraining wages and price increases is our only hope for handling the wage-price spiral and thus combining high employment with reasonably stable prices. Goldberg led off ably but, I suspect, made the President impatient by talking too much. He was still ducking a commitment to price stability; so was Luther Hodges.[23] I pointed out that this was like establishing a Narcotics Bureau but not mentioning drugs. I pressed for a stronger commitment to standards which hopefully would have a continuing influence on the bargaining. The language was improved but I still feel it is too diffuse. But Arthur Goldberg

23 Secretary of Commerce.

sees clearly what it must do. And while I am not satisfied, I did not expect to be.

The President has a gift of power. When a dispute arose as to whether the Secretary of Labor should head the body — by nature too partisan a figure, said Commerce — he quietly and firmly resolved it before it got out of hand. It is curious how quickly and naturally one settles down to a discussion around the Cabinet table.

February 1 — Washington

We had a meeting at the White House this morning to resolve questions on the balance-of-payments message. Most of the conflicts were over things I had inserted to ensure discussion — for example, a section I had drafted calling for immediate study of how we might have a closer association with the Common Market and the free trade area. Everyone agreed on the desirability of the goal and was appalled at saying so. The result: deletion. We were to see the President for final resolution of the points of disagreement but this proved unnecessary. I did have a brief chat with the President in which he expressed great satisfaction that I was going to India. "Otherwise you and Heller would have me expounding a far too radical position. My policy is to be moderate and do much." I denied that I was a radical; only a realist. But I agreed that since I enjoyed stating moderate positions in abrasive form, I might be better in India.

In the afternoon, I went to the press briefing. Sorensen, Bundy and Salinger[24] were also present. We sat around in a circle and covered a great number of prospective questions in ten minutes. Salinger had a list of likely ones, some reflecting the stated intention of a reporter. The President wanted the suggested answers in two or three quick sentences. One could almost see him seizing upon this information and arranging it in his mind. On two or three questions, a State Department memo had suggested evasion.

[24] Press Secretary to President Kennedy.

He expressed impatience: "I can evade questions without help; what I need is answers."

He also made clear that he wanted some "hard news" for each press conference and observed that there was none for this. I dug out some from the forthcoming messages, including the revocation of an order recalling the dependents of GI's from Europe. It had been proposed by Ike to save foreign exchange. The matter had not been finally cleared between Defense and Treasury. This bureaucratic detail was accomplished in about six minutes by Bundy. It dominated the next day's news.

I should think that from half to two-thirds of the eventual questions were at least partially anticipated. The President's answers, as I watched them on television, seemed rather crisper and better than anything said in the briefing. And in most cases he had otherwise improved upon the earlier suggestions.

One unanticipated question was whether he would enter a debate with his rival in 1964. His answer, a simple yes, was uncomplicated and right.

The rest of the day was tediously and wearily devoted to the balance of payments.

February 3 — New York

Here yesterday to address the national Roosevelt Day Dinner, an annual festival of Americans for Democratic Action.[25] The crowd was large and loving and included the Soviet Ambassador. Things have thawed since ADA was considered an association of liberal red-baiters. I was too tired to do well. Also the balance-of-payments message had prevented my preparing as I should. Thank the Lord I am through — I hope — with the message writing.

February 4 — Washington

This afternoon I wound up the balance-of-payments message — the President evidently liked it very much — and had my first talk

[25] The other speaker of the evening was Martin Luther King, Jr.

with Rusk. He expressed regrets over the misunderstanding growing out of his letter. I tried to be handsome. In discussing India,
he told me that he wanted the Ambassador to assert his authority
over the Mission. And to speak plainly to the Department especially
when delays occurred. I promised and suggested that he be equally
candid. It was pleasant and informal in easy chairs on one side of
his office. Also brief; I had been there only a few moments before
the Soviet Ambassador was announced. The latter greeted me
warmly as I left.

Another enormous snowstorm which kept me in Washington.
I had a long talk with Arthur Schlesinger who is unhappy and uncertain concerning his White House assignment.[26] He has a good
address but no clear function. It will soon straighten out, but it
confirms my view that no sane man should ever take a staff position
as distinct from some line responsibility in Washington. One should
get his power, not from the man above but from the job below.
One should be not one of the people the President wants to see
but one that he must see.

February 10 — Washington

The President may not yet be persuaded of my diplomatic
talents, but I am still without rival as the nation's first expert on the
price of hogs. After a few days of teaching,[27] I am back to review a
feed-grain program. The idea, sponsored by Roswell Garst[28] with
the support of Ted Schultz,[29] is to relax controls, convert the increased corn supply so resulting into pork and milk solids — and
replace some of the corn acreage with soybeans (which are more in
demand) by raising their price. I am favorably disposed.

I used part of the day for preparation for India. I had a pleasant
and moderately informative meeting with the Department hier-

---

[26] See page 1.
[27] Pending Senate confirmation, I continued with my classes.
[28] Iowa liberal and hybrid corn tycoon. His was the farm at Coon Rapids which
was visited by Nikita Khrushchev on his American tour in 1959.
[29] Theodore W. Schultz. Professor of Economics, University of Chicago.

archy — Assistant Secretary for Middle Eastern Affairs (which included India) and desk and economic officers. The burden of advice: discretion. Silence is advised for the first six months to be followed by a policy of silence. However, it is considered important that I undertake a strenuous program of speeches to acquaint the Indians with American policies and aspirations. I should avoid advice on Indian economic policy or any commitment on economic aid. Also, a waiting policy on Kashmir. This does not sound too strenuous. More valuable, Robert Fluker, a former economic counselor in New Delhi and an old Princeton friend, provided me with down-to-earth information on secretarial needs, the ideal legman, how to handle the staff, the social life of Delhi, the house.

I had lunch with the Indian Ambassador and George Ball. We talked about Snow's novels, linguistic states, Bombay and Oxford. The Embassy is a cavernous house on Macomb Street — not unpleasant but hardly homelike. We had very good Indian food plus martinis.

After lunch I went back to the hogs. One problem in giving away pork is the number of Moslems in the world. Public Law 480, loosely applied, could set off a nasty *jihad*.

February 14 — Washington

Yesterday the FBI invaded Cambridge. If my loyalty is imperfect, it will be one of the most dangerously delayed discoveries in modern history.

Meanwhile my diplomatic career continues to be subordinate to the price of hogs. I went to a long meeting last night at the Department of Agriculture, followed by one with Mike Feldman[30] and Freeman this morning, followed by a lengthy session with the President.

I had become a little alarmed about the Garst proposals and proposed a compromise — some control this year, a higher soybean

[30] Myer Feldman. Deputy Special Counsel to Presidents Kennedy and Johnson and previously a member of the Kennedy senatorial and campaign staffs.

price, a guarantee on pork. (The danger was of a large increase in feed-grains and a sharp fall in corn and pork prices.) This, in the end, was accepted. It is costly and not very good but better or at least safer than the alternatives.[31]

The President looked relaxed and rested. His new desk, made from the timbers of a sunken ship (H.M.S. *Resolute*[32]) is massive and elegant, and the office is beginning to look rather more agreeable. The bookshelves still contain the public papers of F.D.R. and the complete volumes of reports and testimony of the Temporary National Economic Committee of the late thirties. Such was Ike's reading — just possibly.

I watched the President's reaction to the discussion. He is sharply sensitive to political freeloading. His sympathy for the poor farmers is quick; it is matched by a deep suspicion of those whose case depends on the benefit to their own pocketbooks. "We are being forced to bribe the corn growers to make the cut in acreage that is in their own interest. That is a lot of damn nonsense."

Then he quizzed Freeman at length and in detail on his progress in getting food to needy people in West Virginia. It was fine.

I have learned how to put issues before him in the crisp fashion which he obviously likes. My suggestion that agricultural policy never involved choosing the best, only the least Christ-awful, pleased him. When I told him that the program would be criticized, he immediately asked for specifications. (It costs too much for the acreage retired, and won't be thought to do enough for farm income.)

There was also another long White House meeting on foreign aid — very rambling and inconclusive. More on this later.

One of the most pleasant things in the White House is the Navy-run mess in the basement. The food is good American, well-served.

---

[31] This, in the light of the full later development of the feed-grain policy, vastly exaggerates my role.

[32] The desk was presented to President Rutherford B. Hayes by Queen Victoria.

The telephones also reach in to the tables. Conversation is much like that at the Harvard Faculty Club, perhaps because it involves the same people.

February 18 — Washington–Cambridge
For the last three days, I have employed myself on a variety of matters — economic recovery, India, hogs and soybeans, the Peace Corps, textiles and science. I wrote a strong memo on the need for getting down interest rates. The President was impressed and gave it to Dillon who read it to a gallery of economists and monetary authorities. I doubt that it pleased them. I stressed the "mystic claptrap" of trying to bring down long-term rates while holding up short-term rates[33] and compared it with trying to land the top of an airplane while keeping up the bottom side. I suggested that the people involved did not really want to reduce rates or to offend those who did not want to reduce rates and described the whole effort as, technically speaking, half-assed. I hope it did some good.

We are raising the support price for cotton. And then to insure exports, we are paying an increased subsidy on what we sell abroad. The support price raises the world price. The subsidy then lowers it. At the lower price, the foreign mills have cheaper cotton which they export to the United States in competition with domestic mills. The latter complain bitterly; so we limit imports of textiles. But we are continuing the arrangement in the absence of a better alternative for this year. I included in the program a promise of reform for next year. I would discount the chances for same at a modest rate.

Thursday night we were guests of the Indian Embassy at *The World of Apu*, by Satyajit Ray. It needs cutting but is obviously a superior film. Afterward there was a pleasant party at the Embassy. Good food; quite good wine; very pleasant company. And

[33] To bring down long-term rates would, it was felt, encourage investment and employment. To keep up short-term rates would prevent a capital outflow and an adverse effect on the balance of payments.

many handsome women in handsome saris. Last night I went to a party for a visiting German delegation, an occasion of unrelieved tedium. Germans and Americans, one after another, made speeches of incredible awfulness. All were concerned with improving understanding by one country of the other. I framed a few remarks on the inadvisability of the effort. Leave each country to its own devices; treat the other's ideas with dignity and respect, whether right or wrong. No one ever worries about relations with Switzerland which is why everyone has good relations with the Swiss. Start doing something about them, and this would mean that they needed improvement, ergo were bad. It was one of my greatest undelivered speeches.

Yesterday Kitty, Florence Mahoney,[34] Barbara Ward[35] and I had lunch with the President. The food — mushrooms, a salmon with some rather complex sauce, ice cream and chocolate sauce, with white wine — was disastrously plentiful. When the coffee ran out, the President took the pot around. He remarked, rightly, that no one would ever get thin on his food.

The talk was mostly about Africa, and I was handicapped by my uncertainty as to whether Katanga was the province and Mobutu the man, or vice versa. Barbara today was eloquent and specific. Her tendency is to favor all good things.

The President said that one of the rare and unexpected pleasures of his post was reading the FBI reports on his appointees. No one could imagine how many seamy things were reported about even the most saintly of his men. And no one, he asserted, would ever go into public life if he knew what some second person would eventually be reading about him in these documents.

Kitty and I had entered the White House through the West Wing and strolled along the edge of the gallery by the swimming pool to the House. The view out over the lawns was warm and

[34] Washington hostess and shrewd observer of the folkrites of the capital.
[35] Barbara Ward (Lady Jackson), economist, journalist, currently Professor of International Economic Development at Columbia University.

green, and I was struck again by how southern it seemed. Looking back, we saw the President and Barbara coming out of his office, and we waited and made our way together. One could imagine it as the center of a rather more leisurely way of life. After lunch, we did stroll through the state rooms looking at the paintings. These, incidentally, have deteriorated in quality with the late presidents — especially Eisenhower and Roosevelt. The art of portraiture may be dying out; more likely, control by the patron is raising its ugly head.

February 26 — Washington–Cambridge

This has been a tiring, rather disagreeable week. I spent four days in Washington, none of them rewarding. The economic situation continues to worry me, and I have promised the President another statement. (J.F.K.: "Tell me not what I should do but what I should tell others to do and be specific.") This was during a morning chat on Thursday (February 23) which we also devoted to agriculture and my appointment to India. Senator Bourke B. Hickenlooper[36] is opposing my appointment and has asked for a full field investigation by the FBI. For days, everyone I know, however marginally, has been telling me of a visit by Mr. Hoover's men. The President wasn't pleased by Hickenlooper — "You see how some minds work." I found myself reacting with exceptional amiability — I did say I thought it degrading. The President was deeply annoyed by the objections of the Swiss Government to the appointment of his neighbor, Earl Smith, as Ambassador to Berne. I wonder too; they are usually more sensible than this. Far better to have Smith, who is also an improvement over Henry Taylor, their present blessing, than to anger the President. I doubt that they will suffer much if they get Smith (which they did not). And surely the President's discomposure is the one thing to avoid.

Freeman is urging a Presidential message on his farm program. The final drafts were singularly barren. Farmers were praised for

[36] Former Senator from Iowa.

their productivity and (I think) for their Christian virtue. But there was little else. Presidential messages are not speeches. On the other hand, I thought Mike Feldman,[37] a good and devoted man, was too tough in his criticism. Anyone who is the custodian of the President's power must, I am convinced, use it with the greatest tact. In the end, I fear, I will have to draft this bloody document.

I had a talk yesterday with Walter Heller who, I think, is already doing a good job of building up the prestige of the Council of Economic Advisers. He showed me a memorandum he had just sent to the President recommending against the creation of a "blue-ribbon" committee to propose anti-recession measures. It was crisp and tough and made the essential point, which is that "blue-ribbon" is a synonym for stuffed shirt. I urged Heller not to troop around with his fellow council members on all occasions — people in general, and the President in particular, will quickly tire of visitations by three economists, however good. I also strongly urged against his participation in meetings abroad where he would be sharing the stage with run-of-the-bureaucracy officials. The President's economist should keep himself at the ministerial level; and he should remember that when he is away from Washington, he leaves his rear unprotected, i.e., there is no one with his authority to explain and defend what he may say or do while abroad. And if he neither says nor does anything, he needn't go.

I have been inhabiting the erstwhile office of Secretary Hull (and other Secretaries of State) in the Old State Department building. It is large, dignified and comfortable, with bathroom and kitchen. Today movers arrived to turn me out and to turn it into a conference room. I sent word via the moving boss up through the hierarchy that I much preferred to stay. Word came back down that I could stay.

Last night was the annual White House correspondents' dinner — a vast conclave at the Sheraton-Park. I had an amusing evening

[37] See page 29.

with Richard Rovere and Gore Vidal[38] as guests of Robert Spivak of the *New York Post*. My economist colleagues were there as the guests of the *Wall Street Journal*.

The entertainment was good enough but less than brilliant. The President was brief but amusing — or rather, amusing because brief. Presented with two lanterns, replicas of those on the Old North Church made by Paul Revere, he accepted with pleasure and said it would be one for Judge Smith and two for Charley Halleck.[39] In presenting a watch to some Colonel, he said, "I am happy to give you this *Swiss* watch."

The Chairman was drunk. I did not get the impression that this was as damaging to the content of his remarks as one might imagine.

March 1 — New York

Last night *Life* was celebrating its twenty-fifth anniversary. Harry Luce asked me to attend the festivities; in the interest of my press relations — we have been feuding in public for years and it won't be so easy to respond from New Delhi — I did so. First, there was an incredibly awful television show for which the guests were the live audience. A sequence of banal observations on the last twenty-five years were played out on the stage behind a thick covering screen of cameras and of technicians and workmen, all of whom were taking an exceptionally languid approach to a career in featherbedding. For totally inexplicable reasons, one embarrassing sequence on how a family lived twenty-five years ago was done twice — once live and once on television tape. Robert Oppenheimer and his wife left abruptly at this point. I was too craven to do likewise.

The television treat being over, cars took us to the T-L Building and this was more fun. I shared Harry Luce's table with the Duke and Duchess of Windsor, Perle Mesta, Mrs. William Randolph

[38] Both commentators on the Washington scene.
[39] Two notably conservative Congressmen.

Hearst, Jr., and the John D. Rockefellers III. The Duke is small, pleasant, rather red-faced but not necessarily unhealthy in appearance. The Duchess is showing some signs of wear. "I hear you are going to In-jea," said the Duke. I affirmed the possibility. "A most interesting country," he said. "I had a very good time there in my early youth. You must do the pig-sticking in Rajasthan."

I tried to look like a man who could take pig-sticking or leave it alone and murmured that I had heard very good things about the pastime in those parts.

"Oh, it's excellent," he said. "And you will find the people most agreeable in their own way. They have been most uncommonly decent to my niece." I told him what a wholesome influence he had been in my early life in Canada as the Prince of Wales. We had been told to model our lives on this splendid young man. He looked surprised. At midnight, the Duchess dragged him away explaining that he could have a cup of coffee when he got home.

Perle Mesta asked me to call on her for advice on entertaining. And John Rockefeller, the kindest of men, gave me some useful thoughts on the work of the Rockefeller Foundation in India. I saw many of my old friends from *Fortune* days. I also sense a considerable need to sell *Life*. I wonder if all is well? Has there been some slight diminution in the old self-confidence?

March 3 — Washington–Cambridge

A week ago the President told me that the FBI would finish the following day; and he told Ken O'Donnell[40] to have the State Department obtain the agreement on my appointment from the Indian government forthwith. Yesterday Chet Bowles called to say that all would be settled by the end of next week and they would then clear it with India. He also told me it had been important to mollify Hickenlooper. I went into a black mood, partly at myself for not telling Bowles what the President had ordered.

During the night, I got angrier and was calmed only by two

40 See page 20.

tranquilizers and a sleeping pill. This morning I called Chet to tell him what the President had said. This made no great impression so I called Ken O'Donnell. He got on to the FBI, and they promised to have the report over later today. I hope it is scintillating in its purity. In the process, I wrote a brilliant letter to J.F.K. which I tore up.

Bill Shawn[41] called me to ask if I would write an occasional book note for *The New Yorker*. This was the result of intervention by Dick Rovere. It suits me wonderfully; it is relaxed, nonpolitical and with no worry about deadlines.

March 6 — Washington

This morning we had a long cabinet-level meeting on foreign aid. The present aid organization is diffuse, bureaucratic, too heavily preoccupied with individual projects — dams and docks — and too little concerned with what in some countries are the fundamental things — education and better public administration. It was a good meeting on the whole; Bowles and Walt Rostow greatly emphasized the need for more money. Dillon seemed worried about lending it at unnaturally low rates of interest — "fiscally unsound." He is a liberal-minded man with a lingering commitment to the minor clichés of banking. Banking may well be a career from which no man really recovers.

Later we had much talk about the agricultural message including a session with the President. The proposal is to ask for a broad enabling authority to do almost anything. This would be safe-guarded by according farmers a chance to vote on programs in referenda and Congress the right to reject. Freeman is uncertain; he would like the legislation but is afraid of losing the battle it would involve. On balance, I am for the battle. I spent the late afternoon redrafting the message to make it sound less an arbitrary

41 William Shawn, Editor of *The New Yorker*. In the end, I found time to write only one review, of Ed O'Connor's *The Edge of Sadness*.

bid for power. I did such a good job that Charlie Murphy[42] was momentarily persuaded that the new legislation would leave the Department with less power than before.

Around six, I had a chat with the President. He needed the name of a man with a large reputation for wisdom for a Bolivian mission. I passed on the fears of the people in the Harvard planning project in Iran of a breakup of the government there. We seem to have no ambassador to speak of in Tehran. The President was bone-tired. He offered me a cup of tea and absentmindedly filled the cup with milk and sugar. He referred to Dick Goodwin[43] as "Professor" Goodwin and corrected himself. During our chat, a cabinet officer called and talked at vast length. He put the receiver down once and signed a letter while the talk went on. "Bobby would just tell him to cut the crap. I'm more polite." He claimed to be not so much tired as on the edge of a cold. He mused that with so many countries opting for a neutralist policy, maybe the United States should be neutral too! I suggested that this would be an interesting maneuver but that the term was meaningless. Countries were, indeed, Communist or non-Communist. But the notion that there was a distinction between military allies — many not at all valuable — and non-communist neutrals was one of Mr. Dulles' many contributions to confusion.

In the evening, I had dinner with Newton Minow,[44] Teddy White[45] and George McGovern[46] at the Schlesingers'. The latter have a very pretty house in Georgetown.

Newt is determined to do something with and about the FCC. When he moved in, his office was adorned with a large television

---

[42] Charles S. Murphy, Counsel to President Truman and the new Undersecretary of Agriculture. Since, Chairman of the Civil Aeronautics Board.

[43] Assistant Special Counsel to President Kennedy.

[44] Newton N. Minow. Newly designated head of the Federal Communications Commission.

[45] Theodore H. White. Author and historian of election campaigns: *The Making of the President, 1960, The Making of the President, 1964*, etc., etc. (New York: Atheneum Publishers).

[46] See page 24.

set, the gift of the industry to the former chairman. When it came to removing it, the latter had been overcome by conscience or possibly fear. Newt's first action was one of high prudence; he placed a small seal on it saying, "Property of the United States Government."

Arthur has long been famous for his lofty disinterest in undeveloped countries. Now he is becoming a South American expert. I think he should become Assistant Secretary of State for Latin American Affairs.

Today, at long last, the FBI completed its review of my recent career. I can't think of any obvious impurity that they could have discovered.

III

The Early Education of an Ambassador

March 15 — Cambridge

For the last week, I have been in Cambridge in a condition of recurrent frustration, badly controlled. A week ago Chet Bowles called to say that the FBI had found me virginal — the proper reward of years of conformity — and that approval had been requested from the Indian Government. This, Chagla[1] had told me, took a day or two. But then nothing happened. My patience had deteriorated seriously by the first of the week. As usual, I was imagining all kinds of mistreatment — without quite believing it, I always find the fiction that I am being done in by malign influences strangely agreeable. Yesterday I got on the phone to Schlesinger and Sorensen. Arthur investigated and reported first that all was complete but that my name was waiting along with several others so that it might go to the Hill in a package. Then further and different investigation showed that *agrément* from the Indians had not been received. Arthur, who understands the symptoms, urged calm.

This morning, Reischauer's[2] appointment — for which I had myself interceded last week — but not mine, was announced. My equanimity was further endangered, and I had another talk with

---

[1] M. C. Chagla. The Indian Ambassador to Washington, he later became Minister of Education, and then Foreign Minister in India. He resigned from the latter post in 1967, it was said, because of disapproval of the Indian languages policy.

[2] Edwin O. Reischauer, a Harvard colleague and one of the most inspired of all of Kennedy's appointments, who had been designated as Ambassador to Japan.

Arthur. Evidently someone decided that the situation with Galbraith was getting dangerous; the Indians were cabled. In the afternoon, Chet called me to say I was in. It was announced on the evening news even while the photographers were at work. Louis Lyons[3] gave a flattering account of my qualifications. It improved even on the handout I had written myself, which was a model of unobtrusive praise. My wife responded to the news first by crying inconsolably and then contemplating the problem of clothes.

March 16 — Washington

I arrived in Washington toward noon and had a busy day of press interviews combined with visits from people who would like to work for me. I had lunch with Wallace Cohen[4] and, almost automatically, allowed him to reach for the check. It is wonderful how quickly the reflexes of the public servant are established. Tonight I spoke to a big dinner at the local Harvard Club. I had a rising ovation and a hard time listening to some of the other speeches. Mine must have shown the signs of hasty improvisation; I had spent all of five minutes on it. But outwardly it was well-received.

At dinner, I had a long talk with Chip Bohlen[5] who welcomed me to an "interesting and often ludicrous" profession. He cries a plague on both those who want no peace with the Russians and those who think it easy. This, it must be said, is a position that allows of rapid movement in any direction.

I find it rather pleasant to be called Mr. Ambassador without the previous smirk. At the head table tonight, there were three of us, however. This made it a trifle common.

[3] Then Curator of the Nieman Foundation at Harvard whose evening broadcasts have for many years been a Boston folkrite. "Did you hear what Louis said tonight?"
[4] A distinguished Washington lawyer and old personal friend.
[5] Charles E. Bohlen, career diplomat variously Ambassador to the U.S.S.R., the Philippines and France.

March 17 — Washington

Today I had lunch with John Sherman Cooper.[6] He is tall, good-humored and good-looking and wise without pretense. I had many good tips from him; he urged that I be prepared to talk about Laos which is much on Nehru's mind (and which I do not understand at all as yet) and China. Nehru never wants to talk about American aid. He told me, with some reluctance, that he had made it clear to Nehru when he was Ambassador that his position on the Pakistan arms buildup was not the same as that of Dulles and that he was urging a change. I had speculated on how one learns to conceal obvious disagreement — or how far one goes in revealing it. Perhaps the best way will be to get the U.S. to agree with me.

Tonight I had dinner at The Occidental with Walter Heller. My secretary had booked the table in the name of Ambassador Galbraith. As a result, the headwaiter swept us through the waiting crowd with fulsome assurances that "Your table is waiting, Mr. Ambassador." My pleasure was diluted by the fact that he automatically assumed Heller to be the Ambassador.

March 18 — Washington–Cambridge

This morning we had a long review of the economic situation at the White House. Unemployment is dangerously high; it promises to remain so. Heller wants a tax cut. He is intelligent and attractive but not a tough debater. I am strongly opposed[7] and was not, I hope, lacking in vigor of argument. Tax reduction would remove some of the urgency of needed expenditure programs, be an alternative to starting new ones, and it would underwrite the ridiculous tight money policy.[8] The latter is greatly favored by those with money to lend; for them and their bankers, it is the practical equiva-

---

[6] Senator from Kentucky, former Ambassador to India under Eisenhower and personal friend.

[7] I later became more so.

[8] More precisely, it would be an alternative to reducing interest rates. But so, of course, would be an increase in public spending. My argument here was either wrong or disingenuous.

lent of the farm support prices. Only it is draped with all kinds of pietistic disguises. Few things make me more angry.

In the end, with the support of Dillon,[9] I think I largely destroyed the case for the cut. Arthur Goldberg half opposed me but only because he took his position before he had heard the arguments. Then with Goldberg I made the case for a spending program directed principally in favor of the unemployed — education grants for children, loans for home repair, a youth conservation corps, loans for community facilities. I was well pleased on the whole. But I hate to think, in my modest way, what the bankers will get away with once I am safely in India.

March 20 — Cambridge

At four this afternoon, I saw Mr. Pusey and converted my proposed resignation into a two-year leave of absence. Pusey adjured me that it must be two years and not one extra day. However, he did go so far as to ask me if I looked forward to being an ambassador.

My mail has reached mountainous proportions. Most of it is congratulatory. But a fair sprinkling involves proposals for doing good in India and petitions for posts there. I sense the beginning of a major flow from India asking for jobs or a chance to come to the United States to study.[10]

March 22 — Washington

I made a pilgrimage to Capitol Hill this morning to see J. William Fulbright and my own Senators. I am called for a hearing March 24. Both Massachusetts Senators, especially Saltonstall, were pleased and rather surprised by my courtesy and courtliness. I had a long

---

[9] This was an expedient coalition. At this stage, Dillon opposed a tax cut, not because he preferred increased expenditures, as did I, but because he opposed, or at least questioned the wisdom of, deliberately increasing the deficit. (See pages 381, 393.)

[10] A sound prediction. It continues to this day. One or two letters a week simply ask for money.

chat with Fulbright. He is good-looking, lively and amusing and complains that he is consulted by the Administration just five hours before it takes action. We talked about Laos where he thinks we are paying for past foolishness — we threw out the neutral government of Souvanna Phouma to get an incompetent one that would be on our side — and about John Foster Dulles whom he regards as having been a national disaster. We also talked about Joe McCarthy, against whose committee appropriation his was a lone vote, and about race. He thinks Dick Russell of Georgia is one of the few Southerners in the Senate with deep (as opposed to expedient) convictions on racial issues.

My detailed treatment by the FBI was the result of Bourke B. Hickenlooper's having heard that I had been refused a passport because of my acquaintance with Owen Lattimore. This was imaginary.[11] Also, there was a rumor that I had lived in the same New York apartment house with Corliss Lamont.[12] This is true: it was quite a large apartment house in New York. However, I imagine I might have survived a smaller dwelling without serious damage.

March 23 — Washington

A diplomatic or security briefing consists in approximately equal parts of what one already knows, couldn't remember or doesn't entirely believe. Such was the one by the CIA this morning on China and Chinese-Russian relations. When the geography was being covered and we reached the Tien Shan mountains (which separate Sinkiang from the Central Asian republics of the U.S.S.R.), I pointed out as matter-of-factly as possible that they were burned

[11] I met Lattimore only once or twice, although he seemed an interesting person whom I would have enjoyed knowing better. (Lattimore, a noted authority on China, was randomly accused by McCarthy in 1950 of being a Soviet agent.) The basis for the passport story is wholly unclear.

[12] Corliss Lamont, personal friend, philosopher and son of Thomas W. Lamont, the banker and Morgan partner, is a longtime supporter of left, radical and unpopular causes. Once before, in the early fifties, I had been asked to explain this dangerous cohabitation. I had done so with deeply affronted dignity.

indelibly in my memory because, on their slopes, a dog once bit me on the leg adjacent to the left testicle. This put the briefer off balance, and he never recovered. This afternoon I was briefed on the membership of the Senate Foreign Relations Committee. They are old friends but I listened with all proper patience to the State Department view of their crotchets.

This evening we had a long and interesting meeting on the new foreign aid organization — Labouisse,[13] Rostow, Shriver, et al. Names were reviewed for the organization, and it was decided to break as much as possible with the old bureaucracy. Afterwards I discussed Federal Reserve policy with Sorensen. The Federal Reserve has let interest rates go up in the last week after suspending open market operations. We must bring new pressure, and I am to draft a letter to William McChesney Martin, Jr.[14] That will be fun.

March 24 — Washington

The hearing on my nomination this morning was crowded with almost everyone but Senators. Only Fulbright, Sparkman (of Alabama), Wiley (ranking Republican of Wisconsin) and Lausche (of Ohio) were present — and Hubert Humphrey for a moment. I was tired and in poor voice. I ran interference for the other candidates, and when I left, so did much of the press and crowd.

Fulbright began the questioning by asking — in a voice that implied that he did not have the slightest idea — whether I had had any previous government experience. Then we turned to India, its problems and the relative prospects for industry and agriculture. Sparkman asked me if I were an "egghead socialist." I said that the appellation did not sound excessively complimentary; however, I was for having the government do what needed doing.

Then the shit hit the fan. Senator Wiley asked me where I

[13] Henry R. Labouisse, the first head of the aid organization — the International Cooperation Administration — and later Ambassador to Greece. Not thought quite up to the job of administering the aid organization, Labouisse, a soft-spoken man, eventually gave way to more formidable and less able replacements.
[14] See page 8.

stood on the recognition of Red China and its admission to the U.N. The only acceptable answer was never, never, never. I laid down the modest rule that the Chinese should be recognized and come in when they conceded the independence of Formosa and accepted the Charter. My answer was a trifle wordy. Then I had to repeat it because the Senator's hearing aid was not turned on — or I was too far from the microphone. He roared disapproval and I explained. Then Senator Lausche came in to ask how long I had harbored these thoughts. I found it hard to estimate. Sparkman then rescued me with a few well-chosen questions which made it clear that my position was the same as Henry Cabot Lodge's.[15] I embraced Lodge with unexampled enthusiasm.[16]

I did not feel that it was a distinguished job. But the audience evidently thought better of it. The China part is due for the exclusive play.

At the end, Sparkman, who was presiding, excused me and then Wiley insisted on recalling me to ask about Laos. I came out in favor of a completely non-communist government to be achieved totally without military intervention. This was wholeheartedly approved.

Aside from my distaste for dissembling (the exigencies of Laos apart), there is only one strategy to follow at these hearings. That is to speak, not to the Committee, but to your friends beyond. I might have gained a one-hour advantage by denouncing the Red Chinese and declaring we should never, never, never relent on recognition. But all my friends, remembering what I had previously said, would have known I was a crook. Better to take the medicine.

However, my performance wasn't particularly elegant. Much

[15] See page 6.

[16] There was another exchange which gained interest only as the result of later events. Senator Humphrey eloquently reminded the Committee that I was going to India, a country separated from China by the most formidable barriers of mountain, religion and culture. Therefore, my views on China were singularly irrelevant. There was an implication, at least, that India was the perfect place for a person of my heresy.

of my syntax had the Eisenhower touch. It is so when one is weary. The sentences are the first to suffer.

Later

The evening papers gave exclusive play to my two-China point. Never has common sense been more newsworthy. The Committee lacked a quorum and adjourned after the hearing without a vote.

The Schlesingers had an interesting party this evening which included the Udalls,[17] Denis Brogan,[18] Ben Cohen[19] and others. Brogan quoted Felix Frankfurter at some length. I have never been a great Frankfurter fan; I said his adult life had been poisoned by the need for identification with the great and for applause. Hence his liberal achievements were limited. Brogan cited Frankfurter's support of Sacco and Vanzetti. When I challenged him for more, he could not think of anything else. Udall is annoyed over the proposed regulation by the new Administration prohibiting anyone from accepting cash for articles and speeches. It is a bit rough on the man who needs marginal income of this sort. I could have complained that I had rather more to lose. But my feeling is that some sacrifice is worthwhile in order to have it imposed on J. Edgar Hoover. Any financial disincentive here raises the quality of our literature.

March 25 — Washington–Cambridge

The newspapers gave my testimony a sympathetic play — those, at least, that I saw. A file came in from U.S. Information Service, New Delhi, on my nomination. "The President's flair for getting the right man in the right place at the right time"; "*The Affluent Society* is to democracy what *Das Kapital* is to Communism." I sent it to Al Friendly of the *Washington Post*. If used, it might make me a Senate vote or two.

---

[17] Stewart L. Udall. The new Secretary of the Interior.
[18] Sir Denis Brogan. British political scientist and student of the American way.
[19] Benjamin Cohen, highly perceptive liberal member of the team of Corcoran and Cohen of Roosevelt days.

At eleven, the President had the new Asian Ambassadors in. He seemed unperturbed by my headlines — the *Times* had a front-page story on my testimony and the *Herald-Tribune* gave it two columns. Instead he adverted, half seriously, to my courage on the China issue. He asked if I thought it meant trouble; I replied that I thought not, meaning I hoped not.[20] He questioned the other Ambassadors in turn about their countries — Malaya,[21] Thailand[22] — and Reischauer on Japan.[23] All were exceedingly alert and well-informed and so was the President.

I used the occasion to give him a major economic memorandum including another proposed prod at the Federal Reserve. Sorensen doubts that it will get anywhere. Things are complicated by a column today by Bernard Nossiter in the *Washington Post* on the developing fight over interest rates. I was inadvertently responsible for the leak and hastily got off a note[24] taking the blame. This was not nobility; it was information that could only have come from me, and if you are certain to be blamed, you should at least get credit for candor. I also cooked up a spending program geared directly to the unemployed: payments for the children of the unemployed, loans and grants to out-of-work citizens for home improvement, loans and grants for community facilities in distressed cities. With revival, the people go to work and the spending automatically stops. I warned the President that, unless he took vigorous action, India, under my expert guidance, would catch up. He said he sensed this danger.

Finally, the blow. He wants a personal representative in India promptly because of the Laos troubles. He asked if I could leave in a week. I called Kitty and she was horrified.

[20] The day before, he had thought I had jeopardized my chances of confirmation at least slightly.
[21] Charles F. Baldwin.
[22] Kenneth Young.
[23] See page 40.
[24] To the President.

March 27 — Cambridge–Washington

I left at six this morning, arrived New York at seven, had breakfast at the Century and tried on my ceremonial clothes. I got a bargain, more or less, on a silk hat ordered by J.F.K. for the Inaugural which did not fit.[25] I was in Washington in time for a lunch with Lewis Jones.[26] An afternoon of briefing and appointments and a dinner. Weariness by eleven was total.

Earlier briefing, as I may have said, consisted of what I knew, couldn't remember and didn't believe. Today was concerned with smaller issues and much more valuable. I got into the Nepal, Tibetan Frontier and Kashmir questions. Toward the end of the afternoon, I went over the plans for the new Embassy Residence designed by Edward Durell Stone. It is most interesting and possibly a trifle too grand in the big state rooms. It will be a little like living on a balcony overlooking the main concourse of Grand Central Station.[27] The grounds are nice, and there is a swimming pool.

March 28 — Washington

A long and dreary day of briefing. This is partly a process by which I get information; partly it is an opportunity for agencies which seek to have business in New Delhi to latch on to a piece of the new ambassador for bureaucratic interests. At noon, word came over the ticker that I had been confirmed. The Committee was unanimous, with Lausche abstaining;[28] the Senate then accepted

[25] It cost, as I recall, some forty dollars and I ventured to wear it only twice. I took it as an income tax deduction.

[26] Then Assistant Secretary of State for Near East and South Asian Affairs. A Foreign Service Officer of high integrity and conservative temperament, he greatly impressed me at this lunch by urging the general elimination of clandestine activities (not very important) in my area of responsibility, which (as eventually became known) I carried through and to the general benefit of all.

[27] This indeed proved to be the case. But anyone seeking homelike surroundings does not need to become an ambassador.

[28] In 1968, Lausche was defeated for renomination. Asked to comment, I hazarded the guess that it was the result of the lingering resentment of the people of Ohio over this action. The explanation was not widely accepted.

without dissent. I would not have thought it possible to have escaped so easily. Goldwater, Bridges, Capehart and Karl Mundt[29] all tacitly on my side — a sobering thought. But mostly I did not think but tried to listen to the briefing.

Toward evening I had a visit from Rajeshwar Dayal,[30] the Indian diplomat who has been running the Congo force for the U.N. and who has been in endless conflict with Timberlake,[31] our Ambassador, and various Congolese factions. Opinion on him is bitterly divided, but I thought him very intelligent. I confined myself, however, to comforting him on his woes and congratulating him on having survived a difficult job.

Later I went to dinner with Averell Harriman[32] who is comfortably ensconced in a house in Georgetown. He is just back from Delhi where he pleaded with Nehru to seek the support of Khrushchev on behalf of a neutral settlement in Laos. He seems to think he was tolerably persuasive. Nehru spoke favorably of me but thought me rather outspoken. He adverted to my reference (during an earlier visit) to India's "post-office socialism." I had used this as a way of describing a commitment to public enterprises operated at no profit, hopefully no loss, with no particular efficiency and with no other clear purpose in mind. Everyone proceeded to put his own interpretation on the phrase.

The last thing was the television show on the Inaugural and after. We figured prominently[33] — there was one exceedingly beautiful shot of Kitty. I was shown asking my companions in the car what

[29] All conservative Senators.

[30] Dayal was on leave from his post as Indian High Commissioner to Pakistan. He subsequently resumed his career in the Indian Foreign Service and became Indian Ambassador in Paris and then permanent head (Secretary-General) of the Ministry of External Affairs.

[31] Clare H. Timberlake, a professional Foreign Service Officer, had previously served in India where he had aroused the suspicion of Nehru in connection with sundry Cold War maneuvers. Accordingly, in the Congo, he was much suspected by the Indians. He was soon replaced by Edmund A. Gullion, who brilliantly rescued Congo policy from an excess of involvement with the wrong people.

[32] See page 23.

[33] As noted, we had been selected along with Hubert Humphrey and one or two others as performers for the documentary on the day.

they considered the best phrase in the Inaugural speech. Kitty seemed to answer, "We shall never negotiate out of fear; we shall never fear to negotiate." Since I wrote this, Sorensen and the President will surely think I rigged the show. The answer was, in fact, given by Elaine Steinbeck.

March 29 — Washington

My briefing this morning was by the CIA and on various spooky activities, some of which I do not like. I shall stop them. Then Ex-Im Bank, then a medical examination, and then an endless round of further meetings. While returning from the Ex-Im Bank, I passed through the White House and met the President. We went up to meet a party gathered for the Swedish Prime Minister, Tage Erlander, and the President asked me en route about the show. He had noticed Kitty's seeming answer to my question. He said it was an outrageous exercise in organized self-promotion. He also asked me for a short memo on the Sixes and Sevens (the European Common Market and the European Free Trade Area named for their respective numbers of countries) and our proper policy thereto. He excused me when I pleaded that I was operating at full pressure. Outside, the photographers and newspapermen were sitting in the sun. I told them it must be a pleasant job. They said I was judging superficially.

There was a fine evening party at the Schlesingers' — Harriman, Adolf Berle,[34] Charles Bohlen,[35] George McGovern, Willard Wirtz.[36] Arthur made a pleasant reference to Harriman and Berle, who had been active in 1933 when F.D.R. came to power and still are, "The men who could stay the course." After dinner, we had a vigorous argument over foreign aid. Harriman said we were craven in the amounts asked; he attacked strenuously the ideas in my

[34] Personal friend, Roosevelt brain truster, former Ambassador to Brazil, and at that time Chairman of the Task Force on Latin America.
[35] See page 41.
[36] Then Undersecretary, later Secretary, of Labor.

paper, "A Positive Approach to Economic Aid."[37] I accused him of reasoning too glibly from the experience of the Marshall Plan when money was all that was needed to restore the vitality of states that had underlying organic strength. This was much easier than economic development in, say, northern South America where there was nothing of substance to build on. Here money, without underlying reform, will be wasted. Bohlen strongly supported me.

March 30 — Washington

I had breakfast with the President at 8:20 A.M. He was a little late and raced through orange juice, two or three eggs, bacon and coffee cake. When I stopped eating, he quickly finished up my share. We talked about India and he signed a letter to Nehru. With great amusement, he also suggested a letter to our ten-year-old son, Peter, proposing that he investigate the animal life of India and consider himself a member of the junior Peace Corps. (Peter has been reluctant and unhappy about committing himself to diplomacy.) He stopped a spooky operation of which I disapproved with a phone call — it was an unnecessary risk in the middle of the Laos negotiations (but at the behest of the Cold War bureaucracy, it was later reinstituted) and asked me how I had liked an article about me in the morning's *New York Times*. It described my election memos as "sharp, funny and mean." I said I objected to the *Times* describing me as arrogant. He said, "I don't see why. Everybody else does."

He hadn't read my economic memo (of March 25) but promised to do so. He approved my suggestion that Harriman see Dillon to urge the case for lower interest rates and to point out that Dillon would be the man on the spot if the economy continued to lag. As a conservative in a liberal administration, he (Dillon) would be the natural target. It is a fine strategy, and I don't think it will work.

[37] *Foreign Affairs*, April 1961.

At nine, we went into one of the reception rooms and met the Fulbrights and Jean Smith,[38] and they all took off by helicopter for Andrews Field. I returned to my briefings. Edward R. Murrow,[39] State, the Development Loan Fund, and on and on, ending at eight in the evening with a dinner given by the local Indian press and others. By the end of the day, I was totally done in and had still to fly back to Boston.

I worry about a serious residue of brinksmanlike adventuring in the Administration.[40] The same people who abetted Dulles and discredited the peaceful image of the United States are still about. Very late this afternoon, I talked with Bowles about it. He agrees but is uncertain if he can control it. I am uncertain too; he is insufficiently nasty.

April 2 — Cambridge

Parties in Cambridge yesterday and today. We have gone away so often that the bloom is off a bit. Still, it provides an excellent excuse for a gathering. One important difference between Washington and Cambridge emerges: there the title Ambassador is employed with genuine awe. In Cambridge it is offered, invariably, with a silly grin.

As I have told, when I was breakfasting with the President on Thursday he asked how the family was taking the removal. I mentioned Peter's reluctance. He proposed a letter to him — and one went replete with references to his own younger brothers and sisters when they went to London, the animal resources of India plus an appointment to a Junior Peace Corps. News of the letter promptly leaked out, and Peter has become a celebrity. Here is the letter:

---

[38] Mrs. Stephen Smith, the President's youngest sister.
[39] See page 23.
[40] This was the Bay of Pigs invasion, as it later came to be known, and which I had come to hear about more or less illegally during the previous day or two.

THE WHITE HOUSE
WASHINGTON

March 28, 1961

Dear Peter:

I learn from your father that you are not very anxious to give up your school and friends for India. I think I know a little about how you feel. More than twenty years ago our family was similarly uprooted when we went to London where my father was ambassador. My younger brothers and sisters were about your age. They had, like you, to exchange old friends for new ones.

But I think you will like your new friends and your new school in India. For anyone interested, as your father says you are, in animals, India must have the most fascinating possibilities. The range is from elephants to cobras, although I gather the cobras have to be handled professionally. Indians ride and play polo so you will come back an experienced horseman.

But more important still, I think of the children of the people I am sending to other countries as my junior peace corps. You and your brothers will be helping your parents do a good job for our country and you will be helping out yourself by making many friends. I think perhaps this is what you will enjoy most of all.

My best wishes,

Sincerely yours,

JOHN KENNEDY

I a little wish I were going also

Mr. Peter Woodard Galbraith,
30 Francis Avenue,
Cambridge, Massachusetts.

Last night when I arrived home, he was being interviewed by A.P., the *Globe, Herald* and *Sunday Advertiser*. He conducted himself with much dignity and aplomb although once he accused his younger brother, Jamie, of trying to horn in on his publicity. "I am the famous one, you know." He referred to the Peace Corps as the Corpse Peace.

Kitty and Emily[41] insisted on Jamie's having a place in the pictures. This morning they are on the front page. Nothing has such sentimental news value as attempted communication between the great and the young.

April 3 — Washington

Another formidable day during which I became a plenipotentiary *de jure*. We got up and off at the crack of dawn — Peter, Jamie, Kitty, with my secretary Mrs. Williams[42] as the advance guard. It was bright sunny spring all the way to Washington where it took two cars to move us all to town. I scribbled a speech on the way down and a final letter to the President and Allen Dulles expressing my concern over the surviving adventurism in the government. (This was still the Cuban business.) I put it very strongly to the President — we have had an unparalleled series of disasters, Yalu River, Guatemala, U-2, where we have failed to measure the overall political consequence of failure or (as in Guatemala) even success of military operations or intervention.[43]

I took Jamie and Peter on a tour of the White House in which they were only mildly interested. They sat on the President's chair, tried his telephone, inspected the Cabinet room, recognized the Stuart of Washington saved by Dolley Madison from the British and indignantly refused a gift of some of Caroline's toys. An Air Force officer made it up to them with some model airplanes.

Then at 12:30 P.M. came the swearing in. I had invited a hundred or so people and several Cabinet officers to what is ordinarily a rather sparse and intimate ceremony. Rusk in a pleasant speech recalled that I said in the past that India was less socialist than she

---

[41] See page 2.
[42] See page 2.
[43] However, to my discredit, I did not go to see the President on the matter, but contented myself (and my conscience) with making the record.

professed and the United States less capitalist than we claimed. In my remarks, I doubted that anyone could add anything to the clichés that had been traded on such occasions concerning the function of ambassadors. I pointed out that sometimes jobs had sought the man; sometimes, in less publicized instances, men had sought jobs. Mine was the third case where the two had met halfway. When President Kennedy had called me up to ask me to take the post, I had just begun to wonder how I might properly make a few hints. (This was not true. I had already hinted.)

After my speech, many photographs were taken, most of them of Peter. Now he is horning in on my publicity and I know how *he* felt when he thought Jamie was doing it to him.

Ambassador Chagla also spoke and took us to lunch. En route I had a chat with Heller — urged him to keep pressing on interest rates and to avoid taking too much of the President's time. (No one wants to see too much of an economist.) At lunch, I outranked the Chief Justice, I observed. That, obviously, is about as high as one can go. The Chaglas were charming.

More briefing in the afternoon including a visit to Robert McNamara. He told me that (in response to my petition) I am getting a new plane. A Convair. It is faster, smoother and pressurized and has been detached from a general. A good plane is obviously essential for a decent standard of living.

In the evening, we went to a dinner for Tage Erlander at the Swedish Embassy and distinguished ourselves by arriving a half hour late, during the soup. First, my letter to the President (on Cuba) had to be got off and then our driver got lost. I had great fun questioning Erlander, in front of Walter Reuther and Arthur Goldberg, on the effect on his political fortunes of the sales tax which they have just enacted. The Social Democratic vote increased after they imposed the tax. Finally, at midnight, I had a meeting with Shepard Stone[44] of the Ford Foundation on a program to provide lots of books to be given away by the Embassy.

[44] Director of International Affairs, Ford Foundation, since 1954. More recently President of the International Association for Cultural Freedom.

April 4 — Washington–London

At dawn we turned out of the Hay-Adams. With luggage and other problems, we arrived at the National Airport with only a minute to spare. For a little, it looked as though our mission to Delhi would be aborted by missing the New York plane. But we were put on, and sundry nervous lads from the State Department were greatly relieved.

Peter and Jamie came along with us to Idlewild and the parting there was a trifle tearful. The crossing was perfect, and by late afternoon, New York time, we were in London and on the way to the Ritz. A nice young man from the Embassy named Gordon Chase met us; I am becoming accustomed to being a third person, to wit, The Ambassador.

On the way over, I wrote my arrival speech for India. I cannot say anything. But I must talk. My solution is to be brief and say nothing and to speak ill of those who talk without saying anything.

April 5 — London–Beirut

This is now a very comfortable journey via jet with stops at Frankfurt, Vienna and Istanbul. I polished up my arrival statement en route and otherwise passed the time in a state of weariness. We arrived in Beirut about 7:30 P.M., were met by a formidable delegation from the Embassy and went to a pleasant dinner with Ambassador and Mrs. Robert McClintock. Lebanon looked much as before — partly Mediterranean and partly Oriental. There is much new building out of oil money. The currency is strong, the gold cover huge and there are lots of cars and tourists. After the troubles of two years ago, the political situation is stable with the top jobs carefully divided, in the manner of a New York political ticket, between the various religious claimants — Sunni and Shi'a Moslems and Christians. The Lebanese are the least temperamental of the Arabs — there is a story that at the outbreak of the Israeli war in 1948, they pulled back their army several miles since wars raise the danger of death by shooting. The Ambassador says that this is not so.

April 6 — Beirut

I slept nearly twelve hours and so did Kitty. Both of us feel nearly human again. At noon, I talked to the Embassy staff meeting. Then I went to lunch with the Ambassador and the Indian Chargé, saw some friends and finally went to dinner with a prospective public affairs officer. The Indian Chargé is the Maharajah of Alirajpur, a very small state in central India. At Independence he took a civil service examination and made the transition from despot to bureaucrat with no difficulty whatever. He is charming and so, especially, is his wife.

I spoke to the Embassy staff meeting of developments in Washington from the White House perspective — of the new Assistant Secretary for the area, the new aid program, a new attitude toward the public service, some possible lines of development on foreign policy. People who are a long way from home have a natural desire for identification with high policy — as do people at home for that matter. Modesty is not, in this situation, an unrelieved blessing. One can cultivate both his own vanity and that of his audience by presuming to great knowledge and importance.

By day, Beirut is busy, untidy and reminiscent of a half-finished city in southern California. The sky is clear and the water outside our hotel is very blue. The people have an aspect of well-fed rascality which may not be entirely misleading.

April 7 — Beirut

A bright blue Mediterranean day and one of the most relaxed of recent memory. We did some shopping and then drove out along the coast road to the Dog River to see the old Roman bridge — of three light stone arches — and the inscriptions cut in the rocks. These inscriptions, cut by all the passing armies of history from Darius to the Free French, are in a narrow passage between the hills and the sea. The instinct to immortalize oneself by writing on a wall seems basic; excavations of the primeval privy no doubt prove the point. Actually, much of the romance is gone from the

Dog River. The ancient road once wound along a narrow cor-
niche. It was here, at the narrowest corner, that the armies shaved
a space on the rock and carved their names. Even five years ago
the place had a sparse, barren and romantic aspect. Now a highway
tunnel has been cut under the hill where it juts out to the coast,
and future armies will write their names on the inside of an under-
pass.

For lunch we drove to a restaurant below Sidon and had fish
fresh from the Mediterranean plus various hot Arab condiments
at thieving prices. Then we looked at the Château de la Mer at
Sidon — a small Crusader castle at the end of a short causeway in
the harbor. The soft sandstone walls were stiffened by cross sections of hard granite columns from some earlier temple. It is pleasant in a modest way — but no Krak des Chevaliers.[45] Thereafter
we went swimming and to dinner with the Indian Chargé.

His wife is black-haired, black-eyed, with a lovely face and figure
and a marvelously alert intelligence. Their previous post was in
Nyasaland in the (then) Central African Federation. Here Indians
are classed as "natives." Her husband's diplomatic position and
family origins notwithstanding, they were subject to an endless
and continuing round of indignities. She could not go to a movie
or even purchase a bathing suit in a store without being asked,
"What are you doing in here?" Once when a friend invited them
to dinner, several whites left. "I didn't realize Johnny had Kaffirs
in." Once a plumber came to mend a tap and was about to leave
when he found it a colored household. She persuaded him that
taps were the same whether in white or nonwhite households and
gave him a beer. He was converted and surreptitiously brought
her flowers every week or so thereafter. She is one of the most
beautiful girls I have ever seen so it wasn't entirely the beer. (We
saw much of them later in India, and I never changed my view that

---

[45] The most magnificent of all castles defended by the Knights of the Order of
the Hospital of St. John of Jerusalem — the Hospitallers — to the north and east
of Beirut in what is now Syria.

the Maharani was one of the most beautiful women I have ever admired.)

Their telephone was tapped because they were suspected by the police of being in touch with African nationalist leaders. Later their tapper went to bed at midnight and turned off the phone. After protesting to the government, they were able to get all-night tapping restored.

Neither was bitter about the experience but neither do they take it lightly. A Lebanese businessman who was at dinner said firmly, at the end of this conversation, that he believed that education was more important as a measure of social acceptability than race or color. His liberality was applauded.

On the way to dinner, I visited a display of Indian products and was well-photographed admiring saris which were draped, less indecently than one might imagine, around machine tools and mechanical pumps.

IV

India at First

April 9 — New Delhi

Last night we arrived and not, I am happy to say, without fanfare. I should have preferred arriving, as did the Viceroys, from the sea at the Gateway of India in Bombay and a triumphal train passage to New Delhi, but one must make do with the twentieth century. And it wasn't too bad. Certainly better than an average landing at Logan.

I first came to India in 1956 on Air-India International from Zurich, and on that occasion because of terrible storms in Europe, we were forty hours late. Yesterday, flying in on the same line from Beirut, it became evident that we were going to land about an hour early. I had prepared a statement for use on arrival — mimeographed, with a version on tape for the All-India Radio, and foresaw the likelihood of using this eloquence on a welcoming party of ticket agents and mendicants. But I had the happy idea of asking Air-India to radio ahead, and meantime the Embassy had been advised. So we pulled up to the ramp to a very decent house. (We learned later that the members of the Mission had been rounded up from golf courses, siestas, family outings, and other recreations in response to the crisis caused by our earliness.)

As we emerged on the gangplank, we were garlanded with (literally) several pounds of flowers and met by a legion of photographers. Under the care of the Indian Chief of Protocol, Mr. S. K. Banerji, and Messrs. C. Tyler Wood and Edward Maffitt, the Economic and Political Ministers of the Embassy respectively, we were guided to the edge of the field and to more photographers and to be introduced to the members of the Country Team.[1] They seemed surprisingly glad to see me. Because of my briefing, plus a little extra work, I was able to greet each with some amiable reference to his background and experience.

Then we had more garlands from the Indo-American Friendship Society, the Cambridge Students and Old-Boys Association and numerous other bodies to the extent of, perhaps, another twenty pounds. Finally, after much waving and salutation, we were escorted to our automobiles, and I with Banerji and Maffitt, and Kitty with Ty Wood and Margaret Jones (the wife of the senior Embassy staff member) were brought to the Residence. The latter has a large brass plate on the gate which reads "John Kenneth Galbraith, Ambassador of the United States." This made a favorable impression on me.

The house itself is a one-story bungalow from the days of the British Raj with a large terrace and nice grounds. The walls are white and the furniture is in white and blue and is surprisingly noninstitutional. There are only three bedrooms and evidently the boys and Emily, when they come, are to be housed immediately adjacent to the state dining room which, incidentally, is not very grand and holds only about sixteen people at a maximum. One of their normal explosions of juvenile wrath will have a remarkable effect on a state dinner.[2]

What does an ambassador do when he arrives at his post at seven o'clock in the evening? Well, I chatted briefly with Ty Wood and Maffitt and then with my personal aide, a nice young man named Gil Wing, who stands in some awe of me. Then we had a drink,

[1] The heads of all the Washington agencies — State, USIS (United States Information Service), AID, Army, Navy, Air Force — represented in the country. I made little use of it — most problems concerned only a few of the members and to defer to the body as a whole involved an obvious surrendering of authority.

[2] They had eventually to be housed in a separate house a couple of hundred yards away. See page xi.

had dinner and went to bed. The dinner was a disenchanting experience. The soup, made of bouillon cubes, was normal. This was followed by leathery roast chicken, served in some oleaginous sauce combined with a plate of paris-green pebbles got up to resemble green peas. The excuse for this horror then became evident. The cook had spent his time constructing a dessert in pale purple of ice cream and wafers to resemble the Gateway of India. It was architecturally magnificent and highly inedible.

I slept badly; the late evening alcohol plus the memory of the Gateway had undone me. But it was very nice to have tea and an orange in bed and then have breakfast on the terrace. I had asked for fresh fruit, a scrambled egg and toast. I got canned grapefruit, a poached egg and bacon. It takes some skill to spoil a breakfast — even the English can't do it. But our cook can. His bacon was what turned Islam against pork.

Our garden is better. It is a pleasant L-shaped stretch of brilliant green surrounding the house on two sides and bordered by flowers. Back of the house, it is shaded by a huge tree of still undetermined species. All is trim and modestly elegant. I might have mentioned that the weather was in the cool eighties last night and is still quite tolerable.

April 10 — New Delhi

Yesterday morning we toured the new Chancery. It is an interesting and lively building with its great covered court filled with water, flowers and live ducks. Our official ornithologist, Mr. Bump, was feeding the ducks when we arrived. My offices are modern and comfortable, and the building is well air-conditioned. I am not at all sure it is practical and it is a trifle grand. But why not some modest grandeur? The new Ambassador's Residence[3] is now in the very early stages of construction next door. Everything is strategically located between Red China on the one side and the U.S.S.R. on the other. Portugal was a neighbor but has withdrawn. The Diplo-

3 See page 49.

matic Enclave where all embassies are being built is a dusty stretch of Ganges Plain which is only gradually being redeemed from desert. Near the Chancery is the staff housing — both American and Indian — and the surroundings seem very hot and dusty. The British and Russian Governments afford a swimming pool for their staffs and children but we do not. Children in this climate surely need a place to get wet.

Maffitt came to lunch and we talked until around four. Then Kitty and I walked in the adjoining Lodi Gardens,[4] meeting en route the nineteen-year-old daughter of our Naval Attaché who kept up a running fire of conversation on life among the young in New Delhi. She made it sound both interesting and responsible. Then we took a drive through Old Delhi where the Red Fort, as ever, struck me with its vastness and magnificence. The Moghuls were builders beyond equal and the great wall, facing the old city, is grand and endless. The rich salmon pink is enchanting.[5] We looked briefly at the University which, like so many in this part of the world, is a little too impressive and much too unkempt. Something less should be spent on the new and much more on maintaining the old. A palace is a palace only so long as it is polished to a certain elegance. A shabby and squalid palace is very squalid.

April 11 — New Delhi

Yesterday was my first as an A.E.&P.[6] and, needless to say, I began with a speech. It was on a lawn back of the staff quarters near the Chancery and next to a slight rocky hump known locally as Bunker Hill.[7] Most of my audience consisted of Indian employees who are known as "locals." This term I must reform. I took

[4] A lovely park which contains the tombs of the members of the Turkish Sayyids and Afghan Lodis who ruled in Delhi before the Moghuls. They built their fine domed tombs for their future repose before they died. It was possible that they foresaw that no one would think well enough of them to do so afterward.

[5] The Red Fort, in the view of many, myself included, is one of the greatest sights of India. It was started in 1639 by Shah Jahan who also built the Taj Mahal. The latter, his supreme act of artistic patronage, overshadows the Red Fort in public reputation but not entirely in style and grandeur.

[6] Ambassador Extraordinary and Plenipotentiary.

[7] After Ellsworth Bunker.

the occasion to urge a few worthy beliefs — that civility and good manners are the essence of good behavior even when dealing with Communists, that everyone knows whom we are against but might be less clear about what we are for, and I quoted J.F.K's State of the Union paragraph on the public service as a "proud and lively" career. I was able to do this with exceptional unction for I had written it.

Then I talked with Maffitt and the senior political staff at length on the Congo and Laos. I was tolerably well in the picture from my Washington reading and briefing. Both seem on the way to settlement. The Indian contingent is about to arrive in the Congo. It is well-disciplined and of considerable size. I would think its stabilizing influence would be enormous; the Indians have done the world and the U.N. a big service on this. They should be given much credit.

Then I chatted with my personal staff including my secretary, Margaret Welch, a Foreign Service veteran and obviously a woman of rare competence but, unhappily, nearing the end of her tour here. Then I had lunch with the "senior wives," a group my wife is relying upon for assistance. The wife of my Political Counselor, Mrs. Wallace Stuart, is a Bolivian by birth who speaks agreeably informal English with much intelligence and is greatly reassured by the fact that a foreigner has become an ambassador. (I told her it was better for a diplomat to be foreign-born. It gave him perspective.)

After lunch, I learned about security. The chief security officer is an agreeable man who speaks in a professionally hushed and conspiratorial voice. He suspects much in the way of microphones, other listening devices and assorted bugs, but nothing, I learned on pressing the point, has ever been discovered on our premises in India. However, he told me in justification that in the Curtain countries microphones had been unearthed by the bushel. I propose a policy of strict discipline on all needed rules and a scrupulous avoidance of all unnecessary ones.

Later I talked with Kenneth Bunce, the head of the U.S. Information Service, a diligent but not especially imaginative man, who is leaving. I made it clear that henceforth I would be setting policy. Finally, I had a chat with the Service Attachés. All are mature and pleasant men. The Air Attaché, Colonel Hannah,[8] had just heard that he was getting a Convair. He was suitably impressed when he learned of the fountain from which his blessing flowed. Dinner at home. The food was a little better. Kitty did not have enough to do all day. In consequence, she is planning a vast number of enterprises of which a massive attack on Hindi is the least alarming.

I took home to read, casually, a new bulletin on protocol about to be issued to newcomers. It is an appalling document, full of invidious references to diplomatic rank, ungrammatical and, where not insulting, stupid. Nothing could be better designed to frighten or demoralize the shy newcomer. Employees are told to consort with Hungarians only to a "limited extent" as distinct from Chinese to whom they are only to be polite. On being invited by the Iron Curtain embassies, they are to consult "classified" instructions — this is in an unclassified document. Women are told they may on certain occasions forgo stockings "if legs permit."[9]

April 12 — New Delhi

Yesterday morning was mostly consumed by a photographer from USIS getting official pictures in front of the flag and the new Chancery building. The latter, I discover, is (sometimes) called the Taj Maria — evidently in honor of Ed Stone's wife. She should know that her namesake died producing, plus or minus, her fourteenth child.

Then I had a talk with Ty Wood, Minister of Economic Affairs and head of the technical assistance and aid program.[10] I discovered

---

[8] Colonel George Hannah, Jr., AAF, was the competent and unfailingly agreeable Air Attaché during nearly all of my tour.

[9] A much more civilized version eventually appeared.

[10] And also, by coincidence, an old family friend. As a Wall Street broker, he had years earlier with great intelligence guided my father-in-law's and our own modest investment decisions.

that our diagnosis of past errors and present prospects in the aid program is about the same. A few years ago, all American activities were regarded with much suspicion by the Indians. Accordingly, when we were asked for help — in remedial reading, occupational therapy, flower arrangement — we were delighted and responded enthusiastically. The resulting pattern of technical assistance activities was totally haphazard. We agree that concentration is essential beginning with water, plant and plant production and fertilizer — the things that get food grains. Nothing else is so important; everything else may consume scarce energy.

Ty lives in a vast but ugly house with a large but slightly unkempt garden — ours by contrast is smaller but more elegant. We lunched and thereafter I had a chat with Dr. Earnest C. Watson. Dr. Watson, a former Dean of Faculty at Caltech and a well-known physicist, is the most distinguished member of my faculty. There had been some talk of abolishing the post of scientific attaché as an unnecessary expense. I reassured him.

India has now three reactors and is said to be stockpiling plutonium. There is much talk of an atomic power plant; this is highly controversial and probably unduly expensive. But it is a considerable prestige item, in this respect like jet aircraft — but better.

Later the barber came and cut my hair — the first time I had ever failed to resort to the regular establishment. Then Paul Rosenstein-Rodan[11] came to call. Rosy, at least, was sure the atomic power plant should not be built — 30 percent more expensive than a new thermal plant. He also lectured me firmly on the other of my new responsibilities. Then, though I had a splitting headache, we got through a big buffet for our Embassy staff. The food was not too bad although the chicken took some chewing.[12] Sharply at 10:30 P.M., Ty Wood, the senior ranking guest, departed and everyone else disappeared as though with dysentery. They impress

[11] Professor of Economics at Massachusetts Institute of Technology, specialist on India and old personal friend.
[12] For large occasions, the cook got outside help which was better.

me as an able and devoted group of people and not bad company. Kitty reluctantly allowed the servants to wash the dishes and tidy up.

Later

Today began with a headache from strain, the kind I used to get arguing (in the Democratic Advisory Council) with Leon Keyserling, which kept me in bed until nearly noon. Then I went to the office where I have changed the routine to arrive at the front steps and walk up. Before, the car went into the basement and sent a flurry of frightened functionaries hastening to call the elevator for me.

At lunch, Douglas Ensminger[13] talked about the new intensive agricultural program — selected districts of the country which are being subjected, hopefully, to a saturation of the best in irrigation, fertilizer, improved seed and plant protection; the problem of rehabilitating Calcutta where the Congress Party has at last discovered that something is wrong; the prospect for an entirely new and distinctly better university than any now existing; and arrangements for ambassadorial recreation. He recommends Kashmir which sounds eminently sensible to me.

The new university, he thinks, would render a great service by breaking loose from the patriarchal domination of the present institutions and making a new start. The problems are, apart from money, how to ensure that the old men do not move in here too and how to get better men without merely robbing the existing universities of the present scarce talent. Recall of Indian students from abroad — with the higher pay — would solve the second problem. Keeping out the patriarchs strikes me as more difficult. I think the university location should be high and somewhat cool to attract Europeans.

After lunch, Kitty and I were photographed at great length

[13] Longtime head of the Ford Foundation in India, by training an agricultural specialist.

looking at birds, flowers and each other and at five I called on the
Prime Minister. This involved some ceremony.

First, I went to the Foreign Office where I picked up the Chief
of Protocol. Then we went to Nehru's Parliament office where
we made our way through the crowded antechamber. Then after
a short wait we were ushered in. It was the same smallish, slightly
used-looking and not very handsome office in which I had visited
him two years before. I presented myself as the most amateur of
diplomats. He proclaimed himself an amateur prime minister. I
think that truth will not be a barrier to our association — both of
us were professing a modesty no one else would find creditable.
We then chatted about our respective books, Cambridge University
in our respective days there, and the improvement in India which
I told him I measured by the number of bicycles. He agreed on the
value of this index. He said that he had heard that the new Administration was dominated by Rhodes Scholars. I said that the key
positions in the world were still held by Cambridge men. Then, as
I was about to go, he said he wanted to talk of the Congo. This
continued for half an hour or more — rather to the discomfort of
the new French Ambassador who was waiting his turn. He mentioned the misunderstanding of Lumumba — "not a Communist
and he probably doesn't know what Communism is"; the delays
in transporting Indian troops;[14] the insufficiently hard stand against
the white irregulars and Belgians; the mistreatments of Dayal[15] by
the U.S. papers "with some official inspiration"; the shortcomings
of Timberlake, the United States Ambassador in the Congo;[16] and
the prediction of some unspecified American that India intended
to colonize the Congo. Despite all the briefing, I would have handled myself better if I had been informed. Where I could respond,
as in the case of the reference to colonization, I did: "I am sure you
know that no responsible member of the American Government

[14] For the United Nations force there. Transport had been promised by the
United States.
[15] See page 50.
[16] See page 50.

ever made any such statement." For the rest, I found silence golden but uncomfortable. Afterward, I sent off my first cable to the Department and then went to dinner pleasantly with my chief Political Counselor.

April 13 — New Delhi

I displayed my exceptionally modest administrative talents this morning — I reviewed plans to build offices in the basement of the new Chancery which seemed insane; I considered the Residence which is under construction but on strike — the contractor seems to be chiseling on the minimum wage and is paying something less than two rupees (about forty cents) a day; and I went into the matter of a swimming pool for our staff and youngsters. I also sent a note of congratulations to the Soviet Ambassador on "the epochal journey of Major Gagarin." I was officially advised that the household staff is competent in all matters and included even one or two experts in imaginative larceny. "They stole the Bunkers blind." (This was a grave exaggeration. Ellsworth Bunker emerged quite solvent.) I borrowed some books from USIS for the empty bookshelves at the Residence and had lunch with my Cultural Counselor, and dinner with Maffitt and my old classmate at California, Robert Carr, who is now Consul-General in Bombay. Maffitt's cooking, as also his wine, improves greatly on that of the Residence.

April 14 — New Delhi

At precisely ten this morning I went to the Ministry of External Affairs and began calls — at the rate of ten or fifteen minutes a man — on all the principal officers — the Secretary-General, the Foreign Secretary, the Commonwealth Secretary, the Joint Secretary and the head of the Western Division, a unit which includes Russia, Western Europe and the Americas.[17] From here, the West

---

[17] The Secretary-General, R. K. Nehru, a cousin of the Prime Minister, was the ranking officer in the Ministry of External Affairs. M. J. Desai, the Foreign Secretary, carried the major burden of day-to-day responsibility. Y. D. Gundevia, the Commonwealth Secretary, dealt extensively with Pakistan affairs.

looks smaller and more homogeneous than from Washington. Mostly the discussion was social; all had read with great approval J.F.K.'s letter on my behalf.[18] The problem in getting Indian troops to the Congo did come up. There seems still to be thick confusion on this — some military mix-up — although later in the day a telegram or two came in suggesting improvement, and I am getting off a letter to the Prime Minister. The final draft was full of formal phrases — "my government," "démarche" — and I rewrote it in English.

At noon, I lunched with Ty Wood and G. D. Birla, the industrialist.[19] Birla told me that he had twice read *The Affluent Society* and then asked that I urge the Indian Government to be less severe in auditing the books of American corporations with which the Birlas are associated in India and that it allow Indian businessmen to take their wives abroad on business trips. He explained that under present arrangements the firms from whom the businessmen are buying invite the wives, pay their expenses and then add the cost of the wives to the price of the goods purchased. Since the latter are often paid for by foreign aid, the wives are ultimately paid for by the American taxpayer. Birla believes it would be better to legitimatize this arrangement. I indicated disinclination.

We spent the afternoon on economic matters preparatory to the

[18] A friendly letter of introduction and good wishes sent by the President to Nehru on my behalf which was, I may now confess, a modest tribute to my own drafting skill.

[19] The head of the house of Birla, which with the Tatas is one of the two largest industrial groups in India. The Birlas are Marwaris, which means they originate in the great western Indian state of Marwar (Jodhpur), a part of India enormously productive of businessmen and a desert in most other respects. They are devout Hindus; the Tatas, by contrast, are Parsis, a community that came to India in the seventh century from Persia and which also showed phenomenal business aptitude. All sons of the Birla family, virtually without exception, go into the firm. Sons-in-law do not. Business acumen is thus assumed, in effect, to be inherited, and there is considerable practical evidence to support the view. In strict legal theory, the Birlas are not a company or a corporate combination but a Managing Agency exercising control on behalf of passive owners who, however, would encounter grave difficulty in disestablishing their servants or, in the slightest degree, influencing their actions. Although always keeping a cautious foot in all camps, the Birlas made an early alliance with Gandhi and Indian nationalism, and it was in the garden of Birla House, the New Delhi residence of G. D. Birla, that the Mahatma was slain by a Hindu fanatic on January 30, 1948.

meeting of the aid consortium — of the agencies and countries providing aid to India — to be held in Washington the end of the month. One question is whether we should finance the atomic power plant and also a new steel mill which the Indians badly want. Sentiment is adverse on the part of my staff, but I am more favorably disposed. I shall bring them around by degrees.

Various Cambridge (Massachusetts) friends dropped in for the evening — much like home. Kitty is gradually or not so gradually assuming control of the household. We have not yet discovered how many people work for us. New faces appear each day, some with functions, some without. A vast throng of people pass our door, sign the book and leave their cards. Disguised unemployment in India extends to all levels of society.

April 15 — New Delhi

Almost everyone seems to work here on Saturday although in a rather more relaxed fashion. I spent the morning getting into a variety of matters and sent a clarifying letter to Nehru on our Congo policy. I am still a trifle unclear as to what I clarified, but later in the day the government press secretary said that the U.S. had not been interfering with the movement of the U.N. Indian forces. At noon, the Henry Stebbinses came to lunch; he is a career diplomat and Ambassador to Nepal. Then I slept and slept — blessed knitting of the raveled sleeve.

I end the first week with a fair grasp of my duties. The job itself is amusing and interesting and one for which I have four considerable qualifications — a grasp of the economic situation, considerable ease in written and spoken communication, some knowledge of politics and an unquestioned willingness to instruct other people in their duty. On the other hand, I am accustomed to saying what I think on any question — and of consciously suspecting the official line. To rationalize and explain and cover up as Washington requires will come very hard.

Before I went to bed, I had my first critical look at *Span*, the

USIS magazine for circulation in India, and did not much like what I saw. The articles are poorly selected and editing is poor or absent. But worst of all, the layouts stink. Pictures, typography, captions are an awful jumble. I could correct but it will be more important to get someone out here who can do the job properly.

April 17 — New Delhi

Yesterday morning we went for a drive and then helped open a children's art exhibit. Then we had visitors ending up with Pitambar Pant,[20] his wife Bhanu and their small children for tea. The latter are very cute.

Nothing, I think, so rejoices me as our garden. The lawn has a thick rich pile of deep green; beyond is a garish but bright gay border of flowers. And within and around are majestic trees. It is not large but very adequate. Beyond a back wall are the staff quarters. There I visited for the first time today to see our bearer who is ill. The houses there are small one-room and two-room affairs looking out on a clean brick yard. The youngsters are clean and well-dressed. Still, it obviously makes a considerable difference whether one is born an Anglo-Saxon or an Indian. I wonder how this decision gets made.

✧ ✧ ✧

New Delhi, India
April 17, 1961

Dear Mr. President:

As I once told you, I think, I propose to revive the ancient and admirable custom of an occasional letter from the envoy if

[20] The head of the Indian Perspective Plan, an official of the Indian Statistical Institute and now a member of the Planning Commission of the Government of India. He was an old personal friend. The Indian Statistical Institute is a semi-official data-gathering and research organization in Calcutta, headed by the distinguished statistician, P. C. Mahalanobis, and much frequented in these years by scholars from all lands. I spent some months there in 1956.

not to his sovereign at least to his sovereign source of authority.[21] Since, however, this practice could easily bitch up modern procedure (to borrow from the stately language of Metternich) I will avoid matters where I am in need of advice or action. These I will put in channels or, in high-level emergency, in a special letter. The present communications . . . will be modestly informative and conceivably entertaining and you can read them (or not read them) in the secure knowledge that you will neither encounter (nor miss) any crisis. If I have anything in mind it will be simply to let you see something of India and Asia and of its leaders and its problems through the eyes of your ambassador.

We have been here now for a week. I have lunched or dined with all of my senior officers, had lengthy sessions on the various embassy enterprises — politics, economics, aid, USIS, labor, science and other — spoken to the staff, seen Nehru for a lengthy talk, called on the senior Foreign Office officials and encountered a few of my Indian friends. Some of this is legally a bit premature for I do not present my credentials for another day or two.

We were, of course, given an amiable welcome and the radio carried in full my remarks on arrival which, faithful to the fraud of modern communications, I recorded in Beirut and never gave at all. Some fifteen or twenty pounds of garlands were laid on in a manner that must have rejoiced the local florists. Our physical arrangements are enchanting. The residence, a one-time bungalow of the British raj, is small — only three bedrooms — and the principal wall decorations are some large gilt mirrors left behind possibly by Lord Curzon. Some of the furniture was discarded from the White House by Mrs. Warren G. Harding. But basically it is a charming house with a large loggia and a reach of thick green lawn, floral borders in violent color and great trees that are a constant delight. The staff is of alarming size but

---

[21] This wording implies that the idea of the letters came from me. However, my memory is quite clear that the President proposed them — following, though I am less certain of this, some expression of doubt as to how an ambassador really employed himself.

Arrival with garlands

BEGINNING

Arrival with hat

Hearty welcom

Family deployment: C.A.G., James, Pete
Emily Wilson, J.K.G. (Absent: Alan Galbraith

THE WHITE HOUSE

WASHINGTON

March 28, 1961

Dear Peter:

I learn from your father that you are not very anxious to
give up your school and friends for India. I think I know
a little about how you feel. More than twenty years ago
our family was similarly uprooted when we went to London
where my father was ambassador. My younger brothers
and sisters were about your age. They had, like you, to
exchange old friends for new ones.

But I think you will like your new friends and your new
school in India. For anyone interested, as your father
says you are, in animals, India must have the most
fascinating possibilities. The range is from elephants
to cobras, although I gather the cobras have to be handled
professionally. Indians ride and play polo so you will come
back an experienced horseman.

But more important still, I think of the children of the people
I am sending to other countries as my junior peace corps.
You and your brothers will be helping your parents do a good
job for our country and you will be helping out yourself by
making many friends. I think perhaps this is what you will
enjoy most of all.

My best wishes,

Sincerely yours,

[signature]

Mr. Peter Woodard Galbraith
30 Francis Avenue
Cambridge, Massachusetts

Peter's letter

The Roosevelt House. Finished in 1962

THE SCENE — I

Chancery — central water court

Household saint
(By Jo Davidson)

Great — very great — hall

The housekeepers

considerable competence, and the cook, while in no danger of being stolen by you, is anxious to please. Your new man may be better on sauces but cannot touch mine in reproducing the Taj Mahal in macaroons. The new Ed Stone Chancery is even more of a delight. Some complain that it is highly unfunctional — water fountains, water gardens and even a few ducks but no office space. You certainly can't please everyone.

The new Chancery is located in an uninviting stretch of terrain on the edge of town which has been set aside for embassies. It is flat, dusty and barren. The junior Americans and their Indian staff live in adjacent quarters with slight protection from sun, dust and heat. At this time of the year it is around 90 at midday but before long it will get warm. The Russian embassy and quarters are on one side; on the other side are the British. In both compounds the youngsters splash happily in swimming pools; one was once contemplated for ours but abandoned lest it seem un-American. I have asked for the development of plans. Most of the cost, I might add, will be paid for out of the abundant PL 480 counterpart so that your budget will suffer no more than from a very minor Nubian temple.[22]

The size of the total staff — 300 Americans, 726 Indians — came to me rather as a shock. My preliminary impression is of well-mannered, competent and hard-working people of good morale. From my deputy, Edward Maffitt, I have had firm and courteous guidance and good judgment in the tradition of the true professional. Past experience of the staff with ambassadors has been favorable so it is favorably disposed toward us. We are, to be sure, expected to combine the best qualities of the Bowleses, the Coopers and the Bunkers but that ought to be easy. I am not quite sure where the line falls in this business between dignity and stuffiness. I shall try to combine decorum and disci-

---

[22] I had taken up with him, as had others, the matter of rescuing the Nubian monuments, including Abu Simbel, from the Nile waters rising behind the new Aswan Dam.

pline with a reasonably relaxed attitude toward rank but, of course, without descending to the raffish informality of the White House.

The senior officials of the Foreign Ministry are intelligent and on easy terms with the Embassy. Communications seem to involve a minimum of restraint. My first talk with Nehru was not quite so easy — I am not entirely at home in his presence and I rather wonder if anyone is. (A strong political leader is, I think, one who raises a certain moral threshold against disagreement.) He read your letter with obvious enjoyment (and later circulated it to his officials) and we talked for a bit about books, the number of bicycles as an index of progress, and other trivia. Then he turned to the Congo which is very much on his mind. His principal concern here was the delay in getting the troops from Dar-es-Salaam and getting out the Belgian and white irregulars. (Dayal and Timberlake came up but less centrally.) I have reported on all this to the Department. One general point struck me hard. The Indian Government feels that it has committed itself deeply with this Contingent and is worried about it. The U.N. was faltering and is very important in Indian eyes and to Indian policy. The troops shored up the U.N. position, may well save it, but the domestic risks now seem more considerable.

We talked in Nehru's Parliament office — a smallish, rather shabby room, indifferently furnished, not far from the floor of Parliament. He is usually here when the House is sitting; this is an aspect of his determination to get parliamentary habits firmly fixed during his lifetime. The central Parliament functions at least as efficiently and equably as the Senate. In the provincial capitals, however, they throw things in their moments of truth. I could not see that Nehru had aged since I saw him last — about two years ago. His face is smooth and unlined and handsome. When I left, he asked that my new role not prevent me from continuing as an economic adviser to his government. I told him I hoped it wouldn't but that my voice might now be a trifle muted.

When I was first here in 1956, the tension between the United States and India — and between Americans and Indians — was evident, palpable. Three years later in 1959, things were much easier. Now I would sense a still further relaxation — it is necessary now that at least some members of the government remind themselves that they are neutral. Things being so I doubt that I can make much of a score.

In the next letter or so I will give you among other things some working impressions of the Indian economy — I must find out whether the Central Bank is maintaining its independence or could use Martin[23] — and on some of the strength and weaknesses of Embassy operations.

Yours faithfully,
JOHN KENNETH GALBRAITH

The President
The White House

✧ ✧ ✧

April 18 — New Delhi

Yesterday morning I looked into the USIS and in the afternoon on TCM or USOM[24] as technical assistance is variously called. I did not much care for what I found. Of the two, USIS is the best — but in all its aspects deadly dull. Magazines, books, film subjects — I shudder at the thought of the films — are totally pedestrian. A large and hideous supersonic jet fighter was on display in the entry but most of the effort seems reasonably pacific and restrained. A table showing the collected propaganda efforts of the Iron Curtain countries gave me some comfort. With the exception of a stunning Polish magazine and some East German cheesecake at the *Playboy* level, it all seemed as bad or worse. I

[23] William McChesney Martin, Jr. Currently, as before and since, there was much discussion of the independence of the Federal Reserve System and Martin's insistence thereon.
[24] With the Kennedy Administration, TCM for Technical Cooperation Mission and USOM for United States Operations Mission became AID for Agency for International Development.

have my work cut out here. And the invariable counterpart of dullness is job security — that is the first thing, indeed, that the dull man seeks and gets.

My morning was interrupted by a call to the Ministry of External Affairs to obtain a letter for transmittal to Washington — a reply to my letter of greeting and an expression of hope that things might be kept calm in Laos and Cuba. In the afternoon, I resumed with TCM.

Some of this disturbed me a lot. Vast salaries are being paid to people to teach elementary engineering. It looks to me like a tax dodge for those willing to live abroad for a while. A formidable program by which five American colleges of agriculture — Ohio, Illinois, Missouri, Kansas and Tennessee — assist forty-five Indian colleges seems to be way under strength. Those giving advice work out at the rate of about one man per Indian college. Other parts of the program are also unimpressive — some provide not technical assistance but a substitute for Indian lethargy. That must be costly to supply on a large scale. I am far from happy about this and troubled more by the considerable contentment with it all.

April 19 — New Delhi

I am finally officially an Ambassador. At eight-fifty yesterday morning, the Chief of Protocol from the Ministry of External Affairs called at the Residence where my principal colleagues had already assembled — the military men in an exceptionally high state of polish. We rode in an open procession — motorcycle and patrol car — to the President's Palace (the Rashtrapati Bhavan)[25] at the gates of which we were met by a detachment of mounted lancers on beautifully matched bay horses. They escorted us to an open courtyard where an honor guard of Sikhs was drawn up in two ranks — perhaps the best turned-out soldiers in the world. I mounted the reviewing block while the national anthems were

[25] The President's Palace in Delhi is known as the Rashtrapati Bhavan. The Governor's residence in each state is known as the Raj Bhavan.

played. Then I inspected the guard; nothing seemed seriously wrong. I drew heavily on old newsreels for my protocol, but the Commanding Officer was there to nudge me if I needed it.

After congratulating the O.C., we went into the palace and rehearsed the ceremony. Then we had the ceremony. A slow approach to the President;[26] my speech; his reply; presentation of credentials; then down to his study for a private chat; and finally on to a state room for a public reception for all present. It was exceedingly well done; the Indians approach ceremony as though they meant it, rather than, as in the United States, in a kind of abashed reluctance. And the soldiers, band and military aides were all sparkling by our standards. My speech, in which I urged accomplishment as distinct from conversation and noted that the warmest words of friendship were exchanged just before the breaking of diplomatic relations, was evidently well-regarded. When we emerged to come home, my automobile flag was unfurled for the first time.

After some champagne for the staff, I got into the TCM again and spent the afternoon on routine matters ending up with a meeting with Stebbins. The question is whether I should see the principal exiled leader from Nepal. Obviously I should. He is a liberal and a democrat — and the American Ambassador should be available to any leader of importance.

The Cuban business (the Bay of Pigs) has come and the effect here is not good. I am afraid that even if we win, we will lose. Castro would eventually have died on his vine. His army was not a threat and now we lose prestige and esteem where it counts. This inability to balance small Rover Boy gains against large general loss was the prime weakness of the Eisenhower Administration. The same people who erred before are diligently promoting error again.

26 Dr. Rajendra Prasad.

V

Settling In

April 20 — New Delhi

Yesterday morning, I first took some flowers to the Rajghat[1] — a bouquet of lilies — and then called on the dean of the diplomatic corps, Ambassador and Lt. General Rana of Nepal, one of the Ranas who until modern times were the hereditary governing clan of that kingdom. He is about to be recalled; the Nepalese are said to want someone more anti-Indian. The General told me his military rank was strictly nonmilitary. Officials are promoted from one military grade to another even though, as in his case, they have never spent a day in the army. Then I departed precedence to see Sir Paul Gore-Booth, the British High Commissioner, and Chester Ronning, the Canadian H.C.[2] Both of these visits were mostly liturgical although Ronning (a distinguished authority on China) expressed discontent over the inflexibility of U.S. China policy. He told me that Prime Minister Diefenbaker's stand with India and against South Africa at the recent Commonwealth Conference had been popular in Canada. South Africa is surely not the most popular of nations.

In the afternoon, we went over press conference questions. My staff advocated either caution or silence on nearly all prospective

[1] A chaste memorial area by the Jamuna River not far from the Red Fort where Gandhi was cremated and his ashes committed to the waters of the river.
[2] British Commonwealth nations do not exchange ambassadors but High Commissioners.

queries. Then we went to see the Deshmukhs[3] and look at the new International Center[4] — now building. Finally we went to a big Indian reception where I had pleasant small talk with Nehru. He was delighted when I told him about my encounter with the Duke of Windsor and his report on the amiable Indian reception of his niece.[5] The reception was in the garden of a large dwelling occupied by the Secretary-General of the Ministry of External Affairs.[6] It was summery and gay, and the blend of Indian and Western costume gave an interesting effect of flowing white on somber black.

April 21 — New Delhi

I had my first press conference yesterday morning. I was braced for a barrage of questions on Cuba. It would have been better had I known that the "revolt" (i.e., the Bay of Pigs invasion) was already over. I carefully began with a comment on economic matters. Then a tendentious and tedious chap asked me a long question about military aid to Pakistan which he went on, helpfully, to answer himself. This rather antagonized the audience — which numbered a hundred or more — and I drove home the point by gently noting that he had answered his own question although not wholly to my liking. Then we did get onto economics. I put the fourth government-owned steel plant at Bokaro within the range of American aid. I had no instructions but one should use what freedom he has, for it is evidently a rare blessing.[7] Toward the end, we got to Cuba.

[3] C. D. Deshmukh, a figure of much importance in the life of modern India. A civil servant, he was successively Finance Minister, head of the University Grants Commission and Vice-Chancellor of the University of Delhi.

[4] A handsome combination of hostel, library, dining and conference rooms on the edge of the Lodi Gardens not far from the Residence. It was being built through the generosity of John D. Rockefeller III who had given me a watching brief on its progress. The architect, Joseph Allen Stein, an American, had practiced for some years in New Delhi and was the source of some of its most inspired modern buildings.

[5] See page 36.

[6] R. K. Nehru. See page 70.

[7] This became a highly controversial matter. My position — that public sector plants could be financed by the United States and that this one was eligible in

I was as brief as possible, but I suppose what I say on this will have the headlines. Sympathy for Castro here is very strong.

Then my wife and I went to an exceedingly interesting lunch at the Prime Minister's house. Excepting for us, it was a family party. The Prime Minister, B. K. Nehru[8] and wife, R. K. Nehru and wife, Indira,[9] and, I believe, a daughter of Mrs. Pandit.[10] The house is large with furniture a trifle on the heavy side — the British left a tradition of Victorian overstuffed tropical — but the gardens are charming and wall decorations include interesting old maps and various Indian memorabilia.

First we had fruit juice upstairs followed by lunch in the downstairs dining room followed by a chat upstairs. Indira pressed me a bit on Cuba, and after lunch I used the occasion to ask a question or two — what should be done as between Indonesians and Dutch in West New Guinea — and a few other matters. Mostly the conversation was light and general — whether the arms race might be turning into a scientific contest in space, the possibilities of M.I.T. as an educational institution (B. K. Nehru has two sons there and Indira contemplates sending her son) and similar matters. We have obviously been taken into the fold in a most agreeable way.

Later I spoke briefly to the world-touring members of the U.S. Industrial College of the Armed Forces — obviously a most rewarding junket — and then went for a swim at the Gymkhana Club. The latter, Delhi's most distinguished club to which we have been admitted (for exercise) without the usual waiting period, is a

---

principle — was strongly supported by President Kennedy, strongly opposed by Republicans and a source of great nervousness in the U.S. bureaucracy which, at one time, reversed the President's approval on the grounds that he was running undue political risk. This is discussed on several later occasions.

[8] A cousin of the Prime Minister, then in charge of Indian economic interests in Washington and shortly to become, for a long time, Indian Ambassador in Washington.

[9] Indira Gandhi, daughter of the Prime Minister, to become, of course, Prime Minister herself in 1966.

[10] Mrs. Vijaya Lakshmi Pandit, sister of the Prime Minister, former Ambassador in Moscow and Washington, later to become Governor of Maharashtra and an influential member of Parliament.

place of unimaginable hideousness, but it has quite a good swimming pool. When I dived in, several others climbed out. This evidently was not so much a sanitary precaution as for fear of lèse majesté.

Finally, a call from Prasanta Mahalanobis.[11] In Switzerland in 1955, during the course of a dinner party, he invited me to India. We came, I became interested in India, returned and now again. Obviously I would not have come back had it not been for this first visit. Prasanta thus rightly takes credit for having selected the American Ambassador. In return, he would like me to get him a Univac through AID.

April 22 — New Delhi

I write these notes each morning at breakfast on the large back terrace of the Residence. It is shaded by a large covered awning (in India, a *shamiana*) extending to five steel masts at the outer side. Around the edge is a ring of extravagantly colored potted petunias and ferns. Beyond is the deep green grass, and more flowers and shrubbery on the borders. Two other presences must be noted: most obtrusive are the birds which in this nonviolent land are almost totally unfrightened. They are incredibly controversial — always denouncing each other in the most raucous and angry tones. Indian birds rarely twitter and never sing; instead they challenge and scream.

Less obtrusive by far are two *malis* — gardeners — who sit on their haunches only a few feet away arranging the flowers for the house. These they put in dense globular bouquets dominated by violently painted phlox. The bouquets are turned out at the rate of one every half hour. They try very hard to make every bouquet exactly like every other one and they succeed.

Yesterday morning I held my first meeting with my Country Team[12] who act as a cabinet. I broke the news that meetings

[11] See page 73.
[12] See page 62.

would be held irregularly. Meetings are a great trap. Soon you find yourself trying to get agreement and then the people who disagree come to think they have a right to be persuaded. Thus they acquire power; thus meetings become a source of opposition and trouble. However, they are indispensable when you don't want to do anything.

At noon yesterday, we celebrated the Queen's Birthday at the British High Commission and in the afternoon I had a pleasant chat with Krishna Menon. Most people dislike him; I found him rather attractive on first acquaintance.[13] He is much concerned with proving that he is an intellectual and a socialist. Provisionally it is my conclusion that those who do not like him have never encountered this particular kind of public figure. They might be equally antipathetic to Richard Crossman.[14]

On my return to the Chancery, a demonstration was forming up on behalf of Cuba. It was not very large — perhaps 200 activists with 50 police and 100 spectators — but noisy. We had been advised of it, and I ordered that the gates be left open and that everything proceed in the most unconcerned possible way. If they wanted to present a petition, the leaders were to be invited in.

My offer wasn't accepted. The demonstrators marched around

[13] Later I was to have a more mature and reserved view, as a sound diplomat might put it. V. K. Krishna Menon, born 1897, was at this period the next best known Congress leader after Nehru and by a wide margin the most controversial. Of South Indian origin, he had lived for many years in England and had, indeed, been an elected member of a London Borough Council and was once selected by the British Labour Party as a Parliamentary candidate. From his British base, he was active in the struggle for Indian independence. Following Independence, he became Indian High Commissioner in London and then returned to a political career in India where he finally became Minister of Defence. During these years he became widely known in the United States as the perennial leader of the Indian delegation to the General Assembly of the United Nations and as a participant in numerous other international conferences at all of which he was an eloquent, frequent and unsparing critic of American policy. He was at the peak of his influence as this journal begins. A year and a half later, the border attack of the Chinese and the resulting Indian military defeats began a series of political reversals leading to his disappearance from Indian political life for several years. In 1969 he again won election to Parliament.

[14] British Labour Parliamentarian, Lord President of the Council, journalist and friend.

outside the gate with red banners — I thought a few Indian flags would have been tactful — and shouted, threw some stones and denounced the Delhi police as murderers. They also called for my resignation, although how that would have advanced their cause they did not say.[15] When all the staff had gone home, I drove out with the Ambassador's flag flying. I passed immediately by the little mob and wasn't noticed at all. I analyzed my feelings in this, my first sortie into a hostile crowd, and found them surprising. I would have been much more frightened by departing by the back drive as someone suggested. The fear of being craven, as thousands must have said, is the worst fear of all. However, my courage was greatly supported by the small size of the demonstration and the large size of the police force. We had one broken window in the Chancery — a low score for an all-glass building.

In the evening, there was a long reception at Maffitt's. My feet gave out and also my charm.

April 23 — New Delhi

Diplomacy has its oddities and short cuts. Yesterday morning M. J. Desai[16] of the M.E.A.[17] called me in to give me a draft declaration which the Indians will submit for the approval of the aid-to-India consortium meeting in Washington next week. I had already advised on its composition. Then the Secretary-General called me to give the Indian view on policy on West New Guinea. I had previously asked the Prime Minister for suggestions. The S.-G. had first to ascertain what the P.M. had told me so that he would know what Indian policy was.

---

[15] I've since concluded that more people, on disagreeing with policy, should resign. But I have difficulty imagining myself doing it on this occasion — partly for reasons of courage, partly because the President, not the authors of the enterprise, would have been hurt.

[16] See page 70. One of the ablest civil servants I have ever encountered in any country. After his retirement, he came — by my arrangement — to teach at Brandeis University. A cigarette chain-smoker, he died of cancer in Switzerland in 1967.

[17] Ministry of External Affairs.

In the afternoon, a prime hazard of life in India overtook me —
an affluent attack of dysentery. I went to bed and by dinnertime
felt somewhat better. The doctor came and prescribed total ab-
stinence from Indian food.

That was fortunate, on the whole, for in the evening we had a
vast dinner at the home of the Law Minister.[18] We ate on the lawn
beneath a great red *shamiana* with an equally red carpet below.
The table was ⊏-shaped with perhaps seventy-five sitting down
in all. It was Indian except for the Australians, United Kingdom
and ourselves. Before dinner, I had a gay and pleasant chat with
Nehru. He told me that Diefenbaker[19] had earned his gratitude
for supporting him against South Africa at the last Commonwealth
Conference (when S.A. left the Commonwealth) and that Men-
zies,[19] once a friend of *apartheid*, had now heard enough from home
to be opposed. I told him of Bill Blair's[20] response when he was
asked if he would accept ambassadorial appointment to South
Africa. He said yes, were it understood that he could receive air
drops for the Bantu underground in the Embassy backyard. Nehru
was delighted. We talked of his relations with Churchill; they were
influenced, he said, by the old school tie. He thought Churchill
had been generous in saying that he, Nehru, had forgotten both
how to fear and to hate.

The party broke up promptly at 10 P.M. and we went for a drive.
Our Chrysler, which was made by a man with a bad conflict of
interest,[21] died several times during our tour. Each time it was
revived with greater difficulty and we limped home.

Later

I am badly in need of breath, and today was chosen. After

[18] A. K. Sen from Bengal. The post of Law Minister, conforming roughly to
that of Solicitor General (as opposed to Attorney General), is a comparatively
junior one.
[19] Prime Ministers of Canada and Australia respectively.
[20] William McCormack Blair, Jr. See page 20.
[21] The Chrysler Corporation at the time was suffering a severe crisis from the
conflicting business affairs of some of its executives who were selling products or
services to the Corporation.

swimming this morning — we had to cross a picket line manned by proletarians with a red flag — I got into business matters for a couple of hours. Then we had lunch for Eugenie Anderson,[22] husband, and Kusum Nair[23] and husband, and then read and slept through the afternoon. In the early evening, we visited the Tomb of Humayun,[24] a vast structure of admirable proportion and coloring which inspired the Taj.

Cuba is on the way to being forgotten, but it remains a bad blot on the copybook. I hope Kennedy is not too forgiving of those who led him astray. Unfortunately, the man who makes a mistake usually has a certain commitment to those who get him into it. He shared their bad judgment; he must, accordingly, share their excuses and apologies and in a measure accept them. If you want to put yourself in solid in the government of the United States, you should guide your boss into a big error. Then he is your partner in expiation and apology. Anyhow, to a point.

April 25 — New Delhi

My first protocol visit yesterday[25] was to the Spanish Ambassador, an elegant old aristocrat with noble mustaches under his nose and two more coming out of his ears. He plays tennis, golf, climbs mountains and shoots and is not seriously diverted therefrom by any diplomatic tasks. He did tell me Spain was all behind Franco. Then I saw Walter Russell Crocker, the Australian H.C., who keeps office in an old GI building from World War II (and talks with charm and devastating frankness about his government), and finally had a visit from the Nepalese Ambassador whom I visited

[22] Minnesota Democrat and longtime political acquaintance.
[23] Indian author.
[24] Humayun, 1508–1556, son of Babur, was the second Moghul ruler in India. No visitor to Delhi should miss this monument.
[25] A new ambassador visits and then receives a return call from all the other diplomats accredited to the capital. Often it is the only business an ambassador ever has with a diplomatic colleague. Though tedious, it is for many members of the profession a valuable alternative to unemployment.

last week. I ended up with the Soviet Ambassador, Ivan Alexandro-vich Benediktov, at noon. The latter, a bluff, vigorous male, was formerly the Soviet Minister of Agriculture. He is without English — a considerable handicap, I should think. He welcomed me as a fellow nonprofessional and broke out the caviar and vodka in a highly professional way. Our conversation was given over to elabo-rate compliments — mine of Soviet economic development, his of American automobiles including the Oldsmobile which he drives with pride. In the afternoon, routine business and more calls in-cluding S. K. Patil, the Indian Minister for Food and Agriculture. These calls are losing their interest.

Today's *Times of India* thinks it is a sad sight to see Adlai Steven-son and Galbraith trying to paper over the Cuban business. It wasn't our finest hour. Fortunately, I was in a position to do far less talking than Stevenson.

April 27 — New Delhi

My diplomatic colleagues here, on several of whom I called yes-terday, are not the most salubrious representatives of the profes-sion, I fear. Quite a number live and work out of the local hotels; one Levantine, who is accredited to several countries in this area, is said to be deeply involved in the black market. The others evidently have to get along on very little money. Their houses are hideous.[26]

This afternoon a message came in asking me to inform the Prime Minister that the President had marked him down for a billion dollars for the next two years of the Five-Year Plan. I went over to his Parliament office to tell him. I could not be sure whether

[26] Several months later, a new ambassador from one of the Arab countries called on me. I found him very agreeable and invited him to dinner. Alas, he never came. A few days after his visit, his luggage was being unloaded, I think, at the airport. A container broke open spreading gold, which commands a great pre-mium in India, all over the place. He was disaccredited and returned home after a total tour of around ten days.

he was embarrassed or touched — he made almost no comment. But then, at the end, playing on some statement that I had made at the beginning, he said that this was an occasion when an ambassador did not risk having his head chopped off.[27]

✧ ✧ ✧

New Delhi, India
April 27, 1961

Dear Mr. President:

The last week wasn't the best in the history of the frontier and I haven't found much comfort in contemplating your problems. However I think I can offer a word or two of cheer — and since you know how I felt about this adventure, as well as my mean tendencies, you won't imagine that I am glossing things over. New Delhi was, I imagine, the worst station. The papers had carried the full newspaper accounts of our Cuban involvement with all available exaggeration. There are lots of people here who love to make life difficult for us — and who think we have been doing too well these last two or three years. And, perhaps not less than the Latin Americans, the Indians see their protection (in particular to the North) in the principle of non-intervention. This attitude is a most important force in the unpowerful part of the world, where it is naturally regarded as a vital protection. The result was a bad setting and much pressure on Nehru to give us the business.

We did not escape unscathed but it was no disaster. I kept our explanations simple and short; there is nothing worse than windy arguments. At a press conference, which came as these damn things always do on the worst day, I repeated you and

[27] Nehru's pride was closely engaged with that of India. He recognized the great role played by our help. But it also meant, I am certain, that he saw his country in some slight measure as a beneficiary of charity, and this he did not like at all.

then contented myself with running over our history of alleged misdemeanors in undermining Cuban despots as seen by the latter from the complaints of Spain to the present. Castro I made merely the last troublesome chapter on the list .

As much by good luck as good management I saw Nehru almost every day during the business — once during a long family lunch at his house — and this helped take a great deal of the sting out of the situation. At the beginning he made a rather unhappy statement in the House. But he ended last Saturday with a speech minimizing our role, stressing that no Americans had been involved and citing a point that I had urged in our conversations, namely that 100,000 Cuban refugees were bound to cause us trouble. The episode is now over. Do keep it muted at the Washington end.

In the next few days I am going to write a detailed policy paper on how to balance prospective accomplishment and risk in matters of this sort and on the realities as distinct from the slogans of social revolution.[28] We must be more learned on these matters than we are. Would you have an eye out for these thoughts?

I am engaged, these days, in making my calls on the other ambassadors. This is an incredible waste of time. As you can imagine New Delhi is not the place where (say) Peru[29] sends its best man or the best man wants to come. Paris suits the Latin and Levantine temperament better and so does New York. One Levantine, who is accredited to a half dozen Asian governments, I suspect of being in the black market and possibly in the white slave trade. As a result he does seem rather more affluent than the common run. Many of the other diplomats obviously get along on a shoestring. They live in hideous houses decorated by some expressionist of the rural Nepal school. I do note one redeeming feature: the more underdeveloped the country the

[28] It never got written.
[29] A tactful reference, for Peru does not accredit an ambassador to India.

more overdeveloped the women. Still after meeting many of my diplomatic colleagues I think better of . . . conversations with Foster Furcolo.[30] Nehru suggested that I call on the big countries because of their vanity, the small ones because of their sensibility and omit those in between. However I shall struggle nobly on — for a while. Fulbright should know, incidentally, that the Soviet Ambassador next door, though he understands, does not speak . . . English.[31] He has given me five jars of caviar, and I have given him a copy of one of my books. I hope you do as well trading with Khrushchev.

I did pick up one useful bit of information yesterday. An Indian told me that when they recently played a game of ordinary or non-touch football with the Indonesians in Djakarta, the latter got a medicine man to the stadium early in the morning to insure by incantation and other well-established techniques that the citizen-supporters of our friend Sukarno would win. I asked if it worked. My Indian friend replied, "Of course not. We had the better team and anyhow our astrologists had picked the day."

I am still looking into Embassy operations. Next week after welcoming Sarge,[32] I shall give you a view of this operation.

Faithfully,

JOHN KENNETH GALBRAITH

THE PRESIDENT
THE WHITE HOUSE

✧ ✧ ✧

April 28 — New Delhi

Yesterday morning the Rumanian Minister, who occupies a dismal house decorated with pictures of the politicians of his land, broke out a bottle of excellent wine. It was the only relief in a dull

---

[30] Recently retired Governor of Massachusetts.

[31] Senator Fulbright had long insisted that American ambassadors be competent in the language of the country to which they were going.

[32] Sargent Shriver, Director of the Peace Corps, who was arriving to launch this activity in India. See page 8.

round of visits, although the people were a bit more interesting than the day before. I have now reached the end of my patience with this stupid business. When I finish the appointments I have now made, I will reduce operations to one call a day and take forever to complete my rounds.

At noon, there was a large luncheon to meet the AID staff — unfortunately, there were so many that I didn't remember anyone. But we got fed. Finally I met the American press — half a dozen uniformly lively and attractive men[33] — and, in the evening, spoke some appreciative words at a celebration staged by the USIS for the centenary of Tagore's birth.[34] This was my first large public speech and was sufficiently devoid of content to have pleased even the State Department. The celebration was on a pleasant lawn in front of Bhawalpur House, an ex-maharajah's palace, which houses the USIS. Thousands of lights — wicks in clay dishes of oil — had been spaced around the lawn and the effect was rather good. Children sang and dancers danced and speakers spoke well of Tagore. The program was a marvel of bureaucratic precision. Here is an extract:

8:01   — Ambassador arrives
8:01½ — Ambassador gets out of car
8:02   — Spotlight on main stage
8:02½ — Dr. Bunce[35] crosses platform

All in all, there were fifty-five such steps. Alan Carter, my press officer, said, "My God, if only that man had planned the Cuban affair."

---

[33] Representing the two wire services, the *New York Times*, *Time*, the *Baltimore Sun* and *U.S. News & World Report*.

[34] Rabindranath Tagore, the great Bengali poet, writer and painter. There was something slightly contrived about an American official celebration of the anniversary of a local poet or prophet — a too obvious effort to make capital. Later I would have discouraged it.

[35] See page 65.

April 29 — New Delhi

Alarming messages started coming in from Laos early yesterday — new fighting after the cease-fire and request for authority for U.S. air intervention. Very bloody. I drafted a cable urging caution and was about to dispatch it when a letter came in from the President to the Prime Minister asking him to intervene with the Soviets and the Chinese. Maffitt and I went to see Nehru at 7:30 A.M. at his house. We found him also concerned. I urged the need for his help; he agreed, and while demurring on the Chinese, promised to get on to Moscow and also Hanoi. He also agreed on the desirability of getting the I.C.C.[36] back as quickly as possible. I do not myself quite credit the stories about heavy fighting. More likely only a few guns going off in the general direction of the enemy. The Prime Minister shares this view and reacted with approval when I said that the Laotians had not learned to kill each other like the civilized nations. (This observation had much to do with his favorable response to my request, I think.) Still, it is dangerous enough.

Last night I got the order of battle for a visit of a General (Brigadier) of the United States Air Force. Six colonels accompany him in a Boeing 704. Seven cars are being detailed to get him to town. A long briefing paper has been prepared. This paper deals exclusively with the logistics of shopping and restaurants and has a poignant reference to the existence of prohibition.

April 30 — New Delhi

I had a bad headache yesterday morning, and it was incredibly hot. So after a couple of calls I canceled out and went to bed. At noon, I felt better and lunched here with the TCM group asso-

[36] The International Control Commission, consisting of Canada, Poland and India with the latter as chairman, was established under the authority of the 1954 Geneva Accords to limit foreign military intervention in the Indo-Chinese successor states, and otherwise enforce the terms of the Accords. It had been expelled from Laos by a right-wing government (brought in with the skilled efforts of the then American Ambassador, Mr. Graham Parsons, and the CIA) and was now sitting in India.

ciated with development of the colleges of agriculture. The teams
from our colleges, as I have said, are mostly far below strength. As
usual, the responsibility for this failure is obscure; evidently after
an academic decision is reached at home on an appointment, a
tedious review is required including the Indian state government
and the Union Agricultural and Finance Ministries. This takes
months. What surprises me is the degree of acquiescence of our
people. We should either get a remedy or get out.

In the afternoon, with some Calvinist pleasure, I instructed that
henceforth visitors would not be instructed on shopping or recreation or provided with official transportation therefor.[37] It was
pointed out to me that this would be hard on my Service Attachés
whose generals expected such treatment. I countered by having
the order sent to the Secretary of Defense with a view to having
the position fully understood in Washington.

Later

More trouble in Laos. The essence of my problem is this: The
Control Commission is meeting here; an infinity of meetings is proceeding in Washington; and fighting goes on in Laos. I know something of what is going on here; a little, but not much, about what is
going on in Washington; and nothing of what is happening in
Laos. On the basis of this information, I am supposed to report
and advise. Even the local reports on what the Control Commission
is doing are conflicting. Chester Ronning, the Canadian High Commissioner, told me at lunch that it was winding up its deliberations
in New Delhi, would report and then be all cleared to proceed to
Laos. This morning it seems not to have finished its work, and the
Polish representatives have taken a trip to Agra. This might be
stalling. But from the way business is combined with tourism in
this part of the world, it might be to see the Taj Mahal.

---

[37] This was not wise. While discouraging shopping tours, it was only reasonable that serious visitors be supplied with transportation to go to shops and see
the Red Fort. One should not make capital out of petty economies of this sort.

To complicate life, I am afflicted with some disorder in my foot — my present and presumably not last manifestation of senile decay. As a result, I am hobbling around on a cane. Last night we went to the celebration of the birthday of the Japanese Emperor — a vast gathering at the Japanese Embassy. Japanese lanterns were burning in great numbers around the garden until a violent dust storm[38] hit them a little after the party got under way. Many lanterns are by now nearly back in Japan.

May 1 — New Delhi

Yesterday I busied myself from morning to night trying to arrange a cease-fire in Laos. This morning, to my delight, there is indication that we may have one. There is not the slightest reason to imagine any connection between my efforts and the results.

In addition, we had two long meetings with Sargent Shriver and party on the Peace Corps. They accepted generously my notion which is to identify them pretty closely with agriculture. And I would like to concentrate them. They will be more manageable, and though they won't change the face of India, they might have an effect on their own small corner.

Paul Gore-Booth, the British High Commissioner, and his wife, Pat, came to lunch and told us that Nehru is much opposed to lavish parties celebrating the national days of the accredited countries. I will be happy to oblige him with appropriate austerity. In the evening, we went to a moderately austere party to celebrate the birthday of the Queen of the Netherlands.

The weather is becoming really hot — far above 100° F. in daytime and no longer reliably cool at night. But one goes from air-conditioned house in air-conditioned car to air-conditioned office. It is New England winter in reverse.

[38] A phenomenon of the spring months in Delhi bringing dust from the deserts to the west. They are welcomed, on the whole, for the temperature falls sharply.

May 2 — New Delhi

I am still partly immobilized by my foot. I could not go to Chandigarh[39] with Shriver and Company. In the morning, M. J. Desai called me in for a long talk. Afterward, the reporters swarmed over me to ask questions about Laos. I told them to say that the American Ambassador was enigmatic. Four or five, including Paul Grimes (of the *New York Times*) and Phil Potter (of the *Baltimore Sun* papers) tried flank approaches. "Have you been consulted?" etc. I reproached them for lack of subtlety and, while still talking, escaped.

In fact, Desai and I talked about Nepal. The Indians, as is widely known, are worried about the King who, in their view, is opening the door to the Chinese Communists and assorted local adventurers. (I had little knowledge with which to agree or dissent.) They wanted us to ask the French and British Ambassadors in Kathmandu to join Stebbins in persuading the King to broaden his government. I am not very optimistic. The heads of small states must resist such pressure to show that, though small, they are independent. And the British Ambassador seems to be quite an admirer of the King. When Queen Elizabeth visited Nepal a few weeks ago, he prepared a speech for her praising His Majesty as one of the greatest and wisest since (approximately) Solomon. The Queen's managers reduced this by about a quarter and removed the part identifying His Majesty with divinity. The Queen gave that version; by accident, the Ambassador's version got released to the press. There were delighted comparisons. The Queen is said to have ordered her Ambassador sacked and then to have discovered that, as a constitutional monarch, she couldn't do it.

I used the occasion to suggest that perhaps in the future we might be less enthusiastic than in the past about defending every last rampart against Communism. Mr. Dulles did it out of religious zeal but we are more practical men. We noticed that, as in Laos, if we were too eager we were criticized as belligerent. Perhaps we

---

[39] The Le Corbusier capital of what was then the Punjab.

might try being reluctant and get criticized for that for a change. It made some impression, I think.[40]

An independent American film producer named Rogosin is in town and has just shown his newest product to Nehru — it is on *apartheid*. I had invited him to show it at the Residence and somehow word got back to Washington — in the weekly reports or something. A cable came in yesterday morning saying that the producer was "offbeat and downbeat" and had uncooperatively insisted on showing such films when he had been requested not to do so in the past. I fired back a blistering telegram to Coombs[41] and Murrow, neither of whom was directly responsible. Then I confirmed the showing.

The Washington USIA is horrible. Day after day it belches out dreary and boring attacks on the U.S.S.R. and China in the most repulsive and stinking prose. Nothing could do more to promote neutralism or anyhow total inattention.

May 3 — New Delhi

Yesterday morning Sarge Shriver and I called on the Prime Minister at his office in the Secretariat.[42] His is a large room with one of the famous circular desks, half surrounding the occupant, favored by the British. They are of mahogany or something similar and are almost invariably piled deep in moldy files. (The Prime Minister's is the rare exception.) The general effect is one of neither efficiency nor beauty.

The P.M. was relaxed and handsome and there followed a marvelous miscarriage of plans. I had anticipated great trouble in selling the Peace Corps to him. So we had carefully concerted our arguments; I had instructed Shriver not to ask for too much — a

[40] Naturally I hoped I was right in my diagnosis of the change. A lot of people in the State Department, including the Secretary, did not see things this way and they were more influential than I.

[41] Philip Coombs, Assistant Secretary of State for Cultural Affairs.

[42] The principal building housing, since British times, the senior ministers.

small group working on agriculture with the Ford Foundation and AID in the Punjab. I introduced Shriver: "a friend and political associate." I recalled the President's reluctance to appoint him: "He naturally did not believe his sister showed the same care in selecting a husband that he should show in selecting an official." The Peace Corps had to succeed so as to prove that idealism was still worthwhile — to disprove the case of those who considered kindness to be subversive. Then Sarge took over and made an eloquent and moving plea on behalf of his enterprise. The effect was just right — natural, uncontrived and sincere. And following my advice, he proposed only a small enterprise in the North. The Prime Minister then proceeded to speak of the greater needs of the United Provinces and of other parts of India, his belief that more might be attempted and his personal support for the enterprise *despite* its small scale. We left a little dazed and with my reputation as a strategist in poor condition.

A major crisis arose during the day: The Embassy in a note full of ancient and fulsome language — may the "friendly and cordial" relations between our countries increase and multiply — tells each other Embassy of my arrival and the fact that I am in business. The question: What should we do about the Hungarians with whom by instruction we are by no means friendly? I cut through the problem with one brilliant diplomatic thrust. We shall hope that "cordial relations" with the Magyars "will increase" and no mention was made of their multiplication.

A Calcutta paper tells that the staff of the Embassy has been given "a terrific brush-up" by the new Ambassador and lives in fear and trembling. Alas, were it only so.

We had our first formal dinner last night — a buffet on the terrace. It was quite tolerable. The guests arrived promptly at 8:30 P.M.; left en masse at 10:30 P.M.[43] We were tucked in our little beds by eleven.

---

[43] Entertaining in New Delhi in Western fashion is, for many, not a pleasure but an extension of the day's duty. Half-past ten is the first moment it is considered decent to leave.

May 4 — New Delhi

Yesterday was devoted to a number of things: administrative matters at the Chancery, a visit to the New Zealand High Commissioner, a visit from the Consul of Vietnam, a big lunch at the Residence on the Peace Corps, a meeting on the Peace Corps, a visit to the Planning Ministry, a speech to the Planning Board, a visit to the Japanese Ambassador, a visit with Shriver to the Vice-President, a summons from Desai at the Ministry of External Affairs to talk about Laos, a stalled civilian air negotiation in Washington, dinner and then Rogosin's movie on South Africa. By midday, I was developing a modest headache; by night, it was raging.

At the Planning Board, I used the occasion to express the importance I attach to exports — it enforces cost discipline, shows foreign leaders that India will have foreign exchange to repay loans, and encourages attention to the naturally efficient industries, some of which, like tea and textiles, seem rather old-fashioned and hence are easily neglected. Someone asked at the Planning Board if I would have predicted a year ago that if Kennedy were President, I would be the next Ambassador to India. I said I had and it was simple: In the event of Kennedy's election, I would be more wanted in India than in the United States. Someone was certain to find this out and tell the President.

In the evening, I learned that the Thai Consul was holding up the transit visa for the Polish member of the I.C.C. The Pole being a Communist, the Thai had to have instruction from home. The cease-fire seems about settled and this could cause trouble. Maffitt intervened with all available force, but the little man stood his bureaucratic ground. Finally I cabled Bangkok.

Later still I learned that Harriman[44] might stop here to inform Nehru about Laos. I cabled urging against it. I have asked Nehru for enough appointments this week. And I intend to resist the notion that there is a higher order of ambassador for special or difficult tasks. I plan to be the principal representative of the President hereabouts, and this had best be understood.

[44] See page 50.

We showed the Rogosin film on the back terrace of the Residence. It is excellent and not very subversive except of South Africa. It made a very good evening. It has become exceedingly hot — and all around the clock.

May 5 — New Delhi–Srinagar

Yesterday after taking Shriver, who is departing, to see M. J. Desai and collecting some instruction from the Ministry of External Affairs on the evils of military aid to Pakistan (which I amply understand), Kitty and I took flight for Kashmir.[45] I still had a headache which got steadily worse. But the flight was mercifully cool and restful, and Kashmir was almost as beautiful as I remembered it. The Valley floor is covered with great clumps of large white and blue iris. The lilacs are out, and there are lots of other flowers, most of which were presented to us on arrival.

With great ceremony, we were taken to Mr. Butt's houseboats[46] where we were installed in a series of seven or eight rooms on two handsomely carved and rather handsomely furnished craft. Artistically, the local furniture, of solid carved walnut, is far superior to the gimcrack stuff at the Residence. After a late lunch, I went to bed and awakened in late afternoon to go for a ride on the marvelous coolness of the lake. For our boat ride, which was on a *shikara*, or long, narrow gondolalike craft, we were propelled by three energetic men using shovel-shaped paddles. We went down a canal with rectangular islands on each side about six feet wide and

[45] Srinagar, the capital of Kashmir, is about 420 air miles north of Delhi. The Valley — the Vale — of Kashmir is at an elevation of about 5200 feet and so is strikingly cooler than the Indian capital. The Valley, which contains the enchanting lakes on which the houseboats are moored, is some 85 miles long and 20 to 25 miles wide. It is entirely surrounded by mountain ranges of great height including Nanga Parbat reaching 26,620 feet and, like many lesser peaks, capped in gleaming snow. While the Alps are related to the earth, the peaks surrounding the Kashmir Valley have their association with the clouds. In former times, the access to the Valley was by way of what is now Pakistan and not unduly difficult. This route is now closed and present access is over or through high mountains.

[46] His houseboats on Dal Lake have long been favored by official visitors to their owner's unabashed delight.

some hundreds of yards long and planted to willows. These grow very rapidly; the tops are used for fodder and the rest for firewood. When we returned, I got a telegram saying that Harriman was stopping over in Delhi only for forty-five minutes.

But this morning after breakfast I got a call that he was remaining in New Delhi to see Nehru at the latter's invitation. George Hannah, the Air Attaché,[47] it said, was on the way up for me, so to the airport and back to the furnace. For a moment, it did not seem so certain. Our plane, still the old C-47 (DC-3), was waiting at the airport, but the outgoing flight of Indian Airlines had been suspended because of bad weather in the Pass. (At the altitudes reached by a DC-3, one must fly a complicated dog's leg through the mountain pass. In a fog, since the Pass is narrow and the Himalayas soar on either side, this is not without interest.) George Hannah said we would go up and "take a look." We did after I had told him, with all appropriate casualness, that it was not a matter of life and death. We squeezed between the mountain and a cloud with no difficulty. (In fact, there was a little difficulty. I learned later that at one point there was barely room between a rain squall and the mountain, and Captain Egbert, the Naval Attaché, who was flying as copilot, thought we couldn't make it.) Thereafter it was easy, and as I write this, we are almost back in New Delhi.

May 6 — New Delhi–Srinagar

I took Harriman to see the Prime Minister at the latter's Parliament office. Not much transpired. Harriman described his visit and his impressions of the King of Laos and various other Laotian notables. We discussed the forthcoming Geneva Conference. This Nehru will attend only if it seems to be running into trouble. He thinks even the Laotian Communists may be a trifle suspicious of the Chinese. He told that Ho Chi Minh, on a visit to India, asked him, "How many Chinese do you have in India?" He replied,

[47] See page 66.

guessing, "Oh, about 50,000." Said H.C.M., "You are lucky." I commented that Laos provided the special problem of communism superimposed on a combination of feudalism and anarchy.

Nehru thinks we are in for a bad time in Angola where the Portuguese are said to be getting brutal.

We were with the P.M. for about an hour. After many photographs, we went to dinner, and at 10:30 P.M. I saw Harriman off for the United States. At eleven-thirty this morning I returned, via the Indian Airlines Viscount, to Kashmir.

My companion coming up was a medium-weight Broadway actor (whose name did not get transcribed from my notes). He thought it very democratic for the American Ambassador to be traveling *sans* suite. But he was disillusioned about my standing as a man of the people when he saw my baggage check marked "V.I.P." and the assembly of welcoming officials at the airport.

May 8 — Srinagar

Weariness is something which I am incapable of understanding. Afflicted by it, life becomes less pleasant, one's judgment deteriorates, so does temper and I am conscious that this is so. Yet my judgment deteriorates just enough more rapidly than my perception of this downward trend so that I do not stop and rest. Or not immediately. Then when I do, my eyes and head clear and I see what a dark valley I have been inhabiting. As the result of a couple of days of perfect rest and exercise, I am now, for perhaps the hundredth time, in the midst of such a revelation.

I have always had a curious relation to fish. I like seafood; fishing boats, harbors and, at a decent distance, even fishermen intrigue me. When I have felt the pangs of parenthood afflicting me, I have either taken my children fishing or considered doing so. Yet this affection is unrequited. Fish regard me with distaste and suspicion and certainly as unworthy of their slightest consideration.

I have never shot anything in my life. Indeed, I have never shot a gun without closing my eyes and this, no doubt, interferes with good aiming. For thus resisting blood sports, I should be compensated with reasonable luck as a fisherman. But it hasn't worked out that way. I may be the only diligent fisherman in the world who has never caught a single full-scale specimen. I have taken my children fishing in Vermont in shady pools from which they have pulled very decent trout. When, under the guise of helping them, I took a rod, the trout disappeared down to the smallest minnow. My youngsters sensed the reaction of the fish and from an early age pled with me to confine myself to baiting the hook. Once my wife and I went deep-sea fishing off Nassau where results were absolutely guaranteed. This was no idle promise. I had seen similar boats dashing over the waves in the newsreels and noticed that they invariably caught huge and dangerous-looking beasts. On this day, my wife caught six fish including two lethal barracuda; I caught one tuna but by the time I pulled it out, it had been eaten by other fish so nothing was left but the head. Another time, off Nova Scotia, I went out with two fishermen at five in the morning to lay down a cod line. They should never have taken me for it was the worst day's fishing in forty years — so they told me — and it was their livelihood too. I was so embarrassed that I gave them a bottle of whiskey which, fortunately, they preferred to fish. Once, in studying new and original forms of economic development, I went to a fish-rearing farm. They wanted to show me their prize stock. Two men took a wide net with handles on each end which stretched across the rectangular box stall where the fish were stabled. Another pulled it forward from one end of the box to the other. Then they lifted the net to show me the fish. There wasn't one; all had got through an unnoticed hole in the net.

All of this is by way of preface to today's fishing expedition. It was to a stream about forty-five miles from Srinagar which is reserved for important visitors. The trout fishing in Kashmir is world-famous; this is the best stream in Kashmir. We learned that one only dragged a fly in the water and the fish raced in, each trying his best to oblige.

Fish or no fish, the drive out was worth it. The farmers were at work in the paddy fields, each with his tiny plow and diminutive oxen. In some places, the hillocks were already covered with water, intricately patterned by the green tracery of the dikes. At intervals were the villages; these consisted of high brick houses, thatched and a trifle disheveled but blending into the willow and white and purple iris by which they were surrounded. (Iris often grow on the roofs as well.) On each side, higher than one imagines mountains can be, were the Himalayas. It was a wonderful drive.

The stream, when we reached it, was clear and black and flowed rapidly between low, green banks, closely cropped, with occasional clumps of large, snow-white iris. Every fifty yards or so, the stream tumbled over a low stone dam erected at some distant time to slow its pace and lessen the damage to the surrounding land. Were I a judge of trout streams, I would rate this one as perfect.

I was equipped with a rod and fly and lowered the latter somewhat tentatively into the water. Immediately there was a flash of yellow. I had hooked a two- or three-pound trout some eighteen inches long. Here in the Himalayas the fish hadn't heard about me. Being unknown, my luck had changed.

Alas, it wasn't so. This fish was a fat, mentally retarded fellow. He had been swimming downstream with his eyes shut and blundered into my hook. It was a wonder he had escaped so long.

Until then there had been no real word that I was around. Immediately it was passed and, naturally, I caught no more. After an hour or two, I let the guides cast for me. But my presence in the neighborhood was sufficient. They had no better luck than I. Once one of them hooked a sizable specimen and handed the rod to me to bring it in. (The guide was sensitive to my feelings and an expert in the sort of gesture which makes me ashamed of not tipping adequately.) The fish looked up at me, not with fear but with contempt, and promptly wrenched himself free.

We had a lovely ride back in the rain.

May 9 — New Delhi

We greeted a fine fresh dawn yesterday in Kashmir — blue, green, pink and lamb's wool across the lake and blue and more white fleece above. All this was important for it meant that our plane could get to us through the Pass. At breakfast, we had word that it had. The trip back was fine and smooth with an elegant view of the mountains. Captain Egbert, who was flying, explained in advance his strategy for evading a cloud in the Pass, and it proved sound.

The day's diplomatic business included plans for the arrival next week of Vice-President Lyndon Baines Johnson with a party of about fifty in two planes, including a special signals unit for talking to Washington. Then we had a session on steel with the Minister of Steel, Mines and Fuel, Swaran Singh.[48] He would like us to finance the fourth steel mill under public ownership with no inter- ference by us with construction or operation, although we would have an opportunity to advise. The Indians can be a bit exacting in the requirements we must meet if we are to be allowed to help them.

In the evening, we visited the Saudi Arabian Embassy. The S.A. Ambassador is a vast man, exceeding in diameter even the late J. Falstaff (whom he resembles) and looks just fine in Arabian robes. He was not built for the desert, and all camels should be grateful that he took up diplomacy.

The party proceeded on deviled eggs, cashew nuts and Coca-Cola in the lobby of the Hotel Ambassador where the Ambassador lives. From time to time some rather furtive characters slunk in and out, eyeing each other with what seemed to be well-justified suspicion. Attendance by the more commonplace members of the diplomatic corps was poor. However, the Chinese Ambassador was there, and in a touching gesture by one popular democracy to another,

---

[48] Sardar Swaran Singh, for a period after Nehru's death Minister of External Affairs, was the only Sikh in a cabinet office and, in beard and high turban, a highly visible figure.

my wife, who disdains questions of recognition and nonrecognition among the great powers, was soon chatting happily with his wife. I had a pleasant talk with the Papal Internuncio, an agreeable, well-spoken Australian named Father Knox. I asked him if his name was not a handicap in his line of work. He said it was far from ideal but perhaps better then either Calvin or Luther.

We then went on to an extraordinarily pleasant dinner given in our honor by the Mayor of Delhi. All that happened was that we sat in the garden and talked, drank Coca-Cola and ate in a mild way.

May 10 — New Delhi

I am losing patience with the USIS and even more its mother agency in Washington. They are about to lose the lease on their building here. Yesterday they came up with the third proposal in three weeks for replacing it — to be taken up urgently in Washington. I told them they must settle on a single plan and stick to it.

At the same time, I got word that Washington had selected a new deputy-director without consulting me. I fired off a tough telegram of objection. One curiosity about this job is that you cannot be quite certain about the extent of your authority. Under these circumstances, one can only presume to a great deal and be disagreeable when it is invaded. A bad temper, real or contrived, serves as a "No Trespassing" sign. This causes those who are out to grab some power to go poaching on the more gentle, lovable men next door.

Planning for the big Johnson visit is now elaborately under way. I have opted for the biggest dam in the neighborhood to which we will have to go by special train. Thereafter a tour of the villages where L.B.J. can be surrounded by eager peasantry. The Taj Mahal will be only for the ladies.[49] This is the new Galbraith line enforcing utility and austerity on all official visits.

---

[49] None of this, as will presently be evident, transpired.

New Delhi, India
May 10, 1961

Dear Mr. President:

The last two weeks have been very busy, mostly over Laos. The ceasefire now seems firm. Thus I have my first diplomatic triumph. However, my satisfaction is slightly dimmed by the fact that at no point can I see the slightest relation between my stupendous effort and the result.

I have reached two conclusions as the result of my concern with Laos and the Congo. These jungle regimes, where the writ of government runs only as far as the airport, are going to be a hideous problem for us in the months ahead... The rulers do not control or particularly influence their own people; and they neither have nor warrant their people's support. As a military ally the entire Laos nation is clearly inferior to a battalion of conscientious objectors from World War I. We get nothing from their support, and I must say I wonder what the Communists get. One answer, no doubt, is that the Communists will do a better job of organizing existing leaders out. Nevertheless I am convinced that in these primitive countries we cannot always back winners and we cannot be sure that the winners we back will stay on our side. For the same reason we should never assume that anyone is lost to the Communists. We must above all face the probability of gains and losses and certainly no single loss will be decisive. Most of all we must not allow ourselves or the country to imagine that gains or losses in these incoherent lands are the same as gains or losses in the organized world, that of France or Italy — or India.

A second thought I have been trying out provisionally on the Indian officials. It is that our friends must one day recognize that there has been a change in our attitude toward these regimes. In Dulles' day our efforts to save them from Communism did have elements of a holy crusade. Perhaps there was occasion then for some alarm over our (or rather Dulles') zeal. But we are getting more practical. Those who get alarmed over what we do need to ask themselves whether they would prefer total inaction. Would India be happy were we to wash our hands of Nepal, South Vietnam or the Congo? Would they wish that we were neutral too?

In spite of Laos and the ceremonial preoccupations of this task, I have begun to get a fair view of the operation of this Embassy. I doubt that you would wish to acquaint yourself with all features of all your Missions. But perhaps you should know about one. And India probably reveals the common strength and weaknesses with the further advantage that it is exceedingly important in itself.

With the exception of some [matters] . . . which do not lend themselves to these letters (but about which I will have much to say when I see you and others in June) the affairs of the Embassy can, like Gaul, and most everything else, be divided into three parts: (1) the traditional political, economic and administrative tasks of the Embassy proper; (2) the technical assistance and other economic aid functions; and (3) the United States Information Service. Two and Three, i.e., technical aid and USIS, are very important and very large — the largest, indeed, of any overseas headquarters.

The central Embassy staff, the whole show in your London youth, and including the political and economic ministers, counsellors and secretaries, are hard-working, competent and admirably committed to the interest of the United States without being humorlessly enslaved by any particular line or theology. They respect the Indians and are respected in turn. The political sophistication of the younger officers seems higher than when I knew the Service fifteen years ago. I am well pleased with this part of the enterprise.

The USIS runs libraries, publishes three or four magazines, distributes books, arranges exhibits, books American cultural enterprises and gets your speeches to the intellectually starving masses. It is a large operation; the current budget is $3,466,261.

My impression of this is less happy. The people here are hard-working and dedicated. The various activities are conducted with reasonable efficiency. The libraries handle an enormous traffic. (At the end of the month the McGraw-Hill bakery magazine is grubby from its many avid readers.) What is missing is spirit or lift. The organization lacks excitement. Everyday tasks are not even very expertly done. The magazines and other publications are poorly written and edited with unattractive layouts and fairly dull material. Our upper middle-brow magazine is so far inferior to what the Poles distribute as to make one cry. (The latter very rarely mentions Communism and can even outstrip us on an article on ecclesiastical architecture.) The book presentation program for libraries has not, in the past, thought it wise to distribute your books or Schlesinger's or even very many of mine.

Much of the trouble is from the Washington support. You cannot imagine how bad this is. Each morning, over the air, comes the day's American story. I can no longer read it for simple reasons of health; five minutes of this wireless file and one loses his breakfast and cannot eat the rest of the day. In two weeks it caused me to lose twenty pounds and I have prescribed it for the Saudi Arabian Ambassador who is badly overweight. Apart from some useful speech texts it consists in equal parts of utterly irrelevant pieces about the progress of the grass silage industry, tedious and execrably written articles on the American economy (I attach today's thought which brilliantly likens the nation to a large corporation. You would have saved yourself trouble if you had held out for the Merchandise Mart[50]) — or uninspired thoughts of the lesser members of the bureaucracy, or diatribes against Communism. The latter are perhaps the dreariest feature of all. I cannot read them without pausing to consider whether the Communists have something, and Murrow may well be turning me into a security risk. Lately I have been sending

50 In Chicago. Owned by the Kennedy family.

him samples of this gaseous diffusion with a note of personal congratulation.[51]

I am going to need a new head of the USIS organization here. So far I have been shown only a worthy but broken-arch bureaucrat. Outsiders are opposed in the interest of upholding the merit system. I am puzzled as to why a merit system is important in the absence of merit, but you are President and will understand better. Or perhaps you could ask Larry O'Brien[52] to explain.

The technical assistance program, and related economic aid activities, also produce no cheering. In the old Dulles days, the Indian Government regarded the technical assistance activities — agriculture, public health, education and so forth — with considerable suspicion. It seemed an invasion of sovereignty, a possible cover for cold war penetration. And there was feeling that some of our experts we were sending were less than leaders in their chosen fields — a suspicion that was amply confirmed when at intervals some truly remarkable stumble-bums were off-loaded at the local airport. As a consequence of all this, whenever the Indian Government asked for help there was a great effort to respond — "at least they were asking us." No effort was made to fit the particular expert into a sense-making program or even to be sure that what he did made sense. And the Indians in turn subjected our talent to a scrutiny that regularly took and still takes months. So our technical assistance is a hit-and-miss affair, helping here and missing there, and maybe even doing occasional damage by diverting attention from first essentials. On the essentials, for example technical assistance to improve Indian agriculture, the effort is spread very, very thin — so thin that I can-

[51] The President, as I later learned, read this to Ed Murrow over the telephone in what Ed described as the most difficult single telephone call of his life. It pleased the President to imply that Murrow had written it personally. Presently the file diminished radically in size. Previously anything that might offend a right-wing congressman was deleted. Now anything that might offend me had also to go. Not much was left between.

[52] Special Assistant to President Kennedy for Congressional Relations and since then Postmaster General and manager of presidential election campaigns.

not think it will have any appreciable impact before the Second or possibly the Third Coming. The experts range from very good and very skilled to indifferent. Vacancies remain unfilled for many months and by the time a man is cleared for appointment, if he is any good, he is no longer available. Quite a few experts still come for short tours of duty and afflict the Mission and the government with the divine revelations of every newcomer to India. It may be debated in the matter of religion but no one seems to question the doctrine of immaculate conception where ideas on economic development are involved.

The leadership of the economic and technical aid program, if not inspired, seems sound. I have already asked for a thorough restudy of operation, and I have given my thoughts on needed reform. These include concentration of our energies on first essentials, the elimination of frills, and a clear indication to the Indian Government that we will henceforth provide assistance only when it is seriously wanted. This being so we will expect our judgment on people to be accepted and will undertake to ensure performance. This means we will have to provide people of first-rate ability.

Shriver was here last week and did exceedingly well. The Prime Minister liked him and he seems even to have charmed Krishna Menon whom I sent him to visit. Krishna Menon is an odd and difficult character. But some small part of the problem, I think, is that the Republicans treated him with all the warmth and tact of a Brahmin encountering a leprous untouchable at his table. I am routing all visitors through K.M.'s office.[53]

This includes Lyndon who arrives next week with two airplanes, a party of fifty, a communications unit, and other minor accoutrements of modern democracy....

Faithfully,

JOHN KENNETH GALBRAITH

THE PRESIDENT
THE WHITE HOUSE

[53] See page 84.

May 11 — New Delhi

Some very dreary diplomatic callers came in plus some oil company representatives who have just broken off negotiations with the Indians for exploration rights. I doubt that virtue is all on one side. Indeed, the companies all but admitted that they were being forced to take an unreasonable position with the Indians (who are also unreasonable in their own way) in order to protect their position, also unreasonable, in current negotiations in Iraq. Meanwhile the Soviets are at work. And meanwhile, also, large amounts of the scarce foreign exchange of the Indians go for petroleum products. Whether a country has a balance-of-payments problem or not, as I once observed in South America, depends largely on whether it has or must import oil.

Planning for the Johnson visit goes on apace. In another week, everyone will be involved in nothing else. An international crisis may find us quite helpless, but we will be managing the Vice President well.

May 13 — New Delhi

The neutral countries, led by Yugoslavia, the U.A.R. and with the reluctant consent of India, are planning a summit meeting later this summer. The Yugoslav Ambassador asked me yesterday what I thought the U.S. view of it would be. A little later the U.A.R. man made the same inquiry. My first offhand reaction was "fine" and then I remembered that I had no instructions of any sort so I modified this into a statement about our agreeable view of neutrals. I added that economic development would be a good agenda topic. Economic development, unlike, say, Portuguese colonies, is always a perfectly safe subject. No one can ever quite remember what was said.

I did say that neutrality shouldn't consist of denouncing ourselves and the Russians equally. The U.A.R. Ambassador, who has the slightly non-euphonious name of El-Feki, said that colonialism would be given quite a going-over. I said that I appreciated the nostalgic and tactical appeal of this business and its continuing applicability to the Portuguese. But in a day when the British, French, Dutch and Belgians had all but given up, and in the decade which would always be celebrated for this fact, was it wholly necessary? I asked if in Cairo it was the custom to keep on playing a football game after the whistle even though the game had been won by a considerable score. He granted the force of my argument but said they would like the discussion nevertheless.

Last night we had our first considerable sit-down dinner. It was rather nice. The Burmese Ambassador (the widow of General Aung San who was assassinated) is delightful.

A minor footnote in the annals of diplomacy: A few years ago a French Ambassador had a strong preference for boys and more or less forbade members of his staff to have wives. In the end, he was called home having been told that General de Gaulle did not approve. On receiving this news, he died.

May 14 — New Delhi

I am having nasty headaches and yesterday was one of the worst. A technical assistance mission set up a training school for aspiring foundry workers in my frontal lobes. They banged away, energetically but carelessly, all day. After signing an agreement for financing a new school for American staff and a few privileged Indian students at 11 A.M., I surrendered and went to bed for the rest of the day. It was rather nice.

For the signing of the school contract, several of the local leaders of the American community had filed into my office with some ceremony. It was a major event calling for some important words and flourishes. None came. I must do better.

At dinner night before last, my dinner companion, a famous M.P. and former cabinet member, was talking of the still incomplete progress on women's rights. In some villages bigamy is still the thing. If there are three couples more or less of an age, and one wife loses her husband, she is taken on, as it were, by one of the surviving husbands. I opined that this might be unsettling for the man's wife but rather good for the girl who was bereft. My companion said privately that this might be so. I said I took this position privately and not on behalf of the Government of the United States.

Speaking of marriage, the Hindustan *Times Weekly* lists a page of possibilities every Sunday. Herewith some samples:

For a Maheshwari[54] girl of 23 years M.A. of respectable, well-known family suitable Maheshwari or Aggarwal boy. Only those having modern thoughts need apply. Box 3450, Hindustan Times, New Delhi–1.

Wanted a beautiful, educated and well-accomplished girl for an Aggarwal (Jindal) 24, getting Doctorate in Soil Physics in U.S.A. in couple of months. Elder brother a Civil Engineer and his wife, both doing post-graduate studies in U.S.A. Father Gazetted Officer. Will visit his parents this month. Girl is expected to stay in U.S.A. for six months. Only high class families need apply with full particulars in first instance. Box 29641-CA, Hindustan Times, New Delhi–1.

Accomplished, beautiful, homely[55] virgin from respectable family for Punjabi bachelor, 26 years, industrialist, income 1000/–, Box 31334-CA, Hindustan Times, New Delhi–1.

May 15 — New Delhi

My strategy for getting L.B.J. to the Bhakra-Nangal Dam,[56] with lots of pictures of Texas hats against the background of big con-

[54] Maheshwari, Aggarwal and Punjabi refer to the linguistic community to which the applicant belongs.

[55] As used in India, "homely" means a woman who prefers to cultivate the home or even merely to stay there.

[56] This huge structure is where the Sutlej River emerges from a narrow gorge in the mountains onto the Punjab Plain. It was built by the Indians with their own funds and technicians but under the supervision of the late Harvey Slocum, an

struction, has gone haywire. He will, we are advised, be too tired for the train trip. And the air trip which is recommended would, in fact, be too tiring for it involves some four hours altogether in an automobile. We shall take him to an agricultural college instead.

A telegram yesterday said that even at "some risk of some small offense" to the government he would stay at the Ashoka Hotel instead of the President's Palace should it be impossible to house all of his party in the latter. It is clear that there is not room in the Rashtrapati Bhavan,[57] but it is also clear that we should not be in the business of offending in a minor way. We are a big country and should always offend in a big way. I decided for the palace.

Last night we had a large "at-home" for USIS and AID personnel. The latter included a large number of agricultural experts with vast, useful hands and large shoulders and great cylindrical stomachs. We breed to a strong type here and I was glad to be reminded of it. Some were surprised when I told them of my credentials as a graduate animal and poultry husbandry man.[58] It is not, somehow, the education which they associate with an ambassador.

To add a touch, I hired a violin and accordion team. This was not an unqualified success. After a few fairly lugubrious numbers, they settled down to "Home on the Range" and nothing else. We had some twenty renditions in all. I later learned the reason. Nicolas Nabokov[59] was our house guest, and Ed O'Neill,[60] in a

---

American and legendary builder of dams. His method in working with the Indians, as presumably with all others, was to combine uncompromising candor with a minimum of tact. It was greatly resented, greatly admired and greatly effective.

[57] Designed by Sir Edwin Landseer Lutyens, who also built the British Embassy in Washington, and, begun in 1921, this vast and handsome palace of red sandstone is not lacking in space. There are 54 bedrooms among its several hundred rooms. Nonetheless, it was hardly up to an American official visit at full strength.

[58] I graduated from the Ontario Agricultural College in 1931 with the degree of Bachelor of Science in Agriculture. I specialized in animal husbandry and agricultural economics.

[59] A well-known composer, although not of "Home on the Range."

[60] A former reporter of the *Louisville Times,* an old India hand and general assistant for USIS matters.

good-humored mood, had told them that Nabokov had composed this piece. They had thought it wrong to play anything else.

May 16 — New Delhi

The Polish Ambassador[61] called yesterday to give me a lecture on diplomacy. He is a brief, thick-set man, with heavy glasses and a heavy, swarthy face. He is capable, it is said, of being quite nasty, but yesterday he was wonderfully cynical. The great thing in New Delhi, he told me, is to find material that justifies a telegram home. That shows the diplomat is at work; it reminds the Foreign Office of his existence; and it establishes the value of his post. But getting material for the well-justified telegram is not so easy. And to make matters worse, everyone rushes to the same bait. When I came down from Kashmir to meet Harriman and the Prime Minister, that suggested something pretty important. (I told Katz-Suchy it wasn't especially important, and he said, "Of course. No reason why it should be.") When the I.C.C. was assembling here, the fact that one member was a Pole made the Polish Ambassador important. He handed out appointments at ten-minute intervals. For some countries, news from embassies east of the Iron Curtain — "in conversation with the Polish Ambassador today, I learned" — is especially good. But it has no advantages for other countries within the socialist camp. He advised me to be generous with information. "In conversation with the American Ambassador, I learned . . ." makes, he said, a fine beginning for another ambassador's cable.

Poland he described as a country where peasants live under a form of strongly assisted private enterprise and flourish at the expense of the workers. Polish peasants have never been so affluent. Nor will the situation be corrected — "the next revolution will not come in our generation."

Later the French Ambassador came in. Having in mind the

---

[61] Dr. Juliusz Katz-Suchy. He had served previously at the United Nations. In 1968, having meanwhile returned to a professorship in Poland, he was (reportedly) retired as part of the anti-liberal, anti-Zionist campaigns of that year.

counsel of my Polish colleague, I asked him the latest word from Geneva. He said he had a number of telegrams on the subject from Paris, but unfortunately they were still in code and he did not know what they said.

In the evening, I went over to the Ministry of External Affairs to settle some of the final details of the Johnson trip due to start in four days' time. They were concerned with measuring the minutes that it would take to move him from one ring of the circus to the next. I was soon overcome with impatience and left.

I did have a press conference to promote the visit a bit. So far the Indian papers have accorded it total silence.

May 17 — New Delhi–Bangkok

Yesterday I visited the Saudi Arabian Ambassador who gave me a booklet about his country. It says encouragingly that "public security and stability are prevalent in Saudi Arabia"; it goes on to praise the efficient work of the Bureau for Boycotting Israel which has as its principal term of reference the "suffocation" of the latter state; and it explains that the King does great good by going hunting during which time he distributes food, clothing and money to the inhabitants of the desert. Later I received the Ambassador from Iran. He is busy writing his memoirs. I asked him about the minor revolution now being made in his country. He expressed himself as uninformed but favorable. He said, encouragingly, that everything happens for the best in Iran.

In the afternoon, I called on S. S. Khera,[62] a senior I.C.S.[63] offi-

[62] In India in 1956, I had given him a paper on the organization of Indian public enterprises and the need for according them more autonomy. He had been impressed and had given it to his Minister. Meanwhile I had given a copy to Asoka Mehta, since a member of the government but then, as a Praja Socialist, in opposition. Mehta urged the government to take my views seriously and read part of my paper to the House. The elderly Minister, who had been briefed by Khera on my paper, had heard my name as Braithwaite, the latter being a familiar business name in India. He said he preferred the views of Braithwaite and read into the record different extracts from the same paper. A debate then ensued on the comparative merits of the views of Galbraith and Braithwaite. The matter was never resolved.
[63] Indian Civil Service.

cial, old friend and now head of the Cabinet Secretariat. Then I looked in briefly on a reception at the Rashtrapati Bhavan. The latter is really a place of spacious elegance. After everyone was assembled, the President came in and made the rounds, bowing to the guests. Magnificently attired attendants guided one about. Again I reflected that India, in such matters, is a good deal more grand than Washington.

Then, at 7:45 P.M., I called on the Prime Minister. In his visits elsewhere in South Asia, Johnson will hear much about the need to contain Communism, and about the effectiveness of military measures for doing so. It will sound exceedingly straightforward and simple. If the Indian visit is to be useful, it must redress any such impression. And I thought it well that Nehru not expect a polished expert on international affairs and react adversely if he encountered something else.

However, I could hardly tell Nehru what he should say to L.B.J. So I went into the nature of fact-finding trips; why Johnson was eager to learn; the importance in this connection of a balanced view of Asia and of the problem of containing the Communists. The Prime Minister got the idea rather well and without my overstepping the line. Afterward we chatted about modern art — "my daughter is partial to these things" — and how heads of state should behave — "A most important thing is always to drive at low speed." This grew out of newspaper accounts of Diem's closing off of the streets of Saigon for Lady Bird's shopping, and the P.M.'s recollection of a sixty-mile-an-hour trip through the same city when he visited there a few years back.

He also asked me about what was happening in Seoul where a military coup occurred today. I was able to give him the very latest from Reuters.

Then he went on to a pleasant outdoor dinner by the Chief of Protocol. Quite good Indian food and very pleasant, relaxed, untroublesome conversation. We got to bed about midnight and rose to take off for Bangkok at five. As I write this, we are on our way aboard a MATS Constellation with ancient five-abreast seats in which one rides backward. We were originally booked on a Pan American flight but, because of bad weather, it was half a day late leaving New York. We then were moved to a B.O.A.C. and it came down with engine trouble. But now we are far down the Ganges Plain. It is bleached almost white by the terrible arid heat. The villages are the same color as the soil — of which, indeed, they are made.

VI

Visit

May 18 — Bangkok–New Delhi

Kitty and I arrived in Bangkok about 4 P.M. in moist and incredible heat. The local discomfort index had topped all previous records and then collapsed. We were met by Embassy people and Kukrit Pramoj[1] and taken to the Erawan Hotel which is built in a U around a garden and swimming pool. The Prince is in a relatively hopeful mood about Thailand. The Government is strong and moderately corrupt. This is better than the only alternative which is weak and moderately corrupt. One is struck by how much better housed, fed and clothed everyone seems than in India. As another sign of progress, the automobile traffic is far worse.

At six, I had a meeting with the State Department officials accompanying the Vice-President. The situation is full of despair. The Department people are at their wits' end with Johnson. Johnson's people are similarly furious with the Department. Johnson, in the Department's view, won't adhere to schedule; he identifies diplomacy with a campaign tour; and he is oblivious to the necessities and niceties expected of any visitor from abroad. In the opposite view, he has been loaded with an excessive schedule by people who are more concerned with protocol than performance, are not very efficient and do not appreciate a forthright approach to the people. Evidently I have some work cut out for me.

---

[1] M. R. Kukrit Pramoj, a prince of the royal house, newspaper publisher, local gadfly and personal friend.

Later in the evening, C.A.G. and I went to an unnecessary dinner with pleasant Americans under conditions approximating the inside of a steam boiler. Later I telephoned to New Delhi to take a few items out of the program we had arranged. Part of the problem is that everyone is tired. Now we are all riding in the utmost elegance aboard the official Boeing, two hours late, and I am about to brief L.B.J. on his Delhi duty.

May 21 — New Delhi

It is over and was really a great deal of fun. Everything went off well; by the dubious scorekeeping used for official visits, it was rated a success. I couldn't be sure what was accomplished, but at least everyone left much happier than he arrived.

We got to Delhi a good two hours behind time and got off to a fine start when Nehru made an unscheduled appearance to welcome L.B.J. An honor guard, including some exceedingly handsome Sikhs, made a marvelous display and put Jean Kennedy Smith,[2] who has all the agreeable enthusiasm of youth, into a fine state of excitement. Then we went into town over barren landscape so unpopulated that not even Johnson was tempted to get out and greet any voters. Anyhow, he was riding with Nehru and hence somewhat under control.

Shortly after arrival, there was an afternoon meeting with Nehru. Various officials on each side participated and it was no astounding success. The Prime Minister and Vice-President spoke rather formally on education which they favored, poverty which they opposed, freedom which they endorsed, peace which they wanted and the Third Five-Year Plan which they praised. The rest of us listened with respect and drank tea. The meeting was in the Prime Minister's main or M.E.A. office.

Then with some pomp we called on the President. India is underdeveloped in everything but photography, and each of these stops was fully recorded. Then in the evening we went to the

2 See p. 53.

Prime Minister's house for dinner — the Johnsons, Smiths, Indira Gandhi,[3] R. K. Nehru, the Galbraiths and a few others. This was much better. Before dinner, we went out in the vast garden back of the Residence to see the Prime Minister's two very attractive tiger cubs and then, after the usual fruit juice, on to dinner. I worried a little about Indira and Lyndon who did not communicate in any intimate way. I worried much less about Nehru and Jean Smith who got along very well. Why I should worry is unclear. After dinner, Nehru and Johnson had a long talk, mostly by Johnson, which lasted until nearly eleven. Among other things, they agreed to issue a communiqué which I drafted and returned to the Rashtrapati Bhavan to read to Lyndon about 2 A.M. He approved and I went to bed.

Next morning, L.B.J. and I went to the Prime Minister's house with the communiqué — a literate but remarkably general document — and we discussed it over coffee. Mostly the Indians approved it although they deleted some references to our hope that they would exercise leadership and offer counsel on the problems of South Asia. I made a mistake in handling this. We should have sent a draft in advance and not seemed, as we did, to have presented a document (even as noncommittal as this) for signing on the line. But no great harm was done. The communiqué was much wanted by Johnson, partly for its effect on the Congress — for improving the legislative climate for economic aid — and partly for its proof that the mission was producing useful results.

Then the entire party took off for Agra, the press having already been dispatched in advance. At the airport there, an air base, we were welcomed by a considerable gathering of the citizens and soldiers, and L.B.J. did some electioneering which he followed up a few minutes later with a ride on a bullock cart and by lifting water from a well. Then we went on to see a couple of villages where he campaigned in earnest. At one, a brass band boomed us down the village street to a wedding march with many garlands and mari-

[3] See page 82.

gold petals and an infinity of handshaking. I left the Vice-President to his own devices and time schedule and was comforted by the thought that the campaigning was coming out of his afternoon rest period. There is no doubt that the villagers liked it. And presumably their smiles will show up in the photographs.

The second of the villages, visited at L.B.J.'s behest, was in a state of nature. The houses were of mud and thatch; the streets were as God made them, and the mud must be inches deep in the monsoon. By now, the temperature was around 110°; everything was scorched a light beige.

Later we laid the cornerstone — a board imitating a stone on a bogus brick wall — for a new agricultural school that would not necessarily soon be built and then went to the Taj. It was as beautiful as ever, even under the late midday sun. There was a flaw. One of the minarets was enclosed in scaffolding for repairs, and so much does it depend on purity of line that the effect is more than a little impaired. There were many, many more photographs plus Coca-Cola on the lawns in front. Then we got aboard the big jet and went back to Delhi. By now, it was midafternoon.[4] (Johnson got an adverse American press for giving a Texas yell in the Taj Mahal to promote the famous echo. This was unfair. It is something that guides do for tourists every hour of the day. And the Taj Mahal is a monument, not a mosque as some critics assumed.)

In the evening, I took the Vice-President to visit the Vice-President and then on to a vast reception at the Residence. We did not make him stand in line but guided him around to meet people. At the appropriate moment, I had him announce the anticipated K. & K.[5] meeting in Vienna of which we had just had word.

---

[4] Word had come to me the night before that, because of expected noonday temperatures, the Vice-President's jet would not be able to take off from the Agra air strip. The warmer the weather the more runway required; at the expected 120°, there would not be enough. After contemplating an afternoon with L.B.J. at the airport waiting for the weather to moderate, I chartered a Constellation to stand by to bring us back to Delhi. But it was not needed. There was a cold wave, the noonday temperature did not exceed 115°, and the jet remained functional.

[5] Kennedy and Khrushchev.

Finally, there was a big state banquet at the Rashtrapati Bhavan. This was fine; lancers in full regalia lined the great staircase as we came up to the large hall adjacent to the state dining room. The dining room has a table the size of a small racetrack where the Viceroys once dined in imperial elegance. Their portraits still line the walls. They are so bemedaled that they must have jangled and one or two could profitably have been broken up for scrap. The food was far from bad. The speeches were mercifully short. Jean Smith was seated next to the Minister of Irrigation and Power[6] and thought that the only subject they had in common was sex. I warned against it. The speeches, incidentally, paid warm and well-deserved tributes to the new Ambassador to which I responded with a modest smile.

The following morning, more or less on time, they all flew off to Karachi — much happier than when they came. Kitty went along, L.B.J. having offered her a ride home. I think she had always had in mind going and was not above a hint or two without ever admitting that she was guilty of such wretched behavior. But, in any case, the invitation she wanted was immediately and warmly forthcoming.

I went back to the office, looked briefly at the three days of accumulated mail and came home and went to bed.

May 22 — New Delhi

I have had another visit. Yesterday (Sunday) morning I was taking an early turn in the garden of the Residence when the bearer came out to say that Mr. and Mrs. Levinson were waiting for me. I asked who they were. "Very old," he said.

They were installed in the living room, old but rugged except that Mrs. Levinson was wearing a cast. She had broken her leg in Japan. I repressed a slight feeling of lofty annoyance over this informal invasion and was glad, for I heard a fascinating story.

They arrived in Delhi a few days ago on a round-the-world tour

[6] Hafiz Mohammad Ibrahim.

from their Los Angeles base. With a day to spare, they looked up
a tour-and-taxi man located near the Janpath Hotel, to whom they
had been recommended by someone they had encountered earlier
on their travels. His name, they were told, was Singh; so is that
of every taxi driver in Delhi.[7] On asking a likely-looking taxi man
if his name was Singh, he replied truthfully that it was and they
booked a tour of the city. He then persuaded them to give up their
plane trip to Kashmir and go instead by Singh's tour service —
marvelous scenery, good restaurants, air-conditioned hotels. Only
Rs. 800.[8] They were persuaded and started on the worst journey
since Scott. It was as hot as his was cold. Filthy hotels; filthy restaurants; an appalling vehicle which, six hours from Delhi, was five
hours behind schedule; no sanitary facilities — "He just sent me to
the fields like an animal." Mrs. Levinson did the talking and was
eloquent. Three days out, they made Srinagar.[9]

Here the qualities that have kept her race alive over the centuries asserted themselves even against the Singhs. Singh was given
Rs. 150 for his gasoline and sent packing. The Levinsons later returned by air. But Singh met them at the airport on their return
and has been pestering them for his Rs. 650 ever since. He threatened to garnishee their possessions at the airport when they took
off for Bombay later that morning. Thus their appeal for my protection. I gave them a letter of my own typing asking that Singh
see the Commercial Attaché with any complaint and hinting that
the C.A. would also wish to take the whole matter up with the
Indian Tourist Bureau. I told my guests to reflect on what a good
story they would have to tell on their return. They were somewhat
comforted. (I heard no more of the crisis.)

A crippled child was to have been taken to the United States
aboard the Vice-President's plane for treatment. The Indian Government objected; publicity, they said, and a clear invitation to the

---

[7] All cab drivers are Sikhs, and all Sikh names (virtually) append the name Singh
(meaning lion) to their other names.

[8] About $160.

[9] An hour or so by plane.

Russians to undertake some similar stunt. I think they are too sensitive, but I stepped in and stopped it after exacting a promise they would fly the youngster back by a regular Air-India plane. Then I took the rap (rather mild) with the press. I said, thoughtfully, I feared it would look too much like a publicity stunt.

May 23 — New Delhi

Nothing in the morning; nothing at noon but a swim; nothing much in the afternoon but an official visit to Cottage Industries Emporium[10] and a reception in my honor by the Indian and American agricultural specialists at the Ashoka Hotel. These latter made an empty day unduly full; one shakes hands with a hundred people whom one tries to seem to have recognized — if this is required — or anyhow look glad. Then as the last man arrives, the first leaves. The Indians on leaving all say: "I had a very nice time, Your Excellency." The Americans all say: "Hadavernicetymgbysir." Then it is over. My ankles are swelling dangerously; I think I may claim workman's compensation.

At the Emporium, I bought some nice Benares stoles and arranged to have an edition published to order with a signature, "From the Galbraiths" or "Love from J.K.G." woven into the design. Not a great idea but all mine.

May 25 — New Delhi

Yesterday morning I visited the All India Institute of Medical Sciences[11] and spent an hour going over the new buildings. In one laboratory, a Yogi is being studied. According to the electrocardiogram, which presumably does not lie, he can indeed put off his pulse at will. Also, he can slow down his metabolism and exist in a smallish — $4' \times 4' \times 6'$ — box, hermetically sealed, for up to eight

[10] A fine government-run enterprise, beloved by all tourists, selling a variety of beautifully wrought handicrafts.
[11] A large modern hospital and health complex to which the governments of the United States, New Zealand and others have contributed.

hours. (There is an electric button for him to signal when he wants out.) This strikes me as a peculiarly Indian contribution to science. I wonder if any Indian engineers are working on the rope trick.

The buildings are fine. The maintenance, as so often in this part of the world, promises to be awful. I came up with the idea that a trained and disciplined maintenance corps — painters, janitors, cleaners of all kinds — be organized, uniformed and trained to the highest standards of performance and pride of task.

At noon, we had a long session on USIS; this was the best chance I have had so far to deliver my ideas on how we should bill ourselves. We reach only a few hundred thousand people with our information services in India at most. We must match them in intelligence. And anyone in the group we seek to influence is fairly likely to detect spurious propaganda and be repelled by it. I doubt that there is much to be gained from talking about democracy in the abstract. Our strongest economic case is not the dynamic free enterprise system but our concern for popular welfare. I don't think we should talk much about labor unions; on this subject, I have never encountered anyone who wanted to listen. Our arts, industrial and scientific achievements appeal to a large audience. There was general agreement. This is a pleasant tendency where the views of the ambassador are concerned.

In the evening before dinner, I visited Nehru. The *U.S. News & World Report* had just published my picture with a note saying that I am the key figure in a plan to align Nehru with the West. I asked if he had seen it and felt duly warned.[12]

Then we talked about a dozen or more things. He liked Lyndon Johnson whom he regarded as an intelligent, down-to-earth, practical, political figure;[13] he would like to meet Kennedy but would delay the idea of a visit for he is a little weary; he told me to tell

---

[12] He was a faithful reader of *U.S. News & World Report* and derived therefrom a great deal of alarming information on American intentions.
[13] "The kind of politician I understand," I recall him saying.

the President to have in mind that Khrushchev is a man of exceedingly fast responses. When Khrushchev first visited India, he confided to Nehru his feeling that he must improve British and U.S. attitudes toward the Soviets — in effect, clean up the image left by Stalin, although Nehru did not put it in these words. Then Khrushchev went to Burma. Reacting angrily to a question, he denounced British imperialism and all its filthy works. Back in Delhi, Nehru asked him if this were a wise way to make friends. Khrushchev replied, "We react that way. We were surrounded and subject to siege for forty years."

I told Nehru Roswell Garst's[14] story about hybrid corn. Garst, in the course of selling corn to the Soviets, was questioned at great length by Khrushchev on cultural practices. Finally, Garst interrupted to ask why he was being asked: "This is all in our agricultural bulletins, Mr. Chairman, and it has been explained thousands of times to our farmers or anyone who will listen. I imagine that where our atomic secrets are concerned you have an organization that gets them in a couple of weeks . . ."

"No, no," interrupted Khrushchev, waving his finger vigorously, "one week."

"One week or two weeks," said Garst. "Why do you ask me about something that is in the public domain?"

"The Russian character," said Khrushchev. "When the aristocrats first discovered that potatoes were a cheap way of feeding the peasants, they had no success in getting the peasants to eat them. But they knew their people. They fenced the potatoes in with high fences. The peasants then stole the potatoes and soon acquired a taste for them."

We discussed Laos and I reiterated my feelings that we must have a strong enforcement machinery. Then we turned to more casual matters. Back at home, I had a pleasant dinner party for the planning types.

[14] See page 28.

May 26 — New Delhi

Yesterday morning, I visited the Chilean Ambassador, an agreeable man who writes books, contemplates the Indian scene and avoids overwork. And then I had an interesting chat with the Moroccan Ambassador, one of the most intelligent men in the diplomatic corps, who, in wise defiance of Koranic law, came up with ice-cold beer. I mentioned my mystification over Arab politics, and he told me that he shared it. I recalled a meeting in Moscow two years ago at the Institute for World Economics and International Affairs. A professor told me their Mid-Eastern project for the year was a study of Arab nationalism. I said, "Do you understand it?"

The professor replied, "Of course not."

Some branches of our Mission are still maintaining independent communications with Washington. The other day, by chance, I saw a dispatch from a Washington agency to its local officer discussing my views. I am moving in to tighten up; the key to authority in the field is full control of communications. If you know and clear what everyone is saying to Washington, you are in full control. Sometimes in exercise of authority, one is not sure where it is a matter of dignity, where a matter of discipline. But on control of communications, the requirements of the two happily coincide.

In the afternoon, we had two interesting conferences. One with Krishna Menon and M. J. Desai took up the Geneva negotiations on Laos. I registered our views with some enthusiasm — neutralization with guarantees — for they are sensible. My relations with Krishna Menon continue to be agreeable. His office in the Secretariat — that of Defence Minister — is large and dark and piled with the musty-looking files which clutter every Indian office. It is the combination of age, dust and poor paper which gives the effect. Krishna Menon wears a dhoti[15] and conveys the impression of a severe ascetic. But he also serves excellent tea.

[15] A white cotton sheet wrapped around the waist as a skirt or with one end pulled between the legs.

Later we saw Swaran Singh, the Steel, Mines and Fuel Minister.[16] I had indicated our possible willingness to finance the new Bokaro steel plant in the public sector. The Indians, as I have told, had then laid down a variety of conditions under which we might be allowed to do so — technical direction by Americans and management of project by Indians and other interesting dualities. This is a hangover from the day when we seemed so anxious to help that we agreed to anything. I made clear that if we were providing the money — if we do — we must be able to ensure that a good job is being done. Today at the meeting we got a paper indicating agreement on this point. Diplomacy is easier from a strong bargaining position. The harder test would have been to make these arrangements if we were not the prospective source of the money.

May 27 — New Delhi–Rome

I left at six-thirty last night for Bombay en route for Washington. My briefcase is packed with petitions to Santa Claus — a sugar quota for the Indians, a Deputy Chief of Mission[17] for me, an administrative officer for Madras "desperately needed," a swimming pool for the staff of which Washington takes a poor view, a civilian air agreement (with more Atlantic flights for Air-India and more Indian stops for Pan Am), a solution to or anyhow some action on the power crises in Delhi (where the lights regularly go off), the steel plant. And on and on.

I had to have a press conference in Bombay and by the time it was over, I was violently ill. The people from the Consulate had come out, including my old friend Bob Carr, the Consul-General, and they sat in the V.I.P. room until after midnight to keep me company. In the same room was a marvelous bed. I looked at it longingly but, alas, no chance.

At midnight we took off for Tehran, and I suffered the tortures of the damned — headache, nausea, sleeplessness and all the other

---

[16] See page 105.
[17] Maffitt having reached the end of his tour.

known ills including morning sickness. Tehran, on a shelf just above the desert and just below the mountains, looked clean and beautiful. It was also blessedly cool and fresh. Here I had a piece of prime luck. As we were taking off for Rome, one engine lost power and we aborted. For three precious hours while they fixed it, I was able to get some sleep on a long settee in the airport lounge. I was much, much better when we finally lifted off. Now we are nearly in Rome.

After all the ceremony of these last weeks, I am now an ordinary air passenger again. People see the words "The Ambassador" on my special baggage tags and conclude that it is meant for a hotel.

A young Canadian in the next seat, an electrical engineer, said to me, "What is your line, sir?" I replied that I was working as an ambassador in New Delhi. He said, "Then you must be accustomed to the heat."

This plane is full of handsome young mothers, each equipped with an incredibly fat and noisy baby. They bawl loudly, continuously and with no effort at synchronization. It would be more efficient if they took turns. But they are independent little bastards and will not work in shifts.

May 28 — Rome–Boston

Rarely have I felt such bliss. I was late arriving in Rome yesterday but in time to have a large, elegantly-cooked luncheon with a martini and a good Campania wine, all of which tasted like the nourishment of the gods. I can't be sure why Indian food is, by contrast, so tasteless. E. M. Forster says in *A Passage to India* that it is because the cooks, preparing European food, neither eat nor understand what they are preparing. Certainly they are well advised. I imagine that the heat bleaches the flavor out of many things, and if scientific basis for this is lacking, it should be found. Also, many good materials — beef, veal, tender chicken, varied fresh seafood, numerous vegetables — are lacking.

After lunch, I slept — I am at the Hassler atop the Spanish Steps

— and then went for a leisurely walk to Via Vittorio Veneto where I bought a paper and a novel and read for two or three hours. Then I went to bed again. Several invitations were awaiting me at the hotel which I either declined or ignored, as also the solicitation of a large and exceptionally frowzy prostitute who was doing duty near the hotel.

This morning I awoke utterly rested and with all tissues in a state of exquisite tone and after breakfast went to St. Peter's. The enormous ornamented interior reminded me nostalgically of our first magic trip to Italy twenty-four years ago when we lived in these cathedrals. It being Sunday, Mass was being said in half a dozen chapels and confessions were being heard in a dozen stalls. I was depressed by the thought of so much sin and refreshed by the thought that, were I a Catholic, I would have so little to confess. In one chapel, some thirty or forty priests were gathered for some churchly office. Quite a few were too fat and one was enormously so — he could barely squeeze into pew space allotted for two. Their surplices were none too clean — all looked rather shapeless and unpressed; I had the impression that some needed a shave. Pope John may be too liberal. The next Pope should be more of the spit-and-polish type; Bob Kennedy should be brought in to get a physical fitness program going.

At noon, I went to the new airport, by Ostia Antica, and en route worked on a speech for the University of Toronto and continued with my eating. It was wonderful spring weather all the way across.

June 1 — Washington–Toronto

The consortium for assistance to India — of the countries making loans and grants to the Third Five-Year Plan — met here in Washington yesterday. Because of my rank, I was told I could not attend — it was on "the official level." What nonsense! However, things worked out well. Enough money is in sight for the first year, and a good start has been made on funds for the second year of the Plan.

I spent the day talking on domestic matters with Walter Heller and James Tobin[18] and with Chester Bowles and Arthur Schlesinger on more general matters. The mood of the Kennedy Administration is not what it was when I left in April. Cuba had a profoundly depressing influence, and everyone worries over the extent to which the soldiers and the CIA are making policy. So do I. Bowles struck me as being a bit apologetic and defensive about his role on Cuba. He was at pains to prove that he was doing his best elsewhere for whatever is right and rational. I contemplated urging that he be a little more aggressive fighting but desisted. He is on the right side.

The fundamental division in American politics is coming to be over foreign policy. On the one hand are the proponents of all kinds of direct anti-Communist action. They have a strong military base in the CIA and the support of the Congressional right wing. On the other side are those who argue for the more complex forms of economic and social defense against Communism. By rejecting armed intervention, they invite the suspicion of being appeasers.

June 2 — Toronto–Cambridge

Last night in Toronto we had a family dinner — Alice, Catherine[19] and her husband, nieces — and this morning we walked around Queen's Park and the University. Then at noon I went to a luncheon at Hart House and, in the afternoon, received an honorary degree — it was the thirtieth anniversary of my own graduation. In my speech, I dealt with the possible obsolescence of my animal husbandry education and the increasing polarization of the world as between the unrighteous and the self-righteous. For the rest, I talked about aid and development and how much easier it was to have development in the nineteenth century. For then when debt became burdensome, the borrowing enterprises could always

[18] See page 14.
[19] My older and younger sisters.

resort to honorable bankruptcy. And one did not have to keep bad governments in to keep the Communists out.

It was all very good for my sanity, but I am not sure that any other major purpose was served. It is hard to know what to do with an honorary degree.

Security Note: I had asked that a cable from Washington to New Delhi summarizing the results of the aid consortium be repeated to me through the Toronto Consulate. It arrived in code; no facilities existed for decoding. They brought it out to me at the airport — a mass of numbers. I asked if they assumed I could read it. They said no. I asked how they managed. They said when something arrived in code, they phoned Washington and had the original message read to them.

June 20 — Rome–New Delhi

A diary should be a servant, not a master — or, in any case, it should not be an insufferable tyranny. The last two and a half weeks in Washington have been so tiresome and generally oppressive that I have had to beg off. One reason was the social life. During my stay in Washington, I succeeded in eating by myself not a single night.[20] In that city, a social lion is one who is suitably installed in an important job; who has some mystery apart from his official position, of which the possession of money is the most common, though a literary reputation serves well; and who is not suffering from overexposure. Harold Stassen is not good. For the moment, I am.

My Washington tasks were virtually endless. A new D.C.M.; a new head of USIS; settling policy with Ex-Im Bank and the Development Loan Fund; some problems on the sale of military equipment to the Indian Government; the oil negotiations; some exceedingly confidential air route negotiations; Nepal; a visit of Prime Minister Nehru to Washington; rice for CARE to distribute in Madras; a regional meeting of ambassadors which Bowles wants

[20] My wife being mostly in Cambridge after returning with L.B.J.

to have in New Delhi and which I welcome like a case of amoebic dysentery; the possibility of small-scale power plants for Indian villages which L.B.J. promised to investigate when there; the question of financing the Bokaro steel plant; the swimming pool; the further architectural plans for the Embassy; a social secretary; a secretary; the possibility of a new policy on Kashmir; the Peace Corps; books from the Ford Foundation; paintings for the Residence from the Museum of Modern Art; and more.

On the whole, I am well pleased. Most of all, I needed to establish my authority over all (meaning *all*) Embassy operations. Some operations worried me greatly; the more worrisome are eliminated, and the rest are on ice. Nothing that we now do would cause us impossible embarrassment. These negotiations were rather less difficult than I had expected. Cuba has brought about a healthy excess of caution and responsibility. I am still faced with Chester Bowles's regional conference. But that may perhaps be averted. Bowles may not survive for the President is fixing to give him the heave. I am sorry about this; Chet is a good man. I expressed my general support of him but less enthusiastically than were he more determined. I think he wants office so much that he is now evading criticism.

I saw the President on three occasions. Once he was in the bathtub; once in bed; once we rode to the Shoreham together for a speech. I think he is suffering a good deal from his back. Certainly it is more serious than he admits or wants to admit.

The first of our sessions was in his bathroom. While sitting on a stool, I told him about some iniquitous goings on. Every once in a while, the conversation was interrupted as he turned on the hot water with his foot. Bob Kennedy came in with one of his youngsters — approximately six. I wondered if the boy were cleared by the FBI for we were talking about some very secret matters. The President was properly frightened by some of the activities I outlined. "How," he said, "do these things remain secret? In this town, the only things that are secret are the things I need to know."

I was not able to reassure him that everything would remain secret. Indeed, that is precisely the point.

He asked me how it was being an ambassador. I replied it was easier than being in the White House. "Softer too, I imagine," said the President.

The bedroom meeting was on economics — Dillon, McChesney Martin, Heller, Gordon[21] and Roosa.[22] This was interesting. The Federal Reserve, pressed by the higher interest rate lobby, has been actually raising interest rates of late although unemployment is still around seven per cent. Dillon, who is an excellent operator, entered only a partial defense. But then Martin, who isn't so clever, went all out. "The Federal Reserve," he said, "could not keep interest rates artificially low." They had been doing their best; in the last few weeks, they have been buying government bonds to keep the money market easy. I asked if such purchases were not artificial and went on to ask that he define the difference between natural and artificial action on the part of the Federal Reserve. I did this with great mildness and many assurances of my desire to help Martin clarify his position. In response, only static came out. The President then made a magnificent statement saying he did not want the recovery choked off by premature increases in interest rates. In accordance with the well-known principle of counter-vailing power, I urged a cut in the rediscount rate. Dillon, not being committed, was able to reverse and row vigorously upstream. In consequence, any tendency to a tighter money policy was arrested. Felix Belair of the *New York Times* told me next day that Martin was likely to resign. The work was ceasing to be agreeable.

A vacancy has occurred on the Federal Reserve Board. The liberal economists in the Administration had a long caucus to discuss the new appointment. I said I did not care. The Chairman is the only one who counts. He has two years more if he chooses to stick it out. Planning for what may happen two years hence when

[21] Kermit Gordon. See page 21.
[22] Robert V. Roosa. See page 24.

the appointee might replace Martin is like planning for the Second Coming. In any case, no one of any intelligence should take a job on the Federal Reserve Board because there can be few posts of such unrelieved dullness, and the choice as between unintelligent men does not greatly matter. The only attraction of the post is its service to personal vanity. It takes a certain amount of time and energy to master the intricacies of monetary policy. Those who have done so (as also those who have not) think their knowledge important. They are pleased to have the recognition. Being close to large sums of money adds to the feeling of importance.

Kitty joined me and we ended the visit with two mammoth parties. One was at the Phil Grahams'[23] followed by an all-night dance at the Paul Mellons'.[24] These were in the rolling Virginia countryside some fifty miles from Washington and the Mellon function was a highly affluent affair. There were two orchestras, a specially erected ballroom, fireworks, several bars, Matisses, Cézannes, a tent city to house the young and an elaborate security check for guests. J.B.K. came in late with William Walton[25] and looked very fresh, gay and beautiful. We stayed with the Grahams and got to bed at 5 A.M.

The next evening there was a gay assembly at the Robert Kennedys'. This was enormous fun. We left at 4 A.M. just as everyone[26] began diving, fully-dressed in evening clothes, into the swimming pool. Those who didn't dive were thrown.

[23] See page 16.
[24] Gentleman and civilized patron of the arts.
[25] The artist and general guardian of Washington amenity.
[26] Not quite.

VII

More Education

At 3:30 A.M. day before yesterday, our plane picked its way down through the thunder clouds to Palam. The P.A.A. captain invited me into the cockpit for the operation which was just at daybreak, a particularly bright and beautiful one. I was relieved to see that the landing of a big jet involves a considerable amount of strain and is taken quite seriously.

Apart from staff meetings, I celebrated my arrival in bed listening to the rain which arrived simultaneously. This marked the beginning of the monsoon and brought a fairly substantial fall in the temperature — to the high eighties. Yesterday, when I went to the office to clear up an exceptionally large and tedious file of mail, the landscape had altered from purely arid to slightly tropical.

Yesterday morning I had a press conference. This followed a staff briefing at which, as usual, I was conscientiously advised to evade all questions. I supplied enough answers to make front-page news. There was much interest in a Kennedy-Nehru meeting; I managed to give the impression that one was coming without giving anything more. The rest of the session was on economics in general and the prospects for the Bokaro steel mill in particular. My strategy on the latter is to move toward a commitment without moving so rapidly as to seem to be making one. The local interest is an indication of what a good project it will be.

In the evening for two hours, I talked with Nehru at his house.

He would like to visit the President; September now seems probable. I gave a darkening account of Khrushchev's stubbornness at Vienna on the test ban and on Berlin to which he listened with little comment. Then we went on briefly to Laos, Nepal, Angola and the neutral summit meeting. I also gave him an unadorned account of the Cuban adventure which did not entirely exculpate the Eisenhower Administration. It was a very good talk although (not necessarily because) I did ninety percent of the talking. I might have been wiser to have omitted the Cuban history; it aroused unnecessary memories. After the P.M.'s, there was a very pleasant dinner at Maffitt's for Carol Laise.[1] She is about to return to Washington and will leave a major gap.

I am dissatisfied with the way the Peace Corps is being handled. It should be an amateur enterprise led by dedicated individuals who live at or near the economic level of those being recruited. I fear it will pass under the direction of high-salaried bureaucrats who will inculcate the volunteers with their attitudes.[2]

June 24 — New Delhi

I sent off a long telegram on my discussion with Nehru, taking some slight pains with the drafting. State Department business is conducted in horrible English. As a result, if one takes trouble to write intelligibly, he automatically gets attention. I quoted from my invitation to Nehru, namely that we hoped he might wish to visit the United States informally "without the medieval splendor which has come to characterize state visits in modern democracies." I also sent off a rather nastier response to a circular telegram from Bowles on the projected meeting of ambassadors here. Noting that the proposed agenda would deal with the philosophy of the new Administration and internal problems of embassy administration, I observed that the philosophy, or something meant to be the philoso-

[1] An able and remarkably attractive member of the Embassy political staff, now Ambassador to Nepal and wife of Ellsworth Bunker, who is currently Ambassador in Saigon.
[2] A threat that did not develop.

phy, had been extensively articulated. No one needed more. The internal problems were unavoidable but, fortunately, matters that a good ambassador could solve. I had previously said the Indians would not like the meeting. That rug was pulled from under me when the Indians said they had no objection.[3]

Yesterday afternoon Wood and I had a long session with Morarji Desai, the Finance Minister.[4] I reported at length on my Washington business including my concern over the high cost of some of the aid India is getting. There should be no divine reward for aid from other countries that consists only of commercial loans at 6 percent. Desai is an attractive man of vigor and strength who shares the general awe of the Prime Minister.

There is a private firm in New York which each year organizes a "seminar" in some foreign country. This is attended by businessmen and they meet with cabinet officials and heads of state. It is supposed to bring the members in touch with opportunities for foreign investments. An even more agreeable purpose is to provide members with income tax deductible travel.

This autumn, they are meeting in India and several weeks ago a representative called in to tell me about it. I gave it the minimum of thought. But now they have sent a set of questions to the Indian cabinet ministers they hope to see. These are highly impertinent, or perhaps just naïve. What are the reasons for failure of some industries in the public sector? Isn't there an undue predisposition to Soviet technology in some sectors of the government? And so forth. The Indians are quite exercised and have had a cabinet meeting on it. I must investigate and explain.

[3] I had hoped they might think a gathering of American diplomatic brass unneutral or untactful, or otherwise hint adversely. Instead, as might be expected, they welcomed it cordially.

[4] Long a major figure in the Congress Party and nationalist movement and the dominant political figure in the west Indian state of Gujarat, Desai had a broad grasp of economic issues and a generally, though not invariably, conservative reaction to new proposals. In a country where ideas were more numerous than the means for carrying them out, this was far from a handicap. Following Nehru's death, he was out of office, to return again as Finance Minister and Deputy Prime Minister.

The rains have stopped temporarily and it is much cooler. Everywhere there is a sudden greenness which is all the more pleasing in contrast with the previous desiccation. Yesterday I saw two large black birds splashing like little boys in a puddle before the house. They seemed astonished at their good fortune.

June 26 — New Delhi

Early yesterday morning — at 4:30 A.M. — I went to Palam to meet Kitty. She wasn't on the plane, but the Prime Minister of Barbados was. I was extensively photographed greeting him and will receive high marks for my exceptional attention to duty. (My wife arrived at the same time twenty-four hours later. There was a communications error.) I returned to the Residence, walked for a half-hour in the Lodi Gardens and then slept until noon. It was the first time in weeks that I had all the sleep I wanted. I doubt that a shortage of sleep greatly impairs efficiency. But it does lead to verbosity — one does not have the right single word — and it makes life infinitely less agreeable. A shortage of sleep also makes me more aggressive and has a slight tendency to induce a persecution complex.

Krishna Menon came for lunch to talk of the Geneva conference on Laos where he returns in a day or so. I had several things to urge including an effective Control Commission in Laos and more responsible concern by India for the neutrality of Southeast Asia. I pointed out that India could mediate between ourselves and the Communists in the days when we were collecting military allies against the Communists. She could not do so when we are seeking neutrality too. Krishna Menon is an interesting but hard man to talk with. There is a touch of genius in the way he slightly confuses all issues. Presently you find that you are confusing them yourself.

Nothing repels me so much on returning to India as the food. Yesterday we had a vegetarian lunch for Menon. It was marginally better than some carnivorous concoction that was arranged for dinner. It will be easy to lose a little weight.

The Defence Ministry is obviously according me attention. Late day before yesterday, I had a visit from Sardar Surjit Singh Majithia, the Deputy Minister — a wealthy Sikh farmer and sugar manufacturer. He inquired as to my interest in wrestling, cricket, riding and hunting and asked me to intervene to help arrange to have the Davis Cup quarter- (approximately) finals between the United States and India played in New Delhi. He also offered to make me a member of the Polo Club. We eschewed all military questions.

June 27 — New Delhi

The Ford Foundation is actively contemplating a grant to India to found a new national university. We would supplement it with some of our rupee funds.[5] The idea, as I have told,[6] is to have an institution that is out of the ordinary bureaucratic routine of existing universities and which has a faculty of genuine quality. The problem, of course, is how to achieve this without making the present institutions just that much worse. To retrieve Indians from abroad and add American and European scholars is the only answer and not an easy one. We had a meeting yesterday to consider the matter.

June 29 — New Delhi

One of my problems is my numerous helpers in Washington — those who want to come here and lend me a hand. In addition to Bowles's high-level conference, I have a proposal from Commerce

[5] When food is provided to India under Public Law 480, the Indian government resells the food to the grain trade or otherwise to the people (otherwise local food grains would cost money, those provided from the United States would be free). Most of the rupee proceeds of this sale go into a special account to be used in India for purposes agreed upon between the United States and Indian Governments. But 10 per cent accrues to the United States Government for employment wholly at its discretion. So large have been the food shipments to India that the amounts accrued under this latter provision were very large, although not larger than the ideas as to how they might be used.

[6] See page 68.

for a high-level trade mission. All Indian trade is now controlled by the government. If India had the dollars and no restrictions on imports, we could sell them anything, mission or no mission. With the controls, no conceivable mission could expand our trade. In recent years, there have been six such missions. It is the consensus of the experts that they have accomplished nothing. Nonetheless, another is proposed, and today an approving draft cable came across my desk for my signature. I redrafted it saying the mission should stay home — or go where it would do some good. I reminded Commerce that when we drafted the Balance of Payments message last January, I specified that there should be no stepped-up sales effort when nothing could be sold.

I worry more than a little about Berlin and the position in which it places the President. Obviously there must be some negotiation. But in the meantime the advocates of a hard line, so-called, are having a field day. Their position is strategically magnificent. They can call for everything up to and including nuclear catastrophe rather than yield an inch. For this, they get great applause for their heroism. The President, however, must be more sensible; nuclear destruction is not likely to be popular with the average voter. So he must strike a bargain of some sort. Then the hard men can assail him for weakness. So they are unbeatable.

The rains have stopped momentarily and it is again exceedingly hot. I somehow sleep badly under the air-conditioning.

July 1 — New Delhi

Night before last, we embarked about 10:30 P.M. on the private saloon car of Karnail Singh,[7] the Chairman of the Railway Board, to visit the Bhakra-Nangal Dam in the Punjab and its affiliated structures. The Edward Masons and Richard Gilbert of Harvard[8]

---

[7] His brother, D. S. Saund, was then a member of the House of Representatives from California.

[8] Professor Edward S. Mason, Lamont University Professor of Economics at Harvard University, and long-time personal friend. Mr. Richard V. Gilbert, also a personal friend, head of the Harvard University Development Advisory Group in Pakistan. The group advises the Pakistan planning authorities.

and Tyler Wood were in the party. A considerable crowd assembled at the station to see us off. It was not especially interested but had nothing better to do. India could quickly give a person a wholly erroneous view of his importance. Our equipage was a marvelous Edwardian vehicle exceedingly well-supplied with food and beverages, and an extra long bed had been installed for me. The bed was comfortable enough, but the car combined a roll and a pitch that excluded all sleep until I took slightly less than a lethal charge of sleeping pills. I was still sleeping beautifully yesterday morning when I was propelled into the dining room for a large breakfast. Shortly thereafter, we reached the station where it was pouring rain and agreeably cool.

Bhakra is a vast structure of Hoover Dam proportions set in a narrow gorge where the Sutlej, one of the six big rivers that feed the Indus, emerges from the Himalayan foothills into the Punjab Plain. It is being built in great blocks, something after the manner of a child's block-building set, and is perhaps four-fifths completed. It is an exclusively Indian enterprise, although some sixty Americans (along with Harvey Slocum)[9] were once engaged on the project. I was struck by the way Indian locomotive, crane and bulldozer operators, most of them Punjabis, had acquired the easygoing precision of American workmen in handling machinery. Upstream is a large and placid lake. The dam presents a vertical face to this lake and a sloping one over which the water spills on the downstream side. The view from the top down into the maelstrom of escaping water is most alarming. At the base of the dam are two powerhouses. According to one doctrine, the rock walls of the surrounding hills are not very strong and one day may release their grip on the ends of the dam. This would be in spite of reinforcements that have been driven into the rock. I hope there is nothing in this rumor, for people downstream will surely get wet.

Later we visited a fertilizer plant which seems to be using an inordinate amount of the power from the dam and in all outward

9 See page 114.

aspects appears to set a remarkable standard of inefficiency. The cost of the fertilizer, I was told, is very high. I was puzzled as to how one could know for almost none was being produced.

After lunch on the banks of the Sutlej, which will soon all be captured by an irrigation canal, we drove to Chandigarh, the post-partition capital of the Punjab, designed by Le Corbusier.[10] By the time we arrived, it was hot again but the trip was through the most prosperous part of India — villages made of brick and substantial if not very clean, with lots of bicycles and well-dressed people. I rather like the architecture in Chandigarh[11] — it is imaginative though perhaps a bit fussy. The town itself is intelligently if expensively planned. It is divided into sectors, each with dwellings of varying costs, schools, shopping centers and the like.

The Chief Minister of the Punjab, Pratap Singh Kairon,[12] a fellow University of Californian, had a party for me. We sat around in a large circle at his house drinking fruit juice and tea. To make conversation, I asked the Development Minister, who was next to me, how many of his village-level workers were adequately trained.

"All," he replied proudly.

"Don't tell the American Ambassador such nonsense," said the Chief Minister.

"Eighty percent," said the D.M.

At 7 P.M., we took off on the maiden trip of our new Convair, and by 8 P.M., we were back in Delhi. On the way, I slept on one of the couches and otherwise enjoyed my privileges. To end the day, we had a big dinner for the Masons.

July 2 — New Delhi

Yesterday I took the Masons to see the Chancery and had a long talk about Indo-Pakistan affairs. The Pakistanis are basing their

---

[10] Now in dispute between the two states (Haryana and Punjab) into which the erstwhile Punjab has been divided.

[11] I came to like it less. The legislative building has the aspect of a cooling tower in a chemical works.

[12] He was murdered by a roadside gang in 1965.

case for aid on their military virtuosity. And the decisions are being made these days by those who place most stress on economic aid. Hence, India gains and the Pakistanis suffer. I urged a strong program of civilianizing the Pakistan appeal.

Later I had a long talk on Laos and related matters, first with M.J. Desai and then with Krishna Menon. As usual, not having any instructions, I improvised. The Indians are beginning, I think, to take seriously my contention that as we come to support neutrality in Laos, they must become more concerned to make it work.

Thereafter, I helped celebrate two national days — Canada and Ghana. The Ghanaians, who were more exotic, were all in handsome costume and a vast crowd attended to see the sight — indeed, with band and everything, there was scarcely standing room in the small front yard of the Residence. As usual, I became the center of an ostensibly admiring crowd, many of whom, I seriously believe, attend all of these occasions whether invited or not. After shaking free from the Joint Secretary of the Delhi Indo-Cultural Forum, I was immediately taken up by the Hon. Chairman of the Hindu-American Dental Society. My wife spent her time in deep conversation in Spanish with the Cuban Ambassador whose existence we are forbidden by protocol to acknowledge. (I reproved her. She said she found him charming and also that he was unhappy and needed sympathy. I told her she was being used, obviously, by a very devious Communist.) After a time, we went out to the airport to see the Masons away. I believe Ed began to sense some of the disadvantages of my job when the autograph hunters swarmed in.

July 3 — New Delhi

One thing I like the most about USIS is the way it wins credibility for its news. This morning, the *Wireless File* leads its story of Hemingway's death with the statement that he had shot himself accidentally while cleaning a gun. It ended the story by reminding everyone that Ernest's father had shot himself to death when Ernest was a boy.

I wonder, incidentally, if anyone was ever killed while actually cleaning a gun. In any case, Hemingway's heroes, whom he imitated in life, always handled guns with an exceptional competence.

July 5 — New Delhi

In years past, the American Ambassador celebrated the Fourth of July with a vast party in the manner of most other countries. But some genius reduced it to a picnic and fireworks display at the staff quarters to which the American residents come at their own cost. The profits from the sale of beer and hot dogs are used, in turn, to relieve the Ambassador of the cost of the Christmas party. Altogether, a noble arrangement. I made a mild speech in favor of our independence.

Word came yesterday that on the morning following the Ghana party, the Cuban Ambassador resigned and defected. He left, economy-class, on the early plane for Paris and Caracas. It will not be easy to persuade my wife that henceforth she should abide by the official rules governing discourse with representatives of, as they are called, unfriendly powers.

July 7 — New Delhi

It continues very hot without rain. I sleep badly, and my life is complicated by a touch of the flu. Only a certain intrepid nobility of the soul causes me to struggle on.

Henry Stebbins has been here and we have been discussing Nepal. As the result of recent political convulsions, the administration of the country has gone sadly to pot. On the other hand, the country is so primitive that it doesn't need much administration so the latter isn't much missed. The question is what, if anything, we do. The temptation is to do nothing; it seems certain that this course will find favor in Washington.

I read the press releases each day from USIS and both the English and spelling are bad and they are full of typographical errors. Yesterday there was a touching tribute to Hemingway from James

Thruber (sic). I asked that a competent English-speaking officer read these over before they are issued and learned that we have only "one overworked information officer" to each consular district.[13] I asked if a few minutes' reading of the material for which he is responsible would add intolerably to his duties. It was agreed that it would not.

Our information services continue to pain me deeply. They are by turns petty, petulant and irrelevant. We might be better off if the daily propaganda was never dispatched.

July 8 — New Delhi

About four yesterday, it became very cloudy and dark. Then in the distance we heard cheering; this was followed by heavy rain. People were applauding the re-arrival of the monsoon which had come and departed.

In the morning, I worked on speeches, received the Czech Ambassador in one of our endless exchanges of calls and helpfully gave him a copy of *The Affluent Society*. Then I went on an inspection tour of the building we are to occupy for an industrial fair that is scheduled to open a few months hence. The building, which we built for an agricultural fair, was designed by Minoru Yamasaki and is a delightful thing. Exhibition halls are joined together by walkways protected from the sun by cupolas in a manner reminiscent of a mosque. It was incredibly hot.

The afternoon was given over to visiting businessmen and the young representative of the Protestant Relief Organization. They get food under PL 480 to distribute. He assures me that this involves no problem of mixing church and state. Not half a dozen Hindus and Moslems desert the faith of their fathers in a year. Many more Christians are annually lost.

In the evening, I went to a reception for the Prime Minister of Eastern Nigeria — an admirable and opulent-looking man in the tribal robes of a major chief. One of the prime manifestations of

---

[13] There are four such districts in India with headquarters in Calcutta, Bombay, Madras and Delhi.

national independence is an increasing volume of official travel. Then we had a wedding reception which, however, was called off because of rain and after that a huge official dinner at our house. This was well under way when all the lights went off. So did the air-conditioning, and in no time the heat was suffocating. The rain had stopped so we moved out on the terrace at which moment the power came back on.

I sent Rs. 500 to the Prime Minister's Relief Fund. This is in response to a special appeal for the victims of floods which are now rampant in the south. I now face the question of whether I should have it officially reimbursed which I learn is the custom in the State Department. It is certainly more blessed to give than to receive when one's munificence is fully underwritten by the United States Government.[14]

July 9 — New Delhi

While in Washington, I arranged for a visit by the Prime Minister to President Kennedy at some unspecified future date. Later it was settled for early November to be announced July 10. Last week a cable came from the Department asking us to ask the Indians to postpone the announcement until July 21, else announcement of Nehru's visit would coincide with the arrival in Washington of President Ayub of Pakistan. (This seemed to me excessively sensitive.) Simultaneously, the *Washington Post* carried news of the visit replete with dates. I cabled my intention to release the Indians from restraint noting the "competently executed" leak that made it necessary.

Last evening, Lal Bahadur Shastri,[15] the Home Minister, had a party for his son who is getting married. I had a pleasant chat with the Prime Minister — about news leaks, his trip to the United States and the amount of Indian talent consumed by the interna-

14 Later, as will be evident, I greatly increased my donation but had it reimbursed.
15 See page 482.

tional organizations. The latter is serious. Good and needed men work at routine jobs on high salaries in New York, the Bank and Fund, Geneva and Rome.

For the rest of the day, I worked in a relaxed fashion on speeches and went shopping. For the first time in a very long time, I am unfatigued and in no pressing need of sleep.

July 11 — New Delhi

The Department for the second time in two weeks has become upset over my saying that we are no longer seeking military alliances in this part of the world.[16] (As indicated, we cannot get the Indians fully behind a neutral solution in Laos if they think we are recruiting allies.) I see no way of making the Department happy save to say that we *are* recruiting allies. I have difficulty, incidentally, in controlling my tendency to send biting replies. I am not trying very hard.

One of the undiscovered pleasures of this job is that I have $10,000 to spend at my discretion for charitable and relief purposes which is replaced once I have spent it — a kind of self-refilling financial spring. I learned this yesterday when we gathered to see what we could do about some bad floods in Kerala. Everyone points out, however, that the floods come every year and are always billed as the worst ever by the Indian press.[17]

I am so practiced that I can now entertain diplomatic colleagues, agree pleasantly and have an uninterrupted chain of thought. Two came in yesterday morning and caused me not the slightest distraction.

---

[16] Rusk in a cable had warned me sharply against such statements.
[17] This is an overstatement.

New Delhi, India
July 11, 1961

Dear Mr. President:

I have been back about three weeks and from day to day I have been planning to pass along some thoughts on matters in Washington and here. I must say that the trip was reasonably exhausting with my time divided almost equally between asking for things that I needed and asking not to have things that I don't need. On occasion I am appalled at the money possessed by the United States Government for things that aren't necessary. A few more years and I could easily become as penurious as I learn you already are.

Thus I have just successfully arrested a Commerce [Department] plan to send a high level trade commission to India — officials, businessmen, staff to spend several weeks touring India to acquaint the natives[18] with the virtues of American products. They do not sell, only expound. It was all but settled when I learned about it. I discover that there have been six such missions in the last six years. I learn further that the results of all have been nil or negative except as described by the participants or the unduly polite. The Indians operate a water-tight system of exchange control and import licenses, with our encouragement, to save dollars. However admirable American goods they cannot be bought without a license and licenses are available only to the extent that dollars are. Some dollars do get spent in other countries not because of ignorance but because our goods are too expensive. The cost of our goods incidentally is the major problem of our trade and our balance-of-payments. Ultimately it will be the major problem of our foreign policy for the latter costs a lot of money which we must earn.

I do discover that past missions have raised hopes in the minds

---

[18] This usage, I should perhaps explain to Indian readers, bears no relation to nineteenth century imperial language. It is an American slang form. "You were in Boston. How did you find the natives?"

of numerous Indian entrepreneurs that they might be allowed to import our gear grinders and garter belts — "The Americans must know what they are doing" — only to have their hopes dashed when they sought the licenses. So much for this. I cite it not for its importance but as an example of excessive affluence.

As you may have seen from my cables I discharged your commissions with Nehru on Berlin and testing and, I think, made some impression. More on testing than Berlin, I think. The press dust-up over a new China policy started just as I got back so I concluded that I had better postpone any talk with the Chinese (Com) Ambassador.[19] There is an off-chance that it might have become known with muddying effect. When it seems safe I will raise the matter.

From here the discussions over Berlin have an Alice-in-Wonderland quality which, sadly, I can only suppose is improved by distance. When I wonder about our ability to conduct a successful foreign policy, which is often, it is usually because of our tendency to take an issue and simplify it to the point of absurdity. The two favorite absurdities consist (1) in reducing all matters to a choice between whether we win or lose and (2) to whether we are hard or soft.

In Laos, for example, our problem has long been to escape from an impossible position with a certain amount of grace. Any escape will be good and one may still be possible. But according to the official simplifiers, we have already suffered an overwhelming loss. We never, so far as I can see, had a chance to win — not anyhow since we arrived. And if we are convinced we have lost I can't see how the Communists can fail to take the hint.

In the Berlin discussions the simplification is between hard and soft. Nothing could be more irrelevant. Were the Russians determined to have a war they could doubtless force one upon

[19] A proposal by the President that we open up a new channel of communication with Peking. For various reasons, the matter was not pursued. The "dust-up" refers to rumors that the Administration was moving to revise the China policy.

us. And similarly if we were so bent. So at some point we are both hard. There is no need to demonstrate this point for it is evident. Since the contingency is one which presumably we both seek to avoid the problem is to find a solution tolerable to us in between.

Those who talk about hard solutions divert all thought from solutions by asking only that we advertise our willingness to risk a deep thermonuclear burn. In their souls they know that this is an eventuality which a President cannot accept. And they always protect themselves with their public by saying that, of course, it won't really happen. So they happily exploit the antipathy toward the Russians, strike impressively heroic poses, feel personally secure nonetheless, and, when the inevitable bargain is struck, are free to condemn it as a defeat. It is only when one spells it out that one comes to realize how tactically unassailable are those who argue such tactics. I can't think that you find them very helpful.

This brings me to my suggestion of the day. In making appointments there are three qualifications which, in one way or another, rate a measure of consideration. These are *ability, political acceptability* and *personal loyalty*. It is my impression that in key positions you have put more or less the inevitable stress on political acceptability and that you have stressed ability at the expense of personal loyalty. I would not argue that ability is a wholly negligible asset. But it is often combined with a tendency to think of one's self first, one's agency second and the President last. In the end the best Roosevelt men were not the smartest but those who thought of F.D.R. first and themselves and their agencies second. Hopkins,[20] a man of second class wit, was a case in point . . .

I suspect in these days it is almost as important to know what isn't serious as to know what is. The current flare-up in Pakistan of which you will be getting an earful strikes me as unserious.

[20] Harry L. Hopkins, chief aide to Roosevelt.

Kashmir is an involved and troublesome matter with no solution in sight but I think most of the present flare-up is political posturing.

On the other hand South Vietnam is exceedingly bad. I hope, incidentally, that your information from there is good and I have an uneasy feeling that what comes in regular channels is very bad. Unless I am mistaken Diem has alienated his people to a far greater extent than we allow ourselves to know. This is our old mistake. We take the ruler's word and that of our own people who have become committed to him. The opponents are thieves and bandits; the problem is to get the police. I am sure the problem in Vietnam is partly the means to preserve law and order. But I fear that we have one more government which, on present form, no one will support.

The monsoon has come and it is wet and almost cool. I am starting out next week to make a tour of the major cities and a few speeches. I am avoiding the Indo-American Societies,[21] the Rotary Clubs and the other usual American forums to see if I can make some dent on the university audiences. These are influential and also rather suspicious.

Yours faithfully,
JOHN KENNETH GALBRAITH

THE PRESIDENT
THE WHITE HOUSE

❖ ❖ ❖

July 13 — New Delhi
For the last two or three days, I have had an unaccountable headache every morning. Hence the gaps. However, I continued my endless and futile round of diplomatic calls and have now almost finished. The Turkish Ambassador yesterday must have been about the last of those in town.[22]

[21] Though not, of course, completely.
[22] It was, in fact, many weeks before I had completely finished.

Yesterday I lunched with Peter Thorneycroft[23] and Paul Gore-Booth on the Common Market and learned once more how scrupulously the British pursue the British interest. They see admirably all points of view but do not allow them to interfere with their own in any way.

They have clearly decided to join the Common Market unless repelled therefrom. This means that Indian goods which formerly entered the British market tariff free under the Commonwealth preference will pay the Common Market duty. The need for this sacrifice is now being explained to the Indians. I have urged them not to be too nice about it. When the British did not want to join Europe, they always pled their Commonwealth ties. Now that they want to join, they should be made to worry about it as much as possible. That won't be much but it will dramatize the problem.[24]

President Ayub is now in the United States and making disagreeable sounds about our aid to, and friendship for, India. Last night Foreign Secretary Desai complained to me about these statements. I urged calm. Things would be worse, I pointed out, if we were unfriendly, giving no aid to India and thus providing Ayub with no grounds for complaint.

For weeks, the civil air negotiation between India and the United States (more flights by Air-India across the Atlantic in return for more landings by American carriers in India) has been dragging along. Both sides have been asserting highly theological principles about predetermination, capacity consultation, Bermuda principles, rights to Fifth Freedom traffic. It is a wonderland of words. Last night I got the top Indians together and obtained their agreement to a position reasonably reflective of their interests which I think Washington will have to accept.[25]

[23] British Conservative M.P. and Minister of Defence.
[24] I had opposed our efforts to shove the British into the Common Market. The reasons for our supporting the formation of a tariff club organized to discriminate against the United States escaped me.
[25] This, shortly thereafter, it did.

July 15 — New Delhi

Yesterday I was up bright and early for a trip to Phoolbagh to see the new Uttar Pradesh Agricultural University. It is about an hour distant to the east, and we were off at eight in the Navy plane which is very GI and functional and filled with parachutes and yellow life jackets. All together, there are ten seats including a small compartment at the back where I installed myself.

We flew low to keep under the rather low-hanging clouds and at times were down to 150 feet. With the rain, the Ganges Plain is green (with occasional stretches of gray-brown, muddy flood water) and fresh and in total contrast with the arid aspect when we went to Bangkok two months ago.

I busied myself writing a speech until we were about fifteen minutes from our destination. At that juncture, the ceiling came down to the ground — wispy, non-ominous but very ubiquitous clouds — and there was nothing to do but return. By 10 A.M., I was back at the Residence and spent the day working at home.

Last night, we had a pleasant dinner for the French Ambassador to celebrate Bastille Day. A couple of very handsome Indian girls — an artist and a dancer — showed up and very much raised my morale. I am told that diplomats have not always been men of rigid virtue. A onetime U.S. Ambassador in Europe, astonishing in view of his age, is said to have approached all problems with a closed mind and an open fly. I suspect, however, that being Ambassador to India is the nearest thing yet devised to a male chastity belt. But one can still gaze wistfully.

Krishna Menon has just submitted some proposals at the Laos conference at Geneva which seem designed only to infuriate our people. Everything we argue for is described as indecent. Meanwhile Ayub is in Washington describing Nehru as an untrustworthy character. This is what many in Washington wish to believe. I could do with more help.

July 16 — New Delhi

Chet Bowles's forthcoming conference of ambassadors occupied us in the morning. Four or five papers have been sent out by the Department for preliminary discussion. Some are banal; the rest are insulting.[26] Embassy staff are enjoined to good behavior, morality and unobtrusive automobiles. Several automobiles were requested for those attending the conference, and I cabled back that in the interest of being unobtrusive, they should use the car pool. Only by a magnificent effort do I control my anger over this nonsense.

Last evening, I took Alan[27] to visit the President. The President's staff looked at us in some surprise. We were ushered into a room where several people, including a beautiful girl in a sensational blue and gold sari, were consuming tea. Then after a few minutes we were taken across to the study. This is a large, square room, lined with bookcases and more sparsely with books and furnished with the rather solid, square, overstuffed furniture that the British favored in the days of the Raj. For some reason, the colors are invariably awful. We chatted with the President for fifteen minutes or so and I made a present of some books. Later I learned that through a mix-up of communications, we had not been expected. Expert staff work had kept us from realizing it.

[26] Not to be blamed on Bowles.
[27] John Alan Galbraith, my oldest son, then twenty, recently arrived on vacation from Harvard.

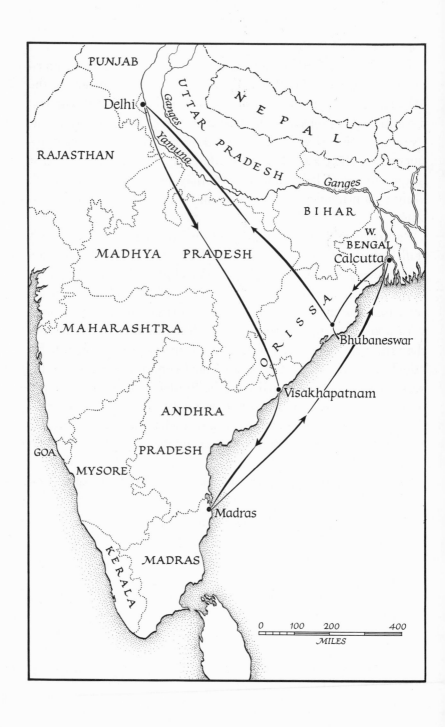

VIII

First Indian Venture

July 17 — New Delhi–Visakhapatnam

I finished my speeches for this tour at noon yesterday. That was my deadline, and I made it to the minute. The writing should control the time. Here the time controlled the writing. If the speeches had been nonofficial, I could have made them twice as interesting in half as long.

In the afternoon, I visited Krishna Menon at the Defence Ministry. As usual, we disagreed and, as usual, I did not feel I had made my case. He can take any position and argue for it ruthlessly, with a certain moral indignation and peripheral vagueness which make him invulnerable. Presently he reduces you, or anyhow me, to impotence.

Yesterday he was trying to persuade me of the importance of getting the U.S. Government behind Souvanna Phouma in Laos.[1] I was urging the importance of an effective charter for the I.C.C. The first was out of my hands; on the second, I made no progress. Once I said that our path would be easier if India would fight for genuine neutrality. He got (seemingly) very angry; were we lecturing India on how to be neutral? I said not the United States, only Galbraith. One should be paid extra for this.

Now we are high over Central India. The thick clouds of the

[1] Which eventually, in the course of our diplomacy — which often involves starting in one direction and moving eventually in another — we did.

monsoon are everywhere below and at 10,000 feet, George[2] is still ducking clouds. But mostly the skies are blue and it is very cool. Our plane is full of newspapermen and photographers who have come along to cover the trip — or for the ride. NBC is doing a film on the education of an ambassador; *Life*, a piece on an intellectual abroad. Not since the Prince of Wales has there been a better-covered journey.

July 18 — Visak–Madras

We got to Visak[3] about noon yesterday, were duly met by the local collector and district magistrate and Caltex officials including the attractive local manager, a Mr. Berdine. Visak, until a few years ago, was a minor port on the Bay of Bengal in an exceedingly backward part of Andhra. The country round about is covered with deep red soil, sometimes piled up in irregular hillocks. The fields are fringed by palm trees; the principal crop is rice. In general aspect, it is much like Jamaica.

I was to have the afternoon for final work on speeches but that turned out to be impractical. So, about three, we left the Caltex compound, full of neat bungalows overlooking the ocean, for a tour of the new industries. The ranch houses of the compound house only eight Europeans, the sole survivors of eighty-eight who launched the Caltex refinery in the area. Both houses and jobs have been taken over by Indians. Our way was through the town, rather dirty, and by a noisome body of water into which goes all the raw sewage and called, in consequence I assume, Lilac Lagoon. Then we passed through an area occupied by Indian houses — conical one-room mud huts, cheek by jowl and thatched with palm fronds. In dry season, they make a lovely fire. A man who has lost his house asks Rs. 60 (about $12) to replace it. Amortized over forty years, the annual cost is not high.

At the shipyard, which with the Caltex refinery and the Naval

[2] Colonel George Hannah, Jr., AAF.
[3] About 1,000 miles southeast of Delhi. See map, page 158.

Station are the principal enterprises of the town, we were taken up the local Olympus to get a panoramic view. What we got was the worst soaking of our born lives. For we had barely reached the top, without umbrellas or coats, when the heavens opened in the manner of someone pulling the chain. In seconds, not minutes, we did not possess a dry stitch. It continued for an hour and, while warm and rather refreshing, it eliminated all chance of seeing the shipyard without a periscope. I ascertained that, in the manner of most Indian industrial public enterprises, it is functioning at unduly high cost.

As we drove to the refinery, the streams were rushing down the hills and cutting new channels across the meadows. The water was a thick, viscous red. I commented that it was carrying away a lot of soil. Someone said, "Yes, and there is erosion too." The refinery was neat, well-painted and competently manned by self-confident young Indians. For some reason, power plants and refineries maintain much higher standards of housekeeping than, say, steel mills.

Later I visited the Vice-Chancellor of Andhra University and narrowly escaped giving a lecture. Students have been reading my books and, as usual, wanted to be assured that I existed. Then there was a reception, a dinner with mercifully abbreviated speeches and then to bed.

July 19 — Madras

We were up yesterday at 6:30 A.M. and off at eight for Madras.[4] On the way, I had an additional and merciful nap. At 10:30 A.M. we were in Madras and elaborately welcomed with a press conference following. I recalled that a young customs collector in 1959 greeted me by name as I was passing through on the way to Ceylon and asked me to elucidate a point in *American Capitalism*.[5] The papers later dug him up.

---

[4] About four hundred miles south down the coast from Visak.
[5] *American Capitalism: The Concept of Countervailing Power* (Boston: Houghton Mifflin, 1952, 1956).

Then we went to lunch with the Governor in a vast, airy Victorian palace some distance from the city of Madras in the middle of a deer park. Deer were everywhere. The great high ceilings, lattice work and wide verandahs were far from unpleasant. The food was less far. The Governor's wife, one of my luncheon companions, spoke no English. But on the other side was the former Mayoress of Madras, very intelligent and charming, who spoke it constantly.

Later I called on the Mayor, a rather diffident man and a member of the D.M.K. party.[6] The latter party, rather strong locally, advocates (in principle) taking south or Dravidian India out of the Union to form a separate state. The threat is more serious than the intention.

Municipal employees gathered by the hundreds to see me come and go. The damage to the public business may not have been irreparable. In India, the difference between working and not working is not always decisive.

In the early evening, the Consul-General[7] gave a reception for several hundred, a fair number of whom were missionaries. I thought the line would continue to file by forever. Afterward, I fell into conversation with an agreeable savior of souls who told me he got forty last year. Alas, he told me, there was also backsliding from among these and also from the earlier accumulation. He figures he and the Lord are lucky in any particular year to come out even.

The reception was to have been held outdoors but this plan was revised by another cloudburst. The day ended with a dinner by the Consulate people.

---

[6] The Dravida Munnetra Kazhagam party. It has since come to power in the Madras State.

[7] Dr. Thomas W. Simons, a highly-informed scholar and close observer of South Indian affairs, distinguished himself that night by introducing hundreds of people by name. Indian names are long and hard for Westerners to remember.

July 20 — Madras

Yesterday was only slightly less long than that of the Last Judgment. At a little after eight, I visited the Consulate[8] which occupies a couple of dingy floors of a loft-type building which are painted a repulsive green. The American officers occupy offices around the edge of a bull-pen; the Indian staff are in the pen. One office is occupied by our intelligence staff whose coming and going is observed with much interest by all. When the chief CIA man was replaced a few months back, a local Indian police officer commented amiably in public on the change to the Consul-General the same day. ("I hear you are getting a new chief spy.")

To get back to the Consulate: I made a speech to the staff, saying some kind words to the Indian members. By an accident of timing, it coincided with a letter from the Indian staff membership asking that the Americans be less arrogant to them. The letter was typed but not signed so I think I may safely ignore it. In outward aspect, our people seem kindly; it would be a serious mistake to interfere on behalf of what are most likely invented grievances.

Next I looked at the USIS library. It looked well-managed but a trifle dingy too. Their losses by theft are appalling.[9]

Next I went to USIS headquarters which is a few blocks away. The staff of this is large and almost exclusively Indian — the application of the principle of indirect rule to propaganda. I made them a speech, stressing familiar points — we have sufficiently established our anti-Communism, so let us say what we are for. Elegance and technical expertise in our publications are extremely important. And we are effective only as we have a reputation for credibility.

Our next stop was Fort St. George on the seafront. It was once occupied by Clive (from where he marched to Arcot) and is one of the few things in India he did not try to take back home. The

[8] The United States maintains Consular offices in Bombay, Calcutta and Madras, as well as New Delhi.
[9] Elsewhere in India I learned that USIS libraries have much smaller losses.

Secretariat, with high ceilings and a flowing breeze, is within the old bastions. Here I talked with the Chief Secretary, a highly intelligent I.C.S.[10] man, much interested in family planning. For India he thinks sterilization, especially of males, is the answer. Then we walked around the verandah to visit the Chief Minister, and then his cabinet. The Chief Minister, K. Kamaraj Nadar, is a highly competent Congressman and a coming influence.[11] He is dark-complexioned, clad in a dhoti and we communicated with difficulty. The visit was largely ceremonial with dozens of pictures.

Luncheon was a large affair at the University — also on the waterfront — with the Vice-Chancellor presiding and all professors on hand. Then at three I visited one of the more promising motion picture studios and watched some shooting, talked with the owner-producer and stars and was photographed from all angles with the latter. Censorship, I was told, is the principal problem. Sex, encouragement to law-breaking and communalism (e.g., conflict between the Hindu and Moslem communities) and doubts about government policy are all kept under close scrutiny. In a telling drama not long ago, a small boy raced for the doctor to save his dying mother. At the railroad crossing, the gates were down; he ducked under and across in front of the train. This sequence had to come out; it incited to disobedience of the law. Some time ago the censor also objected to indecent whistling. Quite rightly, I think.

The female lead was, nonetheless, a bit on the sexy side. One of the male parts was being played by the exact Indian counterpart of Lionel Barrymore. All of the actors told me that they disapproved of the income tax.

At five, I had a lecture at the University. This was in the Senate

<hr>

[10] Indian Civil Service — the highly qualified cadre that ran India for the British.
[11] With the electoral setback of the Congress Party in 1966, however, he lost influence. Then the Chairman of the Congress Party, he shared responsibility for the poor showing. At the same time, he lost his seat in the Madras legislature and his party lost control of that state to the D.M.K.

House, a huge hall of the same style as the Brighton Pavilion[12] and very gay and attractive.

After a walk on the beach, we went to a great formal dinner given by the Governor and Chief Minister. Beforehand, there was much photographing and especially when I shook hands with the leader of the local Communist party who, somewhat unexpectedly, had turned out to do me honor. I hope it won't ruin his career.

The banquet was at one long table in a huge room lined with the British governors in full regalia. I ate adequately of the earlier courses, not knowing the number yet to come. It was over by ten and we left in the middle of another downpour.

This morning I went to see an industrial estate outside Madras. A hundred-odd small firms occupy the factory buildings. Common services required by various plants such as tool and die making and foundry work are provided. Products include glassware, radios, eyeglasses, electric switch gear, bicycles and dozens of others. It is quite impressive although some of the production (as usual) seems to be at high cost. Also, too many managers were around in gleaming white clothes for the occasion. I thought it exemplary to shake hands with the dirtiest of the workers.

A press conference at eleven was divided about equally between questions on the wickedness of Pakistan and speeches affirming it. It provided me an occasion for making clear that we were not stepping up military aid to Pakistan or mediating in Kashmir. I was also asked if Chester Bowles was coming out to reform our Indian policy. I doubted it.

Before lunch, we had a lovely dip in the ocean. The beaches by Madras are wide, and the waves roll in in a stately fashion. Lunch, the highly competent handiwork of Mrs. Simons, was at the Consul's, following which we were soon airborne. Two of my crew have very bad stomachs. The crew chief is stretched out on one of the couches in my cabin and resembles nothing so much as a dog that has recently been run over by a moving van.

[12] An Indian-style palace built by George IV on the south coast of England.

July 23 — Calcutta

This is Sunday. On Thursday evening, we were duly welcomed at Calcutta and installed in a king-size suite at the Grand Hotel. After much debate and consultation, a bed an acre or so in extent was contrived out of the parts of several others. I then settled down to look at the paper.

Therein I came on an advertisement picturing two semi-nude dancing girls, an attraction so to speak, currently being featured at this hotel. Underneath was the line: "Remember also to buy your tickets for the Ambassador Galbraith reception." In my mail was a note from a lady asking whether the girls weren't unfair competition. At the Consul's, I went into the matter and was assured that it was customary to charge for receptions of the local Indo-American Society.[13] I said the custom would have to be changed. They said to do so would destroy the Society. One inventive official pointed out that it was very much like the grand old custom of the $100-a-plate political dinner at home. I told them to invite all members of the Society who had not paid to come as my guests. Also any university students so disposed. The use of a public official as a shill to raise money seemed to me highly irregular. Apart from this unpleasantness, it was a very good dinner at the house of Bruce Buttles, the second in command and acting head of the Consulate. The Consulate is in an old part of Calcutta consisting of large houses, pleasant intimate gardens to which one moves effortlessly through french windows and open doors. In this season, there is a good breeze and the evenings are cool.

On Friday, I met the Consulate staff and gave them a little lecture on New Frontier gospel according to Galbraith. Then we went to visit the Acting Governor of West Bengal in the great palace of the Governors-General of the Company and State. It is a magnificent and vast palace with great high-ceilinged rooms opening on deep

[13] An officially-encouraged organization of Indians and Americans. I always doubted its value. From the outside, the normal view, it looked like a club of affluent (and conservative) Indians and official Americans.

verandahs, marble and teak floors and a fine and moderately well-kept park stretching in all directions. There was some criticism of extravagance at its building in the eighteenth century.[14] However, it is standing up well. The Acting Governor, Justice Surajit Chandra Lahiri, is an intelligent and pleasant former jurist, and we talked for half an hour on the court structure of Bengal and India, the organization of the bar (which in Bengal as in England divides solicitors from barristers) and the problem of the death penalty. This he favors, assuming there is a wide discretion by the judges. He illustrated by recent example in Bengal. A man murdered by slow poison the husband of the woman he loved, or anyhow liked to take to bed. The man was dispatched and according to some of the local religions is by now a low form of insect life. But at the same time a refugee from East Bengal, sheltering without food under the porch of a house, could no longer bear the anguished cries of his starving baby son. He killed him by banging his head against the step. He was given three months.

I demurred on the ground that capital punishment degrades the state. And nothing is so bad as a public discussion on whether someone should be officially murdered. I cited the recent and endless debate in California over Caryl Chessman.

Then we drove along the Hooghly[15] and looked at the ships and the fast muddy water and visited with some Pakistan boatmen. At the Writers' Buildings, the government headquarters and so named because members of the secretariat of the East India Company were called writers, I called on the Acting Chief Minister. Then I visited the USIS and the library and repeated my old plea that everything interesting in American culture be put boldly on display and that unorthodoxy in books, music, painting, news, theater if ever criticized be blamed on the Ambassador.

At noon, I had a press conference to tell of Nehru's visit to the

[14] It was started in 1799 and finished in 1802.
[15] The Hooghly is one of the outlets by which the Ganges reaches the sea. A complex network of waterways extends into East Bengal, now East Pakistan.

United States and thereafter went to a luncheon with newspaper publishers and educators and on to the University for tea with the Vice Chancellor and senior faculty members. Following tea, I lectured to a jam-packed audience for an hour. Not only were the standing room signs out; only a minority had seats. The University of Calcutta has 125,000 students and most of them were evidently there. The lecture was long, but tolerably substantial, and the audience was attentive to the end. Then I was attacked by the autograph hunters. The Government of West Bengal had assigned an unobtrusive but efficient man called Inspector Roy to be my guardian. He got me out.

The day was far from over. On we went to a reception of all the great, near great and officially so designated at the Bengal Club. They filed by for an hour or more after which we mingled briefly in the throng. Again there was a pleasant eighteenth century aspect to it all. The Bengal Club is the ancient headquarters of the British in India, and it is still rather grand although women are now admitted to help pay the bills. The crowd, exceedingly well-dressed and with many handsome women, spread out on the terrace under the stars and seemed very civilized. Afterward, there was a formal dinner at which my ear was bent, twirled and bruised for two long hours by the heroic achievements of one of India's great industrialists. No one could be rich enough to buy the right to be such a bore. Finally in desperation the British Deputy High Commissioner seized the conversation and told me a long and wholly pointless story by way of relief. I was everlastingly grateful to him.

Such is the day of an ambassador. It was relieved by a magnificent sunset across the Maidan.[16] Great fountains of light shot into the sky ending in brilliant saffron and pink. In this admirable setting, in the exact middle, was a large thunder cloud complete with lightning and rain.

Calcutta, despite its squalor, is a city of much magnificence.

[16] The huge park, dwarfing Central Park or the Tiergarten, along the Hooghly and in the center of the city.

July 24 — Bhubaneswar–New Delhi

On Saturday from Calcutta we drove thirty or forty miles into rural Bengal to see a dairy farm and agricultural school. The countryside was lush and green, the fields fringed with palms and at intervals were shady, thatched villages of agreeable aspect. Crops here consist of rice, jute, pumpkins, sorghum and corn and seem to be prospering. The journey was slightly spoiled by an exceedingly talkative official whose technical knowledge, understandably enough, fell far short of his verbosity. He rolled on and on, and eventually I screwed a look of rapt attention on my face and allowed my thoughts to wander at will. Every five minutes, I tuned in long enough to ask a question. Once I asked him if the eucalyptus trees which tower in great stands were indigenous. He replied, "Very indigenous, Mr. Ambassador, very indigenous. They were brought here from Australia."

The farm is one to which they are relocating the dairy herds that are now maintained in Calcutta. (The latter are scattered around the city in stables of indescribable filth — a health menace in a city where to be an added health menace takes effort.) Like so many things in India, it seemed a worthy experiment but on a small scale and at very high cost. At the nearby college of agriculture, the laboratories seemed barren and unused and the library small and unread. Most of the students, I learn, are those who are rejected for medicine and the law. Plans are under way to merge this unpromising enterprise into a larger agricultural university. This could easily mean doing the wrong thing on a larger scale. When we disembarked at the school, someone slammed the car door most painfully on Inspector Roy's thumb. He collapsed. Faced with general inaction, I picked up my protector, carried him into the poultry husbandry building and laid him on a washing board with his head well down in the sink. Presently he came to and reached for his gun. It had fallen out en route. He was much embarrassed.

We drove back to town by way of the jute mills along the Hooghly and stopped to see an open-air barber at work — thirty or forty shaves a day are necessary for a livelihood — and to drink coconut milk amidst an admiring multitude. I questioned one urchin about his aspirations. He replied: "I want to be a business-man and make a lot of money."

At noon in Calcutta, I called on the commanding general of Fort William and we had drinks overlooking the old moat and gate with the embrasures on either side and the Maidan beyond.[17] It is rich and green and very old.

Lunch was with the local AID personnel. I cited my hopes on the technical assistance program — more concentration of energy both geographically and by enterprise, more people in the field rather than in the cities and New Delhi. Then came a press con-ference which went tolerably well but with many efforts to have me award Kashmir to India. I was asked also how I would ensure that the arms being given to Pakistan would not be used against India. Also whether Calcutta is getting dirtier or cleaner. On the latter, I said there was scope for further effort and propounded a law which is that the more intelligent the people of a city, the worse its government. Being intelligent, they believe it obligatory to concern themselves with global issues. As a result, the streets get deeper and deeper in filth. When they notice the filth, they debate the philosophy of trash prevention and collection rather than hiring men to clean up. After the press conference, I went shopping and bought a nice bracelet for my wife and then on to that Indo-American Society reception. The students had taken lit-erally my invitation and turned up by the hundreds. I made a few remarks which included some humor that fell exceedingly flat. There followed a riot of medium proportions as everyone sought my autograph. I must have awarded not fewer than two hundred, Kitty likewise.[18] The day finished with a dinner.

[17] The latter was cleared of buildings, in fact, to provide a field of fire for the guns of the fort.
[18] So automatic did it become that she signed her name on a paper I presented without noticing who it was for.

AN AMBASSADOR AT WORK
Seedtime

Harvest

"Demarche" — or something

Festival rites

Exhibitionism

More of same

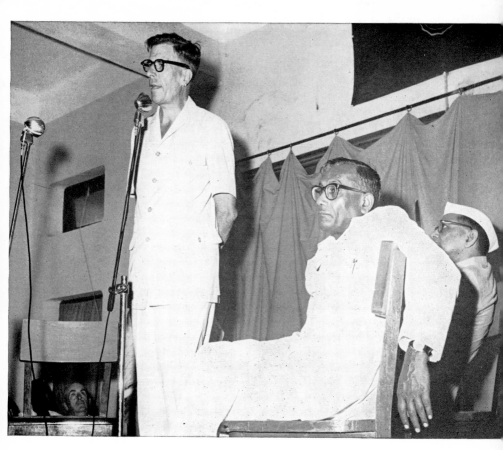

Being a bore

Meeting a friend

Meeting with a future Prime Minister

Arriving (with Mrs. Gandhi)

NEHRU

Descending (with C.A.G.)

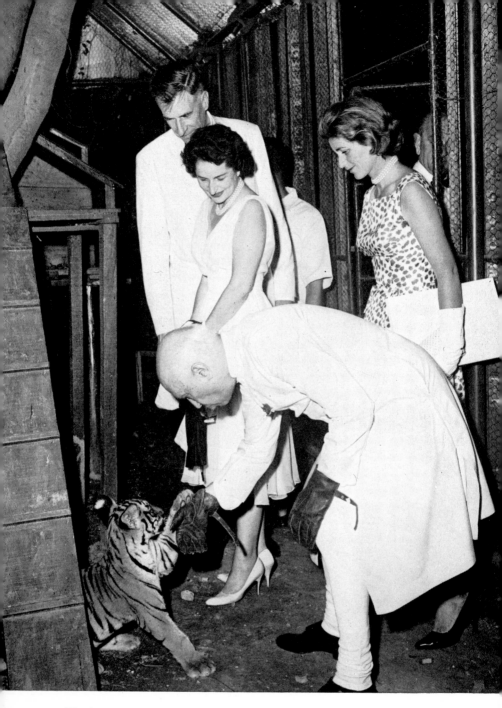

Playing
(In background: Ladybird, Jean Kennedy Smith)

Listening

Presenting (cup for
horsemanship to my son)

Playing —
Holi Festival

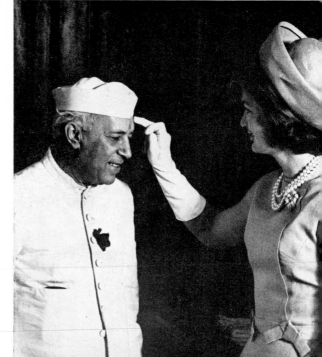

Yesterday morning (Sunday) we flew to Bhubaneswar[19] and arrived mid-morning. We looked at a few of the five hundred temples — mostly of the eighth to twelfth centuries and handsomely carved — and then went on to see the caves. The latter, which were religious centers and hostels, have fine carved entrances. (Once going into one some years before, we met a large cobra coming out. My wife, who saw it first, said jokingly, "Is that a cobra?" Our guide took one look and retreated rapidly saying, "Yes, it *is* a cobra." But the cobra had business elsewhere and paid us no attention.) Then we drove the thirty-five miles to Puri on the coast where we were handsomely housed in the Raj Bhavan, i.e., the governor's palace, on the beach. This beach is one of the best in the world. It is a quarter-mile wide with a high booming surf in which you are protected by lifeguards — one lifeguard to each swimmer. The guard always remains between you and the Bay of Bengal which is reassuring for there is an undertow that operates like a large-caliber suction pump. After swimming, I missed dinner, went to bed at eight and woke at seven. This morning we had a swim before breakfast, then I had another nap, another swim, a drink and lunch. Now we are on the way back to New Delhi. Thanks to the swimming and sleep, I am considerably healed in body and spirit.

Item: At Calcutta on our approach to the hotel, the police made a point of holding back all passersby as we crossed the wide sidewalk to the hotel. It is not easy to go up the avenue so formed with the right combination of democratic nonchalance and diplomatic dignity.

---

[19] Capital of the State of Orissa and about a third of the way along the coast between Calcutta and Madras.

New Delhi, India
July 25, 1961

Dear Mr. President:

This has nothing to do with India. It is on the European Common Market which bothers me a lot whenever I think about it. My recent thoughts have been inspired by Thorneycroft[20] who has just been here to persuade the Indians to make sacrifices they cannot afford so that Britain can join. The British are looking to their own interest; so is everyone else except ourselves. We are looking after the interests of other people. On the Common Market [our] liberals and conservatives are divided in a peculiar way: liberals want to do the wrong thing for the wrong reasons; conservatives want to do the wrong thing for no reason at all.

The drive for European unity caught the liberal imagination in the Marshall Plan days. Partly it was to expedite European recovery and make our aid more efficient. Partly it seemed a way of erecting a new position of anti-Communist power west of the Elbe. It has rolled on under this latter banner ever since. We applaud and encourage. But we view it as a political and economic initiative peculiar to Europe which has no direct meaning for us. It is a unique act of political creation.

There is another possible view which is that modern industry with its ever-increasing scale requires larger and larger trading areas. And access to markets is now more important than protection from competitors. Social security and modern fiscal policy provide the cushioning effect on national economies which were once provided much more imperfectly by tariffs. Low-wage competition such as that of Japan or Hong Kong is still inconvenient. So is *too big* a competitive impact such as could be registered by the United States. But within limits market access is now the thing. This the Common Market provides for Europeans. So viewed the E.E.C. is not a unique act of political crea-

20 See page 155.

tion. It is an accommodation to the facts of modern economic and industrial life.

Such it is in my view. It is a reflection of a trend and Europeans are on the trend and we are not. They are developing market access at our expense. As their internal tariffs disappear they will have duty-free products from each other in competition with our duty-paid imports. No European will pay duty on (say) an American automobile when he wants a foreign car. He can have one from another Common Market country duty free. In the averaging of the internal tariffs we will also get the short end. The low-tariff countries where we now sell will be averaging up their tariffs; the countries with a tariff we cannot beat and where we have no market will be averaging down. Still we say fine. Let us get Britain and the rest of Europe in. Thus we build up Europe against the Bolshevists. In fact we are building up Europe, which is already economically powerful, against the United States.

We must react very soon. The British, once almost as retarded as we are, have seen what is happening. After using the Commonwealth for years as an excuse for keeping out of Europe, they now have their best political P.R. types deployed around the world explaining that British interests now require the sacrifice of Commonwealth preferences for the good of Britain. We must be equally concerned. We cannot continue this policy of ignoring our own interest. I have never been worried about the Pope running the government, but I am genuinely bothered about St. Francis.

We cannot and should not block the E.E.C. Nor is there anything to the idea of organizing our own hemisphere trading community — there isn't enough to organize. To pull in our horns and put up our tariffs as our conservatives would recommend would be fatal. So all that remains is to find a tolerable association with the Common Market. This we must do and we must do it while we can still bargain. I am not quite prepared to say what the form of association should be, but I have some ideas which, at some juncture, I would like to offer. Ahead and required will be some hard and clear-headed trading with our allies. We cannot continue to think first of Europe or foreswear any steps that might upset the present equilibrium or de Gaulle.

The other day Thorneycroft asked me if I thought you could be persuaded, at some juncture, to ask de Gaulle to admit Britain. I didn't answer for you, but I did take the liberty of telling him that henceforth we would . . . look seriously to our own interest. He was obviously shocked but took it well.

This letter incidentally is one of the dividends (or stock assessments) of the new air lift.[21] I am writing it en route from New Delhi to Madras with the monsoon far below. It couldn't be done in a Dakota.

Yours faithfully,
JOHN KENNETH GALBRAITH

THE PRESIDENT
  THE WHITE HOUSE

❖ ❖ ❖

July 26 — New Delhi

Yesterday I worked my way through a top-heavy desk and other things. The Pakistan press is complaining over my Madras press conference. It seems to have found me saying the United States would defend India were it attacked by Pakistan. I didn't. They have confused me with Dulles who, in the process of protecting everyone else, once protected India against Pakistan. I sent off a short, rather nasty telegram to Karachi reporting what I had said.

Then I learned that an aircraft carrier is about to arrive in Karachi to deliver some F-104's — a modern jet plane. They are to be trundled through the streets at night in secret when not fewer than 10,000 people will see them. It will be widely assumed that they represent increased military assistance won by President

[21] The Air Force Convair.

Ayub on his recent visit. I warned Washington to make the matter public — and then be braced. These planes will contribute nothing to our security in the area. They will be another complication in India-Pakistan relations and another source of suspicion so far as we are concerned. There is an obduracy about our determination to do the wrong thing which would be admirable in any other context and preferably by some other country.

Later in the day I saw M. J. Desai who asked me what the "personal" invitation I had given to Indira Gandhi to accompany her father meant. I said the personal was in effect superimposed on official. He warned me in a friendly way to warn Chester Bowles to pay a visit to Pakistan while here. Someone else should have thought of that first.

Finally tea with S. K. Patil[22] who gave me an exuberant and valuable account of his trip to the U.S.S.R., U.S. and South America. I reproached him for saying in London that India had solved her food problem. He denied saying it. Or anyhow the papers had quoted what he didn't want quoted. He recalled an earlier press interview in England when he was asked who would be the successor to Nehru. He had replied, "No one can say. The Prime Minister is like the great banyan tree. Thousands shelter beneath it but nothing grows." He told me that, in consequence, his relations with Nehru had been strained for weeks.

Health note: A fortnight ago our household staff had its annual medical checkup. This indicated three cases of tuberculosis. But yesterday we received the encouraging news that there had been errors in the diagnosis. Instead we have one hookworm, one amoebic dysentery and one case of syphilis. These, rightly, are all considered much less alarming.

[22] See page 88.

IX

More Movement

July 28 — Geneva

Day before yesterday, I got approval from the Department for a fast journey here to get abreast of the Laos problem. So I departed the same evening aboard B.O.A.C. and, miraculously, slept most of the way to Rome. There I got a room at the Hassler, slept for an hour or two and then walked down the Via Gregoriana to the Pensione Suisse and in on Peter and Jamie. (With Emily, they are en route to India.) Both were in bed reading; neither was able to react for a full ten seconds and then they fell on me with great violence. Peter is suffering from a more severe case of homesickness than he chooses to admit. I found I could take a later plane to Geneva without loss so we went to see the Sistine Chapel and Ostia Antica and it was good fun. At noon, I put them plus Emily on a plane for Athens, which we all but missed. Then I went to a restaurant in a grape arbor off the Appian Way and spent an hour enjoying elegantly cooked food and fresh fragrant wine. India gives a whole new dimension to such enjoyment.

At six, I came along to Geneva where Harriman met me. I joined him for dinner, along with two exceedingly able members of his staff,[1] and we talked until nearly midnight. Later I will give an impression.

[1] One was William Sullivan, later to become the highly effective Ambassador to Laos.

July 29 — Geneva

In the morning, I walked along the Lake and down to where it becomes the river and dashes by the islands and the statue of Rousseau. There is still a magic about this deep, glittering water. The morning was gray with broken clouds across La Faucille.

At nine, we went to the conference mission headquarters where there was a long staff meeting. It was a quiet, well-informed affair devoted to noting and assessing new intelligence on the conference, intentions of the participants and the news from Laos and elsewhere. Then I gave a view of India and Nehru (and Krishna Menon) in relation to the proceedings.

At eleven, Harriman and I drove to the Palais des Nations. The conference room itself is a squarish affair with tables also arranged to form a hollow square. Inside the hollow were numerous functionaries; around the perimeter were the participants. It was a little hard to tell who these might be; it being the Russian day to preside, the signs were all in Russian. However, I had the various delegations identified to me. The Asians were, on the average, twenty years younger and much healthier than the Westerners.

Shortly after I arrived, the proceedings began. The British with great politeness and urbanity denounced the Russians. The Russians then denounced the British and Americans. The North Vietnamese joined the Russians; the South Vietnamese came down on the side of the Americans. The Indians and the Burmese remained silent, having the day before, being neutral, denounced everybody. The meeting lasted only two hours. Short meetings are a great aid to the peace, for otherwise the denunciations are longer.

It is Harriman's decision not to participate in billingsgate and recrimination. This is a tremendous innovation in modern diplomacy. (I learned that he was forbidden by the State Department to communicate with the Chinese. I sent an indignant letter to the President on the subject, and this ridiculous bar was removed.)

The subject of the discussions was insignificant — whether a future Lao government would have the right to call on SEATO for protection, although it is agreed by everyone that it shouldn't be allowed to do so.

I talked with the conference staff and acquired a good deal of additional information. Then I had a brief nap, watched the rain over the Lake, bought a large supply of sleeping pills — they are available here without prescription since suicide is a human right — and dined pleasantly with Malcolm Macdonald,[2] Harriman, Chester Ronning,[3] and two or three others. The discussion was extensively, but not exhaustively, on Laos. I am beginning to feel pretty well in control of the problem.

Harriman is conducting the negotiations with patience, skill and a certain magnanimity. Not a suggestion of this appears in the press which implies only a kind of competitive point-scoring with the Communists. They goose us; we goose them back good. They propose; we expose. Conferences, as viewed by the newspapers, are not for accomplishment but to confound knavish tricks.

August 4 — Poona–New Delhi

This last week got far beyond the capacity of a diary. Today is Friday. On Monday, I got back to Bombay from Geneva. I alternately slept and worked on a speech until noon. At that time, our people arrived in from New Delhi and my official visit to Bombay began. The point of departure was Lincoln House, a onetime maharajah's palace on the ocean, which houses the Consulate and Consul-General and does so quite handsomely. The top floor, where the Consul lives, has a spacious view of the waves, which on occasion invade the lawn, and a merciful breeze.

My first speech was at the University and to one of the largest crowds I ever encountered. The papers dealt with it generously and it provoked a good deal of discussion.[4] After the lecture, we

---

[2] Conference co-chairman, former British High Commissioner in Canada and India, holder of numerous other high posts and son of Ramsay Macdonald.

[3] Ronning, detached temporarily from his post in India (see page 80), was representing Canada at the conference.

[4] These speeches were a problem. Traditionally, an ambassador speaks but says nothing. To say something is to make policy and of this the State Department disapproves. I gave a series of lectures on economic development. The subject was

strolled along the waterfront by the Gateway of India and on impulse employed a junk for a sail around the harbor. The latter was muddy and angrily tossed about by the monsoon but we survived.

Tuesday and Wednesday were occupied by a procession of calls, speeches, luncheons, receptions and press conferences which left me in the end in a deep coma. Apart from an occasional hasty nap, there was no relaxation at all. One day I went shopping but was quickly recognized and promptly overwhelmed by the autograph hunters. The conversation was uniformly stuffy. Prince Philip may be better designed for this than I am. Even the press conference questions were stereotyped.

Bombay, more than any other Indian city, has a strong European aspect. The great buildings around the Maidan are of Canadian Pacific Railway Gothic, gone slightly shabby. The waterfront apartments are Bauhaus with some concessions to the Socony service station. Everywhere are the palaces of the rich or the once-rich. These are castellated, tasselated and otherwise ornamented concoctions, the state of repair reflecting the present affluence of the owner. Many are by all indications insolvent.

Yesterday morning we took off for Poona atop the Deccan Plateau and some hundred miles southeast of Bombay. There we passed under military management and into a stately Packard which took us first for a visit to the Commanding General and then on an official visit to the National Defence Academy. The latter, which trains all three services, is on a wide, cool plain some distance from the city. The cadets looked clean and smart, and the curriculum, which ranges from chemistry through gliding to blacksmithing, seemed to make sense. Lunch was in the Officers' Mess, a charming building with a vast swimming pool on one side and cricket ground on the other, and was attended by numerous officers, good-looking women, and helped by a goodly amount of excellent beer. The food was also good. Bombay, except at Lincoln House, was sultry;

---

of great interest in India. Although they dealt with policy, it was not in a field where Washington sensitivity is high or where the average official thought it wise to correct me.

here it is almost invigorating. For a couple of months before the monsoon, Poona is warm. But once an inch of rain has fallen, it is again cool and remains so. It is much like Southern California in winter but — oddly enough — rather less congested.

After lunch, I went to the Gokhale Institute[5] for a visit and tea; to the University for a visit to the Vice-Chancellor and tea; on to have tea with the faculty; and eventually back to a meeting with the press where we had tea. We were billeted in the Turf Club beside a mile-and-a-half track — really four concentric tracks of grass, tanbark, sand and dirt with a great grassy enclave within. So weary was I when it all ended that I fell into bed without dinner. I dreamed fitfully of descent into a Hell that was shaped like a teapot with smoke pouring out of the spout.

The University was interesting. It occupies the residence of the former British governors. The buildings are neat and workmanlike and at the center is the palace. This is high-ceilinged, wide-verandahed and elegantly accoutred with the portraits of erstwhile governors and king-emperors. At one end, as a garish touch, the Indians had introduced the single indigenous note — a huge painting of some ruler aboard a most improbable horse in full charge. The painter's object was to achieve the maximum of motion by using the largest amount of color. My tea companion was an eighty-four-year-old mathematician of wonderful appearance and vigor, a classmate at Cambridge of A. C. Pigou.[6] At the Turf Club, I had a special guard of four soldiers. Someone should have told me what to do when they came violently to attention and presented arms as I passed. One cannot make a very dignified salute in a bush shirt, but something seemed called for. I was preceded by a pilot car, really a jeep, on all movements.

This morning we toured the parts of the city which were damaged by the recent floods — two dams above the city gave way

---

[5] A center of economic and social research of note which commemorates in its name Gopal Krishna Gokhale of Poona, one of the great progressive leaders of the early Indian nationalist movement.

[6] The great Cambridge economist of the last generation.

and let down a mighty wall of water. Some thirty or forty thousand people lost their houses in an hour or so. It was an awful mess. Those affected seemed cheerful, and the mud and debris is being cleaned away with considerable efficiency. A contributing cause of the disaster is the use of mud as mortar in the brick walls and as filler within the walls. This dissolved rapidly in the water bringing the houses tumbling down, sometimes on their occupants. Western-style buildings were little affected.

Then we looked at some feeding stations where the people being fed looked amazingly well-nourished — disaster may have improved on their ordinary slum existence — and at a big school which had been turned into a temporary shelter. Finally I had tea with the Commissioner of the Region, who is in charge of reconstruction, and gave him a check for five thousand rupees or $1,000. As before, I thought how sweet are the uses of charity when underwritten by the United States. However, I made ample point of the fact that the donors were the compassionate people of the United States and not the Galbraiths.

After lunch, I reviewed my guard for the last time and we took off for Delhi at 1:30 P.M. Word has just come of five inches of rain there and considerable floods.

August 6 — New Delhi

A busy and interesting time. Yesterday morning I spent with USIS and its Washington brass and repeated my general directive on information operations — what we are for, competence not quantity, a broad-based ideology to embrace all who like liberty and a full cultural showcase from which nothing is banned for reasons of ideology. I had fine support from Tom Sorensen[7] from Washington, brother of Ted and of the same hard intelligence.

Then I fixed up my brief for Nehru and at 4:30 P.M. called on him at the Ministry. We had a tough argument. I contended that

[7] Deputy Director for Near East Policy, U.S. Information Agency, now a Vice-President of the University of California.

a strong I.C.C. in Laos was essential for Lao independence and sovereignty. He argued that it could do little if the Laotians objected. I countered by saying that they should be persuaded. At one point, I noted that India did approve a good deal of outside interference in the Congo to which the Congolese were far from reconciled. He said this had been occasioned by foreign interference in the Congo and retreated good-naturedly when I asked him if foreign interference had been absent in Laos.

I also pled the case for India, as a neutral, making a strong bid for protected neutrality — "You should be dragging both the U.S. and the U.S.S.R. along in your insistence on leaving nothing to chance." Perhaps I made some progress.

My talk with Nehru prevented me from meeting Bowles who arrived late this afternoon.[8] Later he gave me a generous insight into the efforts to fire him. He attributes his troubles to his liberal stand. I would give a little more emphasis to conflict of style and personality where the President is concerned. But he has taken the lead in getting a good many liberals into the Department and obviously should be supported.

Today I won my battle on telling the Indians about the F-104's we are delivering to Pakistan. (These were only twelve. But rumor and imagination were already greatly exaggerating the number.) Phil Talbot[9] is here with Bowles. He came in and I began by asking him who was running the store in Washington. He insisted that he took full responsibility including the failure to respond to my cables. I then asked him if he took responsibility for the surrender to Pakistan demands that the deliveries be kept confidential. He said no. Then, after I reminded him of his claim that he was in charge, he reluctantly authorized my telling the Indians.

[8] For the convention of ambassadors previously mentioned. See pages 134–35.
[9] Phillips Talbot, Assistant Secretary of State for Near East and South Asian Affairs. He was an appointee of Bowles but quickly made peace with the cold warriors in the Department and tactfully detached himself from his patron as the latter declined in influence. He subsequently became Ambassador to Greece and survived to handle relations with the military junta that seized power in 1967.

I imagine he is worrying a bit about what he has done and will tomorrow wish he hadn't. He told me that he tried to give equal attention to the pleas of all chiefs of mission. I told him brutally that I was to be considered a member of the Administration, one of the policy-makers of the Democratic Party and that a special accommodation to my requirements was in order. He took it well. I hope I have frightened without unduly antagonizing him. It is a thin line.

At lunch today, Teddy White,[10] who is visiting, was exceedingly pessimistic about South Vietnam. So am I.

August 8 — New Delhi

Meetings yesterday. Bowles was interesting and clever. Knowing the tough position he was in, he went over promises with which the new Administration came to power — against military pacts, no fooling with the dictators, against buying anti-Communism, the importance of social solutions. This was unexceptional as history; it kept him clear of positions he was not authorized to take. There followed a remarkably good debate on Chinese policy. No one present objected to the admission of China to the U.N. — the only difference was between those who favored it and those who urged the acceptance of the inevitable. We had lunch on the military pacts, and I think I had some influence on the Pentagon people. My argument: this is what arrests the movement of India in our direction. It could send her to Russia. One must keep things very simple for the soldiers.

In the afternoon, Talbot held forth on the harmony in Washington, the many studies of foreign policy under way, and committed himself to nothing. He will, I think, always be controlled by the most disagreeable person around him. Perhaps I can qualify.

In the afternoon, I saw Krishna Menon for an amicable talk about Laos. Nothing new but I made progress on the art of conversation with him. That is to start first and allow no opportunity

10 Theodore H. White. See page 38.

for interruption until you have finished. However, yesterday was unduly easy for I had just completed some very complicated arrangements to have one of the most popular generals in the Indian army go to the United States with Bowles for cancer treatment including hospitalization at Walter Reed Army Hospital. He is under a six-months death sentence, poor man.

Later I told M. J. Desai the number of planes to Pakistan. He was appreciative, if not approving, and the actual number was far fewer than the rumors already had suggested. The Pakistanis, who naturally appreciated exaggeration, will not be pleased. And they had a promise we wouldn't tell the Indians. Perfidious America.

During the day, word came in from Washington that it was not financing the Bokaro steel plant.[11] I replied before my temper could cool, which is always wiser. The reasons they gave were ludicrous — all old stories here, all obviated in our planning, but all new to Washington. This morning by the grace of a brilliant accident, the newspapers told of possible Soviet interest. This is front-paged along with the Soviet multiple space orbit.

August 10 — New Delhi

Two days of meetings. One was devoted to the new role of women in public affairs. I remained away, stating I preferred the old role to the extent that advancing age allowed me to appreciate it.

Some other sessions were better. There was a spirited debate on the military pacts with Bill Rountree defending rigorously a policy of which he was an author.[12] I led the attack with a surprising measure of support. I pointed out that the pacts identified us with the governments in question. Then legitimate anti-government agita-

[11] See page 81.
[12] William M. Rountree, professional Foreign Service Officer, then Ambassador to Pakistan and later to South Africa. He had served previously in the State Department as Assistant Secretary for Near Eastern, South Asian and African Affairs and was a strong and effective supporter of what, in those days, was called the Dulles line.

tion became anti-American agitation and to some extent pro-Soviet activity. Also, we cannot use military aid as leverage for reform; military men do not exercise much reformist leverage. Also, military aid to Pakistan opens the way to pro-Soviet pressure on the Indians.

Night before last, the Prime Minister had a small family dinner — Bowleses, Galbraiths plus M. J. Desai — and last night he was at our house. Both occasions were pleasant. During the meetings, I had a long talk with Bowles about his situation in Washington which is exceedingly tenuous. He attributes it to the opposition of the F.S.O.'s.[13] I gave him a more accurate view: He is being blamed for the inadequacy of the State Department which is chronic and endemic but which he has made an insufficient show of trying to correct. Instead, he has persuaded people that he is busy writing memoranda and thinking advanced thoughts. He accepted my diagnosis and also my remedy which was to settle down to running the Department or as much of it as possible and do a minimum of talking. He may not be totally persuaded. It took him a very long while to tell me he agreed.[14]

The Prime Minister was late for dinner. He had been addressing a big meeting in Old Delhi. He reported that he had been surprised at the size of his audience and later discovered they were there to see a movie star. Krishna Menon also came to dinner. He was polite and charming but went to sleep after he had eaten.

August 11 — New Delhi
Early yesterday, the Washington captains and the kings departed. I broke my rule and went out to the airport to see Bowles off. Then I returned to a meeting which Talbot, who was proceed-

[13] Foreign Service Officers. President Kennedy had contemplated moving him from his post as Undersecretary of State to another assignment. This, however, had been postponed because of premature publicity.
[14] My diagnosis may well have been wrong. Bowles had initiated substantial reforms and these had run into heavy opposition. The attack on his style and personality was, I now think, a cover for these deeper objections.

ing to Nepal, insisted on having with the ambassadors who are still in town. I had tried to persuade him against it but he was adamant. So I had myself called out after half an hour and went about my business. Talbot told of his strenuous efforts to keep the Peace Corps in its place. I have no doubts that he finds this a more rewarding object of his energies than the Pentagon. Then we had all the surviving ambassadors to lunch. Rountree and I entered into a mutual assistance pact according to which neither of us will have a press conference for the next few weeks. Whatever I say in India or he in Pakistan is used adversely in the other country.

In the evening, the Harvard Glee Club, some sixty strong, came to dinner and made away with prodigious quantities of Indian food and Coca-Cola. I had some Indian music for them and they came out on the garden terrace and did some songs. They sounded fine and the setting — the lights against the trees and the lawn — was quite compelling.

New Delhi, India
August 15, 1961

Dear Mr. President:

I have a variety of matters of interest and amusement including a few of the subtleties in self-advertisement which you must be finding familiar in your communications. I might number them:

(1) I trust your life was . . . enriched by your visit with Baruch.[15] I appreciate your seeing . . . [him] and it liquidates a campaign promise. . . .

(2) We have just had a three-day meeting with Bowles plus one with Talbot.[16] I was admirably instructed on what I already knew, didn't believe or couldn't remember.[17] I can't say that you have done wonders for Chet's morale. In what Lyndon . . . calls a belly-to-belly talk I [urged] him to . . . write no more memo-

---

[15] In soliciting Bernard Baruch's support during the campaign, I had said that, as President, Kennedy would wish to consult him.

[16] See page 182.

[17] I was becoming unduly impressed with this line.

randa and concentrate on making the African, Asian and Latino parts of the Department work. He thinks he has aroused bureaucratic enmities by firing too many people; I said it was my impression he had aroused yours by not firing enough. (Even the Attorney-General would have winced at all the candor.) Chet promised to do his best but says he is boxed. In government people get boxed only when they won't kick their way out. I like Bowles. His only trouble is an uncontrollable instinct for persuasion which he brings to bear on the persuaded, the unpersuaded and the totally irredeemable alike. In my view the State Department needs not to be persuaded but to be told. I think it conceivable that Chet might take hold. He was very good in O.P.A.[18]

(3) If the State Department drives you crazy you might calm yourself by contemplating its effect on me. The other night I woke with a blissful feeling and discovered I had been dreaming that the whole Goddam place had burned down. I dozed off again hoping for a headline saying no survivors. I think I dislike most the uncontrollable instinct for piously reasoned inaction. When the Department does respond to telegrams it is invariably to recommend evasion of issues that cannot be evaded. The result, in the end, is that we get the worst of all available worlds. The touchiest issue here is the shipment of military hardware to Pakistan — arming the present rival and foe and the ancient enemy and rulers of the Hindus. A few weeks ago one of our aircraft carriers brought twelve supersonic jets to Karachi where they were unloaded in all the secrecy that would attend mass sodomy on the B.M.T. at rush hour. Rumors plus Indian intelligence raised the number to 30, then 50, then 75. (This, I learn, is escalation.) The Pakistanis asked that the number not be released in order to keep the Indians in doubt and the Department agreed over my protests. When the thing

---

[18] The World War II Office of Price Administration of which he became the head in 1943 shortly after my own much applauded withdrawal as head of price control.

promised to get out of hand here the Department cabled me sympathy. Eventually, I wrung authority to release the number out of Talbot more or less by physical violence. That then doublecrossed the [Pakistanis] who had been promised we wouldn't tell.

Talbot, who was here with Bowles, spent some hours outlining the excellent longer-range studies that are now under way on our foreign policy. They are being conducted in a cooperative spirit; he says, indeed, that complete harmony prevails. I think he has a good sense of tactics. He took a cautious line on the Pentagon but came out strongly for keeping the Peace Corps in its place.

(4) I liked very much your reference to national interest in your statement on the Common Market. However, I remain unhappy. The British accession will convert the E.C.M. from a step toward political unification, which is the liberal's image, to a tariff club that discriminates systematically against our products. Yet the magic of the word unification will keep us from demanding the concessions the British will get. No one seems to see that we have a large and expensive foreign policy in which money serves as a substitute for intelligence and that we must have the export earnings to pay for it. Indeed we haven't really been paying for it for years — instead we have been drawing systematically on accumulated reserves.

(5) I have just completed a tour of the major Indian cities with an incredible variety of activities including a major speech to the university students in each place. I had large, interested and friendly crowds, and the talks, which were on economic policy and planning, went exceedingly well and are still being much discussed. In short your well-known political prescience is again justified and I am a considerable success.

(6) Laos continues to command a lot of my time. I am trying hard to persuade the Indians that once we accept neutrality they cannot be less concerned to protect it than we. If neutrality

means that Laos goes to the Communists, the word will stink and everyone will attribute the failure to acceptance of an Indian policy. It is an uphill fight. The Department expects me to explain our devotion to neutrality in Laos one day and our supersonic toys for the Pakistanis the next. That is called a policy. The Indian habit of mediating is strong — halfway between the United States and Russia is somehow right — and Krishna Menon is also a major stumbling block. I don't think he is open to persuasion for he owes his position to his hold on the left wing of the Congress Party. But even were he open to conviction I would rather work on Wayne Morse.[19] Incidentally I find Menon the most interesting man in the top hierarchy. I have rarely encountered a politician who is more completely exempt from the wish to be loved.

(7) Two weeks ago I went to Geneva for two or three days to get some more ammunition. I asked Arthur[20] to tell you what a good job Harriman is doing — the really right combination of patience, firmness and dignity and good sense. We have a depressingly weak hand to play and I sometimes wonder why we should expect the Communists to turn in their winning cards. Maybe they are tired of the Laos.

(8) From here I get the impression that your position on Berlin makes a great deal of sense. I predict an outcome that will reflect credit on you and your Administration.

Faithfully,
JOHN KENNETH GALBRAITH

THE PRESIDENT
THE WHITE HOUSE

---

[19] Longtime Senator from Oregon, a man not easily persuaded — fortunately.
[20] Schlesinger, Jr.

X

Berlin, China, Laos, Kashmir

August 16 — New Delhi

Night before last, the U.A.R. Ambassador celebrated something or other. His house was filled with shady-looking characters by the time we arrived. They stood around for several hours, vehemently denouncing each other as stooges of imperialism. Then we went in to dinner which was ample but inedible. (I have never been in a city where it is so easy to lose weight. The Metrecal market is inherently minimal.) I sat with the distinctly beautiful wife of the Yugoslav Ambassador who tasted the wine and promptly pronounced it potable. She said to the waiter, "I will have some more. It is actually rather good." I thought her a bit tactless, but I lean over backwards as befits a big power.

Yesterday was Independence Day. We were up at dawn and soon thereafter seated atop the gate of the Red Fort.[1] Some hundreds of thousands were out in front. An honor guard arrived and presently the Prime Minister and Krishna Menon. Thirty-one guns boomed out, the national anthem was played and the monsoon resumed. The latter was heavy and drenching, and everyone had to put up his umbrella. In front and below was the great lawn which borders the moat of the Red Fort, covered with schoolchildren, and beyond were more thousands with the dome and minarets of the mosque piercing the horizon. At least there was reason to believe that all this was there. In fact, I could see only

[1] See page 64.

the umbrella of the wife of the Afghan Ambassador immediately in front. The water running off its eaves onto my knees was also a major distraction. Nehru spoke in Hindi, with occasional English words, and I followed him poorly. In the afternoon, there was a vast reception at the Rashtrapati Bhavan where, as a center of idle curiosity, I ranked only a little behind Nehru and the Vice-President. The Moghul Gardens at the back are now green and rich and with pools and fountains exceedingly beautiful.

August 17 — Mahabalipuram

Economic aid is ordinarily considered to be a matter of power plants, steel mills and dams. I am concerned to gain recognition for less tangible and equally useful forms. So yesterday I flew down here and this morning at nine went to Madras Harbor to welcome the M.S. *Browind* with a cargo of some four million pounds of powdered milk for the school feeding program. In this progressive state, every youngster gets a free noonday meal — and we are providing powdered milk, rice, cornmeal and cooking oil. The Chief Minister, Education Minister and numerous notables were on hand at shipside under an awning erected for the purpose. I had a perfect speech; partly amusing, partly entertaining and adequately making my point. I also cemented international goodwill by rather elaborately saluting the Soviets for imitating the American and Indian system of providing free food. (This had just been announced as a long-range goal of Soviet planning.) I was bedecked with several pounds of flowers and reflected as usual on the blessedness of giving at the public expense. In this connection, I had brought some books for the ship's library assuming, of course, that it was an American ship. Alas, the *Browind* turned out to be Swedish.

I had lunch with B. K. Nehru and learned that the Bokaro plant was dropped for the time being from the Indian priority list. This undercuts some very nasty telegrams I have been sending to Washington protesting Washington disinterest. However, I am not completely on a limb for it remains on the list.

August 20 — New Delhi

We spent an afternoon, night and morning at Mahabalipuram, south of Madras on the ocean, in a comfortable guest house, and I had the relaxation I get only in Vermont and from ocean swimming. We also looked at the caves and friezes. Here as at Ellora they tackled the living rock. Smallish outcroppings became elephants and cows, larger ones became temples all firmly attached to the earth's core. A great bas-relief, with varying names but usually called "The Descent to the Ganges," is exceedingly fine. It covers one side of a huge boulder and is a vast concourse of men, animals and combinations thereof in movement.

Yesterday I caught up with bureaucratic detail and in the evening was entertained at the Press Club. This is in a rather decayed building and the room was packed and incredibly hot. The first question, predictably, was on arms aid to Pakistan. I noted that I had answered the question in Madras, Calcutta and Bombay and had then been hurt to discover that answers were still wanted from Chester Bowles. My feelings remained so deeply hurt that I could not bear to respond. I told the questioner I respected the deep sense of tradition which caused him to ask. The crowd was rather on my side. The other questions were relatively straightforward. One man asked if there were still a Dulles clique in the State Department. I said no; Heaven will call me to account for that one. After an hour, I escaped without a dry stitch.

I am heading for a considerable showdown with AID. Their activities are still ridiculously dispersed as to subject and outrageously concentrated in New Delhi as to locale. A couple of weeks ago, I asked for two memoranda — one on plans for a greater concentration of agricultural activities and one on the present and recommended proportion of the force to be stationed in New Delhi. The first resulted in a snow job. It agrees that there should be concentration of energies on bread-grains production — the most efficient way of filling stomachs. But rural sociologists and home economists now have their justification for their contribution to wheat-growing. The memorandum on the concentration of talent in New Delhi still hasn't appeared. Suitable disguises for the legion of specialists lodged in the capital are still being invented. Ty Wood is marvelously ambivalent about the whole business. He wants to agree with me; he dislikes defending the indefensible; and he wants to uphold his organization.

August 22 — New Delhi

The other day in Madras, as I may have told, I ironically congratulated the Soviets on their adoption of the American (and Madrasi) idea of free lunches in their new twenty-year program. The point was not lost on the crowd; some of my own people thought I might be getting over the line in an attack on the Soviets in neutral territory which protocol wisely forbids. I worried a bit myself. It was unnecessary. On Sunday at a luncheon at the Yugoslav Ambassador's, Benediktov[2] thanked me effusively in the presence of Nehru for my kind observations. Nehru, who knew what I had been up to, was greatly amused.

Yesterday I struggled on with a terrible cold. But in the afternoon I had an interesting talk with Dr. Homi Bhabha, the head of the Atomic Energy Commission.[3] He is medium-complexioned, stocky and speaks without rhetoric. A most attractive man. He produced figures to show that at Bombay they can produce electricity more cheaply from atomic energy than from coal. Maybe, although most calculations are to the contrary. Speaking of calculations, he wants a computer on the scale of a Univac or I.B.M. 704. I shall try to oblige.

[2] The Soviet Ambassador. See page 88.
[3] Bhabha was killed in 1966 when a plane of Air-India approaching Geneva crashed on Mont Blanc. Both as a scientist and administrator, he had earned worldwide respect. The figures he here presented were first questioned and subsequently accepted by the United States Atomic Energy Commission.

August 24 — New Delhi

A telegram from the President asks why a small U.S. arms buildup gets more attention than a big Soviet one. Why are we condemned for weakness in Laos and belligerency in Berlin? I have replied in detail. I doubt that the Indians think we have been weak in Laos — only sensible. On Berlin and the arms build-up, it is more fun and also more fruitful to criticize the Americans than the Soviets. We listen. There is no similar indication the Soviets do. So it is natural that we are lectured. We cannot be sorry that we are regarded as open to suggestion — not incorrigible. But I also used the occasion to weigh in on noisy U.S. generals, arms aid to Pakistan which is taken locally as indication of our unremitting militarism, and the fact that we could better defend our policy if the Department would get off its ass on various matters and provide one.

August 25 — New Delhi

Day before yesterday, Nehru said in Parliament that our access to Berlin was a "concession" by the Russians, not something we enjoyed by right. This has put the skunk in the air conditioner. Washington is raving; the reaction will bring all who don't like Nehru together with all who don't like Galbraith into quite a coalition. Before I had got around to reading Nehru's speech, my staff had got off a cable asking for material to unpersuade him. My desk will be thick with instructions today.

I got off my answer to the President yesterday on criticism and Berlin. It is crisp, critical and constructive and highlights the need to have an affirmative negotiating position on Berlin if we are to persuade people that we are both firm and reasonable. I suggest as such a negotiating position keeping West Germany atom-free, conceding the unlikeliness of unification, relaxing on the issue of diplomatic recognition of East Germany. On the other side, we remain absolutely categorical on our rights of access to Berlin.

I have also taken exception to the elaborate stratagem currently being devised for keeping China out of the United Nations. It is ingenious and patently bogus — we try to get agreement by majority vote that admission is an important question and then get them rejected on a proposition that requires a two-thirds vote. I sent off a mean cable ridiculing this whole proposition.[4] It crossed one from Washington asking me promptly to take up the stratagem with the Prime Minister. I somehow suspect that the position was approved all the way up to the President.

New Delhi, India
August 26, 1961

Dear Mr. President:

I am a good deal worried about our negotiating position on admission of the Chinese Communists to the United Nations. I know as a politician rather than as a diplomat exactly how difficult this situation is and how difficult you know it to be. Indeed, some years ago I concluded that I would speak my mind on what I deemed to be inevitable and have had some experience of the consequences. I am not reacting now to the merits of the case but to the reputation and posture of the Administration and the United States.

The experts have cooked up a device which they think will keep the Chicoms[5] out for another year. This, as you certainly know, is to have Chinese representation made an "important question" which, if adopted by a majority vote, would make the decision to change from Formosa to Peking subject to a two-thirds majority vote. The tactic is patently transparent. Debate over whether it is an "important question" will straightaway become a debate on admission. We will have gone out on a limb for what seems to be a clever maneuver and will be defeated. At the meeting of the South Asian Ambassadors a fortnight ago not

[4] The major points are in the letter that follows to the President.
[5] An offensive official usage for which I weep.

a soul thought we could promote a majority for exclusion. This morning Maffitt, my DCM, and I discussed the tactic with Desai at the Foreign Office. Since I could easily be considered a prejudiced party I let Maffitt carry the ball which he did very cleverly. He got nowhere. Desai simply said, "There would have to be a majority vote and it is our position that the seat belongs to the Chinese mainland." He was willing to consider charter revision as an interesting idea. But this tactic would greatly alarm me for it would give the Russians a hunting license on the office of Secretary-General.

As I say, I see no chance of lining up a majority. What seems to me inevitable is that we shall have a minority consisting of the more dubious figures in the world — Salazar, Chiang, Sarit.[6] We won't have Ayub. The New Frontier will get credit only for continuing the Old Frontier policy with the difference that with us it failed. And even should we win, we will have the issue back with us again a year hence and an election to boot. There is no happy solution to this problem but wise men have long been told of the proper reaction to inevitable rape. I would urge that we take a passive attitude on the Chicoms, making a token vote against them but no impassioned pleas. Our prestige should not be put on the block. Then let us put our energies into keeping Formosa in the General Assembly. Here we are acting on behalf of an old ally and no one will doubt our good will. We might even get a majority for this although I confess to being uncertain about the precise legal procedures.

I have put all these matters in a pointed telegram to the State Department. The result was not entirely disappointing. It produced one of the rudest responses in the history of diplomacy.

Yours faithfully,
JOHN KENNETH GALBRAITH

THE PRESIDENT
THE WHITE HOUSE

[6] Then Prime Minister of Thailand.

August 27 — New Delhi

My China cable brought one of the rudest and certainly the promptest response in the history of the Department. "To the extent that your position has any merit it has been fully considered and rejected."[7]

Friday I gave a speech at the Indian School of Public Administration to the usual Indian full house. The School has a handsome auditorium, not air-conditioned, and the day was exceedingly sultry. By mid-point, I hadn't a dry stitch, and the sweat was running over my glasses in a minor Niagara. The effort was in part unnecessary for I discovered that not until I was well under way did the amplifying apparatus come on. So I was not being heard. I spoke on "Planning and the Public Corporation" and made a strong plea for having public corporations (such as those producing steel) free from political intervention and supervision and also from the deadening hand of the Civil Service.

My mind was not entirely on the speech for Nehru's comment on the absence of legal right to Berlin has stirred up a hornet's nest. I had determined to try to get him to reverse it before he (a) alienated one and all in the U.S. and (b) gave the Soviets unlimited encouragement.

I went to his house at 7:30 P.M. and, in accordance with previous arrangement, took along the boys for a picture with him. There was one especially amusing shot of Peter, Jamie and the Prime Minister on a couch with Jamie in ordinarily voluble conversation.

When the children left, I moved in on the Berlin question — beginning by saying that my remarks would be unpleasant. This was not merely a gesture; in practice, the unpleasantness never does live up to the promise and your victim thus gets the benefit of a pleasant surprise. I had brought along a corrective statement with me that I had hoped he would release and which my staff was amply assured he would not.

Oddly enough, he seemed not to think he had questioned our

[7] It was, I learned later, drafted — some said almost lovingly — by the Secretary himself.

right of access to Berlin. When I showed his words to him, he was rather nonplused. This gave me an unquestioned advantage. I pressed it very hard and first he offered a new affirmation of our right of access. Then to my great delight he approved my statement. Thereafter, I presented the essentials of our Berlin posture anew: we were quiet; it was the Soviets who had kicked up a fuss. If there is a payoff under these circumstances, there will be a premium on trouble-making. Then I went on to urge our case on the nuclear test ban. We want it. The Russians evidently do not. The world must have it. Would he so impress the Soviets? And would India support us in the U.N. on affirmative proposals which included controls rather than merely resolving for a continuation of the ban without controls? On the whole, I think I made some headway.

Finally, we had our usual word about Laos. As I have noted, the Communists are resisting most measures of supervision and control there because they say it would interfere with Lao sovereignty, whatever that exiguous commodity may be. The Indians have not been very strong to the contrary. Last week Arthur Lall, the Indian delegate in Geneva, objected to a provision on prisoner-of-war repatriation under international supervision on which, actually, we and the Russians agreed. This gave me the opportunity I had been waiting for to press for a stronger Indian position. I hope it had some effect. Nothing I have said so far seems to have got through to Geneva.

All of this took about seventy-five minutes. Afterward, I had an exceedingly well-attended press conference and released the statement that Nehru had approved along with a brief happy one of my own.

Yesterday, although Saturday, was a large day, given mostly to dictating telegrams on my various activities. But at noon we visited M. J. Desai. So there could be no suggestion that I was queering the pitch, I had Maffitt present the proposed strategy on China.[8]

---

[8] Also, I did not want to exhaust my personal influence on a hopeless case. India was then sponsoring the admission of China.

This he did quite cleverly but the transparent character of the effort was immediately evident. Desai promptly said no. Maffitt tried again and Desai again said no. Further accomplishment was negative.

My instructions were to take the matter up with Nehru. These I had interpreted to mean by way of Desai. One cannot argue an honest case and a patently bogus one at the same time without doing damage to the legitimate case. Berlin was too important to allow this.

Yesterday afternoon the rains stopped for a while and in the cool damp of the early evening, we went out to the zoo. There I presented them with three Canada geese.[9] As a reward, I was presented a bouquet of flowers by an elephant as was Kitty when she arrived a little late. The same talented greeter garlanded us with flowers and played us a mouth organ selection to which it danced. Peter and Jamie, to their joy, were presented with a young leopard cub. We then went on a tour of the zoo, which is natural and spacious and situated under the towering walls of Deen Panah, now called Purana Qila, on the site of the first of the seven cities of Delhi.[10] It includes the only happy tigers I have ever seen in a zoo — they roam in large paddocks. Perhaps in consequence of their good psyches, the zoo keeper can fondle and pet them, to which they respond with obvious pleasure.

August 28 — New Delhi–Srinagar

It is hard in this job not to develop a morbid dislike for the State Department. It is remote, mindless, petty and, above all, pompous, overbearing and late.

---

[9] I had arranged for the import of six of these handsome, dignified and exceedingly arrogant birds, three of them for the fountain and pool in front of the Chancery. One shortly thereafter broke its neck disputing the right of an automobile to the adjacent drive. The other two swam disdainfully in the pool for the duration of my tour.

[10] Built in the 1540's, Deen Panah means "Abode of the Modest." Purana Qila means merely "Old Fort." Old Delhi, the city of Shah Jahan, is the seventh city.

These thoughts are stimulated by a circular telegram to various embassies which arrived this morning. It was dispatched an hour or two before my talk with Nehru. Arriving three days later, it told of all the antagonistic reactions that had followed the statement that he had subsequently clarified or retracted.

Although yesterday was Sunday, the only difference was the difficulty in getting a secretary. Various visitors arrived including Dr. B. C. Roy.[11] Recently he has been in Washington where, as one of the most powerful and self-confident political figures in India, he naturally sought a meeting with President Kennedy. The State Department refused to intercede — so did the Indian Embassy which would have had to pass the request through the Department. The President, all the officials assured him, sees only heads of state. They were unpersuaded by the fact that, as regards many matters in Bengal, he so functions. Then he went to the Capitol to visit Fulbright and Humphrey and they told him he should see Kennedy. He told of his efforts. They called and the President asked him over immediately. They had an hour's conversation on the problems of Calcutta, Pakistan and comparative politics. At the end, Dr. Roy told the White House newsmen that he had been primarily interested in the President's back but hadn't examined it professionally because of some doubts about the fee. He does exceedingly well for eighty. To say that he was enchanted by Kennedy would be too mild.

September 5 — Srinagar–New Delhi

After a week in Kashmir, I have got rid of a nasty fungus rash which I cultivate in New Delhi heat, months of accumulated fatigue, my office pallor and several pounds of excess weight, the result of insufficient exercise in the great heat. The weight loss

---

[11] Chief Minister of West Bengal, a tall, vigorous figure in Indian politics for more than half a century, he was Gandhi's personal physician and cared for the Mahatma during his fasts. He once told me that he thought fasting did him (or would do anyone) a considerable amount of good. He died in 1962.

reflects a new approach to the problem which I have derived from Master Tara Singh.[12] Instead of dieting, I find it psychologically sounder to think of fasting. I try to see how little I can eat in order to kill the actual pain. Then I stop. It is also exceedingly important to test progress not by a scale but by the disappearance of the rolls of fat. When you weigh yourself and observe that you have lost a few pounds, you have an uncontrollable temptation to relent. The absence of any visual effect prevents this damaging reassurance.

All the family was here including Emily, and it will be some years before we have another such holiday,[13] for Alan leaves tomorrow for Bangkok, Hong Kong and home. One day we went into the mountains above Gulmarg; on another we went for seven or eight miles above Pahalgam. This latter especially, on the edge of the Great Himalayan range, is fine mountain country and our route lay along a rushing torrent and through thick pines. We took ponies costing Rs. 5 a mount (roughly a dollar); behind us came a couple of men carrying lunch, gear and equipment of all kinds and costing only Rs. 3 a head. Manpower here is cheaper than animals. Against economics, I equalized the price.

We also visited the Prime Minister[14] and I endowed him with a small radio — reception over the mountains is very difficult but this one is supposed to be effective. And on another day we lunched with the Maharajah. His possessions have dwindled in modern times and the main palace is now the principal hotel. But his present quarters are in an airy and attractive house on a high saddle with Dal Lake on one side and Srinagar on the other. The lunch, which was Indian style served in large circular multi-holed plates with a hot water base, was very good. At each corner of the room

[12] Sikh leader who was on a hunger strike on behalf of autonomy for the Sikh community of the Punjab. I doubtless owed something to Dr. B. C. Roy. See footnote above.

[13] Actually, it was not.

[14] Ghulam Mohammad Bakhshi, a rugged machine politician with no very high reputation in Indian political life. He has since disappeared from the public scene save as he continues to defend himself in the law courts.

was a water basin for washing up as the situation required since one eats with his hands.

The Maharajah of Jammu and Kashmir[15] is, along with Mysore, the last of the princes to survive as governor. He is thirty and presently completing his Ph.D. thesis in political science at Delhi University. He says he hasn't minded the transition to his new and reduced status for he had little experience of the old grandeur. That evening he assembled a dozen or fifteen professors and University and Planning Board officials for a discussion of economic policy.

During the week came the news that the Soviets were resuming atomic tests. And the Chinese are also making ominous sounds in Laos. It is not very encouraging.

On the other hand, I have managed to think through a host of major and minor problems. I see much more clearly than a week ago the things I must work for, proving that vacations have a function.

September 8 — New Delhi

Day before yesterday we took the Navy plane on our delayed journey to Phoolbagh.[16] This is in the Terai, in the United Provinces, about 150 miles from New Delhi. It is the site of a new agricultural university. The Terai is an area of subfoothill which lies between the foothills and the Ganges Plain and until recently was jungle. Tigers still roam the area in small numbers.

The University has an area of several thousand recently reclaimed acres. It is being developed with the advice of a team recruited from or by the University of Illinois. The model is to be an American land-grant college. On the whole, it is impressive.

The Vice-Chancellor, a civil servant, K. A. P. Stevenson, is able

---

[15] Karan Singh, who became a good personal friend. He has since served as Minister of Tourism and Civil Aviation in the national government.
[16] See page 156.

and alert, although being a civil servant, there is always the possibility that he will be dispatched next week for another task. Placing these positions under the unspecialized and rotating authority of the civil service is unwise. No one is permanently and professionally associated with a task and with the assurance that the handiwork will be his.

I visited the poultry department, animal husbandry, dairy, veterinary, hybrid corn, horticultural and numerous other establishments and gave a speech to the students recommending that they measure their success in the world by their active assistance to those who engage in physical toil. The students responded to my praise of toil with great applause and loud demands for a holiday from work in honor of my visit. I told them that in the United States distinguished visitors rewarded students with an extra day of study. This I would provide for next Sunday. There were furious groans. Then, in honor of myself and in deference to local custom, I withdrew the extra work. In the ensuing confusion, I escaped.

By 4:30 P.M., we were back in Delhi where I faced another three hours of routine.

I am not very happy about the neutral conference in Belgrade which broke up yesterday.[17] Despite our absence of posturing on Berlin and our desire to get a treaty on testing, we seem to be held equally accountable with the Russians for the current crisis. I am going home to have a talk with J.F.K. about this and other things.

September 11 — Washington

I got to New York at 2:30 P.M. day before yesterday and to Washington about six. It is still a long journey — 36 hours — when taken without a break. I went to a dinner at Scotty Lanahan's[18] but hardly shone. Still, we ate good food in the garden and it was fun.

Yesterday, though it was Sunday, I spent most of the day at the

[17] Called by Nehru, Tito, Nasser and Sukarno. In fact, as Schlesinger notes (*A Thousand Days*. Boston: Houghton Mifflin, 1965, p. 518), the mood there was not unfavorable to Kennedy and the United States.
[18] See page 18.

204   AMBASSADOR'S JOURNAL

State Department and dined with the Schlesingers. Most of the morning I spent with Kohler[19] on Berlin but added little to my guesses or what I could surmise. We want assured access to Berlin; we will negotiate other issues. No one seems to have considered what we negotiate. Intensive discussions are to start this week and I can't imagine what they have been discussing all along.

My own view is that they will, in the end, concede to the Soviets on East Germany.[20] We will be billed as suffering a major defeat; Kennedy will get credit for having lost something we never had.

Lunching with George Ball, I learned — as I had from several cables — that Rusk was deeply seared by my telegram on his China policy. At the same time, it is being revised in accordance with my criticism.[21]

Last night I had a brief discussion with Lane Timmons, my new D.C.M.[22] Then I went on to the Schlesingers' for dinner and a long talk about Washington, New Delhi and Cambridge. Arthur thinks the New Frontier is doing not badly; he is very low on the idea of returning to Harvard a year hence. I could go more contentedly.

September 12 — Washington

At nine-fifteen yesterday morning, the Secretary had his staff meeting. This was over at a little after ten when George Ball had a meeting on operations. Following this at ten forty-five, Phil Talbot, the Assistant Secretary, returned to his office and convened a meeting of his staff to tell them what happened at the two

[19] Foy Kohler, then Assistant Secretary of State for European Affairs, subsequently Ambassador to Moscow, now teaching in Florida.

[20] Some kind of *de facto* recognition. For the short run, this was quite wrong. In the longer period, it reflected the broad trend of events.

[21] Quite wrong. It wasn't.

[22] Whom I had previously selected. A Rhodes Scholar and Marshall Plan economist, he had been Deputy Chief of Mission in Stockholm. Following his tour of duty in India, the State Department proposed him for a minor NATO post in Paris. At President Kennedy's personal insistence, reflecting appreciation of his energy and instinct for accomplishment if not his tact, he was made Ambassador to Haiti.

earlier meetings. There was not much to report for at such big meetings you cannot decide serious matters. But it took until nearly noon. This is an average day in the making of foreign policy.

I am rarely so depressed as after a day in the Department. It is so large it crawls with bodies. And all energies are employed in arranging for so many people to live together.

At noon, I saw the Secretary for an hour. I outlined my ideas for an initiative on Berlin but I am not sure I got anywhere. He seemed mildly impressed by my idea that we are negotiating furiously for things — control of Laos, the way things develop in East Berlin and East Germany, who shall be the government of China — that we never had or have already lost. He did give me some useful suggestions on approaching the Indians on alternatives to Pakistan military aid. I weighed in heavily on the latter as currently the most poisonous factor in our position in the area. I was helped by the fact that the Pakistanis have become rather belligerent on the Afghan border. The idea is to see whether a nonaggressive or mutual security understanding between the two countries is possible as a replacement for our military assistance. I doubt it but any alternative is worth exploring.

After lunch with Phil Graham and others at the *Washington Post* including Joe Alsop[23] who is exceedingly martial, I visited Fulbright, Angier Biddle Duke[24] on the details of the forthcoming Nehru visit, talked to the Policy Planning Staff, went to dinner with Stevenson, Schlesinger and George McGhee[25] at the Bowleses' and finally went on to the Schlesingers'. Fulbright is as depressed as I am at the general state of our foreign policy. He told me that the John Birch Society was making his life very miserable in Arkansas. He looked brown, lean, healthy and much livelier than

---

[23] Then a much-feared columnist.
[24] Chief of Protocol, subsequently Ambassador to Spain, and again Chief of Protocol.
[25] See page 12.

the run-of-the-mill statesman. Bowles, Schlesinger and Stevenson all talked mournfully about our foreign policy without coming up with any affirmative ideas. Arthur was toying provisionally with an idea of Joe Alsop's which is that world public opinion is unimportant in a climate of fear. Power alone counts. Adlai was outraged.

September 13 — Washington–New Delhi

Yesterday I made the rounds beginning at breakfast with Rostow[26] and Bundy, then various people in the Department, then a long lunch with Abe Chayes[27] and Carl Kaysen,[28] then Bill Sullivan[29] on Laos and Bowles on various matters, Roger Jones[30] and, in the evening, a dinner with Wallace Carroll[31] for, among others, Jacob Beam[32] and his wife. Beam, who was in Warsaw for years, told me that he talked with Gomulka only once — at the time of Nixon's visit. Most of the discussion was on Berlin. I urged that we accept and even welcome the existence of East Germany but insist on review after (say) five years; make the strongest claim on access to Berlin; avoid risking prestige on issues we cannot win. On the whole, I had a favorable reception. By the end of the day, I was tired beyond belief. I did snatch a few minutes' rest at teatime but had only dozed off when a messenger came into my hotel room at the Hay-Adams with a classified paper. She was an exceedingly good-looking girl who told me she had got the assignment because she wanted to meet me. I apologized for my attire — a pair of cotton shorts. She was a bit chilling: "Not at all. I have often seen my father like that."

[26] Walt Rostow. See page 12.
[27] Abram J. Chayes, legal adviser of the State Department, subsequently Professor of Law at Harvard.
[28] Of the White House staff, subsequently Professor of Economics at Harvard and later Director of the Institute for Advanced Studies at Princeton.
[29] See page 176.
[30] Then Undersecretary for Administration.
[31] Washington journalist and personal friend.
[32] Former Ambassador to Poland, and later to become Ambassador to Czechoslovakia.

This morning after breakfast in the White House mess, I talked with Haydn Williams[33] about military aid to Pakistan. Perhaps I persuaded him of what aid is costing us. But I fear the Pentagon would really prefer to cure the question by giving it to the Indians too. Defense is drafting a letter urging on State the policy of subsidized sale. I doubt that the Indians will accept.

Then at about ten the President called me in — he looked tanned, relaxed and very healthy and was in the best of spirits. We talked of Berlin. He agrees on the State Department and its elephantiasis. He says it annoys him more than it does me although he thinks I am probably more annoying in return. I told him of my problems on arms aid with which he sympathizes. I urged a tolerant view of the new neutrals; he expressed dissatisfaction with Nkrumah and Tito, approval, on the whole, of Nehru. I asked about a trip by J.B.K. to India which he applauded. I sat on a couch, he on his rocking chair. Behind him through the window, I could see the lawns and gardens. It was very nice and lasted a long time.

Following, I had a chat with Arthur Schlesinger and talked on the phone with Jackie at Hyannisport. She is enchanted by the trip; she wants to come in October or November. I suggested that Berlin cool off a bit first.

I barely made a luncheon at Blair House for the staffs and embassy representatives of Mali and Indonesia. As I was having a drink, I learned that, in fact, I was supposed to be eating at the White House with the Presidents.[34] I made it in lots of time for the Presidents were late. Sukarno is short, uniformed and wears a multiple row of ribbons. The President of Mali was tall and beautifully berobed — exceedingly handsome. Nothing much happened. Sukarno and I exchanged small talk about our disparity in height. In the proceedings, he deferred to his African colleague who was eloquent. The White House food — lobster, a small steak, good

[33] Defense official concerned with arms aid.
[34] Who had come to Washington to inform President Kennedy of the results of the Belgrade Conference.

wine — has improved enormously since last time. It was the first occasion on which I had eaten in the big state dining room. The latter is a shiny green, a bit on the glittery side, but is dominated by a superb painting of Lincoln.

From lunch, I went to see Frank Coffin[35] to weigh in on Bokaro — evidently they thought I was getting too far ahead. I urged its importance; the unwisdom of letting the Russians get the jump on us; and the diffused and anonymous nature of our aid in the absence of such projects. I believe I made an impression. Then I said good-bye to the desk officers, went back to the hotel to throw things into my bag and went on to the airport.

I forgot to say that I had tea with B. K. Nehru last evening. He showed me a letter describing the Nehru-Khrushchev talks. Nehru asked Khrushchev if he would guarantee our access to Berlin; K. said he would. He was agreeable about Kennedy, thought he had been handicapped by his small majority and attacked Adenauer.

September 17 — New Delhi

I got back at dawn on Friday and this is Sunday. By noon Friday, I had slept off the worst of my weariness and cleaned up my desk, held a press briefing for the American correspondents and had a staff meeting. At the latter, I gave a detailed review of my trip — Berlin, atomic testing, reaction in Washington to Belgrade. We hold these meetings in the conference room of the Chancery; the attendance was large and eager. To convey information is the only important function of staff meetings. Nothing can be discussed or decided.

I did not immediately seek an appointment with Nehru; I had nothing urgent to take up and am anxious not to appear too eager. At the airport, I said there would be no change in our aid policy as a result of the adverse press reaction to the Belgrade Conference —

---

[35] Former Congressman from Maine. Then Deputy Administrator of AID and the Managing Director of the Department of State's Development Loan Fund. Now a Federal District Judge.

"We do not change our policies as some fastidious people change their undershirts."

Yesterday I got agreement in principle to a major reform in our TCM operations in agriculture. This calls for concentration of energies on a few subjects concerned with bread-grain production, on a few colleges of agriculture and on a limited range of technical subject matter, i.e., soil technology or pest control techniques.[36] No more home economists or communication specialists, whatever in hell communication specialists are. Wood will see if we can get some of the irrelevant people recalled so that we won't have to wait for reform until contracts have expired.

Saturday afternoon, I slept blissfully for hours and then met the Indian press.

A bright ten-year-old in our staff compound behind the garden is down with what seems to be typhoid. He was left lying on an open cot for four days with an appalling temperature. A witch doctor treated him by tying strings around his neck. We have moved him into the Residence and are plying him with penicillin. He isn't any happier but at least he looks more comfortable.

John Lund, acting head of USIS, told me last night that, in light of the Berlin crisis and the fears of war it has aroused, some of our people are saying that, as compared with the United States, India is a rather safe and comfortable place to be.[37] I told him anyone voicing such thoughts publicly could expect a prompt transfer to West Berlin.

✧ ✧ ✧

[36] This, as previously noted, concentrated attention on the thing — bread-grain production — which would most efficiently counter hunger. It did not confuse simple people, the peasants in particular, by giving them more ideas than they could digest. It did not waste Indian resources on secondary matters. As a reform, however, it was only partially successful.

[37] I doubt, in fact, if this were more than an idle expression of one or two people.

New Delhi, India
September 19, 1961

Dear Mr. President:

Here are some thoughts on the perils of our time, some of which follow the line of our conversation the other morning. You must have discovered that I am considerably less incoherent on paper than in oral exercise, the mark I imagine of a deep but turgid mind.

There is a tendency in Washington to conclude that any serious problem must be infinitely complex. This has never been more in evidence than in the case of Berlin. I can't but think that the Berlin issue is rather simple: The Russians may (1) be concerned with building up the prestige of the East German regime, holding people there, giving it a regular existence and cutting down the general impact of our presence in West Berlin. Or (2) they may be concerned with denying our access and throwing our soldiers out. If the first is their aim things will be worked out. If they intend the second we will have a nasty time — but I don't suggest it will be war except by accident but there will be a lengthy trial of nerves and strength since we both are after the same thing.

In a world where everyone else is sure what the Russians want, I have learned, painfully, to keep an open mind. My guess is, given the weakness of the East German regime and the willingness of the Russians to talk about access and token troops, that the Russians want the first alternative. (Writing to Nehru a few weeks ago Khrushchev said he could not stand the collapse of the East German government, and in Moscow the other day when Nehru said he did not think much of the Ulbricht government Khrushchev said in substance, "Neither do we.")

Access and presence are important to us. Accordingly we should ask for what we have plus the removal of all doubts and irritations connected therewith. Thus my notion of a free and open road into Berlin along which all can travel without let or hindrance with similar security for air, water and rail travel and transport. Where we are on firm ground and our need is clear we should ask, and ask a lot. We shouldn't ask for what we don't have and won't get.

This has a heavy bearing on our position on East Germany. It is now a Washington cliché that we won't go to war over East Germany. But I hold it even more important that our prestige — either that of the country or the Administration — not be put at risk on this issue. It pains me to hear talk about reunification and self-determination for the East Germans as bargaining points. No one can bargain with what he doesn't have except Chiang Kai-shek. All this effort does is build up the importance of what the Soviets will get. We invent a defeat and make it look as bad as possible.

That is why I come out with the idea of a time limit. Let us accept and even (if possible) mildly welcome the idea of a regular status for East Germany in the short run while making it clear that reunification is essential in the long run. And in exceptionally rigorous pursuit of my exceptionally rigorous logic let us make this clear in advance and not reserve it as a bargaining point. Then we won't set up a defeat for ourselves.

So much for Germany. When I wake up at night I worry that in our first year in office we will be credited with losing Laos which we did not have, losing East Berlin which we did not have, losing East Germany which we did not have and (touchy point) with failing to persuade the world that Formosa is China. As an extreme idealist I am in favor of lost causes. But I wonder if we should lose our lost causes more than once.

In coming back to Washington I was struck with how sensible and flexible are the views on the top side of the State Department, not to mention the White House, as compared with those which come to me in the telegrams. And in Washington itself reassurance disappears as one gets to what by some witticism is called the working level. It is very important, indeed absolutely indispensable, that we begin to understand what is wrong with the Department.

It is not that people are dull although quite a few are. Nor are they exceptionally conservative although there is a widespread feeling that God ordained some individuals to make foreign policy without undue interference from presidents or politicians. The far more serious problem is that the Department is simply too large. And with size has come an inflexibility that is as inevitable as it is incredible. The reason is simple: there are more people on C Street than there are problems. Nothing is so serious for a crypto-Talleyrand as unemployment. By common understanding, therefore, everyone insists on, and by common consent everyone is accorded, a finger in every important pie. Every civilized group acts in some degree by unanimous consent. So one cannot get agreement on anything new. When a deadline approaches everyone repairs hurriedly to what was agreed several years ago. Accordingly, the sheer size of the Department freezes it to all of its antique positions.

The problem here is a serious one. Nothing in my view is so important as to get the Department back to manageable size. The Pentagon is not nearly so bad. For while it is larger and much too large most everyone is concerned with operational problems. In State the multitude must all make policy. When I was back this time one of my assistant secretary friends attended the Secretary's staff meeting from nine-fifteen till ten. Then he had a meeting with the Undersecretary on operations until ten-thirty. Then he took until eleven-thirty to inform his staff of what went on at the earlier meetings. Whereupon they adjourned to pass on the news to their staffs. This is, I am told, communication.

> Faithfully,
> JOHN KENNETH GALBRAITH

THE PRESIDENT
THE WHITE HOUSE

September 20 — New Delhi

Yesterday the Department sent me a priority dispatch — a circular — asking in my discretion to go to the Indian Government and point out the urgency of the reunification of Germany. I would gather also that they want the reunited Germany in NATO. This is completely in conflict with Washington top-level thought. I sent it to Bundy who had pooh-poohed my objections to such unrealism by saying, "Ken, you are banging on an open door." I pointed out that the Department dealt to him off the top of the pack and to me off the bottom. There is no resemblance in the cards.

This evening I had a long talk with Nehru at his home. He was in excellent spirits. On the whole, he is optimistic about Berlin: the Russians will give on access. I made it clear in a roundabout way that we were not nailing our colors on Russian nonrecognition of East Germany. If these assessments are accurate, we won't have a fight except either by accident or someone's desire to be a hero.

He is pessimistic about disarmament, but glad to learn that we are taking a new initiative. I am urging that Schlesinger or Wiesner[38] come out to go over our position.

Dag Hammarskjold was killed day before yesterday. This makes great trouble for everyone but especially for the Indians who still have a large force in the Congo. Nehru told me they are still trying to sort out their ideas.

Finally, we had a long and very confidential talk about Kashmir — the first I have had. I shall have to fill in the details of this later.

Bertrand Russell has just gone to jail for disturbing the peace in an anti–nuclear bomb demonstration. Nehru told me with amusement that the Lord Mayor of London had denounced him for saying he wished he were in Russell's place. The L.M. threatened to lift Nehru's credentials as a freeman of the City of London. The sanction did not seem serious.

[38] Jerome B. Wiesner, Science Adviser to the President, subsequently Provost of the Massachusetts Institute of Technology.

This morning Kitty and the boys went by air with Admiral Grantham[39] to Agra and managed to see the Taj, Fatehpur-Sikri and the Agra Fort. All this they accomplished in the space of four hours. The Admiral, who was on his way to meet his command at Colombo, dropped them off at Delhi after the tour and they were home for a late lunch.

A cobra came into the Embassy grounds today and was duly taken in custody by a snake charmer. It was cool enough to have dinner out on the terrace on Monday evening, and we had a large party for Grantham extensively attended by military types. There was a piano player and we even had some dancing. The food, as usual, was inedible.

September 23 — New Delhi

Harriman came through yesterday after his meeting with Souvanna Phouma and a visit to Laos and South Vietnam. We had lunch with the Prime Minister and later a talk at the Ministry of External Affairs. Harriman is reasonably optimistic about a settlement in Laos, his optimism being based on the feeling that the Russians want to forget about the place. Souvanna Phouma seems to him satisfactory. He is a patriot, Harriman believes, and the strongest of the three princes, and anti-Communist. There was much discussion at the Prime Minister's house of the problem of winning agreement between a pro-Communist *prince*, an anti-Communist *prince*, and a neutral *prince*. All princes, incidentally, stress their loyalty to the Lao crown.

The Prime Minister's house was flooded with air and sunshine and the lunch was brightened by some wonderful melons and grapes which he had brought back from Tashkent. Harriman is just seventy; Nehru is seventy-two. Both are young for their age, but Harriman by a considerable margin is the younger.

---

[39] Rear Admiral Elonzo B. Grantham, Jr., commander of the small American naval force, consisting mostly of a seaplane tender, stationed in the Middle East and Indian Ocean.

The United Nations is much on Nehru's mind. With the death of Hammarskjold, the Soviets will press the Troika.[40] Nehru suggested meeting them with the proposal of a rotating S.-G. — a man from each of the major blocs to serve as Secretary-General for a year. I urged him not to propose it. Perhaps, in the aftermath of Hammarskjold's death, the Soviets might not resist the appointment of a single Secretary-General. Yielding might thus be premature and unnecessary. I, of course, had no instructions.

In speaking to an agricultural group the other day, I had suggested that no literate peasantry was unprogressive and no illiterate peasantry was progressive. Nehru read this and thought it a fine formulation.

Each day the weather gets a trifle cooler and more pleasant. The rains are now over and the air is becoming crisp and dry once more.

Our boys have their leopard cub. They are delighted but the cub does not share the pleasure. She sits in the back of her cage and berates them with a remarkable ferocity.[41]

By a combination of persuasion, threats, blackmail, promises to resort to higher authority, appeals to patriotism and promises of what the Soviets will do, I seem to have a provisional approval of our financing of the fourth steel mill at Bokaro. Now we must find a way of building it with competence and distinction.

This project is very important. It is needed, useful and symbolic. Many of the things we are doing are rather anonymous — we provide copper and other nonferrous metals which are needed and useful but not very dramatic. And our past help to private-sector plants, such as Tata's, has evoked the comment, "The Americans help the Tatas and Birlas who are already rich. By contrast, the Soviets or British build plants that belong to the people." Now we are in the same league — provided that we can perform.

---

[40] The Soviet proposal to replace the Secretary-General with three men, representing three blocs: East, West and Neutral.

[41] About this time, Nehru heard of the pet and threatened to have it sequestered. Tiger cubs, he averred, made good pets. Leopards, he held, by contrast, to be mean, untrustworthy and otherwise of poor character.

September 24 — New Delhi

There has been more rain followed by wonderfully cool weather during which, for the first time in months, we have the air-conditioning off. In addition to our leopard cub, an increasingly fearsome thing with a most alarming snarl, my wife has acquired a mare and a colt. They are beautiful.

I forgot to tell that a day or two ago the Prime Minister said that Tara Singh's fast[42] on behalf of a Sikh state could go on indefinitely. I asked him at lunch if that meant he thought T. S. was cheating. "I had something like that in the back of my mind," he said.

My cables on India's U.N. position (on the Secretary-General) have brought a massive response. They imply a bad conscience over failure to keep me posted. However, my extemporaneous position is strongly approved.

September 25 — New Delhi

A conference of Asian economic planners begins today. I have concluded that I should go to the first session even though it means that my day is totally consumed by ceremonial matters. The State Department had wanted me to lead the delegation. I declined (for high-minded reasons) after contemplating the boring sessions I would face. Lloyd G. Reynolds,[43] whom I proposed, accepted and is here along with Byron Johnson.[44]

Last night, I had a session with Sardar Swaran Singh on Bokaro. The question is whether we can have a clear authority to build the steel mill and manage it for a running-in period. First, I must persuade Washington to provide the money. Then I must persuade the Indians I do not have it until they agree to the appropriate conditions. Duplicity is not easily avoided. In this case, I am a little

---

[42] See page 201.

[43] Professor of Economics at Yale and a longtime personal friend.

[44] Former Professor of Economics at the University of Denver, former Colorado Congressman and official of AID.

assisted by the fact that the Indians are on the defensive about the defective operation of the existing publicly-owned mills.

Yesterday President Kennedy made a very good speech in the U.N. He used again my line — "We shall never negotiate out of fear, etc." He also partially detached himself from past positions on the Berlin peace treaty. That crisis is by way of settling itself, I think.

Yesterday morning I spoke to the Fulbright Scholars. In the question period following, one asked me what responsibility the government would assume for them in the event of war. I replied that responsibility for people living in a target area such as the United States might be more difficult to assume.

September 28 — New Delhi

Night before last, the Acting President[45] had a reception for the Asian economic planners in the Moghul Gardens. Enormous soldiers, wonderfully caparisoned, lined the walk to the garden. The fountains and also the band were playing. People strolled and chatted; the Prime Minister arrived in high good humor and was very appreciative of the rumor that our new leopard cub — which still will not eat — had been named Tara Singh by our sons. I introduced him to Byron Johnson who began a conversation about "waging peace." This was fine save that Nehru inspires a general desire among men to prove their idealism.

Yesterday I presented fifty tickets to the upcoming Davis Cup matches to young Indian players. I asked one recipient whom she would cheer for, Indians or Americans. She looked appreciatively at the ticket and said, "Everybody."

Last night we had another of our gay informal diplomatic dinner parties. The women sat in soggy splendor in one corner, the men in another. The food was terrible; however, I didn't notice for the conversation was worse.

[45] Dr. Sarvepalli Radhakrishnan, former Oxford professor and ambassador, author and later President.

September 30 — New Delhi

In the last two days, we have had two vast receptions — one for the Asian economic planners and one for the tennis team. At these functions, one stands for a terrible hour or two while people file in and then for another hour when they go out. In the interim, they stand around and drink mostly soft drinks and consume the greasy and repulsive objects which our cook turns out under the impression they are hors d'oeuvres. Last night, he had French fried potatoes fried in extra deep fat. My wife, who never eats his stuff, strongly defends him.

I have been leading a largely ceremonial existence. Yesterday morning, we visited All-India Radio, listened to the orchestra and watched various choruses and plays in rehearsal. Then Kitty made the draw for the Davis Cup matches.

But I have had a few crises. Krishna Menon in New York has been negotiating various complex quadrumvirates to succeed to the Secretary-General's post. This has outraged Stevenson, and the climax was reached last week when Menon proposed a new collegium with Arthur Lall[46] as the Chairman. I intervened with effect.

We are airlifting some Indian supplies to the Congo. Four big transports are to do it in a matter of ten days. I had proposed sending twelve and doing it in one grand sweep. It would be a dramatic gesture in support of the U.N. and the kind of demonstration of military virtuosity to which no one could object. For my part, I promised to see that no literate adult east of Suez is left unaware of the accomplishment.

For the last three days, India and the United States have been playing tennis in the Davis Cup inter-zone semi-finals. I have been operating in the unnatural role of a patron of sport. It has not been entirely unpleasant. This is the first good tennis I have ever seen in any detail. It is rather agreeable to watch. The leading American player, Chuck McKinley, is famous for his exuberant manners. Accordingly, I had the whole party into the Embassy be-

46 See page 198.

fore the opening and hinted broadly on the importance of mildness, amiability and restraint. It worked wonders, perhaps partly because the American team won.

Lane Timmons,[47] my new D.C.M., arrived. At Balliol, I learn, he was a student of Thomas Balogh.[48] The enlightenment seems not, however, to have done any permanent damage.

The weather continues to get cooler and now the mornings are delightful. We still live under air-conditioning, partly as protection against the noonday heat and partly because of a phenomenal horde of nocturnal insects which not even the screens will entirely exclude. The world also seems for the moment to be better. The Russians talk of recognizing East Germany, we of access to Berlin. So we still do not meet head on. Harriman thinks he is getting a settlement in Laos. Matters are less bad in the Congo. The Russians seem to have moved slightly on the matter of an interim Secretary-General. In this business, however, it is as important to avoid exaltation as depression — neither is ever justified in the slightly longer run.

October 4 — New Delhi

Yesterday I introduced my new D.C.M. to the staff and took him around to see the Ministry officials. I am going to put him in charge of running the Mission so far as possible. I will remain free for ceremony, protocol, speech-making and other important matters.

The State Department has now more or less completely cut off communications. On a dozen important matters from the Secretary-General to the Congo, we would be much better off if we had information as to what is going on. But none arrives.

The Department has drawn up an exceedingly dreary program for Nehru's visit. Many large and heavy dinners; nothing that

[47] See page 204.
[48] Now Lord Balogh. Famous Oxford economist, fellow of Balliol, Reader in the University and personal friend. Subsequently he became a close adviser to Prime Minister Harold Wilson. The reference to damage is, of course, ironical though it would be otherwise assumed in some circles.

seems to be amusing. The Indian Embassy in Washington wired that it is objecting. The Department wired that it had been acting in accordance with the wishes of the Indian Embassy.

October 6 — New Delhi

I am gradually working toward a more satisfactory regime. Two hours' work at the Residence — speeches, other writing — before going to the office at 11 A.M. An hour and a half there and then a swim. The afternoon at the office. This promises to allow me some slight time for writing and thought.

Menon's speech in New York yesterday seems to have shown some effect from my intervention. We are also proceeding with passable generosity to satisfy the Indian requests on planes for moving troops and supplies to the Congo. A fleet of Globemasters is now picking up equipment at Palam and I have told USIS to ensure that it isn't done in secret.

Still, a shockingly large number of things seems always to wait on my action. Old things are done pretty well, but new things are not done at all.

Day before yesterday, I had a press conference and reviewed our policy on a variety of matters — we support Adoula in the Congo, are against group management (the Troika) at the U.N. and for disarmament. If I had followed past practice, it would have been off the record and, I am convinced, a waste of time. Henceforth when I have something to tell the papers, I intend to say it in full for quotation.

October 7 — New Delhi

Yesterday I think I worked out a more or less final formula on the technical assistance program. The industrial training program, an expensive, hasty and ill-considered effort to give some gloss of knowledge of management engineering to Indian recruits, will be lengthened; we will put more energy and resources into employee training in the steel plants. The diaspora of the Delhi headquarters staff will at least begin. And the reorganization of the agricultural program which I have described looks promising. I have learned not to be optimistic[49] about reform and there remains a vast administrative lodgement of sixty or seventy people in Delhi whose function escapes me.

Last night, the local very artistic amateur theater — "The Unity Theatre" — produced *The Lark*. It was very loud, very dull. Twice the power went off and the lights went out. This was a relief. The Vice-President was in attendance but did not stick it out beyond the middle of the first act.

I have taken to sending inedible food back to the kitchen. My wife is outraged by such indecency but admits that it brings improvement.

[49] But not sufficiently. The reforms were less successful than here suggested.

XI

Southern India

October 9 — New Delhi

Yesterday afternoon, we went to the airport to welcome and dispatch the fleet of Globemasters which are flying support for the Indian troops in the United Nations force in the Congo. They are huge and ugly vehicles and I have difficulty imagining that they fly. Someone has called them the workhorses of the Air Force. For oratorical purposes, I renamed them (God forgive) "the bullock carts and tongas of the U.N. command."

Jerome Wiesner,[1] the President's Science Adviser, got in last night. He is somewhat depressed at the battle he has to fight from day to day with the Pentagon. The pressure to resume nuclear testing (before the Russians) is perfectly enormous. I am giving him an earful on needed reforms in our diplomatic representation. Nolting,[2] our Ambassador in Saigon, seems to be lacking in independent judgment or capacity to see the consequences (in the United States) of another Korea. Nor does he appear to put any real pressure on Diem. I worry more about South Vietnam than Berlin.

❖ ❖ ❖

[1] See page 213.
[2] Frederick E. Nolting, Jr., a career officer and Ambassador in Saigon, 1961–63. This judgment is not entirely fair. Though I disagreed with him, Nolting was a brave man of strongly held views. He believed Ngo Dinh Diem to be the only leader capable of providing an effective alternative to the Vietcong.

New Delhi, India
October 9, 1961

Dear Mr. President:

I keep seeing stories that we are to have a serious review of foreign policy. Men of wisdom will applaud this. When things are not good, it is usually imagined that a review, or possibly a reorganization, will make them better. No one ever asks whether the best is being made of a lousy situation. That, on the whole, is my present view of things. However, a good review will create a lot of needed employment for the State Department.

I am sure most people exaggerate the scope for change in foreign policy. The greatest difficulty with Dulles was his yearning for new and exciting variants in policy — massive retaliation, the thumbed nose at neutrals, military alliances with the indigent, were change for the sake of change. They were partly change for the sake of putting on a black tie and proclaiming a new policy to a gathering of the affluent in Manhattan.

Foreign policy, like domestic policy, is a reflection of the fundamental instincts of those who make it. All of us have been reared with the same instincts, more or less — that we should combine courtesy with compassion, suspect pompous or heroic stances, respect our capacity to negotiate, refuse to be pushed and seek solutions in social stability rather than military prowess. Since these instincts cannot be changed not much can be done about the policy that derives from them.

The country is indeed fortunate that our instincts are sound.

I do worry a good deal about the domestic political position in which our foreign policy will be placing us. Ahead of us, in fact, are the same difficulties that beset the Truman Era. The Right, in the United States, will always criticize reasonableness as softness. To be sensible is to appease. And to knock the Soviets or the Chicoms into the gutter is not the least bit warlike. It is the only thing they understand and respect. Democrats are warlike because they are weak-kneed.

The Truman Administration never developed a way of dealing with this dialectic. Sometimes it brought Republicans, including Dulles, into the Administration with the hope that this would blunt the attack. Sometimes it tried to show that it could talk as pugnaciously as the Republicans. Neither worked.

The answer, I am sure, is to pin the label of warrior firmly on these . . . [people]. This is not an emotional reaction but a sound political tactic to which they are vulnerable. When they speak of total victory they invite total annihilation. They aren't brave but suicidal. There is a curious superficial pugnacity about the American people which, I am persuaded, does not go very deep. They applaud the noisy man but they reconsider if they think him dangerous. We must, I feel, make it clear that these men are dangerous. They survive because we have let them have the best of both worlds: they could appeal to the pugnacious as defenders of the peace.

These are matters which, of course, should be handled by craftsmen below your office. One of the major problems with foreign policy, as distinct from domestic policy, is the silence it imposes on almost all of its defenders. Secretaries, undersecretaries and ambassadors, the natural debaters on these matters, are all silenced by tradition plus the myth of bipartisanship. So the attackers have it all to themselves. Sometime I would like to offer some thoughts on how to even up the game.

Bipartisanship, incidentally, is a booby trap for Democrats. We make concessions to the Republicans and appoint them to office. We refrain from nailing the extremists to their nonsense. We mute our own defense or stand down. And, in the end, not only Goldwater but Eisenhower does not hesitate to attack. Cuba is a classic case.

I am going to Calcutta on Monday to identify myself with the efforts to rehabilitate this hideous community. If the Communists were not so stupid it could incubate enough for all Asia. Then I am starting on a ten or twelve day tour of the far South:

a major speech and honorary degree at one of the southern universities, inauguration of a school feeding program in Kerala, a general show of support for the non-Communist forces in this state, a speech at the Defence College in Wellington, a breathtaking display of horsemanship, a visit to the Maharajah of Mysore and the great religious festival of Dasara, an inspection of two industrial plants in Bangalore. When I return it will be almost time to come back for Nehru's visit. I am preceding him by about a week. The Department is preparing a vast number of special papers for you. I think you can safely forego the pleasure and get the whole thing from the highest authority.

I remember once during the war Henderson[3] sent a great bale of memoranda to the President on price legislation. A little later we had a meeting in the White House and the President said:

"Leon, what about the constitutionality of this legislation and why isn't Labor included?"

Henderson said, "Mr. President, I sent you memoranda on both of those points."

Roosevelt said, "Leon, are you laboring under the impression that I read these memoranda of yours? I can't even lift them."

Although at times when I have been rather troubled by Berlin, I have always had the feeling that it would be worked out. I have continued to worry far, far more about South Vietnam. This is more complex, far less controllable, far more varied in the factors involved, far more susceptible to misunderstanding. And to make matters worse, I have no real confidence in the sophistication and political judgment of our people there. Harriman, incidentally, shares my view.

Yours faithfully,
JOHN KENNETH GALBRAITH

THE PRESIDENT
THE WHITE HOUSE

[3] Leon Henderson under whom I served in the Office of Price Administration in World War II.

October 10 — New Delhi

At six-thirty yesterday morning I took off for Calcutta with George Hannah. We spent nearly eight hours in the air, a full day in Calcutta and were back at 10:30 P.M. In Calcutta, I put a shoulder behind the Calcutta metropolitan plan that is being developed and sponsored by the Ford Foundation. I toured the slum areas which are bad but not quite as bad as I anticipated. They were heavily populated with clean and comparatively healthy-looking youngsters. Then I listened to an account of operations of the planning group, lunched, toured the docks, had a session with B.C. Roy[4] and then we made our way back to Dum Dum.[5] The Ford team is working with the government of West Bengal. The Calcutta Corporation, which is utterly incompetent, is playing no part. The urgent problems are to get a water system — much of the metropolitan area is without drinking water, a sewage disposal system and some passable housing.[6]

We filed into B. C. Roy's office midafternoon where he sat like a maharajah behind a great circular desk. His interest in the planning is not extreme. But he is profoundly concerned about the elections next winter and would like some results he could show right now. (Setting up a new model of a low-cost house was much mentioned.) That is the trouble with Calcutta. The politicians have been trying to pull rabbits out of the hat for years. Their concern has been with creating an impression of accomplishment rather than accomplishment.

October 12 — Tiruchirapalli–Trivandrum

We had a dinner for Wiesner night before last which followed a meeting with the Prime Minister. To the latter, Jerry gave a very effective and thoughtful exposition of the disarmament problem. He is handicapped, as am I, by a lack of real conviction that those

---

[4] See page 200.

[5] Dum Dum Airport. Nearby is the Dum Dum arsenal for which the famous soft-nosed bullets were named.

[6] All of which at this writing (1968) are even more desperately needed.

who oppose it, at home and in the Soviet Union, will yield to reason. And disarmament, like economy in government, has become a
cliché. Everyone can be for it without doing anything about it.
I am not sure I have ever done much myself.

Yesterday at 7:30 A.M., we left Palam and got to Tiruchirapalli
(Tiruchi for short) at 1:30 P.M. Then we drove three hours to
Chidambaram, seat of Annamalai University, one of the sizable
institutions of the South. There we had tea and made a tour of the
campus which was rather fun. The students were waiting for us
outside of their hostels or schools and gave us a noisy welcome.
The University has pleasant palm-lined streets and attractive verandahed buildings, some of modest elegance. Then came a vast banquet in our honor — tables were divided as between vegetarian and
non-vegetarian. Dinner was punctuated by the sounds of a considerable student riot in front of the building as the students
struggled to get into a concert and dancing exhibition which was to
be given in our honor. It had in the end to be canceled which made

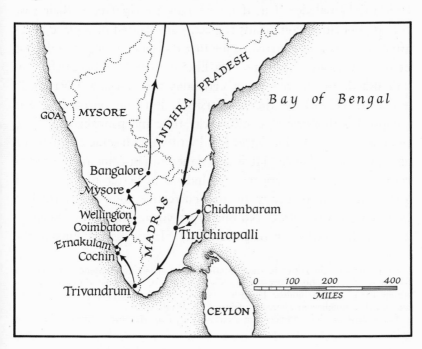

the students more unruly than ever. Our hosts explained that mostly townspeople were involved. Perhaps. But if so the people of this town are remarkably uniform in age.

After dinner, steps were taken to spirit us out the back way. But I had the feeling that most of the students were really waiting to see either me or some similar curiosity. So over our host's objections that it would be exceedingly dangerous, I went out and spoke to them. Of course, it wasn't dangerous at all. The students quieted down, listened and then started for home.

I forgot to say that earlier in the evening we visited the temple of Chidambaram — an enormous thing with numerous sub-temples, tanks, cloisters and some fine early Indian carving. It is a working temple and we were greeted by dozens of priests, a hereditary caste, who by Indian standards have it good. We also met hundreds of postulants, worshipers and plain idlers. A band whomped it up. At various points, before different gods, we were the object of various complex and arcane rites. Briefly, I got some satisfaction from the knowledge that, if the Hindus are right or if their vast voting population commands respect, I am assured of a place hereafter. But then it occurred to me that the surroundings would not be terribly clean — perhaps a bit like the temple. My satisfaction diminished. In a more sanitary ceremony this morning, I was made a D.Litt. (Hon.) of the University.[7] For the purpose, I was equipped with a gay blue and scarlet robe and pancake cap. The price was a speech. The latter I had written with some care but for an American audience. (It was designed to put some of the reciprocal nagging of Americans and Indians in better perspective. I argued that the tendency to give corrective advice is normal as between open societies. No one urges virtue on a closed society. It is not believed open to persuasion.)[8] It was rather outside the

[7] The Indian universities in their citations have an amiable absence of restraint — "Dr. Galbraith's books are not merely treasures of economic thought but are among the glories of modern English prose . . . His abiding love for our country and his true nobility of character shine . . ." Well said.

[8] Published as "The Poverty of Nations" in The Atlantic Monthly, October 1962.

interest of my immediate audience so I gave the text to the press
and a more informal version to the students.

The girl students, many in handsome saris, were often bare-
footed — I think perhaps by choice. One of my faculty neighbors
on the platform also slipped off his sandals and luxuriously wiggled
his toes. The academic attire ran to rather trying purples. Sometimes a bad shade of light purple was superimposed on a worse
shade of dark purple. After lunch, we drove back to Tiruchi —
three hours more — and boarded the plane. Part of the way we
had a police escort which shoved aside the population in highly
offensive fashion. The population did not seem especially resentful
but it made me uneasy.

October 14 — Trivandrum–Cochin

Kerala is a mild and lovely land, decked with coconut palms on
top of red soil, with cool breezes blowing in from the Indian
Ocean, and people everywhere. The people live in palm-thatched
cottages — the best have red tiled roofs — and are clean, handsome,
intelligent and politically contentious. Trivandrum is swept, white-
washed and even painted in places and is by far the neatest city I
have seen in India. It stands on various mounds and low hills covered with palm trees and combines with much that is Indian a
little of the elegance of an English village. In the distance are blue-
green, rather molded mountains. Along with our labors, we got
only a glimpse of these things.

Yesterday morning at six, we did go swimming at a marvelous
beach. A brother-in-law of the ex-royal family of Travancore took
us in tow. He was rather nice and like so many of the ex-Maha-
rajahs, trying very hard to maintain his place in the scheme of
things. (He organizes tennis, golf, cricket, swimming, captains the
flying club, photographs and performs various other entrepre-
neurial services.) After breakfast, we had been summoned to meet
the Maharajah and Maharani. I declined, courteously but with
some firmness. Nothing is less agreeable to the moderate politicians

than such obeisances and more encouraging to the Communists. My action was well received.

Next I called on the government, a highly unstable coalition of Congress, Moslem League and P.S.P.,[9] and with the Chief Minister, Pattom A. Thanu Pillai, from the latter party. We sat around a large table in the Chief Minister's office and discussed industrial prospects (dim), agricultural prospects (better: Kerala is a big producer of cash crops in India), fishing, forestry and education. Some of the ministers left me with the impression that they regarded such discussion as a useful gesture to respectability. As such, it was a permissible interruption to the normal work of a politician which is politicking.

Then we went to inaugurate the school lunch program. This was great fun. Among the palm trees by the school, a white pavilion had been erected and trimmed with pink flowers. Beneath, two or three hundred people were gathered. In a school building next door, some fifty or sixty six-year-olds were waiting patiently on the ground for their noon meal with a palm leaf, plus bowl and cup, to receive it. We had a prayer to some unspecified god, singing, some speeches, and then I served out the first lunch to the children. Everyone seemed very pleased and so was I. My speech stressed, among the more placid banalities of such occasions, the importance of keeping the food we were providing out of the black market. My people thought this would strike a raw note. That, however, was the precise idea.

The day went on for quite a while — a lunch by the Governor, a meeting on local political prospects with the Congress leadership, a visit to the University. I also visited the USIS library during the day, had a press conference and attended a state dinner with dancing and singing afterward.

At the press conference, I was, as always, short of news. What an ambassador knows is always either unimportant or secret, mostly

[9] Praja Socialist Party, the result of a union in 1953 between the Kisan Mazdoor Praja and Socialist Parties.

the first. So I issued a statement based on one by the President saying that our aid was instituted to promote independence. Accordingly, it would not be denied to those who made use of their independence — presumably by way of differing with the United States. It sounded important, I hope.

A reporter for a Communist paper asked me about incidents involving African diplomats in the United States in the last few months. There have been several in which they have been denied restaurant service or rooms. The local head of USIS worriedly thrust a slip into my hands saying he was a Communist. This meant, presumably, that I shouldn't answer.

This morning, we went swimming again and watched the fishermen launching their boats of four squared logs bound together — they are assembled for each voyage. The two inner logs are a little lower than the two outside, providing the semblance of keel and freeboard. However, the principle is that of a raft, and the water comes through and over. We breakfasted and took off at 8:30 A.M.; the latter, because of the short runway, being an exercise of some small interest for the Convair. We had, it developed, a thousand feet to spare.

October 15 — Cochin–Coimbatore

We got to Cochin midmorning yesterday and were housed in the onetime house of the British Resident on an island in the harbor. This was a deep verandahed affair with endlessly spacious rooms and a golf course round about. Two launches were available for our movements. Cochin is rather like a flat San Francisco. It occupies a peninsula protecting a bay and, indeed, the orientation is the same. The gate is rather less spectacular, but the general combination of water, palms and clean streets with tiled-roof houses could not be more lovely. After our arrival, we toured the bay, called the Backwater — a placid, palm-fringed stretch of water — for a couple of hours and then I had a large drink of whisky, lunch and went to bed for several hours. I awoke much better.

At 5 P.M., we were dislodged and embarked for the old city of Ernakulam. This occupies the area equivalent to Oakland and the hospitality committee had prepared a birthday celebration for me. This was a slight mistake; today, not yesterday, is my birthday but it seemed more tactful to avoid correction. A group of girls from St. Teresa's High School sang "Happy Birthday" for me under the guidance of two sisters. While being photographed with them afterward, I asked a member of the choir to tell me who St. Teresa was. A sister hastily interposed, "She wouldn't know; she is a Parsi child." I asked the one on the other side who St. Teresa was. "A saint," she replied.

In his speech of felicitation, the chairman of the hospitality committee compared me in succession to Christ, Moses, Krishna and Alfred Lord Tennyson.

This morning, we went deeper into the Backwater and visited a couple of villages. It is marvelously marine country. There are no roads, only wide stretches of water and palm-covered islands. The people live on their islands in a density of two thousand or more per square mile. The density is also increasing at a phenomenal rate — by 24 percent in the last ten years. The land is absentee owned; even the coconuts do not belong to the people on whom they fall. However, people are now being given security in their tenure. And once they can no longer be evicted, I imagine they will soon learn to be a little careless about paying rent. The Communists do very well out of the general situation.

We saw villagers treading out paddy, making pots, gleaning the fields for the last rice and drinking toddy. Everyone was exceedingly amiable and also remarkably clean. The women are intelligent and handsome. It is an old Kerala custom to go about with the breasts uncovered. Unfortunately, this fine old custom is adhered to only by the very old. Now we are back on our island for lunch and a 2 P.M. takeoff.

October 16 — Wellington

This lovely place is about six thousand feet high and wonderfully cool. The road goes up around a succession of perilous curves each marked Hairpin Turn 1, Hairpin Turn 2, etc. The lower part is through intensely tall, very thin-stemmed palms which yield betel nuts. Higher yet, one passes through the glazed green of coffee and into the tea gardens. Wellington itself is a town of clean white and yellow-tiled cottages, numerous churches of the western faiths and the Staff College of the Indian Defence forces. It is covered with flowers — huge roses five or six inches across and thousands of poinsettias.

This morning, I lectured an audience of a couple of hundred middle military brass on American foreign policy and then we drove to a hunt club a dozen miles or so distant and yet higher up. Here we changed to horses. This was very nice. We had fine spirited beasts used for hunting and racing. The country called the Downs is a high green plain with a sharp contour and brooks in the valleys. We went for several miles, some of it at a hard gallop. Then we paid a visit to the hounds, had tea with the huntmaster at his house — Dingle Dell Cottage on Blue Ash Lane — and came on back to Wellington.

For the second time on this journey, they have concocted special beds for me. These are around eight feet. Not knowing my wife's dimensions,[10] they here took the precaution of making an equally long one for her.

The Indian Army officers are among the more cosmopolitan or at least European people in India, as also their wives. They favor all British Army manners from dress, salute, drill and whisky to mustache. Sport is a serious business. The Queen's picture hangs prominently in the Officers' Mess.

[10] 5′4″.

October 17 — Mysore

If one favors medieval splendor, this may be the last place in the world to sample it. We are ensconced, as guests of the Maharajah (and Governor) of Mysore[11], in the Lalitha Mahal, a large marble-domed palace about two miles from the main palace. The Lalitha Mahal is the guesthouse of the palace. Our suite consists of four or five large high-ceilinged rooms opening at each side on a spacious verandah. We get to it via a vast marble staircase which leads up from the state dining room and drawing rooms, all of suitable elegance.

This, however, is a modest cottage compared with the main palace to which we repaired at a little before seven this evening for a durbar of the Dasara. We were guided into the palace in a diplomatic convoy and, after divesting ourselves of our shoes, were taken by way of various staircases to a balcony overlooking the throne room. This is an enormous rectangular area, closed at the back and on the two shorter sides, and open to the palace grounds on the fourth. One should think of a large rather flat grandstand. In the center back of the grandstand was an enormous golden throne; on each side to the number of nearly a thousand were members of the court. These were in turbans and court costume and, when we arrived, attendants were going up and down policing up the dress of the more informal or indigent members. Few wore shoes. The general color effect was red and gold; the arches to the palace grounds are Indo-Saracen with light tracery and the whole was brilliantly lighted. In the palace grounds were a troop of elegantly caparisoned soldiers, even more elegantly clad elephants, some much-decorated camels and a green-clad regimental band. Beyond were more lights and tens of thousands of people. It was grand.

The Maharajah took his seat on the throne at seven to the vast

[11] Officially, His Highness Sri Jaya Chamaraja Wadiyar Bahadur. A man whose intellectual distinction was matched by his physical bulk, he was (and continues to be) a strong supporter of Indian parliamentary institutions. He subsequently became Governor of Madras State.

excitement of courtiers and crowd, and various retainers filed by to make him a symbolic offering of money tribute which he returned. (In the old happy days, he kept it.)

Then elephants in fantastic attire came forward to throw flowers over themselves and wave their trunks to the ruler. Horses then danced to music as did a number of little girls. Soldiers paraded, trumpets blew and the courtiers were garlanded and given *pan*.[12] So, as a special gesture, was I. After about an hour, the Maharajah left his throne — he conducted himself throughout with an admirably languid hauteur — and the proceedings were over. We were taken down to examine the throne, an exceedingly uneconomical affair of gold inlaid with diamonds, rubies and emeralds and reached by a small golden stair. It even has a wheel for raising and lowering it as the occupant may deem necessary. Tonight's proceedings were at minimum elevation.

Earlier in the day, we drove down to Mysore from Wellington and lunched on the way at the Bandipur Game Sanctuary — a place famous for its tigers, wild elephants, bison, spotted deer, pythons and other livestock. We saw only some spotted deer. A cloudburst came upon us as we arrived and lasted until we had to leave. The animals had wisely sought shelter.

Much of our way down lay through tea gardens and then teakwood plantations and finally jungle. Then we emerged on the high plains of Mysore, a parklike countryside of reddish soil, tree-lined roads and neat villages. When I visited Mysore before (in 1956), I was struck by how spruce and trim was the city and how elegant the parks and gardens. So again.[13]

October 21 — Bangalore–New Delhi

We spent three nights as guests of the Maharajah in the marble and gingerbread palace I have described. We went a second time

[12] Spices folded into a leaf and eaten, usually after meals, as we would eat after-dinner mints.
[13] Mysore, one of the greatest of the Princely States, had also the reputation in British times of being one of the two or three best governed.

to the durbar, this time to be guests in the royal box. This is opposite the throne with a view down on that in one direction and out
on the palace grounds on the other. (One must think of seats on
the outer edge of the grandstand under the roof adjacent to the
track.) It was filled with the royal female relatives, all handsomely
gowned and some with an astonishing burden of rubies, diamonds
and other precious stones. "Just an old piece from the South," one
of the princesses said when I admired a ruby and diamond neck-
piece. It contained perhaps fifty medium-caliber rubies and must
have been worth — well, say, half a million dollars.

The Freemans joined us on the morning of the last day. Orville
is surveying food and agricultural problems on the subcontinent.
Peter, Jamie and Emily came down from Delhi with them. Together we saw the final parade of elephants, horses with leopard-
skin saddle blankets, a silver carriage, soldiers, Rolls Royce cars.
In the evening, we went to a torchlight tattoo a few miles away at
which the Maharajah arrived on elephantback. I also visited the
Maharajah, *cum* Governor, in his palace and presented him with
a book on (American) Indian art. He told me that on his recent
visit to the United States he had been inducted as an honorary
member into an Indian tribe which, for an Indian Maharajah, would
seem to be the culminating consequence of Columbus' mistake. He
gave Kitty a handsome Mysore stole. Since the Ford Foundation
paid for the book, or possibly even USIS, and Kitty got the stole,
there is something slightly wrong about this exchange. However,
it may be within the permissible limits of official corruption. I, of
course, also visited the Chief Minister of Mysore.

After the torchlight procession, we came back to the main palace which was lit on every edge with hundreds of thousands of
lights. The effect was of a wedding cake in fairyland. Very exciting.

Orville is full of his job and I think doing well. He sees very
little of the President who, as always, is unenchanted by agriculture. The farm program continues to get more expensive every

year. This is the feature that principally attracts President Kennedy's attention.

Yesterday morning, with the Freemans, we drove from Mysore to Bangalore. The country looked green and fertile and after Kerala practically unpopulated. The road is wide and straight and the new rice, in particular, gave a quality of lush freshness to the landscape.

In Bangalore, I saw the Freemans off for Dacca, visited the USIS library, the Hindustan Machine Tool Company, had a press conference and a dinner with the Indo-American Society. In between, I found time to sleep off a bad headache.

Hindustan Machine Tool is the best plant I have seen in India. It is conspicuously not overstaffed. Only the manager guided me around — in contrast with the platoon that accompanies one in most places. It has its production costs well below American or European levels and is plowing its profits into expansion. The manager says that he got the idea that public sector plants should finance their expansion from their own earnings from my seminar speech five years ago in Bangalore. Possibly. I was eloquent on the subject for I have strong convictions. Such growth, so financed, is a source of corporate pride; it keeps workers and customers from claiming the earnings for they see how they are being used; and the promotions that go with the expansion rejoice the managerial men and ensure high morale.

I had a huge press conference at which I announced the changes which I am hoping to put into effect in our technical assistance program — concentration on fewer fields, on fewer agricultural institutions, with fewer people in New Delhi. I needed some news and one of the best ways of getting the policy is to proclaim it. Washington will be surprised and may wonder which part of the bureaucracy there authorized the change. However, no one will challenge it.

I told the Indo-American Society that I hoped they wouldn't become a mutual admiration club of well-to-do Indians and Americans. That is what some are and, as I have said, they look better from the inside than the outside.

This morning I looked at an industrial management seminar, an important part of the technical assistance effort, and it seemed to me a very thin operation. It is costing us a great deal of money; the industrial engineer in charge probably stands the U.S. Government about $70,000 a year. He teaches rather elementary simplification techniques such as the desirability of picking up two bolts at a time rather than one.[14] Then we went on to Hindustan Aircraft Limited. This is run as a private company by the Indian Air Force and makes fighter planes, railway coaches, jet engines and has just finished its first supersonic fighter. The latter we saw, and it is an impressive vehicle. Speeds are still subsonic for, while they have the frame, the engines are still subsonic.

Now we are on the way home and I am feeling the wear. But I have made South India aware of my existence for what that accomplishes. I have managed to keep constantly in the papers for ten days.

[14] Later investigation confirmed the dubious quality of this costly activity. It was gradually but still very expensively brought to an end.

XII

Nehru and Kennedy

October 24 — New Delhi

We are to have a visit, private and informal, beginning about November 20, from Mrs. Kennedy and her sister, Lee Radziwill. A Top Secret, Eyes Only, Destroy Before Reading message came in yesterday through army channels. It referred to her as "your girl friend" and asked if a "date" on November 20 would be satisfactory, and if I had received her letter. It was from Tish Baldrige.[1] Colonel Myers[2] who brought it in was blushing. He was relieved when I told him "girl friend" was only a cover name.

Today I served notice on Catholic Relief and Church World Services that they must make greater efforts to keep their relief food out of the black market. They receive it under Public Law 480 for distribution to charitable enterprises with which they are concerned. A considerable part is stolen or otherwise diverted for private sale. In packages marked as a gift from the American people, it turns up for sale in Indian shops. Both organizations denied that they were responsible for the black market stocks and said that rumors of diversion were synthetic and malicious. I yearned to tell them that God would know they were not telling the truth.

Ty Wood has returned from Washington with a proposal for getting U.S. Steel in on the Bokaro mill as a private enterprise oper-

[1] Mrs. Kennedy's social secretary.
[2] Lt. Colonel Clifford L. Myers, Assistant Army Attaché.

ation. Of the $500 million required, $100 million would be subscribed in common stock and the rest as a loan, possibly guaranteed, from the U.S. and India. One-third of the $100 million of common stock would be held by each of U.S. Steel, private Indian capitalists and the Indian Government. Half of U.S. Steel's investment would be cash, the rest in technology and "know-how." This means they would get control of a $500 million firm for ten years — their control is to be guaranteed for that time — for an investment of $16.7 million. A real bargain.

October 28 — New Delhi–London

Yesterday I saw Nehru and thereafter told the press that I hoped that it might be possible to have a meeting of heads of state where nothing astonishing happened. That should keep down hopes. I also tried to get through the myriad of matters which always pile up in the last moments before a departure. Life was complicated by an announcement from Washington of a cut in the Indian sugar quota to the United States. This followed by a few days Secretary Freeman's visit, but he knew nothing about it. A poor way to run things. The sugar was mostly loaded and on the way to port.

Nehru said he was delighted by the prospect of J.B.K.'s visit, asked me to add his invitation and invited her to stay part of the time at his house. Last night the telephone rang at the Residence and the operator said, "Call from Mr. and Mrs. Kennedy." It turned out to be Tish, asking if I could arrange for such an invitation. I told her, quite dishonestly, that a good ambassador thinks of everything first and that it was all arranged.

Last night at Palam, for the first time in my experience of the place, it was cool, and after boarding, I took three Seconal tablets and remained in a coma until after Cairo. Now the sun is just coming up over the horizon and we will soon be in Dusseldorf. I feel only slightly subhuman.

October 31 — New York

I got to Boston Saturday evening, had dinner with Nancy Sweezy[3] at Locke-Ober's[4] — what wonders India works in causing one to appreciate food! On Sunday, I lunched with Alan and a gathering of his friends at Quincy House and then went to a cocktail party at Felicia's.[5] Yesterday I saw Houghton Mifflin and had a luncheon at Harvard for a discussion of the Common Market. Then I went on to New York and to bed at seven and slept more or less until seven this morning. I had lunch with the editors of *Time* who are preparing a cover story on the Kennedy ambassadors. Like other lambs, I cooperate in my slaughter. Later tonight I join J.B.K. on the *Caroline*[6] for Washington.

This morning the White House called and asked me to "step over." I explained I was in New York. The President had assumed I was in the Hay-Adams.

November 1 — Washington

I joined Mrs. Kennedy at the Marine Terminal at LaGuardia about 11:30 P.M. after a terrible dinner party at which I horribly insulted some high German diplomat. He had given a long disquisition on the shortcomings, unworldliness, weakness and naiveté of Americans where foreign policy is concerned. I then asked him who on the record had been wiser in this century so far, Germany or the United States, mentioning the foreign policy of Wilhelm II and Hitler and the consequences. He said this was the first disagreeable thing he had heard on his visit. He lives a too protected life.

The *Caroline* is pleasantly furnished in gray with sundry seats and divans. By Washington, we had covered all aspects of the forthcoming journey. It should be fun. It has also been a remarkably well-kept secret so far. Our prospective visitor is full of

[3] Cambridge friend.
[4] Notable Boston restaurant.
[5] The wife of Professor Benjamin Kaplan of the Harvard Law School.
[6] The personal plane of the Kennedy family.

enthusiasm and it pops out of her eyes. She is also a little worried that we may kill her. She dropped me at the Hay-Adams about 1:30 A.M.

This morning, having slept badly, I breakfasted with Arthur Schlesinger and then went over the trip plans with Tish[7] and staff. This was in the second floor of the East Wing of the White House, whence social matters are managed and which looks a bit like the reception room at a Radcliffe dormitory.

Then I talked with Chet Bowles who feels more and more out of things. Were I him, I would quit. I lunched with George Ball. George is as far up as Chet is down. We reached a broad agreement on the approach to the Common Market: we support British entry and the Market in general in return for a broad reduction on our tariffs and theirs.[8] George especially favors a bulk reduction on industrial hard goods which is good policy.

I saw the President at 5:30 P.M., we being joined by President Truman. It was the latter's first visit to the White House since he left it in 1953. We were to talk of the Nehru visit, but H. S T. carried the conversation back to Korea and forward to some recent political speeches of Ike. He said, amiably, that Ike was unable to think and that had it not been for the guidance of George Marshall, his patron general, he would have finished his career as a lieutenant colonel. He admitted, however, to having liked him once. He thinks he is bored at Gettysburg — where he has "built a house with extra rooms for all of his gifts" — and will be a considerable source of trouble to J.F.K. He was only slightly less favorable to the Communists who he said, simply, were all crazy.

A meeting on Laos intervened and Truman greeted Bowles with the cheery observation that he had surely gained forty pounds. The Laos meeting was on whether Harriman should be given freedom to proceed with negotiations on the basis of a rather unsatis-

[7] See page 239.

[8] I later had second thoughts about this. I felt during the following year that far too much energy and political capital was being invested in getting the required Congressional authorization for what was to become the so-called Kennedy round.

factory compromise on the functions of the Control Commission. Alexis Johnson[9] and Walter McConaughy[10] objected and stated their case with a remarkable lack of conviction. After talking with Harriman in Geneva, the President overruled them but with such tact that I doubt they knew.

November 5 — Newport, Rhode Island

This past week has been terribly busy as always in Washington but also most interesting. In theory, I have been making preparations for Nehru's visit. In practice, I have been interfering with all manner of things but mostly Vietnam. Maxwell Taylor[11] and Walt Rostow are advocating exceedingly half-baked intervention. Not troops but soldiers to do flood control work. Once there, they would use a shovel with one hand and deal with the guerrillas with the other. At a meeting yesterday, I rather frightened Walt at the responsibility he was assuming. And this morning we had a new session at the White House with Bundy. Mac thinks there is no occasion when I would urge the use of force. I have to admit that my enthusiasm for it is always very low.

The State Department could not be in worse condition. Rusk is away. Bowles is feeling very uncertain. George Ball is in fine fettle and has excellent judgment but he is two rungs down the ladder. No policy being available to those below, even the smallest questions come to the White House for Bowles cannot make his decisions stick.

Dave Bell[12] asked me at lunch yesterday for the three reforms

[9] U. Alexis Johnson. Deputy Undersecretary of State for Political Affairs, and an important architect of our Vietnam policy during various stages of deepening disaster. He later became Deputy Ambassador in Saigon and then Ambassador to Japan.

[10] Assistant Secretary of State for Far Eastern Affairs and later Ambassador to Pakistan. Like Alexis Johnson, a committed "hardliner."

[11] At the time, he was serving as military representative of the President. He then became Chairman of the Joint Chiefs of Staff, and later U.S. Ambassador to Vietnam.

[12] See page 13.

most needed at State. I told him: (1) to reduce the number of people; (2) to eliminate the ridiculous specialization as between political officers, economists and planners, making one man responsible for a country; (3) put George Ball effectively in charge, with Chet handling Asia, under Rusk.

One thing that offends me endlessly is the meetings. Everyone assembles several times a day for genteel, aimless conversation. No one seems to have a feeling of responsibility. You serve by being present. And no one is pressed for time. This last I cannot understand. I never attend a meeting without calculating when it will be over.

Life was made better by an amusing dinner party at the Schlesingers' night before last and another good one in the Sterns'[13] affluent new house last night. I should have told that I got Phil and Leni an invitation to dine with Nehru, whom they deeply admire, in return for paying the cost of shipping two bison calves to Delhi. The cost of shipping the bison turned out to be less than expected so I added a raccoon, an opossum, a bear cub, a whistling swan and numerous other beasts.

At noon, I got aboard a Convair at the MATS base and made a pleasant two-hour flight up here, with lunch on the way. Then I was helicoptered over to Hammersmith Farm — the house of Mrs. Kennedy's mother and stepfather — which looks out on heavenly green pasture, trees in late autumn colors and the blue waters of the bay — some bay. It is lovely. The President, Mrs. K. and Caroline were out boating when I arrived, and the President is now taking a nap. I am writing this on the terrace. The last few days have been warm for this time of year although here there is now a slight nip. The sun is bright with a slight haze and it is hard to worry about Vietnam. Nehru is arriving in New York about now.

After infinite pains and trouble, J.B.K.'s visit is now announced and firm. The Pakistanis were unhappy over the allotment of time to India as opposed to Pakistan. Everyone in the White House hinted privately about coming and some asked. At one time, the whole thing looked too tiring. The press coverage still promises to be overpowering. But evidently it will come off.

November 6 — Washington

I think this has been the most interesting day in my memory.

Last night, I dined with the President and J.B.K. and we talked over a vast number of subjects from South Vietnam to civil defense to domestic economics. The food, a light steak, was agreeable as was the Moselle. After dinner, we talked further and then the President settled down to playing backgammon with Lem Billings.[14] We also watched Nehru on "Meet the Press," a most embarrassing show. Larry Spivak tied into Nehru like a prosecuting attorney in a movie.[15] Scotty Reston[16] unwound an elaborate question about Nehru's successor. Nehru squelched him by observing that in a democracy, leaders do not name their heirs. He cited as an unfortunate precedent Churchill's naming of Eden.

This morning, I had breakfast in bed and dictated a speech for the President to give on the arrival of the Prime Minister and did some business for him in Washington by phone.

Then about ten o'clock, we boarded the *Honey Fitz*[17] to go to the Newport Naval Air Station to meet Nehru. There was a heavy fog that grounded the helicopters and it was chilly and damp on the boat. The latter, a fast largish launch, is nicely turned out and we were escorted by two smaller launches. About halfway across, a speedboat overtook us and handed over the typed copy of the speech I had written.

At the Air Station, it was dark but the weather was flyable and

14 Lemoyne Billings, close personal friend of the President.

15Perhaps he was too severe this evening. But I have since come to conclude that Spivak is the best such interrogator in the business. In contrast with others, he knows his subject and he asks and presses the right questions.

16 See page 8.

17 See page 247.

the MATS plane, a DC-6, bearing the Prime Minister, came sweeping in exactly on time. There was a small color guard and a handful of Indian students with bouquets. Nehru was accompanied by Indira and B.K. Nehru[18] and seemed in the best of spirits. After a little photography, we got back on the "H.F." and sailed off for Hammersmith Farm once more. The weather had improved a bit more and Nehru was delighted when the President pointed to some of the Newport palaces. "I want you to see how the average American lives." Nehru replied that he had heard about the affluent society. At the house, Caroline presented the Prime Minister and Indira each with a rose. Mrs. Kennedy said to her husband, "Jack, did you see what Reston said this morning?" The President turned to Nehru and said, "Mr. Prime Minister, my wife does not believe in a free press — and she is right." Nehru was even more delighted.

At the residence, we had a long lunch, mostly on South Vietnam. The President and I pressed Nehru hard on what we should do to put down Communist terror. Could Ho Chi Minh do anything? The U.N.? What about a U.N. observer corps? What could the I.C.C. do? Nehru was rather negative on all of these matters and most interested in making clear that we should not send in soldiers. I agree heartily but we need an alternative with a plausible chance of success.

At 2:30 P.M., we broke up and B. K. Nehru, J.B.K. and I went for a walk. Mrs. K. was having new doubts about her journey to India.

The weather has improved some more so we boarded four helicopters and in a few moments were back at the Air Station. Then we got aboard the President's Air Force jet for an hour's ride to Washington. The plane is large, light and comfortable and done in brown and beige. A forward compartment houses the President and his guests. A rear compartment contains the reporters, lesser but still important members of the White House staff and the supporting proletarians. En route, the President read papers at the rate of one a minute. Nehru read the *National Geographic* and

[18] See page 82.

the New York *Daily News*.[19] Indira read *Vogue*. J.B.K. read Malraux. Soon the plane was making a wide sweep around Andrews Air Force Base.

There we dismounted for quite a show. The diplomatic community was turned out in strength with the support of Lyndon Johnson, Dean Rusk and Chester Bowles. A ten-page folder had been issued for our guidance. The places where we stood on the reviewing platform were marked with our names.

Then guns went off, national anthems were played and a contingent from each of Army, Navy and Air Force rendered suitable salutes. The President gave a highly abbreviated version of the speech I had written. Nehru spoke at greater, and I thought undue, length but I may have been prejudiced because I could not hear a word he said. Then we took flight in another bevy of helicopters and were landed on the White House grounds.

It was dusk as we twirled our way over Washington and came in by the Washington Monument a few feet away and fifty feet or so up. It looks very large and square from that height. I rode over to State with Rusk and gave him a general account of the luncheon talk with my specific arguments against putting troops in Vietnam.

By the time I got to the hotel, I was very tired. I still am.

I think "Honey Fitz" a poor name for a presidential yacht. The President asked what would be better. I suggested "The Dorchester" or "The North End."[20] He agreed but I doubt that he will change.

There is no safe way of phoning from Hyannisport or Newport to Washington. All secretaries were housed on the base twenty minutes distant.

The President promises me he will not talk any more about the balanced budget. This sets up an impossible test which cannot be met. The keynote should be that the budget is under control, as it is. That standard can be met.

[19] Noticing the latter, the President asked if I wouldn't get him on to a friendlier sheet.
[20] For two notable Boston purlieus. Honey Fitz is for Mayor John F. Fitzgerald, J.F.K.'s grandfather.

November 7 — Washington

The talks began at ten in the President's office with Nehru, B. K. Nehru, M. J. Desai, Rusk, Talbot and Rostow present. We were disposed on the two couches with the President rocking between on his rocking chair. The sun was bright outside and the french doors were open. Caroline and playmates were running about and once J.B.K. almost came wandering in wearing purple slacks.

As talks, they were a brilliant monologue by the President. This was not intentional — Nehru simply did not respond. Question after question he answered with monosyllables or a sentence or two at most. I thought the President found it very discouraging but he kept his good humor and kept on trying. The subjects included Berlin, South Vietnam, nuclear testing and Indo-Pakistani relations, and only the latter elicited any real response. On the other hand, it gave me a good insight into the President's views on a wide variety of matters. As usual, he was incisive and totally candid — even as to the role of the Pentagon and its friends in promoting arms appropriations.

After the meeting broke up around 12:30 P.M., I strolled out on the back lawn with the President. He was very discouraged and so was I. He thought he had done badly; I fail to see how he could have done better.

In the evening, I went to a big reception at the Indian Embassy — the Indians are on to my techniques of social escape and M. J. Desai warned me I would be missed. Then on to a dinner at the White House.

The latter was attended by about thirty at one long table — the Bunkers and the Coopers[21] were there plus Schlesingers, Lyndon Johnsons, Rusks and Orvil Dryfoos of the *Times*. The gold plate was out and the flowers, which included an assortment of orchids, were very light and gay. The food was far from inadequate. The band made far too much noise for the rather limited space.

We assembled in one of the middle rooms and on the arrival of

[21] See pages xi, 42

the President, filed by and on into the state dining room. I sat between Lorraine Cooper and Harriet Bunker,[22] both very nice.

The President's toast was superb — "I can add little by way of welcome, Mr. Prime Minister, to the one you received from Mr. Lawrence Spivak."[23] The Prime Minister, who had sat between Mrs. Kennedy and her sister and with the light of love in his eyes, was obviously delighted. His response, rather long, was a touching account of how Gandhi had affected the Indian character. After dinner, the men gathered in a circle around him for nearly an hour. The talk was mostly on Communist China, Tito, the new African countries, the relation of innocence to isolationism. On the whole, it was very good. Incidentally, Walter Reuther was there and was very vivid and lively as usual.

It broke up about midnight. Toward two in the morning, the President called me to inquire how I thought things had gone, to talk about South Vietnam and to tell me that Jackie had postponed her trip until January.

November 10 — New York

Day before yesterday, in the morning, the Prime Minister and President met alone at my suggestion and things went much better. In private, the conversation became much more relaxed. Meanwhile Talbot, Desai, B. K. Nehru and I sat out in the Fish Room. It was the first relaxed hour since coming to Washington. After the President and the Prime Minister broke up, the President and I strolled for a few minutes in the sunshine on the terrace. He was much happier and said he had caught some of the Nehru magic.

Lunch was at the John Sherman Coopers'. I sat with Mrs. Gandhi and Lyndon Johnson. Lyndon was just back from an electoral victory in Texas and talkative as usual. But I like him more and more. He is genuinely intelligent and wants to do things.

[22] The wives of my two predecessors as Ambassador to India.
[23] The version in Arthur M. Schlesinger, Jr.'s *A Thousand Days* (Boston: Houghton Mifflin, 1965), p. 525, is, I believe, more accurate.

That is worth ten Talbots — men who are wise, well-spoken and inactive.

The Cooper lunch was downstairs at small tables with the garden in the background — all very intimate and civilized. Walter Lippmann was on hand and had a long talk with the Prime Minister.

I rode back with the P.M. to Blair House behind a motorcycle escort. I suggested that democratic heads of state should not travel in such totalitarian fashion. He agreed. Angier Duke[24] pointed out that some, notably Sukarno, measured their welcome by the number of outriders they had.

In the afternoon, having taken over Chet's office and staff, I struggled manfully with various chores and then went home to the Harrimans' at six to catch a nap.

At eight, I went to the White House for a dinner in my honor, my distinction being shared by Ormsby Gore,[25] the new British Ambassador. Present also were the Bundys, the Schlesingers and Lee Radziwill.[26] We ate in a small room upstairs, and so fast and agreeable was the conversation that I failed to notice the food. Latin American affairs came up. Evidently Robert Woodward, the present Assistant Secretary, is believed to lack the energy so a new man must be found. Arthur urges Dick Goodwin;[27] the President thinks he is too young and I agree.

Vietnam is still very much on everyone's mind. The President does not want any overt intervention but desperately needs an alternative. The Indians have not been very encouraging. At the close of the evening, we had a private talk, and I told him that for my own satisfaction, I would like to go home via Saigon. He jumped at my suggestion.

Jackie and Lee both looked especially lovely. I missed a dinner of the Secretary of State but with an excellent excuse.

[24] See page 205.
[25] Sir David Ormsby Gore (later Lord Harlech) was Ambassador to the United States from 1961 to 1965.
[26] See page 239.
[27] See page 38.

Yesterday I had breakfast with Averell — he is back from Geneva and I am staying with him. Then I worked on a booklet on civil defense,[28] a speech for the President and a hundred other details. Toward noon, I read the draft communiqué that would be issued in the afternoon on the talks. It was a marvel of lugubrious formality wholly inappropriate to such literate men as Nehru and Kennedy. It had already been agreed to on both sides. I intervened, killed about a third, rewrote the lead and then compelled acceptance. Communiqués, I discover, are usually written well in advance of such a visit.

In the evening, there was a most agreeable party at the Indian Embassy with a dancing troupe. The latter had run into bad trouble in the American South. It was excluded from restaurants and once had considered canceling the tour. But they forgive and forget. The Kennedys were there in force. Eunice Shriver[29] asked the Prime Minister why he did not have bags under his eyes as in his pictures and would he increase the size of the Peace Corps. The President called me afterward to say he thought she had probably set back Indian-American relations about five years. He also worried me more about South Vietnam. I am having a further major try at the Indians. I wish they were more concerned.

Yesterday was an appalling but very interesting day. We had a full honor guard at the MATS terminal for takeoff and came here to New York in the *Columbine*. Arrival at New York was routine. A representative of Nelson Rockefeller was present and told me afterward how sorry he was that the Governor could not welcome Nehru. I said I thought the public reaction would be bad. He said the public wouldn't notice. I said I was sure it would, that in fact I was having a press conference that afternoon and would mention

---

[28] The booklet on civil defense, a pictorial job, greatly worried the President. It made the whole idea of nuclear attack seem rather jolly. One family was shown putting out to sea, following the warning, in their cabin cruiser. Another picture showed a happy farm scene with everyone decontaminating the cows. I wrote a comment on the political aspects of nuclear defense designed especially for Republicans. A sharply edited version eventually emerged.

[29] Mrs. Sargent Shriver, the President's second oldest sister.

the Governor's absence. In the evening, Rockefeller was waiting at the Carlyle for Nehru. I asked Nehru later how they got along.

"A most extraordinary man. He talked to me about nothing but bomb shelters. Why does he think I am interested in bomb shelters? He gave me a pamphlet on how to build my own shelter."

To get back to the day. At noon, Nehru spoke to a big audience of radio, press and advertising men. It was a two-dais affair — honored and highest honors. I announced the formation of an engineering university consortium to help the new Indian Institute of Technology at Kanpur. I called it a "small souvenir" of the visit from the President. Nehru did not react. His speech was passive, though pleasant.

After the speech, he went on to address the U.N. in a performance that was far from distinguished. I was not there — I shopped for lawn bowls for New Delhi, saw Jim Perkins[30] and held a press conference. The latter produced the usual questions about Krishna Menon, which I evaded as usual, plus some interesting ones on Indian economic development.

After the press conference, we went to Gracie Mansion for a reception by the Mayor, newly elected after a triumphant campaign against the bosses who once supported him. I like Bob Wagner, but his house is the most hideous in the world. The people there, all New York liberals, gave Nehru a rousing welcome. Ambassador Richard C. Patterson[31] welcomed the guests. He had everyone's name in phonetic fashion. He checked them with me: Prime Minister Nay-Rew, Mrs. Gan-Dee. Mr. Dess-sy was missing. Later we went to dinner at the Council on Foreign Relations, where Nehru and I shared the limelight. Most everyone of note was there, a fine turnout of the American Establishment. Nehru spoke for the nth time, rather interestingly on Indian history. The questions were genteel and predictable, except for one about

[30] James A. Perkins (See page 4). He later became President of Cornell University.
[31] Then Commissioner of the Department of Public Events in New York City.

how he thought we might arrest the advance of the John Birch Society (Nehru had never heard of the J.B.S.). Afterward, I went to a party at Marietta Tree's[32] which was great fun, save that I was feeling the wear. I described the day, and my account of Governor Rockefeller pleased all present — which included the Jonathan Binghams,[33] Mrs. Jock Whitney[34] (exceedingly good-looking) and the Canadian Ambassador to the U.N. The Binghams came back to the hotel afterward for a chat.

This morning, I remained in bed until noon, more or less. I labored on an article for the President for *Look*. He helped *Life* to celebrate its twenty-fifth anniversary with a piece and thus was hooked by *Look*.

[32] Then a member of the U.S. Mission to the U.N. and later to have the rank of ambassador in this post.

[33] Bingham was then a member of the U.S. Mission to the U.N., later with the rank of ambassador, and later still a member of Congress from the Bronx.

[34] Wife of the Ambassador to England.

XIII

Saigon

November 14 — Honolulu

This is Tuesday. My notes came to an end last Saturday when time failed. No more was to be had.

Last Saturday afternoon, I took leave of Nehru — "I suspect you of seeking to avoid Disneyland, Ambassador" — and rode the air shuttle to Washington with Adlai Stevenson. (He had lunched with Nehru but complained that Krishna Menon had taken over the conversation.) Adlai is only moderately happy about his job.[1] Too many detailed instructions from Washington — the State Department advises him, more or less, at what hour to see Gromyko, when to interrupt to go to the men's room and how long to stay there. He thinks the New Frontier is too much like the old one. I agree on foreign policy but pointed out that the domestic policy was broadly in line with what he had once considered the dangerously left positions of Harris, Hansen and Galbraith.[2] At State, I stopped off for an hour or two to read the Taylor-Rostow[3] Report on South Vietnam. It is a curious document. The recommendations are for vigorous action. The appendices say it cannot possibly succeed given the present government in Saigon.

[1] See page 3.
[2] Seymour Harris, Alvin H. Hansen and J. K. Galbraith, all Harvard professors and economic sages of the Stevenson campaigns. Stevenson, the product of Princeton economics of an earlier era, viewed his economic advisers in 1952 with some misgivings.
[3] For General Maxwell Taylor and Walt Rostow both recently returned from Vietnam.

Then to *The Party* at the White House — eating regularly there is a great saving over going to the Hot Shoppes and pleasant too.

This was a grand bash. A hundred or so were there, and the President led us into the small dining room which was given over to small, round tables. I sat next to Eunice Shriver[4] and with Tish Baldrige and some lady who is doing the White House furniture. The food I failed to notice. But I did notice the women, all of whom had spent hours and days on their dress and with remarkable results. This and youth made for sensational effect. Everyone had also that fine glow that comes from being "in." A jazz band made a nerve-curdling but pleasant racket. It lasted until 4 A.M. I drank a great deal of champagne and remember telling Gore Vidal[5] on the way home that Shakespeare was almost certainly better than he. Gore was mortally insulted but took it well.

Sunday I went to the White House at nine. Mac Bundy went over his desk three times in search of a paper we were to discuss, failed to find it and finally asked me why I had come in. He had also been at the party. I spent the morning doing final chores, talking about India and briefing myself on the hideous mess in South Vietnam. Mac says the President has not made up his mind. The State Department (Alexis Johnson) assures me a modified intervention is settled.

In the evening, after a short nap I went on "Meet the Press." Despite my weakened condition, I was in excellent form. Lawrence Spivak[6] was not there, but I made reference to the unique tact with which he had questioned Nehru the week before. The questions — on aid, neutralism, Menon, birth control — were not bad, partly thanks to Elie Abel and Carroll Kenworthy of the United Press who knew what they were asking.

Afterward, I went to see Scotty Lanahan and brought her a scarf which pleased her very much. She had missed "Meet the Press"

4 See page 251.
5 See page 35.
6 See page 245.

and I complained bitterly. As always, she was succinct and intelligent. Then I went to dinner with Harriman after which the Schlesingers came in. Arthur thought well of my performance but believed I was unwise in an exchange which went as follows:

"Mr. Ambassador, do you agree with Nehru that America and Russia can be dealt with on the same moral plane?"

"No. If I did, my security clearance would surely be lifted."

He said it was too ironical for my public.

Harriman is to become an Assistant Secretary of State for Europe or the Far East. I urged the latter.[7]

Monday I went through more business including Bokaro, real estate, and more South Vietnam and said goodbye to the President by phone. I borrowed Bowles's Cadillac, lunched at the White House Mess, said goodbye to Mac and called on Arthur. He was talking to a good-looking girl who turned out to be Angie Dickinson, the actress whom I had last seen as a missionary in Africa in a film which we showed at the Residence in New Delhi. She had campaigned for Kennedy and had been in town for a dinner to promote either T.B. or cancer; I forget which. By coincidence, she was leaving for Los Angeles from Friendship Airport at almost the same time as was I. I made a quick shift and we drove out together. By halfway to Los Angeles, I was deeply in love. She has fair, pure skin, blond to vaguely reddish hair, merry eyes and a neat, unstarved body. She also has a bubbling sense of humor and a quick interest in life. I never had a lovelier companion and the trip went in a minute. I was heart-broken when Los Angeles came up under the wing and invited her to come on to Honolulu. She declined and I kissed her tenderly, put her in a cab for Hollywood and got glumly aboard my flight. There I learned that if I had not changed planes to go with her, I would have missed my connection. I am by love both possessed and protected. After another several hours, I was in Honolulu, met by Ed Martin[8] and lodged in the

---

[7] He got it, as noted on page 265.

[8] Edwin Webb Martin, Foreign Service Officer, Asia hand and political adviser to Admiral Harry Felt (see page 257).

Royal Hawaiian Hotel. I was almost too tired to dream of my lovely girl. However, I concentrated. She told me, incidentally, that she is owned body or anyhow soul by a contractor; that her African film almost tempted her to turn down the script which meant she would have neither worked nor been paid for several months; that people do not ask for her autograph, unfortunately; that Bette Davis and Myrna Loy have grown old gracefully, but most actresses have not; that she does not allow the movie magazines to deal with her psychiatric problems of which she seems to have few; that she refuses invitations which are inspired by the fact that she is decorative; that she works twelve hours a day when making a film of which time for makeup takes two-and-a-half; that she does not think that her parts affect her character which is fortunate "since so many of them call for my being, in a manner of speaking, a whore."

This morning, after a remarkable sleep I went out on the beach for an hour or two of swimming. The water is placid and green and moderately warm, and the scenery is a controlled tropical with considerable damage from new high hotels. Surfboard riders could be seen in the distance.

At eleven, I went to see Admiral Felt[9] and spent an hour talking with him about South Vietnam. He has little confidence in the Vietnamese Army and not much in Diem. But in his view all can be improved. I got the feeling that everything is complicated by Diem's fears of being thrown out. The soldiers of his army get almost no pay, no leave, their relations starve and they spend a lot of their time guarding the politicians. The latter double in brass as the army brass. It sounds like a Christ-awful mess. I will keep an open mind.

[9] Admiral Harry Felt, Commander-in-Chief, Pacific.

November 17 — Hong Kong–Saigon

Admiral Felt's headquarters were in Camp Smith on a hill more or less overlooking Pearl Harbor. On the way down, I had my first glimpse of that famous spot — a large roundish body of water with a big island in the middle, many ships about and all very blue in the bright sunlight.

I slept all the way to Tokyo, a meal apart. We landed at Wake Island but I got only a glimpse of it as we soared off.

At the Tokyo airport, I told an officer sent out by Ed Reischauer of the Nehru visit so far as it might have a bearing on a forthcoming visit by the Japanese Prime Minister to India. Then I slept for another four hours until we were coming in at high speed over the lighted hills and around the islands of Hong Kong. In a moment or two, we were through customs and on the way to the Ambassador Hotel — very new and comfortable in the best Hilton-Sheraton tradition. I slept, this time on a bed for a lovely change, for another eight hours. I awoke with the feeling that I had finally made up the cumulative deficiency.

Yesterday, in the morning, I added enormously to my wardrobe — two suits, a gabardine overcoat, the latter very light and, even by the standards of Hong Kong, a trifle expensive. I also bought presents for the youngsters, mostly electronic, and lots of luxurious silks for Kitty.

Hong Kong must be the most effective economic community in the entire world. The British provide law, order and government, the latter something the Chinese pioneered but never wholly mastered. The Chinese provide economic energy beyond anything any European has ever imagined. The world supplies capital; raw materials and merchandise come at sea-borne rates. The place reminds one of a vast Sears, Roebuck store, replenished from every corner of the world.

At noon, I took the ferry by the drowsing ships and junks to the Island — the hotel is on Kowloon or the mainland — and had lunch with a group from the Consulate plus Professor Kirby from the local University, and a man of above average interest from the colonial government. We talked about the economic situation in China proper. This, I am persuaded beyond the impact of official wishful thinking, is fairly bad. The farmers are beating the regime as they have usually done when exposed to pressures beyond their endurance. Agriculture is the least manageable of the several forms of economic life.

The Consulate, very large and important here, had a further program for me but I persuaded them to cancel it. At the end of the afternoon, I strolled, had a luxurious Chinese dinner, did some more shopping, had a nap and finally went to bed. This morning I got up, packed and, after a modest delay at the airport over a burnt-out spark plug, we are now sailing southwest over the clouds to Saigon.

Saigon (later)

I arrived here about noon and was met by Fritz Nolting,[10] the Ambassador. Trimble[11] from Cambodia was also here and we lunched at the Residence. The latter is a spacious house with pleasant rooms and high ceilings and an incredible traffic noise pounding by outside.

Saigon itself is very lively and agreeable in a French sort of way. The women are handsomely dressed in *ao dais,* these being high-waisted pajamas with flowing panels of white silk fore and aft. They are also very good-looking and especially so on a bicycle. The city shows little sign of the terror in the countryside and few soldiers are in evidence. There are reminders though. A few weeks ago, someone tossed a bomb at Nolting.

I settled down immediately to talks with Nolting and General McGarr, the head of M.A.A.G[12] On this, more later.

[10] See page 222.
[11] William Cattell Trimble, U.S. Ambassador to Cambodia and thereafter Deputy Assistant Secretary of State for African Affairs.
[12] Military Assistance Advisory Group. This designation of our military mission in other countries has the connotation of an alliance — and also, in some instances, inconvenient independence of the ambassador.

November 19 — Saigon

Yesterday morning I spent reading background papers at the Embassy, a shabby six-story building near the Saigon River. Then I had a long talk with members of the Embassy staff, followed by lunch with Arthur Gardiner, the head of USOM (United States Operations Mission), the AID mission here. After two or three hours, we drove for an hour or so into the country. More talks with Nolting followed, then a formal dinner at the Residence and then still more talk. Before dinner, I decided to have a few minutes' nap and nearly succeeded in sleeping through dinner.

Saigon is busy and bustling; a French provincial city, say Toulouse, comes to mind. People are clean, well-dressed and well-fed, and one is struck by the stylish-looking women in the *ao dais*, which I have mentioned.

But one learns that the city is also in a modified state of siege. The Ambassador and senior officials are followed everywhere by a car filled with gun-bearers — one went along with us into the country yesterday and was never more than a few feet behind. The members of the USOM cannot go or anyhow are not allowed out of town without an escort consisting of two or three carloads of soldiers. This makes extension work, say a visit to instruct some farmers on how to improve rice production, rather labor-intensive. In fact, to the number of about two hundred, they are all penned up in Saigon. Gardiner says they are busy; I imagine that means they are extensively advising each other.

The Vietcong has long been active on the Mekong Delta to the south of Saigon. In recent weeks, they have been attacking villages in some force in the highlands to the south, and they control countryside up to thirty miles from Saigon. Food, especially rice, no longer comes here in satisfactory quantities for the farmers are being terrorized into not selling. Rice exports have fallen to zero. This problem is not especially eased by a bad flood on the Delta.

The countryside, to the north, over which we drove yesterday on a new multi-lane highway, is green and rather sparsely populated. Rice fields alternate with stretches of low jungle. Soldiers were much in evidence although they are little to be seen in Saigon itself. I couldn't help wondering if a super-highway of this sort — it was built with American aid — was the most urgent need of the country.

I have discovered that to get to New Delhi with any promptness I must return to Hong Kong today. This is much like going to Chicago from Boston by way of Dallas.

Dinner last night was for the Economics Minister and the Health Minister, a full-dress affair. Neither seemed much perturbed by their state of siege, although if they lose, I imagine, they will either be hanged or forced into exile. The atmosphere of this city begins to leave a horrible taste in my mouth.

November 20 — Bangkok–New Delhi

Yesterday morning, I had a briefing on the military situation. I can't entirely get over the fact that there are 250,000 organized forces on the government side and maybe 15,000 in opposition. Anyhow, the briefing was held in a large auditorium-like building at the M.A.A.G. headquarters. A few young officers attended and it was geared to the mentality of an idiot, or, more likely, a backwoods congressman. The presiding general became embarrassed at one point and told the officers they were telling what I already knew. Much of it bore only a limited relation to the known or demonstrable truth. One officer said that since the beginning of the year, the Vietcong had suffered 17,000 casualties at the hands of the government forces. This was the equivalent of losing their entire force and some fifty percent more in ten months for they started the year with many fewer than the 15,000 just mentioned. I asked for a figure that reflected the officer's own judgment. The general supported my request but the officer had none. One briefing officer said the jungle had no underbrush and made for easy passage. Another said it was impenetrable except on the trails. One had to remember each moment that Vietnamese divisions on the war map were not necessarily divisions in practice.

In the afternoon, I had a political discussion, much more valuable, although even the military information was so wrong as to be, in its way, a clue to the state of things. From the political briefing, I left to get the Cathay Pacific plane for Hong Kong. The latter came in a little late while I was talking with Nolting and Irving Brown.[13] We continued to talk and presently I got aboard and waved goodbye. It was unnecessary for one engine would not go. After a time, we were unloaded and, after waiting a couple of hours, back I went to the Residence. There we had drinks and dinner, and this morning the Air Attaché at the Embassy flew me over to Bangkok. Over the Delta we saw the floods.[14] I am sure they are doing much less damage than is imagined. These rivers flood regularly, get billed for being the greatest disasters in history and then the mud walls are put back and the rice grows better than ever. The flood is supposed to play a big part in the misfortunes of South Vietnam. I much doubt that it has been a serious factor.

We took off steeply. The Vietcong snipers sometimes sit a few hundred yards from the end of the runway. On the previous takeoff, the pilot had collected some bullet holes in his wings. This time none.

Bangkok was hot and sticky as usual. I dispatched a report to the President too sensitive for present discussion[15] and had lunch with Unger.[16] Then I visited Kenneth Young, the Ambassador,[17] who verified a number of my impressions on Vietnam, and had tea

[13] American union official with a wide charter to help the noncommunist labor movement in Asia.

[14] Of importance, for the Taylor-Rostow Report had proposed that American combat forces be introduced on the excuse of doing flood control work.

[15] Urging, in general, no armed intervention. I stressed the unpopularity and inefficiency of the Diem Government and urged detachment therefrom. We would let it be known that an alternative to the dictatorship would be acceptable but initiate no coup. I did not, I regret to say, urge a prompt pull-out.

[16] Leonard Unger, Deputy Chief of Mission. Later Ambassador to Laos and then Thailand. Unger was a former student.

[17] See page 48.

with Kukrit Pramoj.[18] Following this and a major struggle with
the Bangkok traffic, I managed to buy some silk and even, more
surprisingly, to reach the airport. The traffic in this peaceful oriental city is possibly the world's most hideous. Big cars, small cars,
midget cars, motorized tongas, motor bikes, scooters and bicycles
compete madly for the space.

Pramoj has just completed the assembly of three ancient Thai
houses as a residence. They stand on a platform of teak about six
feet high held up by round teak logs on which one sits in the breeze.
One house is a bedroom, one a study and one a shrine. They curve
gracefully from eave to sharp peak, are wonderfully carved and
altogether delightful. He was careful to observe that it wasn't a
museum.

He says Thailand as an ally should be considered a committed
neutral.

November 24 — New Delhi–Mysore

I had only three days in New Delhi before taking flight again.
One I spent reporting on Saigon. I am well pleased with what I
sent in. I am persuaded that the Department is wrong, I right and
that I was persuasive.

One day I spent at the office, including a background briefing
for the press, a press conference, a staff meeting and a reception for
the Japanese Prime Minister. One day was Thanksgiving. I arose
at dawn and, as a pagan, enjoyed reading a proclamation by a
Catholic President of a Puritan festival. The proclamation, incidentally, was much too long. J.F.K. enjoined all parents to tell
their children of the first Thanksgiving, including, presumably,
some expression of regret that the Irish would not show up for
some years. I spent the day working on a speech for Mysore which
promises to be much better than one would expect, given the time
available. For Thanksgiving dinner in the evening, we had the

18 See page 120.

Nathan Puseys, Charles Taft,[19] the Keith Kanes,[20] a Bishop and Henry Morgenthau, Jr.[21] All of these virtuous men (except Henry) were attending a meeting of the World Council of Churches in New Delhi. I gave silent thanks instead of grace for the ability of the United States to function without so many good people.

I arrived home very tired and I am still far from rejuvenated.

November 25 — Mysore–New Delhi

This morning, clad in gleaming white silk with baby blue facings, I received the degree of Doctor of Letters, *Honoris Causa* from Mysore University.[22] There was a time when my vanity would have been deeply engaged. But it is the third this year. Honorary degrees have a rapidly diminishing marginal utility. And my pleasure is further weakened by reflection on how respectable I have become and how unnecessarily ahead of Schlesinger I am.[23]

My speech, on foreign policy, was leaden. The students chattered agreeably throughout and paid it not the slightest attention. They were a vast conclave, with many handsome girls, and they cheered loudly when I finished, obviously because I had finished.

We went shopping after the convocation and then had lunch. Thereafter I paid a farewell call on the Maharajah-Governor-Chancellor[24] and we drove to Bangalore, a long two-and-a-half-hour ride. We are now well on our way back to New Delhi.

En route to Bangalore, we stopped at a roadside vendor where a ten-year-old boy, wielding a wicked-looking knife, chopped the ends off drinking coconuts for us. He did it with great dexterity and seemed bitterly disappointed at the price he was paid by our

---

[19] Lawyer, civic reformer and personal friend from Cincinnati. Son of President William Howard Taft.

[20] He is a lawyer and member of the Harvard Corporation.

[21] Of Cambridge. Pioneer figure in the development of educational television and personal friend. Son of the former Secretary of the Treasury.

[22] From the citation: "Galbraith is a great man: Behind the greatness of a great man is the influence of his silent and unseen wife."

[23] My rule on honorary degrees had once been to always have one more than A.M.S., Jr.

[24] See page 236.

Indian guides. I secretly added a rupee on the side and left him all smiles. Bribery, I continue to believe, is the true foundation of friendship.

While we were drinking our coconuts, a large audience of monkeys assembled. As we discarded the shells, they moved in quickly to appropriate them.

Mysore at this time of year is warm in daytime but quite cool at night. The grass is drying up, but it is still parklike and beautiful and the city is most spacious and elegant. As before, we were housed in the spacious precincts of the Lalitha Mahal. Communications with Delhi on various matters during the evening cost $75 — an astonishing sum which seemed to be related to the priority employed. If one places an "immediate" call, the price is very high.

November 28 — New Delhi

Sunday I saw M. J. Desai and encouraged him to a more active attitude on Vietnam — especially a more active role for the I.C.C. which, however, I don't think will make much difference. I told him also that the overall result of the Prime Minister's visit to Washington was a feeling that the Indians were not very responsive on issues and places not immediately relevant to their borders. They become functional only when Pakistan or Kashmir come into the conversation. He protested but I said I was giving impressions. Sunday evening Jamie recited a poem in Hindi at a public exhibition.

Yesterday I visited the industrial fair. Our exhibit has lots of things that weld, machine, grind, retread, move, repair, print and otherwise process, and I think it quite good. The building by Yamasaki is pretty and so are the girls who act as guides. One rode with me to the maximum reach of a fork-lift truck.

Today word came of a change in the top command of State. Ball as Undersecretary for Bowles; McGhee as Undersecretary for Political Affairs; Harriman on the Far East and various lesser changes. It is all excellent and not a moment too soon. I had reached the breaking point with Alexis Johnson who had moved into the vacuum left by Bowles's decline, leaving the situation still somewhat empty. Yesterday he sent me a cable announcing a decision on a secret matter on which I had been firmly promised consultation and possibly affecting India.[25] I promptly put a block in at the White House and sent him a few homely truths. I have rarely been so angry.

✧ ✧ ✧

New Delhi, India
November 28, 1961

Dear Mr. President:

You will already have had sundry more official communications from me on South Vietnam. This is by way of giving you something of the informal flavor and color of the local scene.

It is certainly a can of snakes. I am reasonably accustomed to oriental government and politics, but I was not quite prepared for Diem. As you will doubtless be warned, whenever anyone reaches an inconvenient conclusion on this country, he has been duped. My view is derived neither from the Indians nor the Saigon intellectuals but my personal capacity for error. One of the proposals which I am told was made to Max Taylor provides an interesting clue to our man.[26] It was that a helicopter be provided to pluck him out of his palace and take him directly to the airport. This is because his surface travel through Saigon requires the taking in of all laundry along the route, the closing of all windows, an order to the populace to keep their heads in, the clearing of all streets, and a vast bevy of motorcycle outriders to protect him on his dash. Every trip to the airport requires such arrangements and it is felt that a chopper would make him seem more democratic. Incidentally, if Diem leaves town for a day, all members of his cabinet are required to see him off

[25] Some intelligence operations in the Asian vicinity which I regarded as unnecessary and dangerous — as did the President. Eventually they were abandoned.
[26] Meaning Diem.

L.B.J. and friend

L.B.J. and feet

Rusk and the wary eye

R.F.K. — thinking

LOW-COST HOUSE FOR 100 LAYING HENS
- INCREASES EGG PRODUCTION
- MAKES WORK EASIER
- REDUCES DISEASE

George McGovern — felicitating

Henry Robinson Luce —
listening (with Barry
Corthian)

Angie Dickinson —
framed

By yacht

TRAVEL

The practice of modern diplomacy requires a close understanding not only of governments but also of people. . . . Therefore, I hope that you will plan your work so that you may have the time to travel extensively outside the nation's capital.

> — The President of the United States
> to Chiefs of Mission, May 29, 1961

The hire of boat, automobile, taxicab, aircraft, livery or other such conveyance will be allowed if the use of such facilities is authorized or approved as advantageous.

> — Standardized Government Travel
> Regulations (as amended). Page 4

By man-powered marine

By elephant

By train

Through the air
Through the ground

Something Edwardian

ENVOY ENDS BHUTAN VISIT

Kingdom Builds A Village For Galbraith Trip

By PHILIP POTTER

[*New Delhi Bureau of The Sun*]

Camp Galbraith, Manas River, Bhutan, April 30—Camp Galbraith was dismantled today as Ambassador John Kenneth Galbraith completed a two day visit to Bhutan—the first ever by an American ambassador to this Himalayan kingdom of 700,000.

Commissioner J. B. Pradhan, administrative agent for the Maharaja in southern Bhutan, who looks after the welfare of five sevenths of His Majesty's subjects, had mobilized 300 men and women to build the camp, using native timber and bamboo for walls and floors and corrugated tin for roofs, the latter hauled up by small boats on the Manas, high at this season with melted Himalayan snow.

Took 14 Days

It took the Bhutanese mountain people fourteen days to build the camp in a forest clearing, its dozen buildings temporarily making it one of Bhutans largest villages.

There are no cities in this state lying between the Indian and Red Chinese frontiers, the
~ai~   ~out fro~ ~ ti~

tive tribal people who maintained the camp, catering in various ways to the needs of their guests, there was no sign of it in today's farewell.

As the boats were poled away from the bank and out into the swift-flowing Manas, Pradhan stood on a rock with tears in his eyes, waving until the current took the visitors out of sight.

There had been two nights of talk with this "wise man," as Galbraith aptly described him, while giant cicadas clustered around the lamps in the mess hall.

"Wise Man"

There had been a five-hour ride on six elephants, including a giant tusker, through the dense jungle of the Bhutan foothills, where mahouts hacked paths with their kukris; through the high elephant grass of the Terai, where the Himalayas flatten out into the Gangetic plain; and across streams where the huge pachyderms cautiously picked their way over a boulder bottom.

The party saw deer and crocodiles, but there was no shooting. Galbraith opposes "blood sports," although he ate the venison stew from a samba killed the day before his arrival by Jerry Hyde, Anglo-Indian transportation officer of the Calcutta consul general's office, a congenial and efficient logistics man in the Galbraith safari into this part of the Indian Subcontinent.

In Every State

Galbraith, here as Ambassador for only a year, has traveled over it more than any of his predecessors.

Hi~   ~ ° inch ~   ~ been

Journey's end

For the weary — rest

and welcome him back although this involves less damage to efficiency than might be supposed.

The political reality is the total stasis which arises from his greater need to protect himself from a coup than to protect the country from the Vietcong. I am quite clear that the absence of intelligence, the centralization of Army control, the incredible dual role of the provincial governors as Army generals and political administrators, the subservient incompetence of the latter, are all related to his fear of being given the heave.

The desire to prolong one's days in office has a certain consistency the world around and someday somebody should explain this to the State Department with pictures. I would love to have come up with the conclusion that our man would be reformed and made into an effective military and political force. It would have given me similar hopes for . . . [some people nearer home].

Saigon has a curious aspect. It is a rather shabby version of a French provincial city — say, Toulouse, as I remember it. Life proceeds normally and it has the most stylish women in all Asia. They are tall with long legs, high breasts and wear white silk pajamas and a white silk robe, split at the sides to the armpits to give the effect of a flat panel fore and aft. On a bicycle or scooter they look very compelling and one is reminded once again that an ambassadorship is the greatest inducement to celibacy since the chastity belt. Restaurants, nightclubs and hotels flourish as they seem always to do in cities *in extremis*. Yet one moves around with an armed guard and a group of gunmen following in a car behind. The morale of the Americans seems to be rather good although I wonder a little bit about our technical assistance program. The people assigned to the country are confined almost exclusively to Saigon since travel has become too dangerous. I can't imagine that the agriculturists, for example, are of much value under these circumstances. The Ambassador there, a decent man who is trying to obey orders, has been treated abominably by the State Department. He first heard of Max's[27] mission on the radio. He had no chance to comment on the orders resulting therefrom. I would reluctantly tell you who is responsible for this management were steps taken to overcome my natural grace and charity.

I liked both your Seattle and Los Angeles speeches. People were rather waiting for a word against wild men[28] and even here I heard quite a number of relieved comments. It is necessary, as I think I argued once before, to nail these people as dangerous and warlike and once this has been done they wither rapidly. In the past they have had it both ways. They could appeal to the heroic stance so beloved by our countrymen and at the same time say that theirs was the path to peace.

Incidentally, I would urge that the radical right be kept in perspective. I have a feeling that at any given time about three million Americans[29] can be had for any militant reaction against law, decency, the Constitution, the Supreme Court, compassion and the rule of reason. They will follow Huey Long, Bill Lemke, Gerald L. K. Smith, Father Coughlin, Fritz Kuhn, Joe McCarthy . . . depending entirely on who is leading at the moment. A particularly able demagogue or an especially serious mood of national frustration, such as that of the Korean War with its help to Joe McC., will increase the ceiling on this Christian army. Tranquility or the availability only of some road company demagogue like Gerald Smith will reduce the numbers. But this fringe is an inescapable aspect of our polity. The singular feature of liberals is their ability to become aroused over each new threat as though it were the first. Perhaps this is good for it becomes the countervailing force. In my view, however, the Birchers, being rather more improbable than most reactionary rally points of recent times, should perhaps be kept and encouraged.

[27] Maxwell Taylor. See page 243.
[28] I.e., the contemporary hawks.
[29] An estimate of mine which appears to change from time to time.

I am going to see Nehru in the next day or two and will perhaps have some comments on how he enjoyed his visit. I have told Desai that while everybody says these visits are a great success they should not be carried away. I said I thought Nehru's visit left you and Washington with the feeling that the Indians were rather irresponsible in their view of events in Southeast Asia and elsewhere. He protested strongly that this was not intended and in nowise the case. . . .

Incidentally, the visit was an enormous success from my point of view. I vastly enjoyed the visit to Newport, hearing you for the first time on foreign policy and, most of all, the highly agreeable parties in the White House. As I have written Jackie, the latter were exceptionally enjoyable after the austerity of the New Delhi society and prepare me for a winter of fruit juice receptions, curry, and intense conversations on the political prospects of Mr. Krishna Menon.

I have been dictating this in the plane coming back from Mysore where I have been getting an honorary degree. My rule on these used to be to have one more than Schlesinger. However, I am caught up in an uncontrollable flood of academic distinction.

Yours faithfully,
JOHN KENNETH GALBRAITH

THE PRESIDENT
THE WHITE HOUSE

XIV

Goa

November 30 — New Delhi

I am gradually catching up with the paper shuffling after my travel. J.B.K.'s trip is now firm and we shall soon have a schedule. It promises to be fun. The Indians are worried about a trip to Kanarak lest she be photographed in the middle of a set of highly pornographic statues.[1]

Yesterday we got the technical aid program settled for the next year or two — I have far less time for this than I wish — and I got into the future of the Peace Corps. I also spent some time plotting against the State Department on various matters.

A North Vietnam minister is coming here in a few days. The Indians thought I might see him to hear his story and tell him of our policy in South Vietnam. The Department predictably said no, noting that it might hurt Diem's feelings. Meanwhile Diem is busily attacking the United States for interfering in internal affairs of his country — this being his reaction to the reforms we have requested. I shall see how Harriman feels for the responsibility is about to be his.

At noon yesterday, we had a lunch for the Puseys and Harry

---

[1] The famous Black Pagoda on the sand near the coast, north of Puri, between Madras and Calcutta, is the greatest artistic monument of Hindu India. It rides on great carved wheels, as a heavenly chariot, and is covered with hundreds of intricately carved figures, many of them exuberantly erotic. Indeed no known or imaginable design for lovemaking is thought to have escaped the attention of the artists.

Luce, who were convening with the World Council of Churches, and the Maharajah of Mysore. Harry gave me an attractive portfolio of *Life* photos taken at various times on my journeys around India.

In the afternoon, we had the churchmen of the world who are in convention here. We invited 300, and 380 showed up, indicating that even men of God can do a little freeloading. However, they were very pleased, had all read my books and were, on the whole, most agreeable guests.

Our social life continued on into the evening — Yugoslav National Day and then a departing party for John Lund.[2] *Blitz*[3] has recently said that I am firing him because of his Dulles-ite views.[4]

December 3 — New Delhi

Yuri Gagarin, the Soviet space man, has been visiting New Delhi. One or two of the more militant NATO ambassadors proposed to me that we show the solidarity of the western alliance by boycotting the parties for him. I vetoed this nonsense and turned up at the Russian Embassy reception. One should be grand about these things. The Soviets were prepared for my arrival with a battery of photographers. No caviar.

All this was last Thursday. Yesterday — Saturday — I took the Navy plane and Harry Luce to Jaipur.[5] It was good fun — a press conference, lunch with the Vice-Chancellor of the University, a visit to the City Palace and then to Amber. The City Palace is a gay building of pink stone which covers an enormous area. It is now mostly a museum and has a wonderful collection of Rajput

[2] Acting head of the United States Information Service.
[3] The remarkably erratic but generally anti-American weekly tabloid published in Bombay. President Kennedy and I were generally exempted from its onslaughts.
[4] The statement was not true; Lund had completed his normal tour of duty. However, it is true that I was seeking stronger leadership more sympathetic to my views.
[5] Jaipur, about 150 miles southwest of Delhi, is one of the most interesting cities in India. The present capital of Rajasthan, it was the capital of one of the greatest of the Princely States. Its rulers, Hindu Rajputs, were the sword arm of the Moghuls and, thereafter, strong supporters of British rule.

miniature paintings, costumes and weapons. The great court looking on the gardens with the walled and fortified hills beyond is
very grand.

Amber palace,[6] which we approached by elephant, is five or ten
miles from Jaipur in a region of low, barren hills which are en-
crusted with fortifications. Small editions of the Great Wall march
uphill and down and back of them lie varied fortresses. Amber itself on a low hill overlooking the plain is a warren of courts
and chambers with some exquisite low relief marble carving. The
most amusing part is the elephant ride up to the palace. Three great
beasts convey you there at a stately rolling pace something like
that of a large sailing yacht in a low wind. The elephants are elegantly painted and take obvious pride in their work.

In the evening, we all had a gay dinner at the hotel at which I
consumed some highly indigestible material and, as a result, suffered the tortures of the damned all night. This morning I was,
literally, too weak to move. The rest of the party started on to
Udaipur without me, only to find that the airplane had sprung a
gas tank leak. So Kitty and Harry Luce went back to Delhi by
car. Later in the day, when the airplane had been repaired and
time had worked similar improvement on me, we flew back. They
have rigged a bunk in the Navy plane and I made the trip in comfort.[7]

December 5 — New Delhi

I dictated a speech yesterday morning — they are much worse
that way but time imposes its limitations — and then tried to cope
with a variety of frustrating problems in the office. Because of the

[6] The Amber palace was started by Raja Mun Singh in 1600. In 1728, his
descendant, Maharajah Jai Singh II, left this palace in the hills to create the present
city of Jaipur. This, with its wide streets and consistent rectangular design, is often
described as the first modern city in the world. It remains a center of jewelry and
metal crafts of a high order.

[7] Although, in one way or another, the effects lasted for some months. It
developed, evidently, into some form of hepatitis. I have (though it will be difficult to believe) deleted numerous references to my disability. Sinus attacks, later
mentioned, seemed to have been intensified by this disorder.

new regime in the State Department, or perhaps because of normal habits, they have ceased entirely to answer my cables. I would especially like to know about the new steel plant on which I cannot keep the Indians waiting much longer. I am sending Wood back to find out what is going on.

The afternoon and evening were a dreary waste. At 2:30 P.M., I went out to Palam and waited an hour for the arrival of President Frondizi of Argentina, who was a half-hour late. I had previously skipped these airport welcoming ceremonies but this time concluded I should show solidarity with the American system.

At 3:30 P.M., Frondizi arrived in an Argentine Airlines Comet with an appreciable percentage of the Argentine population. (Someone explained that this was necessary. He could not safely be absent unless he took with him all conceivable rivals.) There followed shooting of guns, presenting of arms, a short speech by the Vice-President and a long speech by Frondizi. The Argentine national anthem was rendered. It takes slightly more time than a symphony.

In the evening, there was a large state banquet at the Rashtrapati Bhavan that was worse. Frondizi made an interminable speech in Spanish, but in the middle allowed the interpreter to go on in English without the benefit of the original rendition. It favored peace, self-determination, noninterference, improved terms of trade and better breeds of livestock. Both the Prime Minister and the Defence Minister went sound to sleep.

Afterward, there was a cultural program. I checked out and was caught in a jam of others trying to do the same. A very arid day.

December 6 — New Delhi

Yesterday I sent a long telegram on the Portuguese colonies. It drew attention to the contrasting stance of Kennedy on Angola and Roosevelt on India and recommended the Roosevelt example. It will infuriate Rusk, which was part of the purpose, I fear. He is so firmly fixed in my mind as a cautious, self-constricted man that I delight in actions that will disturb him. Doubtless I do him an injustice.

Yesterday was a long and busy day. In the morning, I worked on a speech for Rajasthan University. Then I met some Indian journalists, lunched with Tyler Wood and went through a long afternoon of conferences on matters from Bokaro to Mrs. Kennedy's visit. Everyone in India wants to see her which promises to be a trifle difficult to arrange.

December 7 — New Delhi

Yesterday was another disagreeable day. In the morning, we had a reception at the American exhibit at the Industrial Fair. Then at noon I got word that Washington had overridden my resistance on a (secret) matter which I thought peculiarly foolish.[8] At lunch I fear I was rather abstracted as I contemplated my further reaction. I do not now expect to win, but I must make it clear that they can't disagree with impunity. In the end, I wrote the President and briefed Ty Wood to conduct a final campaign. In fact, I might win.[9]

In the afternoon, I called on the Japanese Ambassador, a quiet, pleasant man, conversationally a little like the Buddha. And then in the evening there was a banquet by Frondizi. The food for this was at least a little better and with wine. But the anthem was as long as ever.

Afterward I had a long talk about South Vietnam with M. J. Desai.

December 8 — New Delhi

The Indians are fabricating great excitement over Goa.[10] Coincidentally, early this week I got off a long, elegantly constructed

[8] See page 266.
[9] Eventually, as earlier noted, I did.
[10] Goa, which occupied some 65 miles of the west, or Malabar, coast of India to the south of Bombay, constituted, along with the two small enclaves of Damao and Diu, the Portuguese Africa in India. There was no obvious reason, its greater

telegram urging our final detachment from Portugal, or at least from its possessions. My technique was to imply that none of the really touchy points could be taken seriously by any sensible man. Only those inexperienced in association with paper strongmen and dictators would be uncontrollably anxious to support Salazar. I imagine one effect will be to immobilize Washington, at least temporarily, on any moves *toward* Portugal.

The Indians' cause, which has my sympathy, also includes a high component of contrivance. The casual reader could conclude from the papers that Portugal is about to take over the entire Indian Union. Aggression is charged although it amounts to little more than the firing of a rifle in the air — and it is not clear by whom.

At noon yesterday, we entertained Joey Adams, the comedian, and his troupe for lunch and last evening saw them at the Fair. They were rather good although vaudeville is not to my taste. Even in its day I always found it boring.

In the evening, we dined at the Indonesian Embassy. It was very nice and civilized with good food and surprisingly searching talk.

December 11 — New Delhi

This was a rather unquiet weekend. I went to Jaipur on Friday for the second time in a fortnight, this time to give a convocation speech. The latter was held under a huge marquee where several thousand got their degrees. It was an attentive and responsive audience. I talked in nonpolitical fashion on education and economic development. Too many political pitches dissipate one's influence. The Raj Bhavan, where we stayed, is covered at this time of year by multicolored bougainvillea, and with lawns and

---

antiquity (from 1510) apart, why it should not have become part of the Indian union, along with British and French India and the partially independent Princely States at the time of Independence. The failure of the Portuguese to yield was a major annoyance to the Indians as was the use of Goa as a center for smuggling on a considerable scale including the whiskey that was banned by the formidable dry laws of the adjacent state of Maharashtra. Though extensively converted to Christianity, the Goanese are not ethnically distinct from the other people of India.

rose gardens is most agreeable. Unfortunately, it is also a little cold at night and a crack in the toilet seat had a ferocious bite. I comforted my companions by noting that this was where the Queen was housed and she had made no public complaints.

While there, I extracted J.B.K. from the Maharajah. He was naturally anxious to have her as an exclusive visitor — not only for the normal reasons but possibly also because the Maharani is running for office on the Swatantra (Goldwater) ticket.[11] Mrs. Kennedy had cooperated admirably; political comprehension is automatic in this family.

Meanwhile in Delhi the Indians have been continuing to create a dust-up over Goa. Every morning there are incidents, all more or less imaginary. However, the impression is rapidly getting around that the Portuguese are about to march on Bombay.

Early last week, as I have mentioned, I sent an elaborately argued cable proposing that we drop Portugal, so far as her colonies are concerned. This has produced a wonderful blast from our Lisbon Embassy which asks that we stand four-square by our Portuguese ally. I have written a brief but infuriating response. They say that Nehru is dusting up the trouble to get elected. I noted that this is not so. However, I urged that the error of our man in Lisbon be excused since life there allows of no experience on elections.

In my view, the Indians will decide in the end against the use of force. I have taken the position, no instructions having come, that we oppose force. But equally we must show that we are opposed to colonialism. This our recent U.N. stand makes clear. And I have dismissed as nonsense the notion that Goa is not a colony.[12]

[11] The present Maharajah, Sir Sawai Man Singh Bahadur, became ruler in 1922 at the age of eleven. A notable sportsman, in particular a polo player, he is (at this writing) Indian Ambassador to Spain. His third wife, Aisha Raje, of the princely house of Cooch Behar, is regarded by the discriminating as one of the most beautiful women in the world, a judgment I endorse. In the ensuing election, she won a seat in the Indian parliament. Mrs. Kennedy's visit to the Jaipur palace (see page 327) was later to cause me some concern related mostly to my deficient perspective on such matters.

[12] In 1955, in a uniquely regressive gesture, Dulles had agreed with the Portuguese Foreign Minister, Cunha, in calling Goa a province, that is to say an in-

December 12 — New Delhi–Karachi

I saw Nehru yesterday afternoon and, after detaching myself from support for the Portuguese, pleaded they not use force. The threshold against marching armies must be kept high. India has a large stake in settlement without violence. I doubt that I made much impression.

I talked with Nehru at Parliament and we went on for an hour-and-a-half on the Congo, South Vietnam, Mrs. Kennedy's visit and many other matters.

Late in the evening came reports that Indian plans on Goa are becoming very serious. We had a series of meetings of the staff and, during the night, I determined to send Nehru another letter urging restraint. This I did this morning.

I quoted an anti-Portugal editorial from the *New York Times* saying the latter's colonies would soon go anyway. Then I renewed my case against force. It was a fairly eloquent letter but I doubt that it will shift the balance much. I still hope that there may be second thoughts.

December 14 — Karachi–New Delhi

The sun is just coming up and we are already an hour out of Karachi on the way back to Delhi.

Night before last, we arrived late afternoon and I had a long talk with Rountree.[13] He is hard-working, intelligent and conservative. He divides the world in excessively simple fashion between the aligned and the nonaligned (when in fact there are only the self-concerned) but he has brains and is not stuffy. The Karachi living standard is well above Delhi. They have a fine, large house with tennis court and a new and extremely efficient-looking Chancery. Karachi, once the ugliest of cities, is enormously improved. The

tegral part, of Portugal. This endorsed a latter-day constitutional amendment adapted by the Portuguese in 1951, which so described the overseas territories and thus made them exempt, hopefully, from anti-colonialism. Secretary Rusk enthusiastically continued, both in Spain and Portugal, what liberals in the Department, some at least, called the *Iberia über Alles* policy.

[13] See page 184.

refugee hutments seem virtually to have disappeared, the streets are clean, the pavement is improved and of the wall-to-wall type. Even the camels and camel-drivers, of which there are many, look sprucer and better. Perhaps they are in hopes of a trip to the United States.[14]

In the late evening, we went over to dine with President Ayub. He lives in Karachi in the palace of the British governors of the Sind — a gracious, comparatively modern building with large rectangular rooms, a nice garden and terrace. Ayub is a tall, self-confident man of intelligence and a good deal of charm. We had drinks on the terrace and chatted until 8:30 P.M., then went on to dinner — the components of which I again missed.

I told Ayub of my talks with the Prime Minister on Kashmir and of the discussions in Washington. I told of our hopes for a settlement, our willingness to mediate but, at the same time, our dislike for the waste of resources from having two armies face each other and draw sustenance from economies we are aiding. Since he is very anxious to get talks going again with Nehru, this was welcome news on the whole. I spoke in very grand terms of the possibilities of bypassing the territorial issue (where no one can move) by some arrangement by which the Pakistanis have access to the Valley of Kashmir, a suggestion I had previously made to Nehru. He seemed not to be averse although he was noncommittal.

He was pleased to hear that Nehru had said a settlement would help quiet communal troubles (i.e., Hindu-Moslem friction) in India. He noted that this was a point he had made. He agrees that nothing can be done until after the Indian election but he hopes for a meeting, based on a real desire for settlement, soon thereafter. I am encouraged and I think one consequence may be to keep the question out of the United Nations. Were it to go there, it would involve a hideous debate between the Indians and Pakistanis with the maximum of damage to all concerned.

---

[14] In a notably expansive gesture when visiting Pakistan earlier that year, Vice-President Johnson got out of his car to greet a camel-driver by the roadside and invited him to visit the United States. The driver naturally accepted.

Yesterday I slept until nearly ten, a welcome luxury, and then we met on various matters, none of much moment, until noon. Then I received a succession of reports on the worsening of the situation in Goa and finally a message from the President asking me at my discretion to express his concern and to state his specific approval of my letter to Nehru. After some reflection, I got off a message for Timmons to take to the Prime Minister —later discovering that, by the fastest routing, it would require around six hours to get it from Karachi to New Delhi as also vice versa. However, if the Indians are marching this morning, it will be too late in any case. If they aren't, a few added hours won't make so much difference.

I had lunch with G. Ahmed,[15] a friend and deputy chairman of the Planning Commission, and after more afternoon meetings on military matters, the Rountrees had a big dinner. Recurrently during the day I contemplated going back and finally ordered a plane for early this morning.

Last night Rountree told me he has trouble with black-marketing of rupees. They can be bought abroad at a low price and smuggled in and their purchasing power is high in Pakistan. I must see what is going on in India. He also asked me if I had heard what might be happening to him. I told him that I had heard that he was to be replaced by Eric Johnston[16] but had some personal doubts that Eric would be given the job. In the event of such a change, I said, I assumed he would be in line for another mission. None of this was pleasant, but I have learned not to lie — eventually he would probably learn I knew. There is another point. Some knowledge, even troubling information, is probably better, and more in keeping with one's dignity, than uncertainty.

[15] Later Pakistani Ambassador to Washington.
[16] Diversely active figure, former head of the United States Chamber of Commerce and then head of the Motion Picture Association. The Johnston appointment did not materialize. Rountree went on to serve as Ambassador in the Sudan and South Africa.

December 15 — New Delhi

I got to Safdarjung airport at eleven yesterday morning, only a step or two away from the house, and was handed several pounds of telegrams. I went to see the British who are much divided. Portugal is an old ally; India is a member of the Commonwealth. They have to be nice to both. They are really taking no positions and hence getting the worst of it from both sides. I am persuaded of the virtues of a clear position — against force, not for colonies.

I saw M. J. Desai and thought I made some progress with him. He told me to be sure to see the Prime Minister tomorrow which means we have another day. Since I must have something to say to him, I telegraphed several suggestions to Washington: e.g., tell the Portuguese to save what they can by negotiating — the Indians would give quite a bit; wait and put the matter up to Macmillan and Kennedy in Bermuda next week; possibly suggest a nonviolent takeover, the Indians proclaiming sovereignty and then asking all friendly vessels to respect Indian customs and immigration but no military action.

In the evening, I had a talk with Nehru at a reception and he seemed very upset and disturbed. I pressed him again and told him of my pressure on Washington. I believe he has decided, probably for Saturday, December 16, but much dislikes the decision. The Department will have to give me something fairly good to stop it.

December 17 — New Delhi

Friday morning, December 15, I had another talk with Nehru. (There is some disadvantage in doing business at receptions. It has been generally noticed that last night he gave equal time to Krishna Menon and to me.) He was much more relaxed, listened appreciatively to my arguments and we parted in friendly fashion. I strongly stressed the point that India, having rid herself by peaceful means of the British and the French, would be showing real weakness if ever she had to use force to be rid of the Portuguese pimple. I came away with the feeling that the operation might be put off and also that my arguments had something to do with it. I had the meeting with none of the cards I had asked. Overnight the Department had specifically told me that it will do nothing. Still, I did reasonably well without.

December 18 — New Delhi

The record of any important event must be a good deal more incomplete than that of a minor one for no person will have time to tell of it. I have fallen far behind in my accounts of the Goa business.

Last Friday was the last of the three days in which, according to rumor and better information, the operation was to be ordered. Having got by that, I felt fairly optimistic. Friday afternoon the Soviet President, L. I. Brezhnev, arrived, and I went to another stereotyped reception at the airport. In the evening, there was another vast state dinner at the Rashtrapati Bhavan. Kitty suggested that we try the vegetarian food for a change, the other being not good. Accordingly, we mentioned this preference in our response, and a flower was put in front of our plates to proclaim this. For a change, the meat looked rather good.

Brezhnev compared me in physical stature to Peter the Great. I protested comparison with a feudal figure. He said I should not worry, Peter was a progressive. I said I was conscious of that but anxious to avoid anything that smacked of right deviationism. He said I was in no danger. The Indians were highly amused. It was the only amusing aspect of the evening.

We managed to slip away before the cultural show. As usual, many others had the same idea.

Late Friday the Portuguese went to Stevenson in grave alarm to say an attack was imminent. The latter got U Thant who drafted a letter to Indians and Portuguese calling for talks within the framework of the U.N. Charter and Resolutions. Since the latter are anticolonial, the Portuguese protested violently. So the letter was dispatched by Thant with the proviso that the Portuguese did not accept the anticolonial provisions of the Resolutions. When it got here, the Indians exploded at the reservation.

I went over to see M. J. Desai but they had already answered. The answer was long, argumentative but negative. I tried very hard to get Desai to reconsider, pointing out that the Portuguese were inherently at a disadvantage if they had to seek the support of the U.N. while excluding it on the matter of anti-colonialism. All this talk took place last Saturday; transmission delay and the difference in time accounting for the time in reaching me. Desai was extremely tired and finally promised to mention the matter to the Prime Minister. I repeated my old arguments once more about using force adding, of course, a few new ones, but Desai finally and wearily told me that matters had passed to the political level.

I had planned to issue a public statement clarifying our whole position and noting that we had argued that the Portuguese Empire would soon fall and that this could be hastened in the U.N. rather than by violence. (The language was more agreeable than this but such was the gist.) I had wired my position to Washington, and without, as usual, getting any response. (I then took this to mean approval although in fact it means indecision.) When you have a good position, it is well that it be known; and I thought it might help the Indian moderates who would be arguing for a nonviolent alternative. I told Desai that I couldn't issue this statement if they were about to move. He gave me the impression that I could do so but it had best be soon.

There was one other discouraging development during the day. A telegram came in reporting a conversation between Rusk and Nogueiria,[17] the Portuguese Foreign Minister, at a NATO meeting. It was an appalling conversation. Rusk had sat passively while Nogueiria had made the most preposterous proposals — one was that a couple of Pakistan divisions be moved to the border to frighten the Indians. Here Rusk did reply; he said mildly that they

[17] Dr. Franco Nogueiria.

weren't available. They also discussed ways and means of bypassing the U.N. with its inconvenient anticolonial attitudes and how
more pressure might be brought on the Indians to desist. Foy
Kohler[18] told the Portuguese that he regarded it as an election
stunt[19] and designed to divert attention from the Chinese Communist penetration in Ladakh. Although Elbrick,[20] our Ambassador
in Lisbon, had earlier been told to persuade the Portuguese to be
slightly reasonable, Rusk uttered not a single word of reproach.
No question of anticolonial principle obtruded. I had not expected
any great support with the Portuguese. I hardly imagined that I
could be undercut in such a flaccid and incompetent manner by our
own management. Had I not been earlier assured of the support of
the President in such a strong fashion, I should have had no idea of
where I stood. I sent off a comparatively restrained commentary
in which I directed my anger more specifically at the Portuguese
than at the Secretary; however, I did not allow the latter entirely
to escape. I have in mind providing him with some whole truths in
a personal letter.

Yesterday, which was Sunday, I wrote and polished up my public
statement of our position on Goa and we had a meeting at noon
to go over the general situation. Indications of impending action
were beginning to accumulate. The Ministry of External Affairs
was holding a briefing that afternoon. Perhaps as significant as anything, Lieutenant General B. M. Kaul,[21] who was giving me a dinner
the next night, left town for the south without canceling the dinner. This must have presented him with an interesting problem.
Had he canceled the dinner, it would have given away the show.
But to leave town as he did with no possibility of returning in time

[18] See page 204.
[19] Nehru was in no need of such action to win the election. He would have
been startled by the suggestion. Prior to the takeover of Goa, there had been
much discussion in India of Chinese incursions in the disputed area of Ladakh on
the extreme northern frontier. Goa did divert attention from this area.
[20] Charles Burke Elbrick. Later Ambassador to Yugoslavia.
[21] Chief of the General Staff of the Army. He was second ranking officer of
the Army in Delhi at the time.

and without canceling dinner was equally suspicious. The conclusion is that generals who are planning military operations should never give dinners.

We went to a rose show in the afternoon to which the Prime Minister came somewhat late. Then later in the afternoon the Department provided me with a card which, had it come two or three days before, perhaps would have saved the situation. It was a telegram saying that George Ball and George McGhee had called in B. K. Nehru, urged the disastrous effect on American public opinion, damage to Nehru's reputation and chain reaction of violence which would result from the Indian action. Then they proposed that Prime Minister Nehru announce a six-months' suspension. They would then promise to make a major effort with the Portuguese. The nature of the latter effort was unspecific and badly hedged but it did mean in effect that we would do something to bring the Portuguese around. They promised to try to get the British involved in the business — a rather distant hope.

I took the telegram and sought an appointment with the Prime Minister, whom I finally reached at his house at eight o'clock. In the summertime, the house is hot with the exception of an air-conditioned room or two. In the winter, it is rather clammy. The rugs and furniture are rich and agreeable but slightly tarnished.

The Prime Minister wanted to postpone the conversation; he brought up the proposal of a magazine publisher for a Sunday supplement in various Asian papers and then we talked briefly about the economic conditions in Hong Kong. However, I soon got the conversation around rather urgently to the Ball-McGhee proposal. He had already heard about it from B. K. Nehru, but he listened attentively and asked me a few questions. The six months stuck immediately in his throat. I retreated from that to a plea only for sufficient time to put the arm fully on the Portuguese. But, in the course of the discussion, it became plain to me that the zero hour had passed. He cited more newsprint atrocities by the Portuguese that morning though when I pressed, he conceded that no one had been shot. He said disorder was imminent and thousands of Indian volunteers were waiting to march on Goa. I suggested waiting until the fact of the march; however, in the end, it became fully evident that it was no use. I asked if I should cable his rejection and then withdrew the question to make the Indian reaction seem less absolute. I asked him if he changed his mind to call me. I came home and cabled the Department that the operation would begin at dawn. Actually by the time I got the cable out, it was probably under way.

If I had had this proposal of the Department two or three days earlier and some indication of the Portuguese movement, I am sure I could have saved the situation.[22] However, it is remarkable how little people want to be saved. With the loss of Goa, the Portuguese Empire will dissolve increasingly in violence, and the Indians have badly tarnished their reputation. Had Rusk shown any backbone, the Portuguese would have been told the consequences of their action and urged to accept the inevitable here against the chance that it might be postponed elsewhere. This, of course, the Indians would have bought.

December 20 — New Delhi

On Monday shortly after I talked with the Prime Minister, they jumped off. The Indian army moved into Goa. We had a meeting in the morning to go over the situation which was principally distinguished by the total lack of information on the part of everyone as to what was going on. The Army, Navy and Air Attachés had all requested briefings by the Indian defense establishments, and all their requests had been declined. I asked for military estimates as to how long it would take, and the answers generally were two to three days with the prospect of some fairly stiff fighting. I then gave as my nonprofessional estimate one day and no casualties to speak of. Indians, Germans, Americans and Russians can be or-

[22] In retrospect, I am much less sure. This was a moment for *non mea culpa.*

ganized and trained to accept death. But one can assume that the Portuguese and native Goanese will be more resistant. And likewise the Angolans, who are reported to be present. (In fact, there were none.)

I also got off to Washington a strong telegram urging them to keep their reaction as temperate as possible but above all to make clear that against the Indian use of force was the Portuguese persistence in colonialism. In other words, Washington should follow the line that has so far produced the best results here and which is one on which we can stand. The British went over to the Ministry of External Affairs to file a protest. I kept away even to the point of calling off a planned meeting on Mrs. Kennedy's trip.

Yesterday the thing was in fact wound up. Late Monday evening, we had word that the Indians had occupied all of Goa except the city and had suffered no casualties except in the course of some mishap on Anjidiv Island. Dispatches from Lisbon told of heavy fighting and All-India Radio occasionally spoke of the troops being locked in combat which, however, turned out to be unmortal. We had another briefing by Colonel Curtis[23] which showed where everybody had moved with great sweeping arrows. There would have been the same military significance to a map plotting the movement of the governor through the Iowa State Fair.

There was a meeting of the Security Council in New York, and Adlai Stevenson made a very stern and, I think, unfortunately emotional speech. He talked about the death of the U.N. and used the occasion to spill some of his anger at Krishna Menon. He made no mention of Portuguese colonialism. The question of why this handful of white people emanating from a small European despotism should rule several million Asians and Africans does not seem to impress anyone in the government. There was bound to be criticism of anybody who made this speech, but Stevenson let himself in for it worse than need be.

[23] Colonel Clifford A. Curtis, U.S. Army Attaché of the Embassy, an excellent and highly sensible officer, as I was later to learn.

I also got a long telegram from Rusk expressing appreciation for my efforts and asking for counsel on the next steps. I have an unhappy feeling it also reflected a bad conscience over his flabby handling of Nogueiria.[24] Lane Timmons, in the manner of a good deputy, finally persuaded me not to send the answer that I first drafted — which told generally of the situation here, forecast Stevenson's bad press, urged more stress in Washington on the colonial issue, advised pressing B. K. Nehru on the problem of American public opinion, and then went into the faults of the Department. It pointed out the incompetence of various members and urged discharge; I also indicated my discontent with the Secretary's handling of the Portuguese. In the end, my complaints on the Department were toned down and put in a letter and the rest was sent in a telegram. It was a good thing that the telegram was not terribly urgent. The weariness and strain of the whole business had begun to tell, and last night, since life goes on, we had a dinner for José Ferrer, who is here to make a film. In consequence, this morning I found the draft of the message still on my desk still unsent. I had completely forgotten to give it to my secretary. Needless to say, had a member of my staff been so negligent, I would have contemplated sending him or her home on a jute boat.

The party last night was actually rather amusing — very different from the usual New Delhi assemblage. It was pleasant to see Hollywood people again with their good clothes, obvious posturing and whatever it is that gives charm to theater people. I had an engrossing conversation with a gorgeous person who is playing the part of a Punjabi harlot in the film.[25] At first, I thought she lacked intellectual depth. But then I wondered why it was needed.

Today exhaustion overtook me and I had to come home. The American reporters came back from Goa very much annoyed by Indian propaganda. They have all filed stories which are going to be taken very much amiss locally. They verified that there had

[24] See page 282.
[25] *Nine Hours to Rama* about the assassination of Gandhi.

been no fighting and very little shooting. Evidently some bridges and culverts had been demolished. There seems to have been a considerable gunnery duel between a Portuguese sloop called the *Albuquerque* and an Indian cruiser. It continued for several hours, but the aim was so bad that neither of the principals seems to have got hit. A British freighter in the harbor did get a hole in its side from one of the many wild shots.

As I expected, the papers here are pretty brutal about Adlai. Several of them remind people he was a defender of armed action against Cuba. I reported this back and I am afraid that it won't be exactly music to his ears.

One of the interesting features of this whole episode was the large number of pressing messages from Washington asking me to authorize or order the evacuation of Americans from Goa. This is the first thing we think of when there is trouble. Actually, there seems to have been only one American there in addition to the correspondents. I took a chance on the theory that he would be safer in Goa than on the New Jersey Turnpike on an average day. (An evacuation order would have shown that we did not expect our arguments to prevail. And given the shortage of news, the order would have been much publicized.) I suppose if someone had got killed, I would have had to answer for it. But none did. All the reporters got back safely with the exception of Phil Potter.[26] They said that at last report he was personally leading last ditch resistance.

Another interesting thing in the newspapers today was a statement by the Ministry of External Affairs that, in deference to my arguments, they had held the operation off for several days. I think this may be so. It also suggests that the whole miserable episode might have been avoided by a little planning.

---

[26] New Delhi correspondent for the *Baltimore Sun* and a veteran of many news beats. A man of strong convictions and a ruthless aversion to cant, he not only reported the news but took full responsibility for the moral rectitude of those who made it. I regarded him as one of my most valuable friends in New Delhi. Being indestructible, he naturally returned safely a day or two later.

What was needed was a tough approach to the Indians on the matter of force and a tough approach to the Portuguese on the issue of colonial rule. There needed to be a full and coordinated understanding of the problem between here, Lisbon and Washington. In fact, Washington made no policy until the last minute; until the thing got above the level of Talbot, there was nobody capable of thinking and acting in such terms. Embassy Lisbon, of course, had no policy except to keep the Portuguese happy. There was one mild approach to them but nothing of any consequence. The Secretary did not pursue any strategy with Nogueiria. I had a plan which would have worked, but I could only put into effect as much of it as was under my control. That was not enough.

The Danish Ambassador came in to see me today and told me that it has always been the policy of Denmark to sell its colonies to the highest bidder; thus, they long ago sold some possessions in India. Also, of course, the Virgin Islands; and, if they didn't sell, they at least traded off the Hebrides.[27] As compared with the Portuguese, they saved themselves and the world a great deal of trouble.

December 21 — New Delhi

The Goa business has simmered down to defensive explanations and an attack on Stevenson. All of the papers have jumped on Stevenson as the defender of the attack on Cuba. The *Times of India* attacked his speech but went on to say that intellectually he perhaps wasn't at his best. In a cable to Stevenson, I gave a general account of matters pointing out that on the matter of not being at

---

[27] I reported badly what the Ambassador told me. The Hebrides were not under Danish rule. And when I checked the matter with him, he proffered the following reply:

"I am afraid I could not well have said that we traded off the Hebrides, the history of these Islands being unknown to me. What I said probably referred to the Shetland Islands and the Orkney Islands, which Islands were mortgaged for the dowry, when King Christian I in 1469 gave his daughter Margrete in marriage to King James III of Scotland. The mortgage was never paid off and in 1590 the Islands were finally ceded to the Scots."

his best, I would tactfully explain that he never was.[28] I made a good deal stronger point of the jam that they got themselves into by not disassociating themselves from the colonial issue.

All sorts of rumors are going around that Mrs. Kennedy's visit may be canceled. Maybe it is good that there should be some worry.

Today of all days, the Indians approached us to buy some military equipment. This was still informal but it seems to have some sanction from Krishna Menon. A representative of the Lockheed Aircraft Corporation is here looking for the business. I sent word to the company that they couldn't have picked a worse time to come and centralized the whole problem in my hands. Menon until recently was in considerable trouble over the Chinese border incursions. The Goa business had boosted his stock at the expense of alienating American public opinion and considerably damaging the capacity to get aid. If he could now pull off a purchase of arms from the United States, it would prove he can do business with everyone. Any such action would, of course, be very badly received by the Pakistanis.

I am impressed, incidentally, with the way his Department[29] wastes money. He has developed a supersonic plane which, unfortunately, does not have a motor to propel it. Also a transport aircraft which flies but is already obsolete and of no military value. These have been done at great cost and, of course, are extremely impressive to some of his countrymen. All such military equipment is in some measure a toy. Were it successful, the cost would still be a decisive objection.

I may have mentioned that Krishna Menon has gone to New York. The Security Council is no longer seized of the Goa problem

[28] This was meant to be amusing but was taken rather amiss by Stevenson. In retrospect, it doesn't seem very funny and my sympathies are with Stevenson. Harlan Cleveland, the Assistant Secretary of State for International Organization Affairs, was also greatly perturbed and later, with ponderous solemnity, so advised me. The fact that Cleveland did not think it funny led me, erroneously, to suppose for some time that it was.

[29] Department of Defence.

and the General Assembly has adjourned. Portugal wouldn't dare take it to the General Assembly anyway so I can't quite see why he has gone.

Yesterday morning at dawn, or slightly before, the Peace Corps was due to arrive. Considering the name, it gets here in the nick of time. These last few days have been quite cold in New Delhi — light overcoat weather — and yesterday morning there was a thick ground fog. The Peace Corps plane could not land and in the end went on to Calcutta. There, according to a USIS press release, they deplaned "bright-eyed and eager." They will be back here tomorrow; I am having them for lunch.

December 26 — New Delhi

There has been a certain gap in the record resulting partly from the Christmas weekend and a sinus infection. A telegram came in from Stevenson objecting to the strictures that I had laid upon his U.N. speech. He asked if I were aware of the strong stand he had taken against Portugal on Angola and Mozambique at the U.N. with, he added, the full support of the Department. I wired back that I was fully informed and that my complaints extended beyond him to a wider field of policy and action. Then I cabled Adlai, personally, the pertinent extracts from a dispatch from Lisbon telling of the warm praise there for his U.N. speeches against using force in Goa. I pointed out that the Portuguese response would scarcely have been so ecstatic if he had been as critical of their colonialism as he claimed.

Last Friday evening we dined with Prem Bhatia[30] who offered a new and interesting and somewhat elaborate interpretation of the whole affair. It was that the military services are deeply fearful of the Chinese incursion. Goa represented a serious diversion of national attention. Those who want to let China off the hook —

[30] Leading Indian newspaperman. Then Delhi editor of the *Times of India*, and later of the *Indian Express*, as well as being the correspondent for the *Manchester Guardian*. He has since become Indian Ambassador to Kenya.

including the fellow-travelers — could steam things up over Goa whenever pressure on the northern frontier became too great. Therefore, the Government had to get rid of the Goan diversion. Now India will be able to concentrate to the point of true national concern.

Saturday I had to keep to bed all day although I rallied sufficiently to read and reply to another telegram from Stevenson. This was a most curious document in which he said that he could only conclude that I hadn't read his speeches. He then went on to say that I evidently did not know that an adverse reference to colonialism in his speech to the Security Council had been taken out of his main speech by the State Department. Of course I hadn't known and I immediately wired back saying that his quarrel must be with his editor and not with me. I fail to see how he could object to my missing what had been taken out over his objection.

I also concluded Saturday that I had better take a few days off. My equanimity is less than perfect, and I shall not throw off this sinus trouble without getting away from Delhi. I wired the Department that I thought I would go to Switzerland for eight or ten days and then come on to Washington. By that time, I hope Goa will be mostly forgotten.

On Sunday, Christmas Eve, only a mass application of codeine removed the pain. It also brought the first report from the Department on reactions to Goa. This was a document of unparalleled banality; it said that those who disliked Nehru were pleased while Nehru's friends were dismayed. However, it did not have the advantage of being quite this brief. Also came a query via Bundy from the President asking whether J.B.K. should go ahead with her trip. On balance, I think she should come but were I to recommend this too unequivocally, it would not be very influential. I would be thought indifferent to American opinion in order to have an interesting visitor. However, were she to cut out the visit entirely, this would be taken as a terrible slap. After some reflective discussion with Timmons, I recommended that she come but, if possible, a little later and perhaps for a shorter trip. (She might have to cut out the visit because of the illness of her father-in-law, Joseph P. Kennedy, who has just suffered a severe stroke.) I took the occasion to outline in some slight detail my reaction to events here and the way I believe we should proceed. We should try to make the Indians rather more aware of American public opinion and of the problems which the U.S. political leadership faces on such issues as aid where their own interests are much involved. On the other hand, India is the strongest of the non-Communist countries in this part of the world and we cannot avoid doing business with her. It would be easy but not wise to react in anger.

Christmas in New Delhi is about the temperature of late October in New England. It is fairly sharp at night and the wood and cow dung fires lay a thick smog pall over the city. This is mixed with Kipling's clammy fog in the morning.[31] However, toward mid-morning the sun comes out and it is quite pleasant. The flowers at this season are exceedingly brilliant, especially the roses.

For the festivity, our children slept up at the Residence, and Kitty had shown considerable ingenuity in finding them presents. I found her a rather nice emerald and ruby necklace — very Christmaslike colors. After we opened gifts and stockings, the staff came in from the Compound to the number of twenty or thirty to garland us and, more than incidentally, to receive their Christmas tips. The latter neither compensated nor tax-deductible — I am not quite sure of the latter — came to some $300 without making any single individual very rich. The Timmonses came for Christmas dinner along with the Dexter Perkinses,[32] and we had a huge roast beef which my wife had foresightedly brought over from Karachi.[33] Not much business came in and I can't see that the world

---

[31] "O the white dust on the highway! O the stenches in the byway!
O the clammy fog that hovers over earth!"
From "Christmas in India," by Rudyard Kipling.

[32] He is Professor of History, Emeritus, University of Rochester, and was Professor at the School of International Studies in New Delhi in 1961.

[33] Beef, derived as it is from a sacred animal, is difficult to buy in India. Since Pakistan is Moslem country, there is no problem.

was any the worse for it. My sinus was much better although I was still a bit wobbly from the antibiotics. One thing I can say for my disorders; they took me completely out of the vast circuit of Christmas parties to which I would have been committed. Kitty covered them nobly.

Bright and early this morning Jamie, our youngest, popped out with a highly decorative case of chicken pox. This took him out of the tiger hunt which had been planned originally for everyone and was eventually reduced to Kitty and the two boys. Kitty, Peter and Jiwan Singh, our driver, departed midmorning and I got down to clearing up the debris of the weeks preceding.

I had a meeting of the senior staff to lay down the line to be followed in the days ahead. This followed the general tenor of my message to the President. Nothing vindictive. The historical perspective is rather different from the immediate view. I also got off a telegram to the Department along the lines of my letter to the President noting that, subject to instructions and suggestions, this would be the policy of the Mission. The chances of such instructions or suggestions are, of course, nil.

During the day, I also got a rather sharp letter from McGeorge Bundy complaining that I have been insufficiently pleasant to some of the more pompous people in Washington. He says that both Rusk and Alexis Johnson have come to suspect that I do not have a very high regard for them. This does credit to their perception. He pleads with me to moderate my mood and not use "Acheson's[34] techniques on an anti-Acheson position." I replied, drawing attention to some of the shortcomings of the Department but conceding his point. I did note that there was one difference; namely, that Acheson was wrong. However, it is plain that in the last two or three weeks I have unduly aroused the pigeons.

[34] Dean Acheson, Secretary of State 1949–53.

December 27 — New Delhi

This morning at long last I finally got some extra sleep and on awakening, read the proof on the several lectures I have given on economic development. These are being published by the USIS.[35] I had lunch with my stricken son and spent much of the afternoon giving the general line on Public Law 480 food to the senior Mission members. This has become a very important part of our aid program. We provide it almost completely in secret. Surpluses were once greater than they are now and so it was possible to imagine that countries were doing us a favor by taking the stuff off our hands. Now only wheat and corn are in surplus. Soon we shall face the question of whether we grow cotton, soybeans, rice and some other products for free distribution abroad. Such assistance can be just as important for the development of a country such as India as foreign exchange. It is as good a form of saving as any. Views on this whole matter must be much clearer.

[35] And later by Harvard University Press as *Economic Development in Perspective* (1962). It was a non-book of the kind which I have urged all and sundry to avoid. A revision, *Economic Development* (1964), is marginally better.

XV

In Sickness and Poor Health

January 20, 1962 — New York–London

During the last three weeks, there have been no entries. There is little point, I discovered, in keeping a diary if, as I frequently hoped, you are not going to survive to see it published. I was also depressed, I thought, by the resort to violence in Goa; in fact, it was my liver. I first tried physical rehabilitation in Switzerland.

I stayed with the McKinneys in Gstaad — he is an amiable, intelligent, highly hospitable Democrat from Santa Fe whom (I believe) Lyndon Johnson got rewarded (*vice* Earl Smith[1]) with the post of Ambassador to Switzerland. They have a nice chalet,[2] and were pleasant hosts and are not overworked. The snow left something to be desired, but I managed to ski incompetently for a couple of days. Otherwise I walked with Bob McKinney, slept a lot and read some not very interesting books. In the meantime, I was pursued by the poisonous post-Goan issues including the determination of the Pakistanis to haul India into the Security Council on the Kashmir issue. Timmons handled matters very sensibly, but the thing weighed rather heavily on my mind — more heavily than for good reason.

Still, it was not unpleasant. Gstaad was full of our friends, idle and otherwise, of old. McKinney thinks they are a justification for

[1] See page 33.
[2] Belonging to Yehudi Menuhin. I have spent a great deal of time in Gstaad over the years and wrote much of *The Affluent Society* and *The New Industrial State* and all of *The Triumph* there.

revolution. It would be hard to say they are useful, but there was much good partying damaged only a little by my alcohol-free diet. Once or twice we walked to Saanen to eat blue trout, better there than anywhere in the world, and once to Gsteig for a vast dinner of fondue. I thought at the end of a week that I was much better, although still unaccountably depressed. I stopped over a night with Graham Martin[3] in Geneva, a competent member of the Foreign Service who is inadequately employed in Geneva, and came on to the United States. The plane had to refuel en route at Goose Bay which was caught in the full bind of Arctic winter — it was so cold we were not allowed off the plane — and then, happily, the flight terminated in Boston. Alan came to dinner. I saw Edward Mason[4] and, in a state of mental and physical disrepair, said I doubted that I would remain indefinitely in New Delhi — perhaps only until September. Then on Sunday I went on to Washington.

In the end, Dr. Travell[5] dispatched me out to the Naval Medical Center in Bethesda — a great skyscraper of a place and marvelously managed by a mixture of admirals, doctors, nurses and corpsmen. There is nothing like the armed services for a plethora of manpower and nothing like manpower for comfort. I was put to bed.

Eventually they came up with an infected sinus, a bad liver and some suggestion of amoebic dysentery. I had had the more obvious symptoms in Switzerland. There is evidently some connection between the liver and the brain — when one is jaundiced, so is the other.

The first morning I was there, Raymond Swing[6] called me to say that Carl Rowan[7] who is, of course, a Negro had been rejected for

[3] Head of the Mission to the U.N. Agencies in Geneva; later, for a long tour, Ambassador to Thailand. There he was, perhaps inevitably, a strong supporter of our military role in Southeast Asia.

[4] See page 143.

[5] Dr. Janet Graeme Travell, President Kennedy's physician, 1961–63.

[6] Early and famous radio commentator. Then political commentator on the Voice of America.

[7] Prize-winning journalist and then Deputy Assistant Secretary of State for Public Affairs. Subsequently Ambassador to Finland, head of the U.S. Information Agency and now again a newspaperman and columnist.

membership in the Cosmos Club. This provided me with an interesting problem for I was currently (with James B. Conant[8]) the sponsor of the President for membership. His application was pending. I called Salinger[9] and told him I thought I should resign to get the President off the hook. He agreed but advised that I not do it for that reason — just resign and let the President's role be passive.

He announced my decision at the White House press briefing and for the rest of the day, I was bombarded with phone calls. To make matters more inconvenient, I had no phone in my room although presently one was rigged by the Navy. I kept my explanations short and stressed that, of course, the President was an innocent bystander. I added that all ex-clubmen — Robert Kennedy (exiled from the Metropolitan), Ed Murrow, Harlan Cleveland, Arthur Schlesinger[10] — could now be found hanging out around Sholl's Cafeteria, an excellent watering place. The whole incident was front-page news the next day. Rowan behaved with great dignity. The press uniformly praised his qualifications and identified the action with his race. This is probably correct but, inevitably, there are some who are not race-conscious but who are not overly fond of Carl.[11] Not everyone can command universal love — especially in the newspaper business.

CBS asked to come out and film me in my bed. I declined.

I got out a week ago last Thursday, went back for a checkup Friday and had to return Sunday in serious pain to have my sinus opened up. By Tuesday of this week, I got a final discharge. Meanwhile, efforts had been proceeding to prevent the Pakistanis from having a dust-up in the Security Council over Kashmir. On my

[8] Former President of Harvard and Ambassador to the Federal Republic of Germany.
[9] See page 26.
[10] All having declined membership or resigned on the issue of segregation of Washington clubs.
[11] The issue was especially embarrassing for the Cosmos Club which stresses the scientific, intellectual and public dignity of its members. In the end, it opened its doors to Negroes. I (and I believe others) then reapplied for membership. (I had belonged for some twenty years.) But this was going too far. It decided to remain segregated as regards those who resigned over the issue.

liberty on Thursday, I went to the White House meeting where it was decided to send letters to Ayub and Nehru inviting them to forgo action in the U.N. and, instead, ask Eugene Black[12] to come out and use his good offices. There was also talk of a proposal to get aid into Afghanistan by way of Iran to avoid giving the Afghans the embarrassment of having it go through Pakistan. The added cost was fantastic. I urged that it was silly to pay large sums to bypass an ally, Pakistan, to which we were giving large sums of money as part of the strategy of defending that same ally. Were the Soviets to become threatening in Afghanistan, then Pakistan, perceiving the further threat to herself, might be more agreeable. The President agreed, but the State Department persisted, and so the President was overruled (though the Department later relented).

The next day, Talbot held a series of meetings on Afghanistan and finally, at six o'clock, convoked a vast Estates-General to consider the letters to Ayub and Nehru. Overnight they had produced a long, argumentative and rather silly letter to Ayub which did not mention the proposal to send Black and produced no letter to Nehru at all. However, I had drafted a letter to Ayub and Nehru, and on Saturday George Ball offered it as his own. Then he got in touch with Eugene Black in Europe and persuaded him to accept.

As of this writing, the Pakistanis have responded saying they will accept Black but demanding the Security Council session too. The Indians haven't been heard from but obviously aren't happy. They may accept if the Pakistanis forgo recourse to the U.N., and that is the problem in persuasion I now face.

Yesterday, Friday, I came up to New York with the President by plane, leaving at 11 A.M. and we had a good chat. I urged a serious study of the payments balance of the coming five years, pointing out that he needed to be sure he would have enough foreign exchange to last seven years.[13] He said he was unwilling to face so

[12] Then head of the International Bank for Reconstruction and Development.

[13] It was undertaken and eventually published by the Brookings Institution in 1963: *The United States Balance of Payments in 1968* by Walter S. Salant with Emile Despres, Lawrence B. Krause, Alice M. Rivlin, William A. Salant and Lorie

extended a prospect. I do not believe it. He is also very annoyed by the needling he receives from the *New York Times* and is not inclined to accept my argument that it is better to have it from the liberals than from the right. Today, keeping a promise to him, I had lunch with John Oakes[14] and chided him for complaining more about Kennedy for doing something than about Ike for doing nothing. He rather admitted the charge but pointed out there had been a change of administration at the *Times*. The President also warned me with great good humor that I had as yet unexplored experiences in traveling with Mrs. Kennedy. He thought I was going back to India too soon and urged I go to Florida for a few days' rest on the *Honey Fitz*. I told him I couldn't forsake my family indefinitely.[15]

We arrived at noon. Some twenty motorcycle outriders and two helicopters guided us into town. All the protection was against nobody whatever. The occasional bystander paid no appreciable attention.

In the afternoon, I had a long talk with Adlai and used the occasion to repair damage from our various misunderstandings and recriminations over Goa. His relations with the President are much better. He was pleased to hear the good things Kennedy had said about his U.N. leadership. (The President had commented on the plane that morning that Stevenson's appointment was one which really made a difference.) I also went over the problems of the Black mission, including a lengthy discussion with Plimpton.[16] He is a man of intelligence but insufficient force. I quickly became impatient.

I had dinner in bed. I am still a bit wobbly.

Today I did last-minute telephone business, talked briefly with

---

Tarshis. The purpose of the study was to avoid domestic action based on adverse short run factors, were the long run prospects favorable. And, ultimately, it would help ensure the requisite action, were the long run prospects unfavorable.

[14] Editor of the editorial page of the *Times* and a personal friend.

[15] An excuse, actually. I dislike boats of all kinds.

[16] Francis T. P. Plimpton, Stevenson's deputy at the United Nations.

Eugene Black and, after lunch, caught the plane. I am glad to be away from Washington and especially from the State Department. It suffocates me with its endless, undirected meetings, its prideful commitment to the clichés of foreign policy and its pomposity. Especially annoying is my desk officer who combines a great verbal felicity with a remarkable inability to accomplish the most minute task, a considerable reluctance to try and a total unawareness of any inadequacy. I must find out if there is some way of filing an inefficiency report on him.[17] Yesterday when I called to ask him to rearrange my travel to India — I was originally going on Sunday — he advised me that there should be a travel office in my hotel. I assume he had once been in the Biltmore.

January 24 — New Delhi

Day before yesterday, following my early morning arrival, I managed to sleep most of the day. Then at 10 P.M., I saw Nehru to urge a favorable reply to our proposal on Black. The Indians are not enthusiastic about it, but they are also as anxious as we to avoid another disagreeable session in New York. They will answer the end of the week.

Krishna Menon is always interesting. He told Henry Kissinger[18] that it was American policy to separate him off from Prime Minister Nehru and President Kennedy — not possibly an unbearable deprivation for the President — and he described me as too pro-Indian. An Indian Ambassador who was equally pro-Lebanese he said would be recalled. Maybe he is trying to save me from my affectionate nature.

Yesterday I had a staff meeting and told them that, on the whole, we had been favorably regarded for our work on Goa. I appended the observation that I had done everything possible to further this view. I lunched with Sir Guy Powles, the New Zealand High Com-

[17] On future trips, the Department kept him out of my line of sight. He is quite possibly doing well.
[18] Political scientist and Harvard colleague who had been lecturing in India.

missioner, in honor of Sir Leslie Munro.[19] The latter is a bluff, intelligent man who had been more impressed than was I by my "Meet the Press" performance.

Last night we had a big party with Indian music for Yehudi Menuhin who is visiting here. The food and company were good and, all in all, it was an agreeable occasion.

February 18 — Hong Kong–New Delhi

A long gap will be noted. At the Republic Day reception amidst a vast crowd at the Rashtrapati Bhavan, I was assailed by extreme dizziness and a sinking feeling which together could have conveyed the impression that the U.S. Plenipotentiary was stoned. I took to bed, the doctor came and gave me the choice of the Holy Family Hospital on the edge of New Delhi or getting out to Germany or Hawaii. The latter sounded best so I was bundled aboard Pan Am at a nasty hour Sunday morning (January 28) with Kitty in attendance and the Embassy staff looking on with more sympathy than they could reasonably have felt. Amoebic dysentery, hepatitis, sinusitis, malingering and various other complaints were put on the label attached to the remains. It was a most tiring and disagreeable trip and we arrived next day at noon, although in fact much earlier, having regard for the time. Tripler General Hospital had sent an ambulance but I got to the hospital under my own power. I was given a most attractive two-room suite overlooking Pearl Harbor from a considerable height. They then proceeded to repeat the indignities I had undergone at Bethesda. The hospital is a huge one, beautifully equipped and well-staffed, and, in the end, my complaints turned out to be unclear but mild. I have a feeling that a surprisingly large number of illnesses come down in the end to a bad stomachache. Meanwhile, the papers carried the stories of my imminent demise. Letters of condolence (including a few vaguely

---

[19] Then the U.N. Special Representative on the Hungarian Question and Secretary-General of the International Commission of Jurists. He had previously been the New Zealand Representative to the U.N.

implying satisfaction) came in from around the world. So did Bob and Ethel Kennedy one day on their trip around the world. They were marvelously vital, just having gone sailing outside Pearl Harbor and tipped over their dinghy. I proposed they say they had been cut down by an enemy destroyer with stress on the fact that Bob had saved the whole crew. He could then be President. After his visit to the hospital, we had a press conference and said we had been discussing the President's fitness program.

After ten days, during which I managed to do a little writing and a lot of reading, I was paroled to Kauai and Kitty went back to New Delhi. Kauai, the westernmost of the Hawaiian islands of importance, is small and mountainous with cane and pineapple on the flatlands — of which there isn't much. It is sparsely populated, quiet and beautiful in a heavily green way. The hotel at which I stayed, the Hanalei Plantation, is on the northern shore, rather remote, and consists of a double row of separate houses extending down a slope for a quarter of a mile from the dining room. They are connected to the latter by cable car. The rooms have a magnificent view over the bay and surf. A hostess asked me if I were "happy, happy" and a cocktail bar is called "The House of Happy Talk." Such happiness. The place cost close to two million, I was advised by the editor of the local newspaper who came out to interview me. Joel Fisher, an old New Deal lawyer friend from Washington, was there with his wife and we walked and swam together. One day we went fishing. I caught several bonita and a thirty-pound tuna. All of us — the Fishers, myself, the fish — were utterly astonished.

Yesterday I got up at dawn or a bit before, drove to the airport on Kauai, flew to Honolulu, met with Admiral Felt[20] and attended his staff briefing. Officers were present in division strength to learn what they could have learned better in ten minutes of reading. However, it gave me an opportunity, for which I was grateful, to get a sense of how matters in South Vietnam and Laos are viewed.

[20] See page 257.

They prefer fighting, feel it is the only solution, but bow to civilian restraint. Felt and Harriman are possibly heading for a clash. And Rusk has just agreed to putting a full general co-equally in charge in Saigon with the Ambassador.

I met Fritz Nolting in the airport just now — he is heading for Honolulu for a conference — and he is most unhappy about the general. I celebrated the first day out of medical jurisdiction with the worst sinus headache in weeks. Fortunately, I was well supplied with pain-killer.

This morning I bought a watch (I have one that doesn't keep time and another that you can't see without spectacles), a suit and some luggage. This shopping along with a shave, haircut and massage filled in the morning and now I am on the way back to Delhi.

February 19 — New Delhi

We got in at nine-fifteen last evening. My seat companion on from Bangkok was the Chairman of the Uzbek S.S.R. State Planning Board. He had no English and my Uzbek is shaky, but we managed to carry on a very decent conversation after I won his heart by arranging to get him a second and third martini. He waved his hands violently when I told him I had once visited Tashkent.

At the airport, we were welcomed by Arthur and Marian Schlesinger[21] who are here, plus a sizable Embassy delegation. The Schlesingers have had a good time in India, although I evidently overscheduled Arthur a bit. We returned to the house for dinner and a pleasant chat. He thinks the Punta del Este Conference[22] was the best of a bad job. Peru introduced and pressed strong anti-Castro resolutions and thus forced a showdown on grounds other countries could not accept. Arthur agrees that Rusk is a dull

[21] Arthur Schlesinger was on a brief speaking tour of India in company with George McGovern.

[22] On the Alliance for Progress. The Conference sought generally to increase confidence between the United States and Latin America.

foundation type, necessarily dependent on the military and a passionate and indiscriminate exponent of all the Establishment clichés. But he is in, which is the basic position of all Establishmentarians.

February 21 — New Delhi

Day before yesterday at noon, we loaded the Schlesingers on the Embassy Convair and we all went to Calcutta. It was a gay and agreeable flight with lunch en route and I had a long talk with Arthur on life in the White House. Ken O'Donnell, as I have long suspected, is the most practical and uncompromising liberal on the immediate White House staff. Ralph Dungan[23] is at last becoming aroused over the number of Republican appointments. On all honorific boards and bodies, it is imperative to be either a Republican or Ralph McGill.[24] However, this does not matter excessively for honorific and unpaid bodies never accomplish anything.

In Calcutta we did a bit of sightseeing, had a pleasant dinner at the Consulate and went to Dum Dum Airport to dispatch the Schlesingers who were joining the Bob Kennedys on the plane there. Bob looked very tired and his press conference was uninspired but intelligent. Ethel seemed unchanged by the round-the-world campaigning. She spoke appreciatively of the art and culture of Japan, Indonesia and Bangkok with special reference to President Sukarno's collection of nude paintings.

Arthur had written a speech for Bob to give in Berlin. I had thought it all right. Bob immediately pinpointed its faults: strictly conventional praise of the bravery of Berliners, strictly conventional damnation of the Communists. On second thought, I was forced to conclude, as did Arthur, that the criticism was sound.

They departed and we came back to the Grand Hotel where I slept badly. In the morning, I had a further briefing on the Calcutta metropolitan plan and went over Mrs. Kennedy's schedule.

[23] Special Assistant to President Kennedy. Later Ambassador to Chile.
[24] Of Atlanta. Publisher of the *Constitution*.

Then we flew back to New Delhi. On the way, I answered forty or fifty letters and had a brief nap.

The Ford Foundation planning team on Calcutta is doing a good job, I think. I proposed that they work out a new approach to schooling — a subsidy in the form of salary to every teacher that sets up in business at any possible place and passes a given number of pupils through carefully conducted examinations each year. If we must wait for a highly organized school system along western lines, we will wait forever. There must be something better adapted to the needs of the very poor country. I also urged that, as the planning operation comes to an end, we have a huge conference to publicize and utilize the whole operation and put Calcutta on the conscience of the world.[25]

February 22 — New Delhi

A horde of workmen are at work in the yard on various structures under which will be celebrated George Washington's Birthday tonight.[26] The garden is full of flowers at this time of year and the lights thereon make a very nice effect. The colored bulbs in the shrubbery and elsewhere, a much beloved Indian decoration, are less rewarding.

Yesterday was a rather dismal day. I am basically in sound health,[27] but I tire rapidly and sleep badly, the latter involving a pathological collection of dreams.

February 23 — New Delhi

The other day, I wired Dr. Travell for some barbiturates with which she is supplying me. I got back an answer, not from her but from the President, saying, "Lay off that stuff. Do you want another Goa?"

---

[25] Nothing came of either proposal.

[26] In New Delhi for climatic reasons, this, rather than the Fourth of July, is the occasion of major national festivity.

[27] An unduly sanguine diagnosis.

I had a long meeting yesterday morning with Banerji[28] on J.B.K.'s visit. This has become the major preoccupation at the Embassy. It promises to be very interesting. Most of yesterday was devoted to dealing with requests for visits — the Girl Guides, Girl Scouts, Associated Virgins, League of Fallen Women and others. At noon, I had a press conference marred, slightly, by the absence of any important news and by excessively desultory questions from the press. The *Times of India* describes me this morning as "looking tired but displaying sparkling good humor."

Last night was the big national day celebration — held here on Washington's Birthday. Because the Indian elections are the principal local preoccupation, it was celebrated largely by non-Indians. We had the Baird Marionettes, who are on tour, and they gave a splendid show. Guy Powles, my New Zealand colleague,[29] said henceforth it would be impossible for any other Mission to give a party. That seems to me wildly optimistic. But the Bairds are indeed gay, amusing and highly intelligent.

We had floodlights playing on the flowers in the Residence gardens which are at their brilliant best and the effect was very striking. As usual, the food consisted of potatoes and stale grease.

By the end, I was exhausted and could not go to the airport to greet the Bowleses who arrived shortly after midnight.

February 26 — New Delhi

There are times that try men's souls. Early yesterday a telegram came in postponing J.B.K.'s trip for a week. Thousands of man-hours and more rupees have gone into it and the first effect looked sheer disaster. I was told to see the Prime Minister pronto and tell him. The telegram came from Tish Baldrige in Rome and referred vaguely to health. I postponed the visit to Nehru until evening and, after great difficulty, talked with the President in Palm Beach. He ticked me off in a way that would have made Dean Rusk rejoice

[28] Chief of Protocol. See page 61.
[29] See page 301.

for not acting on orders. (I mustn't be so hard on Rusk. He is a traditionalist and thinks that because foreign policy was bad under Truman and bad under Eisenhower it should be at least mediocre under Kennedy.) During the night, I figured out ways and means of softening the blow and then took four sleeping pills. As a result, this morning I feel mildly euphoric.

During the last couple of days, the horse show has been in progress before the Red Fort. It is a marvelous setting with the horsemen on the greensward in front and the tremendous façade of the Fort to the rear of the stage. Some of the exercises, such as the tent-pegging (spearing of a two-and-a-half-inch peg while going flat out) are quite dramatic. Jamie entered Sandstorm[30] and to his uncontrollable pride got third in a class of twenty. Last night, he received his cup from the P.M.

Chet and Steb Bowles have been visiting the last three or four days. They have not had much business, but they have been renewing acquaintances in a large way. I don't think Chet is very happy. If anything happens to me, I can always quit and write. It must be rough to be without such an alternative.

February 28 — New Delhi

Government only in rare moments involves making progress. Most of the time one spends retrieving losses. I think I have eased the local pain over Jackie's postponement fairly well — careful explanations to the P.M., letters from the President to the Governors who were deleted, press statements stressing her illness. I even have some big loans to announce — nothing like redirecting attention from the spirit to the flesh.

Day before yesterday along with the Bowleses, we had lunch with the Nehrus. Delhi gardens are a dream at this time of year and theirs is beautifully groomed with the most elegant of borders. Ours is lovely too — one side is extravagant with color and not without some harmony.

[30] Kitty's recently acquired, handsome and recurrently very self-willed mare.

The Bokaro steel project has also been off the rails and Bill Gaud did an excellent job of getting it back on again. He is a fine, intelligent, proficient figure and a great asset as AID director for this part of the world.[31] We have agreed on getting a mission to establish the feasibility from the American viewpoint. Once that is under way, I think we will be pretty well committed.

Yesterday I had a sudden recurrence of sinus pain and staggered to a meeting with M. J. Desai and to lunch. He thinks we might get a deal in South Vietnam. Hanoi is becoming frightened; it fears equally that we will move in, or the Chinese will move in to prevent our coming, and in either case, they lose. He also wanted us to go to the British on the activities of their Ambassador in Nepal who, he says, is inciting the King against the Indians. I suggested that he might more appropriately go to Gore-Booth, the British High Commissioner. Finally, he asked that we warn Bowles — who will be seeing Ayub — that the Indian offer of settlement in Kashmir on the cease-fire line cannot be open very long. For the Chinese will assert the same right to a settlement on the line they claim. This the Indians cannot accept. I see this as a way to associate the Indians' position on Kashmir with an anti-Communist pose. Anti-Communism is always considered hot stuff for Americans.

March 1 — New Delhi

I had a press conference at noon yesterday to announce some new loans. It was well-attended with good questions. I also had the imminent arrival of the animals to announce — the large collection of North American fauna for the National Zoo for which Phil Stern[32] is paying. Included are bison, raccoons, porcupines, opossums, deer, bears and many others. I described it officially as the largest such cargo since Noah.

New Delhi continues cool at night and not very hot in the day-

[31] After 1966, he became the head of AID.
[32] See pages 18, 244.

time. Surprisingly, there have been very heavy rains in the last few days.

✧   ✧   ✧

New Delhi, India
March 2, 1962

Dear Mr. President:

I think the rearrangement of Mrs. Kennedy's schedule has gone fairly smoothly. There has been a little pettish comment and of course disappointment in the South and Calcutta. Americans are supposed always to confine themselves to the Ganges plain and thus they never see the most attractive part of India. But certainly she can count on a warm and agreeable welcome. Nehru, who is deeply in love and has a picture of himself strolling with J.B.K. displayed all by itself in the main entrance hall of his house, was entirely agreeable. Do tell Jackie that she could have no disorder better calculated to arouse my sympathy than a sinus infection. It still knocks me out at about the same intervals that alcohol used to level my Uncle John and in much the same way.

The tone of Indian-American relations, as viewed from here at least, has improved a lot in the last few weeks. Apart from any beneficial effect from my absence, they have now got over their guilt about Goa, some of which they were taking out on us. And Krishna Menon has been out of town getting reelected. There was never any doubt incidentally about his reelection. The only two political organizations in his district are the Congress and the Communists and he had the support of both.

When I am not worrying about your wife, I worry about Indo-China. (Ross once told Thurber in 1940 when he was losing his eyesight: "Thurber, I worry about you and England!") I had a long talk with Felt in Hawaii and have been over the papers and documents again. I continue to be sadly out of step with the Establishment. I can't think Diem has made any significant effort to improve his government either politically or administratively or will. We are increasingly replacing the French as the colonial military force and will increasingly arouse the resentments associated therewith. Moreover, while I don't think the Russians are clever enough to fix it that way, we are surely playing their game. They couldn't be more pleased than to have us spend our billions in these distant jungles where it does us no good and them no harm.

Incidentally, who is the man in your administration who decides what countries are strategic? I would like to have his name and address and ask him what is so important about this real estate in the space age. What strength do we gain from alliance with an incompetent government and a people who are so largely indifferent to their own salvation? Some of his decisions puzzle me.

But it is the political poison that is really at issue. The Korean War killed us in the early 50's; this involvement could kill us now. That is what the military and the Department will never see. But I must learn to be easier on the State Department. It has a sense of tradition. It believes that because we had a poor foreign policy under Truman and Eisenhower we should have a poor one under Kennedy. No one can complain about that.

There is one ray of light. I think that Hanoi may now be getting worried. The Indians keep saying this — that the North Vietnamese feel they will lose their independence either to the Americans or to the Chinese defending them against the Americans but that in any case they will lose. However this may be, and knowing your distaste for diagnosis without remedy, let me lay down four rules that should govern our policy in this part of the world. They are:

1. Keep up the threshold against the commitment of American combat forces. This is of the utmost importance — a few will mean more and more and more. And then the South Vietnamese boys will go back to the farms. We will do the fighting.

2. Keep civilian control in Saigon. Once the military take

over we will have no possibility of working out a disentanglement. I have been disturbed, incidentally, by indications that
Harkins[33] might have a standing more or less independent of the
Ambassador. That was what cost us so heavily in Korea. Without Brown[34] as boss we would have had no chance of working
our way out of Laos.

3. We must keep the door wide open for any kind of political
settlement. In particular we must keep communications open by
way of the Indians and even the Russians to Hanoi. If they give
any indication of willingness to settle, we should jump at the
chance. Any form of disentanglement is going to bring criticism
from fighting Joe Alsop as it has in Laos. But the one thing that
will cause worse damage and more penetrating attack will be
increasing involvement. Politics is not the art of the possible. It
consists in choosing between the disastrous and the unpalatable.
I wonder if those who talk of a ten-year war really know what
they are saying in terms of American attitudes. We are not as
forgiving as the French.

4. Finally, I hold to the view, whatever our public expressions,
that any alternative to Diem is bound to be an improvement. I
think I mentioned once before that no one ever sees an alternative to the man in power. But when the man in power is on the
way down, anything is better.

Yours faithfully,
JOHN KENNETH GALBRAITH

THE PRESIDENT
THE WHITE HOUSE

✧ ✧ ✧

[33] General Paul D. Harkins.
[34] Ambassador Winthrop Brown who helped brilliantly to extricate us from
Laos.

March 4 — New Delhi

Last Friday — this being Sunday — the animals arrived, a whole Constellation full of them and exuding a frightful smell. I extended an official welcome and rode down on the fork lift with the bison. Peter and Jamie made several round trips on the same conveyance. As intended, the papers were full of it.

Speaking of publicity, we also have the announcement of nuclear test resumption. Washington would like to make a major exercise in explanation of this. The more we explain, I am convinced, the worse we will be — it will keep the subject alive and show a bad conscience. Here, at least, I am going to maintain a severe silence. I don't much like the decision.

One of the worst features of this job are the evenings when everyone sits around for hours before dinner — if Americans, drinking; if under Indian auspices, doing nothing at all, sometimes not even talking. I am passing the word to the American community that a half-hour of cocktails is enough. The time to talk is after dinner and the merit of that is that after dinner one can go home if he wishes.

Business continues principally to concern Mrs. Kennedy's visit. It is too bad it has become such a production. Indian election results have been coming in all week with the predictable win for the Congress Party. This is, essentially, a one-party country.[35] The Congress is an omnibus organization which works out its compromises within the party structure. The elections are a ratification process and a check to ascertain that the solution is within the general range of acceptability. The elections show it is, although with indication of more dissent on the right than on the left. The Jan Sangh and Swatantra[36] parties have scored some gains. The Communists seem to have shown no increase in strength.

My health continues to improve and I have taken up riding again.

[35] Now, 1968, no longer. However, the Congress Party remains by far the most powerful grouping.
[36] Respectively, Hindu traditionalist and economically conservative.

March 5 — New Delhi

The weekend was remarkably quiet and yesterday, Monday, was the first in months devoid of ceremonial occasion, or almost so. I rode in the morning at six forty-five — cool and fresh on the riding grounds of the President's bodyguard, returned for breakfast, wrote for an hour, worked at my desk for an hour and dictated some telegrams and read the incoming ones, held one of my rare staff meetings, had lunch, napped briefly, had a couple of brief meetings at the Chancery, arrived a little late in the closing session of a U.N. seminar on human rights and freedom of the press — it took a stand in favor of them — where the P.M. was speaking, bought some materials for some shirts, took a walk, had dinner and then investigated the lighting arrangements at the Chancery for Mrs. Kennedy's dinner. After studying various improvements on Ed Stone's lighting, we went back to things as they were, save for some lights on the flower beds. Some had wanted a great array of Indian Diwali[37] lights (wicks floating in dishes of oil) and I had favored a succession of rising and falling electric floodlights on the building. The first were rejected by me — they clashed with the other lights as a candle clashes with an electric bulb. I was reluctantly talked out of the changing lights as too gaudy. Thus the day.

March 9 — New Delhi

Henry Stebbins is here for more talks on Nepal. This could be the next Laos although somehow I doubt it. I am still holding back our eager people from protecting the country on behalf of the Indians. What happens there is, primarily, India's responsibility, not ours. The Indians for their part are being blamed for raids on the border being conducted by the Nepali Congress Party.

Last night I saw Gundevia[38] who produced a major bill of complaints on American policy in South Vietnam. I told him I agreed but asked him what we should do. He said he did not know. I

37 The name comes from the Hindu festival of lights held in October.
38 See page 70.

asked if we should pull out. He said no. I asked if India could get the Vietcong to call off its forces. He said they couldn't.

B. K. Nehru is back for consultation. By querying him on a recent conversation with the President and Secretary, I got an improved view of American policy. One must use the available channels.

Night before last, we went out to the Zoo to see the animals. They seem quite happy and are attracting a reasonable volume of attention. A pair of tiger cubs as pets are being put in the house Mrs. Kennedy is to occupy. I propose they be called Ev and Charlie.[39]

March 11 — New Delhi

Friday evening we had a rehearsal dinner at the Chancery, a preview of the grand occasion for J.B.K. On the whole, it was beautiful — the table on the second floor in the form of a gentle crescent was stunning and so also the view out over the water garden. Some things needed improvement. The music was a penetrating screech, the service was sloppy and we had mulled (i.e., lukewarm) Rhine wine and champagne.

Outside, the floodlit flower beds were a small fairyland.

For the last two or three weeks, we have had a rash of weddings. January and February, which are the normal months, could not be used this year because of most unfavorable astrological indications. (The world, indeed, was scheduled to come to an end. Only the fact that this was foreseen by the astrologers who thereupon resorted strenuously to prayer and incantation prevented the catastrophe.) So there is a marital backlog. The attendance of the American Ambassador is considered an important sacrament. We

[39] For Everett McKinley Dirksen and Charles A. Halleck (see page 35). The two had a weekly television conference nicknamed the "Ev and Charlie Show." The suggestion here as to names was a joke. However, it did get into the press, and Mrs. Kennedy by no means approved. She was scrupulously concerned that nothing associated with her activities cause the President any political embarrassment. The cubs were to go to the White House. A day or so after she left India, they both sickened, sank steadily, suffered stoically and died.

arrive and make our way under brilliant colored lights and through a great gathering of friends and relatives of the bride and bridegroom in the honoring presence of numerous officials to greet the couple and be photographed. Then we get out. The whole operation consumes some fifteen minutes. The celebrations continue for several hours.

March 12 — New Delhi

Yesterday we went to see the Shankar art contest.[40] Hundreds of little tykes were busily painting away. Some of it very good, some very children's painting. Indian children are rather more representational than Shady Hill. However, I saw a highly impressionistic airplane with four propellers attached.

I inspected the guesthouse down the road which we have arranged for J.B.K. and it is very chic. It has been rented from Gerry Gerold, the local head of Pan American. The lawn is like green velvet with a backdrop of dark red flowers against a wall and a gay border. The house itself has been refurnished with wonderful charm — all with borrowed furniture. It is very clean. Now we must go to the airport and greet the lady.

[40] The name is from the sponsoring magazine, *Shankar's Weekly.*

XVI

Great Fun

March 13 — New Delhi

As we started out for the airport yesterday morning, we discovered that every door of the Queen Elizabeth[1] was locked with the keys inside. Jamie had got out of the car after absentmindedly pressing the knobs that locked it. He was heartbroken. We got to the airport in a Ford.

The Air-India jet came in, handsomely on time, and I went aboard to find J.B.K. full of life and looking a million dollars in a suit of radioactive pink. With her was Lee Radziwill.[2] There was a big crowd at the foot of the ramp including Nehru, Krishna Menon, various other ministers and a thousand children. The road in from Palam through the desert was lined with people most of the way. A better house than for Lyndon Johnson, I am obliged to say.

Before anything else, we went to see the President return from opening Parliament in his open carriage with horseguard — it made a noble sight viewed from above from one of the cupolas by the Secretariat and looking down the Rajpath — the wide central mall of New Delhi — toward the War Memorial. Then in the afternoon we visited the President — neither he nor J.B.K. were especially articulate[3] — and went for a walk in the Moghul Gardens

---

[1] The more modern of two vast Embassy cars; the other was the Queen Mary.

[2] The compact party also included a pressman, personal maid and, of course, the Secret Service.

[3] The late Rajendra Prasad was a distinguished but notably untalkative statesman. See page 79. J.B.K., more than most women, is a gifted listener.

which lie back of and are partly enclosed by the wings of the Rashtrapati Bhavan and which at this season are magnificent. They are beautifully manicured and the combination of color and water is brilliant.

Then we went to the Rajghat to lay roses for Gandhi and to the Chancery to greet the Indian and American staff. This was rather brief and unhappy — everyone was gathered outside the Chancery or inside around the pool. The pool has islands and stepping stones and, seeing the chance for a memorable photograph, I turned her across the stepping stones before she had completed the circuit. Some of the officers and their wives missed their *darshan*[4] in consequence and were sadly disappointed.

J.B.K. brought Kitty a handsome gold monogrammed pencil and to both of us a nice picture of herself with the President. One judges them to be the best-looking heads of state in modern history.

March 14 — New Delhi

Our guest slept late yesterday and I managed to give condolence to the Embassy officers who had missed meeting her. Then at noon we went to the Rashtrapati Bhavan for a huge and glittering lunch tended by the President. The guards, table, saris and view of the Moghul Gardens were in fine color. Nehru and the Vice-President[5] kept J.B.K. well entertained and, all in all, it was an excellent show. Then in the afternoon we went to the All India Institute of Medical Sciences where a huge crowd was out. The children were delighted and the pictures of them with J.B.K. were compelling. More than incidentally, we got attention for an enterprise into which we have put a great deal of money.

In the early evening, I went to the press briefing where there was far too much attention to the subject of clothes, designer, dress, handbag and so forth. I asked Jackie afterward if she wanted all

[4] *Darshan* is the beneficial glow from being in the presence of the great. Sought in all societies, only the Indians are candid enough to endow it with a name.
[5] Dr. Sarvepalli Radhakrishnan, about to become President of India. He was in nowise inarticulate. See page 217.

this and she said no. So I have issued instructions that questions of clothes be answered only when asked — no details volunteered. Also, I have asked Jay Gildner,[6] her press officer, to develop a bad memory for designers and materials.

In the evening, we had a nice party at the Prime Minister's.

March 15 — New Delhi

Yesterday I faded into the wallpaper which, given the alternative feature, was exceedingly easy. Mrs. Kennedy visited the Prime Minister's home for waifs and strays in the morning. After that, I visited her on the porch outside her suite at the Prime Minister's house to which she had moved from the instant Embassy guesthouse. As we chatted, we had an elegant view out over green lawns, bright flowers, bright saris and, in the near distance, the hovering press. A feature of this trip is beautiful women in beautiful gardens. The combination I find highly agreeable.

I wrote Jackie a six-line speech which she memorized expertly and used in presenting a children's art exhibit to Indira Gandhi, a ceremony which also included garlanding by a baby elephant and a reception by local artists. In the afternoon, she visited the Cottage Industries Emporium where Kitty surprised her and everyone else by emerging as one of the models. It was a sari dress of sari material selected by me; alas, my taste was unsung. Then in the evening we all went riding at the exercise grounds of the President's bodyguard. J.B.K. circled and jumped beautifully. Though it was all private, I had smuggled in a cameraman and I hope he was good. I was very nervous over the jumping. Had his wife broken a leg, the President would, I imagine, have broken me — with some justification.

While proving to Kitty that her horse was exceptionally tame, one of the officers — "Bubbles" Jaipur, the son of the Maharajah — was thrown and somewhat damaged.

In the evening, the Prime Minister rounded up the gayer mem-

---

[6] A diligent but not highly resourceful man rather unhappily cast in his role as Mrs. Kennedy's press protector. In the end, I largely took over.

bers of the community, all in best clothes, for a large dinner followed by singing and dancing on a floodlit stage in the garden. J.B.K. was wearing a long dress of pale turquoise which responded brilliantly to the lights. I am having a signal lack of success in soft-pedaling emphasis on clothes. Indeed, in cabling a general account of the journey to the President, I said this effort promised to be the biggest failure since Stassen tried to ditch Nixon. Last night's dress was adequate explanation.

The scene on the Prime Minister's lawn last night would last in anyone's memory. You must imagine chairs stretching across the lawn and lit by the half-moon and the reflection of the stage lights. These flashed on a stunning array of saris — every woman present had chosen from among a great number and spent hours on the choice. In front of the chairs was a little canopied area for the supreme guests, the canopy being made of flower petals. Finally, before all was the stage, dancers, musicians in vivid or sometimes wild costume, the women being especially sinuous as they turned and twirled.

At ten this morning, we met Jackie and Lee at the Prime Minister's and, the P.M. and Mrs. Gandhi accompanying, we went to the V.I.P. railway station in New Delhi — the one where, in imperial times, the Viceroys entrained and detrained. Here, after numerous farewells, we got aboard a special train for Fatehpur-Sikri.[7] The train — the President's and once the Viceroys' — is a brilliant red outside and pleasant fawn within. It includes drawing room, bedrooms and dining room, and is unquestionably the proper way to travel. We went at a leisurely pace across the Ganges Plain with a late lunch and, by some special dispensation, drinks and wines, and much agreeable conversation. B. K. Nehru was in the party and was a most entertaining addition. At three,

---

[7] The great, brooding capital of red sandstone near Agra. It was built by Akbar the Great in 1569 and occupied for fifteen years. Then its magnificent palaces, walls, mosque, courtyards, mint, treasury and tanks (ponds) were abandoned forever. In the dry, hot climate, they have deteriorated but little. One sees them today much as they were when Akbar marched away.

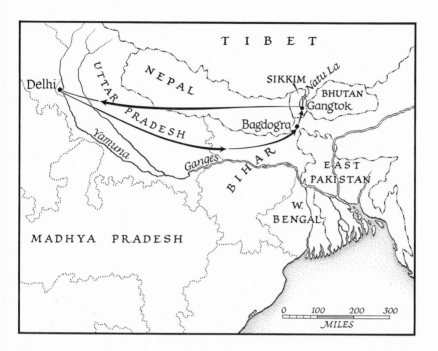

we reached Fatehpur-Sikri station, were loaded into cars and toured the city and palace for just short of an hour. It wasn't the best way to see it. Photographers dashed in front, reporters crowded around and quite a few others struggled with more determination than skill to get into any available pictures. Still, it was fun and we saw the palaces of the various queens where Akbar played parcheesi in the moonlight using live maidens as pawns, and the great Gate of Victory with the tank below. An exceptionally large number of loincloth-clad exhibitionists were on hand to jump from high on top of the Gate into the tank some 170 feet below and they were rewarded by at least five different Embassy officers, each of whom separately concluded that this was one occasion when Americans could not afford to be niggardly.[8] The sight of first one or two and then great

[8] A number of athletes are always on hand to entertain tourists with this fearsome plunge.

numbers jumping wildly into the tank was not without effect.

After leaving these vast red sandstone buildings, we reboarded the train and went back to Agra. Here we had a big welcoming crowd and duly toured the Taj Mahal. As a sightseeing tour of the world's most gracious and majestic monument, this was also a bit like making love in a cageful of monkeys. Photographers were jumping everywhere to get into position, reporters crowded in and, all in all, it was pretty much of a riot. But J.B.K. didn't seem to mind and I think rather enjoyed it.

After the Taj, I decoyed the press with a press briefing and she went jewelry shopping. When I got back to the Circuit House where we were resting, I got the news that a propeller-feathering mechanism in the Embassy Convair which was to convey us to Benares was in default. Unless a part could be procured by Indian Airlines, and happened to fit, we had no airplane.[9]

To make matters worse, at the Circuit House people were having drinks and otherwise milling around in a party mood and it was difficult to get anyone's attention. However, I worked out a plan to use the Constellation which was carrying the press as a shuttle — first it would carry J.B.K., then the reporters to Benares. And as an alternative, we sent a request to borrow the Prime Minister's Viscount. However, at this point someone suggested taking the train to Benares, and B. K. Nehru tracked down Karnail Singh, head of the Railway Board, and found it to be quite practical. At the moment the train became available, news came that the repaired Convair was landing in Agra. Meanwhile, Indian Airlines had heard of our difficulty and sent a plane. The Constellation had arrived, and the plane of the Embassy Naval Attaché had also come in. We now had enough planes to start a medium-size airline. J.B.K.'s preference was to proceed by train, so we did. We got aboard about eleven o'clock. She was in good form. My situation

[9] The possibility of such a mishap should have been foreseen. The Air Force crew had been polishing the plane for this duty for weeks. It is possible that the absence of a back-up plan reflected their conviction that every conceivable part had been double-checked.

was one of total exhaustion. Food, bedrooms and all were beautifully ample.

I forgot one incident as we left Fatehpur-Sikri. Mrs. Kennedy walked down to be photographed against the locomotive and to exchange a word or two with the engine driver. A member of the Embassy staff came hurrying up to point out that she was being photographed against the name plate of the locomotive. It showed the locomotive, a posh black and green machine, to have been made in Poznan, Poland. I managed to quiet his alarm. A few years back under Eisenhower (more properly, Dulles), this would have been a grave error. At least we do make some progress.

March 16 — Benares–Sarnath–Jaipur–Udaipur

By the device of taking sleeping pills every time I woke up, I had quite a good sleep at the price of a nasty hangover. We breakfasted and arrived at Benares[10] at around 10:30 A.M. I was struck by the thought that this part of the Ganges basin, more or less midway between Delhi and Calcutta, is the dark land of India. The peasants are poor and thin and you have the impression of being much further from home than in Delhi or Agra.

From the station, we made our way to the city and on to the ghats (the great steps leading down to the water) and boarded a launch. The press followed us at some distance in a barge. This distance, I discovered later, was a source of considerable anger. We made our way the length of the city, some three or four miles, waving to the great numbers of people who had swarmed down to the waterfront. With her excellent sense of theater, J.B.K. had put on a lavender dress which could be picked out at any range up to five miles. The burning ghats were not in operation but one widow in her wedding sari was waiting for the pyre to become properly warmed up. I used part of the trip to explain to Lee the great

---

[10] Religious capital of India, one of the seven sacred cities of the Hindus, a main center for the worship of Shiva and the goal of some million pilgrims every year.

advantage of dying in Benares. You proceed to heaven forthwith and without any intermediate ceremony or diversion. She said she wasn't sufficiently persuaded to seize the opportunity.

The river trip was hot and actually less interesting than I had remembered it. One reason was that the ghats were swarming with people to welcome Mrs. Kennedy. Before, people had been going about their ordinary business of bathing, washing clothes, praying or otherwise occupying themselves.

After landing, we went to a silk-weaving establishment where there was a near riot as photographers fought to take pictures and the merchant sought to assure that every single piece in his shop was shown to J.B.K. She made a number of purchases, including at my behest a length of raw silk for a jacket for the President. I am fairly certain he would not be seen in it, but it seemed a good idea at Rs. 19 ($4.00) a yard. Then we sent the press to the airplane and visited Sarnath[11] which was rather pleasant. Jackie was photographed in detail by the Asoka pillar.[12] Then we saw the great *stupa* and visited a Buddhist temple where Mrs. Kennedy listened to various arcane but indubitably non-Catholic rites. By turns, we all banged the great temple bell. Then we boarded the Convair for Jaipur and had a merry party consisting of J.B.K., Lee, B. K. Nehru, Kitty and myself. The crew of the plane had gone to such pains to prepare lunch that it was a couple of hours before we had anything to eat, but when it came, it was very good. We left the Convair at Jaipur and came on to the smaller Udaipur field in an Indian Airlines Dakota. Here we have had the most impressive welcome of the trip. The crowds were massed along the streets for miles and Mrs. Kennedy stood up in the back of an open car to greet them. There were loads of welcoming arches and much enthusiasm. The population of Udaipur is about 110,000 and I would guess that there were twice that many along the road today. Now

[11] An even greater religious center than Benares in some respects for it was here that the Buddha first made his doctrines known to the world.

[12] The pillar surrounded by lions appears on the Indian crest and flag. The *stupas* are solid structures of great antiquity and religious symbolism.

we are ensconced in the Maharana's palace. This is a vast marble affair by Pichola Lake — most impressive. Tomorrow hopefully is an easier day.

March 18 — Udaipur–Jaipur

Udaipur[13] is the superb result of major exactions from the local poor over many generations; it is a city of marble palaces around Pichola Lake, itself an artificial creation. The heights of land around the city, as near Jaipur, are surmounted by great Rajput crenellations in the manner of the Great Wall. The main palace is some 1½ miles in length although the first mile or so is in a state of acute disrepair. The Maharana is a handsome man in his forties, in the good graces of the government, and an extremely good host. Yesterday was a highly agreeable day, much of it devoted to physical and mental repair. J.B.K. slept until nearly noon and the press came up to the palace courtyards and walked around in the sun in evident good humor. Phil Potter and I went for a long walk around the lake; it was the first exercise I have had in weeks. After a family lunch, we made a private visit to a palace in the middle of the lake. This is being converted into a hotel to hold some thirty or forty couples. If carried through according to present plans, it will be one of the most charming in the world.[14] It has lovely intimate courtyards and the walls are decorated in inlaid glass of superb workmanship.

Following the visit at the hotel, we came back, picked up the rest of the party and then made a major tour of the lake by boat with the press and cameramen following in yet other boats. It had something of the appearance of a regatta. As we got close to the

---

[13] Udaipur, capital of the ancient Rajput state of Mewar, lies some 250 miles southwest of Jaipur in what is now the modern state of Rajasthan. Its ruler, styled a Maharana, is traditionally the premier prince among the Rajputs. Unlike Jaipur, its principal rival, Mewar resisted the Moghuls in a succession of bitter struggles. As an earnest of their opposition, the Mewar Ranas swore never to go to Delhi, the Moghul capital, and only in the last few years with Indian independence has the vow been relaxed.

[14] It was and has so become.

town, the buildings were laden with children who shouted greetings to the "American Maharani."[15]

Once we contemplated landing to walk and greet the crowd.
J.B.K. gave me quick instructions not to get permission of the
Secret Service which is organically negative. However, on this
occasion the Indian police intervened in opposition and kept us
afloat.

Correcting the errors of Benares, I let the press come in very
close for their pictures. They remained profoundly dissatisfied. It
is a rule of the press always to be dissatisfied and thus always hope
for something more. This is sound policy — and something it is
well to understand. Dissatisfaction may lead to more privileges;
satisfaction confirms the status quo.

In the evening, there was a reception in the durbar room of the
palace with Rajasthani dancing. The boat trip had been very heavy
with princes, so I got J.B.K. around to chat with various modern
officials — Additional Chief Secretary, Chief Justice, head of a
college of agriculture and some AID technicians who were on
hand. The conversation between J.B.K. and the agricultural dean
was less than technical — her opening gambit was, "What is your
annual rainfall?" However, I did better for democracy in a press
release designed for home consumption. The dinner following the
reception was in the State Dining Room of the palace and very
pleasant. It was also rather heavy with courtly figures, but it was
soon over. The rest of the party went boating and J.B.K. to bed.

Today was the day when things went wrong on a considerable
scale. It began innocently enough with Mass for Jackie and a visit
to the old palace by the rest of us. The latter, which has glass inlay
work, marble audience chambers and a roof garden, is a storehouse
for court treasures. It is very interesting and has a marvelous view
out over the lake. It also has fifteen or twenty Moghul or Rajput
miniatures of the finest sort.

Thereafter came a long, hot and dusty ride to the airport and a

15 A Maharani being the consort of an Indian ruler.

hot and dusty ride from the airport at Jaipur. The welcome at Jaipur was pleasing enough with thousands of children and Rajasthani maidens in bright dresses dancing and singing for Jackie's arrival. The arrangements for the motorcade were appalling and in the end Kitty, B. K. Nehru and I got left under the porch while the Maharajah went off at the head of the column. I was very angry. Eventually we reestablished our position at the price of some rudeness. We were in the middle of a constitutional row. The Maharani of Jaipur has just been elected to the Lok Sabha, the equivalent of the House of Commons; the Maharajah is expecting to go to the partially appointive upper house, the Rajya Sabha. He is a great friend of Lee's and thus of Mrs. Kennedy's and is suspected by the Indian Government of wanting to make political capital of the visit.[16] The Indian Government has been determined to thwart this effort. I have been in the middle and most unpleasantly so. The Maharajah had planned a round of activities — cocktail parties, polo and above all a visit to the City Palace. The latter is his personal property; the Government feared it would provide an occasion for a triumphal tour through the city of Jaipur.

In fact, the civilian authority got in first. J.B.K. was met by the Governor of the state and brought by him to the Raj Bhavan. She was later his guest at a large dinner last night attended by all the civilian notables of the state. A chef had been brought from Delhi. It could have been a case of mistaken identity. Before dinner, I had several of the leading jewelers and merchants telephoned and they set up an impressive array of merchandise on the lawn outside the guesthouse. This part of the evening was interesting.

March 19–21 — Jaipur–New Delhi

Monday, at least until noon, also belonged to the civilian authority and so far there has been no major explosion. The Maharajah, however, is a figure to be reckoned with. It was the Government of India plan to have Mrs. Kennedy stop at the City Palace on the

16 See page 276.

way to Amber Palace this morning. However, the Palace is the personal property of the Maharajah. It was, in consequence, closed for cleaning and repairs. So this strategy collapsed. The trip to Amber, however, gave an ample opportunity to the government forces to show off their visitor. The route lay dead through the city; the schoolchildren were let out for the occasion; there must have been two or three hundred thousand people on hand. Also triumphal arches including a magnificent one with the legend, "Long Live Mrs. Keneddy (sic) — the Wine Merchants of Jaipur."

We went by car to the Palace yard at Amber, having in my case to make the trip in a borrowed car for the Embassy Cadillac would not negotiate the turns. At the top were six or seven magnificently caparisoned elephants and the party was taken on an elephant ride around the courtyard. The cameramen had a field day. These are the pictures that will make the greatest impression in the United States and, needless to say, bear the least relation to India as it really is. The number of reporters and photographers touring the Palace with Mrs. Kennedy was kept down to a modest size and it was, I think, a fairly agreeable visit. As I have told before,[17] the setting of the Palace on the Rajput hills with the fortifications marching up and down the peaks all around is magnificent.

At the end of the tour, J.B.K. met and was photographed with the members of the Peace Corps, one of whom had a magnificent Sikh beard and turban. They all looked well and healthy and claimed without exception to be enjoying themselves. At two o'clock I delivered her into feudal custody at the Palace. I then returned for an hour-long session with the Peace Corps.

Then I went over to a press briefing. But the press was so replete with news that they asked no questions. While I was there, J.B.K. called up with a new crisis. Her hosts had invited her to go to the City Palace that evening. They suggested to avoid embarrassment she go alone. It had been polished, cleaned, lighted, and she

17 See page 272.

naturally wanted very badly to see it. I concluded the time had come to decide in favor of her. But I urged her not to go surreptitiously. I said I would try to get approval from the Indian Government for her to go with her hosts. I decided that I would also go so that any Indian press criticism would not be of her but of the U.S. Government. This is a somewhat less specific and vulnerable target. I took the matter up with Mrs. Kochar[18] who has been a wonderful help on the trip. She argued strongly against it, but with a certain underlying lack of conviction. So I was able to persuade her to call the Chief Minister of Rajasthan who first argued against it and then said he would have no objection if Delhi didn't oppose. Mrs. Kochar got on to Delhi. After failing for over an hour to reach the Chief of Protocol, I went off to dinner at the Palace. On her own authority, Mrs. Kochar called to say I should authorize the visit. This I did.

The dinner was pleasant and lighthearted, although scarcely my particular social specialty. The conversation was on horses, mutual friends, social events and polo. I did have a long talk with the Maharani. She is in favor of free enterprise and also more and better government services; for protection of all existing feudal privileges but also more democracy. She is vivacious and extremely good-looking, and I detect a certain determination to inform herself.

About midnight, we drove into the City Palace and spent a couple of hours roaming its environs — the various courts and audience chambers, the gardens where the fountains had been turned on, the armory and the museum with its wonderful miniature paintings. The lights gleamed on the red walls, the swords and also on the saris of the party. And rugs and tapestries which are a bit vivid in the daytime seem fine and subdued at night. It was all most romantic, and it was plain that Mrs. Kennedy enjoyed it enormously.

[18] Sonnu Kochar, liaison officer from the Ministry of External Affairs to Mrs. Kennedy.

The next morning, Tuesday, Mrs. Kochar woke me up at about 7:30 A.M. for a report which I gave to her. And then I sent a note to J.B.K. urging her to do no more traveling that day. She was extremely tired and Dr. Purcell[19] had given me a slightly alarming report on her health. Whether in response or otherwise, she didn't stir out of bed until noon. I picked her up at 2:30 P.M. and we returned to the Raj Bhavan to say goodbye. She rode with the Chief Minister and Governor out to the airport, and a pleasant group of Rajasthan ladies and schoolchildren were there to chant her away. We rode back in the Convair and in about forty-five minutes, she was back in No. 12 Ratedone Road, the guesthouse, for a rest.

I forgot to say that a number of interesting things came out of the discussion with the Peace Corps. All are in good health; all seem to be enjoying themselves; and all have engaged cooks on their pay as volunteers. Those engaged in agricultural work are finding a good deal of difficulty in bridging the academic and very theoretical preoccupations of the Indians and their own practical desires for results. One or two seemed a bit discouraged on this point. Their recommendations were: (a) a better preliminary language instruction and (b) a better balance between the sexes. Most of them do not find the Punjabi girls, beautiful though they are, a sufficiently available substitute. The point is a good one and I will take it up with Shriver. Youngsters of this age cannot be expected to take kindly to monastic chastity, however good the purpose.

In the evening, we had our grand and final gala. At eight, I brought Mrs. Kennedy, dressed in queenly white, to the Residence where several hundred senior citizens of Delhi had assembled. We

---

[19] Harry Purcell, M.D., a very able St. Louis physician who had been serving a volunteer tour of duty in New Delhi. He was unofficial medical adviser to the Embassy, and I had attached him to Mrs. Kennedy's party over the objections of the State Department which had proposed importing a staff physician for the tour. I said I would not be responsible for her health unless Dr. Purcell was in charge. Before it had occurred to anyone that I wasn't responsible in any case, the tour was over.

had gone all out with a vast *shamiana*,[20] food, drinks and two orchestras. One of these was installed in the front yard under the flag and
consisted of ten or twelve pipers and bass drums. J.B.K. came in to
"Over the Sea to Skye." The decibel count was somewhat above
the opening day of the battle of the Somme. She passed through
the house, received a picture of herself, some art books and made
a tour of the garden, greeting on the way most of the local men of
distinction. Then with Kitty, who had on a fetching dress in yellow brocade made from a present I had got for her in Hong Kong,
we went to the Chancery for dinner. This was a wonderful success.
The Vice-President, Nehru, two or three other senior Ministers,
the members of Nehru's household and a fair selection from the
academic and artistic community were present to the number of
about forty-five in all. The water garden looked fine, and we had
installed a small string orchestra on one of the islands. The balcony
dinner table was handsome. The food was good and hot; the wine
was cold; and we had lots of champagne. The toasts were com-
mendably short, J.B.K. proposing one to the President of India and
Vice-President Radhakrishnan responding with one to the President. There were no speeches at all. We went downstairs afterwards for coffee and more champagne around the pool and the
party showed every intention of extending far beyond the Prime
Minister's departing hour of 10 P.M. However, Kitty, who has
considerable control over Dr. Radhakrishnan, managed to suggest
our promise to J.B.K. that she could be in bed soon after ten-thirty.
It was in good style and, I think, quite a good climax to the tour.

Today at twelve o'clock, I called for J.B.K. and took her to the
Prime Minister. She was to have recorded a farewell message that
morning but begged off and I did an account of the trip instead.
It was the morning of Holi or the Festival of Spring. While recording, I was showered with red paint (which, with much spraying of
colored water, is the main expression of festivity) and thus had to
see her off in a disreputable sport shirt and splashed trousers. Every-

[20] See page 83.

body came on out to the airport to see her away. The Prime Minister bade her an affectionate farewell and went back to make a glowing speech about his guest to a press conference. Kitty and the boys joined the plane, a Viscount belonging to President Ayub. They are going to the horse show at Lahore. In an excellent example of official confusion, most of the press baggage remained behind and we had to get a special plane to fly it over.

I went back to the Chancery and drearily made my way through a vast quantity of business. Toward the end, I spent less time deciding matters than wondering how they might decently be postponed.

The President had told me that the care and management of Mrs. Kennedy involved a good deal of attention, and he is quite right. I found myself worrying constantly either about the Indian press reaction, the American press reaction, that of the people she was visiting and her own state of contentment. The last perhaps was most important because had she become tired and unhappy, the rest of the effect would have been certainly poor.

I was also more than a little troubled by the very practical fact that anything that went wrong on this trip would go very promptly to the White House. One can hope to conceal some errors or mistakes but not when they have to do with the President's wife. Finally, as I have implied before, there was the shocking incompetence of her entourage. The head of her Secret Service detail was an amiable and agreeable officer. But he had the very limited imagination of a policeman. The other Secret Service men seemed to have their energies largely occupied by their communications apparatus and with talking to each other over it. However, they were in the main attractive and intelligent men. Her Press Attaché was less than adequate. He was short on imagination and sadly involved with his own pride. Finally, Tish Baldrige, who is good-hearted and extremely energetic, has a certain agreeable feeling that confusion is a manifestation of femininity.

One of the minor footnotes of the trip was some shopping in Benares. On my advice, J.B.K. bought a couple of handbags and, while she was looking at the textiles, she whispered as to whether she should buy something. I urged her to do so and she hastily bought some silk brocade and a couple of jeweled brocade bags. In the rush, neither of us inquired the price. I assumed they were 200 or 300 rupees. In fact, they were Rs. 3000. The papers made something of the fact that she had spent some $600 in less than five minutes. Actually, it couldn't have been more than ten seconds. She was annoyed at my carelessness.

March 22 — New Delhi

Today was officially a holiday. With all of that, I had to go wearily in to clean up my desk. Pearl Buck[21] came for lunch along with G. D. Birla[22] and one or two others. P.B. is still very much occupied by China and still hopes to make another visit to the mainland. Perhaps because I was tired, I didn't find it possible to develop much of a conversation.

March 25 — Ahmedabad–New Delhi

I had promised to visit Ahmedabad in Gujarat in January but had to cancel it because of my illness. I had a firm promise outstanding to Governor Jung, whom I had met years ago in Hyderabad, to come as soon as possible. So, with a break of only a day or two after J.B.K.'s departure and with my own departure for Washington also imminent, I took off last Friday morning, picking Kitty up in Amritsar. She had driven over from Lahore in the early morning. We had to wait about a half-hour for her because of the usual delay in the Pakistan-India customs and immigration formalities which are conducted with great deliberation on both sides. How-

[21] The Pultizer Prize-winning novelist and longtime authority on Chinese life.
[22] See page 71.

ever, it was an opportunity to work on my speech. I am still following the theory that fewer good speeches are much better than many bad ones. Most American diplomats, I have discovered, give so many speeches they serve only to establish the fact that they have little or nothing to say.

We got to Ahmedabad about noon, a textile center from ancient times and now, with Bombay, one of the two great centers of the textile industry. There are some eighty or ninety mills in the vicinity of the city and their chimneys have the appearance of a forest as one approaches. The city itself bears a curious resemblance to a southern U.S. textile town. For an Indian city, the streets are wide and well-paved and it is comparatively quite clean.

We had lunch at the Raj Bhavan with Governor Jung. The house is on the banks of the Sabarmati and pleasant and colorful. It was built as a residence by Shah Jahan in the style of a Moghul villa and is full of balconies, terraces and screens. The ancient style is well preserved by an interesting collection of traditional furniture.

After an afternoon nap, I went to lecture at the University. The Governor acted as chairman and we had an excellent house. I had my usual problem of having written the speech for the newspaper audience and finding it was much too condensed to be grasped by the students. However, I made generous use of interpolation and, on the whole, it was well received. An Indian audience, particularly a student audience, does not hesitate to depart wearing a deeply pained expression if a speech is not to its liking. This is sensible. I lost only a handful.

After the speech, I went to the household of Ansuyeben Sarabhai and Shantilal Banker. Miss Sarabhai is the daughter of the largest, or certainly the most famous, mill owner in Ahmedabad. Banker in 1918 was a relatively young labor leader and active in the great strike that was led by Gandhi in that year. Miss Sarabhai deserted her father to take sides with Gandhi and the strikers, and her life with Banker has continued ever since. Now in their seventies, charming, lovable and wise, they live in one spacious section of the vast Sarabhai mansion which, in turn, stands in some twenty acres of grounds which have a little of the appearance of a tropical rain forest. The mansion itself goes on for two or three hundred yards — courts and fountains, guest rooms and apartments, dining rooms and terraces having been added as the family expanded over the years. And in recent times various of the offspring have built additional houses to their particular taste at various spots on the grounds.

I tried to talk a bit with Ansuyeben Sarabhai and Shantilal Banker about Gandhi but they had read my books and felt obliged to turn the conversation in that direction. However, the conversation was rather less important than the chance to watch this charming, elderly couple dressed in white khadi with their wonderfully gentle manners.

Dinner followed at the Raj Bhavan, buffet and informal, and attended by the leading citizens of the city. Thereafter there was Gujarat dancing by a troop of fifteen or twenty girls — quite gay and energetic — and the evening was over by ten.

Yesterday in the morning we went sightseeing and saw the Mosque of Sidi Saiyad with its marvelous stone tracery in palm and parasite design. Then on to the zoo and children's park where we were taken in tow by a remarkable zoologist by the name of Reuben David. In the last three years, he has created one of the most charming zoos in the world on a little hillside by a tank and he lives on most intimate and agreeable terms with his animals. The latter collection includes two or three tigers which charge their cage walls with inspired viciousness and another so gentle that, after being further tamed by playing with a favorite dog, he was available for petting and photography. I was duly photographed stroking him with highly tentative affection. The photographs, which were prominently featured in this morning's paper, look a good deal braver than they really were. Everyone was prepared to evacuate at a moment's notice.

At eleven, we went to visit the head of the trade union. The local textile unions were organized by Gandhi in the early twenties and he worked out a system of arbitration with the mills. There have been no serious strikes since 1923. This has become the mother union for the rest of the I.N.T.U.C.[23] or Congress trade union movement. The principles are those of nonviolence and coopera- tion between management and workers with an elaborate grievance procedure and all wage disputes going to arbitration. I had a little of the feeling of the company union. However, given all prob- lems, including the importance of competitive prices, it may not have worked too badly.

For lunch, we went back to the Ambalal Sarabhais' where the whole clan was assembled. It is a devoutly Hindu house, strictly vegetarian, but also remarkably cosmopolitan. There is also a small, or, to be more precise, not so small museum of Hindu art. The conversation turned partly on Gandhi who is still a living figure in the city but partly also on the practical problems of the textile industry. These I continued to discuss in the afternoon in a meet- ing with the textile mill owners' association. They complained that the government is not allowing them to proceed as rapidly as they should with modernization and is also restraining the mill-cloth producers to protect the hand loom industry, both obviously valid and sound complaints. I managed to convey sympathy without seeming to side with their attack on the government. We talked also of the effect of the Common Market on textile exports and the upcoming cotton famine. This year's cotton crop in India is going to be small and it will be difficult to find substitute stocks in the U.S. Our own surpluses for the moment are also small.

There were various other activities during the day and at six o'clock, the Chief Minister gave a large reception. This was at his house and included anybody who was anybody at all in Gujarat.

[23] Indian National Trade Union Congress.

But instead of standing in line, various people were brought over to chat and one got some slight impression of the most interesting figures. It was, in fact, rather enjoyable. The Chief Minister himself, Dr. Jivraj Narayan Mehta,[24] was a physician by training, formerly head of a medical school and a handsome Gandhian figure in his mid-seventies. I would sense he was also a fairly shrewd politician. In the last elections, Congress suffered some setbacks to Swatantra which was also represented at the reception.

The day's business came to an end with a large formal dinner at the Raj Bhavan followed by some motion pictures on the beauties of Gujarat. Gujarat may have some great beauty spots but evidence was not available from the motion pictures. I have rarely seen such a consistently hideous technique. The narration of one was in Indian English and barely intelligible. An Englishman had been obtained to do another, and it was impossible to believe that he missed a single cliché from "the glory that was Gujarat" to "a silent dream in stone."

This morning, we went back to visit the tiger again and see if we could get a more authentic picture. With some delicacy, he was maneuvered outside the cage and with even more delicacy, a quick picture was snapped in my company alone. Then there was a press conference, after which we went to lunch at the mansion of another of the great textile houses, this time the Kasturbhai Lalbhais'. This was also vegetarian and also assembled quite a number of the clan, and the house, no less of a treasure than that of the Sarabhais, had some quite magnificent bronzes. I was greatly struck, in spite of all the magnificence, by the down-to-earth and practical judgment of the textile business that governed the conversation. There was no dilettantism; all of these men know the business in great detail. I discovered, for example, that the Sarabhais have been thrown out of the mill owners' association because they have learned that by work incentives, scientific management and three-shift operations, they can go substantially above the going wages

[24] Later Indian High Commissioner in London.

while still keeping costs somewhat, and I expect considerably, below the average level. The discussion of how this was brought about was highly professional.

After lunch, we went back to the Raj Bhavan, said goodbye and are now (midafternoon) about half way to Delhi. One detail that I should mention is that until now the heat in India has been quite tolerable. At Ahmedabad these past three days, the wrath of the furnace has again been upon us. This is what now lies ahead.

March 27–April 8 — Washington, D.C.

I have been in Washington for the last ten days to testify before the House Foreign Relations Committee. That occupied one morning and was not worth the trip. A goodly number of members were present but it was an executive session and an expensive form of education. However, it gave me a good impression of the Congressional mood which is less vitriolic than I had anticipated. There were a few questions about Goa and many about Krishna Menon but they were not especially bitter. I followed my usual practice of assuming the absolute friendship even of the most perverse bitterenders. In about four cases out of five, whereas hostility invites hostility before a Congressional Committee, amiability induces amiability. I invented a good answer on Krishna Menon. The Harvard Department of Economics, it used to be said, was dominated by liberals. In fact, there were exceedingly solid and satisfactory conservatives — Burbank, Williams, Haberler.[25] Only it was the liberals like Galbraith who did the most talking. Hence the unfortunate reputation.

In executive session, the members and witnesses sit around a cluttered table, more or less in order of seniority. Each member has five minutes to put questions. Hostile members must be answered at length but without the discrimination being obvious. Members

[25] H. H. Burbank, John H. Williams, Gottfried Haberler, all distinguished economists with no valid reputation for radicalism.

who come in late and ask the same questions must be kept from feeling their lack of originality.

On Sunday last, April 1, I drove down to Glen Ora, the Kennedys' rented country place, with the Schlesingers. It is a modest plantation house, comfortable and unpolished, in the trim countryside of the farming and non-farming rich. Protection is highly inconspicuous; Caroline in bright red boots, bright red slicker was out paddling in a water puddle beside the house and John, Jr., was getting the air in his baby carriage. The President and J.B.K. were asleep. Arthur and I strolled about the grounds and presently went in to tea where we were joined by Jackie. She looked a bit tired but manages to be handsome and compelling without benefit of makeup or hair-doing.

I should have said, incidentally, that I had seen her briefly on her arrival in Washington. She phoned from New York asking me to come out to the National Airport and rewarded me in the receiving line with a well-televised and widely reported kiss. The Herter Committee on Foreign Affairs Personnel had a brilliant thought. It passed a formal resolution of thanks for what she had done to encourage public officials. They sent it to me.[26]

In the evening, we all watched an hour-long NBC color spectacular on her tour — it was very gay and quite good but somewhat deficient in editing, I thought. The President was visibly impressed by J.B.K.'s general political grace and style; he was moved to a particular and well-meant compliment by her speech presenting the children's art carnival. She had commented on the similarity of children's art the world 'round — "In a world where there is quite enough that divides us, let us cherish whatever unites us."

For the rest, we had a family dinner around one end of a small table. Caroline came in with a volume called *Taffy* to demand some reading. The President disappeared to keep a promise. She

[26] Here is the text: "Public embrace enormous encouragement in recruitment high level officials for Foreign Service. Congratulations on initiative and bravery obviously beyond call of duty and in highest traditions of the diplomatic elite. James Perkins for Herter Committee on Foreign Affairs Personnel."

had already had an hour or two, he observed, during the afternoon.

We talked also of the Common Market, South Vietnam as usual, and appointments, also Massachusetts politics — "Let the Republicans keep the corrupt place. The Catholic Church is a dominant influence and it should be ashamed of what it dominates." I find that I am far less effective as an adviser than a year ago. The President knows much more, has much greater confidence and I know less from being out of touch. I asked him how long he wished me to remain in my exile. He said another year.

We talked until eleven at which time he announced he was turning in. J.B.K. referred repeatedly to her trip; I think she is sincere in saying that they were very good days indeed.

An amusing thing happened as regards my Pakistan colleague, Walter McConaughy.[27] Ayub had not been especially anxious to have Walter, urging that someone, a professor he said, with my general political standing and assumed access to the White House be sent. The President would have concurred but Rusk insisted on McConaughy, an old friend, and prevailed. During J.B.K.'s stay in India, Bundy wired me asking that I impress on her the need to show special attention to McC. I was asked to remind her that the Ambassador and the President were friends of even longer standing (I wondered at this) than in my case. This would overcome any impression that McC. was any less in. I followed instructions and impressed J.B.K. with her duty accordingly. At tea soon after arriving in Pakistan, she took the opportunity of telling Ayub in McConaughy's presence what an old friend the Ambassador was of her husband. McC. who was unbriefed promptly corrected her, saying that he had only recently become acquainted with the President. Then she presented pictures to Ayub and the Ambassador; the latter was inscribed from the President, "To my old friend, *William* McConaughy." At Glen Ora, J.B.K. was eloquent on the episode, blaming Bundy. "How can you trust a man like that on atomic weapons when he can't get names straight?" I later told

[27] See page 243.

Mac about it with pleasure. He was furious at such ineptness, his fury including Rusk.

At the President's suggestion, I had a long talk last Tuesday with Bob McNamara.[28] I discovered that he is deeply sensitive to the dangers that I foresee in our involvement in Saigon. For the rest, he was glad to have some pressure from my side. I left the President with a memo on our policy on South Vietnam, which, however, added little that was new.

April 5, 1962

Dear Mr. President:

I have put in a lot of time the last three or four days on the scene of my well-known guerrilla activities, namely, South Vietnam. This included a long and most reassuring discussion with Bob McNamara. We are in basic agreement on most matters and for the rest I think Bob appreciated having some arguments from my side of the fence. I also had two or three long discussions with Averell and the attached memorandum, which is of no breathtaking novelty, comes close to reflecting our combined views. I think I can safely spare you another eloquent restatement of what you have already heard from me several times before. However, I do pray that in addition to reading the attached memorandum you see Governor Harriman at some early date.

I am leaving this afternoon for New York and tomorrow night for India. There are no pressing Indian issues I need to cover with you. Kashmir will continue to simmer. This is not the time for any brilliant initiatives and the best we can do is to press both sides to keep their behavior in low key and keep above the obscene politics ourselves. As I told you attitudes on the Hill toward India seem mellower than I had expected. I am coming back on a very brief private trip in early June to get an honorary degree and make a speech. I will try and give A.I.D. and India

28 See page 1.

a lift before the Senate if, as Fulbright and some others believe, it may then be needed.

Last, but not least, I must tell you how much I enjoyed the other evening at Glen Ora, our survey of the problems of the nation and the world, and the chance to reflect on the unique capacity of your advisers to solve them.

Affectionately,
JOHN KENNETH GALBRAITH

THE PRESIDENT
THE WHITE HOUSE

April 4, 1962

MEMORANDUM FOR THE PRESIDENT
Subject: Vietnam

The following considerations influence our thinking on Vietnam:

1. We have a growing military commitment. This could expand step by step into a major, long drawn-out, indecisive military involvement.

2. We are backing a weak and, on the record, ineffectual government and a leader who as a politician may be beyond the point of no return.

3. There is consequent danger we shall replace the French as the colonial force in the area and bleed as the French did.

4. The political effects of some of the measures which pacification requires, or is believed to require, including the concentration of population, relocation of villages, and the burning of old villages, may be damaging to those and especially to Westerners associated with it.

5. We fear that at some point in the involvement there will be a major political outburst about the new Korea and the new war into which the Democrats as so often before have precipitated us.

6. It seems at least possible that the Soviets are not particularly desirous of trouble in this part of the world and that our military

reaction with the need to fall back on Chinese protection may be causing concern in Hanoi.

In the light of the foregoing we urge the following:

1. That it be our policy to keep open the door for political solution. We should welcome as a solution any broadly based non-Communist government that is free from external interference. It should have the requisites for internal law and order. We should not require that it be militarily identified with the United States.

2. We shall find it useful in achieving this result if we seize any good opportunity to involve other countries and world opinion in settlement and its guarantee. This is a useful exposure and pressure on the Communist bloc countries and a useful antidote for the argument that this is a private American military adventure.

3. We should measurably reduce our commitment to the particular leadership of the government of South Vietnam.

To accomplish the foregoing, we recommend the following specific steps:

1. In the next fortnight or so the I.C.C. will present a report which we are confidentially advised will accuse North Vietnam of subversion and the Government of Vietnam in conjunction with the United States of not notifying the introduction of men and material as prescribed by the Geneva accords. We should respond by asking the co-chairmen to initiate steps to re-establish compliance with the Geneva accords. Pending specific recommendations, which might at some stage include a conference of signatories, we should demand a suspension of Vietcong activity and agree to a standstill on an introduction of men and material.

2. Additionally, Governor Harriman should be instructed to approach the Russians to express our concern about the increas-

ingly dangerous situation that the Vietcong is forcing in Southeast Asia. They should be told of our determination not to let the Vietcong overthrow the present government while at the same time to look without relish on the dangers that this military build-up is causing in the area. The Soviets should be asked to ascertain whether Hanoi can and will call off the Vietcong activity in return for phased American withdrawal, liberalization in the trade relations between the two parts of the country and general and non-specific agreement to talk about reunification after some period of tranquility.

3. Alternatively, the Indians should be asked to make such an approach to Hanoi under the same terms of reference.

4. It must be recognized that our long-run position cannot involve an unconditional commitment to Diem. Our support is to non-Communist and progressively democratic government not to individuals. We cannot ourselves replace Diem. But we should be clear in our mind that almost any non-Communist change would probably be beneficial and this should be the guiding rule for our diplomatic representation in the area.

In the meantime policy should *continue* to be guided by the following:

1. We should resist all steps which commit American troops to combat action and impress upon all concerned the importance of keeping American forces out of actual combat commitment.

2. We should disassociate ourselves from action, however necessary, which seems to be directed at the villagers, such as the new concentration program. If the action is one that is peculiarly identified with Americans, such as defoliation, it should not be undertaken in the absence of most compelling reasons. Americans in their various roles should be as invisible as the situation permits.

✧ ✧ ✧

Last Sunday for lunch, I went to the Philip Sterns' and thanked them for the animals they shipped to the Delhi Zoo.[29] Monday, I dined at Bob and Ethel Kennedy's. I had a long talk with Jean Kennedy Smith who is tall, slender and very good-looking. She and Eunice are coming to India in February next. I must move it to January for Republic Day and the Beating of the Retreat.[30]

On Tuesday evening, Florence Mahoney had a large, gay party — the Bells, Ralph Dungan[31] and wife, Scotty Lanahan and husband, the Alfred Friendlys.[32] Scotty, under the fairly transparent excuse of interviewing me for the *Washington Post*, managed to stay behind after the others had gone. We spent an agreeable hour or two. She has the uninhibited joie de vivre of her parents of the legend and is highly amusing into the bargain.

Wednesday night, my last in Washington, I went to a dinner at the Brazilian Embassy for President Goulart, who is on an official visit. I took on all the solemn men. Don't stabilize until you have confiscated the feudal revenues of the landlords. Otherwise there won't be enough revenue to go around and stability will be at the expense of the economically weakest group, namely the workers. But though economically weak, they will be politically strong enough to throw you out.[33]

Following a long defense of Brazilian neutrality by the Brazilians and a strong argument by Rostow for alliance, more or less, with us, I pointed out that each was only a different technique for exerting pressure on the United States. The ally says: "Agree with us because you are our friend." The neutral or nonaligned power says: "Woo us because you need our support."

[29] See page 244.
[30] The trip did not materialize.
[31] See page 305.
[32] See page 47.
[33] Later, I received frantic word from Lincoln Gordon, our Ambassador in Rio de Janeiro, saying that my comments had been taken by the President as endorsing unlimited inflation. I got off a corrective letter saying, in effect, that the customary 60 percent a year price increase was enough.

Goulart is a square, well-tailored, rather handsome man without much to say.

Day before yesterday, I came along to New York and Alan came down and we went to see *How to Succeed in Business*, etc. He liked it immensely and so, I confess, did I. It is sophisticated slapstick. We remained overnight amidst the splendor of the Harrimans' impressionists. In the morning, Ersi Breunig[34] came down to see them and me, and at noon I lunched at Time, Inc. with Harry Luce, Bill Furth,[35] Teddy White and Emmet Hughes[36] — a freewheeling occasion during which Harry did most of the talking.

[34] Handsome wife of Leroy Breunig, Professor of French at Barnard College, formerly of Harvard, and a longtime personal friend.

[35] Executive Editor of *Fortune* in my time on the magazine and then general editorial assistant to Luce. He died not long after.

[36] Author and journalist.

XVII

Mountain Journey

April 15 — Bombay–New Delhi

I put in three or four days catching up on the things at the Chancery and then early Wednesday last, today being Sunday, took off for Trivandrum. I spent the six hours en route desperately and rather wearily contriving a speech to be given later before the Council on World Affairs in Bombay. We arrived at Trivandrum in the early afternoon and went to the Raj Bhavan and thence to an old palace on top of the hill where the Chief Minister, Cabinet and Members of the Legislature were assembled and where I announced our approval of aid to the Pamba-Kakki hydroelectric development, a scheme for letting water down from the mountains to the Indian Ocean in an exceptionally complicated way. It will cost about $60 million and we are lending both the dollar and rupee amounts, the latter from counterpart funds. It will rather more than double the existing supply of power for the State of Kerala. It is oddly the first large-scale aid project we have ever had in this State.[1] Almost no notice would have been taken of the loan had I not gone down to make the announcement in person. As it turned out, however, it was front-page news in all of the Indian papers.

After the speech, we went swimming out at Kovalam in water which at this time of the year is about body temperature. Then

[1] Odd because Kerala was considered Communist-prone and the mystique of the time made extra attention likely.

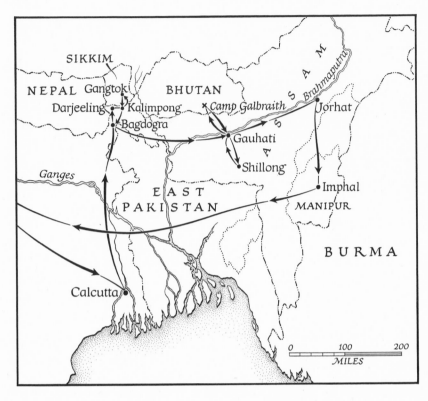

we went on to a State dinner by Governor Giri and the Chief Minister. It was pleasant seeing Governor Giri again.[2] He is one of the
most active and intelligent of the older Congress figures. I am not
so impressed by Pillai,[3] the Chief Minister, who heads the Kerala
coalition. There have been some complaints that the food we are
giving to Kerala school-feeding programs[4] is going into the Black
Market and, indeed, I learned that the CARE representative may
be on the point of resigning as a result. I spoke to Pillai about it,
and he told me to have no fear; they would allow no leaks. I spoke
to the Governor who said the situation was serious and he would

[2] Varahagiri Venkata Giri, previously Governor of Uttar Pradesh and later
Vice-President of India. He is a distinguished authority on labor relations.
[3] See page 230.
[4] See page 230.

do what he could to impress on the local government the importance of cleaning it up.[5]

Kerala at this time of the year is usually extremely hot and sticky.
But there had been a couple of days of rain so it was not too uncomfortable. The dinner was over early so we escaped to bed
about 10 P.M. We got up at six-thirty the next morning for another swim and while at the beach learned that the Convair was
suffering from the same propeller disorder that had afflicted it during J.B.K.'s visit when it was supposed to carry her from Agra to
Benares. Only this time there was no spare part closer than Delhi.
I took the commercial airline, by way of Cochin and Bangalore, to
Bombay, missing an afternoon trip to the Atomic Energy Commission at Trombay. It was a long, slow journey but gave me time to
work on the speech which was in need of attention. I did arrive in
time for a dinner by Dr. Homi Bhabha.[6] The party which included
in the main engineers, plus the visiting head of the Canadian Atomic
Energy Commission, was interesting — very intelligent and informed discussion of prospects for atomic power and the possibility
of desalination of water. Bhabha is among other things a competent
collector of modern art and does some painting himself.

The next day, which was Friday, I gave the speech some further
and final attention and then made a courtesy call on Y. B. Chavan,[7]
the Chief Minister, and then on the Mayor of Bombay. I met
Chavan at his house, and, as before, he impressed me as a self-confident, able and effective leader. We talked about a possible trip to
the United States and of the noonday school-feeding program in
Maharashtra. The visit to the Mayor was purely ceremonial. The
Town Hall is not more beautiful than Boston City Hall,[8] which in
general architecture, mustiness and clamor it resembles.

[5] Although nominally without executive authority, an active Governor of an
Indian state may have considerable influence.
[6] See page 193.
[7] Later to become Defence Minister (see page 492) and thereafter Home
Minister.
[8] The old City Hall, that is.

I had lunch in the Consulate — a routine gathering of Americans of the community. I was again annoyed by the habit of assembling an hour or two for drinks before lunch or dinner. By the time the dinner is served, one is exhausted and some women stoned and silly. In Delhi, I have passed the word that these pre-prandial soaks should be greatly abbreviated.

The speech was at the Council on World Affairs, Sir Homi Mody presiding, and not too bad. The theme was the excessive role of sad and weary men in international affairs and the importance of sustaining nonetheless a conviction that progress toward amity and law is still possible. (I had some suggestions.)

There was a good crowd, and the first question brought reality back in with a thump; I was asked if we intended to supply more cotton to India under Public Law 480. Bombay is a mill town. There was a fairly routine dinner with the officialdom of Bombay and Maharashtra. The visit was a heavy burden for Bob Carr, our Consul-General, for his wife, alas, is mortally ill with cancer.

Yesterday, Saturday the 14th, Angie Dickinson came in the early morning hours on a special Air-India inaugural flight on which she had been invited to freeload, and looking fresh and handsome in spite of the two nights on a plane. We had breakfast and then I went out to see the Tata Institute. This is a handsome building on the water looking out over the Arabian Sea. I met briefly with the staff members who are known to be first-rate, looked at the computer installation which is of their own design and seems a highly creditable piece of work, saw something of their cosmic ray and high altitude instruments, and generally spent a most instructive two hours. One can tell the quality of Indian academic institutions almost from the moment he walks in the door; they range inevitably from extremely good to sadly bogus. The latter have various formulae for concealing their inadequacies. One is to have some work of some slight complexity and interest which is shown to every visitor. Since few visitors come twice, no one realizes that the same alleged research is trotted out for all comers. Lunch was with some film people, and in the afternoon we were to visit a film studio. Fortunately, I discovered it was shooting a script on the liberation of Goa and took evasive action at the last moment. The papers this morning made considerable point of the fact that Kitty went. It would have been major news[9] if I had shown up.

In the evening, we had a vast reception in the seaside garden of Lincoln House (the Consulate) followed by a buffet dinner, followed, in turn, by a showing of Arthur Miller's *A View From the Bridge*. My main idea of the evening was to establish some contact with the film community. This in India is large and influential and in some quarters more than a little anti-American. No ambassador has ever paid much attention to it. However, Bob Carr had interpreted the words "film colony" liberally, and it included a very large number of his Consular opposite numbers from other countries, the entertainment of whom I consider a total waste of time. A fair number of the Maharashtra political figures were more usefully present, including the Chief Minister. I was a little worried about the use of representation (i.e., official) funds for a bash of this sort, and it was rather expensive. So I picked up the tab myself rather than try to explain its public value. I was being unduly cautious.

Arthur Miller's screenplay had an almost stunning effect on the crowd — and for that matter on me. It is engrossing, and by the end of two hours one is almost weary from paying such attention. It was also very good for the occasion — a fine example of screen and dramatic techniques in which the Indians were professionally much interested.

One of the problems encountered yesterday was that all the projection equipment available in Bombay for 35 mm. films is of Russian manufacture. The Consulate thought it would be inappropriate to borrow this. It would, of course, have been quite all right. But a humorless official could give a subordinate who borrowed such

[9] For a day but harmlessly so except as Washington would have scored it adversely.

equipment a severe blast; in consequence, subordinates run no risks. At the last minute, a good red-blooded American-made sound projector was discovered. Two of the USIS men told me that they thought *A View From the Bridge* showed an unduly seamy side of American life. They want our friends, I gather, to see healthy Iowa maidens making pies in the kitchen.

This morning we took the Port Admiral's barge and went to Elephanta. This is about forty-five minutes across Bombay Harbor and involves a most pleasant trip by the ships and docks. The caves have marvelous sculpture, somewhat damaged by Portuguese Christians who cleaned them up sexually speaking. The statue of Shiva with his three faces, which forms the center piece, is especially wonderful. However, the general effect of the caves, after Ajanta and Ellora,[10] is not sensational. One should see them before, rather than after, one has seen the others.

At 1 P.M., we boarded the Convair which, after some tribulation, had been repaired in Trivandrum, and after a stop at Agra to show Angie the Taj and vice versa, we are now coming into Delhi.

April 21 — Calcutta–Bagdogra

The past week since returning from Bombay has been one of the busiest that I can remember. There was a vast accumulation of tasks around the Embassy plus a considerable concentration of social and protocol activities. On various nights we had a lot of chairs put out in the garden to show films including another run of *A View From the Bridge*, plus *Judgement at Nuremberg*, plus Angie Dickinson in *Jessica*, with Angie present herself. For the latter, we invited the Peace Corps and, in their present state of complaint over the absence of women and considering the content of the film, we could hardly have done more. I had to leave Angie to be introduced by Ty Wood, for this was also the night of the

---

10 Two of the great sights of India near Aurangabad some 200 miles east of Bombay. The Ellora caves are magnificent temples cut from the living rock. The Ajanta caves are famous for their painting, a great landmark in the history of Indian art.

State dinner at the Rashtrapati Bhavan for the King of Nepal. The dinner was laid on with the usual pomp. But I had Mrs. Thapar[11] and Her Highness of Bikaner for dinner companions and the first was agreeable to talk with and the second to look at. Before dinner, I had a long and difficult discussion with the King. The problem was not the subject matter but the difference in height. After I had mentioned the weather and the trip down, I was about to ask him how things were in Nepal. Since they aren't entirely good, this seemed open to misinterpretation. Meanwhile, the Indians, assuming we were on some deep diplomatic discussion, tactfully deserted us and I had to signal desperately to Kitty from behind my back to come and help me out with some small talk. This she, having been to Nepal and being more nearly his height, was able to provide.

Earlier that day at the airport, the French Ambassador had expressed great anger at not being invited to the dinner. He is accredited to Nepal and pointed out that it was a grievous discrimination that he, an accredited representative, was denied while I, with no such accreditation, was allowed. I handsomely offered him my place.

Last Thursday night, today being Saturday, Kitty and I took Angie over to have Rhine wine with the German Ambassador and then went on in the early evening to see Nehru. He seemed to be making a good recovery from his illness and was much pleased by the visit. There are few men, myself possibly excluded, who more enjoy the company of good-looking women, and as he relaxed and expanded, the five-minute call ran on to thirty or forty minutes. I noticed, incidentally, that in his upstairs sitting room where he has pictures of the really important people in his life — Gandhi, Motilal Nehru (his father), Tagore and Edwina Mountbatten — there is now a significant addition, to wit: Mrs. Jacqueline B. Kennedy. It is the picture of J.B.K. and the Prime Minister walking arm in arm in the White House garden.

[11] The wife of General P. N. Thapar, the Chief of the Army.

Early yesterday morning, after a bad night — accumulated weariness — Kitty, Angie and I took off around eight o'clock for Calcutta on the Convair. On the way down, I composed an address on coal washeries and power plants for use at the inauguration of work on the Bandal power plant outside of Calcutta. This will be the largest thermal power plant in India and we are picking up the full tab. We got into Calcutta around noon, had lunch and a brief meeting with the Consulate and USIS staffs. Then I joined Dr. B. C. Roy for a trip out to Bandal which is some thirty-odd miles north of the center of Calcutta. It was a long ride through very congested streets. A motorcycle escort helped only slightly, because the traffic cannot be ordered out of the way if it has no place to go.

The inaugural ceremony was one of the most disastrous events in diplomatic history. Some three or four miles from the site, which is on the banks of the Hooghly, a terrific storm which had been building up from the north burst upon us. There were high winds (of near hurricane force), hail and literally inches of rain. The downpour was so dense that we could not see from the windshield to the front of the car, much less to the pilot car in front. So we had to stop. After twenty minutes or so, the rain and wind abated slightly and our procession resumed. But in approaching the plant site, most of the cars bogged down in mud as sticky as any at Arras. Dr. Roy and I were transferred to a jeep and we finally made it to the site, from which the wind had removed the *shamiana*, tea tables, microphones, decorations and all of the other preparations. A few people waded in through the mud and stood on the porch of the Superintendent's house, the only available building. And since it seemed too silly to read my prepared speech, I asked the newspapers to print it as though read. I then proceeded to plant a tree to commemorate this historic moment. While doing so, I broke into two pieces the silver spade that was given to me for the digging. Then, feeling exceedingly silly, I symbolically watered the tree with a small silver sprinkling can amid the continuing torrential downpour. After that, Dr. Roy, with all the authority of his eighty-two years, proposed a prompt return to Calcutta. And promptly we returned.

The one agreeable feature of the journey was our conversation on the way back. He told me of his role as Gandhi's attending physician at his fasts. In the end, Dr. Roy became quite an expert on the medical aspects of non-eating, and he thinks there is some positive merit in an occasional fast. His case is that the body only barely keeps abreast of the task of eliminating waste material from the food that is absorbed. A fast allows it to catch up and even get going on the backlog. If this isn't scientifically sound, it certainly should be.

Last night, there was a dinner at the Consulate which I barely got through. Now we are on our way to Darjeeling for what I hope will be a slight break.

April 24 — Gangtok, Sikkim

We arrived in Bagdogra about noon last Saturday — today being Tuesday — and shifted to jeeps and Land Rovers for the journey up to Darjeeling.[12] This climb up through the tea gardens was as pleasant as I remembered it from earlier travel. The road parallels a Tom Thumb railroad which must be one of the busiest in the world. Every few minutes the tiny mountain engines, each with a few cars, puff up and/or down. A brakeman rides on each car; the brass-bound engines with the coal tender atop the boiler are loaded with operatives.

We lunched at a Dak bungalow[13] along the way and got to Darjeeling about midafternoon. Kitty and I were quartered in moderate comfort in the bungalow of the manager of the Mount Everest Hotel; the rest of the party was hideously confined in small rooms at the back of the hotel. The Mount Everest, a great

---

[12] At 7,146 feet, it was the summer capital of Bengal in British times, and the Governor of West Bengal is still in official residence there in the hot months.

[13] Houses for accommodating traveling officials.

barracks of a place, combines a maximum of space with a minimum of charm. After a stroll through the shops, Kitty and Angie betook themselves to bed. I joined the male members of the party at a Chinese restaurant which, though dirty and endowed with a hideous orchestra, had exceedingly good food. Perhaps it was only by contrast with the cooking at the Residence which by common agreement has now reached a stage of awfulness imperiling the whole American position in the free world.

Sunday morning, Kitty, Angie and Al Carter[14] went up Tiger Hill to see the sunrise on Mount Everest. I contented myself with Kanchinjanga[15] which was on the western horizon in all of its magnificence. It is forty-five miles from Darjeeling but still seems to soar far above your head. After breakfast, I visited the peddlers of jewelry before the hotel. They quote fantastic prices, cut them drastically, sorrowfully surrender half that amount and still cheat you unmercifully. They clearly enjoy the bargaining. One was quite pleased when I asked him if it wasn't a major disadvantage for him, an indubitably honest man, to have such a dishonest face. I had correctly identified half of his problem.

Toward noon, we procured horses, quite tiny ones, and rode for a few miles to a water tank on a hilltop near the nearby town of Ghoom. I instructed Angie in proper riding — back stiff, lean forward on the saddle. She protested that the position was difficult for a woman and should be impossible for a man. But vanity triumphed; it obviously looked more professional and this was decisive.

In the evening, we had a merry party at the Chinese restaurant and came back to moderately more hideous quarters in the Mount Everest proper. Next morning at about nine we departed for Kalimpong.

The road from Darjeeling to Kalimpong lies through high foothills up to five or six thousand feet and once down to cross the river

[14] See page 92.
[15] 28,146 feet. Everest adds only another 882.

at about a thousand. It is open with fetching views of Kanchinjanga[16] and neighboring mountains and one passes through tea gardens which give the impression of a whole hillside of terraced and
sculptured green and then lovely teakwood forests interspersed
with great stretches of rich fir.

Kalimpong, where we arrived at noon, is the point of access for
Bhutan, Sikkim, Tibet and India — all of which, in a manner of
speaking, meet here. It has a famous reputation as a resort of spies,
thieves, smugglers and multipurpose rascals. A certain number of
people on the streets have faces that affirm their reputation. However, the reputation unquestionably exceeds the reality. The town
is perched on the side of a hill with a bazaar and a market, the latter
not being currently in operation. After lunch at an exotic and
highly uncomfortable hotel run by three sisters of Indian, Tibetan,
Scotch, and possibly other ancestry named Macdonald, we went
to the shops. These were strikingly without interest, but the people
in their variety of costume — Buddhist, Sikkimese and Tibetan
monks, numerous Indians, and a variety of secular mountain costumes — were colorful and enchanting. They are also very gay
and agreeable people and evidently liked being photographed.
After a strikingly pretty girl in dark red Tibetan robelike costume
had posed with us, she said, quite without warning, to Angie in
wonderfully precise English, "I saw you in *Rio Bravo*. Your hair
was darker then." Angie assured her it was.

In the midafternoon, I went to call on the Prime Minister of
Bhutan, Jigme Dorji,[17] who has a house on the hill above the town.
The P.M. is a small, very sensible, well-spoken man greatly inter-
ested in horseracing. His house somewhat resembles a small Long
Island country mansion of the late twenties — gray stone with low
gables in a well-tended garden. We talked of his kingdom which

[16] Once, some years earlier, making this trip I had pointed to the mountain and
said to the guide, "Everest?" He had replied, "No, Kanchinjanga." Impressed by
its great height, I had said, "Are you sure it isn't Everest?" He obligingly replied, "O.K., it's Everest."
[17] A year or two later struck down by an assassin.

has around 700,000 people but is devoid of cities (the largest has only one or two shops), telephones, electricity, newspapers, public opinion, sanitation or any of the other encumbrances of modern civilization. It does not even have a capital. The P.M. functions mostly from Calcutta and Kalimpong in a kind of external or correspondence-school administration. The Indian political agent operates from Gangtok in Sikkim. The Maharajah moves from one to another of seven Dzongs — half fortresses, half monasteries — and wherever he resides (as where McCrimmon sits) is the capital.

However, Bhutan does have some modern features. A big road-building program is engulfing him — so the P.M. told me — in paperwork he does not understand. He has also asked for a little American aid. That will complete his submergence in paper, poor man, and make him wholly modern.

In the late afternoon, we moved, this time to Mundsong, a West Bengal cinchona plantation of some ten or eleven thousand acres almost immediately adjoining the Tibetan border. The last stages of the road clung perilously to the mountainside and we were housed complete with guard of honor in a cottage on a high saddle, a good halfway to heaven. We had a magnificent view across a wide deep valley to mountain ranges in India, Sikkim, Bhutan and Nepal. Our bath consisted of pouring over oneself from a jug. Kitty and I washed our faces in rotation in the same water and the beds were more than firm, but I have rarely been so happy.

We were given a heroic welcome for dinner at the plantation. A delegation of children met and garlanded us, and a gay band of dancers and musicians led by an eloquently whirling drummer led us in procession to the plantation. There we were fed local beer in huge bamboo-stem steins. As one drank it down, someone with a teapot filled the stein with water and the water became beer. There is some fairy tale in imitation of this. We then had a program of children's folk dances with one particularly admirable number in which a villain of twelve, richly painted and costumed, put an alarming hex on all hands. We watched from the porch by lantern-light and afterward went down to inspect the barbecued carcass of a sheep that had been butchered that afternoon. Then we returned to the porch for a dinner of rice, curry, the barbecued sheep and assorted condiments, all served in a banana-leaf bowl on a low bench. At about nine, we were taken back up to our eagle's nest.

This morning, we had breakfast in the distant company of Kanchinjanga and looking down on more of the world than one can see from any other hilltop. I took the salute of our armed guard with great dignity in my pajamas. At half-past nine, after a good deal of unnecessary and pleasant confusion, we made our way down the mountain once more, bade farewell to our host, Anthony Fizelle, the plantation manager, and drove along the Tista River to the Sikkim border. For a moment, it looked as though our permission to enter Sikkim had been withdrawn[18] for we were waved back but only, we discovered, because the bridge was under repair. A fair-weather Bailey bridge was serving as substitute a little downstream and soon we were safely on the road to Gangtok.

This runs for fifteen or twenty miles along the river and initially through a succession of Indian army cantonments located here, presumably, to discourage the Chinese. The valley then widens, and the sides up to a height of two or three thousand feet are terraced and sprinkled with thatched cottages. People live out on the land; villages are very rare.

After a time, the road begins to climb and one gets glimpses of a town clinging to the mountain peaks far above. After a further climb, we arrived in what must be the most agreeable capital in the world. It is nearly six thousand (5,800) feet up the side of the mountain and consists, in principle, of one street making its way along the mountainside. We passed along this and up to the yellow-roofed palace, the gates of which are protected by two men in beef-eater hats, bright red jackets, white shirts and khaki leggings — all

[18] For various reasons, military and political, permission to visit Sikkim must be obtained from the Indian Government, but except in rare instances it is readily obtained.

in all, the most exquisitely attired soldiers I have ever seen. To add to the effect, not one is over five feet — only a trifle taller than his rifle.

We skirted the palace gate and came to the guesthouse. This is, perhaps, the most civilized building within a thousand miles of New Delhi — a modern, attractively designed little house with wide windows, good beds, taps that give out water and a surpassing location on a promontory with all the world below.

We had lunch pleasantly and privately in the guesthouse, looking out on the world beneath us. And toward the end of lunch, a thunderstorm came out of the mountains with violence. The mountain peaks on the way to Tibet were immediately covered by a thick coating of snow which we later learned was, in fact, hail. The storm was over almost as soon as it started and I then began, given the size of the town, a very substantial round of activities. Our first visitor was the Prime Minister, Baleshwar Prasad, known to the community as Diwan Sahib, who is the effective administrative head of the government and an Indian. He is a man with twinkling eyes and of medium height and impresses me as a very efficient operator. I can readily believe, as rumor suggests, that his efficiency may not be entirely matched by tact.[19] The top administration in Sikkim is by Indians. After we had chatted briefly, we made our way first to the handicraft center to see rug- and other cloth-weaving. The rug design seemed to be very good, and I bought two or three. It was my impression, however, that the participants in the enterprise had been conserving their energies for several days and went to work only as we arrived. Next we drove with the Prime Minister at breakneck speed down the main and only street of Gangtok to the Institute of Tibetology, about a mile-and-a-half distant on another peak. This interesting establishment, still rather sparsely stocked and populated, was opened by Nehru in 1958 as a cultural center for Tibetan refugees. It has an extremely rich collection of *thang-kas*[20] and a large number of

[19] Other Diwans have since succeeded him.
[20] See page 361.

Tibetan manuscripts, together with a less distinguished collection of Tibetan bronzes. It is a repository of scholarly and literary material brought out by lamas and lesser refugees.

From the Institute of Tibetology, we made another breakneck run back to the palace where we met the Maharajkumar,[21] his sister Princess Pema Tsedeun and other members of the ruling family. The Maharajah, a man of sixty-eight, but looking decidedly more ancient, is an enthusiastic and moderately competent painter who is interested in little else. I made a long and by no means uninteresting tour of his studio. His son, who is about to marry an American girl from Sarah Lawrence, is well-spoken, intelligent, handsome and most attractive. Even more so his sister who, like her brother, was dressed in Sikkimese costume, a most stylish, flowing robe with a high mandarin collar and, in her case, the symbolic protection of a silver dagger in her belt.

The palace is a comfortable hilltop affair, spacious without being especially ostentatious, and is also endowed with a handsome collection of Tibetan art including an even more attractive collection of *thang-kas* than in the Institute of Tibetology. *Thang-kas*, incidentally, are delicately wrought paintings on silk brocade. The dyes are usually ground stone of different colors. In another, and to me less attractive version, they are worked out in embroidery. The figures, especially in the paintings, are very sharp and delicate. I have bought two or three excellent specimens. From the palace, we went up to another hilltop — everybody of importance has a hill to himself — to visit the Indian political agent. The present agent, I. J. Bahadur Singh, is an old China hand, and we had a pleasant talk in the large house which he inherited, I imagine, from the British Resident. His duties extend also to Bhutan. In neither country are they currently feeling any severe Chinese pressure and there have been no incursions in recent years. Both countries, however, since they were once tributary to the Chinese empire, are considered a possible object of Chinese aspirations.

After a nap, we went back to the palace for a Tibetan dinner —

21 Meaning the son and heir of the Maharajah.

rice, curries, condiments — and afterward we entertained everybody with the film of J.B.K.'s visit. The latter was well received.
We were back for bed about eleven. However, the rest of the
party stayed on at the palace until four in the morning. There was
much dancing and merriment, and several members this morning,
including Phil Potter who is one of the two newspapermen covering this tour, showed signs of wear.

April 25 — Sikkim–Assam

We had breakfast on the terrace this morning, with the world
again spread out at our feet, and watched the guards being changed
in their twinkling red uniforms. At nine, the Prime Minister and
the Maharajkumar came down to bid us goodbye. The latter lent
us his Mercedes for the trip to Bagdogra, which was a big improvement in comfort over the Land Rover in which we arrived. Once
or twice we had to make our way on foot because of the extensive
road-building enterprises. The trip down was rather less spectacular than going up and much of it was through dense forest and in
the latter stages through jungle. We are now, at two o'clock, airborne and on the way to Shillong.

April 27 — Assam

Gauhati, when we arrived day before yesterday, was hot and
uncomfortable. And we had missed the gate on the road up to
Shillong — this is an arrangement by which traffic up and down
the mountain moves one-way with a change of direction every two
hours. We waited in the Circuit House on the banks of the
Brahmaputra where, as compensation, I had a good sleep.

In midafternoon, we drove out of the lowlands of the Brahmaputra — a great, winding river with a broad Mississippi-like aspect,
and up into the Shillong hills. Evidently, one cannot be completely
confident of the one-way arrangement for we did meet an occasional down-coming lorry. But it is a rather good arrangement
for a winding mountain road. As to the winding, there is no doubt.

Guest cottage — Maharajah of Mysore

THE SCENE — 2

Cottage — built for American Ambassador in Bhutan

Bungalow — Gaekwar of Baroda

Palace — Mysore

Palace — Udaipur

Another palace — Udaipur

Wheel on which rides temple of the Gods — Kanarak
(Adjacent carvings repay study)

AMBASSADOR'S WIFE AT WORK

Dancing

Posing

Consuming

Modeling clothes (for Mrs. Gandhi, Mrs. Kennedy)

Communing silently (with President Prasad)

Ship of the desert

By the time we got to Shillong, Kitty and Angie, both of whom are subject to car sickness, had a complexion consisting of bright green and yellow stripes.

The countryside coming up the Shillong hills is rough, tropical and much less densely populated than most of India. The soil is deep and red, and the prevailing rural architecture is a bamboo hut roughly resembling an overturned basket.

We arrived about eight at the Raj Bhavan, a low, rambling house — half-timbered with deep gables — of English vintage and were installed in the guest wing. My bed was extended to a full eight feet; arrangements could not have been more comfortable. The Governor canceled an official dinner and we ate privately and well and went early to bed.

Yesterday morning at dawn, we discovered the full advantages of our surroundings. We are in a lovely English park of perhaps fifty acres, with good landscaping, fine trees and lots of bright flowers. It is very green and also very cool. Birds are available in remarkable variety, color and song.

In the morning, I dictated the inevitable speech and strolled in the park. We lunched with Governor Shrinagesh[22] and family — he is a former Army Chief of Staff. Their daughter was predictably stunned by Angie in real life.

In the afternoon, I met with the Assam Cabinet for informal discussion of the economic problems of the State. It feels very disturbed and neglected. Yet, with comparatively ample land and resources (including oil) and good cash crops (tea and jute), its prospect would seem to be brighter than most parts of India. Next came a press conference at which a local correspondent tried desperately to arouse my outrage over the installation of some Czech equipment in an American-aided power plant near town. I told him we had more important worries. Another asked me to specify

---

[22] S. M. Shrinagesh. He is a member of a family noted for its service to India in numerous and varied capacities. (See page 414 for reference to his brother, J. M. Shrinagesh.)

which was the best-governed Indian state — I seem now to have visited them all. I replied Madras but uncourageously placed my answer off the record.

Then we had a small dinner with the Governor and family and then films. We had Mrs. Kennedy once more including a speech by me about the architecture of our Chancery that I cannot stand to hear again. I said government buildings should always be too small to keep down their population. Then we had some excellent local movies on the wildlife sanctuaries we are about to visit. They are by a local naturalist named Gee and are genuine works of art. We may have gone a little overboard on animals on this trip.

April 29 — Camp Galbraith, Bhutan

The Governor had a luncheon for us day before yesterday — today being Sunday — with the principal citizens of Assam attending. Then in the afternoon we climbed up through a forest to have tea at his mountain hideout. This was a quiet and pleasant exercise followed by a speech at the Rotary Club on export policy and designed at least partly to prove that I am the kind of man who speaks to Rotary. The President-Rotarian introduced Phil Potter (of the *Baltimore Sun*) as Mr. Baltimore. The Governor had asked us to coffee at nine and on the excuse of this beverage, I managed to be away an hour ahead of time.

At coffee, I presented books. We, in turn, were given stoles, an embroidered jacket and a silver pipe.

Yesterday morning at dawn, we mounted the cars for the tiresome and twisting journey back to Gauhati. There we arrived toward noon. After a few minutes at the Circuit House and a stroll along the river — straw huts and exotic river craft — we embarked on an ancient ferry for the twenty-minute ride across the Brahmaputra. This led into another four-hour drive to the north, broken once for a picnic lunch by a dried-up and dusty stream and once when a vast throng blocked the road to read me an address of welcome. It was precisely thirty seconds from the moment when

I was aroused from sleep in the car until I was making a speech. For the rest, it was one hot and incredibly dusty mile after another.

However, the end was happy. At about five, we reached tea gardens and the first foothills. Then, after some more road dustier than any we had seen, we came to the Manas game preserve and a Dak bungalow atop a small bluff overlooking the Manas. Numerous dignitaries were assembled to welcome us. When they had done so, our party was transferred to a long, narrow boat poled by men fore and aft. We sat in armchairs of some splendor and made our way up and across stream for a mile or so. By now, we were in Bhutan and our boats were guarded by two handsomely caparisoned men — a loose, red embroidered robe and cap — and by the Forest Officer and Assistant District Commissioner of Southern Bhutan.

We disembarked at a specially constructed floating landing place where we were welcomed a second time and here we mounted five elephants — Kitty and I on a colossal beast who must have been a full ten feet high.

We proceeded for another mile, the last half through double rows of prayer flags — red, white and blue atop high bamboo poles — and into our camp.

The visit of an ambassador to Bhutan does not happen every day — indeed, it never happened before — and this may be just as well. Some three hundred men have been toiling for the last fourteen days to prepare for us and they have cleared the jungle and built nothing less than a small village of houses.

These stand on a high bluff over the river. They include an octangular pavilion something like a bandstand immediately above the river; a two-bedroom and two-bathroom, center-hall-and-porch bungalow for Kitty, Angie and me; a large dining room in the center of the compound; five or six smaller cottages for the rest of the party; and a cookhouse and various outbuildings.

The houses are made of basket-weave bamboo on a heavy wooden frame, the weaving of white, green and brown strips being so accomplished as to make a rectangular design. The inner walls are lined with cheesecloth as is the ceiling. There is no glass; dark green curtains cover the windows. The floors, which are also of bamboo, are a foot or so off the ground and have a marvelous springy quality as well as a wholesome crunch and crackle. It is, in fact, like walking on the bottom of a basket.

Great pains have gone into contriving plumbing — pails and great tin tubs — and a wooden toilet which a diligent man watches and cleans out after each use. We even have extra-length beds and mattresses and they are far from uncomfortable.

After passing under a welcoming arch — orchids and greenery — and through smoke fires to deter the evil spirits in the vicinity, and which were operating most satisfactorily, I was officially greeted by the Commissioner for Southern Bhutan, a girthful, courtly man of sixty-six dressed in the red embroidered garment above mentioned. I returned his welcome and asked that President Kennedy's official greetings be extended to the Maharajah. President Kennedy was unaware of the courtesy he was thus dispensing. This the Commissioner promised to transmit forthwith by wireless, there being no postal system in Bhutan. He told me he had never dreamed of welcoming the U.S. Ambassador to Bhutan. Then we went to the pavilion for beer and thereafter went down the bluff for a swim in the river. The river is brisk and cold, and one can have a good swim keeping even with the current. It was a great relief after the heat, dust and other tortures of the day.

At 7 P.M., we gathered with the Commissioner and Forest Officer in the pavilion and at seven-thirty for stewed venison, rice and chicken in the dining room. At nine, we made our way along the graveled walks that have been laid out around and across the compound to bed. Giant June bugs were buzzing around the oil lamps and ignoring two small men who were energetically pumping Flit into the air. But when the lights went out so, evidently, did they.

My sinus assailed me by night, and I slept fitfully when at all. At five, I gave up the effort with relief and at six, we mounted elephants — half a dozen this time — for an inspection of the game.

Of the latter we saw little but the cruise through the jungle had its points. Our massive beast of the previous day led the way, occasionally tearing off a branch or bringing down a tree that compromised our passage. He also picked up and stored between his tusks a great quantity of a favorite forage that grew at intervals along the path. This he then ate with relish when he had the opportunity to enjoy it properly.

The jungle is not very exciting — sparse trees and a badly burned forest floor. Once we came out on the river and saw a wild buffalo and a couple of sambar — largish, handsome deer. Then we crossed belly-deep to an island, our procession looking very impressive indeed. After a couple of hours, I had enough and detached one elephant and guard — a rifle to contend with a possible tiger — and came home. Much of the passage back was down the river — again belly-deep at times. Once my elephant saw a foreign object on the shingle. He stopped, picked it up and gave it to the mahout.[23] It was a film container or spool.

April 30 — Gauhati–Jorhat

After lunch yesterday, we subsided for an hour or two and then went for a swim. The current is very rapid with strong eddies and once when I ventured out too far, I was quickly sucked under. As will be evident, I came up. Then we took boats upriver for a mile or two, poling against the current. Once the boatmen got out to pull us over a ledge. Eventually, we came out on a low beach with the heavily wooded banks rising abruptly on each side. The view is pleasant but not stunning. We looked at a school of crocodiles sunning themselves on a rock across the river and three or four hundred yards upstream. The trip up took close to an hour; we were back in a little more than ten minutes.

On return, I had a press conference with the two newsmen, Phil Potter and Pat Killen of U.P.I., so they could date a story from Camp Galbraith, Bhutan. I told them much of what the Prime

---

23 The chauffeur of an elephant.

Minister had told me in Kalimpong — no post office, no city large enough to sustain more than one shop, no telephones but radios, details of the road-building program, the request for economic aid which we are clearing with the Indians. We were considerably worried about Angie who seemed to have some fever, a complicated form of dysentery and a state of general exhaustion.

Dinner was ceremonial. The Commissioner and I sat opposite each other and, after a formal discussion of Bhutan and its prospects, I thanked him for his hospitality and he responded. In the light of the flickering lamp and in the specially built state dining room of triangular lattice bamboo and cheesecloth, it was quite mysterious.

This morning, aided by the nine o'clock bedtime, we were up at five and Angie to our relief was quite recovered. We had a fine breakfast by courtesy of Lowrie Campbell's[24] cook, whom we hope to hire for the Residence. Prior to breakfast, we had accomplished a quick swim.

The trip down the river and back to Gauhati went quite rapidly and we were an hour or so ahead of our ferry. We made it across on a launch and after a good lunch took off for Jorhat. We dropped Angie in Gauhati for Calcutta, Bombay and Europe. She won everyone's heart with her good looks, high spirits and rugged delight in the experience. We were sorry to see her go.

May 1 — Jorhat–Imphal

We arrived in Jorhat late yesterday afternoon and embarked in cars for a long twilight ride to Khaziranga, the most famous game preserve in eastern India. Actually, as so often in India, it was more a matter of time than mileage. The latter was only about sixty miles but it took more than two wearing hours of continuous horn-screeching to make it. The road, through tea estates for much of

---

[24] A highly intelligent member of the Embassy staff and authority on the mountain peoples and their languages who had managed this part of the tour. We did not, in the end, steal his cook.

the way, is not unpleasant but it was dark well before we arrived. At the sanctuary, we were housed in an airy, two-story guesthouse — very comfortable. I was very weary and we went to bed directly from dinner in the room.

This morning, we got up at four-thirty and mounted eight elephants at the rate of three to a beast plus mahout. The animals were soon visible in abundance — single-horned rhinoceros, the leading exhibit, plus hog deer, swamp deer and wild buffalo. The rhinos are vast, heavily-armored, lumbering beasts and quite tame. One or two shamelessly mugged the camera. They were visible everywhere singly, in pairs or families of three or four. I am told that they are not very fierce. In the old days, they were tamed for plowing, and a few months ago an old bull developed the habit of following the elephants whenever they came out, giving the tourists a poor impression of his native savagery. One in the stockade was sold some time ago to the Paris Zoo for Rs. 20,000 (about $4,000) — the price is now Rs. 40,000 ($8,000). An elephant, incidentally, costs only about Rs. 4,000 ($800).

May 2 — Imphal–Gauhati

At about eight yesterday morning, we returned from our safari and drove back to Jorhat and made a rough and bumpy flight to Imphal, capital of Manipur. Manipur is not a full state but a centrally administered territory under a Chief Commissioner reporting to the Home Ministry. There was some question about getting into the valley at Imphal and some question whether we might not come down before reaching it for we ran into a most violent thunderstorm en route. But with some shake-up, we got through the storm and when we arrived over the valley, it was clear.

Commissioner and Mrs. Raina,[25] a highly civilized couple from the United Provinces and originally from Kashmir, gave us a warm welcome and launched us on a major program of activities.

While Kitty went out to visit villages, I caught an hour's sleep

25 J. M. N. Raina.

and then went to a large reception at the Imphal Municipal Corporation. I was presented ceremoniously with sundry local textiles and an ivory walking stick. These were given to me on big brass platters; I learned a little later, to my embarrassment, that the platters were not part of the package and returned them.

Then we went on to the exhibition of Manipuri ballet dancing. Mrs. Raina is the choreographer, stage designer and producer, and it was colorful, lively and amusing. The costumes were exceedingly gay. There was also a rather interesting story line of young love, jealousy, tiger-killing and the like. We showed the inevitable movie.

It was ten before it was over and an hour-long party ensued before we finally went to dinner. I was very tired. Kitty, having done the villages, was more so.

This morning, we slept until seven — since leaving Shillong, we have turned out not later than five every morning — and went strolling in the garden of the Commissioner's House. The latter is a hideously-painted red brick inherited from the British Raj and includes a cemetery full of the subalterns, lieutenants and I.C.S. officers who succumbed to the climate — often in their twenties. Many of them worked hard for the well-being of the people. Their reward is to be remembered as imperialists.

At nine-thirty, we went to a polo game. Here the game is played by all available horsemen and the concern is only that the number on each side be equal. Most other rules have been dispensed with and, until recently, it was sufficient to hit the ball over a line at the other team's end of the field. The horses are tiny as are the men who wear leggings but go barefoot. Some suggest that polo originated here. In accordance with custom, the chief presented my wife with his horse; she, in accordance with custom, returned it.

Next we made a ceremonial visit to a couple of villages with more dancing, offers of refreshment, rice beer and other edibles, all of which one must seem to eat. We were presented with various gifts and I made an offsetting contribution to the village cultural association. Finally lunch and takeoff. The latter was a little uncertain for the field which we had planned to use was not in service and the new one was a thousand feet shorter. But we did it with something to spare. Now we are landing at Gauhati for the fuel we had to unload at Imphal.

Manipur is divided as between the plains people who are mostly Hindus and the tribal peoples of the hills — some of whom also live in the valleys — who were largely Christianized in the last century, in the main by Baptist missionaries. The Nagas are the leading tribal group and they are currently in revolt against the Indian Government. They wish a separate Naga state. An estimated two or three thousand are conducting active operations and causing the authorities a great deal of trouble in Assam and NEFA[26] as well as here in Manipur. They are armed with weapons left behind from World War II. Support is smuggled in from Burma and, the Indians allege, from East Pakistan.

Manipur is remarkable, among other things, for its clean and tidy countryside, tidy villages of bamboo and thatch, all of which may reflect the decisive role of the women in the society. Women do the work — plant, cultivate, fish, cook — and also manage, conduct business and entertain. Since they earn the money, they manage it too and keep their husbands on a retainer. If a man wants a bicycle, a bush shirt or a battery lamp, consumer goods that are all in high demand, he petitions his wife. If she deems him worthy or is otherwise in an affectionate mood, he gets it. Perhaps as an insurance of an adequate living, a great many men have two wives. The latter do not object. The market stalls are dominated by women who arrange things with neatness and grace. When the day is over, they don their good clothes and dance. The tribal women wear bright red and black sarongs which wrap around the breasts just above the nipples leaving the shoulders bare. They are supple and pretty.

[26] North East Frontier Agency, the wild mountainous area north of Assam and east of Bhutan.

May 7 — Bombay–New Delhi

Following my return last Wednesday, there were many weary tasks, all characterized in common by their total absence of interest. A large amount of dull mail had accumulated.

Last night, my plane being out of commission, Timmons and I took the Indian Airlines Viscount to Bombay. After a highly un-comfortable ride, we reached Lincoln House which we occupied by ourselves, Bob Carr being in the United States. His wife has now an advanced stage of cancer. This morning, we went out to the airport and at nine-thirty, the huge Boeing came in taking Dean Rusk on to Australia. We talked in the airport lounge for about an hour-and-a-half on all available topics — Berlin, Pakistan, China, aid legislation, trade legislation, atomic energy. I learned nothing new. Rusk was intelligent, unforthcoming and wary. We were advised on a lot of matters — Berlin, the reaction to Mrs. Kennedy's visit, summitry, aid prospects — on which I was already tolerably well-informed.

✧ ✧ ✧

Bombay, India
May 7, 1962

Dear Mr. President:

It is some time since you have had one of these reports, a gap to be related more or less equally to the state of my stomach, the pressure of other tasks including most recently the need to com-plete some travel before the heat here becomes unbearable, and the absence of any information for which, by my best assessment, you could have an incontrollable thirst.

I am writing from Bombay where I have just spent an hour or two with your Secretary of State. We had a useful and agreeable session. While I still do not find him the easy, confident, forth-coming, eclectic and commanding figure with which in my imagination I associate the diplomacy of the New Frontier, we get along much better than hitherto. This is partly because, in some indefinable way, our foreign policy does seem to me to show increasing evidence of thought. But as you are aware I grow mellower by the month.

My most recent major worry has been over testing[27] and the danger of a major anti-American explosion with some serious effect on fundamental public and political attitudes. However, we have come through all right. We are getting only a few strictly C.P.[28] demonstrations. The press, politicians and public are not aroused even in this congenial environment. Partly it is the general good management by the Kennedy Administration. We have managed to establish our reputation for good sense and restraint; we obviously responded to the Soviet initiative with reluctance; we have managed to keep in focus the simple fact that the Russians did it first.

I suspect also that this is the reward for a lot of patient and tedious effort. Clearly the government, press, students and pundits do not want to embarrass us on the issue. And one reason is that our cultivation of the universities and press, your unrewarding hours with Nehru last autumn, Jackie's visit and other efforts have persuaded the Indians that we are good people and they have no righteous obligation to embarrass us.

Incidentally, I hope the series will be run as rapidly through to conclusion as possible. Time deepens the effect and engages passions. I also strongly endorse the policy of the minimum of needful publicity and avoidance of comment on the destructive virtuosity of the gadgets we are testing.

One of my current problems is Ayub's compulsively repeated statements that he will use American arms against India if the need arise. He said it again last week and, naturally, the Indian press reacted joyously. It greatly helps those who want to buy Soviet aircraft, an enterprise I am trying to stand off. There was never such a drastic misadventure in modern diplomacy as

[27] The reference here is to the resumption of nuclear testing.
[28] Communist Party.

these minor alliances of Dulles. Machiavelli warned weak princes against joining with a strong one. In my forthcoming revision of his work, I will warn all strong states against weak ones. Since weak states are weak, the strong state gets no added strength out of its alliance. But the weak state can use its stronger ally for its own purposes. Since the state is small and weak, its purposes will be small and undignified. To these the large state becomes a party and such is our present fate. From the Portuguese to General Phoumi our indigent allies are principally concerned with how to use the U.S. to promote their puny affairs.

In fact the United States should stand in majesty and grandeur above such matters. Involved we lose our influence. Above we could have great influence. The major N.A.T.O. powers apart, I cannot think of anything so important as that we have a gradual but inflexible will to remove ourselves from special relationships with the Albanias of the world and be prepared, instead, to help and treat all alike. There is of course nothing in the experience of being Ambassador to India which argues against this view. But this was always our instinct and it shouldn't surprise us that we were right.

One feature of the State Department mind on which I find I have not mellowed is its profound moral conviction that established policy is to be preferred to the one that is best for the United States.

I am coming back more or less privately for a few days in early June to get an honorary degree and possibly get some more of the medical advice for which I am becoming a kind of global customer. I plan in a speech to develop the point you raised at Glen Ora; namely, what, on candid view, are the advantages and disadvantages of communism as compared with our mixture from the viewpoint of the new and developing country. Thought, as distinct from *obiter dicta*, will show I think that we do have some important advantages and more than incidentally, that we have some faults that if remedied would add to our margin of advantage. In accordance with established procedures, I will send you a copy.

My recent travels have taken me up along the Chinese frontier and back to the Burma border. In addition to their better-publicized problems with the Chinese, the Indians are having very serious trouble in living with people within their own borders. This is an area with a large number of ethnically separate groups and all are unhappy in their present relations with the Indians. The Nagas are in open revolt and tie down a couple of divisions but they are only the extreme case. A half dozen other ethnic or linguistic groups are asking what they can have in the way of independence, autonomy or self-determination.[29]

Yours faithfully,
JOHN KENNETH GALBRAITH

THE PRESIDENT
THE WHITE HOUSE

[29] A final untactful sentence was deleted from this letter.

XVIII

Interlude — Mostly Dull

May 19 — London–Boston

A fortnight ago, I was struck simultaneously by the prospect of a drastic cut in economic aid by the Senate Foreign Relations Committee and a proposal by the Indians to buy a couple of squadrons of MIG-21 interceptors from the Soviets. The timing of the combination could hardly have been worse. The Senators thought the MIG purchase was a reaction to the cut. The Indians thought the cut was punishment for the MIG deal. Since the latter leaked out, no one could say which came first. And then the Pakistanis moved to reopen the Kashmir dispute. They also opened negotiations on the Kashmir boundary with the Chinese, infuriating the Indians and adding to our problem.

After long discussions with M. J. Desai, Morarji Desai[1] and a bitter interchange with Krishna Menon, the MIG purchase was postponed for a month. I also urged the principle that purchases for rupees from the Russians at concessional rates was military aid no less than procurement for rupees from the U.S. The Administration meanwhile has moved to win restoration of the aid cut. Now I am on my way back at Fowler Hamilton's[2] behest to help on that. Meanwhile, I urged the Indians to behave as agreeably as possible on Kashmir.

---

[1] See page 140.
[2] New York lawyer and then director of the Agency for International Development.

All of this has been in the context of a bad stomach and no sleep. The doctor finally told me I should have another round of medical investigation. My plan is to start that in Boston tomorrow. I would like to spend as little time as possible in Washington for I have been there too much.[3]

May 29 — Newfane, Vermont

I have had a very good week in Vermont and once more am sleeping like a lamb. Brilliant spring day has succeeded equally brilliant spring day. My study commands a world of emerald green and blue. Ena Gladden[4] has provided me with meals of astonishing size and quality.

The only flaw in this Elysium has been the stock market. Monday it took a terrible plunge, and as the Thucydides of the 1929 crash, I was immediately called by the President. To his annoyance, I had not heard about it. I was getting no papers and not listening to the radio. Our conversation was on a well-populated party line which allows of a very helpful measure of mutual surveillance. My neighbors must have felt the President needed better-informed advisers. The President was thinking of going on television to calm fevered nerves. I persuaded him not to do so. He would put his prestige on the line. The fact that he spoke would give the impression that things were serious. Speculators, as like as not, would say now that the President is persuading everyone to hold on when they should sell. Thus a worse debacle.

In the afternoon, the market rallied and the question became academic.

June 2 — Washington–Baltimore–Portland

Two days in Washington have had a drastic effect on my health but a better impact on my psyche.

[3] During my first year in India, there was some discussion by the Republicans of the time I spent in Washington. Some, it was said, felt not that I was neglecting India but that I was insufficiently neglecting the United States.

[4] Family friend and frequent helper.

I have been working hard on the Tarapur, MIG's and on paving the way generally for military aid. The first — a loan for a big new atomic power plant near Bombay — is going very well. It was a pleasure to meet with Glenn Seaborg[5] and Henry Smyth[6] and to see how efficiently they responded to the thrust of good ideas. The plant was discussed a year ago but then seemed too expensive in relation to coal. Now the process has become much cheaper and coal (in India) more costly. And when the Chinese start exploding nuclear devices, a big peaceful atomic plant will bolster Indian self-esteem. If the Indians want Tarapur, they will have to accept controls on the fissionable material; if they do that and the costs check out in a reasonable way, they will evidently get it.

The problems posed by the MIG deal are more difficult. Everyone or nearly everyone agrees that the Soviets should not become the main suppliers of the Indian defense forces. But no one wants to face either the congressional objections to granting military aid to the Indians or those of Pakistan. So they just keep wishing I would not press for a decision. Last night, I extracted a letter to Macmillan asking the British to offer Lightnings at concessional rates. I must still get permission to talk about other military items with a reasonable prospect of being backed up. The Indians get Soviet equipment against rupee payment — costs being highly arbitrary and presumptively subsidized. This is said not to be aid. On our side, sales for rupees are classified as military assistance. As noted, I have made it clear that this is a distinction we cannot accept. But the point is only worth making if we have something to offer.

The Senate, led by Stuart Symington, cut the aid authorization 25 percent but has now restored it. However, I am seeing Symington and meeting the Committee for a general briefing next week. A question is how much of Symington's reaction was caused by

[5] Former Chancellor of the University of California at Berkeley and, by appointment of President Kennedy, Chairman of the Atomic Energy Commission.

[6] U.S. Representative, International Atomic Energy Agency. Previously a member of the Commission and author of the famous Smyth Report on *Atomic Energy for Military Purposes*.

my failure to get him an appointment with Nehru when he visited India last autumn. The *New Republic* so says. He says no.

Last night, the Kennedys gave me a highly agreeable dinner and dance at the White House. J.B.K. asked the Brooks Becks and the Alexander Ellises.[7] The party, about forty in all, emphasized good and sometimes sultry looks. For dinner, I had as partners a Swedish-French screen actress who is also a model for a dress designer and Lilly Pulitzer, granddaughter-in-law of Joe Pulitzer, who has a rich Palm Beach suntan and admirable shape.

The President toasted B. K. Nehru, Hervé Alphand, the French Ambassador, and myself and noted that no three envoys in history had produced such a disastrous effect on the relations between the countries represented. I responded with a poor joke about my speech material, my intended book on the care and maintenance of Presidents' wives and how J.B.K. had applauded a speech she had dictated to me. (The reverse had been noticed.) Dancing lasted until 5 A.M. I departed at three to protect my reputation as an invalid. I drank much champagne and woke up at nine with a remarkably clear head. Diana Michaelis,[8] looking very blond, fresh and chic, came for breakfast. She is unenthusiastic about Washington and is coping with difficult problems of aging parents. It was something of a scramble to organize my departure and get the plane I am now on at 1:15 P.M. I arrived at Friendship without my ticket (which remained at the Hay-Adams) but emergency substitutes were arranged.

June 4 — San Francisco–Washington

Much travel signifying less than it should. I got to Portland latish Saturday afternoon and dined at the Waverley (I think) Country Club which was wonderfully green and fresh. Then I had

---

[7] Friends from, respectively, Canton and Concord, Massachusetts. Brooks Beck is my lawyer. His wife, the daughter of Samuel Eliot Morison and an admirable scholar in her own right, and I were graduate (research) students together at Cambridge University.

[8] Cambridge friend and a highly distinguished producer of television programs and motion picture films. A documentary on VISTA produced under her supervision by Edmond A. Levy won the 1966 Oscar.

a long night's sleep followed by a pleasant morning stroll through downtown. The streets were clean and the trees in their boxes along the sidewalks give a gardenlike appearance to what elsewhere is harsh and urban pavement. In the suburbs, the rhododendrons are a rainbow of color.

I visited the Jebbie Davidsons who had invited Monroe Sweetland and wife[9] to their elegant house on top of the city. Then on to a press conference:

"Do you expect to be Ambassador to Russia?"

"No."

Then I went on to Lewis and Clark College for lunch, a speech and an honorary degree. Commencement was in the gymnasium and my audience was attentive and responsive. I am not sure either their education or my honors entirely justified the journey.

Then, after a tedious reception — "We enjoyed your message a lot" — I caught the plane to San Francisco. Much of the country en route is lush and green and reassuringly unpopulated. The Commonwealth Club where I am to speak does not put itself out in hospitality. I made my way to town, to the Palace Hotel and on to Chinatown for dinner. This morning, I got up late, talked with Aaron Gordon[10] and Clark Kerr,[11] made my speech and rushed for a car to connect with a 2:15 P.M. plane. (Lunch 12 noon, speech 12:30 P.M. to 1:00 P.M., questions 1:00 P.M. to 1:15 P.M. An hour to the airport.) However, the plane was an hour late.

The speech, on the comparative advantages of Marxian and non-Marxian development, was fine in text. As a speech, I had to condense it too much. It may be better in *The Atlantic Monthly* where I plan to publish it.[12]

[9] Oregon Democratic leaders and friends. Mr. Davidson is a former Assistant Secretary of the Interior; Joan Davidson is a devoted liberal and devoted friend. Monroe Sweetland is a former Oregon State Senator.
[10] Professor of Economics at the University of California at Berkeley.
[11] Then President of the University of California.
[12] October 1962. "The Poverty of Nations."

June 15 — Washington–Rome

On return from the Coast, I was immediately involved in a series of meetings on the state of the economy. Everyone, including the President, is prematurely alarmed about the economic prospect and the antagonism of business generated by his recent condemnation, and forced reversal, of steel price increases. At a meeting in Walter Heller's office the night after I returned from San Francisco — Heller, James Tobin, Paul Samuelson, Robert Solow, David Bell, others[13] — everyone was for an immediate tax cut to give a boost to the economy, myself and possibly the Budget people excepted. The next day, Wednesday, I deliberately missed further meetings including one at 5:30 P.M. in the Cabinet Room. But I saw the President beforehand and weighed in heavily against the action. It is premature; money from tax reduction goes into the pockets of those who need it least; lower tax revenues will become a ceiling on spending; there will be a nasty contrast if Congress cuts taxes but does not extend temporary unemployment compensation. I also stressed to the President the importance of realizing that in economics, the majority is always wrong. The tax cut was postponed until next year.

The same day — June 6 — I testified before the Senate Foreign Relations Committee. Only a handful of Senators were there with Albert Gore[14] presiding. By sticking to my usual rules of answering all questions with all seeming candor and assuming the friendly tendencies of every Senator however hostile, I got by very well. There was the usual adverse reaction to Krishna Menon. I conceded that he might be trying to drive a wedge between the U.S. and India and urged the importance of not falling into the trap. This would be the effect of cutting aid and similar punitive action.

By the end of the two days in Washington, my feeling of well-being from Vermont was gone. I put in one more day — Thursday

---

[13] Paul Samuelson is a professor at Massachusetts Institute of Technology; Robert Solow, also an M.I.T. professor, was on the staff of the Council.
[14] Old friend and Senator from Tennessee.

— helping the President with his speech for the Yale Commencement. Arthur Schlesinger, Mac Bundy and Ted Sorensen also participated. In the end, not much of my draft survived — something on the arrogance of insisting that a President earns business confidence by always agreeing with them and a few phrases. A sobering form of literary expression, this. One expends much effort and never reaches any audience whatever.

Thursday evening, I went to New York and was met by Jean vanden Heuvel[15] and her father's Rolls Royce and went out to Ruth Field's estate where she had rented the Winter Cottage for the month. The estate is of several thousand acres and about to become a park. Confiscation of such properties for the people — parks or development — seems as inevitable in the U.S. as in Poland. The only difference is the reason. In our case, taxes and the impossibility of organizing the requisite staff at any price are the compelling causes.

For a week, I slept long and without a troubled thought, swam, walked and was surrounded by a succession of attractive guests, mostly from the theater, including a reassuring number of good-looking women. Jean was a constant, attentive and agreeable hostess. Bill was present for most of the time in equally agreeable masculine version. I found myself able to drink a little again without damage. I also wrote a story under a pseudonym, which *Esquire* promptly took for $1,000.[16] Joan Fontaine (who had recently been in India) told me in great confidence that Emily exposed many of the details of our family life to our friends in New Delhi. I tried to seem surprised and alarmed.

[15] William vanden Heuvel has long been active in New York State Democratic politics. Thereafter he was on Robert Kennedy's staff in the Department of Justice and more recently a member of the State Constitutional Convention. His wife, Jean, a sensitive if unprolific writer, is also much interested in theater and television. Ruth Field is the former wife of the late Marshall Field.

[16] The first of the McLandress series by Mark Epernay. *The McLandress Dimension* (Boston: Houghton Mifflin, 1963).

June 18 — Beirut–New Delhi

This is early Monday morning and my last chance to come abreast. While in Washington, we worked out an arrangement with the British to counter the MIG offer of the Soviets. We would underwrite part of the cost of British fighters and the development of an engine for the Indian supersonic fighter. Needless to say, we would put up most of the price. Thursday morning, my having come to the Dorset in New York the night before, the President called to say he disliked the deal. Why should we spend $40 million to save the Indians from a foolish bargain? Ersi Breunig[17] had come over to visit me; the President rudely switched me back to the hard truths of existence. I pointed out that the problem was to support our friends in the Indian Government and give them an alternative. Less friendly people were hoping to throw a hooker into U.S.-Indian relations by this action. In the end, I canceled my New York appointments — Adlai Stevenson and James Perkins of the Carnegie Corporation[18] — and took the plane back to Washington.

At a six o'clock meeting at the White House — McNamara, George Ball, Walter McConaughy and James Grant[19] — we got things straightened out. Bob McNamara proposed an offer of fewer fighting planes and more heavy transports which suited me.[20] The President's resistance had meanwhile melted. I had thought for a while I might have to go back empty-handed and designed a strategy for this. A strong letter from the President — one politician to another — asking for postponement of the deal and urging the irrelevance of the weapons. The latter is an important point.

[17] See page 346.
[18] See page 4.
[19] Deputy Assistant Secretary of State.
[20] I now look back on this effort to stop the MIG deal, its congressional public relations aspect apart, as unwarranted. The planes were a great waste of money, as were the F-104's for Pakistan, but that was the Indians' business. The foothold they provided to the Soviets in supplying military goods was not important.

Supersonic planes go so fast they can neither see nor find anything without ground radar which the Indians do not have. Were they used in ground support operations, they would hit the ground before they hit the enemy. However, with an alternative, my position is much stronger.

After the meeting, I called J.B.K. who asked me over to supper. We sat talking at the west end of the great hall upstairs which they have made their living room. (Perhaps it always was.) The President came in and presently came an invitation to go to Jean Smith's for dinner. The President had his rocking chair packed up and we adjourned there. It was a gay dinner party in the garden — the Peter Lawfords,[21] Rowland Evans and wife, Ben Bradlee and wife,[22] Robert and Ethel Kennedy — with speeches, records, dancing on the grass and much fun. J.B.K. was my dinner partner and we exhaustively reviewed Washington life to the disadvantage of all participants.

Next day, Friday, I wound up business at State and in the evening, flew to Rome. There I slept twelve hours, got up early this morning, walked to St. Peter's and caught a noon plane to Beirut. With four hours to spare, I had a nice swim. At Karachi, Bill Hall[23] filled me in on MIG negotiations. I am now near New Delhi. My firm resolution is to keep this diary more fully abreast.

June 19 — New Delhi

I got back at dawn yesterday. It was already hot and uncomfortable at the airport and I was besieged by reporters wanting to know about MIG's. After a couple of hours' stop, I had a meeting with Duncan Sandys[24] who is here to talk about the Common

---

[21] Sister and brother-in-law of the President.

[22] Reporters, respectively, for the *Herald Tribune* and *Newsweek* and friends of the Kennedys. Evans is now a columnist and Bradlee the Executive Editor of the *Washington Post*.

[23] William O. Hall, Deputy Chief of Mission, American Embassy, Pakistan.

[24] Political leader in the Conservative party, and head of the Commonwealth Relations Office. He is a former son-in-law of Winston Churchill.

Market and to try to stop the MIG deal. He is not popular with Nehru. He is exceedingly self-confident and reminds the Prime Minister, I fear, of the kind of Englishman who put him in jail.

Kitty is up in the Kulu Valley with the boys and has put Bim[25] in charge of me. After lunch, I cleaned up the desk accumulation — not excessive — and in the evening, saw M. J. Desai. I thought it well to ask him how he would handle the problem which the MIG deal poses for our congressional relations. He will tell Nehru I asked him. That will clear the way for me to raise the matter.

The Indians have developed an interesting theory that MIG's, since no one knows the cost, are not subsidized. "It is inherent in the system." I asked if that would still be true if the price got down to (say) eight annas (10¢).

June 20 — New Delhi

Yesterday the British went back to their Lightning offer for reasons which had mostly, I would judge, to do with cost. This came in a letter from Macmillan to Kennedy and crossed up Sandys whom we had finally persuaded to offer something definite. Sandys got off an indignant letter to Macmillan. After some reflection, but prior to learning of this, I sent a NIACT[26] to the President proposing another effort at the British. My own guess is that the Indians are settled on the MIG's in any case but I cannot be sure. I asked for an appointment with the Prime Minister yesterday but without any suggestion of urgency. We shouldn't seem to worry.

June 21 — New Delhi

I weary of MIG's. Yesterday the British came part way back on the track. Sandys had had some effect on Macmillan and we sent

---

[25] Bimla Nanda, now Mrs. John Bissell, who became a much loved family friend, was the Social Secretary of the Embassy.
[26] Night Action (or urgent) cable.

a further letter offering to pay a larger share. (The latter will be very persuasive.) I then saw Nehru in the evening and produced adequately eloquent arguments — problems of the President with Congress, our belief that any rupee sale was aid, desirability of considering alternatives, the specific British alternative, the fact that the planes aren't very relevant to Indian defense anyway. It lasted about an hour. In the end, he said no decision was imminent and the British alternative would be considered. I enjoy presenting an argument such as this and suspect that I am getting rather good at it. I hit especially on the theme that the word MIG has become a highly evocative term like U-boat and thus especially likely to arouse emotions.

We shall see what happens when Krishna Menon comes home. I would guess that the project is shelved, at least for a while.

The monsoon is approaching. Yesterday was hot and very sticky. As usual after one of my trips, I have trouble getting my sleeping habits turned around. I can sleep well during the day. Night is something else again.

June 22 — New Delhi

Katz-Suchy,[27] the highly intelligent Polish Ambassador (and also effective exponent of the Soviet line), came in yesterday to say goodbye. He is an old Bolshevist intellectual. I have kept him supplied with books and he has enjoyed talking politics with me. I asked him if the Poles couldn't be more careful in their semantics and thus give us less trouble in supplying them with food. Reference to us as fascist hyenas does harm. He said much could be done along these lines and he would try some missionary work on his return.

At noon, I signed some $275 million worth of loan agreements. I worried a little lest they be reported in the U.S. immediately on top of the MIG discussion with congressional static. "They buy

[27] Dr. Juliusz Katz-Suchy. See page 116.

MIG's; we lend money." So I tried to make my speech very dull and succeeded beyond all expectations.[28]

Kitty returned from the Kulu Valley at twelve. The sun has now largely disappeared as the monsoon approaches. It is getting even more sultry.

June 23 — New Delhi

The State Department, by trying to please everyone, usually ends up offending all available clients. Hard on my labors on the MIG purchase has come the Security Council debate on Kashmir. Krishna Menon has had considerable success in reducing support for the standard United Nations resolutions calling for a plebiscite.[29] We and the Irish were the only ones left in favor; and the watered-down version we supported doesn't seem particularly attractive to Pakistan. The new Pakistan Foreign Minister, Mohammed Ali, is currently under attack for being too pro-American. The Indian newspapers are having an anti-American field day over our support of the Security Council resolution. However, it will soon pass.

Yesterday I met with the U.S. Steel team which is investigating the Bokaro steel mill and had them to lunch. Their appearance here is a ritual.[30] One or two good men could have gone over the engineering and clerical data and passed upon the plausibility and need for the mill in a couple of weeks.

[28] However, the President, with good reason, did not like the timing and for several months kept a tight hold on such announcements.
[29] The United Nations resolution of April 21, 1948 on the Kashmir dispute called, among other things, for a U.N. supervised plebiscite to decide the future of the State. The Indians have always contended that the Pakistanis never met the preconditions for the vote. However, their enthusiasm for this solution had long since evaporated, to say the least.
[30] This was not so. Their work proved valuable.

June 24 — New Delhi–Kulu Valley

This morning the papers are in a rash of protest on Kashmir and the U.N. debate. And Nehru has taken exception to our pressure on the MIG's. I don't know which I find more difficult — our mistakes or the Indian reaction. During this past year, we have twice outraged the Indians by our support of two allies, Portugal and Pakistan, and neither of them has responded with the slightest approval. On the other hand, the Indians made no overtures to American opinion.

I am en route to Kulu to see the boys who have been there for the last two or three weeks. I must be back in the cauldron tomorrow night.

June 25 — Kulu–New Delhi

The Kulu Valley is a narrow crease in the Himalayas in the range from 3,000 to 5,000 feet. The boys and Emily were at Mandi at the upper end and no great distance from Tibet.

A strong mountain stream flows through the Valley which is covered by massive trees somewhat resembling Douglas fir. The main mountain torrent has a large number of small offshoots, a yard or less wide, which dash through the meadows on each side of the stream. Here and there they turn small millstones housed in tiny stone buildings, all on the scale of an overgrown doll's house. The millstreams flow through beds of wild iris and between the great trees, and it is one of the loveliest places ever.

The surrounding mountains are high — up to 20,000 feet and snow-clad — but this is all hearsay. They are now quite invisible behind the clouds.

June 26 — New Delhi

President Kennedy is unhappy about the Indians. Nehru made a speech in Parliament suggesting that the West was invariably unfriendly on Kashmir (and not clearly confining his charge to this) and complaining of our pressure on MIG's. This reached the White House with resounding effect.

Last night we had a big party for George Kistiakowsky[31] who is visiting here on his way to Indonesia. At about dinner time, the lights (and air conditioning) went off and we were expelled outside into the insufferable heat. Dancing made it warmer. Eventually the lights came on and the evening to a close. Everyone assured us that they had a wonderful time. This could indicate a highly undiscriminating approach to social life.

June 27 — New Delhi

The papers still complain that we are out of step with India. Prem Bhatia[32] has the remarkable thought that the United States might be losing the art of gracious giving.

In the evening, I saw M. J. Desai. I bored in heavily on my strong points — diplomacy requires essentially the same tactics as arguing with your wife. Did the Prime Minister not know that the F-104's were given Pakistan by a previous administration? Could we not talk about matters of common concern, such as the effect of Indian actions on Congress and the aid program without being accused of threats? Does the P.M. really think that we are invariably hostile?

June 28 — New Delhi

The papers continued bitter yesterday but with some sign of mellowing. I dined last night with Morarji Desai who was angry about Kashmir and depressed about other things. He is about to leave for Europe in search of aid — a mission which will show how difficult it is to come by money except in the United States. I continued to press on the Prime Minister's statements about hostility

---

[31] Brilliant and popular Professor of Chemistry at Harvard and former Science Adviser to President Eisenhower. A great personal friend.

[32] See page 291.

and his failure to distinguish between policies under Kennedy and under earlier Presidents. On this, at least, my friends are a trifle defensive.

Douglas Ensminger,[33] local head of the Ford Foundation, came in during the afternoon. He was very bitter about the Kashmir debate. He thinks we do vast damage by supporting an outdated and irrelevant resolution. He feels we must become more practical soon. I agree.

July 3 — Hyderabad–New Delhi
This is Tuesday. Friday last we left Delhi early for Bhubaneswar, the capital of Orissa, where I made a courtesy call on the Governor and something slightly more than that on Patnaik,[34] the Chief Minister. The latter is an able operator, much younger than the average, much interested in education and much too concerned, I think, about how to find jobs for the educated. Whatever their misfortunes, they are better able to care for themselves than the uneducated.

Then we went on to Puri on the seashore arriving in time for a swim and this we followed by several more on Saturday, Sunday and before departure on Monday. The monsoon having not yet broken, the weather is good and the sea is not excessively high. On Sunday, we drove over to see the black pagoda at Kanarak. It was as good as I remembered it but hard to see in all its erotic glory in an official capacity. An ambassador cannot enjoy statues celebrating active love in all its infinite Indian variety without wondering who is watching or photographing.

Monday at noon, we went to Hyderabad for the usual round of an official visit — call on Governor, dinner (canceled by death of B. C. Roy), press conference heavily committed to Kashmir and MIG's, meeting with AID people and wives, call on Chief Minister, trip to village to start a noonday lunch scheme, luncheon with Chief

[33] See page 68.
[34] Bijayananda Patnaik.

Minister, airport. The symbolic free lunch fed only about fifty youngsters. Two or three hundred equally hungry were onlookers at the feast. I disrupted the routine by having them fed too.

Saturday I woke up fresh and interested in new ideas and sent a telegram to the Department asking if I could announce formal abandonment of support of the plebiscite on Kashmir. It is out of date; we do no one any good by keeping it alive. The Department will have had a hideous day trying to decide what to do for I left some hint that, in absence of instructions to the contrary, I might proceed.

July 5 — New Delhi

The President enthusiastically turned down my proposal for ringing the bell on the Kashmir plebiscite. I don't think he quite realizes what I am up against here. The proposal was probably premature in any case, but my making it may work against our support of another round on the subject in New York.[35]

Last night was the annual Fourth of July picnic, my second. I spoke and said little quite well. I am mastering the technique of the totally minor speech. There has been much worry about the Prime Minister's health. S. K. Patil told me this morning that the Prime Minister is suffering from no specific disease, just the general wear and tear of age. It should be noted for history that S.K. said I had done a remarkable job of holding things together these last six months. I hope he is right.

July 7 — New Delhi

A very quiet day. I did some personal writing in the morning. I am rather interested by the group of characters I have invented — Dr. Herschel McLandress, Brighton (later Allston) C. Wheat and

[35] The suggestion was undoubtedly ill-timed. However, the U.N. debates on Kashmir exacerbated rather than eased feelings between the two countries and served no useful purpose for either.

Mark Epernay who tells about them.[36] Then I cleaned up my desk and worked on a telegram to the Department on the political prospect. Lunch, swimming, dinner, nothing else.

July 8 — New Delhi

The monsoon has struck with great drenching force. A yellow lake appeared yesterday in front of the Residence in which great numbers of infants were splashing muddily and happily about. My morning was taken up with a paper on the balance of payments for the President which I promised to get on the wires today.

July 9 — New Delhi

Everything remains very quiet here but I detect a slight mellowing in the atmosphere. I had a quietly amiable letter from the Prime Minister in response to one from me inquiring if there was anything we could do medically for him.

Rusk has made a good defense of Indian aid — and said many of the right things. There is more tension along the northern, i.e., Chinese border. This creates the suspicion that India may be a bit too concerned with angering everyone at once. Meanwhile my psychological warfare onslaught against the Department is having some result, I think.

July 10 — New Delhi

Much of yesterday was for planning the American Forum. This is to be a big discussion, speech-making, concert show in Madras the third week in November. In the past, we have dribbled in our efforts and with second-rate people. My idea is to have all efforts at once, in one place and have them good.

[36] See page 382.

New Delhi, India
July 10, 1962
Dear Mr. President:

I read with a good deal of concern about the pressure that is mounting on taxes. I also sense that your instinct is to resist and I hope you continue to do so. I submit the following thoughts:

(1) A very large part of American conservative and business opinion is simply against taxes regardless. It will thus argue with great enthusiasm for tax reduction, quite apart from the consequences fiscal and otherwise about which they couldn't care less. Of course, after the taxes are reduced, these people will not hesitate to attack you for an unbalanced budget. Some of them may be sophisticated enough to hope the new lower tax revenues will set a new lower ceiling on spending. The rest welcome the liberal initiative as assistance from an unexpected quarter.

(2) The momentary alliance with my friends is more apparent than real.[37] The people who are simply anti-tax will want an across-the-board and upper brackets reduction including, though less urgently, the corporation tax. The liberals and unions will want relief in the withholding brackets and here, of course, it would have its effect on spending. (The effect of upper bracket and corporation tax on business outlays and spending will be slight or negligible.) So a proposal to reduce taxes, while it looks simple and fast, will produce a nasty Congressional brawl with a disagreeable aftermath. What will satisfy the liberals will outrage the rich and vice versa. Both, in the end, will be angry at the Administration.

(3) From this distance I don't see that the condition of the economy is all that bad. Personal income seems to be holding up very well. The investment plans seem not to have been seriously revised. The stock market is steadier for the moment at a safer level. Unemployment is, to be sure, substantial. But without

[37] Meaning the conservatives mentioned in paragraph (1) above, with the Keynesians in the Administration.

excusing it, it remains that we have been living with something like this volume of unemployment for a long while. Once we would have thought it creditably low.

(4) Most of what I read on the politics of this situation makes no sense at all. While you are aware of my reluctance to lecture you on this curious subject, perhaps I could make three points: (a) No tax cut has the slightest chance of having the slightest effect on the economy by November. (b) The unemployed are (to their misfortune) a small minority and few can be so silly as to suppose they will do better under the Republicans. (c) The unemployed stiff may have become extremely well educated in recent months, but I still can't imagine him applauding the Kennedy Administration for helping him by reducing the taxes of the guy who has a job or the fellow he would be working for if he had a job.

(5) I needn't remind you (but nevertheless I always deem it wise) that the glories of the Kennedy Era will be written not in the rate of economic growth or even in the level of unemployment. Nor, I venture, is this where its political rewards lie. Its glory and reward will be from the way it tackles the infinity of problems that beset a growing population and an increasingly complex society in an increasingly competitive world. To do this well costs the money that the tax reducers would deny.

If the economic outlook for next year is not good, this means that economists and planners should now get down to work on how men can be employed if jobs are needed. Then when next year comes there will be no reason to say that spending for the things that society so desperately needs is too time-consuming a remedy.

With this, I turn my thoughts back to the local scene.

Yours faithfully,
JOHN KENNETH GALBRAITH

THE PRESIDENT
THE WHITE HOUSE

July 12 — New Delhi

More trouble on the Chinese frontier. This time, however, Krishna Menon seems to have turned it a bit more to his advantage. For one thing, the Pakistanis have been negotiating on their frontier with China. For another, the Indians have reacted promptly and not after a long and embarrassed silence. Part of the trouble, indeed, stems from Indian troops taking up more advanced positions.

No one has pointed out that the dispute is over some of the world's most worthless territory.

Esquire seems to be enchanted by Mark Epernay. I am sending a piece on "The Confidence Machine"[38] to the President.

July 13 — New Delhi

The Prime Minister returned yesterday from Kashmir. His pictures in the paper look rather bad. There has been a decision to play down the Chinese crisis. The Indian press is free but highly cooperative. I spent the day on office routine which was far from heavy and doing some writing.

✧ ✧ ✧

New Delhi, India
July 13, 1962

Dear Mr. President:

Carl[39] has sent me a letter with a penetrating item by Ruth Montgomery which could lead me to hope that you might cut off the *Journal-American* too. However, my further thought is that perhaps I should give you a succinct view of exactly what

[38] This was a machine which, by playing speeches of Herbert Hoover and Barry Goldwater in a subdued hum, was designed to sustain the confidence of business executives. See *The McLandress Dimension*, pp. 75–88.

[39] Carl Kaysen (see page 206). The enclosures criticized the Administration for too much aid and attention to India for too small a reward. I was asked to comment, the implication being that the President partly agreed. The President some time before was said to have banished the *New York Herald Tribune* from the White House.

I am doing here. I sense a remote but discouraging tendency for you to imagine (a) that I have become a financial arm of the Indian Government; (b) that my task is to defend the Indians to the United States; (c) that I yearn to be loved. None, not even the last, reflects in fact my preoccupation. In fact, I find Indian politics depressing and not less so on continued contact. The thought crosses my mind more often than you might think as to why Galbraith cultivates this particular vineyard. I also spend my time trying to persuade the Indians of our problems and point of view, but, since I need no particular help in this, it is not in my recurrent advice to the State Department. Here is what concerns me:

India is a peasant and bourgeois, property-owning and, in the aggregate, conservative community. It is held to the West by ties of language and tradition of considerable strength. Most of the effective political leaders are on our side — a distinct oddity as the world goes. Their position depends on their history in the independence movement, the inherent conservatism of the country, the fact that our food eliminates the desperation that would result from hunger, and because planning plus our aid gives a semblance of progress.

Working against these conservative influences is a combination of the Communist, the angry, the frustrated, the xenophobic, and the anti-Moslem. Increasingly in recent years, and rapidly in recent months, they have been coalescing around Menon. And Menon with great brilliance has made himself the custodian of the particular inflammatory issues — Goa, arms aid to Pakistan, Kashmir — which put us automatically on the other side.

A disaster in this part of the world, as I see it, would be considerably worse not only for the United States but for the political reputation of the New Frontier than a disaster in Indo-China. Accordingly, as your man hereabouts, I assume I should seek to prevent it. Aid is a substantial part of my armory and that is my interest. I don't exclude a certain compassion for poor people.

If one lacked compassion, he would not see the full importance of our assistance.

I am equally concerned to arrest the impulse of the State Department and my old friend Adlai Stevenson to show mighty indignation on irrelevant issues. That is why I was so anxious to cut our losses on Portuguese colonialism. It is why we simply cannot have another debate on Kashmir and State must be prevented from drifting on in to it. It is also why our arms aid to Pakistan is a two-edged sword that cuts principally on the wrong side.

Yours faithfully,
JOHN KENNETH GALBRAITH

THE PRESIDENT
THE WHITE HOUSE

✧ ✧ ✧

July 14 — New Delhi

More excitement on the frontier. The Chinese are said to have surrounded, and are also said not to have surrounded, an Indian post. The Indians have orders not to fire unless the Chinese come within fifteen yards — a modern version of the whites of the eyes.

I talked yesterday with Humayun Kabir[40] about the India-American Forum in Madras. He is much attracted by the idea. There is some danger, however, that it might be smothered by government assistance.

At a business lunch yesterday, I initiated a discussion on why everyone is so depressed about the Indian economic prospect. The balance of payments has been partly responsible. People don't know what it means. But they think it must be bad. I suggested that in solving problems, such as coal, India is the victim of increasingly orderly administration. All must be done under the aegis of

---

[40] Then Minister for Scientific Research and Cultural Affairs. A personal friend and a most attractive member of the Indian Government. He subsequently left the Congress Party to lead a group of his own.

a regular ministry. Better plunge in with men and money even at the expense of upsetting things elsewhere.

July 16 — New Delhi

A quiet weekend with a dinner at M. J. Desai's. Newcomers' tea and a dinner here last evening. All dull. In addition to therapeutic swimming, I amuse myself with McLandress and I don't know how I would get on without him. He has just finished automating the State Department.

July 18 — New Delhi

Day before yesterday, I left at noon for Madras. Part of the trip was through the monsoon and the Convair bounced around uneasily. We were there about six. After some lively bickering with the reporters at the airport I went to a reception marking the opening of the National City Bank and on to a handsome dinner with the Simonses[41] and to bed.

Yesterday I met with the Consulate staff, Vice-Chancellor of the University, Minister of Education and a group of civic and cultural leaders to talk about the proposed India-American Forum. This we propose for the end of November.[42] Everyone seemed enthusiastic. I worry only that it may combine with some crisis in Indian-American relations. A bad conflict in Delhi; a big show here. That is a risk that must be run. I left Madras at 2 P.M. and was home comfortably for dinner.

I have cleared USIS to work in a minor way in Kashmir and Goa. The Department would have taken weeks to reach an affirmative decision. My deciding will save a great deal of trouble and discussion.

[41] See page 162.
[42] It was postponed after the Chinese attack and never resurrected.

July 19 — New Delhi

Yesterday an incredible telegram came from the Department washing out the C-130 offer I was to come back to India and try to sell as a substitute for MIG's. And likewise any suggestion of military aid. All in craven reaction to the Congress and, I fear, to the President's displeasure with India. The Department was so obviously off base that I decided on a soft answer and spent most of the day on it. For the rest, I am beginning to contemplate a quiet withdrawal.

July 20 — New Delhi

A long but not very difficult day. Having written out a letter of resignation in the morning, I put it away permanently in my desk and felt much better. Then I visited the Indian Investment Centre, an organization which works to bring Indian and American (and other foreign) investors together in joint enterprises. I made an encouraging speech. This may have been needed for they seem to have worked for a year and consummated only two marriages.

Then I had a meeting to consider how to keep relief milk out of the black market to which a shocking proportion goes. The Catholic Relief Services and the Church World Service are a kind of heavenly gate to an enormous black market. In Calcutta, the milk descends from C.R.S. and C.W.S. through a hierarchy of distributors and each level sells half, more or less, and passes half on to the next grafter for the next division. Not much remains for the ultimate poor after this geometry.

We had lunch with the Harry Schwartzes of the *New York Times* and then heard about the hotel troubles of Pan Am — they are part owners of an enormous hotel here in Delhi which has remained unfinished for many months awaiting government permissions. Then I had an evening press meeting. This was for background and quite successful. The technique is to be interesting and candid and prove the latter by conceding handsomely the sour but unimportant. Then you get on to the relevant sweet.

July 23 — New Delhi

The weekend was quite busy. Saturday night, we had a dinner for C. D. Jackson of Time, Inc. I made a speech recalling, among other things, our last meeting during the 1960 campaign when he told me Nixon was in. He came back with a moving account of how Americans buried the hatchet on the day after elections. The embarrassment was general.

Last night, we had a dinner for Karnail Singh, the Chairman of the Railway Board. It followed a film showing at the Rashtrapati Bhavan to see the John Glenn astronaut film and the visit of Mrs. Kennedy. The Prime Minister was there and a goodly crowd. Everyone seemed to enjoy them both.

Saturday, the first shooting occurred on the frontier — according to the Indians, the Chinese fired on an Indian patrol. Our policy (mine) is to keep silent and seem to take no satisfaction out of this manifestation of the Cold War. It is embarrassing to Krishna Menon. Much better that we be the devils than the Chinese.

July 24 — New Delhi

The Indian papers are considerably excited about the firing on the Chinese border. Meantime this morning's English-speaking papers all feature a picture of Krishna Menon tipping glasses in Geneva with Gromyko and Chen Yi. Such drinking with the enemy could cost a man his job with us. I expect V.K.K.M. will survive.

Yesterday a high cabinet officer[43] warned against our national tendency to be excessively nice to people. In Geneva, Stevenson had complained to him bitterly of Menon's operations but concluded by saying he was able and brilliant. My friend said he asked Stevenson to omit the compliments. Menon comes home to make use of them.

Congress has passed the aid authorization bill, and the prospects

[43] As elsewhere on occasion, I have here deleted a name which, to mention, might even after the lapse of time seem to violate a confidence.

for the Aid India consortium seem fairly good. I must say that the Indians have not done everything possible to help themselves.

I am getting a slightly bad press in the U.S. on excessive homeward travel.[44] It is not entirely unjustified and I will stay grounded for a while. Epernay provides me with a good source of interest.

B. P. Bhatt, Director-General of All-India Radio, came to lunch yesterday and S. K. Dey[45] for tea. Both are anxious about Indian-American relations. Bhatt told me that the Russians have protested my speeches being on the Indian radio. They were told that equally good ones from their side would be eligible.

July 25 — New Delhi

I talked yesterday with Nanda,[46] the Planning Minister. He is a nice Gandhian, much worried about planning prospect and MIG's. Last night, Phil Potter came over with a theory that the deal is decided and that they are leaking it out to indicate good faith.

This morning, the papers are rather rough on Menon, and also the P.M., for being excessively friendly with the Chinese. There is another note of protest from the Indians to the Chinese. Someone must grind them out like sausages.

July 30 — Srinagar–New Delhi

Last Wednesday, I had lunch with T.T.K.[47] who brought me up to date on the MIG deal. A committee is to go to Moscow. There is still no decision but presumably if reports are favorable, there will be. I wonder how the Russians will react in light of the recent outburst with the Chinese. The AID consortium is to meet on Monday — today.

---

[44] See page 377.
[45] Minister for Community Development.
[46] Gulzari Lal Nanda, Minister for Labour, Employment and Planning. Following the death of Prime Minister Shastri in 1966, he was interim Prime Minister.
[47] T. T. Krishnamachari, a veteran of Indian politics, previously and subsequently Finance Minister and then Minister without Portfolio. Wealthy and highly westernized, his career was marked by a spectacular succession of ups and downs.

For the last four days, we — myself and family — have been on Karan Singh's (the Maharajah of Jammu and Kashmir) island in Dal Lake in Kashmir. This is a tiny square acre surrounded by various species of lotus. The cottage is small but quite comfortable; the cook is excellent. This time of year, Kashmir is hot in the daytime but cool enough by night. The atmosphere is a trifle dry, but the land is soft in color and as beautiful as ever.

I spoke to the All India Management Association which is meeting in seminar here. Seminars are obviously an international habit. And we lunched and dined variously with the Karan Singhs. For the rest, I amused myself with some more of the works of Epernay — and swam. With great success, Peter fished consistently for carp, each larger than the last. We are now at 13,000 feet and still going up to get over the cloudy pass on the way home.

August 1 — New Delhi

The papers carry news of my probable resignation. Yesterday the *Boston Globe* called to ask if it were true. I issued a statement which was not without escape clauses but firm in saying I had not yet resigned and did not intend to go to work in Washington.[48]

Lane Timmons returned generally encouraged about the Washington mood. The President is still angry with the Indians. However, both he and others seem to be making suitable distinctions between Krishna Menon and the rest. They advocate gradual detachment from our opposition to the MIG deal which I favor.[49]

I worked yesterday on a speech which I am giving before the Constitution Club, a popular local forum, in a few days. I face the problem of whether to clear it with Washington. In the end, I decided against.

---

[48] This was not, as I recall, related to my poor frame of mind of a few weeks earlier but the result of more or less aimless speculation. See page 399.

[49] In retrospect, as I have earlier noted, I should have taken this much more in stride. I was motivated in the matter partly by the fear of seeming to acquiesce in Soviet arming of the Indian forces. Nothing is so bad in diplomacy as to be activated by fear of criticism back home. Nor is anything more common.

August 3 — New Delhi

Everyone is still in a poor mood. As I have noted, we are contemplating a loan for a large nuclear reactor to produce power and have asked the Indians to accept the international safeguards of the International Atomic Energy Agency in Vienna. They prefer our inspection on a bilateral basis. Today's papers ask if we would forgo a "sale" of the reactor in order to establish the principle of international inspection. Were it the other way around — were we asking for bilateral rather than international inspection — the indignation would be equally great.

The lights go off each evening at the time I would like to start reading.

August 12 — New Delhi

There has been a considerable gap in this report reflecting the undoubted fact that nothing has happened. I made a speech this week to the Constitution Club putting our policy toward India somewhat on the line. Under staff pressure, I eliminated most of the content so that it got only the slight attention it deserved. I did say we were not in competition with the Soviets to serve the Indians — a recurrent point in the papers.

A plane carrying two Americans and the Nepal Ambassador to India disappeared somewhere between here and Kathmandu. Timmons has been masterminding the search in which our Embassy plane is participating. For the rest, Washington is on vacation and we could well be.

I do have the feeling that the Indians may be running into some trouble on the MIG's. The subject has dropped out of the papers. At the same time, the Soviets are pressing the Indians and the Chinese to talk about their border dispute. It would be illogical for them to sell MIG's to the Indians in the middle of efforts to compose this dispute.

August 16 — New Delhi

Yesterday was Independence Day, a holiday involving an early morning trip to the Red Fort. Nehru spoke to the multitude. In contrast with the prevailing opinion, I noted sadly that his face looked puffy and rather unhealthy to me.

Parliament has been debating the Chinese border. The Indian Government wishes obviously to switch from shooting — though no one yet gets hurt — to talking. But in the past it has always said that this required restoration of the status quo ante, meaning mostly Chinese withdrawal. Now it is proposing to talk anyway and this has stirred up the most violent opposition since I have been here. No backsliding is involved. In the kind of distinction which politicians love, the government distinguishes between talking and negotiation. It is properly indignant over the inability of some retarded people to see the difference.

Last night, we went walking in the garden in weather that was almost cool.

September 18 — New Delhi

A considerable further gap during which the weather has been fetid and politics likewise to the extent they have not been dormant. A surprising number of ceremonies have been repeating themselves after a year — presentation of safe-driving awards, speech to the opening session of the American Women's Club, Independence Day at the Red Fort. They suffer on replay in much the manner of a Mort Sahl record.

The Kennedy Administration at this distance seems also to have lost momentum. The record in Congress is very bad — the most remarkable success was with the satellite telecommunications bill where the opposition was from the liberals. However, the President did stand firm against a tax reduction. That, unfortunately, is regarded by most as conservative.

On the plus side, my health has been better than since coming to India. This past weekend, I have been to Kasauli, a flower-bedecked hill station in the Punjab. There I walked and climbed and slept some eighteen hours a day. It is weeks now since I have needed any drugs to sleep.

Yesterday I spent the day doing sewer inspection[50] in the Punjab — Agricultural University at Ludhiana, Ford-AID Package Programs, Peace Corps. The Punjab at this time of year is thick and rich-looking although it is evident that most of the crops are under-fertilized. The public management of the State does not quite come up to the natural endowment. Politics intrudes itself on everything and as elsewhere there is too much government and not enough that is good.

The Package Program, so-called, is an imaginative enterprise by which in a selected area all necessary credit, fertilizer, improved seed, technical guidance is provided as a demonstration of what can be accomplished. It is not, however, getting through to the farmer. And the Chief Minister, who is badly in need of money to match his quota from the central government, is using a large proportion of the personnel for collecting small savings. The collection unquestionably involves a certain metaphorical squeeze on the testicles. So even when the technician appears with benevolent advice, the farmer cannot be sure this is his purpose. As a result, he heads for the local boondocks to be on the safe side.

The Chinese are active again — most recently in NEFA. However, it hasn't kept Krishna Menon from going to New York. Nehru is in London and Morarji Desai is in Washington. So if the Chinese decide to take Delhi, they will find few important captives.

September 24 — New Delhi

New Delhi is still devoid of important prospective prisoners and the Chinese and Indians are still firing in NEFA.

Last week was our 25th wedding anniversary and on Thursday I planned a huge party. A band and dance floor in the garden, Japanese lanterns, great gaiety. This was the night the monsoon

[50] A phrase of President Kennedy's for looking at public monuments.

ended in an enormous downpour. The Japanese lanterns collapsed and guests waded in through a sea of muddy water. But by improvisation we got the party into the house and it was moderately good. Kitty returned from the Kerala Onam[51] festivities with a bad cold and chest and could appear only briefly.

We were to go to Nepal this weekend but the monsoon settled into northern Uttar Pradesh interrupting all plane travel. It kept some seventy-five Nepal-bound Peace Corps volunteers here in Delhi. Weather is now, when not raining, almost cool again. Last night, we turned off the air conditioning.

October 1 — Kathmandu–New Delhi

Saturday morning at eight in the Navy plane, we took off for Kathmandu and arrived about 11:30 A.M. Weather was fine and the high mountains were in full view and shining white with monsoon snow.

The Kathmandu Valley is green and vaguely yellow with ripening rice. The Stebbinses welcomed us and installed us in their highly agreeable Residence — two stories and spacious and only slightly in the debt of the designer of Esso service stations.

The Indians and the King of Nepal are bickering over a series of border raids and almost everything else. We are trying to calm things and the Department has asked for our joint assessment. Stebbins and I agreed on the admirably obvious course — persuade the King that he cannot use us against the Indians and persuade the Indians to be as conciliatory as possible. We will continue to urge the King to make concessions to the Nepali Congress Party, some eighty of whom he has under arrest.

In the evening, the Stebbinses had a pleasant party which I failed to grace because of a merciless attack of sinus trouble. Yesterday, however, it was better and we took a Jeep station wagon on a morning tour of the Valley and Kathmandu. The weather was perfect, sun bright and air cool with the mountains visible between the

[51] Their Thanksgiving celebration.

clouds. All traffic is on foot and people were on the way to market under great loads of freight. The towns are of brick and most of the houses are of three stories, the first story being a shop. There are many pagodalike temples, much decorated, several of them celebrating the theory and practice of fornication in a wealth of imaginative detail.

At noon, Henry and I saw the King at the Palace. This is a large, rather pleasant compound in the center of the city. The buildings are of low white stucco with pleasant flowers and grass and — in contrast to the world outside — quite civilized. In a fine example of instant diplomacy, Henry and I braced him with the same proposals we had just, after discussion, turned in to the Department. The King gave his full diplomatic assent to all we suggested.

Kitty and I lunched with the Indian Ambassador in the ample house of the onetime British Resident. Then at four we took plane, arched up and out of the Valley. We were here at eight.

XIX

Aid Train

October 5 — Lucknow

We had dinner last night in Delhi for visiting firemen including Tom Griffith[1] of *Time* and then moved on to the Old Delhi railway station at 10 P.M. Our special train, shiny red with an elongated steam locomotive engine, was waiting at the platform. Kitty and I have the car of the General Manager and it is comfortably equipped with living room, bathroom and extra-length bed. About thirty members of the press are on the train plus fifteen or twenty from USIS, AID and the Embassy. This is to be an elaborate effort to draw attention to AID operations in Northern India.[2] Through the night, we made our way to Lucknow[3] and arrived here at around nine this morning.

This morning was taken up by ceremonial operations including a call on the Governor and then on the Chief Minister. The latter, C. B. Gupta,[4] a politician of minute stature — some four or five feet high — presides over Uttar Pradesh. Indians usually describe it as the worst administration in India. One of his political techniques is to create a cabinet post for anyone who might be troublesome or a dissenter. There are so many troublesome people.

[1] A friend and now Editor of *Life*.
[2] See the letter to President Kennedy on page 424.
[3] Capital, before the British, of the Nawabs of Oudh and thereafter, with Allahabad, of the United Provinces. (The United Provinces were renamed Uttar Pradesh in 1950.) During the Mutiny in 1857, the British garrison was subject, as in Kanpur, to a notable siege. Unlike Kanpur, Lucknow was eventually relieved.
[4] Long since out of office.

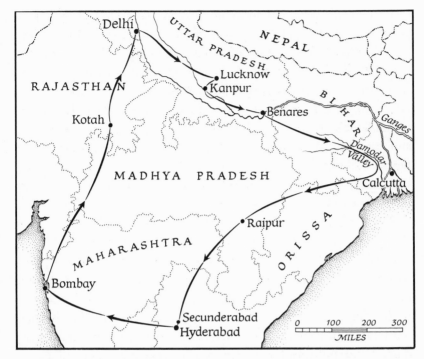

The Governor's Palace retains some traces of its majesty of British times. It is spacious and cool and situated on vast grounds. The Secretariat building, also tracing to British times, is in an advanced state of shabbiness.

The day's operations, which were handled by our people with inspired incompetence, were subject to various shifts in accordance with threats of student rioting. It was over a university issue, I believe; anyhow, we were not the target. We were taken in to see the Governor by the back way because of student demonstrations at the front door. However, by mistake we were taken to the front door where, so far as I could see, there were no demonstrators of any sort. At noon, we went out to Literacy Village run by Welthy Fisher and devoted to teaching people to teach reading and writing. Mrs. Fisher, now eighty-three (the widow of a long-vanished Episcopal prelate), is of undiminished vitality, and the whole place is serious, imaginative and amusing. Lunch was followed by a puppet show, the puppets being one of the Village specialties, which was devoted to the virtues of family planning. These were very great. One of the unwanted children vomited with great realism. The father was narrowly and perhaps unwisely kept from suicide. After lunch, I slept for an hour and then went to the University for an hour's discussion with the students. This had been scheduled and rescheduled several times during the day in accordance with news of rioting but eventually was on. In the end, it had all of the sanguinary qualities of a Y.M.C.A. seminar. The questions were intelligent and not especially tendentious.

After this came a faculty tea and an early nighttime speech in the University quadrangle. The latter was well-attended by students and an especially broad cross section of the local insect population. At one critical passage in my discourse, one flew right past my tonsils and on down. I had a speech for written distribution with a simplified version for the audience. It is by all odds the most satisfactory procedure. The difference between speech and writing is great and multiplied when language or accent are unfamiliar.

Following the speech, there was a state dinner at the Raj Bhavan, better on the whole than most such extravaganzas. We ate soon after arriving, the food was good and it was over by ten.

I forgot to tell that yesterday afternoon we had a party for the workers on the new Residence in New Delhi. About four hundred Rajasthani women, Punjabi craftsmen and assorted foremen, engineers and functionaries showed up with their families. The idea caught the attention of the Delhi press, and cameramen and reporters were there in force. The Punjabis staged a fine wild dance in which Kitty and I joined, and the papers this morning have a full and highly favorable account of the whole proceedings. From all superficial evidence, ambassadors would be well advised to do less talking and more dancing.

October 6 — Kanpur

Our train laid overnight in Lucknow and about 6:30 A.M., made the run to Kanpur,[5] arriving a little after 9 A.M. There we were welcomed by the members of the consortium of numerous U.S. technical institutions — M.I.T., Purdue, Case, Carnegie Tech — that is developing the Indian Institute of Technology, and drove out first to a power station which is adding to its capacity with a small American loan. It wasn't the best possible exhibit for nearly all of the equipment came from Switzerland or England. However, it was as good as we could do here for the newspapermen on short notice. Then came a heavy round at the Institute — a private meeting with the top management, then a faculty meeting in which the speakers sought to impress the audience with the depth of their academic perception. Harvard faculty meetings have the same tendency. I stressed the importance of faculty independence, student discipline and a few other grave fundamentals. I would trust the faculty on selecting faculty more willingly if I thought they were better themselves. However, the Americans, of whom there are eight or nine, with more to come, seem an exceptionally competent group.

Then there was a reception for several hundred people on the temporary grounds of the Institute (these are part of an old agricultural college) followed by lunch under a big *shamiana* followed by another speech. Then we drove out to the new campus where the first buildings — workshops and student hostels — are under construction. The student hostels in particular are of quite interesting design and show good architectural judgment. Then I presented some books, addressed the students and came back to stroll about the gardens of a Marwari[6] industrial magnate, Sir Padampat Singhania. These include artificial waterfalls, a swimming pool with special apparatus for creating waves and an

---

[5] About fifty miles south and west of Lucknow, also in Uttar Pradesh.

[6] Meaning that his ancestors came from the state of Marwar, later Jodhpur, a famous breeding ground for Indian businessmen.

attractive museum collection of ceramics and china including, I would judge, some very fine Chinese polychrome pieces. Then came cocktails and dinner with the Norman Dahls.[7] All in all, it was a good day.

The Institute is, I think, a fairly promising one. Some of the faculty are far from impressive, but the students seem keen and interested. Something depends on whether the politicians can be persuaded to keep their hands off. Our people face considerable problems in recruiting the necessary American staff for the best talent is likely to be busy with research or in the child-rearing brackets or otherwise immobilized in the United States. I have written to the heads of all of the participating institutions warning them of the trouble they will encounter in recruiting. These overseas enterprises look very romantic and attractive in the abstract. But getting good faculty members to go to India is difficult.

The women of the American families learned soon after their arrival that telephones were not available. Electrical engineers from M.I.T. and elsewhere set about devising a system of radio communication between the houses of the newcomers. At this juncture, Mrs. Norman Dahl discovered that a boy could be hired with a bike to make the rounds every half hour and not only carry messages but parcels as well. The cost of keeping him in orbit was Rs. 70 per month or about $14. The electronic system could not compete. The first message she sent was: "What Hath God Wrought?"[8]

October 7 — Benares

The train got into Benares at breakfast time and we disembarked thereafter to the usual crowd of welcoming officials. This

---

[7] Popular and extremely able professor at Massachusetts Institute of Technology in charge of the American group. He is now deputy head of the Ford Foundation staff in India.

[8] I subsequently sent an account of this to *The New Yorker* where it appeared. (The message was, of course, the one sent by Samuel Morse launching the electric telegraph.)

is my third trip here and the first when the weather was even moderately agreeable. Today it was bright and sunny but not excessively hot. After calling on the District Magistrate, we drove ten miles out on the other side of the Ganges to the Ramnagar Fort of the Maharajah of Benares. This stands on the banks of the Ganges, indeed more or less in the Ganges, and is a vast, sprawling and greatly decayed structure in which the Maharajah still spends most of his time. This prince was once one of the most important on the Ganges Plain. However, the domains were greatly curtailed by Warren Hastings and later by the Mutiny. Sardar Patel[9] took the rest. His Highness is left with his palaces, retainers and not much more. We returned to visit a couple of silk houses, including one operated by the Mayor of Benares. This is a highly progressive establishment which uses somewhat modernized equipment and is well up in the techniques of public relations. I discovered after we arrived it was the same one that, not coincidentally, had been visited by Mrs. Kennedy.

We had lunch with the Maharajah at his city palace — I am not quite clear why we were so much in royal hands today — and then went out to the Benares Hindu University for a long campaign which included a visit to the museum, most attractive and containing some of the best Indian painting (marvelous Rajput and Pahari miniatures), then to a modern and not very beautiful temple, the new medical school which seems quite clean and promising, the house of the founder, Dr. Malaviya,[10] a great friend of Gandhi and the other early Congress leaders, and then, finally, to a tea with the faculty.

Then we returned to the train and proceeded almost immediately back to Ramnagar Fort to see the Rama Lila Festival. This goes on

[9] Sardar Vallabhbhai Patel, who brilliantly negotiated the princes out of their domains following Independence.
[10] Pandit Madan Mohan Malaviya. An orthodox Hindu, he was ceremoniously reborn when some eighty years old but, unhappily, died soon thereafter. See W. Norman Brown, *The United States and India & (sic) Pakistan* (Cambridge: Harvard University Press, 1963), p. 245.

for thirty nights and each night celebrates a different episode from the *Ramayana*.[11] Enormous crowds attend and there are subsidiary markets for a wide variety of merchandise. Some six or eight elephants were turned out for our party and we observed a somewhat obscure transaction between Rama and Sita from a distance of around one-fifth of a mile. An abnormally farsighted observer with field glasses might have got more out of the plot. We stayed about an hour and then made our way back to Benares to the train for an evening departure at nine. While this is a special train, we are still running on a very close schedule for evidently if we do not move on time, we can do great damage to the railway operations.

October 8 — Chandrapura–Raipur

At six this morning we stopped at Chandrapura and picked up a covey of Damodar Valley Corporation[12] and Hindustan Steel[13] officials, the latter headed by J. M. Shrinagesh, the Chairman and one of the distinguished tribe hitherto encountered[14] which functions in various aspects of Indian life with additional members in the United States and Germany. The train then proceeded to the proposed site of the Bokaro steel plant, a half-hour distant, where we disembarked. The air was fresh and almost cool and the countryside, which is gently rolling, was a bright lush green. After an introduction to the various young engineers who are being assembled for the project and a lecture on plant layout, sources of raw material and the like, I went with Shrinagesh to a flight strip whence we took off for a half-hour trip over the site and the Damodar Valley. The Valley is underlain with coal and scarred by open cast pits, tipples and piles of waste but nonetheless rather attractive at

---

[11] One of the two great Sanskrit epics, traditionally considered the earliest of poetic literature.

[12] A regional power and development organization in Bihar and West Bengal modeled on the Tennessee Valley Authority.

[13] The government-owned corporation which manages the publicly owned steel mills.

[14] See page 363 for reference to his brother (S. M. Shrinagesh) who was Governor of Assam and is now Governor of Andhra Pradesh.

this time of year. We circled an adjacent mountain about 5,000 feet high, the back and saddle of which are spotted with tiny white temples.

After returning to the airstrip, we made our way to a large coal washery financed by an Ex-Im Bank loan. The coal of the Damodar Valley is of irregular quality. The washing floats off the higher quality coal and the rest remains for consumption in a power plant which is also under construction, with an AID loan. The trip through the coal washery was made at a half trot but the loss was not great. A coal washery may well be the least engaging industrial enterprise thus far invented and not more beautiful from being so useful.

Following the visit to the coal washery, we took a ride on a diesel locomotive that was standing in the yard — also an American endowment with a placard attesting to our generosity — and then went on to the Chandrapura Guest House for a pleasant lunch. I was struck as often before with the effect of industrialization on creature comforts. The showers in the guesthouse spurted ample supplies of both hot and cold water, and the meal was well served and attractive with an unlimited supply of cold beer. Also, quite a few of the men had brought their wives or had been requested to do so. After lunch, Kitty and I planted a couple of ceremonial trees and then went to see the Chandrapura power plant where the lower-caste coal is to be burned. This is in a very elementary stage of construction but when finished will be the largest thermal plant in India. Construction seemed to be going ahead at a good pace, and I did my best for public relations by talking with as much amiability as I could muster with any minimally responsive workmen and then climbing into the high steel. Unfortunately, people seem to like this sort of thing, and, what is more appalling, so do I. By three, we were back at the train where we went for a brief exhibitionist ride down the track on a railway motor car, and I then had a press conference followed by three or four hours of blessed relaxation, the first since the trip began. It was heaven to lie in the bed and look out the window without some appointment approaching in the next half hour.

At 8:30 P.M., we assembled the press and staff in the dining car for a Dasara Festival dinner and I made the sixth or seventh graceful speech of the day.

October 9 — Raipur–Hyderabad

I forgot to tell yesterday about an interesting episode at the coal washery. It is supposed to have a capacity of 8,000 tons a day and is currently processing about 6,000. Shrinagesh told me that the process worked out by the American contractor was not yet fully satisfactory. Later in the presence of the contractor and the Indian plant manager, I asked whether they had reached capacity. The plant manager said no, they were about 2,000 short and went on to say the trouble lay in the contractor's process. The American promptly said the process was just fine and that the trouble lay in a shortage of railway wagons to haul away the coal. I thought they would come to blows but a few moments later they were deeply protesting their friendship. The only thing that did not emerge was the truth.

This morning, we got to Raipur in Madhya Pradesh at six and disembarked at eight to be welcomed by the usual platoon of officials. At the Circuit House, we had a two-hour discussion of agricultural development in the area. The Raipur District is the home of one of the package programs where, as I have noted, all relevant agricultural techniques are brought to bear to increase agricultural production. It is one of the more successful and the discussion which was presided over by the State Minister of Agriculture was lucid and good. Madhya Pradesh is one of the less densely populated states of India and the farms by Indian standards are fair-sized — about three acres on the average. The land is almost exclusively in rice; there is enough moisture to produce only one crop a year. A vastly excessive population of livestock, particularly of cattle, eats any available fodder and lives in a state of semi-starvation. Irrigation would make possible a second crop and there is considerable possibility for this from the repair of the thousands of tanks and from equipping them with sluice gates. Presently the water is stored in the tanks and let out by opening a hole in the tank which gives one uncontrollable flood and nothing more. Something could also be done to increase forage production in the dry season but this would only mean that useless livestock would eat better rather than worse. Animal slaughter, I was told, was out of the question, although there is some possibility perhaps from castration of useless bulls. The whole subject is approached with the same restraint as the discussion of birth control in a Catholic cathedral.[15] At 10:30 A.M., we were joined by S. K. Patil and a party from Delhi and made our way by auto cavalcade out through the villages for several miles to see the progress in fact. Our passage was truly triumphal. Each village had erected an arch, sometimes of flowers, evergreens, brass pots and wheels and, at each stop, we were garlanded to the extent of twenty or thirty wreaths per stop. We also had a quick look at the prize cultivators including a poultryman with some remarkably prosperous white leghorns and a fisherman who had stacked dozens of ample fish along the road. Eventually we reached the village which was to receive us and this had all the aspects of a major carnival. Several thousands of people were there including the local youth organization, the village-level trainees, farmers, dancers, etc., and we were brought down a two- or three-hundred-yard triumphal avenue to a platform whence we spoke. More garlands were piled upon our necks, flowers were thrown at us and there was a general aspect of excitement reminiscent of the reception that might be accorded a winning World Series team. Various people of the village gave speeches of welcome followed by a speech by S. K. Patil and by me. Then Kitty made a speech in Hindi which was the best received of the day — partly because of the language and more because of its unique

[15] Depending on the cathedral, no longer.

brevity. Thereafter we returned to Raipur for lunch and an early afternoon departure.

The country around Raipur consists of plains, overgrazed as I have said, and the soil is very red from high iron content. The monsoon had not been good this year and at every stop a few practical souls not engaged in the welcoming festivities put their heads in the car to urge the need for irrigation.

We left Raipur and came out by the Bhilai steel works, a project financed and built by the Soviets. These look exceedingly vast with the soaring stacks and in striking contrast with the unchanging villages. The new town of Bhilai stretches over several miles confirming my recollection that the planners had been much too prodigal in use of land. In the late afternoon, we had a press briefing on the Nagarjunasagar irrigation project and are now on the way to Hyderabad. Tomorrow, by great good fortune, we do not arrive until nearly noon.

October 11 — Hyderabad to Bombay

Yesterday morning about ten-thirty, we arrived in Secunderabad where I was invited to dismount and inspect the station. It was a pleasure to do so for it was spruced up remarkably for the occasion and was probably the cleanest station in all India. After appropriate admiration, we re-boarded the train and a little after eleven dismounted in the adjacent city of Hyderabad to find the usual congregation of deacons and elders of the diocese. We then drove nearly one hundred miles southeast across high red plains, green at this time of the year, but generally short of rainfall and planted almost exclusively to castor beans. This is not especially fertile country and at intervals there are high rock outcroppings and, even more prominently, great weathered boulders sometimes standing two or three on top of each other. It was a pleasant though warm day and the trip was made at high speed. Mostly the Indian drivers are very moderate in their driving but this was the exception. About 2:30 P.M., we arrived in the construction area of the

Nagarjunasagar Dam, an enormous structure more than twice as big in bulk as the Bhakra-Nangal Dam[16] and, indeed, the largest masonry dam in the world. It has been under way for five or six years and is being built almost exclusively by hand. Cement and rock are carried up the face of the dam on ramps in a continuous line of people crawling up and down like ants and the operations look in fact exactly like the imagined pictures of people building the great pyramids. Over 100,000 are at work on the dam, canals and supporting quarries. We first drove through a two-mile tunnel hewn in an egg-shape through one of the surrounding hills. It will carry water from the lake behind the dam to the left bank canal. Then we went to the guesthouse for some tea — lunch had somehow got missed on the way — and then to look at a model of the dam and then on to visit the actual construction. We climbed up the bamboo ramp (which zigzagged up the downstream face) and the workers by the hundreds swarmed up behind us proving in a somewhat alarming way the strength of the basketlike construction. I ensured a picture in the newspapers, if no other form of immortality, by carrying a dish full of concrete on my head from the bottom to the top of the dam. I borrowed it from one of the ladies engaged more durably in this toil. It wasn't, in fact, especially heavy. By the time I got it to the point of deposit on top of the dam where it is the masonry between granite rocks, a quite considerable part had been lost down my neck.

The dam is being built in sections. During the monsoon, they work at the edges and water pours through the middle. And yesterday it was pouring through with great power and force. As the dry season approaches, they build up the center. The lake, when it is filled, will flood some fine Buddhist ruins back of the dam — a capital of an ancient city. We were scheduled to visit the diggings but time was running out. All in all, the Nagarjunasagar Dam is a famous sight and especially something to see with the incredible lines of workers lifting its substance into place.

[16] See page 114.

After the dam, we visited a heavy equipment training center nearby where, with American aid, some forty young Indians are being trained in the operation and, more important, the maintenance of bulldozers, graders and earth-hauling machinery. The boys in the school were dressed in khaki-colored clothes and had a pleasantly grease-splattered and workaday appearance. One is almost always escorted around Indian industrial projects by men dressed in sparkling white clothes. It was pleasant in contrast to see people who gave the appearance of getting down into the job. This heavy equipment training center impressed me as first rate. The leaders also impressed me in no mild way with their desire for money and more machinery. I think they should get it.

We left at 4:30 P.M. and made another high-speed run back to Hyderabad, arriving about 7:30 P.M. Speed is again a relative matter; the average was probably far from high for we had constantly to slow down to allow cattle, sheep and goats to cross the roads. There was, however, no other traffic.

We had fifteen minutes to bathe and dress and then went to have dinner with the Governor of Andhra Pradesh. The latter is General Shrinagesh whom we had previously visited when he was Governor of Assam and, as I have noted,[17] a brother of the Chairman of Hindustan Steel. His house, once the palace of the Nizam's Prime Minister, is spacious with large rooms and very attractive gardens. A police band provided Gilbert and Sullivan from the garden and, this being our first meal since early morning, it was far from unwelcome. At nine-forty-five, we left for the Hyderabad station to be greeted by assorted Fulbright students and teachers and thence aboard the train and to bed.

October 14 — New Delhi

We got to Bombay midafternoon on the 11th, Thursday, and drove out through the increasingly stifling traffic of the city to the Central Training Institute on the edge of town. This is de-

17 See page 414.

voted to the education of young Indians in the mechanical arts —
draftsmanship and handling of machine tools, job layouts, etc. The
Institute is still under construction, as indeed is everything in India,
but the students looked alert and industrious and I came away with
a favorable impression of the place. In any event, they were all
functioning with exceptional industry for my visit. Every lathe
was turning over, every hammer was hammering and every mill was
milling.

In the evening, we gathered the journalists of our party and the
staff of the Consulate for dinner at Lincoln House. American folk
songs were rendered by an accomplished young Indian who learned
his repertoire while a student in the U.S., and thereafter we had a
movie on the lawn.

The next day, Friday, was the longest of the trip. I went
down to the docks at eight o'clock to see a ship unloading PL 480
wheat. This latter, a 19,000-ton tanker, sucks wheat in and out by
pumps, and a great crew of Indians in the godowns on the wharves
sack the grain as rapidly as it is blown out of the ship. We then
inspected an impressive group of AID diesels which had just been
unloaded on the wharf and were still covered with the protective
boxboard.

Then we made our way across Bombay and out the one access
road, which is the focus of all traffic congestion, to the construction
site of a big fertilizer plant that we are aiding at Trombay, perhaps
ten miles from the center of town. This will supply urea and am-
monium phosphate. A huge office building was put up first and it
is now full of clerks and functionaries. The construction, which is
under the guidance of an American consultant, seems, however, to
be proceeding fairly satisfactorily. In the course of the tour, I
saw a ten- or twelve-year-old boy handling platters of earth on his
head despite a knee that had been patched up with a very dirty
bloodstained bandage and which was so stiff he could not bend it.
He was quickly withdrawn from sight when I called attention to
his need for medical aid. Later I sent him twenty rupees as a supple-

ment to his salary while he was laid off. I hope this wealth assures him attention. One of the depressing things about public sector plants is the number of officials who accompany one on inspection. There must have been fifty on this tour.

Next we stopped at the Esso Standard plant a mile or so away — very clean, trim, nicely landscaped and most efficient in appearance. This was a bow by me to private enterprise and private investment. To round out the morning, we went to Premier Automobiles, Limited which has been the recipient of various loans from the U.S. and various assistance from the Chrysler Corporation. They manufacture heavy trucks and — a broad-minded gesture since the financing is American — small Fiat automobiles. I thought the plant compared favorably with one I saw outside Moscow two or three years ago — in any case, like the Russian plant, very much overpopulated by American standards. Most of the final truck (about 87 percent) and a somewhat lesser percentage of the final automobile (50–60 percent) are of Indian origin. A nonprivileged buyer has to wait about four years for an automobile. Ty Wood and I took an experimental spin in one of the cars and then we all had lunch in front of the factory. The lunch had damaging consequences. I got back to Lincoln House about half-past two to find the Wyatts (Woodrow[18] and Lady Moorea) installed there and we went swimming in the Consulate pool. The latter had just been commissioned and was full of refreshing but very dirty water. Woodrow, who is here to show his wife India and vice versa, is lively, full of ideas and, as usual, involved in controversy. He doesn't like Hugh Gaitskell[19] who reciprocates. Lady Moorea is as lovely as ever. At four-thirty, I left for a press conference which lasted for about an hour and went quite well. The questions were lively and the repartee quite good and for once nobody tried to get me onto dangerous territory. After I had suggested that Nagarjunasagar was the most interesting project we visited, one

[18] Labour M.P. of irregular aspect and close personal friend.
[19] Then the leader of the Labour Party.

reporter asked which had been the worst. I said this was a question designed to elicit not information but indiscretion.

In the evening, we had a fairly stately dinner for the Wyatts at Lincoln House with Mrs. Pandit,[20] and various people from the motion picture or lighter artistic community in attendance. We drank a great deal of champagne, toasted Mrs. Pandit's prospective appointment as Governor of Maharashtra, listened to Woodrow on the dismal future of the British Labour Party and had a good and gay time. A little before eleven o'clock, we adjourned to the railway station and made an appropriately ceremonial departure.

Yesterday was one of the less happy days of the tour. Ty Wood, Jack Christy, Jim Stevenson[21] and a couple of the Indian newspapermen all woke up violently ill, a select company of which I was also a prominent member. My insides, responding to the same lunch, had disintegrated and largely disappeared. I had a fever and numerous other symptoms too repulsive to mention. Fortunately, the train did not get into Kotah until 3 P.M. and we had a tolerably good doctor on board to dose us all with nasty but quick-acting remedies. By Kotah, I was mobile again. We embarked in cars for the visit first to another center for training in operation and maintenance of heavy equipment similar to the one at Nagarjunasagar and then out to a barrage which diverts water to two large canals for irrigation of several lakhs (hundreds of thousands) of acres in Rajasthan and Madhya Pradesh. The training center, under a highly energetic American, George D. Childs, who has been the sole American resident of Kotah for the last four years, is a first-rate institution. And the barrage is an impressive piece of engineering for which we supplied the rupees. It was pleasant to see one dam that is indubitably completed.

We came back through Kotah,[22] a walled town and once capital

---

[20] See page 82.
[21] All members of the AID staff.
[22] Famous, among other things, for a school of painting featuring exceptionally vigorous hunting scenes. See *Indian Painting*, by Mohinder Singh Randhawa and John Kenneth Galbraith (Boston: Houghton Mifflin, 1968).

of this Rajput state. The right bank canal now cuts a spectacular moat along the foot of the old wall. Most of the people live beyond the wall as for the past hundred years or so have the Maharajahs. The palaces and grounds are vast and as usual elsewhere — Jaipur is a prominent exception — in a state of melancholy decay. The day was hot and, aided by a mild fever, I had no difficulty keeping warm. At six, I made a short speech to the Indian Council on World Affairs and then got back on the train and into bed. I managed to sleep for nearly twelve hours or until our arrival at the New Delhi station between six and seven this morning.

✧ ✧ ✧

New Delhi, India
October 16, 1962

Dear Mr. President:

I remember when I was running price control the only news ever passed up to me was of major disasters. The intelligence reaching your office must be much the same. In recent weeks things here have been going sufficiently better so that it requires a major act of will to talk about them. However, perhaps you need a moment's relaxation.

My policy on the border conflict[23], in the convenient absence of instructions, is to express quiet sympathy, make clear that we hope for settlement here as elsewhere, and not to feel any urgency about offering help. It will be far better if the Indians have to ask. They must not think we are yearning for an opportunity to line them up on our side and save them.

I have just completed an interesting and rather encouraging experiment. I took some twenty or thirty Indian newspapermen and photographers plus two American television crews and a newsreel crew on a ten-day tour of American-aided projects in India. We traveled by special train — a delight in itself and, I hasten to say, at no expense either to balance of payments or the

[23] Between China and India then in incipient stage.

United States taxpayer. (We have enough rupees available for United States use to last well into John Jr.'s second term.) Apart from a major University speech at Lucknow, another center of antipathetic attitudes toward the United States, the hegira included (by way of illustration) the new Indian Institute of Technology at Kanpur, support for which we announced a year ago; several power plants which we are financing; two coal washeries, which may well be the least fascinating industrial processes in the world; a huge dam near Hyderabad which is being financed by Public Law 480 rupees on which 100,000 people (sic) are employed; all kinds of agricultural betterment; a big fertilizer plant; an automobile and truck plant; a school for training mechanics and draftsmen and two schools for the training of young workers in the operation and care of bulldozers, steam shovels and the like.

Everywhere there was a lively appreciation of the source of the aid. Invariably there was a sign saying it was being done with the cooperation of the United States. And there was a good deal of enthusiasm on the part of those who were on the payroll. The tour got a great deal of national attention and it blanketed the local papers. I held a more or less continuous seminar on economic development which must have been highly rewarding to all listeners.

Many things about AID still worry me. While I have been trying to do fewer things and making sure that these are the most important, there is still room for further concentration. We still need to move more of our people out of Delhi — it is like pulling teeth to accomplish this. Some very odd people get recruited. The Indian industrial management is highly bureaucratic — at a big fertilizer plant outside Bombay they had — characteristically — put up a vast office building before they had started excavations for the plant itself. Still there is much that is good. A lot of the projects selected by my predecessors were exceedingly sound and the program could easily suffer from too much reform. Out in Kotah (a Godforsaken[24] desert community in Rajasthan) I encountered a Californian by the name of Childs married to a Japanese wife who for four years has been the only American in town. He has done a superb job of organizing a school for training in the operation and maintenance of bull-dozers, graders, heavy trucks and so forth and is just about ready to turn it over to Indian direction. There are many other such cases.

I have been following the aid legislation in the Congress this year with a good deal of misgiving. I would gather there is even more serious trouble ahead in the future. I have a suggestion for giving it a new lift which I will put to you when I am back — that is, if I can catch you for a few minutes between whistle stops. I am in Washington week after next — October 30 to November 6.

The Mississippi affair[25] seemed from here to have been superbly handled. Without question it greatly raised our stock in this part of the world. Not even the Communists now seriously accuse us of evasion.

Yours faithfully,
JOHN KENNETH GALBRAITH

THE PRESIDENT
   THE WHITE HOUSE

✧ ✧ ✧

October 18 — New Delhi

Kitty was damaged last Sunday — October 14 — when a strap broke and she was thrown from her horse, Sandstorm. She is in Holy Family Hospital with a cracked pelvis bone and badly torn ligaments but, fortunately, is less injured than first expected. A

24 An unkind adjective justified only by the bad state of my digestive tract that day and for which I apologize to all citizens of that city. I do not believe that God has forsaken it.
25 The insertion of James Meredith into the University of Mississippi.

precise accident of this sort is, on the whole, less worrisome than vague, natural and possibly cancerous pains but sad enough.[26]

The Chinese still make trouble in the North — now in NEFA. A few days ago there were several more casualties, wounded and killed, which suggests that the fighting must have been in near battalion strength. The Indians are reacting more vigorously and Krishna Menon made a speech the other day that sounded almost fierce.

One problem is that in the disputed area, the border line — the famous McMahon Line — runs in principle along the peaks. But when it was drawn on the maps, these did not show where the ridge was. So the line was drawn south of the ridge. It is in this area between the natural geography and the line on the map that the fighting proceeds.

The weather is again perfectly delightful. In the morning, the air is vaguely crisp and ideal for walking. As a result, I am getting much more exercise. In the last few weeks, I have shed fifteen pounds which gives the illusion of ten less years.

[26] It entailed a month of immobility but eventual full recovery.

XX

Border War I[1]

October 23 — New Delhi

Over the weekend, I had one of the greatest exercises in continuous aerial navigation since Lindbergh. I left Friday evening for Bombay by Air-India and caught the jet to Geneva, Paris and London, arriving a little before midday. I was met and went to the

[1] Fighting broke out between the Chinese and the Indians in two areas — in the high, arid, mountainous plateau region of Ladakh at the extreme northern point of the Indian diamond, and far to the east near Burma in the mountains north of Assam and the Brahmaputra River and just east of Bhutan. This territory, not organized as a state, is called the North-East Frontier Agency or NEFA. In Ladakh, the Indian defenders fought stubbornly but their performance was blanketed by the disastrous collapse in NEFA.

My concern, as these pages will show, was about equally divided between helping the Indians against the Chinese and keeping peace between the Indians and the Pakistanis. The latter had grievances against the Indians which they considered, not without reason, to have substance. The nightmare of a combined attack by Pakistan and China, with the possibility of defeat, collapse and even anarchy in India, was much on my mind. The later outbreak of hostilities between India and Pakistan showed these fears to be real.

This chapter has been edited in one important respect. I was not fond of Krishna Menon, the Defence Minister — a feeling that was deeply reciprocated as his own recollections of these days amply tell. But my feelings were unimportant, and as compared with the antipathy and suspicion with which he was regarded in Washington and equally in Indian political circles, they were almost benign. Krishna Menon was an extraordinarily resourceful politician and I was afraid that were we too forthcoming in giving the Indians military aid, he would take credit for it. He would then present himself as a transcendent figure who was respected by the Americans as by all others. This would cause great trouble in Washington and great trouble for the Indians in getting further military help, should there be a long period of hostility.

I have deleted most of the references to the problem. Mr. Menon is now an old man. It would be wrong, I think, to reopen these old wounds — especially to repeat the angry comments about him which flowed in on me at the time from other Indian political leaders.

Ritz where I successfully negotiated myself into rooms away from Piccadilly and slept until about six. I then strolled down to Piccadilly Circus, canvassed the available theaters and settled for a Peter Ustinov production. The latter, which began at eight, held my attention through the better part of two acts but then dissolved in a miasma of words. I went home to bed and woke up in the early morning hours to a telephone call from the Embassy which had a raft of messages for me. These had principally to do with the outbreak of violent fighting in the Thagla Ridge[2] area of NEFA but also in Ladakh, with the Indians being driven back and heavy casualties. This was no longer a minor skirmish but a major Chinese push. Also included in the messages when they arrived was a Top Secret Eyes Only from the President. It suggested, in terms that allowed of no argument, that I dispense with the Guildhall lecture I was to give the next day on behalf of Granada Television and get back to Delhi immediately. The lad from the Embassy was appalled that anyone could get so outspoken an instruction from the President of the United States and seem able to go back to sleep.

B.O.A.C. had a Boeing leaving at 11:30 A.M. With less difficulty than might be imagined, and time to spare, I made it, leaving the Embassy to cancel numerous engagements. My lecture sponsors were unhappy but naturally did not argue with a war. By six yesterday morning, I was back in Delhi.

I am again reminded of the rule that I formulated in offering this diary. There is no reason to spare any American. But an ambassador is hired to maintain good relations with the country to which he is accredited. Even after due elapse of time, as in this case, he should keep to the spirit of this obligation.

As elsewhere, I have made cosmetic changes in the next two chapters. But it has seemed to me of some importance to give, this once, the full account of how an ambassador reacts to a war. So I have avoided excisions that elsewhere, on grounds of pure unimportance, I might have made. I am more than prepared to be told that in preserving this record, I am comprehensive at the expense of being . . . well, too comprehensive.

[2] High mountain country near the officially demarked border between India and China, i.e., Tibet.

The London evening papers, I remember, had disturbing headlines about the fighting. I remember deciding, as I walked home, to begin worrying when I awoke next morning.

I spent the morning going over the military and diplomatic situation. The Chinese are continuing to push forward on all fronts and giving the Indians a bad time. I still don't believe this is more than a border conflict but it seems evident that the Chinese intend to take possession of the territory that is anciently their claim and establish themselves before the winter sets in. Then they will negotiate from this position of strength. They are far superior to the Indians in arms, manpower and possibly also in determination. I got back to the Department a statement of our policy. It is far safer to propose a course of action to the Department and ask for confirmation than to wait for the latter's instructions which may either never arrive or be inconvenient. My general line is to give quiet sympathy and encouragement to the Indians, let them know who are their true friends, be receptive to requests for aid, but also to have decently in mind the pounding we have been taking from Krishna Menon.

Yesterday's cables included ambiguous references to the need to justify to the Indians our course of action in Cuba.[3] This became plain during the evening when notice came of a Presidential speech plus the proposals to quarantine Cuba and take it to the U.N. In the course of the evening, I got an execrably drafted letter from the President to the Prime Minister plus a copy of the speech that came in during the night. The letter had been so badly drafted for the President that I had to get permission from Washington to make some changes in the interests both of reasonable tact and syntax. There is a quality[4] about the Cuban action which does not appeal to me, but I think on the whole the Indians will be reasonably agreeable.

Today at noon, I saw Nehru and strongly urged him to see how sensitive the issue was for us and to support our efforts in the U.N. to have U.N. inspectors go to the Cuban missile sites. I don't think

[3] The Cuban missile crisis coincided in time with the Chinese attack and was the reason, in fact, the President ordered my return.
[4] The reference here, I assume, is to some aspect of the blockade as described by the cables.

he entirely missed references to their similar reaction to a similar situation in, say, Nepal or Bhutan. I had a well-prepared case and I think it was effective. In the afternoon, I made my case again to M.J. Desai and he gave me to understand that we could pretty well count on their restraint and U.N. support.

At the same time, Desai gave me a full account of their troubles. They have lost contact with the troops fighting in the Thagla Ridge area and their only hope is to hold the Chinese at high passes farther south. This will leave the Chinese in possession of a substantial additional area. In the past few days, the Soviets have taken a tough line with the Indians — including advice to them to settle on the Chinese terms. They have very little hope, accordingly, of the Soviets restraining the Chinese. In the next few days, he said, they were going to have to turn to us for substantial assistance. He said he hoped we would not force them into an alliance or impose security inspection procedures for the arms they received which would be inconsistent with their sovereignty.[5] I reassured him on both points but commented that there are more serious problems in the way in which Krishna Menon has alienated American opinion in the last year and also the very bad state of their procurement organization.

October 24 — New Delhi

Today was equally divided between India's problems and our own. On the whole, I thought India's problems easier to handle.

Fighting continues in the NEFA area and the Indians are falling back to positions well south of the McMahon Line. Evidently they lost heavily in the area of the Thagla Ridge. Probably as the result, the bell seems to have tolled for General Kaul;[6] it is

[5] The Indians had, in fact, previously agreed to such inspection. It is to ensure that arms sold or otherwise supplied are used as intended. Though a commonplace feature of military aid agreements, the inspection is perfunctory and ineffective.

[6] Lieutenant General B. M. Kaul, see page 283. He was commanding in the NEFA area. He was not, in fact, removed until a little later.

rumored that he has been heaved out. There are also indications that Krishna Menon is in some trouble. The Indian Army is without equipment, it is being said, partly because resources have gone into his highly advertised supersonic and transport planes and other gadgets, none of which are available to the soldiers on the frontier.

First this morning I went over the rather meager communications from Washington, the latter having been much reduced by limitations placed on telegraphic traffic as the result of the Cuban crisis. Then we had a staff meeting at which I brought people more or less abreast of policy and gave them the line — quiet support[7] on China, minimum comment on Cuba.

During the morning, I also had a visit from one of the more modest heads of state, Mr. Jigme Dorji, the Prime Minister of Bhutan. He told me there had been no Chinese penetration of Bhutan, but he was worried about concentration on the border. Some of the passes are closed by snow in the winter but others, unfortunately, are open. The Bhutan Army numbers about 1,500 armed men and about 4,000 more who can shoot. The Chinese minority consists of two Chinese army deserters and is not expected to be troublesome. There are some hundreds or thousands of Tibetan refugees who might panic.

Military strategy in the event of a Chinese invasion will be to take promptly to the hills. This seems to me very sensible. Also, hills in that state are readily available. I advised calm and a neutral posture. The Chinese would then have the disadvantage of attacking a small neutral country.

The Prime Minister thanked me on behalf of the Maharajah for a letter he had received from President Kennedy — the first such communication ever indicating knowledge of the existence of Bhutan. This was a letter of thanks for my good treatment there last spring. He also asked me for a small cut in any arms that we supply to India, which I did not encourage.

[7] The original, which was garbled here, says "firm comment on China." The intention was as stated.

Paul Gore-Booth came in and told me that the Prime Minister had been almost tearfully thankful for the warm words of support he had had from Macmillan. He told me, as others have during the day, that Krishna Menon is being sidetracked, and, on military matters, the line of command runs from the Prime Minister to General Thapar.[8]

During the course of the day, the Chinese offered to stop fighting, have a summit conference between Nehru and Chou En-lai and pull back twenty kilometers from their present position. I thought the Indians, given their troubles, might be tempted. But they promptly rejected the offer. They are becoming quite thoroughly aroused. And it is rather cynical of the Chinese to take the territory and then negotiate over it.

This afternoon we met to consider policy on military aid when we have a request — which I assume is only a few hours away. I asked for a full exploration and a careful paper on the subject. It would take Washington far too long to decide on this matter, so we must make up our minds here and then go back for the decision we need.

Next I had a meeting with C. Rajagopalachari,[9] now in his eighties and just returned from a trip to the United States — his first trip there. He is articulate, charming and had been captivated by President Kennedy.

Then I had a press briefing for the Indian press. They were very touchy about Cuba and seemed to have considerable doubts about the legality of our position. I was not very persuasive to the contrary but I hoped I quieted some of their misgivings. I would have been better if I had been free of (legal) misgivings of my own. I stressed the Communists were looking for trouble in installing their missiles. This was the initial act of aggression.

Finally, we had a meeting regarding the festivities of the opening

[8] General P. N. Thapar, Chief of the Army Staff and senior ranking military officer.

[9] Governor-General of India following Independence, and the most famous of elder statesmen. Known as Rajaji.

of the new Embassy Residence designed by Edward Stone, which is nearly completed. We decided for a program of austerity.

October 25 — New Delhi

The Cuban crisis seemed to have eased slightly today. The Russians seemed unwilling to challenge the blockade — or at least are a bit hesitant —and much talk goes on in New York. I would guess some compromise would be found. The Prime Minister made a relatively mild comment today and the papers have cooled down. The Communist Party is said to have debated whether it can profitably picket the American Embassy on Cuba before it pickets the Chinese Embassy on NEFA. This is not fantasy; it seems to be a serious report.

This morning, I sent off a telegram which evened a few scores on the subject of alliances. I have had my nose twisted several times by Rusk and the old Dulles group[10] because of my misgivings over alliances and the trouble which arms aid to Pakistan causes us in these precincts. At the moment, Pakistan is a member of SEATO, CENTO,[11] and is forming some kind of axis with Peking. Meanwhile, neutral India is seeking, however ineffectively, to stand off a Chinese Communist invasion. Next time I question some shipment of new arms to Pakistan, it will not be so easy to send me the usual reminder that this is important for defense against Communism.

Except for the British, everybody has been ambiguous in their support of the Indians. In my view, they would be helped — and would respond warmly — by a clear expression of support. I had in mind making one today but encountered concern on the part of my subordinates. I have postponed it for twenty-four hours. One should probably be guided by one's instinct on these matters and not seek advice. A conference never raises decision to the highest level of intelligence. It is far more likely to lower it to the lowest common denominator of caution.

[10] See page 150.
[11] Southeast Asia Treaty Organization and Central Treaty Organization.

Word came in during the morning of more fighting, more Chinese advances and of a meeting of the Prime Minister with the Congress Party leaders. The latter were protesting that Menon was not a fit man for the Defence Ministry. Nehru said, in effect, that he was now handling this Ministry. This he cannot do.

This afternoon I visited Chester Ronning, the Canadian High Commissioner and an old China hand. He shares my view that the Chinese objectives are limited and we need not be concerned about their descending into the Indian plain. He thinks the Chinese can defend a claim to the Aksai Chin Plateau in Ladakh — they occupied it for two years before the Indians seem to have discovered they were there. The Indians might let them have undisturbed possession in return for the McMahon Line in NEFA.[12]

Krishna Menon, whom I have not seen for many weeks, has been in touch with Ronning on arms — he is evidently still very reluctant to talk with us. When Ronning saw Menon last Friday, the latter talked about a ten-year war and implied that the Chinese might head for Madras. Ronning had seen Menon today and found him somewhat more calm.

This evening I had a further talk with Morarji Desai. Desai is deeply worried and we talked (I thought informally) about the ways and means of providing military assistance. I am concerned that we get some contingency planning under way in Washington against a request for help.

October 26 — New Delhi

This has been a long but interesting day. Washington continues totally occupied with Cuba. For a week, I have had a considerable war on my hands without a single telegram, letter, telephone call or other communication of guidance. The single exception was a message that came in today warning me that I could not endorse the McMahon Line. The subject, it was said, was under study in Washington. I have been sending off telegrams on various urgent

[12] This is, in effect, what has happened.

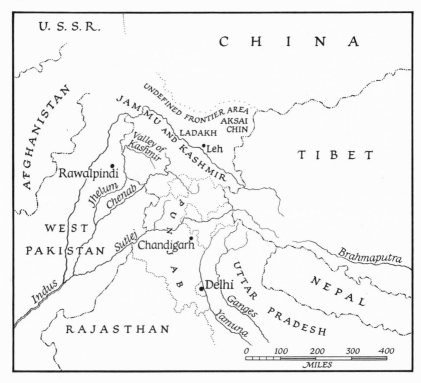

matters without the slightest knowledge of whether they are being received or acted upon. It is like marching troops out of the trenches and over no-man's-land without knowing whether they get through or get shot down en route.

This morning we had a long session on the military scene; the Chinese have taken Tawang, some twenty air miles south of the border, and by cutting across through Bhutan could quite quickly get to the plains. The Indians have taken very heavy casualties — some 4,000 in all (mostly missing) of whom fewer than 400 have straggled back. I continue to revise my estimate that this is purely a border affair. Conceivably they may intend to take all of NEFA. In any case, I must keep my mind open to this. The worst course is to make an estimate and then be so proud of it that one cannot accommodate it to the changing evidence.

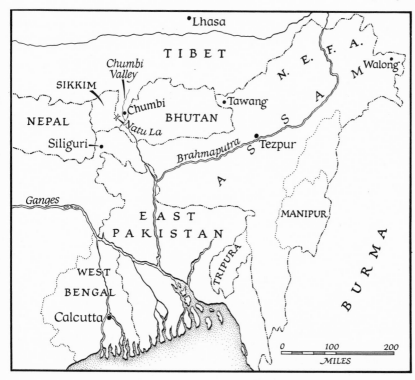

My most pressing concern at the moment is Pakistan. They continue to make pro-Chinese noises and no fewer than three Indian divisions are being kept along this border. This continues to poison feelings here, and McConaughy in Karachi and Talbot in Washington have both made approaches to the Pakistanis. Unfortunately, both men are exceedingly soft. The Pakistanis would not be aware that either had talked to them.

After lunch I had a long talk with Rajeshwar Dayal[13] about these matters. He has just taken over from Tyabji[14] in the Ministry of External Affairs. After all the criticism of our role in Pakistan, there is now hope that we can be a restraining influence. I let

[13] Dayal was now Special Secretary in the Ministry of External Affairs. For further details, see page 50.

[14] B. F. H. B. Tyabji. A Moslem, he was leaving to become Vice-Chancellor of Aligarh University, an important center of Islamic study.

it be known that we never thought that the Pakistanis or Indians were so foolish as to attack each other.[15]

Later this evening I had a long talk with President Radhakrishnan. I had some misgivings that he might want to talk about Cuba; however, like everyone else, his mind was totally on the Chinese.

The criticism of the Defence Minister is everywhere acute. He is held to have played politics in the army, failed to provide supplies, created dissension among the officers, damaged morale — "sending men to fight with highly-advertised supersonic planes that do not exist." All members of the cabinet have now petitioned the Prime Minister to dispense with Menon and it is the general view that he will soon go.

The President told me that later on tonight they are proclaiming a state of emergency. The stated purpose is to check rumor-mongering and seditious activity. The further intention is to restrain the Communists from peddling "the Pravda line" to the effect that India and China should agree on Chinese terms.

The President also asked me to bring influence to bear on the Pakistanis to take a friendly course.

We talked in his upstairs room in the Rashtrapati Bhavan and I have never seen him so tough and angry. Earlier I had dropped in to a party there. The President's bodyguard in all their regalia were deployed along the stairway in the usual fashion.

Various matters occupied the evening and I used the report on the visit to the President as a peg for an urgent telegram especially on Pakistan matters to the White House. Earlier in the day, I sent a highly private telegram to Bundy to see if any of my messages were getting through. Beginning tomorrow, I imagine I will start hearing again from Washington.

October 27 — New Delhi

This was Saturday. I slept badly and under the influence of extensive narcotics, and woke up late. We had what is now a regu-

[15] Another case of imperfect foresight for in the summer of 1965 they did.

lar meeting at ten — D.C.M., Senior Military Attaché, Ty Wood, and Barry Zorthian[16] of USIS. All knowledge of our war came from the newspapers and seems to indicate that the Chinese are stationary in Ladakh but still moving forward in NEFA, both south of Thagla Pass and in the far east. It is appalling in these matters how much action one must base on how little information.

By the time the meeting was over, my complaints to the Department about lack of communication had resulted in a flood of action. I was wisely disagreeable about the failure of communications in the Goa matter a year ago. Everyone, as a result, is now rushing to preserve his reputation. There could be no better demonstration of the Machiavellian dictum that it is better in diplomacy to be feared than loved. Specifically, I got approval of our stand supporting the Indians on the McMahon Line; got assurance of contingency planning in the event we are asked for aid; and received guidance, unhappily already somewhat out of date, from the President on dealing with Nehru vis-à-vis the Russians and Krishna Menon.

Pete Lakeland,[17] one of our junior officers who speaks Hindi and has an unlimited acquaintance with local politicians, came in around eleven with a raft of news including that the Congress Executive Committee had demanded the retirement of Krishna Menon. It was the view of those attending that the Prime Minister has made up his mind to let Menon go. I then dictated a long roundup of the situation for Washington in which I appealed again for restraint on offers of assistance.

At lunch, I came home very weary, but instead of napping found myself reflecting on various matters including whether to get out a public endorsement of the McMahon Line as approved by the Department. This would eliminate all ambiguity and be a great source of support to the Indians. I also wondered if Washington might have second thoughts or might yield to the pleas of Formosa.

---

[16] Later to become the chief spokesman for the U.S. Mission in Saigon, perhaps the most trying single non-combatant assignment of the Vietnam War.

[17] Albert A. Lakeland, Jr., Second Secretary (political).

So I typed out a statement and got the press officer to gather the press for a release at five o'clock. After it was mimeographed and safe in their hands, a frantic message came in from Taipei protesting bitterly against the endorsement of the Line. (Though Taipei's control of the territory has been a bit tenuous, what with British, Indians, and Reds all having been closer, it regards it highly.) My statement was already out.

I have cut protocol activities to the bone since in New Delhi these are largely a form of disguised unemployment. Accordingly, this afternoon I substituted a note of apology for a pilgrimage to the airport to meet the Prime Minister of Malaya. Instead, I worked on the roundup message to the Department and then had a long talk with G. Parthasarathy, who is about to go to Karachi as High Commissioner. Parthasarathy is a reasonable man who will work for Indian-Pakistani reconciliation. Another development of the day was a promise from Washington to support me on this general effort and information that Mohammed Ali[18] had told Duncan Sandys[19] in London that they would not make India's path more difficult, that India was in no danger of attack from Pakistan. Our military attachés were told today they henceforth would be given good working knowledge of developments. Until now, they have been held strictly at arm's length. This has been hard on them. Washington wants reports and they have had nothing to report.

Another problem of the day was Nepal. It came to me that Stebbins has been sitting there on the Chinese border with almost no information. I solved that by putting a junior officer on an airplane with all the telegrams that had come in or gone out in the last seven days.

To complete the day, we had fireworks for Diwali on the lawn, and both Peter and Jamie were afraid that amid all the explosions the Chinese could creep in unnoticed.

[18] See page 387.
[19] See page 384.

October 28 — New Delhi

Today was a busy Sunday with much action from Washington.

We met at 10 A.M. to review the situation. There was very little new on the military front. Some advances in Ladakh threatened Chushul and there was more pressure in NEFA but no very dramatic changes. As usual, our military intelligence had been drawn firsthand from the newspapers.

Ty Wood had seen Morarji Desai early this morning at my instruction to give him general background information on what could be done to finance military aid. Morarji, it turned out, was under the impression that he had already requested aid from me on behalf of the Indian Government — in principle.[20] The Indian Government is loose-jointed and it shows at times like this. He was leaving for Bombay and will not be back until Tuesday morning. By that time, events will have outrun this particular misunderstanding. If they haven't, Wood will tell him we must have a more specific request.

After lunch, I had a sleep for about half an hour. Then I was aroused by two telegrams on the Pakistan situation. McConaughy had been to Ayub to urge a quiet and restrained policy and to ask him to send assurances to Nehru that they wouldn't do anything to embarrass the Indians in their time of trouble. Ayub had been stiff. McConaughy had then fallen back on a suggestion of mine; to wit, a letter from the President to Ayub. This was fine but his telegram on the contents of the letter suggested among other things that if Ayub would assure Nehru as regards China, we would take a strong stand on behalf of Ayub on Kashmir. This alarmed me. It would seem that the Americans and Pakistanis were working together to seek the surrender of territory just as the Chinese were grabbing land. All would seem to be grabbing.[21] I got off an alarmed telegram to McConaughy and the Department endorsing the approach but asking for God's sake that they keep Kashmir out

[20] See page 435.
[21] This, not the merits of the Kashmir question, being of course the issue.

of it. Then I got Timmons on the telephone to Karachi to urge the same in guarded language over the unguarded wire. The Department had got the point and had already warned McConaughy of the danger.

Meanwhile, the Department thought it would be helpful to McConaughy if he could tell Ayub that Nehru would welcome the assurance that there would be no embarrassment from Pakistan. I was asked to seek an interview with Nehru to obtain this assurance. This I succeeded in getting at 6:45 P.M. Nehru was frail, brittle, and seemed small and old. He was obviously desperately tired. The habit of a commanding role, the man who gives or refuses, is almost automatic, and when I asked him if we could tell Ayub that he, Nehru, would welcome these assurances, he said in effect that he would have no objection to our saying so. I then moved in very hard on saying this would not be sufficient, that we must be able to say that he would warmly accept such assurances. He looked a little stunned, then said of course we could say it and went on to add that such a gesture from Pakistan would be important not only in the present situation but in the future harmony of the two peoples. Taking advantage of a strong position, I then asked if I could be assured that he would respond to such assurances. He said on some appropriate occasion he would, and then I pressed that this was a time for generosity and he should be immediately forthcoming. Again he agreed.

We talked a little about the military situation and I left with the comment that as usual we were adhering to the policy of the quiet, steadfast friend. He shook my hand warmly at the top of the stairs.

The other development of the day was a visit from General Kaul at noon. He has recovered more or less and is on his way back to Tezpur.[22] There have been innumerable rumors these last days about him, and a high External Affairs official even told me that he had had a heart attack. I do think he has been under some emotional strain; certainly he was in a rather emotional mood today.

[22] The Indian headquarters in Assam of the forces defending against the Chinese in NEFA.

He spoke in the most urgent terms of the need for arms.

While I was meeting with Kaul, Colonel Curtis, our Army Attaché, was having a session with various Army intelligence people. Our military relations with the Indians, always rather distant, have become extremely intimate these last days. Orders of battle and other military information are being provided. Arrangements are being made for Curtis to go to Tezpur if he wishes. And I have just brought up from Wellington, for such advice as he can give, an American specialist in guerrilla operations who happens to be attending the staff school there. A week ago, of course, all this would have been unthinkable.

We are about to have an influx of the American press. Indeed, it has already begun and I am very dissatisfied with arrangements for handling it. My present man, the replacement for Alan Carter, is a pleasant and likable chap who is lacking in self-confidence and, perhaps for that reason, in firm judgment. The whole burden of press relations, accordingly, is falling on me. I proposed, even before this crisis, to replace him but was talked out of it on the grounds that it would ruin his career. Today I acted — taking on the mutual protective apparatus of USIS. It is better for the man that he go now than that he establish a reputation for failure in a critical situation. We have worked out some partial face-saving arrangements.

The one other development of the Sabbath was to put Colonels Curtis and Hannah to work drawing up a movement table for elementary weapons for the Indian Army. I want to know how quickly and from where we can get such basic requirements as automatic rifles, mortars and shells. Once we are asked for aid, if we are asked, I hope we can have something come here within a matter of three or four days.

October 29 — New Delhi

This was the longest of all days but, I think, the last of the worst. Things that had been pending for a long while got settled in the

Indian manner of speaking. Everything also went according to script. When I got to the office around nine, Menon was on the phone asking to see me or come over to the Chancery. Protocol never allows a minister to call on an ambassador; Menon, to his credit, is not scrupulous about such matters. The decision had been made to request American arms. Menon wished to show that he was persona grata with the Americans and get the credit.

Fortunately, a letter had just come in from the President to the Prime Minister giving comfort and offering help. I had also been firmly instructed by the President that I should in general do business with Menon. But I did tell Menon that I had a letter for the Prime Minister that had to be delivered first. He immediately offered to get my meeting with the Prime Minister deferred. In a series of telephone exchanges, too numerous and oriental to record in detail, I got through to him the idea that I knew he was going to ask for aid and felt that the request should come first from the Prime Minister. Then I agreed to see him after I had seen the Prime Minister.

At ten, we had a brief roundup meeting on the situation and at eleven, I went to fill in Agha Hilaly, the Pakistan High Commissioner,[23] on the background of our efforts to calm the Indian fears of the Pakistanis. He spoke of Indian provocations on the Pakistan border in recent months and suggested that we propose to the Indians a reasonable position in Kashmir in return for a guarantee from Pakistan. I said this would be taken as a form of blackmail in a time of weakness. We discussed the matter reasonably. Hilaly is both a strong defender of Pakistan interests and a concerned citizen of the subcontinent. Another problem of the day was that the troop movements of the Indians along the Pakistan border, even though they represent a thinning-out and redeployment, are disturbing the Pakistanis.

The Prime Minister, when I saw him, looked well and received the President's letter, an exceedingly good one, with gratitude. He

23 Now Pakistan Ambassador to the U.S.

told me he had that morning addressed a letter to the President and to Khrushchev congratulating them on the Cuban settlement. I then told the Prime Minister that if the President's letter produced a request for aid, as I gathered it would, I hoped it would come from him. I told him I was not playing on his vanity — but was not above doing so — but he must know he is loved in the United States as no one else in India. The American people would respond to a request from him as they would not to anyone else.

The Prime Minister said they did indeed have to have aid and it would have to come from the United States. He went on to say they wanted to avoid irritating the Soviets as much as possible. The Soviets had indicated that they realized that assistance from us was inevitable, but hoped that this would not mean a military alliance between the United States and India. I told him of course we insisted on no such thing. He ended up with a warm and affectionate inquiry about Kitty's injuries.

Then shortly after noon Timmons and I saw Krishna Menon. He was obviously under great tension. He spoke about long-range mortars, tanks, and said that they must have machine tools to equip their arsenals. I told him that we were prepared to help him with the things the soldiers needed in the hills, including quartermaster supplies for I had heard that some were without proper clothing for the violent climate of the border. But the time for illusions was past; the Chinese were not being driven back by the supersonic aircraft so much publicized by his Department. He barely controlled his anger at this particular point; under any other circumstances, it would have produced a towering explosion. I then asked that he designate somebody to work with Timmons to get up a list and we would get the first request in to the United States this evening.

Then I saw M. J. Desai. I stressed that in briefing the press, they should make clear that their request for aid had come from the Prime Minister. He told me that in a meeting in the afternoon, steps would be taken to organize a Ministry of Supply or some kind of special supply committee. This is none too soon.

By this time, I was late for a luncheon by the head of the President's bodyguard, a purely social affair. However, it was not a wholly unwelcome interlude and gave me a chance to fill in the Canadians on the events of the day. After lunch, I saw Paul Gore-Booth and gave him a full account of the activities. He warned me in turn that we would find the figures on Indian military needs in poor shape. This proved to be the case and the Indian Defence people and our military people worked all the rest of the day and until midnight putting them in order.

The American newspaper corps which was down to three or four this summer is already back to ten or more, and at 4 P.M. I had a background press briefing. These encounters with the press are, in some ways, the most troublesome problem I face. One can outrun his communications, but not if the press highlights the fact in Washington. For then a lot of people in the bureaucracy read what is happening before they get the cables and become excited. There was particular danger in this today. Washington has been wholly unclear how this military help is to be paid for and I could seem to be offering very generous terms. Accordingly, I kept things very much on the dry side. The press release (on our agreement to render help) was a mere three or four lines, not much considering the great questions involved. Finally, about 5:30 P.M., I got home and slept for an hour with great beneficial effect. Some time during the day, I had also dictated a three- or four-page telegram describing the day's developments.

In the evening there was a big dinner at the Hotel Ashoka by the Malayan Prime Minister for Nehru. This was an appalling waste of time for everyone there and even the most perfunctory conversation was, at times, beyond me. It did give me a chance to see Ministry of External Affairs officials and impress upon them the need for taking the Pakistanis into their confidence. One of the officials, on whom I wanted to press my idea with especial vigor, said, "Oh, those silly fellows. What do they really think we are up to?" I told him this was not a time for criticism but for remedies. Rajeshwar Dayal moved in very hard on my side and I think something will be done.

Finally, after the meeting, we wrestled with the list of requirements and the telegram asking for air shipment of the most urgent things. I was really weary beyond the point of no return. Eventually I let the telegram go off in very inadequate form. Some of the things requested I know we do not have. There was no statement of the quantities to be shipped immediately by air and those which could come more gradually by surface. However, I had reached the end. So, very nearly, had Timmons.

October 30 — New Delhi

Life eased today as I expected. After a usual morning walk in the Lodi Gardens, where I work things out for the day, I got to the office about nine. After the pressures of yesterday, the cable traffic had slackened off and the new personnel that we had requested was on the way — a new press officer, a specialist on military aid organization and three army officers who are competent on military requirements. The telegram announcing the latter had a slightly ominous tone. It was noted that the leader was to be a member of the Country Team[24] and there was a slightly ambiguous comment about his being subject to the authority of the Secretary of Defense. I returned a NIACT telegram saying that I was controlling the whole operation through a much smaller group than the Country Team, would designate their man a member of this group after his arrival, and that all of his communications would, of course, go through me. From all around the world, people seem to be converging on New Delhi and I foresee that I will spend considerable time in the next few days standing off help that I do not need. Today's offering included a Marine Corps specialist on guerrilla warfare and a deluge of Congressional delegations for whom India has obviously become a place of interest and excitement.

At 10 A.M., we met as usual to go over the situation. There has

24 See page 62.

been very little military activity in NEFA but a couple more posts are under attack in Ladakh. In NEFA, it is not quite clear whether the Chinese are still advancing but not coming into contact with the new Indian defense line or whether they have slowed down. The safest assumption is that they have yet to reach the next Indian defenses. Yet I am not sure. From the other side of the hill, the Chinese must begin to wonder if they are arraying a great deal of the world against them.

At noon with Ty Wood, I went to see Morarji Desai. As an indication of how important events can be handled or mutually mishandled, the Finance Minister was under the impression that, when I visited him last week, he had made a formal request for aid. Since neither items nor amounts were mentioned, this had not registered on me. But apparently he had been told by the Prime Minister to approach me. This, in turn, explained some statements by the Prime Minister over the weekend that major countries, including the U.S., had been approached.

In the course of the day, I learned the fate of the famous MIG's. In principle, the Russians are committed to supply a squadron and go in for their manufacture. In practice, they have told the Indians that, because of the serious international situation, they may not be able to keep the commitment. The Indians do not know whether it is Cuba or China that is serious. They think it is Cuba; I would guess it is China.

I had a noontime nap and at three, Sudhir Ghosh[25] came in to urge me to present a paper proposing a major rapprochement with Pakistan. There was no mention as to how Kashmir is to be handled and this, of course, involves territorial pride that is just as great as in NEFA. However, it is a step in the right direction and I told him in general terms of our effort with Pakistan. I used the occasion to urge improvement on the Indians. I recalled that within the last fortnight in Bangalore and in a speech in Connaught Circus

[25] A friend of Gandhi's and Member of Parliament from West Bengal, now dead.

here in Delhi, Krishna Menon had reminded his audience that Pakistan was the major enemy, and produced a telegram which had just come in from our Consulate in Calcutta regretting that the Bengal broadcast still included five or ten minutes of anti-Pakistan propaganda. He promised a prompt look. We also considered suggesting to the Indians that they ask the Pakistanis for rail transit rights across East Pakistan. This would greatly improve their communications to NEFA and be otherwise a useful gesture of confidence. In this connection, some 250 Americans live in the Assam and NEFA area — mostly missionaries. They are becoming nervous and there is some talk of evacuation. I think this is premature. We can get them out quite rapidly by airplane when the time comes. And, as always, I dislike the thought that Americans should always be the first to cut and run. Anyway, I worry about the spiritual salvation of the people that the missionaries would leave behind. Some of them also must be physicians which could be even more serious.

Most of the Dakotas (DC-3's) of the Indian airlines have been taken over by the Army and, in consequence, the schedules are badly disrupted. This raises the question of what we should do about tourists coming here, and I am pressed to urge the Department of Commerce to advise tourists not to come. I think this is premature. It would be a heavy blow to the international airlines and hotels and would lose the Indians much-needed dollars. In any case, we need to know whether the majority of the tourists get much beyond Bombay, Delhi, Agra and Calcutta, to all of which communications are still adequate.

In the late afternoon, I had a background briefing with the Indian press. They were inclined to blame Pakistan for being unhelpful. I used the occasion to suggest exploration of the Indian responsibility. I also gave them an outline of developments in the last few days. One or two reporters said we should have made Menon's departure the price of granting aid.[26] Incidentally, Sudhir Ghosh

---

[26] Needless to say, I did nothing to encourage this line of criticism.

also told me that Menon is about to go. The Parliamentary Congress Party has met three times with the Prime Minister in the last week, and at the last meeting, the only person opposing Menon's departure was Menon himself, and even he was more reticent than usual on the subject. Everybody else denounced him. For a proud man, this must have been a rather difficult proceeding.

The day ended with a brief call at the R. K. Nehrus' who had planned a big send-off reception for the new Indian Ambassador to Moscow. This had been cut under the influence of austerity to a dozen or so including Ambassador Benediktov. In view of the difficulties with the Communist world, he was being rather conscientiously ignored so I congratulated him warmly on the stand Khrushchev had taken on Cuba. He accepted the congratulations and said he thought Kennedy had handled the matter rather well too. He regretted the fact that I had had to cancel my visit to Moscow,[27] and I told him I shared his regrets but that the blame rested on his Chinese ally. He then asked me for my estimate of Chinese intentions. This struck me as a subject on which I could not really be helpful.

The last act of the day was a long roundup telegram to the Department in which I began to signal our changed attitude toward the Indians. Where until now we have been very delicate in our support, I am suggesting that we can now be much more obvious. Before, we did not want to make it difficult for the Chinese to negotiate with them. Now our policy must be to give the Chinese an impression of the strength that will deter them.

October 31 — New Delhi

Today was another of the days when things fitted into form. One of the great problems of the world is that all crises are almost certainly handled by tired men. I slept badly last night but managed to get abroad this morning and the Lodi Gardens had their usual

27 I had planned to return from Washington by way of Norway and the U.S.S.R.

restorative effect. Washington is still reacting helpfully and plans seem well advanced for military shipments; questions of payment, inspection, security, all seem, from the morning cables, to be dwindling in significance. B. K. Nehru,[28] who is an intelligent but dutifully cautious man, is behind New Delhi in his feel of the situation. As a result, he is sticking on such things as the inspection of the use to which the arms are put (a requirement under our law) which aroused no problem here. However, when the ponderous machinery of the U.S. Government starts to move, it does so in a remarkable way. The danger remains of a deluge of generals, colonels, majors and second lieutenants. But that is another story.

After I got over the morning cables with Timmons, I had a half-hour meeting with the American press. Then I did a brief television interview. CBS met me coming into the Chancery and asked a few routine questions. I had some misgivings about this for I am not fond of the role of a professor masterminding a war.[29] I was also afraid that it might appear with a film that Krishna Menon had just done — he had talked for twenty minutes to the American television audience. It could be damaging and I would share in the liability. However, I concluded that a brief interview would not hurt. To keep my shirt-sleeve reputation with Lyndon Johnson, I appeared in a bush shirt.

We had a meeting of our small steering committee. The military situation shows no change and the Indians indeed seem to have mounted some kind of artillery counterattack. I am of two minds as to how aggressively the Chinese are moving but still assume that they have not yet reached the Indian defensive positions. We unloaded a good specialist on military-aid planning from Washington in the early hours of this morning.

Some things do not change even in moments of crisis and, following these meetings, I went to the dentist. The trip far across town gave me a chance to catch my breath, and I returned to a large

[28] The Indian Ambassador in Washington. See page 82.
[29] To be more accurate, I was fond of the role but did not want to seem so.

staff meeting in which I brought the whole staff of the Embassy into the picture. Such meetings are useful only to give people a sense of participation in great events and for transmitting information quickly and with informality. By way of illustration, I instructed against any gloating on the Cuban situation and the Khrushchev-Kennedy accommodation, urged putting entertainment and festivity in low key but not being so dramatic as to cut out all social life. I then shared my lack of information on the military situation and outlined the organization for planning military aid. And so forth. Lastly, I saw a newspaperman and got home about 1:45 P.M. for lunch. After lunch, I had a half-hour nap and, in a modest further state of weariness, went back to my desk work — dictating cables, saluting some touring Indian farmers at four and meeting with Rajeshwar Dayal on Pakistan problems at 4:15 P.M. McConaughy has been doing a notably energetic job with the Pakistanis and has won from Mohammed Ali a promise to put their negotiations with the Chinese in low key and to take a benign attitude on our military aid to India. They will still press their Kashmir claims. The Indian papers are still far from helpful on our efforts to calm the Pakistanis. Their tone is: It is time someone told these fellows what to do. I pressed Dayal to remind the newspapermen that a plea for soul-searching on Indian attitudes would be more helpful. I also asked a calming down of the radio.

I then had a talk with T. N. Kaul, the new Indian Ambassador to Moscow. He thinks that on any showdown the Soviets will always support the Chinese. The best he could do is get some measure of neutrality and perhaps preserve the flow of economic aid. That seems to me to be a good solution. He asked, as many others have, if we will continue to accept the Indian policy of nonalignment. I must make this point clear in some future speech. It would seem obvious that we are not trying to recruit new military partners but evidently the point must be made. This touchiness also emphasizes the importance of not having a vast influx of our own soldiers.

At 7:15 P.M., I saw M. J. Desai. He told me the interesting news that Krishna Menon has been sacked. The Prime Minister is taking over the Defence Ministry himself. Menon has been relegated to a new Ministry of Defence Production, which will not have to do with overseas procurement. This is a stopgap arrangement of great inadequacy. Timmons thinks Menon will use his new position to fight back up. My guess is that the jackals will now close in. We had an indication that something important was in the making when, about five, Barry Zorthian[30] had tea with R. N. Karanjia, the editor of *Blitz*.[31] Karanjia told Zorthian that their next edition would signal a major change in policy — a strong pro-U.S. line, great praise for Kennedy and Galbraith. The CIA, one gathers, will henceforth be the spearhead of American-Indian friendship. This means that Menon, whom *Blitz* supports, is in bad shape. The honor among thieves can be of a very high order as compared with the alliances between politicians. It has been hard in these last few days for me to avoid preoccupation with Menon. I have told our staff to confine all comment to saying that these were internal arrangements of the Indian Government.

November 1 — New Delhi

The pressure abated a bit more today. A team of supply experts arrived, as also a new Press Attaché, and so, for the moment, I have most of the people I need. The lull in the fighting continues and this gives us a chance to match up Indian needs with supplies that are available from American depots. This last is some task. Almost everything we sent for on our first list is unavailable. I am also shocked at the cost — sixty to seventy million dollars.

At the morning meeting I again laid down the line on Menon's withdrawal — no expression of satisfaction, however difficult this is to enforce on the soul. Then we talked a bit about press problems. It is important to get reporters up to Tezpur and the other

[30] See page 439.
[31] Militantly anti-American tabloid of Bombay and previously a strong supporter of Krishna Menon. *Blitz* had made a career out of uncovering highly imaginative and imaginary plots of the CIA.

fighting areas as soon as possible, otherwise they will boil over in frustration and criticism here in Delhi. The Indians are naturally secretive about the sad state of their supply. Even on elementary quartermaster equipment, this apparently is pretty awful and the incidence of frostbite seems to have been very high.

Following the morning meeting, I got off a series of telegrams, including one to Admiral Kirk[32] in Formosa thanking him for his forbearance on the McMahon Line, and I sent another long assessment to the Department on the discharge of Menon. It helps Pakistan relations, eliminates ambiguity in the defense policy, eliminates a divisive figure in the organization of defense procurement, and removes the symbol of anti-Americanism. Menon may not be so important as the change of policy which his departure signifies. However, it is also true that one determined man can do more in the Indian Government than in the U.S. Government.

At noon, I saw some press people and learned from G. K. Reddy of the *Times of India* that a supply minister is likely to be created tomorrow under T. T. Krishnamachari.[33] That will be good even if not quite perfect. All of this kept me very late and we had a relaxed luncheon with the Wyatts[34] who have just come back from Srinagar. Then I went to bed. I have reached the state of general tension where I cannot really sleep but on the whole I feel better after a couple of hours of trying. Then Timmons came in to talk about the day's business — not a great deal new.

I have begun to worry about Indian plans for training and use of the arms we are providing. Many times in the past help has gone to a country only to be stacked up until some newspaperman discovered it was not being employed. I have asked the Indians to submit a plan. In the next few days, I am going to Tezpur and also up to Leh to see what is going on. Zorthian, Weathersby[35] and

---

[32] Alan G. Kirk, Ambassador in Taipei.
[33] He later became Minister of Economic and Defence Coordination. See also page 401.
[34] See page 422.
[35] William H. Weathersby, Counselor for Public Affairs and Head of USIS.

Rosenfeld, the latest and highly competent Press Attaché, came in to talk about press matters and then, as a last act, I saw Karanjia of *Blitz*. He told me with engaging and scrupulous frankness that they were indeed converting — popular opinion would no longer allow them to be anti-American. I took the occasion to ask him to tone down their anti-Pakistan propaganda. I do not know how successful this will be and *Blitz* is not all that important. Still, it is better to have it on the right side, I suppose.

A dinner for the Wyatts this evening at the Gore-Booths'. I have told the Wyatts that the Gore-Booths are strongly opposed to any Englishman in India drinking alcohol,[36] and accordingly advised that they take full precautionary steps, which they did.

November 2 — New Delhi

Menon at Tezpur said, "I am still sitting in the Defence Ministry; nothing has been changed." He is said to be putting up a major fight to preserve some position. I am not at all sure that his strategy is good. He may succeed not in saving himself but in casting doubt on the authority of the Prime Minister.

There is still no fighting to speak of. The Indian intelligence says the Chinese are regrouping. This from a military man means "I haven't the slightest idea what is going on but I'd better assume it is something."

We have received word that the first planes are arriving tomorrow in Calcutta. These are C-130's loaded with infantry weapons and light artillery. This is a fine achievement when one considers we asked for the arms only four days ago. My first notion was to go down to Calcutta to meet them. I was also concerned that there might be a major "snafu" and it would be better if someone at our end on a responsible level were showing an interest. However, I decided it would make too much of a production of it.

In the afternoon, I saw M. J. Desai on a large number of matters and impressed upon him again the importance of relaxing the flow

36 Not true, of course, though the High Commissioner was himself a teetotaler.

of news and letting the correspondents have access to operations. Then I saw Gore-Booth to exchange ideas with him and went on to a press conference. I announced the arrival of the first planes and also some large electric projects. The questions had mostly to do with the airlift, but there was one inquiry about our efforts in Pakistan. I replied with considerable firmness that although I was not asking the Indians to negotiate under duress, I was mostly concerned with their efforts to avoid a clash.

I also impressed on all and sundry that American arms were not all the difference. This was so that we would not be blamed if there were further defeats. It was quite the easiest press conference I ever had in India. And it was also the best attended.

In the evening, I skipped the dinner for Archbishop Makarios. I don't think His Beatitude missed me.

November 3 — New Delhi

Today was another long day. The papers gave prominent display to the arms shipments arriving in Calcutta — there were major headlines. Timmons left at 5 A.M. to meet the transport planes, and I spent much of the day wondering if the arrival would result in some major snarl-up. The papers also carried news of a Russian note and in midmorning, M. J. Desai told me it contained nothing new. I learned during the day that Menon is hanging on by his teeth. The Tezpur statement was a final bolster to his ego. All the papers this morning condemned the statement and called for his final departure.

Just before noon, we got word that the first two planes had arrived — somewhat early in fact — and two more came in this afternoon. (Timmons got back late this evening and reported everything went smoothly; the unloading began at once and plenty of lorries were available to move the cargo.) At noon, there was a big lunch for visiting firemen led by Eric Johnston.[37] And during the afternoon, I managed an hour's sleep. But, with Timmons away,

[37] See page 279.

a variety of problems kept crowding in on me, including inescapable questions on Pakistan. B. K. Nehru has said in Washington he hoped Pakistan would not stab India in the back. To suggest such things is, in some sense, to increase the danger.

My other tasks of the day included a reception for Princess Beatrix of the Netherlands, who is touring India — an agreeable young lady; a long talk with Hilaly, the Pakistan High Commissioner;[38] another talk with Homi Bhabha who is turning on heavy pressure for the nuclear power station. The question also arose as to whether the Indians were trained in the handling of the mines we are providing them. There is a certain likelihood that some Indian soldiers will be blown up, but the Indians insist that this will not happen.

In the evening, I had a visit from K. K. Lee, the saddest event of all. He is a quiet, soft-spoken Chinese who was born in India and whose father came here either in 1904 or 1914. He is an expert shoemaker, as are all of his family, who number some twenty. All are self-supporting except those too young to work. Now rowdies are making life impossible for them and he wants to migrate to some other country. I gave him a letter saying he should be considered under my protection[39] as my friend. He was profoundly grateful. I imagine it might be possible to get him a visa for some South American country — Colombia or Brazil.

November 5 — New Delhi

Yesterday I took the day off which I badly needed. Delhi at this time of the year is delightful and the day was bright and cool. The Wyatts were to go to Kabul in the morning but the plane did not take off. Moorea and I went for a walk in the morning and I slept again in the afternoon. Eric Johnston came in about six. During the course of the day, I declined a dinner that I had promised to attend at Morarji Desai's. Unfortunately, in my weariness, I ad-

[38] See page 444.
[39] A highly unofficial protection, needless to say, but it worked and he survived.

dressed the declination to M. J. Desai. No irretrievable damage was done.

Today my desk was inches thick in telegrams, most of them having to do with the arms lift. There is an incredible variety of problems, from the fact that some of the mortar ammunition is rusty to the problem of getting jet fuel to the Calcutta airport for the planes. Anyone in the Indian military services who needs anything files a request. In the afternoon, we set up a procedure by which everything will have to be cleared centrally. I am also swamped with American proposals for committees, teams and advisers to come here to help the Indians win their war. I am standing most of them off.

Under instructions from the Ministry of Defence, the papers are playing down the news of the arms lift. This, I believe, is in response to a Russian request. However, quite a few of the papers seem not to have got the message.

Today Menon was formally reduced to a small section of the Defence Ministry. The rest was taken over by the Prime Minister. After he had denied that anything had changed, he had then denied his denial. It is not pleasant to see a man engaged in a death struggle of this sort but perhaps more tolerable in the case of Menon than anyone I have seen before.

Edgar Kaiser[40] came in during the afternoon. A Bombay firm with which Kaiser Industries is cooperating is making about twenty-five jeeps a day. There is great urgency in stepping up this number and production of light trucks. Finally, toward evening, General Forman, who is in charge of the airlift, came in. He is charged by the Air Force to see what good he can do. He has done a fine job of organizing the airlift and I must show that I am grateful for that without inviting a heavy influx of Air Force officers. I sent him around to the Indian Air Force to see what he can learn about internal air transport requirements.

The Indian line on Pakistan is improving quite a bit. Unfor-

[40] American industrialist. Son of Henry J. Kaiser.

tunately the Pakistanis are being rather tough. I fear their view of the situation is very shortsighted. They have no chance of getting any concessions under pressure. By adopting a more generous attitude, they could lay the basis for future negotiations and not alienate American opinion.

XXI

Border War II

November 6 — New Delhi

At today's morning meeting, the news looked slightly more disturbing. The Chinese are believed to be gathering in the Chumbi Valley, to be developing more strength in the far east of NEFA and to be massing in front of Chushul in Ladakh.[1] All of this information, as usual, is sketchy and unreliable. Few Indian officers have been in the neighborhood of the present fighting in NEFA. Neither, of course, have we. As a result, knowledge of the terrain, since the maps are also exceedingly poor, is theoretical. Not even the weather has been pinned down — partly, I suppose, because it is different at different heights. According to the official lore, it will be intolerable in the next two or three months. I am pretty well satisfied myself that it is favorable to fighting, and General Shrinagesh,[2] the former Governor of Assam, who is one of the few people who has been in the area, confirms this.

McConaughy is making a brave try on the Pakistan front. Ayub holds, however, that the Chinese have very limited intentions and that the Indians are using the dust-up as a way of getting military aid. But a wire from Karachi today says that the Pakistan papers are beginning to reflect the more conciliatory mood of the Indian press

[1] The Chumbi Valley is in Tibet opposite Sikkim on an old trade route between India and Lhasa. It is directly north of the narrow neck of India that connects the main part of the country with Assam. NEFA is to the east and Ladakh, of course, far to the west. See maps pages 436, 437.

[2] See page 420.

and adopt a better tone. Obviously one can be a stalwart defender of the freedom of the press while still seeking to restrain its inconvenient instincts.

The Communists and their allies here have a new line. It is that we will use the Chinese to attack nonalignment, hitch India to a military alliance and prolong the war. I stamped on this during the course of the day with a well-designed statement saying that we accepted nonalignment in bad times as well as good. I noted that one of the largest recipients of our military assistance in the past had been the Soviet Union. She had, nonetheless, retained a considerable measure of independence. I recalled that several weeks ago at the Constitution Club, I had said that our policy was to be quiet on Chinese misbehavior and do nothing to aggravate conflict. It was something to have been for peace before the Chinese attack rather than after.

I think the statement will clear the air. The cut at the Soviets, which, generally speaking, is against my usual policy, seems justified. After I released the statement, it occurred to me that it could run into some trouble back home. The right-wing press, which has been saying that Nehru's policy on nonalignment is now shown to be foolish, will say that I am guilty of equal shortsightedness. At least this is possible. Still, most of my statement will probably be lost in the election news tomorrow, and I have covered myself with a wire to the Department.

Today was, in fact, heavily involved with public relations. News of the airlift is still being played down in order, I suspect, not to arouse the Russians. But, in consequence, the American correspondents will say that our help cannot be mentioned because the government we assist is so sensitive about the Soviets. I raised the problem with M.E.A. and was assured the purpose of the silence was to prevent saboteurs from having knowledge of where arms are being unloaded. I argued that American public opinion was far more important. Better let the saboteurs (who, in any case, are imaginary) blow up a lorry or two. I was promised favorable action.

The Pentagon is sending in fifteen or twenty American reporters as hitchhikers on the airlift. They could mill around in the Calcutta slums, unable to see anything, and give the Indians a bad press and us for helping them. I won agreement on this and for a press camp at Tezpur[3] within distant range of the conflict. I then dispatched Bill Weathersby[4] to Calcutta to see to their care and nourishment. Something can be done to calm their reactions by providing billets, communication facilities, briefings and other help.

Small matters join up with the large. Two large Congressional parties, including Mike Mansfield,[5] are arriving in a fortnight's time. We are also about to open the new Residence. In the last few days, the general public has been allowed to wander through it at will. Its homelike qualities are much like those of the Taj Mahal.

What will happen if we have a big Chinese push continues to worry me. Though tired, I must take time to think about that tomorrow. It could bring the British and ourselves into some kind of military action. One can't talk about this because it is the kind of decision that is only taken if the Chinese push transpires. Until then, everybody will say that any such involvement is impossible.

I continue to have more offers of help from Washington than I need. Could I put all of the proposed military technicians, trainers and advisers into combat units, I would have a considerable army. One of the details of the day was a raft of telegrams referring to the new Indian MAAG.[6] We asked that this language be dropped wherever it occurred.

November 8 — New Delhi

A trickle of intelligence material through the Indians indicates a step-up of activity, or more precisely of intentions, on the front. The Chinese are massing in front of Chushul in Ladakh. There is

[3] See page 442.
[4] See page 454.
[5] U.S. Senator from Montana and Senate Majority Leader.
[6] Military Assistance Advisory Group. See page 259. The term has the connotation of a mission to a military ally.

sniping in the Walong area in the east. But my mind is principally occupied with an ominous concentration in the Chumbi Valley. Opposite, on this side of the Himalayas, is a wide, wooded valley letting down in the direction of Siliguri in India — I saw it all last spring when I was in Sikkim. The pass which carries the ancient caravan trade into Tibet cannot be high.[7] A drive down here would cut off all of eastern India — NEFA, Assam, Tripura, Manipur. At the morning staff meeting we decided on a new and more serious estimate of Chinese intentions which includes the Chumbi Valley attack. The latter would be not on territory claimed by the Chinese but directly against India. The appreciation when it came late in the day was very stodgy and I redictated it. I spend a great deal of time redictating telegrams to Washington so they are in language that will get attention there.

The Pakistanis are having conversation with the Chinese and there is even mention of a nonaggression pact. Ayub has said he would not attack India but has complained about the weapons we are moving. Washington has asked me to talk with Nehru about some new conciliatory gesture toward Pakistan, but I am a little in doubt as to what to ask for. It is my instinct that more will be possible later and that I am expending my fire too soon.

I have had our man in charge of military aid check to make sure the Indians are getting the airlift material to the front promptly. It would still be bad were it discovered that it is piling up somewhere. I'm also getting in the people that we would require were there another big push. The Pentagon and State know my problem in having too many soldiers here, but, on the other hand, I cannot seem to be running the war by myself. We have just had a highly complimentary message from State and Defense on the agility with which we are making our way down through the eggshells.

I have shuffled the nit-picking on the military aid negotiations off to subordinates. I am also leaving arms requirements to the military and letting others worry about the airlift.

[7] About 14,000 feet at Natu La. No attack developed in this area.

But I am still handling the big press invasion. Today I wrote a long letter to the Prime Minister himself on this. Its burden was that the American press is a fixed factor in life. It can be managed or mismanaged but has to be accepted. I urged him to be forthcoming. I told of their reaction to Indian reticence designed to spare Soviet feeling and said it was better to lose a truckload of ammunition to the saboteurs than to have a shipload not arrive for political reasons.

In the early evening we got news that the Chinese had presented a new offer — this was for both sides to move back twenty kilometers from each side of the McMahon Line, leaving the situation as it is in Ladakh. I held up the assessment for Washington overnight because I thought the Indians would accept. This turned out to be a wrong judgment and this morning's papers — I am dictating this at a little after eight — make clear it will be rejected.[8] If the Chinese are planning a new push, their obvious strategy would be to make one more gesture. I feel now that we are in for some very bad news. It was announced during the evening that Krishna Menon had been finally relieved of all jobs.

News also came during the course of the evening that another expendable politician was gone. Nixon was defeated in California. Meanwhile, Chub Peabody has been elected Governor of Massachusetts. I have contributed to Chub's campaigns over the years, spoken for him and generally considered him to have one of the less promising careers in politics. He never had any program. I once urged him to admit the fact and run on the simple platform, "Vote for Peabody, he don't steal." He doesn't have to conform to very high standards[9] to be a relatively successful governor in Massachusetts. George McGovern was elected to the Senate in South Dakota, as were most of my friends elsewhere.

[8] As will be guessed, I was avoiding any query that might have tempted me to offer advice.
[9] His achievements were modest.

November 9 — New Delhi

I sent off my glum appreciation yesterday morning with particular emphasis on the danger of an attack through the Chumbi Valley. This is perhaps the one place where a great deal of harm could be done in a short time. It would cut off the east of India and be a mortal blow to Indian prestige. A defeat in Ladakh, by contrast, is far from any fundamental center of Indian life. I am by no means sure that the Chinese have these militant intentions. But it is better to be braced and it is better also for one's ultimate reputation — a matter on which I take a high-minded but not wholly negligent view.

Yesterday morning, I got back a reply from the Prime Minister to my plea on behalf of press relations, and through the day came indications that they were cranking up to do a good job. The hitch-hikers who come in on the airlift will be flown up here on a C-130 and we are arranging briefings, a visit to the Prime Minister and, I hope, some sort of journey to Tezpur. Last night, the Maharajah of Alirajpur was withdrawn from the staff college and put in charge of the operation. He is attractive and energetic.[10]

After the morning meeting (in which I have successfully broken with the leisurely discourse of the Department), I decided to call up reserves. The Defense Department has a brigadier general and staff waiting impatiently in London. I summoned him on. He will scrutinize Indian military requirements, inspect the use to which the stuff is put and will be in charge of any training operations that may develop. If a push comes, he will be needed and I won't be charged with keeping out necessary people in order to run the war myself. I am now fairly certain that I can handle any general that comes this way. I have been having an intricate minuet with the Defense Department over communications. They keep saying he will have independent channels to Washington but will coordinate with me. My power lies in being fully astride of communications — as Timmons puts it. Yesterday I finally said I would retain full

[10] See page 58.

control but would combine it with sufficient flexibility and delegation so that the general could do his job rapidly and well. I said he would be very content with the arrangement.

At noon, Parliament assembled and I went over to hear Nehru's speech. I made my way through a vast crowd assembled outside — partly to cheer Nehru; partly, it turned out, to thank me for our aid; mostly, it developed, to be hard on Krishna Menon. Menon arrived through another door.

The chamber was crowded and Nehru's speech was a good deal less than Churchillian. It was long, at times vague, a little repetitious and not inspiring. Speeches are the art form of the politician and it is a constant source of surprise to me how bad those of even the greatest politicians can be. Nehru defended Indian border claims, alluded at length to the perfidy of the Chinese and explained away the shortcomings of the Defence Ministry. This last effort was interrupted many times and occasionally the Speaker had to call for order. There was also an uproar when he defended General Kaul. I had to leave before he had finished.

Yesterday, to add to other things, was moving day and a vast army of peons swept into Ratendone Road and by nightfall had dumped the contents into the new house. The latter, being immediately adjacent to the Chancery, is much more convenient and certainly not without grandeur. It is also in a sad state of confusion. We had sandwiches on the terrace for lunch. For dinner, an emergency detachment had to be sent out for dishes, none being locatable in the unopened boxes. I tried out our newest luxury, which is a swimming pool.

The house itself is high-ceilinged with wide porches, so white that one needs snow glasses, and makes much use of the famous Edward Stone screens. It is lacking in warmth but not in beauty. A fountain runs constantly below the stairway and gives the impression everywhere of a toilet out of control.

My last task of the day was a visit to the Prime Minister at 6:45 P.M. I found him deathly tired and I thought a little beaten. It was a most unsatisfactory session. I told him of our efforts in Pakistan and then passed the ball over to him as to what he thought might be done next. He had no thoughts — only silence. This left me stranded. I suggested that Parthasarathy, their new High Commissioner,[11] who departs today, might take along an agreeable note, but got nowhere. I then gave him our somber assessment of Chinese intentions on the border. To this he listened quietly, but I think he may have considered it an intrusion. Perhaps it was, but given our predictions, it would have been negligent to stand down. We ended with a little conversation on the elections and the endorsement they gave Kennedy and on this, he brightened up a bit. I had the feeling I accomplished almost nothing.

November 10 — New Delhi

There is a meeting this weekend in London of our middle-level officials, assistant secretaries and the like, to look into the war. They have asked for our views on top of everything else. I spent much of yesterday thinking about the longer-run situation. If the Chinese make another big thrust, it will have profound repercussions here in Delhi. The Prime Minister will be seriously undermined; there will be a plea for full protection by the United States. Perhaps strong words from us will deter the Chinese, but, in the end, we may have to back them up. As usual, I dislike raising the question of using American troops. If, on the other hand, the fighting simmers along, or is confined to the seizure of Chushul, our response can be a good deal more deliberate. Defensive infantry weapons will be all we need supply while pressing the Indians to a more responsible posture on Pakistan, and ultimately some sort of a defensive relationship. We should show not how anxious but how reluctant we are to extend our commitments.

Otherwise, yesterday was the lightest day since the war began. We ran through the morning's business rapidly and I had an hour or so to catch up on routine matters. It is psychologically beneficial

11 See page 440.

to get everything off one's desk, even though you don't do anything with it.

Late in the morning, I went over the plans for the big invasion of newspapermen which is occurring this weekend. After lunch, I managed quite a decent nap. I then worked on the aforementioned estimate of the situation and had a session with the United States Steel Corporation team which is studying the Bokaro steel plant. They have done a good and sympathetic job. They find the site acceptable and do not question the need for the plant. They are rightly critical of the management of Hindustan Steel[12] and the existing plants, and they have uncovered some serious deficiencies in the planning on raw materials.

In the evening, we had a film, and Colonel Preston Cannady, who is bearing the brunt of the planning of the airlift activities, came marching in, very erect, and walked directly through Ed Stone's goldfish pool by the spiral stairs in the living room. He did not break step but was quite embarrassed, and more so when I recalled the publicity that Ethel Kennedy's guests had received from going into the water fully clothed. The new house is handsome, indeed elegant, but exceedingly noisy. The most subdued conversation in one place echoes through with magnified effect. Still, it is much easier to live in than the old place.

Barbara Ward[13] came in last evening for a few days. She is here to lecture to a convention of doctors. Much of her conversation — the dimming prospects for success of the Third Five-Year Plan — seemed a little out of touch with reality. These Plans were, in fact, budgets for the expenditure of money. Things were well or badly done in accordance with the difficulty of the task and the competence of the particular minister responsible.

Blitz has, indeed, come out with the discovery that I am enlightened, productive and considerate. For the first time in some years, there is not a single mention in the entire issue of the CIA.

12 See page 414.
13 See page 32.

November 11 — New Delhi

Yesterday was Saturday again, three weeks from the time the Chinese came down in force. There hasn't been much military activity in the last ten days, but I have decided to keep alive the estimate of something more serious, at least for a while. My warning to the Prime Minister did indeed get through. I think I have succeeded in drawing their attention to the Chumbi Valley threat without greatly weakening their reaction elsewhere. Tomorrow the first phase of the airlift comes to an end with the delivery of everything needed by air that we could supply. At noon, I briefly celebrated the birthday of the King of Sweden and then went on to have lunch with a cabinet minister who would like to be Defence Minister. In reflecting favorably on his qualifications, he observed that he was adequately pro-American. He thinks that if the Chinese mount another major push, the Prime Minister's position will be in jeopardy.

I doubt that things will go so far. The Prime Minister is a great figure. I much dislike seeing him under attack as must others. Moreover, while more energetic men might take on the task, they might not be as sensible in seeking an accommodation. The Prime Minister realizes that they cannot force the Chinese off the Aksai Chin Plateau but I am not clear that others see this.

After lunch, I had a nap, worked further on the appreciation and then relaxed for an hour looking at paintings. The dealer had recently been in jail for robbing temples. Then the newspapermen and women who are traveling on the airlift came in and I gave them a lecture. They were an interested, sympathetic and not very distinguished group. The *National Geographic* had a representative, which for this war would seem eminently appropriate.

After dinner, we had the annual Marine Corps Ball. The Marine detachment of the Embassy, numbering about ten or a dozen, save their money all year to celebrate the birthday of the Marine Corps. After the speeches of praise of themselves by the Marines and the message on the same theme from the Marine Corps Commandant, there isn't much the imagination can devise and no other topic is in order. I did note that their descent on the Barbary Pirates had robbed that part of the world of one of the few viable industries it had ever had.

Then I went on to a party for the U.S. Steel team.

November 12 — New Delhi

Yesterday was Sunday. The front was still quiet and we transacted more or less routine business at the morning meeting. I slept through the afternoon and in the evening had a party for the visiting journalists.

Things continued very mild today. There is some exchange of artillery fire in the Walong area. The Chinese are supposed to be still building up strength before Chushul but there is no actual fighting. If this continues for a week or two, I think I shall revise my estimate of the longer-run prospect.

This morning, I put John Fobes[14] in charge of wartime activities of the local American community and also over suggestions as to what well-meaning Americans at home might be guided into doing. I also pressed him as to how the AID program might be remodeled in the light of the new requirements. Both he and Wood were very reluctant to suggest any changes. I think they are right in avoiding anything spectacular. But with the new requirements, there is a presumption now against new long-run enterprises and in favor of investment in the serious bottleneck areas such as coal, transport and, no doubt, the metallurgical industries.

At noon, we had a big luncheon abominably served on the terrace. In the afternoon, I drafted a letter to the President and learned from M.E.A. that the Indians are requesting arms from the Communist countries, presumably excluding China and Albania. This was for the record; they had no expectation of getting them. The Indians are worried about the formation of an arms aid consortium of the supplying countries which would pass on needs and be a formidable power with which to deal. I said this was inevitable

[14] Deputy Director of AID in India.

unless they organized their requests and made sure each of the western countries knew what they were getting from the others.

I also discovered that my meeting last Friday with the Prime Minister was rather more successful than I had imagined. He took my estimate of the danger of the situation very seriously — perhaps too seriously. And he has sent a long and sympathetic letter to Ayub which, among other things, proposes ministerial-level talks. He told American reporters today that the Russian MIG's and the facilities to manufacture them would still be forthcoming. Also that they were seeking all kinds of aircraft from the U.S. This is not true and I had the delicate job of denying it without seeming to do so.

November 13 — New Delhi

We are facing a serious problem as to what arms we should give the Indians for their protection. Until now, it has been a few million dollars' worth of items for immediate use by their infantry. But they are about to come in with requests for arms manufacturing capacity, most of the raw materials to run it, tanks and other armored equipment and an air force. All this will total some billions of dollars. Pakistan will want similar amounts; we will then have the absurdity of arming both sides, partly against each other. On the other hand, we can't leave the Indians to themselves to be overrun by the Chinese — at least as they will see it. My present thought is that we shall have to help them equip their armed forces but somehow make a settlement on the subcontinent part of the arrangement. How else?

My immediate problem is what to do with these requests. If they are transmitted to Washington in the present form, the size and resulting shock effect will do more harm than good. So I must stall a bit by asking the Indians to put them in proper form.

There has been very little fighting and as the lull continues, opinion is gradually shifting back to the assumption that the Chinese have limited aims. The U.A.R. Ambassador gave a luncheon in my honor today and he is of the opinion that Peking still has the door open on the U.A.R. proposal — that is to return to the positions of September 8 (before any serious fighting) and negotiate. My feeling is that the Indians would be well-advised to buy this bargain. However, public attitudes are becoming more belligerent. In a little while, these may make it difficult even for Nehru to accept such an arrangement.

The Indians are asking us for help on presenting their side of the dispute to the world. The New China News Agency is getting an enormous amount of stuff out through Hong Kong; the Indians feel their side of the story is not being told. Perhaps we can give them some help in monitoring the Chinese propaganda and they could then send someone to Hong Kong to get out an answer. And we can get more of their position on Voice of America. Maybe we should lease them some time on V.O.A. I am not greatly impressed with the importance of this sort of thing, but everyone else is.

Late this afternoon, we met on strategy for controlling our own military invasion. The Pentagon keeps suggesting the need for separate communications and more and more people. I am defending against both and intend to continue to do so. Other ambassadors have let matters out of control partly, I think, because they did not have the energy.

This evening, there was a major hassle which may still not be settled. The Indians have laid on transportation for the party of visiting correspondents to Leh. Naturally, the resident correspondents wanted to go and felt aggrieved. I finally worked out an arrangement by which both the visitors and the local men went.

A minor footnote on the domestic architecture of an ambassador: this house has no room with four walls except a very small study and the ladies' room. There is, accordingly, no place where even a semiprivate conversation can be carried on — the small study and the ladies' room apart.

✧   ✧   ✧

New Delhi, India
November 13, 1962

Dear Mr. President:

I have been wanting for the past ten days to give you a more detailed and intimate account of our affairs here. I have been sending rather full dispatches to the Department, some of which you have doubtless seen. But as you will have discovered, few Ambassadors have ever been completely candid in such reporting. There is truth and there is also what one must have believed. I merely try to minimize the difference.

These past three weeks have brought great change here — no doubt the greatest change in public attitudes since World War II. The most treasured of preconceptions have been shattered. The disillusion with the Chinese is of course total. So, save at the top, is that with the Soviets. And the other unaligneds are not very popular. Nehru remains an exception. Even he is now hoping only for friendly neutrality from the Soviets rather than active support. But with him there is another factor. All his life he has sought to avoid being dependent upon the United States and the United Kingdom — most of his personal reluctance to ask (or thank) for aid has been based on this pride. He did not like it because it advertised what hurt his pride. Now nothing is so important to him, more personally than politically, than to maintain the semblance of this independence. His age no longer allows of readjustment. To a point we can, I feel, be generous on this. . . .[15]

One thing much on my mind these last days has been the American press. We have had a great influx of correspondents plus a large itinerant delegation covering the arms lift. . . . Were they bottled up here, the Indians would get a bad press and so,

[15] There followed a long discussion of Indian political personalities which, along with some later references, I have deleted for reasons of taste. Another change has been made in this letter. In the private language of the State Department, the Pakistanis are sometimes referred to as "the Paks." It is not, I think, an agreeable usage.

inter alia, would we. I have now pretty well broken through on this, though I had to go to the Prime Minister himself. There will be many stories on the infirm character of his leadership, but that is not our business. I think Nehru is still playing down our role to protect the sensitivities of the Soviets and perhaps, more especially, to protect his own feelings. I have told him this was something we couldn't take and have pictured the repercussions in the American press. We cannot decently help someone who is afraid to be seen in our company. There will be some damage along these lines, I fear.

The great question is what the Chinese intend. In the beginning I thought that this was essentially a border conflict. The Chinese have a serious claim to the Aksai Chin Plateau in Ladakh. It provides them with a strategic access to Sinkiang and they had been building their road there for two years before the Indians reacted. By getting a good foothold in the east, they could establish a claim for the area they really want. In addition, no doubt, they are motivated by jealousy and dislike plus the feeling that Indians are the world's safest object of animosity. So with their superior ready manpower and equipment they could show the Indians and the Asian countries that in military affairs at least they had superiority. All this could be accomplished by a major border demonstration. I have not entirely discarded the above theory. But last week the trickle of evidence on forces north of the frontier, the concentration in the real danger areas which are the Chumbi Valley and back near the Burma border, the incursions and patrol actions in new places and the drift of Chinese propaganda caused me to conclude that we should assume something more serious. The Indians have consistently underestimated Chinese intentions. In one way or another our estimate influences them. And, of course, we are in less danger if we have to withdraw from a too somber estimate than if we must revise a too sanguine one. In the former instance we shall have at least done some of the right things. My recent estimates have reflected the above considerations. Deep in my own mind I am not persuaded that the Chinese are as ambitious as this implies or that they can be so indifferent to the deterrent effects of our position.

If the Chinese should really come down the mountain in force, there will be more political changes here. Much so-called nonalignment [has already gone] out the window. . . . Popular opinion and our military assistance has worked a further and major impairment. The problem in face of a really serious attack would be how we would react to the prospect of a new, large and extremely expensive ally. I personally hope the Chinese do not force this choice. The Indians are busy worrying about the end of nonalignment. It is we that should be doing the worrying on this.

Generally speaking, I think our affairs here are in good shape. We have managed to appear as a solid and steadfast friend. Even the left press has not seriously pinned on us the charge that we are seeking to entangle or otherwise exploit the situation. On most matters our course has seemed clear. During the Cuban affair I moved ahead but with a fairly good sense of what would be in your mind. The period has not been without interest.

We do have a serious problem next door and this has been much on my mind. The Pakistanis have not taken the attack very seriously and have seen it as the great opportunity to get concessions from the Indians. As I am sure Ayub himself saw, no one could press the Indians in their moment of despair. But instead the Pakistanis were pressed themselves for assurances. And our weapons, in an action not too gracefully cleared with the Pakistanis, started coming to India. Their disappointment is understandable. I have worked hard and I think with a certain measure of success here. The Ministry of External Affairs at my behest has asked the press to be very quiet in response to the Pakistan fulminations. I have given strong encouragement to a Congress Party group which is urging reconciliation with Pakistan. I have pressed the Indians to give the Pakistanis information on Indian troop movements and I succeeded last week in getting Nehru to write a long and friendly letter to Ayub on the situation, while their new High Commissioner is proposing the resumption of ministerial talks. Meanwhile McConaughy has been doing noble work in Karachi to calm the Pakistanis and make them see that the threat is to the subcontinent. My sense of the situation is that we should not press the Pakistanis any more in the immediate future. However I should continue all moderating efforts here. Eventually but not too soon the Indians must be asked to propose meaningful negotiations on Kashmir. This should not, incidentally, raise the question of a plebiscite, an idea in which there is no longer any future. The only hope lies in having a full guarantee of the headwaters of the rivers. Each side should hold on to the mountain territory that it has and there should be some sort of shared responsibility for the Valley. I really don't think that a solution on these lines is impossible. It may be wise incidentally when the time comes to have the British do it as a Commonwealth exercise.

With the great advantage of perspective, I regard the election results as a strong endorsement of the Kennedy Administration, your Cuban policy and the persistence of Mr. Endicott Peabody.[16]

> Yours faithfully,
> JOHN KENNETH GALBRAITH

THE PRESIDENT
THE WHITE HOUSE

❖ ❖ ❖

November 15 — New Delhi

The main task yesterday was to get straight the problems that arise as we receive massive requests for aid from the Indians. I have my mind fairly clear. We must insist on a sensible defense design. And India must assume a measure of responsibility for the Pakis-

[16] See page 464.

tan problem. The latter is exceedingly important. Until now, the Indians have, in some sense, thought of Pakistan as *our* problem. Attacks on Pakistan have been regarded as a political pastime. It is now an Indian problem. We can't arm both sides of a dispute. Our role must be to get the Pakistanis to accept reasonable Indian terms. I think there is a very good chance of progress. All of this I have put in a series of drafts and I hope to get a telegram off today.

President Kennedy, as I suspected, is less than enchanted by the news stories coming out of Delhi — Nehru's insistence that non-alignment is as good as ever; that this is the policy that we really want; and that our aid is being played down to protect the sensitivity of the Soviets. I foresaw this and forestalled it with a detailed letter (on background, the need for patience and my offsetting efforts) last Tuesday. So, in reply to a query from him through Carl Kaysen, I was able to refer to what I had already written.

Yesterday I had a large background news conference and larger because of the failure of the trip to Ladakh to go through. Nobody seemed to be too angry and I told them candidly the nature of my calculation on the journey. I could not afford to let those coming in on a brief junket have precedence over newsmen with whom I had to live. So, partly as a result, the whole trip got canceled. Then I had a large staff meeting to bring the Mission as a whole abreast of developments. I have increased the number of such meetings during the crisis not only because there is something to talk about but to satisfy the natural curiosity of our people.

The Karan Singhs[17] came in for lunch. He has just been re-elected Governor of Jammu and Kashmir and wonders if his state will last out the five years. The Chinese are taking big bites out of one part, the Pakistanis claim another. He is a very charming and good-humored man and has a famous collection of the very finest Pahari miniatures.[18] They were given to him by an old Hindu

[17] See page 202.
[18] The painting of the Punjab hills. It flourished in the eighteenth century when artists fleeing Delhi after the collapse of the Moghul dynasty found refuge and patrons here. See *Indian Painting*, cited on page 423.

scholar who wanted, he said, to endow his father's old ruler.

Mrs. Pandit, the Prime Minister's sister, came in to see me in the afternoon. She has just been appointed Governor of Maharashtra[19] She says her brother feels the world has turned against him in forcing him to reject Krishna Menon, his friend of thirty years. He still works until twelve and one o'clock in the morning, though yesterday was his seventy-third birthday. However, a lot of his time is wasted on visitors seeking jobs or people presenting bangles of gold for the Defence Fund.

We worked out final details during the afternoon for a big Congressional visit headed by Senator Mansfield, which arrives this weekend. I was supposed then to dine with Subramaniam, the Steel Minister, who was saying farewell to the U.S. Steel team. However, too much is too much. So I begged off dinner but then dropped in for an hour afterward.

November 16 — New Delhi

The meeting of minor bureaucrats, including Talbot, in London has composed mild and pleasant documents which assume that the Chinese have no disagreeable intentions. They warn thoughtfully that we must not get the Indians into any military activities they cannot afford. This is very sensible given the assumptions. Unfortunately, it assumes the Chinese will be nice. And I have reluctantly come to conclude that the Chinese are going to take NEFA.

We talked a couple of times today about our reaction. I have written a number of long and learned essays on the situation. Now, to be influential, I must be short, specific and concrete.

We continue to uncover minor defects in the new house. One is that the halyard slaps all night against the flagpole. Another is that the Embassy parking lot, which was meant to be on the obscure side of the Chancery, is now in the front yard of the house, the latter having been built on the obscure side of the Chancery. While

[19] I.e., of the state including and surrounding Bombay.

I was trying to get some sleep after lunch, there was a hideous maneuver of scooters and motorcycles into the lot.

This afternoon, I had a visit from a highly articulate onetime teacher of Arthur Goldberg. She gave me an account of his upbringing. For a Supreme Court Justice, he had a shockingly uninteresting youth.

Then Pete Lakeland[20] of my political staff brought over an elderly Congress leader for a long discussion of Congress Party policy in light of the war. Like everyone else, he told me they were busy reconsidering the nonalignment policy. As to everyone else, I told him that we might find alignment with India too expensive.[21]

My last visitor of the day was T. T. Krishnamachari who has just taken over as the coordinator of supply. He worried about the danger of Calcutta being bombed and asked for interceptor aircraft. Being sanguine about our generosity, he also thought it might be good to have an additional loan of, say, one-half billion dollars. He left with fewer illusions.

Finally, word came tonight of heavy fighting in the Walong area in the far east. General Kaul has been stirring up some patrol action here to prove that the Indians can take care of themselves. The Chinese, as usual, have reacted in great strength to prove the reverse.

At the staff meeting this morning, Colonel Curtis thought that the Indians might be asking for trouble, and it would certainly seem that he was right.[22]

[20] See page 439.

[21] This also reflected my view, elsewhere noted in this diary, that one of our errors both in India and elsewhere has been excessive wooing. One's position is far stronger if, on occasion, one must be pursued or persuaded.

[22] However, there is no evidence that the major attack of the ensuing days was a riposte to Indian action, as this might imply. It occurred along a broad front and, obviously, had been in preparation for some weeks.

November 17 — New Delhi

This was a singularly unrelaxed Saturday. It began about four o'clock this morning when Timmons called me to say that a telegram was going out from Karachi to Washington asking for assurances that arms coming to India would not be used against the Pakistanis — information on arms shipments to India would be passed to Ayub; we would also agree privately to raise the question of Kashmir. The telegram could have waited until morning. However, Timmons greatly enjoys crises and naturally wishes to make the most of them. Since the position here is comparatively strong, I wired Washington that they could do what McConaughy asks. However, I see no reason for having the assurances private assurances. What Ayub or any political leader needs is public support, and that I proposed.

I spent the morning drafting a comment on the London meetings. These, as I noted, produced exceedingly mild, gentle and scholarly proposals based on the assumption that the Chinese are going to nibble at the border and then stop. Even if so, Indian public opinion will no longer allow of such an assumption. They are determined to tackle their defense in more formidable fashion and will want help. None of this is envisaged. I made this point with considerable clarity and persuasion, adding that after lecturing the Indians for years on the aggressive tendencies of the Chinese Communists, we cannot now turn around and explain that these chaps are really lambs.

With a few revisions, the telegram got off about midafternoon. My problem in writing documents is not to get the agreement of my staff but to elicit the requisite exchange of views. There is an excessive and even dangerous tendency to defer to my draftsmanship. For lunch, we had the Maharani of Udaipur. She is a handsomely saried woman, a princess of Bikaner. She has very little to say, but above a certain level, beauty is an excellent substitute.

Howard Rusk of the New York College of Medicine came in during the morning and again for tea this afternoon. He is here on various medical enterprises. The American community is looking for an outlet for its energies, and I think I shall put them onto a medical project for helping to develop a prosthetic and rehabilitation center. If men must lose their legs, the least one can do is to help them get another set.

At 3:45 P.M., I was called to an urgent meeting with M. J. Desai. There has been another military disaster. A couple of crack Indian battalions in the Walong area advanced on the Chinese and cleared them off a ridge. The Chinese reacted in division strength and gave them a terrible beating and now threaten encirclement. Yesterday the news from the area was very cocky and good — now tonight it is clear there has been a major defeat. All civilian air flights have been stopped. The Indians want us to supply them with transport aircraft.[23] In further modification of the nonalignment policy, the Indians also wish pilots and crews to fly the aircraft. However, old habits die hard. When we went back at seven o'clock to work out details and get information on the need to support the request, all of the senior air marshals were unavailable. It was Saturday evening.

My problem is that Washington is psychologically unprepared for these requests. Talbot, of course, is unable to react. The part of the State Department to which I report is accustomed only to scholarly and enlightened issues in this part of the world. Accordingly, the London meetings, which concluded only at the middle of the week, assumed the mildest of Chinese ambitions. They couldn't handle anything else although today's disasters make them already out-of-date. With more experience in government, and also a better knowledge of history, I have kept my assumptions on the dismal side. It is far easier to pull back from a dismal prediction than to move on from a sanguine one.[24] This, indeed, is the lesson on which Joe Alsop has built his reputation.[25]

But the Indians are beginning to see the need for persuading the

[23] To move troops from the Punjab, on the Pakistan border, to the threatened area. I had previously, though very quietly, suggested doing this.
[24] See letter to the President, page 473.
[25] Failure to follow this precept in Vietnam, where he relentlessly predicted victory, also cost him his reputation.

United States of their problems and perils. I had a long talk about the difficulty this afternoon and I think they are going to send a mission, possibly headed by Lal Bahadur Shastri,[26] to explain their predicament.

Shastri would be good. He is a nice, gentle man, very Indian in appearance, and is known to have the complete confidence of the Prime Minister. He is also very reasonable where Pakistan is concerned.

I omitted to tell of another visit in the last few days from Jigme Dorji, the Prime Minister of Bhutan. He was just back from Bhutan and still hopes to get some arms with which to equip his miniature army. They have about 5,000 recruited of whom only 2,000 have anything with which to shoot. He told me that in recent weeks 1,800 Indian soldiers have come into northeast Bhutan as stragglers, all hungry and most of them suffering from terrible damage to their feet. There have been no Chinese penetrations, although an unarmed party has come a little over the border. He said, in contrast with Indian thinking, that this is the very best time of year up there for movement, fighting, travel and, indeed, the time when the Maharajah does most of his touring along the northern border. I sent the latter my sympathy, having very little else to offer.

I should also report for posterity that two or three hundred medical doctors have been here from the States attending a World Medical Conference. We had a reception for them. They filed in and shook hands and a remarkable number wanted pictures shaking hands. I was glad to be a support to their vanity which in a number of cases seemed adequate without it. This was the first large reception in the new house, and I must say it is remarkable how two or three hundred people can disappear from sight. One doctor told me how he had been trying all day to get to see Bill Weathersby of

---

[26] Home Minister, later to succeed Nehru, and soon thereafter to die in Tashkent of a heart attack (on January 10, 1966) just after signing the Peace Declaration between India and Pakistan.

USIS and wished now to mention the problem to me. The problem: "The message of democracy is not getting across in this country." His evidence: he was able to buy quite a few Communist pamphlets around town. I explained to him that this was because all of our literature was so much in demand you couldn't buy it. Incidentally, the *American Reporter*, our official propaganda sheet, has just come out with a remarkable misprint saying the purpose of our aid is to entangle India in military alliances.

November 18 — New Delhi

Sunday again. General Kelly[27] came in although I haven't seen him yet. So did Carol Laise.[28]

Today the dream underlying the London meeting dissolved. The Chinese have taken Walong, are moving in the area of Sela in NEFA and are shelling the Chushul airfield in Ladakh. The latter is probably unusable. (The predicted push, in other words, had come.)

I went for a long walk this morning, the first serious exercise for a week or ten days, and then went over the military situation. I then had lunch with Carol Laise who defended out of loyalty the anodyne conclusions in London but is otherwise disposed to agree with me. She will be all right in a day or so. Then at four o'clock I met the Senatorial delegation, Senators Mike Mansfield, Ben Smith, Claiborne Pell, Caleb Boggs,[29] who will be here for the next couple of days. They were weary and somewhat distressed by the program we had outlined for them; however, I cut the latter drastically and they felt better. I also arranged for them to go to Agra.

Late in the afternoon, I squeezed in three-quarters of an hour to look at paintings at the Indian Arts Palace. They have a collection

[27] Brigadier, later Major General, John E. Kelly, head of the United States Military Supply Mission, India.

[28] A former political officer of the Embassy who had returned to Washington a few weeks before. With the invasion, we had borrowed her for service in India again. See page 139.

[29] The last three from Massachusetts, Rhode Island and Delaware respectively.

of about 25,000 of irregular quality but one can always find something new. Today I encountered some fine erotics. The eroticism is subordinate to the execution of the profiles, costumes and architecture. Men and women engage in the most extraordinary intercourse with the greatest composure and equanimity.

At six, Paul Gore-Booth came in to be brought up-to-date. He got stalled in Bombay when all the Indian Airlines flights were canceled for diversion of the planes to the airlift and would still be there except that I sent our Army liaison plane for him. A trip to India by Duncan Sandys to discuss the Kashmir issue is, I think, being postponed. Ayub doesn't want to see him. If he came to Delhi alone, he would seem to be confining his pressure to the Indians with bad effect.

A dinner for the Senators is still to come.

XXII

Climax

November 19 — New Delhi
This was a day of unbelievably dismal developments. I spent the morning talking with the Senate group, which was interested, intelligent, even penetrating. About eleven o'clock, several members went off to Agra after inquiring whether they could look at a village or two en route. Their conscience bothered them about sightseeing; I explained that the villages adjacent to Agra were the most representative in all the country.

At noon, I spoke to the Press Club. I had had no time to prepare a speech so, as sometimes alleged of the Prime Minister, I was unaware of what I was going to say until I had said it. And thereafter I was largely unaware of what I had said. But I did arrange to be asked a few questions on points that seemed important including one on where we stood on India's nonalignment policy. To this I replied that I was very tired of the question, for it seemed to imply that there was something extremely dangerous in being helped by the United States. We were, in fact, quiet and steadfast friends. I noted that for eight years we hadn't asked for any new military allies.[1] On Pakistan, I again said I wasn't concerned with Pakistani behavior, but with improvement on this side of the line.

I had very little sleep last night so I managed to get half an hour this afternoon, which did a world of good. Then after tea for

[1] See page 150.

Howard Rusk,[2] I saw M. J. Desai. From him I learned of the day's new catastrophes. The Chinese have taken over most of NEFA and with incredible speed. The Indians at all levels are in a state of shock. Not one but two pleas for help are coming to us, the second one of them still highly confidential.[3] The nonalignment I was asked about at lunch is far out of date; the Indians are pleading for military association. They want our Air Force to back them up so that they can employ theirs tactically without leaving their cities unprotected. I am not sure that there is any very useful conception back of this. I would think it would be very unwise for them to initiate any air action.[4]

The Secretary sent me a very firm telegram on the Pakistan situation, supporting my effort to get the Indians to take a conciliatory view. I showed the telegram to Desai. He proposed, in response, an agreement to negotiate a settlement once the Chinese are under control. The Pakistanis will fear that this will be forgotten once the Chinese are thrown back.

The Senators plus Frank Valeo, the Administrative Assistant to the Senate Majority Leader, dined this evening with Morarji Desai. The Finance Minister, not unnaturally, was sunk in gloom. Into the conversation came the most improbable rumors. The Chinese were getting oil from Russia — the fact that there could hardly be a pipeline into Tibet did not seem persuasive. A Polish ship had been seen in Calcutta with suspicious maps of the Bay of Bengal. This affirmed some design by Poland in the area. It was a hideous evening and I brought it to an end as quickly as possible.

---

[2] See page 480.

[3] These requests, which sought full defensive intervention by our Air Force, were transmitted through the Indian Embassy in Washington. My notice from Desai enabled me to warn Washington that they were coming — especially the second and more serious request for air intervention.

[4] In the ensuing days, I urged against doing so in the strongest possible fashion.

November 21 — New Delhi

Yesterday was the day of ultimate panic in Delhi, the first time I have ever witnessed the disintegration of public morale — and for the first time, I began to wonder what the powers of resistance might be. The wildest rumors flew around the town, the most widely believed being that a detachment of 500 paratroopers was about to drop on New Delhi with, in addition to taking over the town, the even more engaging task of reinstalling Krishna Menon. Rumors of the advance of the Chinese reached massive proportions and at one stage, they were said to be virtually on the outskirts of Tezpur. Several told me during the day that General Kaul had been taken prisoner. This was denied rather succinctly in the evening by President Radhakrishnan, who said, "It is, unfortunately, untrue."

The day began with an emergency meeting of our Embassy planning group, at which I came up with several overnight measures — most of them devised with the benefit of insomnia. The three of importance, all designed for their morale-stabilizing effect, were to suspend the detailed military calculations on which we are engaged and get in some American-piloted air transport right away. Somewhere in the neighborhood of a wing, i.e., twelve, of C-130's is needed and we decided they had better start arriving. I also proposed that we ask that elements of the Seventh Fleet be sent into the Bay of Bengal, although this violated my rule that we do nothing the Indians did not request. In view of the loss of matériel by the Indians, I also asked for the cranking up of the airlift again on a regular schedule.

Meanwhile, on the other side, I affirmed my intention to keep the Indians from using their Air Force with the associated expectation of our support. Their air arm is not highly effective. The cities of the Ganges Plain are accessible from the airfields of Tibet. There is no chance that the Indians could retaliate to China and there is nothing in Tibet. And there is no technical chance that we could accord them immediately the protection that Nehru asked. The

Indian purpose in putting in the Air Force was the hope that this would stem the Chinese advance. But the Chinese walk through the woods and at night. We learned in Korea that even with complete control of the air, we could not keep them from supplying their forces or advancing.[5] These considerations were new to the Indians. The telegram outlining these actions was quickly approved, although Captain des Granges,[6] who had been rather out of touch with the situation and whose reaction time involves deliberation, was stunned by the reference to the Seventh Fleet. He had not realized that things had moved quite that far.

Then at 10 A.M., I took the Senators over to see the Prime Minister. As usual in the morning, he was in good form, gave them a scholarly account of the background of the troubles with China and then a grave view of the present situation. He did not entirely escape from his habit of understatement.

I then had a hasty session with M. J. Desai after which we went on to the Parliament. This was filled and when we arrived, the Prime Minister had just finished giving a brief account of the latest disasters. There was some heckling and a great deal of highly original military advice from the back benches. The arming of elephants was not proposed but only because no one had thought of it. There were various demands for a military administration for Assam. Still, given the state of affairs, it was an impressive example of the vitality of Parliamentary rule in India.

Next we had lunch with the Prime Minister, a much too leisurely affair in light of the tension, following which I had hoped to get a few minutes' rest. But just as I had taken my clothes off, a message came from President Kennedy proposing that he send a high-level mission to assess the needs of the Indians, and what we should do to help, and asking my reactions. I accepted. The same message brought the promise of airlift, the air movement of spares for In-

[5] A lesson that had again to be learned in Vietnam.
[6] The Naval Attaché. Naval matters not being much involved, he was not a regular member of the group.

dian transport planes of American origin which are urgently needed and proposals of three other teams to help the Indians run the war. I no longer have any political objection; the Indians yearn for the sight of American uniforms and about tomorrow I will allow our officers to wear them.

I then went with the Senators to see R. K. Nehru, the Secretary-General of the Ministry of External Affairs, and on to hear an account of the difficulties of the Indian armies from his colleague, M. J. Desai. This last was lucid and clear-cut. I had managed in a few minutes while they were in R. K. Nehru's office to give him an account of the upcoming mission and tell him of the prospective arrival of the C-130's, the spares and the rest. (It later developed that, in my haste, I had given the impression that we were making a gift of the C-130's. I recovered them.) Then I took the Senate group on to see President Radhakrishnan, who was in high form. He gave a stirring and vehement account of the perfidy of the Chinese and said that if India went down, so would all of Asia. He did not spare past Indian policy, saying that they had been plowing in sand. Everyone came away much impressed. I got in some further work, the nature of which I now slightly forget, and took Mrs. Mike Mansfield to a party at the R. K. Nehrus'. There was some sorrow that the Senator did not show up. In moments of crisis, one is astounded by the amount of business that goes on as usual.

I had dinner with the children and meanwhile a long telegram from Rusk had come in. This was in response to the Prime Minister's second midnight letter and was largely devoted to asking questions that I had answered before. Would the Indians take a sensible view of Pakistan? Would they be more concerned about problems of Communism in South Asia? (No one hereabouts has thought about South Asia for weeks.) What about mobilizing the resources of the Commonwealth, etc.? What about the United Nations? I dictated a lengthy answer to all points and then ended with the prediction that the Chinese would not, as the Indians assumed, press forward on all fronts. I noted that even they were not magicians and could hardly hope to sustain a supply line over the whole mountain spine. I told of my concern to keep the Indians from unconsidered escalation.

I got to bed about midnight.

November 22 — New Delhi

Yesterday, like a thief in the night, peace arrived. Nobody had disturbed me during the night and so the morning papers provided me with the first news of the Chinese promise to stop shooting within twenty-four hours and then to withdraw on December 1. It would all have been extremely confusing to Napoleon. My first reaction from the incomplete information in the papers was to suspect small print and hidden clauses. But given the fact that India has no army left in the area and has lost extensively of matériel, any breathing space is incredibly important. Yet in the present aroused mood, there seemed to me a danger of outright rejection, and indeed there was. Accordingly, I got hold of Gore-Booth immediately after breakfast and he saw M. J. Desai to urge that whatever the eventual reaction, they now maintain silence. Then, in the process of seeing the Senators off at the airport, I saw an M.P. who was shortly seeing the Prime Minister and had him convey the same message. We had a detailed discussion at the strategy meeting at 10:30 A.M. and I found that my sense of the situation was generally borne out. Our military people in particular believed the Indians badly needed time and strongly endorsed my views. Accordingly, I saw the Prime Minister at Parliament at noon. In line with my urging, he had made a very noncommittal response on the Chinese proposal although M. J. Desai (when Gore-Booth had seen him) was a good deal more hard-nosed. This resulted partly from a tendency to count on us for far more help than we can provide.

The Prime Minister was inclined to think that the Chinese offer of cease-fire and withdrawal was real. He cited two factors as inducing the Chinese offer. One of these was the unexpected anger

Arrival

VISITORS — 2

At Rajghat (where Gandhi was cremated)

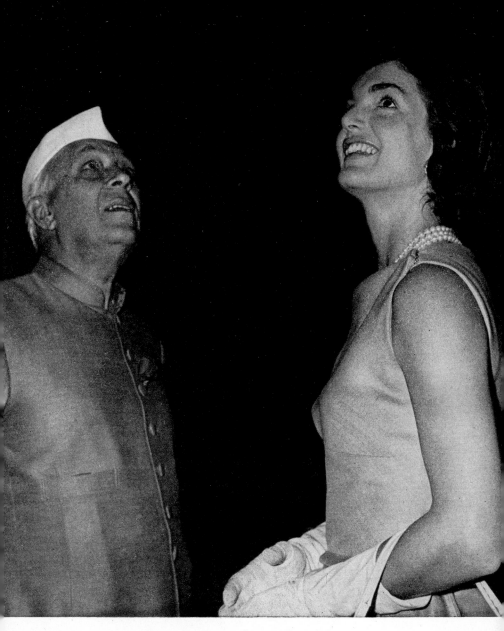

Star gazing

Experience of splendor (with her sister)

Enthusiasm of alcohol

Leh in Ladakh

WHERE THE WAR WAS FOUGHT

The mountain waste

In Leh

Instant Eisenhower

of the Indian people when aroused — an anger that was unfortunately unmatched by military effectiveness. And the second factor was the speed of the American response. He said he thought the Soviets had a little peacemaking influence but not much. This latter is consistent with his idea that the break between the Soviets and Peking is very great. In any case, he told me that the Indians would stand by for a few days. I sent off word to Washington. All of this caused me to miss most of a luncheon for a visiting admiral, but I got in on the end of it and made a touching speech on sea power. There is a point here. It is good that the Chinese cannot come by water into the Bay of Bengal.

I had a meeting with General Chaudhuri, the new Commander-in-Chief, after lunch. Chaudhuri is an intelligent and aggressive man who fought with the British during World War II and whose most recent military experience was commanding the operation against Goa. It would be more convenient to have the Portuguese now.

Then I had a press conference with the American newspapermen. They were in a bloody mood. Many of them have come halfway round the world for what looked like a very promising war. Now suddenly it had disappeared or seemed likely to do so. This is very inconvenient. Naturally they wanted something done about it. Half of them wanted me to advise the Indians to refuse negotiations and resume fighting; they did not say what with. The rest wanted me to throw in American troops. The rumor has got around that I have told the Indians to play for time. I made it clear that I had not advised negotiation or non-negotiation. I had only urged the Indians to keep their counsel for the moment. Phil Potter associated me, as a defender of appeasement, with Joseph P. Kennedy.[7] On this charge, I should be able to arrange some high-level protection.

The cease-fire came into effect today, so far as anyone could tell,

[7] At least such was the elder Kennedy's public reputation after Munich. The merits of the charge have, of course, been debated.

although a lot of Indian troops — perhaps a division which was at Sela — are behind the Chinese lines. The Chinese are supposed to go home December 1. There are still almost as many interpretations of why as there are people in Delhi. I am adhering to the rule of not advising the Indians while advising them to maintain silence. And on this I think I have been influential. Today's papers express some suspicion of the Chinese designs, but there is no outright rejection.

I didn't realize until I got to the office that today was Thanksgiving. There were few cables of any significance and most of them had to do with the worsening situation in Pakistan. The National Assembly is meeting with a lot of inflammatory anti-Indian and anti-American speeches. Delhi by contrast is much calmer and the rumors have died down. One today caused an alarmed call from a highly placed leader who had just come back from Tezpur. She had heard there that the Pakistanis and Chinese had entered into a secret deal according to which the Brahmaputra Valley in Assam was to be ceded to East Pakistan. In keeping with this bargain, the Hindus were leaving the area and the Moslems were staying. I calmed the situation by suggesting that it would have been rather difficult for the Pakistan Government to have communicated a secret deal to all of the illiterate Moslem villagers.

Arthur Smithies[8] arrived this morning on a visit and attended the Thanksgiving services with me. These are held in the little garden outside Bhawalpur House, and for once I had a Presidential Proclamation to read which was in tolerably good English.

I had a nap after lunch, the first time in several days that I have managed this luxury and at four o'clock called on the new Defence Minister.[9] He agreed generally with what I had to say. That was mostly that the Indians keep quiet, win time and be suspicious of the possibilities of air power. However, he was surprised when I told him that it would take six months to move in American inter-

---

[8] Professor of Economics at Harvard University.
[9] Y. B. Chavan. See page 349.

ceptors[10] and two years to create a modern Indian Air Force.

At 6 P.M., a large mission arrived from Washington, some twenty-four people in all, headed by Averell Harriman and including Carl Kaysen, Paul Nitze[11] and a clutch of colonels. We went over to see the Prime Minister almost immediately on arrival. He seemed tired, but very grateful for our prompt reaction and then the party came on to the Residence for dinner. Carl told me that their first plan had been to have U. Alexis Johnson head the mission. I expect I could have survived. He also told me that my telegram anticipating Nehru's second plea for planes had come in during a meeting on the first request. It was handed to Rusk who never got around to reading it.

This mission is so large that there doesn't seem to be any way of arranging conferences with the Indians short of hiring a church. However, I have hit on the idea of scheduling a great number of conferences at the same time. This cuts down the number that can attend any one.

[10] This was an exaggeration based on the time needed to install fairly elaborate radar and communications.
[11] Assistant Secretary of Defense for International Security Affairs, later Secretary of the Navy and then Deputy Secretary of Defense.

XXIII

Peace . . . Wonderful and Bureaucratic

November 25 — New Delhi

I missed day before yesterday. The arrival of a big Washington mission is worse than a war. The Harriman mission is far too large; all the bureaucratic divisions of the State Department plus Defense are represented and each man feels he must uphold his unit at every meeting. When a whole battalion descends on an Indian official, he naturally clams up. When you cut down the size of these visiting delegations, the excluded become angry, hurt or depressed. Yesterday I solved the problem by sending Harriman off to talk to various people alone.

The day's business for me included calls on the new Defence Minister, Y. B. Chavan, T. T. Krishnamachari who was in remarkably good form, an amiable lunch with Barbara Ward here at the house, an afternoon meeting with the British including Duncan Sandys, an evening call on the President, and a late evening session with the Pakistan High Commissioner. One of the major pieces of news was the collapse of the indestructible Timmons who is now in Holy Family Hospital suffering from acute fatigue. He has been working twenty hours a day although partly because he so much enjoys it.

Chavan was impressive yesterday and I used the occasion to settle an old score. One of the senior secretaries of the Defence Ministry has been carrying on the old policy of making life difficult for me. Day before yesterday, he banned pictures of our military people in uniform talking to their Indian opposite numbers. This was considered rather disgracing by our brave men. I told Chavan of this in the honoring presence of the official yesterday without indicating that I knew who had issued the order. Chavan promised to reinstruct whichever official was involved.

T. T. Krishnamachari went over the problems of mobilizing the Indian economy with great felicity and intelligence. He described the most cherished of past defense projects — supersonic fighters, for example — as toys. He said India should make its own ammunition and simple infantry equipment and import the sophisticated matériel.

At lunch, Barbara proposed a program of mobilizing the villages. She was so eloquent on the subject that everybody approved and nobody thought to ask her what it meant.

In the afternoon, Duncan Sandys[1] arrived and came in for a visit. He regards the whole argument with China as being over a few acres of desert in Ladakh which he would have the Indians surrender. Opposition to alteration of boundaries by force, as a matter of principle, doesn't appeal to him. I pointed out that the loss of several thousand square miles might cost Nehru his job. He was only mildly impressed. I then tried to persuade him that he shouldn't talk to Nehru about Kashmir.

At 6:30 P.M., we went over to see the President. The whole party went. Our military people would have preferred their uniforms. On reflection, I decided for civilian clothes. Better that we lean over backward in this respect. We sat in two circular rows. The President made an impressive speech about the principles for which India was fighting and the moral as well as strategic consequences of her defeat. It was admirably designed for the purpose; you could have heard a pin drop during the proceedings.

We had a family dinner, after which Harriman, Kaysen and I had a long talk with Hilaly, the Pakistan High Commissioner. He was

[1] He was leading a British mission paralleling that of Harriman with Lord Louis Mountbatten as the senior military member.

much concerned about the Pakistan position but, underneath it all, reflected a genuine concern for peace and, I thought, gave Harriman some useful advice about how to conduct himself in Rawalpindi[2] to which the mission is proceeding after it finishes here to discuss matters with Ayub. He especially urged plain talk, not smoothing platitudes. Yesterday the Chinese proposed a nonaggression treaty with Pakistan and the general tone of things there is not good. I've wondered if we shouldn't take some dramatic action to ensure the peace such as guaranteeing the Indo-Pakistan border. However, I came away slightly relieved. I have asked our Embassy in Karachi to send over an officer to give us a reading on the situation.[3]

Life is varied. Timmons is quite ill and may be in the hospital for some time. A Soviet sailor, clad in his shorts, jumped ship in Calcutta and took refuge aboard an American freighter. The Russians demand his return. Duncan Sandys says with great certainty the Indians should give away most of Ladakh to the Chinese because it has no commercial value. I reminded him that roughly the same point was once made by Englishmen about the Sudetenland. An American medical team is going into the problems of cold weather survival, an important subject in Ladakh. Another team is helping the Indians on military communications. An Indian cabinet officer attributes the Indian Army collapse to conspiracy between Krishna Menon and the Chinese Communists.

Today I first did a television interview which took an hour or so. Then I took Senator Bourke B. Hickenlooper[4] to visit the Prime Minister. The Senator gave the Prime Minister a thoughtful lecture on the dangers of aggressive Communism. The Prime Minister wondered to me afterward if the instruction at this time were neces-

---

[2] In West Pakistan.

[3] My concern over some kind of outbreak, stimulated by anger and excitement, on the Pakistan frontier remained considerable, and given the pressures on the Indian Government, the effect at this point would have been especially demoralizing. See page 428.

[4] Then senior Republican member of the Senate Foreign Relations Committee, he was on a short visit to New Delhi. See page 33.

sary. Then I finished up the television interview, had a meeting with my immediate staff, attended various other meetings and had a luncheon here for the British visitors. The discussion afterward was long and pointless. I tried to organize talk around a proposal for a joint guarantee of the Indian frontier by the British and ourselves in return for a promise by the Indians to negotiate seriously on Kashmir. Then I met with the medical and communications teams, had a series of meetings on various intelligence matters, and about seven o'clock collapsed in bed. However, by eight I was mobile again and we had a pleasant dinner. Harriman then went for a personal talk with Nehru. I went out to see Timmons who, in addition to fatigue, has bacillary dysentery, a touch of amoebic dysentery and pneumonia.

November 27 — New Delhi

Most of yesterday was taken up with the meetings of the Harriman mission and that was true also today. We have been pressing the Indians as much as possible on the Pakistan issue and meanwhile the Pakistanis are being exceedingly stubborn. I wrote a new appreciation in which I raised for the first time — as a possibility — a new Chinese thrust with the disintegrating effect in the east and accompanied by Pakistani trouble in the west. However, I do not expect this. The Pakistanis are more reasonable. And the Chinese must have some impulse to caution; they can hardly be contemplating a war which might involve the Americans with their supply lines stretched over the high Himalayas. To add to this caution, I revived an idea yesterday which has been in the back of my mind for some time — that of having a carrier make a courtesy visit to Madras. This would have a calming effect on India and a deterring effect on China. This morning with Harriman's, Kaysen's and Nitze's concurrence, this was recommended.[5]

A new large Congressional delegation came in this afternoon — a

[5] However, I later concluded that it was not necessary and withdrew the suggestion.

rather unalloyed junket so far as I could tell. They seemed annoyed that we had not provided automobiles and a special air trip to Jaipur. Duncan Sandys is now safely on the way to Rawalpindi. Much time has been spent saying that he did not say what he really did say. Among other things, he proposed that India enter a military alliance with the West and come under the protection of a NATO nuclear deterrent. The Indians were aghast, and it was fuzzed over. Had they been pressed seriously along these lines, they would have been forced into an accommodation with the Chinese. Gore-Booth is perturbed but defends his Minister in the finest traditions of the British Civil Service.

The problem of press relations seems solved. Chavan is calling in a group of the American newsmen to see what they want. They won't be satisfied, of course — they make progress only by complaining. But at the moment, they have grounds for complaint.

This evening, there was a small dinner at the Ashoka Hotel for the visiting British and American defenders. It was sensibly small and ended at a sensibly early hour.

November 28 — New Delhi

On this day, the captains and the kings, or anyhow the kings, departed. In the morning, I took the Congressional delegation over to see Nehru; they were mostly concerned with having pictures taken with the great man and I had thoughtfully provided for this wish by having Ishar Dass Beri[6] there. The meeting was brief; there were no lectures on the danger of Communist aggression. In fact, Congressman Barrett of Pennsylvania said rather touchingly, "We hear you are in trouble and we hope we can help you." Then I gave the Congressmen a briefing and had a staff meeting. Some of the American residents in the Kalimpong-Darjeeling area are becoming unsettled and the Consulate at Calcutta is again wondering

---

[6] A highly skilled Indian photographer with his own studio who served also on the staff of the United States Information Service. See photographs following page 586.

about evacuation. I again decided against it — my usual concern about the effect of a general exodus of Americans. At eleven, Carl Kaysen and Hollis Chenery[7] and I took time off to visit the Red Fort (where I gave them a highly beneficial lecture on Shah Jahan as a builder and art patron) and at twelve, I went to see the Prime Minister again with Harriman. We talked again about Pakistan but without much that was new and specific. Nehru told Harriman of his concern for a settlement that would make possible common defense of the subcontinent, and there was some talk of terms. We had lunch at the house and then General Adams[8] and I went back to call on the Defence Minister. I took the occasion to draw attention to yet another public relations problem. The Indian Army in the east has public orders to hold and throw out the Chinese. But privately it is understood they can give up land if needed in order to save forces and maintain tactical mobility. However, if this is the tactic, as it should be, it is important that the public know it; otherwise, any and every retreat will be viewed as a defeat and there will be violent criticism.

While I was at the Defence Ministry, Harriman had a press conference. In response to questioning by the *Dawn* correspondent, the leading Pakistan paper, he said some sharp things about Pakistan which I fear will cause trouble there.

At three, George Hannah took Harriman off to Rawalpindi along with Paul Nitze and Kaysen. With Luther Hodges[9] who had meanwhile arrived on the scene, Kitty and I went over to visit the C-130's. These are large and workmanlike craft. The crews have taken over a hangar, and everything, including a couple of spare engines, is stacked against the wall. It is all very spruce and operative. Then I came back to the office and cleaned up matters and listened to an estimate of Chinese intentions from the Department's

[7] Professor of Economics at Harvard, then with the Agency for International Development.

[8] Paul Adams, co-leader of the mission with Harriman and head of the STRIKE Command.

[9] See page 25.

China expert. He doesn't think there is any danger of the Chinese attacking out of the Chumbi Valley and thinks they will stick to NEFA. On the other hand, he seems to have been associated with the London telegram that came in just before the last push and which promised no further Chinese action.

At 6:30 P.M., I went to see Nehru about matters that are rather too secret even for these confessions. Then I went on to a party for Luther Hodges, and we ended with a big dinner here in the middle of which the Hamish Hamiltons[10] arrived.

November 29 — New Delhi

Early this morning, Gore-Booth called up to say that Sandys was on the way back from Rawalpindi. He and Harriman had got Ayub's consent to a common statement calling for talks on Kashmir — first between ministers and then between Ayub and Nehru. The statement struck me as very close to what Ayub and Nehru might accept. It occurred to me also that there could be a better messenger. Sandys is the man best calculated to shove Nehru into his shell. All of the careful preparation that Harriman and I had done would now be spoiled. The same dismal thoughts had occurred to our people in Pindi and a few minutes later Kaysen called to see if I could insert myself into the conference or go to Nehru first to soften him up. Neither was feasible. However, Gore-Booth is going to impress on Sandys with all power the importance of a conciliatory line.

G.-B. and Sandys met Nehru at 11:30 A.M. and it did not go so badly. The fact is that a stubborn man, when he has his eye on the ball and his own political career, sometimes does better than more cautious people. Nehru considered the statement carefully. With the exception of a few words, to some of which I would have objected had I been in Nehru's position, the proposal worked out in Pindi was accepted. It got down in the end to some fine hairsplit-

---

[10] He is a wealthy London publisher, legendary in his generosity in royalties and advances to authors. Longtime personal friend.

ting over the telephone. The agreement in Pindi was to talk about Kashmir. The Indians wanted "Kashmir and other matters." Eventually, they compromised on "Kashmir and related matters."

During the morning, I received substantial approval from Washington for the courtesy visit by one of our big carriers to the vicinity of Madras. I then went back to the Ministry of External Affairs to be assured that both the Prime Minister and M. J. Desai had fully discussed it. I do not want it said that we forced it on them. But if the Chinese are retiring, it is presumably out of concern for the American reaction.[11] The carrier will be a visible manifestation of this corrective influence.

All in all, today was one of the busiest days since I came to India. Luther Hodges learned that one of his old friends was being held up on an aluminum contract and concluded that he should go to Morarji Desai or even to Nehru to get it unfrozen. While no impropriety was involved, I pointed out the dangers of allowing businessmen to think that any American visitor to India could be so used. I stopped the Nehru part in its tracks; the session with Morarji I let go. Later in the afternoon, I had a detailed press briefing on the whole Kashmir-Pakistan situation with the Indian press. I went over our position in detail — no pressure, a clear concern that Indian arms aid not be wasted in this quarrel and that India herself be able to concentrate energies on the most important front.[12]

November 30 — New Delhi

Nehru both gives and takes away. After agreeing yesterday on talks on "Kashmir and related matters," he said in the Lok Sabha[13] that he had made it clear to everyone that to upset the present

[11] I no longer believe this to be entirely so. They retired when they had shown beyond any doubt that they could defend their claim to the areas they held or sought to hold in Ladakh.
[12] These briefings were very valuable. Our position was strongly reflected next morning in the reporting on the Ayub-Nehru agreement.
[13] See page 327.

arrangements in Kashmir would be very bad for the people there. And, in response to a question, he said, reasonably enough, that he would not be pushed around by Mr. Sandys or anyone else. The whole speech wasn't too bad. However, P.T.I. (Press Trust of India) picked out the worst possible sections to go out over the wires. Gore-Booth being away, I had a talk with the number two man in the British High Commission. He in turn went to see M. J. Desai. The issue is this: Pakistan has always insisted on talks on Kashmir without preconditions. The Indians have always asked, as a condition, that the present territorial situation be recognized which, of course, is to confirm them in the ownership of the Valley. We settled the matter by agreeing that, in the interpretation to the Indian press, the Prime Minister's statement would be described as no precondition. Then I got through to Harriman who was in Karachi and pretty angry. Perhaps no irreparable damage has been done but it gets the discussions off to the worst possible start. The principal problem is that Nehru dislikes and mistrusts Sandys. Hence his statement that he would not be pushed around. Had Harriman and I handled the matter, it would have been much better.

I got a note from President Kennedy this morning asking if he could ask President Pusey of Harvard to have my leave of absence extended.[14] I replied that I thought it would be more dignified if I negotiated directly. I am probably rather useful here at the moment — I have a certain steadying and tranquilizing influence. And I cannot leave in the middle of a war merely to protect a lifetime appointment. Maybe Harvard would be reluctant, in the circumstances, to have it known that it was insisting on my return. But this sensitivity I doubt.

In any case, I dispatched a letter to Pusey putting the problem before him and, meanwhile, asked the President through Bundy not to intervene.

The President is meeting Macmillan mid-December. I told him

---

[14] It was for two years, the Harvard maximum, and the period of service on which the President and I had agreed.

I would welcome seeing him before or during that meeting. This would give me some added leverage here which is always useful. If the cease-fire holds and especially if the Chinese go back up the hill as scheduled tomorrow, the President will probably call me back for a conference. If the Chinese stay or advance, of course I will have to remain here.

Dave Bell has just been made head of AID and Kermit Gordon, Director of the Budget. Both are former teaching associates of mine and I certainly hope I was nice to them.

At 7 P.M., the captains, more precisely the colonels, also departed for Karachi. Everything is now exceedingly quiet. Before they went, I took the precaution of looking at the report they are writing. It is an excellent elucidation of the commonplace. There is not a single new idea but all of the old ones are benign.

December 1 — New Delhi

I have made an important discovery in the field of experimental medicine. When one is working under high tension, it is better to rely on a small amount of natural sleep than a larger amount induced by barbiturates or sedatives. Not only do you feel better in the morning but you feel a lot better if you have to wake up in the middle of the night. Thus, night before last, after the Harriman group departed, I decided to have a long night's sleep with the aid of a massive dose of sleeping pills. I had just downed them when the phone rang from Karachi. There had been a great upheaval there over Nehru's statements in the Lok Sabha. Sandys was flying back to get a statement from Nehru — saying clearly the Indians would negotiate without preconditions. I had to contend with all of this in the middle of the night under a kind of drugged haze. The latter lasted well into yesterday morning.

At noon, I had lunch with General Kaul who is in a poor state of mind, having just been fired from his command. He told me he had always been a stalwart pro-American, was now a determined advocate of any alliance we would accept, and that the Indian defeat had been the result of failure to take his advice. This may not all be true. However, the mental situation of an ambitious but defeated general is not easy. I comforted him, but not completely, by telling him that all generals who commanded peacetime armies in peace-loving countries had terrible trouble when they were struck by the shock of war.[15] We dined in the sun out on the porch and he did most of the talking. He is not sure whether he will resign from the Army or assume command of some nonexistent formations on the Punjab border.

M. J. Desai raised with me the question of a tacit air defense pact. The Indians would prepare airstrips and radar; if the Chinese came back, they would commit their tactical aircraft and we would undertake defense of their cities. This is a very considerable proposal with very major implications. It would also completely pattern our long-term relationships with India.

In the evening, we went for dinner with H. H. Maharajah Karan Singh and his wife — a very pleasant party. He was celebrating, having this day received his Ph.D. Finally, we went to Palam to see Luther Hodges away.

December 2 — New Delhi

This morning, I slept late and woke feeling more rested than in weeks. So far as we know, the Chinese are going back up the hill a few steps at a time and everything is better on the Pakistan front. I might be able to catch my breath.

We had a long meeting of the staff group to discuss the possibility of a joint air defense policy with the Indians. This is very important; it would provide the basis for a close working relationship with India. We would contribute the planes; the Indians, the fields and ground support. The planes would come into the field in emergencies. I have completed a long telegram to the Department on the subject. I have difficulty in seeing myself as a negotia-

[15] Including Douglas MacArthur who, however, survived his disasters.

tor of a semi-military pact. But this is a time of change and we should take it by the ears.[16]

Mrs. Charles Collingwood[17] came to lunch along with Bob Sherrod[18] and his wife, and I learned that Fighting Joe Alsop[19] is coming to town. He will be very angry with the Indians for making peace. I slept this afternoon, studied some paintings, and then we had a party for several hundred Air Force officers and men. Some girls of the Mission came in to do the twist and everyone greatly enjoyed the occasion. We had rum punch which disappeared by the gallon. One Air Force Sergeant said it was the first time in a two-and-a-half-year hitch that anyone had entertained him although "a few tossed stones at his house." Another discriminating guest observed in my hearing to a friend, "They say this Ambassador is the thinking type." The Air Force is an organization of considerable informality. After I had led off with an approximate twist, the commanding Colonel took over and was cheered heartily by his men. Tomorrow morning, I leave for Tezpur.

December 3 — New Delhi–Tezpur–Siliguri

For the first time in weeks, I am away from Delhi and it is a great relief. At dawn, we took the Convair to Tezpur and I managed to sleep five hours. There we were met by General Manekshaw, new Commander of the IV Corps replacing General Kaul, General Sen of Eastern Command — the rare case of a Bengali in a high Army post — and a platoon-plus of newspapermen and photographers. It was warm and pleasant and in a few minutes we were in a French Alouette helicopter (the rest of the party following in a Russian number) and heading for the front.

At the front, we spent an hour or two inspecting a fortified position on the plain just below the hills. The Chinese are in the

---

[16] Too enthusiastic. I later came to see the arrangement as a substitute for expensive military aid.
[17] Wife of the radio and television commentator. She was touring, as I recall.
[18] Then editor of *The Saturday Evening Post*.
[19] See pages 205, 481.

latter, but how near no one knows. They are supposed to be re-tiring.

The soldiers were trim, professional and in good spirits and had prepared their position with evident competence. I thought their tactical conception rather static and easily capable of being by-passed. I discovered later that General Kelly[20] had reached the same conclusion. The old-fashioned rifles the men carry are clearly an anachronism and must give them a feeling of military inferiority.

The villagers watch the military positions and the latter are un-covered by either wire or mines. Both of these defects are going to be remedied. If so, I fear there will also be mine accidents.

We went back to Corps Headquarters at Tezpur, where I talked with some men from the Fourth Division who had just come in from Sela. About 10,000 have now filtered back. They showed the effects of some ten days without food but, nonetheless, looked exceedingly fit.

After lunch at Corps Headquarters, we went back to the airport. I gave a brief press conference and we came west to Siliguri. Here we went over the maps in the operations room — a garage — and reviewed the campaign and its problems until about 10 P.M. As usual in military gatherings, the business conversation was inter-rupted with golf scores and accounts of past battles. We had din-ner and turned in — I on two army cots placed end to end.

December 4 — Siliguri–Hashimara–New Delhi

At 9 A.M., we went over to the headquarters of the 33rd Corps and had a briefing by General Harbaksh Singh. I took the occasion to inquire what would keep the Chinese, should they come back, from simply walking around the Infantry Brigade whose position we inspected yesterday. The question was a good one. There is nothing. Some of the generals are hoping that the Chinese will change their ways and attack along the roads like civilized people.

[20] See page 483.

They will seek out the Indians rather than outflanking and bypassing them. However, General Singh was quick to say that the disposition made no sense and they had every intention of correcting it.

All of this confirms me in my view of the Indian Army. It is competent and professional, but in some parts tragically old-fashioned.

Later in the morning, we flew twenty minutes back east to Hashimara, where we were taken on a full-scale tour of the 17th Division. The Division, consisting of four brigades, was concentrated in the main in a large forest reserve. They were putting on a feverish show of activity for our benefit; it was a snow job in the best international military tradition. Infantrymen were engaged in violent bayonet practice; mortar teams were moving their equipment around with incredible speed; other units were working their way through the bush in a remarkable combination of attack postures; machine gun crews were moving forward and backward; bazooka teams were knocking out hundreds of imaginary tanks; an artillery battery was going through lavishly intricate maneuvers; one company was feverishly digging slit trenches by the airport.

In fact, the troops looked very rugged and competent. The same could not be said for their equipment. They had a battalion or two of tanks, most of them Shermans in high polish, but in an advanced state of wear. These are also too heavy for most of the bridges in the area, and should the Chinese come down, they would need fast lateral movement. And I could not make any real sense of the Divisional Commander's plans and slightly suspect he had none. Certainly he had not been guilty of giving any neurotic thought to Chinese tactics. He told me that they would have difficulty supplying themselves once they reached the plain, unless they could seize an airfield. It was evidently his view that they could supply a considerable operation from one airstrip. He could be an excellent officer. One has also to allow for the possible existence of the kind of peacetime general who proves such a disaster in war.

By about one, we were back at the airport and returned to Siliguri, where we had a pleasant lunch at the Corps Headquarters and then took off again for Delhi. Despite some sinus trouble, I managed to add another couple of hours' sleep to my total and got back to Delhi feeling more rested than in months.

December 5 — New Delhi

A gathering of the uncommitted nations in Ceylon is filling the Indians with despondency — Burma, Cambodia, U.A.R., Indonesia, Ghana and Ceylon are attending to make peace between India and China.[21] We considered this meeting today and then the whole position on Pakistan and the possibility that Swaran Singh may be the negotiator. Finally, there has been much talk of the role of the U.N. in this dispute. We decided to encourage the Indians to go to the U.N. but only with information on the Chinese attack. They should not be encouraged to go to the Security Council where they would have to confront the Soviets and force the latter to decide between them and the Chinese. There is no advantage in this game.

I saw M. J. Desai in the afternoon to tell him that Washington was still wondering if the Indians were serious about negotiations with Pakistan. He assured me they were. He also pled with me to take steps to keep Sandys out of discussions. During the day, I struggled with sundry long telegrams and a detailed letter to the President. Word came in from Bundy that Harvard is willing to dispense with my services until autumn and I am to be summoned back to see the President in the next few days.

December 6 — New Delhi

Things are almost back to normal. Indeed, this has been the lightest day in six weeks. I got a formal summons back to Washington

[21] This was the so-called Colombo Conference, the task of which was to find a formula for peace between the two Asian powers.

and will leave next Monday — four days' time. I completed a long letter to the President on the local political and military situation and received news that Burr Smith, the Economic Counselor, is being recalled. It is unlikely that he can be replaced by anyone very good. No first-rate economist wants to make a career in the State Department.

Rumors came in that Stevenson may leave and that Rusk will take his place at the U.N., while Mac Bundy becomes Secretary of State. Pierre Salinger has denied it. It sounds like a White House trial balloon. There are many stories that Stevenson was at odds with Kennedy during the Cuban crisis.[22] And the President has never much liked Rusk. So it has elements of plausibility. The news having come out, it must, of course, be denied.

I had an idiotic instruction from the Department today on the air defense proposals. I had, of course, reported the Indian suggestions.[23] It is an economical basis for a continuing relationship provided, of course, they consult with us on any action that might lead to our involvement. I got a worried cable back from the Department telling me to make no commitment, not to raise the subject with the Indians and saying that the President wanted to make it clear that the Commonwealth should take the lead on any such scheme. I sent back an angry reply saying that on the night of the panic, I had stopped the Indians from employing their air power because it would either have committed us to back up their defenses or forced us to refuse to do so and that either decision would have been equally unfortunate. Having been aware of the danger of such commitment in the middle of the night two weeks ago, I hardly needed to be instructed now. I added that there were only two-and-a-half cities in the world where the Commonwealth was taken seriously, namely, London, Washington and Canberra.[24]

[22] This was not true. Various positions were taken but both opposed the bombing of the missile sites.
[23] See page 504.
[24] Secretary Rusk, then and later, was the habitual author of suggestions that the Commonwealth could be exhumed for useful work.

During the afternoon, an ophthalmologist from Garden City, Long Island, read me a short speech about what the ophthalmologists of the world were doing for international understanding. We had a lunch for Luke Battle,[25] Assistant Secretary of State for Educational and Cultural Affairs.

✧ ✧ ✧

New Delhi, India
December 6, 1962

Dear Mr. President:

I think I should give you a somewhat more intimate view of developments here than you will be getting from the cables. I assume that you are probably suffering from a considerable surfeit of information on India at the moment — that you are hearing more about penguins than you need to know. However, the changes here continue to be great.

On the military side I am just back from a two-day tour of the front. I went up to the forward positions to look things over for myself. As on all things having to do with the military, it is a great deal better to be observant and intelligent than to be professional if you can't be both. The Indian Army has now recovered its balance, morale is improving, the soldiers are rough, hard and well-trained and discipline is good. Nevertheless, it is well that the Chinese stopped. While there was (and is) no question of their invading the Ganges Plain, they could do a great deal of damage if they decided to come on again. That is because the Indian Army in its command, organization, tactics and equipment is extremely old-fashioned. The individual soldiers carry personal arms that are sixty years old and this can hardly give them the feeling of equality with opponents carrying modern light automatic weapons. The tactics are stuffy and rigid. Success depends to a considerable extent on the hope that the Chi-

[25] Lucius D. Battle, later Ambassador to the U.A.R. and thereafter Assistant Secretary of State for Near Eastern and South Asian Affairs.

nese will reform and fight on the roads like Germans and not bypass fixed defenses. I visited one unit north of Tezpur which was admirably placed and dug in. It would give the Chinese a very bad time if they came that way. When I asked the C-in-C what would prevent the Chinese from giving it a miss right or left, he said "nothing." On these plains they should have a great advantage over lightly armed Chinese with their armor. Unfortunately, the latter is antique, starved for parts and cannot be easily deployed because of poor bridges.

Some of the commanders are very good. More are still the amiable frauds that rise to the top in any peacetime Army. Fortunately, I think they have one of their best commanders in the area of greatest danger — the so-called Siliguri Gap below the Chumbi Valley in Tibet. This is the most accessible route into India from China and the one that could most easily cut off Eastern India and threaten East Pakistan. I am sure we were right to urge them to use the ceasefire to play for time.

However, while I assume that the Chinese have not given up their evil intentions, my instinct is that the danger of a new and major adventure is receding. They have dealt India a very heavy blow, which is certainly one thing they had in mind. They have also established a strong position for bargaining in Ladakh. And I am inclined to think they took Nehru's talk about nonalignment seriously and were honestly surprised at the speed with which we reacted. If they move again, they must wonder what they will provoke and what will happen to their very long supply lines.

So the immediate military phase may well be over. The Indians will be very cautious in their reaction while continuing to make clear that their long-run intentions toward the Chinese are exceedingly lethal. This is probably the right policy. Nehru would be thrown out if we made peace even on fairly favorable terms. But they are in no position to make war. This brings me to the political situation, which is exceedingly interesting.

The Chinese cost Menon his job. But they have also driven a considerable wedge between Nehru and the people. By strongly coming to India's support, but at the same time giving no grounds for suspicion of ulterior motives, there has been a simply enormous enhancement of American prestige. The press, Army, politicians, indeed the country as a whole, has come almost overnight to regard us as a first friend. As I predicted, even the word nonalignment has disappeared from everything but Nehru's speeches and the left-wing press, and there is a lively discussion as to whether we will insist on it. U.S.I.S. has for years conducted a poll on attitudes toward the United States. In October, 1957, 2.5 percent reported a "Very Good" opinion of the United States. In mid-October, 1962, it was 7.0 percent. Last week it was 62 percent. Eighty-five percent of those asked reported an improved view of the United States.

Less distinctly, there is a great desire for some kind of reconciliation with Pakistan. This has survived all of the loud and angry misbehavior of the Pakistan press and politicians these last weeks. Popular opinion would reject any outright ceding of the Valley. But it is well ahead of Nehru in the desire for some other form of settlement and with the ceasefire many feel that concessions can now be made without indication of weakness. . . .

However, if we handle ourselves with intelligence, we can deal with the situation. We must work with Nehru in spite of his present mood. Any punitive tendency could consolidate and alienate the very great forces that are still on his side. We must avoid this and meanwhile let public opinion work on him. This means in practical terms that we must be responsive to their defense needs and thus to their major source of anxiety. When the Chinese subside we will want to take a good look at the more Napoleonic plans of the Indians for defense. It would be fatal, however, to show hesitancy at this moment when they are relying on us and when the fear of the Chinese is so great. Now that we have got the Kashmir issue out in the open — a significant achievement in itself — we must press it but in such a manner as not to involve ourselves in the inbuilt antagonisms between the two countries. We must continue to make it clear to the Indians that it is their task, not ours and not Pakistan's. In my view, incidentally, Kashmir is not soluble in territorial terms. But by holding up the example of the way in which France and Germany have moved to soften their antagonism by the Common Market and common instruments of administration, including such territorial disputes as that over the Saar, there is a chance of getting the Indo-Pakistan dialogue into constructive channels. . . .

Finally, you will have seen my telegrams on the problem of air defense and the opportunities I see here. In my view it provides a long-run foundation for a political association of the first importance. There are also costs and dangers and I gather that my telegrams are at least producing adequate attention to these. The Department also assures me that you are firmly committed to the notion that the British should look after India in this department. This is perhaps a little like urging that they resume a long-run interest in Ireland. However, I shall postpone discussion of this until I get a full view of what I shall require by way of argument. We can hardly deplore the fact that people have faith in us as they do not in our cousins.

More seriously, I think the liberal West in general and the New Frontier in particular have remarkable opportunities in the realignment that is going on here. It is indeed perhaps the kind of opportunity that comes once in a generation. To seize it involves neither boldness nor caution but only an intelligent reaction to events.

Yours faithfully,

JOHN KENNETH GALBRAITH

THE PRESIDENT
THE WHITE HOUSE

P.S. One problem which I more than slightly fear is this. As the Chinese threat recedes, the communists and fellow-traveling left will try to reassert itself. Their line will be obvious. The Chinese tried to take the mountains in NEFA. However, the Americans in cooperation with the Moslems tried to take our far richer heritage in Kashmir. This could be serious. I have protected this flank by always saying that we aren't urging the surrender of Kashmir or any other particular solution. We are urging the importance of a settlement as a prime goal of Indian foreign policy, for that makes our military aid both possible and effective. I don't think we have run any serious risk here so far. But we must move with care.

✧ ✧ ✧

December 7 — New Delhi

This was Friday and the tension is still off. It seems clear that the Chinese are retiring and I fear that we face a new political danger. The left will coalesce around the idea that the Chinese are retreating in NEFA while we are trying to take Kashmir for the Pakistanis in the West, and that Kashmir is more valuable than NEFA.

I had a well-attended press conference this afternoon and met the idea head-on.[26] I noted that we were pressing for progress in both Pakistan and India and both seem to think we were doing too much. I went on to say that we did not force our friends in either country but we were concerned with the whole defense of the sub-continent. Tomorrow we rise at dawn for an excursion to Leh in Ladakh.

December 8 — New Delhi–Leh–New Delhi

We got up this morning while it was still dark and were at Palam at 7:30 A.M. About a quarter to eight, we climbed aboard a loaded C-130 and I noticed not without interest that the cargo consisted of TNT, detonators and land mines. Kitty (her back still in a

---

[26] In accordance with a well-proven theory that it was much more difficult for our critics to raise these matters after I had discussed them as possible opposition gambits.

brace) and I were installed in armchairs on the flight deck. I thought perhaps she had not noticed the cargo so I did not tell her until we were disembarking at Leh. However, she had seen the letters TNT also.

After a meticulous check of everything from brakes to hydraulic pressure to communication gear, we trundled out and took off, on almost no length of the runway. We turned north over the Ganges Plain in perfect weather, climbed high over Simla and the Kulu Valley, then on over a hundred miles of high Himalayan plateau, snowcapped with hundreds of great sharp peaks. We were flying at 25,000 feet, the plateau was about 5,000 feet below and the peaks, I would guess, about 2,000 above that. After an hour and twenty minutes, we dropped down into an arid valley with the Indus River, a small stream here, on one side and, after some highly intricate maneuvering between the valley walls, came into the airport at Leh. At each end of the valley are hills that are topped by monasteries which are extensions of the landscape itself like the great lamasery in Lhasa. The town of Leh is a collection of prayer walls, sheep pens and mud huts together with a small mud fort. Tibetan monks pass along the roads with shepherds. It is an eerie and distant, but by no means unpleasant, place. We are among the comparative handful of Westerners who have seen it.

The air here at some 11,000 feet at this time of the year is fresh and clear and, out of the sun, very cold. In the sun it is not uncomfortable. Officers and a great group of soldiers were on hand to welcome us and we were jeeped first to a brigade mess and headquarters where we met more soldiers and I went on to the divisional operations office to be briefed on combat dispositions and prospects. Kitty went to a hospital which was more interesting. Then we made our way back to the airfield to discover that two Chief Ministers — of Punjab and Rajasthan respectively — had come in, changed to helicopters and gone on to Chushul. One of the helicopters had then been forced down (without damage to the occupants) some twenty-five miles away so only one Chief Minister remained. We climbed aboard the now empty C-130. The checks were repeated, we trundled out again and took off. There had been some talk of circling Chushul but the crew was discouraged by the thought that the Chinese had some anti-aircraft batteries in the vicinity. I did nothing to encourage them. (In fact, they had orders to stay away.) We went back over the equally astonishing peaks and then down into the Ganges Plain and were back in Delhi by one o'clock. From Chandigarh in the Punjab to Leh, the round trip by motor lorry takes twenty-six days.

We had a pleasant luncheon with Arthur Smithies[27] who had come with us on the trip and then I found that various things had gone wrong. The White House, through Kaysen, had declined to accept some amendments I wanted in a letter that the President was sending to Nehru. I wired back asking that my recommended changes, or my reasons for them, be sent to the President himself.[28]

Almost simultaneously, Timmons, who is mobile again, came in with a copy of a letter which he had obtained from the British, which had been written for the President to Macmillan. This, an outgrowth of the Harriman mission, made a number of idiotic proposals — a British mediator on the Kashmir dispute and a quite impractical solution to the air defense arrangements which the Indians would never dream of accepting. They had not only not consulted us on it, but had neglected to send us a copy. Moving in heavily on this blunder, I got off a private telegram to the President and Bundy and a less exclusive one to Harriman. Tomorrow should produce some interesting reactions.

December 10 — New Delhi

Yesterday was Sunday and we had planned an excursion to Khajuraho;[29] however, I stayed home and spent my venom on Washington. I got off two long cables, one denouncing the pro-

[27] See page 492.
[28] Since getting his attention was difficult, the alternative would be to accept them. So it happened.
[29] Ancient capital famous for its graceful and erotic sculpture.

posal for a British intermediary, the other condemning the proposals for air defense.

The Pakistan-India talks as now planned are heading for a crack-up. Pakistan wants the Kashmir Valley; so does India. They can't both have it and India must have the Valley in order to have a base for operations in Ladakh; otherwise, Ladakh would, presumably, be handed over to the Chinese. So now we have a summit with every chance of a confrontation and no progress. Washington had not seen this. And the British intermediary might even be Sandys. It is all quite disastrous.

The air defense proposal is that we would do the dull job of providing the radar and the fields. The British would put in the squadrons and get credit for providing the protection. This seems to me a fantastic arrangement. Also, the proposals as sent to Macmillan would seem to contain no safeguards by way of consultation. So we would have a unilateral commitment to the Indians with no chance to pass on the type of action which might precipitate conflict.

In the evening, I had a long talk with Nehru who seemed to be searching genuinely for a solution on Kashmir. I tried my ideas. He mentioned a number and rejected them and then rather seized upon the proposal I made for something on the European track of the Common Market.

He was also in a very angry mood about the Chinese and said he had lost all confidence in their *bona fides* and would not trust them to reach any sort of bargain. He thinks they may attack again. Nehru looked much younger and more vigorous than at any time in recent months and told me that the tension of the crisis agreed with him.

A telegram came in from Bundy and Kaysen explaining that my irritation should be attributed to the British who had shown to their staff a confidential cable meant only for Macmillan. And their staff had sent it on to India and thus to me. This is hardly an answer. If the British consulted the relevant people, why did not we? And in any case, I objected to the decision. I think my friends were a bit embarrassed.

The Chinese have made some very new and very threatening noises, and at the staff meeting this morning, there was a good deal of debate as to whether I should postpone my trip to Washington or not. In the end, I concluded that I should but wired Bundy for his advice. He wired back urging me to come. His response came too late for me to catch the plane.

December 11 — New Delhi

This morning Smithies and I went for a long walk. The air is fresh and cool and a great pleasure. Following, we had a meeting and a review of the general situation. The Chinese could be again losing patience with the Indians and it may be only a matter of time until there is some new military demonstration — perhaps against one of the frontier posts in NEFA, or in the far east, or against Chushul. I am a trifle more pessimistic than my people but we got out a telegram expressing our new fears.

An amusing telegram has come in giving the conclusions of the Harriman mission. It contains every cliché in the book. I dictated a spurious word of praise and then took biting exception to all the clichés. Thus, I noted that it asked for a Kashmir settlement but said nothing of the nature of the settlement. This is an important question for it could be that none is possible. The report also said we should encourage the trend toward new and younger men in the Indian administration. With a straight face, I pointed to the difficulty in approaching Nehru and suggesting that he hire more men of the New Frontier vintage. There was also a lot of romantic nonsense about the Commonwealth. None of this, I am sure, was Harriman's own work.

On the whole, however, it was a leisurely day. I met with the press this afternoon which I find also shares somewhat my pessimism. However, the press is always pessimistic. Disaster is professionally advantageous.

Then we had a roundup on the supply situation and ended the day with a party for the new members of the Mission. I leave at four-thirty tomorrow morning.

December 15 — New York–Washington

Today is Saturday. I arrived in Washington Wednesday evening and, as usual, have had trouble finding time to write. The journey over, right through on Pan-Am, was long but not as wearying as sometimes. I slept a great deal of the way.

On arrival, I joined the Arthur Schlesingers at a party and we went on to his house for a chat. He has become much more sanguine about the New Frontier; and the papers have rather forgotten that he was meant to be the whipping boy. Charles Bartlett[30] and Stewart Alsop[31] have published a piece attacking Stevenson's role in the Cuban missile affair — it charged him with being an appeaser. It was really an operation of the hard-liners who had wanted to bomb the missile sites in Cuba. The President was not involved in it. Neither was Mac Bundy.

Everyone, I was assured, believes that I handled the Indian-Chinese war in a masterful way. This does not, however, mean that I am universally loved. Rusk, I gather, continues to regard me as a major inconvenience in an otherwise placid organization.

Thursday, I tried with some success to catch up on my sleep. I had a meeting with Phil Talbot in the morning and more on some highly secret matters in the afternoon. The latter, principally calculated to appeal to someone's sense of adventure, struck me as singularly useless. They were stopped.

I had early dinner upstairs at the White House with the President, J.B.K. and the Shrivers. The President looks tanned and brisk and in the best of form. Talk was varied and gay and covered everything from India to the tribulations of Adlai Stevenson — the

[30] Columnist and personal friend of President Kennedy. This friendship led to the suspicion that the President was involved.

[31] Then Washington editor of *The Saturday Evening Post* where the article appeared.

President thinks he complains too much. Then we went to see a French play at the National Theatre. We took regular seats and it was only after we were well-installed that people began to whisper. The stir ran audibly through the crowd ending in vigorous applause. I enjoyed it very much though by the end of the evening, I was very tired and concentrated on the play with considerable difficulty.

Yesterday I had a press briefing. The questions were good and sympathetic. Most had to do with the fighting and the ambitions of the Chinese. I was late, for the President had asked me to look at the speech he was giving in the evening before the Economic Club of New York. It was terrible — terribly written and full of Republican clichés. It dealt at length with tax reduction, cast doubt on the performance of the economy, complained that taxes were handicapping investment and undermining incentives and promised rigid economy. Unfortunately, it was beyond retrieval and I effected little improvement.

At eleven, I met with the Joint Chiefs. They sat at one side of a big table in brilliant beribboned uniform. Talbot, Harriman, Alexis Johnson and McConaughy sat at the other. Various military support was in the background. I spoke for five minutes on India, Phil for the same length of time (which had been specified) as though to a court. Harriman and McConaughy then spoke for about half an hour each. Nothing new or important was said by any of us. But the occasion had an appearance of power.

I left early and joined J.B.K. for lunch. We went to a restaurant called The Jockey Club and she told me it was only her second lunch out since she entered the White House. For once, I faced a headwaiter with equanimity; indeed, he was a little shaken. Apropos the meetings with the Joint Chiefs, she told me that General Lemnitzer[32] had once made the terrible mistake of coming to a Saturday morning meeting at the White House in a sports jacket.

I had various meetings in the afternoon including one with

[32] Chairman of the Joint Chiefs of Staff, 1960–62.

George Ball for a major roundup on Indian matters and then went
to New York. I dined at Marietta Tree's[33] and went on to Mary
Lasker's[34] for a dance. Ambassador Boland (formerly Irish Ambassador to England) and I talked at length about Mrs. Cecil Wood-
ham-Smith's new book on the Irish famine.[35] I danced a bit but, on
the whole, was too weary to enjoy it as I might. Toward one-
thirty, I returned to the Dorset and went rapidly to sleep.

December 20 — Nassau–Washington

During the past week, I have been going through the usual round
of Washington talks and consultations. Very depressing — a very
large amount of unfocused talk. Also, there is too little talk of the
danger of Chinese attack on India and much too much of the need
for a Kashmir settlement. I have gone to various celebrations and
parties which are as always a pleasant relief from the austerities of
New Delhi. Everyone in Washington knows everyone else and
entertains everyone else once a week.

On Monday of this week — this is Thursday — we had a big
roundup at the White House. The Executive Committee of the
National Security Council was the forum — meeting in the Cabinet
Room. Rusk, Ball, McNamara, Bundy, Bell, Stevenson, etc., etc.,
were there. If this is only the Executive Committee, I shudder to
think of the size of the full Council. But happily that never meets.

I attacked the proposal from the Joint Chiefs to divide the air
defense package for India — we taking the radar and the other
donkey work and the British providing the air squadrons. The
President, after listening to me, stamped on the Joint Chiefs with
both feet. One enjoys arguing a good case — and also winning.

In the subsequent days, everyone started paring away at this
decision. By today, a proposal for associating our air power with

[33] See page 253.
[34] Philanthropist, art collector, health promoter, horticulturalist and friend.
[35] *The Great Hunger; Ireland, 1845–9* (London: Hamilton, 1962).

Indian defense had been watered down almost to one of sending a military mission to India.

Early this morning, Phil Talbot picked me up at the Hay-Adams and at 7 A.M., we took off from Andrews Field for Nassau. Passage was in a Boeing 707, the one used until a few months ago by the President, with breakfast en route. In two-and-a-half hours, we were in Nassau where we were met and taken to the club where Macmillan and Kennedy were in conference. The latter, which includes a hotel and settlement of houses, is flowered and beautiful; present were McNamara, Ball, Nitze and sundry Britishers.

Before noon, the President and I went swimming and then we lunched at the President's house with Macmillan and company. Thereafter, we had a long talk on Indian and Chinese matters with the British being very reluctant. They do not believe the Chinese are a major threat. They are mostly concerned with holding operations to a level of cost which they can afford to share. Sandys was there and talked a great deal. Home was not impressive.[36] Nor was Macmillan for that matter. I did not feel that our people recognized the full magnitude of the task or the opportunity. It was a cheese-paring operation throughout.

By late afternoon, all imagination had been removed from the exercise. A great opportunity to bring India into much closer working association with the western community (and to save a great deal on independent Indian defense expenditures), an opportunity sensed only by the President, Talbot and myself, had been largely dulled over. I felt very discouraged.

By twilight, a dismal paper had been agreed by the group — one that largely missed the point. We took off for Washington again.

I arranged with the President to return home about June. He may appoint Chester Bowles in my place although he also has Walter Reuther in mind.

---

[36] Rt. Hon. Sir Alec Douglas-Home, then British Secretary of State for Foreign Affairs, and later Prime Minister. In recalling the meeting later I thought this less than fair to Macmillan.

December 27 — New Delhi

I returned three days ago. During my absence, things have slipped a certain distance back to normal. There has been some sniping at us for the pressure we are applying for a Kashmir settlement. I moved vigorously to explain our concern[37] and with the usual result that we received much more sympathetic treatment. I have actually not brought back very much in the way of military assistance — about $120 million divided between ourselves and the British. But it shows how concern is diminishing that this seemed fairly adequate. Nehru was not especially disturbed. The Indians are still anxious to get ahead with an arrangement on air defense but some of the urgency has gone out of this as well. I asked Nehru if we could count on India to help contain the Chinese should they break out somewhere else in Asia. He told me this would be a matter of great concern to them and they would help.

Talks are starting at Rawalpindi today on the Kashmir settlement. There are slight but no high hopes of a settlement. Swaran Singh is leading the Indian delegation. The Pakistanis ushered in the negotiations by announcing they had reached a border settlement with the Chinese.

[37] Namely, and as before, that we would not be arming both sides of an India-Pakistan dispute.

XXIV

Butting Heads

January 4, 1963 — New Delhi

This is Friday and it has been some days since I have dictated any notes. Not a shortage of time but a shortage of activity is the reason. A week ago today, I went down to Calcutta, visited the new Chief Minister and held a press conference to say once more that we are not attaching any wicked conditions to our military aid and that, while we wanted a settlement with Pakistan, we are not making this the price of "protection" from the Chinese. (The Communists, fellow travelers and the generally susceptible were toying with both points and, as usual, I was seeking to stop them before they got started.) Then on Saturday morning we took the Convair on to Madras. We had lunch there and went out to Mahabalipuram: The guesthouse there is close to the beach which is very flat with a mild surf, and the famous sea temple is half a mile to the south. The weather was perfect and I slept twelve hours a night, again after breakfast and after lunch, and swam the rest of the time. One could feel the nerve ends knitting. We were there for New Year's Eve and New Year's Day and on Wednesday, we came back to Madras where I held another press conference on the same theme as in Calcutta. It was not so pleasant. The Pakistan negotiation with China was the cause. When you urge settlement with Pakistan, you get the question: "Do you want us to give them Ladakh so they can turn it over to the Chinese?" History can be idiotic. A staunch American ally against Communism is negotiating with the

Chinese Communists to the discontent of an erstwhile neutral. I hope that Dulles,[1] from wherever he is, is being required to watch these developments.

After the press conference, I met with the Consulate staff, called on Chief Minister Kamaraj and got back to Delhi late Wednesday evening. The temporary aid program on behalf of the Indian Army goes well. General Kelly, my new military chief, is a diplomat a little in the tradition of Rocky Marciano but he gets things done. Orders are now in for matériel for some two divisions. Kelly has been told (I think) by Max Taylor that he must uphold the military as against the civilian authority. But he is also heavily dependent on the civilian authority so we get along well.

For the rest of the last two days, I applied either contraception or abortion to proposals from Washington for teams to visit India. Everyone in Washington wants to send us a team and be on it himself. And if anyone is uncertain what to do, he proposes a team to find out what team should be sent. Some things slipped out of control in the last two weeks, but they are pretty well in hand again.

January 5 — New Delhi

This morning, I had very secret matters and then Austin Robinson[2] and Ty Wood came for lunch. Austin is here on a big power survey[3] which Ty is promoting and which I hope does good. Ty is a former businessman and nobody is more committed to academic studies. After two years of struggling to get the Tarapur power project — the large nuclear power plant near Bombay — off the deck in Washington, some of my own staff had complained that the economic justification was inadequate. I made short shrift of my own objectors.

M. J. Desai told me about Indian thinking on containment of the

---

[1] I.e., John Foster, the author of these alliances.

[2] Professor E. A. G. Robinson, greatly distinguished economist of Cambridge University.

[3] This one, led by Walker Cisler of Detroit Edison, was, I believe, truly valuable.

Chinese. They are willing to work with the United States both politically and militarily in the rest of Asia. This is quid pro quo for our assistance and quite a remarkable advance. Nehru a week ago hinted that their thoughts were moving in this direction. I cabled this to Washington but achieved no reaction. I sent off another long cable this evening. I marked this one for the White House and I imagine I will get some response.

Following the foregoing, I had a press conference with the American press. And thus the day. Dave Bell is coming in later on tonight and Kitty and I are going out to meet him.

January 6 — New Delhi

Today was Sunday. David Bell came in at midnight last night on a quick trip around the world before taking over as AID Director. He was traveling tourist class as befits a former Budget Director. Happily, I have no compulsion to save money in this way, which is a great comfort.

This morning, I saw Hilaly, the Pakistan High Commissioner, who was in a troubled frame of mind. I pressed him on the bad impression that the Pakistan–Chinese Communist flirtation would arouse in the United States. Ayub's claim to consideration in the U.S. was his firm soldierly reputation as a staunch non-Communist. Recent behavior could only lead to a reputation for ambiguity. Hilaly seemed impressed. He was less impressed by the effect on Indian public opinion.

We went on to a briefing at the Embassy. I then lunched with the Maharajkumar[4] and Princess Pema of Sikkim. Pema's conversation ranged from Lhasa, where she spent three years after she was first married and where her children were born, to New York whence she had just returned. When she lived in Lhasa, it took about eighteen days to reach there from Gangtok in Sikkim; there was no telephone; there was only one Sikkimese doctor, attached to the British Residency; but the warm summer months were one continuous house party.

[4] Later to marry Hope Cooke. See page 557 and following pages.

After lunch, we went to a civic reception being given by the Delhi Municipality at the Constitution Club for the air crews of the C-130's. Only there was no one at the Constitution Club except a few elderly Hindus who seemed to be holding a prayer meeting. Someone had blundered. So we went for a walk around Humayun's Tomb. It seemed both vast and graceful in the evening light. Tonight we are having a dinner for David Bell.

I was ill at this time a year ago, as I have sufficiently reported, and therefore may not have reported on the pleasure of Delhi at this season. The sun is bright and warm — just warm enough to eat outside. The nights are brisk and cool; and it almost gets down to freezing, but not quite.

January 7 — New Delhi–Benares
This morning, we took the Convair to Benares where we left Kitty and the boys for sightseeing. David Bell and I then transferred to the Navy C-47 and flew for another hour to an airport somewhere in the jungles of the southern U.P. Then we went for another hour over very dusty roads in the company of G. D. Birla, the industrialist, to the Rihand Dam. Here in a wild and jungly area the dam creates the largest artificial lake in Asia — China not excepted — and produces a substantial amount of power which is fed into an aluminum plant. We have financed both — first the dam in the public sector and then the aluminum plant in the Birla sector.

On the way, Birla told us about the major interests of the Birla family, a very large tribe which combines moneymaking with a strong external aspect of virtue.[5] All members of the family are expected, literally, to be born businessmen. Only one — that was some years ago — ever turned out to be unqualified. He drank. On the other hand, the daughters are not trusted, and as a result, the sons-in-law are not given positions with the firm.

At the dam, we had long speeches (mostly in Hindi) by the Prime Minister and others and then adjourned to a pleasant rest

5 See page 71.

house complete with living accommodations, swimming pool and tennis court, with an adjacent school. Here we met the members of the Kaiser establishment[6] who are bringing in the aluminum plant. We then went in to an ultravegetarian lunch (a passion of the Birlas) which even excluded eggs. The P.M. spoke, as did I, and we then mounted the cars for the airport and on to Benares and thence to Palam. The Prime Minister had neglected to mention our contribution. I reminded him of it good-naturedly and said one should have a decent respect for money when it was in adequate quantity.[7]

I had a good deal of time to talk business with Dave Bell. He considers integrating AID operations closely with the State Department. This would work fine if the State Department were an efficient organization. But it is capable of slowing all progress to a walk or less, and this will be its impact on AID. I hope I persuaded him. Fortunately, he is doubtful of the leadership of the State Department. Rusk he described as being in the clouds; George Ball he considers a highly intelligent one-man bottleneck.

January 9 — New Delhi

The winter continues, the air remains cold and clear and the Chinese continue to be quiet. Madame Bandaranaike, the Prime Minister of Ceylon, is arriving in a day or two with peace proposals. I have a feeling that one way or another the Indians and Chinese are likely to start talking.[8] However, I don't think anything much will be settled very soon.[9] The Indians, one imagines, are approaching both the upcoming Pakistan talks and the upcoming Chinese negotiations with the hope that talk will be a substitute for action.

Yesterday I took Dave Bell to see Nehru. On my urging, Nehru promised silence on Pakistan until after the talks. The Pakistanis

[6] See page 458.
[7] This, I learned later, was well reported in the United States.
[8] Wrong.
[9] Right.

continue to make up with the Chinese in a way which causes great sorrow all around. McConaughy must be in terrible distress. He is an old Chinese fighter; now he must be nice to a government which wants to be nice to the Chinese.

Last night, the German Embassy had a musicale followed by dinner. I managed to arrive five seconds before the music ended. The dinner itself was agreeable with good cooking and excellent wine. I promised to trade a box of golf balls and a box of tennis balls with the Ambassador's wife for a case of Piesporter. Dave Bell left for Karachi early this morning, and I sent over to the Pakistan PX for my part of the bargain.

Today I talked with the architect of the Indian Pavilion at the New York World's Fair. I urged him to show Indian sculpture, Indian painting, handicrafts and textiles and forget about their industrial virtuosity. There is no chance of impressing any American with an Indian machine tool. I also went to the Ministry of External Affairs to explain that the portentous proposals on joint defense had still produced no reaction from Washington. This afternoon, Chester Ronning and I went out to Palam to welcome a couple of Caribou aircraft just in for delivery to the Indian Air Force. These are planes which carry quite a heavy load to very small airfields. The Canadians produced them and we paid for them, an arrangement which must suit my erstwhile countrymen very well.

Then I went on to New Delhi University to open a science exhibit. The occasion called for a speech on the relation of science to humanity; I said that so many million speeches had already been made on the subject, including C. P. Snow's, that nothing remained to be said. Then I contributed some banalities on the ambiguous modern position of the scientist. Half the world thinks he will drastically shorten life; the other half believes he will unnecessarily prolong it. The science exhibit itself, a USIS creation, was dull. However, there was a Geiger counter which responded well to the radiation from my watch. An Indian Chief Minister came in to see me on some matters so secret that we never really talked about them. He did ask me if our house was bugged.

January 10 — New Delhi

Washington still hasn't responded on the Indian proposal for a defense bargain so I sent another needling telegram. This delay approaches irresponsibility. For years we have tried to get the Indians to agree that we shouldn't carry the burden in this part of the world alone. Now that they are willing, I can't even get an answer to cables. The problem, of course, is that there is no one who can or is willing to take a lead on the matter. I did get a stupid cable on the Pakistan negotiations. It asked what progress I was making on a campaign that had been proposed some time before Christmas to see various ministers and military chiefs to stress the importance of a settlement. Had I tried anything so obvious, it would be said that the American Ambassador was "mounting a campaign" and it would be highly self-defeating. I will take a leaf from the Department and not bother to answer.

Following the morning meeting, I did fairly routine business and had a pleasant academic lunch with Lloyd and Sue Rudolph,[10] Professor Norman Brown, the leading Indianologist from the University of Pennsylvania, and others. Then I went over to Old Delhi to the onetime Hotel Cecil, now taken over by a Catholic school, where I addressed a visiting seminar group from New York University. This is another junket on Public Law 480 rupees. Somebody asked me where I stood on birth control, evidently thinking I would have to evade the issue in these Catholic precincts. I asked if that was why he asked.

I returned to a meeting on the housewarming which, since we are calling the new Residence The Roosevelt House, we propose to have approximately on Roosevelt's birthday; then on to the airport to greet Mrs. Bandaranaike. She is here from Ceylon as part of her

[10] Students of all matters Indian, then members of the Department of Government at Harvard, now professors at the University of Chicago.

effort to bring peace between India and China. These welcoming ceremonies usually take place on the Air Force side at Palam, but that is now given over to the operations of the C-130's and, anyhow, she was coming in by commercial airlines. Not having other useful occupation, the members of the diplomatic corps were there in force in seats suitably distributed around a large heated tent. There can be few public exercises more banal than these welcoming pilgrimages by the diplomats to the airport. Yet those involved, or some, set great store by them. The Chief of Protocol greeted me and then, in what was meant to be a very pointed remark, said he had not seen me for a long while. That is certainly true. It will be a long time before he sees me there again.

January 12 — New Delhi

New Delhi continues cool in the morning but once again the suggestion of heat is coming into the midday.

The Bandaranaike Mission is here but has brought nothing new. The Chinese have made no new offer and are contenting themselves with efforts to get India around the table. The Indians are being stubborn. In the absence of Chinese concessions, they say they will not agree to discussion. "Unless," Desai told me yesterday, "you let us down." I told him we were not disposed to do so.

My effort to get the Indians to promise a more cooperative role elsewhere has struck a few snags. Someone in Washington gave a rather exaggerated version to B. K. Nehru. The impression was of a virtual alliance. This he reported back. As a result, the Indians here have climbed back. Washington is a highly non-secretive place and I should have counted on this.

The President has wired me expressing considerable skepticism about the idea — he referred to it as GATO — Galbraith's All-Purpose Treaty Organization.[11] I told him it was in the tradition of Dulles, and that I had my eye on a commemorative airport. Then I stressed a point with which I think he will agree — that we should

---

[11] An invention of Carl Kaysen. The skepticism had merit.

deal with the Indians on the basis of equal concern over security and stable relations with China, that this is the basis for a self-respecting relationship, and that this point needs to be tied down. (I also reminded him that I was reflecting his desire for a more widely shared concern for peace and stability in Asia.)

Last night we had a showing of the President's television review of the first two years of his Administration. It was extremely well-received and admired as, indeed, it deserved to be.

Today we reviewed the prospect for the Pakistan talks and the Chinese outlook. General Kelly questioned whether we should sell the Indians arms for rupees at a time when the British were providing them free. I explained that the two came to about the same thing — that the Indians merely printed the rupees and didn't really do that but only credited the figures to an account. Back of this was a plan to assert the independence of the military operation. Free arms would be something between the Indian Ministry of Defence and our Department of Defense. I kept the transaction between the Indian Government and U.S. Government, which obviously does things for the Ambassador.

January 15 — New Delhi

The crisis continues to simmer down. The Bandaranaike Mission has now departed, the Indians having accepted most of its proposals. As long as the Indians thought the Chinese had accepted the proposals in principle, they rejected them in principle. When it became evident that the Chinese had largely rejected the proposals, the Indians accepted in principle, rejecting only the things they didn't like. (They learned these techniques, no doubt, from our dealings with the Soviets.) I predict continued bickering, but no real fighting. The Pakistanis are coming in tomorrow. Similar tactics may be in order. What we applaud in the case of the Chinese, we regret in the case of the Pakistanis.

It is remarkable, incidentally, how hard-nosed one becomes on

China. I used always to take a relatively tolerant view. A few more months and I will be as warlike as anyone.

The Stebbinses have been here for the last few days from Nepal. They have been partly on vacation and are in high good spirits. Relations between India and the Kingdom of Nepal have taken a turn for the better. The border raids that were so troubling to the King (and which the Indians could not prevent) have been stopped.

Last night at ten o'clock, I was called to Air House — the Indian Air Force headquarters — to talk about assistance on air training. This looked forward to large-scale offensive operations which made no sense whatever. Plans were for eighteen months hence and could as well have been for eighteen years — or never. Equally exaggerated ideas were in circulation about the efficacy of air power. These are the occupational illusions of all air generals of all nations and especially of Americans. I delivered some useful education.

The Indian Chargé in Peking, an intelligent man, came in to see me this evening. He talked in an interesting way about life in Peking. Food is scarce but there is no absolute starvation. There are few consumer goods in the stores and the priority is now first on food, second on light industry and last on heavy industry, a complete reversal in the last couple of years. Diplomats have to get permission to travel more than twenty miles out of Peking, and the Indians go everywhere under surveillance. Chinese must have an identification ticket to visit the Indian Embassy. The Chinese Foreign Office does its business between ten o'clock at night and the small hours of the morning. Altogether, it doesn't seem to be a pleasant post, but he seems to thrive on it.

This evening with the Stebbinses, we went over to the Rashtrapati Bhavan and strolled in the Moghul Gardens. The fountains were on and the gardens are at their most brilliant. All the beds are in full flower — pansies, roses, nasturtiums, foxglove. It is quite grand. The garden façade of the Rashtrapati Bhavan is low, almost

Italianate in appearance, but with Moghul touches in the towers and dome and, of course, in the salmon pink sandstone.

I have been bombarding Washington with telegrams. I want to keep them from pressing me so hard on Pakistan that I force the Indians to make peace with the Chinese. Actually, I have no intention of going that far. But Washington will have no excuse for being unaware of my thinking on the subject.

January 16 — New Delhi

I met with Z. A. Bhutto, the Pakistan Foreign Minister and leader of their delegation, this morning. He is an intelligent man of conciliatory mood, I think.[12] I braced him on the importance of keeping the talks with India going, not walking out in frustration. The day went on in routine fashion with a lunch for various ambassadors whom my wife thinks we have been neglecting and to which I added Dr. Sabin of the vaccine. In the evening, I pressed the Indians on keeping the Pakistan talks going. Then I went to a Pakistan reception and on to one for the Premier of Lebanon. Our Ambassador in Lebanon had wired asking me to tell the Premier what a straightforward and honest man we thought he was. This, I thought, might imply that these were exceptional qualities in Lebanon. It seemed more tactful to be silent.

I am a little uneasy about being away tomorrow in case the negotiations blow up. I have a long-standing date to welcome our Indian Ocean fleet, or at least its flagship, to Bombay. The flagship is a tiny seaplane tender without seaplanes. I think I can safely go.

January 18 — Bombay

Yesterday morning, we took off at 8 A.M. for Bombay and en route I did a new article on the researches of Dr. McLandress. This concerns the class system in the United States; it seems sensible. We got to Bombay at 11 A.M. and Milton Rewinkel, the new Consul-General, had arranged a schedule of appalling magnitude.

---

[12] A fellow alumnus of the University of California at Berkeley.

At the Consulate-General, I made some final arrangements connected with the new Tarapur atomic power plant, received Admiral Semmes and then returned his call on shipboard. There, after being piped on, I reviewed an honor guard, chatted in the cabin for ten minutes, was piped off and then, standing to a hundred yards or so off the ship in the Admiral's barge, received my nineteen-gun salute. I learned later that at this precise moment on shore, a fairly low-level British cabinet minister was making a call on the Governor of Maharashtra. He heard the nineteen guns, thought they were for him, was greatly pleased and came smartly to attention.

Back at the Consulate, there was a largish lunch. An hour of drinking preceded the food. As noted, in New Delhi I have eliminated this barbarous (and drunken) custom but there has been backsliding in Bombay. The lunch itself was pleasant enough, with good food. I had a long chat with Sir Homi Mody, a brilliant old reactionary who is great fun. He accused me of giving comfort and support to Nehru who, he believes, will later make a deal with the Chinese. At a later press conference, I declined to answer a question which, I said, was designed not to elicit information but to score points off Pakistan. This got mild applause — a considerable change.

A few days ago, Senator Russell of Georgia said that India shouldn't get arms aid because she would promptly lose the weapons to the Chinese. This has aroused great anger. I calmed nerves by saying that I wouldn't dream of protesting any statement about the United States made by any Indian legislator. Then I urged reciprocity.

Back at the Consulate again — it takes about half an hour to cross Bombay — the Rewinkels had organized a vast reception for some five hundred people and we stood in line for a weary hour or two as people filed in and out. Then we took off for the Gateway of India, the Admiral's barge and the U.S.S. *Greenwich Bay* for dinner. This was completely pleasant. We sat on easy chairs on the foredeck which was draped with signal flags. Mrs. Pandit was there; so were various naval types. Dinner was hearty and good, and Kitty and I were comfortably housed for the night on board. However, either fatigue or the proximity to the water brought on a terrible attack of sinus. I woke up this morning suffering the punishment of the justly damned.

We took off from Santa Cruz Airport at 8 A.M. and were back in Delhi at 11 A.M. I went to bed for a few hours to work off the effects of the codeine. Then at 3:30 P.M., I called on Swaran Singh to persuade him to be more forthcoming in the India-Pakistan talks. I gallantly pointed out that ten years from now people would not remember who gave what away. They would remember only the names of the men that made the settlement and ushered in the new era of goodwill and prosperity. Then I went to see Bhutto on the Pakistan side to persuade him. I had no effect on either. But at this moment no one wants to break off the talks. I then sandwiched in an hour at my desk and have yet this evening to dine with the straightforward and honest Prime Minister of Lebanon.

January 19 — New Delhi

The talks between India and Pakistan resemble badminton. The arrangement was to talk a few days first in Pakistan, now a few days in India. The thing is to get the shuttle back in the other court; so I have concentrated my efforts to get through these three days without disaster and to get out a communiqué promising another meeting. So much I have achieved. A few minutes ago, the negotiators announced that they would meet again early next month in Karachi. I must invent some way of carrying things a step further before they assemble again. Although the Department won't like it, perhaps we should come up with some proposal and perhaps also somebody who would act as mediator. Deep in my heart, I know nothing will come of the effort, although new pressure from the Chinese might have some effect.

The Department has found one of the Jo Davidson busts of

Roosevelt for the new Residence. It is one of ten purchased from the Davidson estate.

I face some problems with General Kelly. He is an energetic, determined and thoroughly excellent officer, and he is untroubled by any commitment to tact or diplomacy. The Indians are about to declare war on him in the absence of any Chinese to shoot at. Our own military attachés are very unhappy. I am going to see if I can get him to be a little more conciliatory.

The Chinese are talking about Indian provocations out of Sikkim. This is dangerous and must be watched. If they were ever making a serious attack on India, they would do it there. But I have trouble supposing that, having retired, they will soon come back. Still, nobody expected them to come in the first place.

Today was Kitty's birthday. I bought her a ring shawl[13] and a very nice brooch. Tonight we are having a party, the first really festive event in the new Residence.

January 22 — New Delhi

The Polish Foreign Minister, Rapacki, has been visiting here. Last night I got word that he wanted to talk to me about Vietnam. I met him, along with the Secretary-General of the Polish Foreign Office, at M. J. Desai's house. They told me while we probably couldn't lose in South Vietnam, we couldn't win. Meanwhile, we are forcing North Vietnam to look more and more to the Chinese for protection. This is bad. Why not get a liberal government in South Vietnam which all could support? In return, Ho Chi Minh would call off the insurrection. I had to improvise for, of course, I was without instruction. So I countered by asking why not call off the insurrection for six months and with this manifestation of good faith, we could then withdraw. They said that North Vietnam could not get peace in the south so long as Diem was in charge. They said (approximately), "You know enough of Marx yourself

13 Made of material so fine and so finely spun that a large shawl can be drawn easily through a small wedding ring.

to know about popular movements."[14] I responded, "But you should be good enough Communists to know about the international leadership of the Communist movement." They replied that, under present circumstances, given the split between Russia and China, any reference to international leadership was to a myth. I noted that if it were easy to throw out leaders such as Diem, we would have thrown out Castro. But we weren't that powerful.[15]

I had another less important session on Iron Curtain matters today with the Bulgarian Ambassador, Lubomir Popov. He came in in an ebullient mood and gave me his life history. It was much more interesting than most. He told me that he was a Communist by birth. His father had been a Communist, so was his mother, and so, accordingly, was he. His father, a shoemaker, was shot in 1923. He is leaving India after four-and-a-half years and hopes — like almost everyone — that his next assignment may be in the United States.[16]

In an otherwise humdrum day, I had lunch with Lord Bridges, the former chief of the British Treasury (and thus of the Civil Service) who now runs the British Council, and had a long talk with some of the Indian participants in the Kashmir talks. It is just possible that the Indians might give the Pakistanis the northeastern end of the Kashmir Valley and right of access to the rest with vice versa rights for India in the Pakistani part. And this might be accepted by the Pakistanis. Thus, there is a bare chance of settlement. I don't think it is good, but neither is it completely impossible.

Interestingly, a telegram has just come in from the Department

[14] The reference is to my *American Capitalism: The Concept of Countervailing Power* (Boston: Houghton Mifflin, 1952, 1956), which is regarded by some Marxian scholars as showing enlightened Marxist influences.

[15] This conversation was, of course, promptly reported. It was ignored by the State Department but picked up from the cables by President Kennedy. He told Harriman to have me pursue the matter as he was much interested. By the time his instruction came, Rapacki had departed.

[16] It was. On arrival, he enchanted President Kennedy with an equally entertaining account of the life and education of a Bulgarian Bolshevist.

with roughly similar proposals. I would feel a little happier if the next round were here rather than in Karachi. I don't have much confidence in McConaughy as a salesman. He is rather nervous.

January 24 — New Delhi

This morning after a long walk, we reviewed the Pakistan proposal and the Colombo proposals. I then had a background briefing for the American press. Very often at these sessions I have little to say that the boys don't know. This morning, however, the air defense proposals had come suddenly to their attention — a team to study the matter was announced last night in Washington and here. I said that this was in response to a request by the Indians. I then volunteered the information that the Indians had been thinking of an arrangement by which American squadrons might be called in for the protection of Indian cities in the event of attack.[17] Although this idea of an "air umbrella" has been talked of around town, and has come up in press conferences with the Indians, it hit our correspondents a mighty blow. They plunged into it avidly, more avidly than I had expected. They wanted to know whether the Indians had discussed it with the Soviets, if it meant a military alliance, an end of nonalignment. By the end of the press conference, I had become considerably alarmed about the impact on Washington, and, to a lesser extent, on the Indians. Accordingly, I quickly dictated a telegram to Washington giving an outline of the conference and sent it NIACT to arrive at the same time as the morning papers. There won't be any cheers over my releasing this news. However, it was bound to creep out step by step. And silence was playing into the hands of the British who were systematically watering down the discussion.

[17] During this time, there was new talk of the need by India for supersonic planes. These would, as I have noted, be vastly expensive, would arouse Pakistan and would soon be obsolete. (Few things are more absurd than impoverished countries spending millions a copy on these gadgets.) I was increasingly interested in the air defense arrangements as a highly economical substitute. However, I doubt that I was entirely immune to the activist aspects of such diplomacy. This delight in "doing something" is a constant threat to good sense.

My concern about the Indians was not justified. I showed M.E.A. a copy of the telegram I had sent to Washington and they were unperturbed.

Speaking of double-dealing, there is a mild measure of this in an operation such as today's. The telegram in which I reported the press conference to Washington faithfully recited the exact information that had been conveyed in the press conference. Nonetheless, in the press conference, I gave the impression that this was a proposal of dramatic importance and I managed in the telegram back to Washington to imply that my whole comment had been extremely quiet and innocuous.

These activities took all morning. However, we had a pleasant and relaxed lunch with Kenneth Kauffman,[18] the Brzezinskis[19] and Joan Robinson.[20] Joan is teaching here and it was like dropping back twenty-five years to a Cambridge conversation. I asked Joan how she was managing to keep her famous pro-Chinese sympathies under control in India. She said her support of China did not extend to its foreign policy.

We had a lively discussion of Chinese-Russian relations. Ideological differences are not the problem. Where popular interests diverge, so must governments. This is especially so of countries of considerable size. Possibly the Poles can conform their interests to those of the Soviets. The Chinese cannot — and need not.

Next, I had a press conference with the Indian press. They were interested in the air defense proposals but less so than the Americans. They are now so disciplined that almost no one will raise the subject of Pakistan. When somebody did tonight, I said we were seeking a settlement for the same reason that the Chinese Communists and the C.P.I. (Communist Party, India) were seeking

[18] Of the AID staff, formerly instructor and associate at Harvard.

[19] Zbigniew and Muska Brzezinski of Columbia University, friends and former Harvard colleagues. He later served with vigor, not unmarked by controversy, on the Policy Planning Staff of the State Department.

[20] The famous economist of Cambridge University and wife of Professor E. A. G. Robinson, see page 525.

to divert attention to Pakistan and thus to drive a wedge between the two countries. Everyone subsided.

I went to see the Prime Minister at 6:30 P.M. at Parliament where we discussed some fairly secret defense matters. Then I congratulated him on the progress last week on the Kashmir settlements. He said Swaran Singh had done a good job and I asked him to extend his approval to Bhutto. I told him of a $250 million loan to India which we are announcing next week and asked that it not be treated by the Indians with excessive secrecy. He said it wouldn't be. He expressed great satisfaction over the name of our new house.[21]

January 28 — New Delhi

This was Republic Day weekend. The actual celebrations took place day before yesterday and included a lengthy parade. I missed it last year but its reputation was very good. This year, austerity had set in. Folk dancers and other colorful adjuncts were omitted. There were some very impressive bands at the beginning, then some schoolchildren in costume. Then for an hour or two, the citizens and students of the community strolled by proclaiming their civic duty. It was comparable in both interest and discipline with a crowd moving away from a Harvard football game.

As I have indicated, the State Department has come up with a rather sensible compromise on Kashmir. They transmitted it, along with the detailed strategy for selling it to the Pakistanis, to Karachi the other day. Some genius allowed it to go by commercial cable without encoding it. The Pakistanis must have read with interest how they were to be seduced.

My friend McConaughy lives in constant fear of President Ayub. Today he sent a telegram proposing that the air defense

[21] The name, The Roosevelt House, was my idea, but it had President Kennedy's warm approval. There are very few official monuments to F.D.R. For a long while, to name a school or park for him was to invite a hideous row with the Roosevelt-haters. So controversy was avoided. I had rather hoped that naming this house for him would provoke a minor outbreak on the Congressional far right but, alas, it went unnoticed. Or, more likely, memories have now dimmed.

team, which is to arrive Wednesday, stop over for a briefing by Ayub. This would mean that if the recommendations do not come up to Indian hopes, all can believe it was because the Pakistanis exercised a veto power. I put my foot down.

The opening of The Roosevelt House tomorrow has stirred everybody to great effort. New trees have been planted in the garden and it has taken on a nice leafy aspect. Flowers have been brilliantly distributed around the front of the house and a large stage has been erected at the back of the swimming pool for a performance by the Robert Joffrey Ballet that is here. Less spectacularly, I have ordered a general clean-up of the staff — coats to be brushed, trousers to be pressed, shoes to be shined and shirts to be cleaned. All we need now is good weather.[22]

February 6 — New Delhi

I have missed these notes for several days. Over the weekend, we went out to Udaipur to be present at the opening ceremonies of the new Lake Palace Hotel. This is a white marble palace in the middle of the lake. Nearby is the island with a beautiful palace where Shah Jahan once lived. Opposite is the big palace on the shore. It is the nearest thing to a child's fairy castle anywhere in the world — at least the nearest that is habitable. The hotel is still highly incomplete[23] and we stayed as the guests of the Maharana on the shore in the big round bedroom allotted a year ago to Mrs. Kennedy.

I spent most of the time in bed with a virus infection. We did go briefly to the opening ceremonies on Shah Jahan's Island where there was dancing, a band and cold pork in the grease. And we took a trip around Pichola Lake and looked at the great variety of water fowl and also some massive alligators which inhabit the local

---

[22] The weather was excellent and the house duly and ceremoniously declared open.

[23] See page 325.

water. The latter are a priceless asset for they will greatly discourage water skiing.

I was also visited by the local dealer in Rajput miniatures. He sells originals and copies quite indiscriminately. Some of the copies are sufficiently competent to deserve a higher price than the originals. The first tourists at the hotel were snapping up his imitation Kishangarhs for around Rs. 700 ($140.00). If the hotel succeeds, this man and his fellow forgers are in clover.

I got back Monday morning and was put to bed, but then I stirred out from time to time for conferences with the Prime Minister and Swaran Singh. Phil Talbot was here last week and he left the Pakistan negotiations in a gluey state of confusion. Dealing with him is like playing badminton with a marshmallow — you don't know whether he is going to stick or bounce. The Pakistanis, perhaps because they had read our proposals on the Valley, have decided to go back to their old stand for a plebiscite. Talbot doesn't have the courage to conclude that a settlement is improbable — a stand that would invite criticism from the uninformed in Washington. He also feels that to admit this might cause me to relax my efforts. So he and McConaughy have arranged to believe that the Pakistan position is still malleable. Meanwhile, toward the end of the week, the Pakistan Ambassador in Washington went in to see the President and told him that the only hope for a settlement was for us to jump in with both feet and tell the Indians they must surrender the Valley or have a plebiscite. The President declined. Talbot has now moved on to London. There, in one of his random-thought conferences, it has been decided, against the weight of all evidence, to try and sell the partition idea.

Accordingly, I got out of bed and went to work on Swaran Singh and Nehru. Gore-Booth supported my efforts. Perhaps we made some progress. I don't think the Indians entirely rule out giving the Pakistanis some position in the Valley. Nehru's face did not brighten perceptibly this evening when I brought up the idea, but he did not throw me out.

February 7 — New Delhi

It has proved impossible to stay in bed so I simply ignored the doctor and feel no worse for doing it. The higher the rank, the more you are protected. A junior Foreign Service Officer suffering from my present malady would probably be told only to wear dry socks.

One of my visitors today, who looked interesting at first glance, was a girl who is doing a book on the beauties of India. The only one of which she had ever heard was the Taj Mahal.

General Clay is heading a committee to review the AID program. He has decided that there must be no assistance to Bokaro as long as it is in the public sector. In other words, for blatant ideological reasons, he is going back to the policies of the Eisenhower Administration. These were a grievous failure. Nothing substantial was done to advance private investment; and they talked about it enough to cause everyone to suppose our concern was to sustain capitalism rather than help the Indians. I have shifted to a purely pragmatic policy of doing whatever works. This even relaxes the tension on private enterprise.

I have written a careful rebuttal to Clay making it clear that he would lose sadly in any effort to carry his case to the public. I sent the message unclassified so that he won't be in any doubt as to my willingness to do so. He has just joined Lehman Brothers in New York and will not want to start his banking career there with a public brawl. As for me, I would welcome it.

I am having a dinner tonight for Henry Alexander. I worked with him nearly twenty years ago in the war and have seen almost nothing of him since. In recent years, he has been head of Morgan's and laterally Morgan-Guaranty Trust. In 1945, he told me he found banking a bore. Now he has had two decades more of it.

February 11 — New Delhi

Over the weekend, there was another round of talks on Kashmir in Karachi. Timmons went over. He has not yet come back, so we are only indirectly aware of what happened, but evidently after numerous perils, they managed to agree on a fourth round in Calcutta. And they seem in a vague way to have got down to looking at maps. The Indians are, I assume, closing in on the Khyber Pass and I expect the Pakistan claim stops just short of Tokyo. However, in the end, agreement can only come by some such process as this. Both the *New York Times* and the *Herald Tribune* carry stories from Karachi to the effect that the Indians are willing to give Pakistan a foothold in the Valley. If this is so, it is proof of the success of my salesmanship here. I don't quite believe it.

We are out of touch with Karachi because our communications depend on a link somewhere in Iraq. Yesterday morning the *Principal Officers Summary*, a document sent out each day by the State Department on developments in various parts of the world, carried a thoughtful estimate from our Embassy in Baghdad of the local situation. General Kassem, it told, had just consolidated his position by an effective action which disbursed and disposed of opposition officers. The local newspapers simultaneously carried slightly later news that Kassem had been killed and his government thrown out. For the next several months, every ambassador will warn his staff against reaching any conclusions. However, the immediate effect of all this, as I started to say, was to interrupt our communications with Karachi.

The first shipload of furniture for the new house arrived today. It is quite light and gay and goes very well with the main drawing room. However, one or two borax numbers in shiny veneer are straight from Sears circa 1920.

One of the problems we will face this summer is what to do about our personal zoo. It now consists of a dog, two deer and two horses. I am especially fond of the deer and they of me. I visit the larger one every day and he comes stalking over to meet me with great dignity and grace. He is learning to stand up on his hind legs in a kind of salute.

Last evening after dinner, we drove over to see Humayun's

Tomb by full moon. This, the precursor of the Taj Mahal, is made of a combination of white marble and red sandstone. The scale and proportions are roughly comparable with the Taj. The moonlight picks out the marble and lets the sandstone slip into the background. While it is a handsome structure by day, after dark it is a glittering gem. Few people ever see it after dark, which is a pity.

The local newspapers carry a certain amount of static about the air defense arrangements. Some left-wing Congressmen have seen their Prime Minister to tell him of their misgivings. Inspired stories in the opposition press say that Nehru has not made up his mind (even though he requested the arrangements) and warn that no foreign planes may be stationed in India. They warn further that the nonalignment policy is threatened. One must help defend India in a properly neutral way.

February 13 — New Delhi

During the morning, I had a session with a group of men who are here at the Indians' request to advise the Indian Army on the techniques of special warfare. These are the informal, but not secret, tactics for dealing with unconventional enemies in an unconventional way. It naturally attracts adventurers and bounders of various sorts. I gave them a firm lecture on the need for the utmost tact, restraint and diplomacy. I said they should prove to the Indian Government that its well-justified suspicions of them are somehow erroneous.

A man came in to present me with a pile of Tibetan literature, which I sent to Harvard. I was interviewed for half an hour for a radio network; then we had lunch for several visitors including a peripatetic poet and a woman of evident distinction whose purpose in life I did not get.

This afternoon was equally rushed, ending with a press conference and a big reception for newly arrived members of the military mission. I had no idea we had accumulated so many soldiers. I am always struck with how shapeless colonels look in civilian clothes.

One gave me the encouraging news that, although forty-five and with a notable middle-aged spread, he is still able to fly Mach 2 fighters. He says he improves with age. Several younger officers jeered audibly at his contention.

In the late afternoon, Mr. Sharma, my art adviser (i.e., a dealer), showed up with six beautiful Kulu Valley paintings. I bought four of them. I also bought a marvelous blue Kangra, early nineteenth century.[24]

February 18 — New Delhi

Kitty and the boys and I went up to Jammu for the weekend and stayed with Karan Singh[25] whose palace is situated on a ridge above the city with a magnificent view of the Himalayas. The palace itself is rather unattractive. An adjacent Victorian palace, of Canadian Pacific Railway Gothic, houses a fine collection of miniatures. One afternoon, I lectured to the graduate students in economics at the University and another afternoon we went on a picnic. It was a quiet and highly agreeable interlude.

The Maharajah's wife is a Nepali Rana (Class A)[26] and one of the most beautiful women I have ever met — black hair, a strange fair coloring and rich dark eyes. She is also very intelligent. She was married when she was fourteen; the Maharajah's father selected her and the bride and groom met twenty-four hours prior to the marriage. The father selected very well; these matters should be left to men of mature judgment and taste.

This morning at the airport, a brake drum on the plane seemed to be loose, and we had to make a trial run to see it did not freeze up. It did not, and the fire engine that greeted us at Palam also turned out to be unnecessary.

[24] Not quite this good. Indeed, it did not wear well at all.
[25] For the account of our previous visit to him, see pages 200–202.
[26] This family, the ancient de facto rulers of Nepal, sensibly classify members in accordance with the degrees of legitimacy of offspring, i.e., of wives, concubines, etc., etc.

Over the weekend, disaster overtook the air defense proposal. The left opposition hit the P.M. very hard. In fact, they do not like it at all. The Prime Minister detached himself from the proposals; the idea of an "air umbrella" was an invention of the press. An air defense team was here, he said, at his invitation to consider how to strengthen the defenses of India. All this has caused endless harm in the United States or could. By this morning, I had assembled a chronology of the various requests from the Indian Government, all of which were quite categorical, and this afternoon, I took them over to M.E.A. They agreed that the team was here at the invitation of the Indian Government but hedged on the idea of American and Commonwealth squadrons having been asked to come in. They were having, they said, to be very cautious because of the Russians. I urged that that was no reason for being rough with us. We couldn't seem to be insisting on moving in. We were only responding in good faith to requests for help made at a time of great danger. It was agreed that the Prime Minister would clarify things in the Lok Sabha in the next day or so.

Today was the opening of Parliament and I attended. As usual, it was a highly colorful gathering with many varieties of costumes and turbans. There was some static in the beginning while various members demanded that President Radhakrishnan speak in Hindi. He persisted in English and was accorded a round of applause when he thanked the United States and the U.K. for their prompt response to India's pleas for military assistance.

February 20 — New Delhi

The air defense business seems to be back on the rails. The Prime Minister said it wasn't an "air umbrella" but an armada that would come to the defense of India. Washington seems not to have been too perturbed, perhaps because I managed to get things put right in time.

The last three days have been intensely busy, much of the time with superficialities. I got off a long airgram to the Department

putting General Clay right on Bokaro[27] which I again sent unclassified so that it would have the largest possible readership with every
possible threat of leakage. I noted again that the previous administration had talked about supporting private enterprise while
financing the public sector. They thus got the worst of both
worlds. We were stopping the talk, cooling the debate over private
and public enterprise and had done very much better as a result.

I also got off a long telegram to the Department of Defense inquiring into the rationale of the present distribution of military aid
funds. These go principally to Korea, Formosa and South Vietnam, the places we hold after defeat by the Communists. The one
place where we have had a modicum of success has been India.
Here we are determined to economize. I asked the Joint Chiefs of
Staff if it is a new canon of military policy to reinforce failure
rather than success. I ventured the prediction that if the Chinese
should come back and drive the Indian Government to the Anda-
man Islands, we would then unquestionably see India as a bastion
of the free world and finance it heavily. I wondered, would it not
be better to spend less money and hold the mainland. Such telegrams do not get action but they recruit a certain number of
advocates.

This afternoon, in accordance with a well-considered plan, I
made the first speech in some months. Our critics on the left are
stirring out from under their stones. So I reacted. I said we are
not offering the Indian Government anything which they have not
asked for. This was particularly true of air defense. I gave our
reasons for seeking a Pakistan settlement. We seek to narrow differences as the Chinese seek to widen them. By mild implication,
I suppose, anyone who fosters dislike for Pakistan is mildly pro-
Chinese. It was a good audience and a good crisp speech and I
enjoyed giving it.

This morning, I had a long meeting with the President and lunch
with G. D. Birla. I bent Birla's opulent ear on the Pakistan issue

[27] See page 544.

and persuaded him to have a word with the P.M. on the importance of keeping the talks going.

I ended the day at the inaugural session of the Congress on Diseases of the Chest. A few weeks ago, there was a great conclave of ophthalmologists in Delhi. I did not get there, being heavily engaged with the Chinese at that time. Later they went home and one eye doctor complained bitterly of my neglect to Everett McKinley Dirksen.[28] I had already heard of some dissatisfaction and the probable complaint so I got to Dirksen first with a letter of explanation. But I decided to be nicer to these visitors. Following the opening, there were inaugural awards to some fifty people. In the confusion of people going up to get their scrolls, I managed to duck out. Both the President and the Prime Minister were there, a remarkable tribute to chest diseases.

The *Indian Express*[29] this morning carried the news of my departure and prospective replacement by Bowles. I told the papers that I am most likely going back to Harvard in the fall and also told my staff. The latter accepted the news with commendable equanimity.

February 22 — New Delhi

This morning, *The Statesman*[29] carried a simple factual item from Rawalpindi stating that Bhutto, the Pakistan Foreign Minister, would go in the next few days to Peking to sign a border agreement. Later in the day, it was confirmed. It means once again that the Chinese have moved with great skill and audacity to drive a wedge between the Indians and Pakistanis. And the situation is now extremely difficult. If we press the Indians too hard or even press them at all on Pakistan, they will see it as pressure to sell out to China or so describe it. However, in discussions this afternoon, the Indians seemed to be less put off than I expected.

The air defense team has finished up its work. General J. B.

[28] Minority Leader, United States Senate.
[29] English language papers.

Tipton came in today to report. He is a boyish-looking man just turned Major General and not very articulate. At the end of an hour, I got the general idea that he thought it practical to have squadrons come in to defend Indian cities. They could bring radar with them or the Indians could set up the requisite radar screen. It is going to be expensive. I am not sure that the Indians will agree to the idea of joint practice, and this seems to be an essential feature.

Nehru issued a clarification of the whole idea to the Parliament yesterday, which was a masterpiece of accommodation. He assured the left that there would be no foreign bases. (None were ever intended.) He denied that there was any project for an "air umbrella." (This was quite safe. No one has ever said what an air umbrella was.) He promised new planes to the Indian Air Force but said that strips would be prepared so that in an emergency, friendly countries could help India. This of course was the main point.

Yesterday I left at 10 A.M. and flew down to Phoolbagh[30] where I participated in a workshop on agricultural universities and gave a lecture on the relationship between science and service in an agricultural college. It was nice to get back to old familiar topics. After lunch, I met with the Peace Corps who are making friends and doing a very good job in poultry husbandry. They presented me with an egg filled with sand and inscribed with their names. It is a nice-looking egg but not very edible. We left at three and were back at four. We had planned to go to Ranikhet[31] for the weekend, but there were too many problems.

[30] See page 202. Site of the Agricultural University of Uttar Pradesh.
[31] A hill station in the Himalayas once greatly favored as an escape from the heat of the Ganges Plain.

XXV

Kashmir and Hope Cooke

March 4 — New Delhi

These notes have lagged because nothing of great consequence has happened in the last ten days. The State Department convened a meeting in London to talk about the Kashmir talks. Those attending talked for some twenty hours and agreed on doing what was already being done. I got a long and elaborate and meaningless telegram which said I should do what I had told them I was already doing.[1]

A week ago in a mild fit of synthetic anger, I said I was not going to attend any further meetings on Kashmir. The Pakistanis have a mission in China negotiating a border settlement. This makes it hard to press the Indians. So I said I would steer clear of the Calcutta session. Everyone has since been around trying to persuade me to go. In the end, of course, I agreed.

On Saturday, Kitty and I took the new small Army plane, which we have had for several months but with no occasion to use, to Bikaner. This is far out in the desert and was a large and relatively well-administered Princely State. The palaces are handsome and well preserved. The oldest is a pleasant Moghul-type red sandstone fort, of great extent, with fine stone carving and a commanding view out over the desert. A large residential palace built circa

---

[1] These meetings of middle-level officials, held in great solemnity, are among the world's more ceremonious boondoggles. It is a great mistake to imagine that only congressmen enjoy travel. So do officials, great and small, and they are far less frequently criticized for their pleasure.

1920 is also pleasant; a smaller one in the country in Esso Modern of the 1940's is totally hideous. The medium-age palace is densely populated with trophies. The grandfather of the present Maharajah is reported as having shot some one hundred and thirty tigers, plus or minus, and the carcasses of all are displayed, along with deer, black buck, rhinoceroses, lions and others without number. It is a remarkable example of how man enhances his vanity by matching his skill against animals. One wishes the animals had won just once.

One is also struck (as later at Jodhpur) with how princely prestige still depends on identification with Britain and the Royal Family. Pictures proving intimacy are everywhere displayed and deeply prized.

Saturday evening, we went out to yet another small palace some fifteen or twenty miles from Bikaner by the side of a lake. Here we were taken on a chase (benign) of black buck and deer by jeep. The black buck can outrun the safe speed of the jeep, but lack the staying power. They start out with great long leaps of ten or fifteen feet, but these get shorter and shorter and eventually they are overtaken.

At noon on Sunday, the plane picked us up and took us to Jodhpur, also capital of the erstwhile Princely State. In the afternoon, we visited a vast new palace, a massive pile of 250 rooms begun, partly for work relief it is said, in the twenties, and in the evening, drove out to the ancient capital at Mandor and the gardens of the Maharajah by a tank — all very pleasant. Jodhpur struck me as one of the most prosperous cities in India. The people are well dressed, the shops good. There are masses of bicycles and quite a few cars and the standard of living must be far higher than in, say, Benares. While the land is far less fertile, there are proportionately far fewer people to compete for its product. Malthus is evidently a greater enemy of Indian prosperity than a shortage of water.

This morning, we got up early and went out to the tank for a swim and then spent another hour-and-a-half clambering over the old fortress. This is an enormous pile on top of a large mesalike hill near the center of the city — the whole combination of rock and battlements being several hundred feet high. Some of the stone carvings are magnificent and the battlements command a spectacular view. No castle I have ever seen is more grand with the single exception of Krak des Chevaliers in Syria. More remarkably, it is still the property of the Maharajah and still used for ceremonial purposes. (The Maharajah, a boy in his teens, is at Eton.) In this part of Rajasthan, feudalism is only about fifteen years in the background. At noon, after a visit to the University and to the museum, we took off and were back in Delhi by half-past two.

March 7 — New Delhi

Today was University of Chicago day at the Residence. Theodore Schultz, the Milton Friedmans and Charles Hardins all came.[2] We had a pleasant and lively conversation on the excessive discipline in the Indian academic community. It is a fact. The universities are a tight hierarchy and the man who sticks his neck out may not get promoted. Habit has something to do with it. Also, the universities are new and the people lack the assertiveness which goes with self-confidence as well as competence. However, I think the decisive factor is the extreme importance of a job. Anybody who risks his job risks starvation. This induces a great caution. The same thing was true until at least recent times of land grant colleges in the United States. The man who exposed himself and lost his job had to become a farm machinery salesman or go back to the farm. Accordingly, he played it safe.

I have made the rounds and have persuaded the Indians of the importance of patience in the forthcoming talks. But I have little hope of progress.

[2] All professors or former professors at the University of Chicago. Professor Friedman is the world's foremost friend of the free market. I suggested to him that nowhere in the world, the Soviet Union excepted, would he do less damage than in India. He seemed pleased.

March 12 — Calcutta

The fourth round of these dismal talks on Kashmir are now on. We left Delhi yesterday afternoon about four o'clock and got to Bhopal at six. Bhopal, now the capital of Madhya Pradesh, was once the capital of a Princely State by the same name. It is a rather neglected place scattered around the shores of a couple of lakes. After a suitably ceremonial arrival, I called on the Governor, whose guests we were at the Raj Bhavan, and then on the Chief Minister. The latter is a stolid Congress politician. The food at the formal dinner at the Raj Bhavan left something to be desired. One of my dinner companions, however, was Her Highness, the Begum of Bhopal. This house has been dominated by women for many generations. She is lively and intelligent and still retains what must have been phenomenally good looks — dark hair, slightly silvered, and a strong aquiline and amused face. She was wearing last night, as again this morning, a totally plain, very rich white sari. This is a Moslem house; she inherited it when her older sister after Independence went to Pakistan.

This morning, there was a ceremonial breakfast at the Chief Minister's — raw spinach and cashew nuts. We then went back to the Raj Bhavan, where I made a speech announcing a loan of $25 million for a hydroelectric project. I urged conservation of electric power by charging adequate prices. This was followed by a press conference at which everyone wanted to talk not about power or even about China but about Pakistan. A representative of *Link*[3] dominated the scene from the front seat; he subsided only after I had pointed out, as so often before, that if the Chinese came back this spring, everyone would wish for a settlement with Pakistan. No one would then remember who had scored points in the current debate.

From the press conference we went to the airport and had a pleasant drink and lunch on board and after a couple of hours' sleep we were down in Calcutta.

[3] A newsmagazine reflecting the views of Krishna Menon.

Selig Harrison of the *Washington Post* came along with us on the plane, and I gave him a fill-in on recent developments. The British High Commissioner in Pakistan, in consort quite possibly with the Pakistan Government, has suddenly come up with the idea that the Valley of Kashmir should be internationalized. McConaughy has been pulled into this idea. The proposal plays immediately into the hands of the Chinese. Susceptible Asian and African powers would become involved in the administration, upon whom the Chinese could work. And, in any case, the Indians can hardly be expected to defend the Valley if it is under international control. I told Harrison about this; some version will doubtless appear in the *Washington Post* tomorrow. This will deeply dismay the State Department. But, as a common consequence of revealed truth, it will also kill the idea. Since arrival, I had a talk with Gore-Booth this evening and gave the idea another severe knock, and now I am on my way to see Bhutto[4] and have dinner. The day is just beginning.

March 15 — Calcutta

The Kashmir talks have ground through another session. They just barely avoided being ridiculous. Nothing was accomplished except an agreement to consider the eviction of Moslems in Tripura. Yesterday afternoon, the Pakistanis came over to say they were going to make a new proposal. But it could only come if the Indians would be responsive. The offer was of a small area around Jammu now held by India. The prospective response was less generous. In the end, the Pakistanis never got around to making their offer, and the Indians, therefore, did not have to respond. Impressed by this progress, the conferees set another date for late in April and adjourned.

Selig Harrison played my leak killing off the internationalization idea; I was reported as opposing it.

Last night, Bhutto had some interesting things to say about his

[4] See page 534.

recent visit to China. Much as they dislike us, he said, they dislike
the Indians more. They are about to go in for birth control in a
big way. There is great drabness and uniformity, but no evident
shortage of food. The Soviets protested to the Chinese against the
signing of the China-Pakistan frontier pact. Mao told Bhutto that
in the event of trouble with India the Chinese and the Soviets would
stand together. Bhutto could not square this with the anti-Indian
bitterness of some of the lesser Chinese officials.

March 22 — Gangtok–Bagdogra

During these last festive days, we have been marrying off Hope
Cooke. We left Tuesday morning after I had crowded a week's
work into Monday and got to Bagdogra around noon. I had asked
various ambassadors and M.E.A. officials to ride with us only to
find that our Convair was out of action. So I had to borrow emergency transport from Karachi.

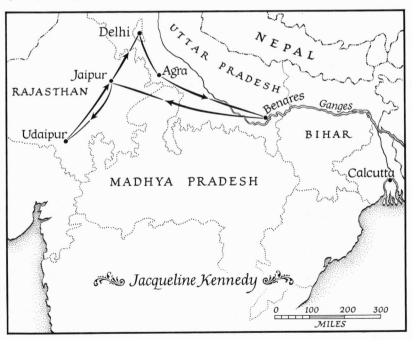

From Bagdogra, we motored and jeeped to a forest rest house in the foothills of the Himalayas where we entertained the party at a picnic lunch and then went on up the Tista Valley to Gangtok. Here we arrived late afternoon and were duly housed in a *basha*. A *basha* is a woven bamboo cottage complete with palm thatch and woven bamboo bathroom. The Gore-Booths were next door; through the bamboo partition, we could hear everything except silent prayers. It was very cold. I shivered throughout the night and woke up feeling fully exercised.

The wedding was in a temple near the palace and was riotously colorful with cherry red robes, furniture and decoration. The Maharajah presided from a high throne; the Maharajkumar, the bridegroom, from a lower one and Hope, the bride, from a slightly lower one still. The ceremony consisted of lengthy intoning of what seemed to be prayers and the ceremonial serving of various foods including rice and tea. It took, cover to cover, about an hour, after which I signed the register as official witness. Then the three principals were presented ceremoniously with silk scarves and the total score was several hundred. Hope disappeared gradually behind the pile. Afterward, my silk hat, which extended my height to something over twice that of the average local citizen, attracted universal derision and much photography.

Following the wedding, a large ceremonial lunch was served in a big marquee on the palace grounds. The food ran out before we arrived, but we got some tea and toast at our *basha*.

In the evening, there was a reception at the palace followed by another dinner and audience in the big tent. Again we missed the food. The dancing was good fun; my arthritic twist got generous attention from the press.

Yesterday I got up at six and at seven, swathed in skiing clothes and with heavy boots, left with the local Divisional Commander for the border. The latter is at Natu La (La means pass) about thirty road-miles from Gangtok. The road must be the most exciting in the world. From Gangtok, which is at 5,000 feet, it goes up the mountainside in wide loops and at times — the so-called gallery section — it is a shelf cut out of the mountainside. Some score or more vehicles have been lost in recent months. The road crosses one pass at twelve or thirteen thousand, drops slightly and goes up to the final pass which is around 14,500. Long before this, the vegetation had given way to sparse mountain firs. Then we crossed the tree line and into an Alpine wilderness. The snow on the road added interest to proceedings although the jeep had chains fore and aft. The general drove himself, not entirely out of democratic instinct.

We had a second breakfast at brigade headquarters by a frozen lake at 12,000 to 13,000 feet and then went on to the top but could not quite reach the pass itself because of the snow. It was cold but not bitterly so. I found I could move at 14,000 feet quite well even in the snow.

I inspected a company of soldiers on the rifle range and looked over numerous other troop dispositions. All of the soldiers — Sikhs, Dogras, Jats, Gurkhas[5] — looked very tough and professional, clean and well-fed and one supposes they would make things difficult for the Chinese. The positions are fairly well dug-in, protected by wire and should be quite hard to budge or pass.

We had lunch again at the frozen lake and then made our way down through the clouds. These on occasion reduced visibility to a few feet; this happened, so it seemed, wherever the road was narrowest and most breathtaking. But in Gangtok, when we reached it again, the sun was shining. I had a nap and then we went on to yet another dinner and dance. At this, we got food and I did another stirring exhibition on the dance floor with the bride. More photographers were attracted, I would judge, than to any dancer since Astaire.

This morning, we got up at six, embarked in autos for Bagdogra and there removed ourselves and diplomatic cargo to the Convair which meantime had been mended. One engine had been recorded

[5] Various of what once were called the martial races of (or serving) India.

as not delivering power. The fault lay, as it developed, with the instrument. This is a clear case where the remedy is to tinker with the thermometer. We are now nearing Delhi.

April 5 — Kathmandu–Delhi

These notes continue sketchy. The Department and the White House have been struggling for the last weeks on Kashmir. I have told them that I will move the Indians if they will promise military aid. That has put the shoe on the other foot. Previously, they have been saying that the Indians must be noble to get aid.

We have had numerous visitors including, most recently, Walt Rostow and Robert Komer.[6] I did not get hold of Rostow's schedule until they arrived. Then I discovered he was here to help me persuade Indians in general and Nehru in particular to be good. This was a waste of time. The Indians heard again from him what they had already heard from me. But it wasn't too bad.

The State Department has four faults:

(1) Rusk is an amiable Chairman of the Board, but not a leader. And he is singularly devoid of any desire to accomplish anything.

(2) Individuals are intelligent. But they are so numerous they cancel each other out.

(3) The senior officers preside but do not work. Thus, telegrams and papers get drafted by cautious subordinates and approved by superiors. One should not dream of delegating even the first draft of an important cable.

(4) Finally, there is an endless faith in oratory and high level representation. I have put in some fine cables on this. I have just noted in a telegram that they have now reduced letters from the President to Nehru to the level of Confederate currency. The President will see and remember this.

Yesterday morning I came up to Nepal in our beat-up Navy plane and on a stretch of wild country outside Kathmandu yesterday afternoon delivered the third commencement address of the Uni-

[6] Member of the National Security Council staff of the White House.

versity. The King functioned as Chancellor and the proceedings were in Nepali. I had no time to write a speech, but took off from one I gave a year ago in Jaipur and it went well enough. The distant mountains, dusty meadow, tents and bright upland sun all were in contrast, not wholly unfavorable, with Harvard Yard.

At ten, I had a long talk with His Majesty who was communicative as compared with earlier occasions. Nepali Congress attacks on his border have ceased and he feels much more secure. Later we were given a dinner in the big palace of the Rana Prime Ministers[7] — it has some 2,000 rooms in four giant units — and is now used mainly as a Secretariat. It is an imaginative place combining marble staircases, crystal chandeliers, red silk furniture, art-metal ceiling and the kind of funny mirrors that you see at a carnival.

This palace once housed some hundreds of wives and concubines and the parties were possibly more interesting. I had a long talk with Tulsi Giri, the Foreign Minister. He complains of our pressure for land reform in a country where the whole foundation of government is the unreformed landowners. I urged that they begin with the handful of very large ones. Their holdings are appreciable and their number is negligible. Thus you divide the landed power. It was thus that India knocked off the princes, *zamindars* and very large landlords — while not alienating the smaller landowners who are stalwarts of the Congress Party. In fact, the action played to their cupidity by providing some with land. Giri noted, as one difficulty, that he was one of the largest landowners.

Barbara Adams, a charming friend whom I had not seen for several years, is here in Kathmandu. She is a handsome, intelligent girl in her late twenties who arrived here a couple of years ago with her Italian husband. They were later divorced and she, in turn, settled down as a member of the royal family. Stebbins considers her a fine influence.

---

[7] The Ranas, until modern times, were the hereditary rulers of Nepal, through their possession of the office of Prime Minister, among others. The King was their captive. See page 547.

In sari and out of context, I did not recognize her immediately when we met at a reception. Gradually I got her identity straight and invited her over later in the evening.

April 15 — Ahmedabad–Baroda–Veraval–New Delhi

My life is currently divided between Kashmir and Bokaro, two problems inherited and on my hands for nearly all of these last two years. Today or tomorrow I am seeing Nehru for the climactic session on Kashmir. I have prepared the way in every possible fashion, and I have some hopes of a fairly generous and forthcoming proposal for the Valley.

On Bokaro, my problem is Lucius Clay.[8] He has come out against aid to publicly owned enterprises. However, he says there is a commitment on Bokaro which we should honor.

I can't accept a decision that is based on a presumptively unwise

[8] See page 544.

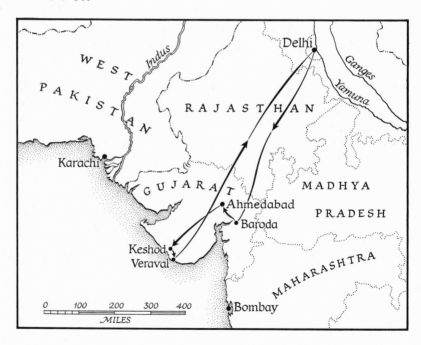

commitment. So over the weekend I issued a statement to the American press saying there was no such commitment and that the issue should be decided on its merits. I left no doubt what I believed these to be.

I have written a long memo on the subject which I would also like to have Washington release. Their hope, as always, is that the controversy will blow away. I can't see why people are so afraid of a little fight. It does wonders for my disposition.

On Friday morning last, we took off early morning for Baroda where I visited the University, opened a General Education Center and lunched with a Maharajah (in his role as a university official) in a vast, deteriorated palace of Victorian magnificence and much gingerbread. Baroda, along with Mysore, was the best managed of the Princely States. It is a clean and prosperous part of India and the city is modern and attractive. The University is American in organization with tightly knit faculties rather than loosely affili-

From Baroda, we went on to Ahmedabad where we spent the ated colleges and is a serious enterprise.
night at the Raj Bhavan. It seemed as gay and attractive as ever — as I have told, it is a kind of garden pavilion from the time of Shah Jahan. From Ahmedabad, with the Governor, we went to Keshod and by car to Veraval on the Arabian Sea. Here we stopped in a nice Circuit House with a cool smooth breeze from the water. Apart from opening a rayon factory on Saturday and attending a civic reception yesterday, there was nothing to interfere with sleep and bathing.

This part of India, Zoroastria of old, was the domain of a great number of princes — some two to three hundred. Only a handful were large enough to rate a gun salute — "the salute states" — and some were tiny. One rajah possessed a well and little more. The Maharajah in whose state we have been residing, A Moslem house which removed to Pakistan after Independence, was exceedingly fond of dogs. At one time he had three hundred and staged a rather elaborate marriage ceremony on one occasion between a favorite dog and bitch. Hence, just possibly, the phrase, "Putting on the dog." The British deposed him for a few months until he reduced his dog population to reasonable proportions.

April 22 — New Delhi

Another round of talks on Kashmir is on in Karachi. I brought my careful buildup of persuasion here in India to a climax. Carefully I persuaded everybody on the idea of a concession in the Valley. Then I saw Nehru and he turned me down flat. Then I saw him a second time and he turned me down even flatter.

At the same time that I was making these efforts in Delhi, McConaughy was conducting a similar campaign in Rawalpindi and Karachi. The results were the same. We succeeded in bringing the Indians and Pakistanis into a new opposition to ourselves. Nothing else was accomplished.

Actually, one thing was accomplished. Until last week, the Department had felt I was dragging my feet. In the course of the week, there was increasing alarm that I was pressing Nehru too hard. A telegram questioned my "all or nothing" approach. They felt I left inadequate room for retreat. This is one of many cases where the element of personal strategy enters diplomacy. My instinct was against pressing Nehru too hard. We stood to lose some of the character we gained last fall, make cooperation on other matters more difficult and probably accomplish nothing. But if I did not press hard, the failure would be blamed on me. "Galbraith was reluctant to come to grips with the great man; another ambassador protecting his client." Apart from being bad for me personally, this would have meant pressure for a new effort later on. So I made the best of a bad situation and tried too hard. I won't be blamed for failure, and won't be asked for more effort.

I have a feeling these may be the last of the talks.

Saturday, after seeing Nehru, I flew to Patna where a two-day program had been condensed into approximately four hours. That included the usual calls on Governor and Chief Minister, a lecture at the University to an enormous audience of five or six thousand, the opening of a cultural center, a press conference and a state dinner. All of this was finished by about ten o'clock and I went out to Jalan's Museum, a private collection of great magnitude and once a famous local sight. At one time it contained a fine collection of paintings, but it has been rifled by various procurers and those that remain are of no real interest. So it is elsewhere. Fortunately much of the really good painting has found its way into the museums.

About midnight, the railway having provided a nice private saloon car, we left for Benares. Patna was hot and Benares almost equally suffocating. We arrived there about eight o'clock yesterday morning. I had a delightful two-hour visit to the museum — this is the second time. There I saw some of the paintings that had once been at Jalan's. I had a chance to check museum prices against some I have paid the same dealers.[9] I have not been robbed as badly as might be expected.

From the museum I went to a new Diesel locomotive factory to which we have made substantial loans, made a new loan, a speech and got aboard the railroad car at noon. During the afternoon, we rattled agreeably across the dry and hot Ganges Plain and early this morning reached Delhi.

Back in Delhi, I discovered we had, indeed, brought about the first agreement in some years between Pakistan and India. Both have joined in denouncing our proposals.

[9] These were, at the time, from Rs. 100 to Rs. 1000 ($20 to $200) with only a slight relation between price and quality. One consequence of the low price was that many were sold essentially as trinkets, often by jewelers and tourist shops. A prodigious number of bad paintings were so sold but also some good ones which were lost forever. After returning from India I joined with Cary Welch and Milo Beach of the Fogg Museum at Harvard to get greater attention for this art, an enterprise in which we had the highly effective help of Mrs. John F. Kennedy and B. K. Nehru, the Indian Ambassador, who joined us to launch a series of exhibitions. (The catalogue for them was *Gods, Thrones, and Peacocks: Northern Indian Painting from Two Traditions, Fifteenth to Nineteenth Centuries* by Stuart Cary Welch and Milo Cleveland Beach. New York: Asia Society Inc., 1965.) One related consequence is that this painting is now better appreciated and its value has also greatly appreciated. (I am avoiding the modest personal benefit of this not wholly unearned increment by giving my acquisitions, those of any importance, to museums.) I told of this aspect of my life in India some years ago in an article in *Esquire*, "Art, Diplomacy and Vice Versa." It is reprinted in the Appendices. Few things I have ever done, association with lovely women apart, have ever been such a source of unalloyed delight.

May 1 — Tokyo–New Delhi

Last Friday, this being Wednesday, I went to Hong Kong. I was weary and slept most of the way. After a handsome Chinese dinner I slept some more and on Saturday did routine shopping, bought watches for the boys, had a talk about China/India problems at the Consulate, lunched with Marshall Green, the Consul, and went to Tokyo. Ed and Haru Reischauer were at the airport and we went along to their vast Coolidge-Tudor residence — graceless but not unpleasant — and to bed.

Sunday morning with my Japanese host, Mr. Takeo Miki, M.P.,[10] Dr. Saburo Okita of the Planning Board and an Embassy Officer, we went by plane to Osaka and then by car to Kyoto. There I was given a civic luncheon in a rooftop restaurant and a tour of various gardens, including a gentle two hours at Katsuru Rikyu, a most wonderful villa, tea house and garden on the edge of the city. This is one of the most sophisticated of Japanese gardens — every view is designed to be precisely perfect and is. Bridges, hills, lakes and brilliant flashes of azaleas are all in wonderful harmony and have been for some four hundred years. The garden of a small Zen Buddhist temple is almost as nice in its austere way.

Then we went to the recently opened and somewhat more florid gardens of a rich businessman. There I was duly grilled on world conditions and treated to Japanese dancing followed by an elegant dinner complete with geishas. One is astonished as always to have a girl kneeling before you throughout the evening with the principal function of smiling and being admired and admiring and filling your sake cup. Pavilion, garden and all were stunning. I spent the night at a Japanese-style hotel. I couldn't have been more comfortable and again woke up to a view of a lovely garden still moist in the early clouds of morning.

Kyoto is less beautiful than I had remembered it. Like all urban Japan, it is being made hideous by economic progress. But the gardens are better than I could have believed.

[10] Later Foreign Minister and later still (in 1968) a candidate for the Prime Ministership.

On the way back to Tokyo, we circled Mount Fuji at a distance of perhaps six hundred yards. It was somehow less impressive than I had remembered from seeing it by moonlight in 1945 from the nose of a B-17.[11]

That afternoon, Monday, I suffered total exposure. First, there was a luncheon interview for a daily newspaper. Then a magazine interview. Then a television show. Then I had a nap, missing a reception at the palace for the Emperor's birthday. Then the leading businessmen and educators assembled to ask my views on India and the world at large. Then came an elegant dinner in a most beautiful and stylish Japanese restaurant with more geishas, more talk and also badly cramped legs. My dinner companion was the Foreign Minister.

Yesterday was equally severe. First, a call on the Foreign Office and talks on India and China. Then my main lecture to open the National Policy Institute. It was a good lecture and is reproduced in the *Japan Times* this morning in toto! Then lunch at the Institute and then another university lecture with many questions. Then a call on the Foreign Minister followed by a dinner and discussion with Japanese Parliamentarians. The latter, a strikingly gay and amusing group, let me away about nine. I escaped back to the Embassy to find my room stacked with dolls, vases and tie pins from various interviewers, all of whom, evidently, were rewarding me for free copy.

As everyone observes, the traffic in Tokyo is incredible and promises to get worse as everyone becomes able to afford a car. The city is valiantly building subways to cope — four are under construction. So is a new high speed railway to Osaka (about the distance from Boston to New York) designed to keep traffic both off the roads and out of the sky. Trains will run at 125 MPH and the time (city to city center) will be no greater than by plane. They describe it as a last major experiment to see if railways are obsolete or not.

[11] En route, as a passenger, on a mission from Tokyo to Shanghai to Manila to the South Pacific just after World War II.

It is something of an experience after India — or the United States — to be in a country where so much is being done with such dispatch.

May 5 — New Delhi

Late Thursday, the Secretary of State arrived in the President's new plane with the Raymond Loewy decor. It was very hot and according to advance notice, we met the party in bush shirts. However, the State Department was not captivated by our informal diplomacy. They all disembarked properly dressed in diplomatic uniform. Rusk and Talbot went off to the Rashtrapati Bhavan as official guests of the Indians; Bob Manning[12] and Bill Bundy[13] stayed with us at the Residence. We had a pleasant evening, dinner in the garden beside the swimming pool with colored lights, to the music of what, I discovered, was a fantastically expensive Indian orchestra.[14] For variety, we made a midnight visit to Humayun's Tomb.

Friday, which was the main day of the Secretary's visit, was full of a number of things. He made the usual trip to the Rajghat to honor Gandhi, followed by the usual greeting to the Embassy staff on one of the islands in the water garden, followed by a visit to the Prime Minister at his Parliament Office. I am now a connoisseur on speeches by outsiders on Kashmir. Rusk's was pretty good. He was less eloquent on the great geopolitical formulations than Rostow. He was very good in describing the anguish which conflict between Pakistan and India causes us, including the problem of fueling both sides of the dispute. Then he heard the Indian side. Toward the end, I moved out with the bureaucrats, and in private, Nehru confirmed to Rusk his willingness to accept a mediator.[15]

[12] Robert Manning, the Assistant Secretary of State for Public Affairs and now editor of *The Atlantic Monthly*.

[13] William Bundy, then in the Department of Defense, since Assistant Secretary of State for Far Eastern Affairs.

[14] One is not recompensed for entertaining Americans. Thus the impression of cost.

[15] A proposal previously resisted by the Indians. See page 299.

This decision had previously been communicated to us by M.E.A., as I should have told. They had used the phrase "good officer." Nehru was untroubled by the word mediator.

We then had lunch at the Parliament building with a group of M.P.'s, some of whom belabored the Secretary for our efforts to get a Kashmir settlement. Then we visited the International Center which Rusk financed when he was President of the Rockefeller Foundation. And this was followed by various news conferences. The Indian journalists are harder on strangers on the Kashmir issue than they are on me. They have learned that I am hardened to their assault. In the evening, we had dinner at the Prime Minister's — one of the more interesting and, on the whole, amusing social functions of my Indian years. A lady M.P. from Calcutta and Y. B. Chavan were my dinner partners, and we had a good deal of lighthearted persiflage. After dinner, our troubles began.

Duncan Sandys was also in town, also seeing the Indians. And he had heard of the mediation proposals. He decided he should go to Rawalpindi and sell them to the Pakistanis. Thus he would have another inning as peacemaker of the subcontinent. But this violated our understanding with the Indians that the idea would be developed unobtrusively. It would seem, moreover, to suggest that we were selling something that had been cooked up here in Delhi. This would arouse suspicions. Sandys was nonetheless adamant at a post-dinner meeting at the British High Commission. I then had to leave to go to a short session with the top Indians at M.E.A. who affirmed their objection to any initiative by Sandys. The discussion was resumed at the Rashtrapati Bhavan, and the Secretary and I, both in the last stages of weariness, took turns in trying to dissuade Sandys from his journey. He professed to be unable to see the point of our objection. Rusk kept his temper and, following his admirable example, so did I. In the end, it was left that Sandys would not go for another day or two, and meanwhile James, the British High Commissioner in Karachi, and McConaughy would go to Rawalpindi and try to sell the idea to Ayub.

I had to report all this to Karachi and the Department and, as a result, got very little sleep. In a state of considerable weariness, I saw the Secretary off at nine on Saturday morning, and then went back to bed for an hour or two. Still weary, I had a quiet lunch with Bill Bundy. He has done a very good job talking with the Indian defense people and we see eye to eye on nearly all matters. We will proceed with military aid but gradually, and letting the Indians know that it will ease our path substantially if they are forthcoming and reasonable on Kashmir. And we will discourage the idea of a vast and burdensome army. A small, efficient and not excessively expensive force is needed to guard the passes.

After lunch, I looked at some paintings brought to me by a collector from Jaipur — a very large number of which, unhappily, were culls from his collection. Then I went to a wedding of one of our secretaries. Meanwhile, Sandys had seen Nehru again and had come up with another idea. It was that he get an agreed paper on mediation. He would first get the support of the Indians, then the support of the Pakistanis. Unfortunately, also, it would wreck all possibility of getting a mediator. The paper, having been agreed by the Indians, would arouse intolerable suspicion in Pakistan. Worst of all, the Indian officials had persuaded him to take out of the mediator's terms of reference any mention of Kashmir. The mediator would have only the task of getting a broad agreement between the two countries. The Pakistanis would rightly dismiss the paper as a transparent stall that bypassed the only issue of interest to them. I heard about this when I got back from the wedding. Sandys had already telegraphed the proposed terms of reference to Karachi. Gore-Booth was correct but distraught. I was extremely angry and decided under the circumstances that anger was probably my best weapon. I told Sandys that agreeing to such a paper was a major error since it suggested collusion with the Indians. It was also a breach of faith on his part, since we had agreed the night before on the more informal procedure of having our people in Karachi go to Rawalpindi to seek agreement. Not for years have I had such a bruising clash and I enjoyed it. It was at the British High Commissioner's and the two professionals, Gore-Booth and Timmons, were wringing their hands in agony over all the hard words. It came to an end when the Britishers had to go visit Shastri. I said I would go back to the house and try to sort matters out. When I got back, M. J. Desai called to say they had signed the paper only under pressure. Sandys had wanted something to show to his High Commissioner in Karachi and they wanted to oblige him with something he could release. Desai also indicated that at a later stage they probably would be agreeable to putting in some reference to Kashmir.

Armed with this knowledge, I went back to the British High Commission. There I found Sandys, who had been reflecting on my insults, ready to fight a duel. I grandly withdrew the charge of bad faith, said he had been guilty only of maladroit performance. This did not please him as much as might have been expected. But eventually he agreed that the statement was a mistake and agreed to cable Karachi that it had no standing. So things were back on the track as before. Crossing the cable to Karachi came an anguished plea from James, the Britisher there, saying they couldn't possibly sell the Sandys formula to Pakistan. Thus the joys and accomplishments of diplomacy.

General Kelly was having a dinner in the evening for Bill Bundy. I managed it for about an hour and then came back and cleared the cables and fell into bed. I was almost as weary as at any time since I have been in India. I think it probable that the problems of the world owe more to human vanity than to human folly.

May 10 — New Delhi
This has been a quiet week and by some curious freak of nature, it has been almost cool. What you expect in Delhi in early May is nature's nearest approach to a furnace. Today it has rained and one

could almost wear a jacket. The cool effect has been heightened by our new house. The air-conditioning system in fact accomplishes mild refrigeration.

As my last reports indicated, the Indians agreed to mediation of the Kashmir dispute. This does not mean that they have agreed to give up anything. But it keeps the discussion going. Talbot had gone back from Karachi to Beirut and had remained poised there in case he needed to return. He read in the telegrams that the Indians had talked Sandys out of any reference to Kashmir and, not yet knowing I had corrected the omission, sent me a solemn telegram regretting the Indian slippage. Both Robert Komer[16] and Carl Kaysen have urged me to be kind to Talbot on the grounds that his heart is in the right place. This does not excuse him for being fatuous. When I needed help in keeping Sandys passive, he was inert. But he was quick to advise me of the damage Duncan did.

I sent him a thoroughly informative telegram on his shortcomings. Since he dislikes this sort of thing, I imagine it's the last time I will hear from him. I must not allow such people to bother me.

The other occurrence of the week was much more pleasant. The President came out strongly on the side of helping the Indians build the Bokaro steel plant and he said it should be supported in the public sector. It was a marvelous no-nonsense statement. For weeks, the AID people have been worrying about Congressional reaction. Characteristically they have been seeking to protect the President on matters where he doesn't need or, one gathers, especially want protection. Now he has moved in and settled matters. He made the statement in a press conference. I followed it up here with a brief press conference in which I drew attention to the President's answers. I also noted that the Congress still had to act and there were many technical and administrative details to be worked out. The papers this morning are full of it.

For the last few days, *Blitz, Link* and the left generally have been

[16] See page 560.

busy assuring India that the U.S. is seeking to undermine Indian socialism. The President's action is an unfair blow to these constructive thoughts.

Tonight we take the children off to Simla and then I come back by way of Jaipur and Kishangarh. This will be our last family journey here. Kitty and the children leave next week for home by way of Japan.

May 15 — New Delhi

Last weekend, Kitty and the boys and I got a special car by courtesy of the Indian Railways and went overnight to Kalka where we shifted to a small gasoline car and took the narrow gauge up to Simla. It was the first time any of us had been there. Simla was cool and moist and still has the great Victorian Gothic palace of the Viceroys and large buildings which once served as the secretariat. (It was the summer headquarters of both the Government of India and the Government of the Punjab.) Although situated in the Punjab, it is now the capital of the adjacent mountain state of Himachal Pradesh. This is the height of the season with lots of women parading on the Mall in handsome saris. The main occupation of Simla is to see and be seen. I thought it a little less shabby than some of the other hill stations of the British Raj.

We lunched with the Raja of Arki, a local political leader whose nearby fief was once a minor center of painting. It was all quiet and moderately restful, save that we had to depart at 5 A.M. It was very pleasant coming down the hills with the Himalayas in the distance and heat coming up to meet us. We drove to Chandigarh and here I parted company with the family and took the plane to Jaipur where I spent the afternoon combining art and duty. I had lunch with the Chief Secretary and afterward we looked at some paintings and after that had tea with some legislators and M.P.'s and then I opened an art exhibit. I spent the night at the palace where the Maharani was in residence. She is deep in politics[17] and very handsome.

The next morning, I met Randhawa[18] who was joining me in Jaipur and drove down to Kishangarh to look at more paintings for our book. This is a couple of hours south of Jaipur by car and was once the center of a most important school. We saw a few specimens and had lunch at the summer palace. The palace and the fort, which are by a lake somewhat in the manner of Udaipur, are quite romantic but in a sad state of disrepair. The lake has been partly drained and planted to rice; the palace moat which is still filled with water has a highly malarial appearance. All in all, it is hard to imagine it was the scene of the great romances of Radha and Krishna. But there are traces.

We came back to Jaipur in the early afternoon and were back in Delhi by five o'clock.

This week, we have a new round of talks underway between India and Pakistan. I gather it will be the last. Having applied every possible pressure to the Indians for a settlement, I am now detaching a bit. It is now only a maneuver for position and to see who will be blamed or not blamed for the breakup of the talks.

May 19 — New Delhi

The Pakistanis have accepted mediation, subject to conditions which can never be mediated: we should freeze long-term military aid to India while mediation is in progress; mediation should not take over three months; it should assume the validity of the United Nations resolutions providing for a plebiscite in Kashmir; and the terms of reference should confine discussion rigorously to Kashmir. McConaughy thinks this is quite a bargain, subject to a few minor changes. Washington rejected even things that I was disposed to

[17] See page 327.
[18] Mohinder Singh Randhawa, naturalist, scientist, soil conservationist, civil servant and leading authority on Indian painting. Our decision to write a book on the subject had been taken some weeks before during a tour of the Kangra Valley.

accept — I thought, for example, that we might live with a time limit of six months. In the present state of incompatibility, these efforts lead not to pacification but only to more combat.

Yesterday, Saturday, Randhawa and I drove down to Rampur. This was a Moslem state in the United Provinces, a hundred-odd miles north and east of Delhi. The Nawab lives there in a vast teak-paneled palace with great ballrooms, banqueting rooms, drawing rooms, hideous furniture and even more hideous nineteenth-century copies of European paintings. The palace is not a great deal smaller than Buckingham Palace and stands in a great unkempt park.

We had been told that there was a very good library there and a fine collection of Moghul paintings (for our book). The library is in another palace, fort and compound in the center of Rampur. Like the other, it is of brick and plaster and strongly reminiscent of the buildings of the Columbian Pacific Exposition. The paintings were a mixed lot. Among numerous erotics was one of a massive open-air orgy which was highly imaginative and, in its approach to intercourse, exceedingly athletic.

I did notice one thing. The women in the Moghul paintings have a deep, almost luminous skin quality which is part of their charm. The women of the Nawab's household, particularly the wives of the sons, have the same beauty.

Both the son and the son-in-law of the Nawab have converted themselves to Congress politics. This is fairly common among the younger generation of the princes. The Raja of Arki told me the other day that his disestablishment had been a great piece of good fortune for him. Otherwise, he would have spent his life collecting rents and doing little more. Forced into politics, his life has some purpose.

John Strachey,[19] here with a group of Labour M.P.'s, came over to visit me this afternoon and we had a long chat. He finds India

[19] Late Labour M.P., author and close friend. We had visited India together in 1956.

less exciting than when we were first here. So with me. A great deal has been accomplished in these last few years. But a great many enterprises which once seemed very dramatic — community development is a notable case — now seem much less promising.

XXVI

Recessional

June 15 — Rome–New Delhi

For the last three weeks I have been in New England and Washington. President Radhakrishnan has been on a state visit to the United States. I went back a few days before, and, as I have said, Kitty took the boys back by way of Japan. After a few days in Washington, we all assembled over Memorial Day in Newfane.[1] It was as green and lovely as ever. I had dinner the evening before with the President and J.B.K. but reluctantly missed his birthday party in favor of Vermont. The President is much occupied with civil rights and his concern for India is at a very low level. He recognizes that this is partly because I have kept it off his desk these last two years. He offered me the Moscow Embassy if I would learn Russian. Perhaps I should accept. But I am very tired of the State Department. And of Rusk.

From Vermont, following Memorial Day, we went to New York where we met President Radhakrishnan at Idlewild. The Air-India Boeing discharged its passengers and then took us on to Langley Field whence we motored to Williamsburg. Arrival ceremonies — bands and salutes — were in a heavy downpour of rain, an American monsoon. Williamsburg was also drenched but fresh and green and very colonial. It is modeled too much on the postcards.

Next morning, still in heavy rain, we went by helicopter to

[1] See page 377.

Washington for further ceremonies on the north portico of the White House. Bands played and raincoated soldiers saluted and speeches were made and, all in all, I found it less exciting than before. In the afternoon, the two Presidents talked about very little for an hour — the problem being that President Kennedy is an operating chief executive while President Radhakrishnan is an intelligent but essentially ceremonial figure. Following was a huge state dinner at which the President paid off a phenomenal number of political debts. In his speech, he congratulated India on having a professor for President and then assured everyone, "in the presence of Professor Galbraith," that we would not follow India's example.

They met further the following day and discussed even less. Then on the third day of the visit, President R. (with my wife) went out on a tour of the nation, and I remained in Washington to lobby for foreign aid and Bokaro. I put in three very tiring days on the Hill and saw some thirty or forty members of Congress. This is much more useful than appearances before committees. I think I did some good.

There were also the usual parties.

Following the lobbying, I went to Boston and drove with Alan to Newfane. Then after a highly agreeable letdown, we drove to Amherst where I got an honorary degree at the University of Massachusetts and gave a Commencement address. The latter was on the American tendency to quarrel with success — TVA worked so well we decided never to do it again; foreign aid is accomplishing much, hence severe opposition. Then I went on to New York and welcomed the Radhakrishnan party back from Philadelphia, Cape Canaveral (now Cape Kennedy), Denver, Disneyland and assorted other boondocks. They had had a good time and had not needed my company to enjoy themselves.

I then accompanied the party through a day in New York including a visit to City Hall for various proclamations of friendship, preceded by a ticker tape parade. The ticker tape was rather sparse since it isn't much used in the tickers anymore and the City has to supply substitute clippings. Then a luncheon, a speech at the U.N. and a rather touching dinner by all the Asiaphiles at the Waldorf.

The following day, last Tuesday, I went back to Washington for a meeting on military aid to India. The proposal is to dribble out a thoroughly inadequate amount. Instead of being able to ask for something in return, we will have only an argument on its adequacy. I argued for more but with no support.

After the meeting last Tuesday, I came back to Boston and met with Houghton Mifflin on my various publishing enterprises including Mark Epernay and the book with Randhawa on painting. Then on Thursday I went to Harvard for Commencement. It was perfect weather and the Yard was gay and agreeable in appearance. Rusk, George Kennan and U Thant were given honorary degrees. In accordance with ancient habit, Chub Peabody arrived by carriage behind the Lancers and looking very pleased with himself. The current view, alas, is that he is doing a very poor job as Governor. Chub's view of politics has always been that the Irish are great politicians. Hence to be successful as a politician you must be like an Irish politician. This is a mistake the Kennedys never made.

There is something very ridiculous about honorary degrees. A grown man stands and tries to look modest in the presence of immodest and (as in the case of Rusk who got marks for courage, skill and decisiveness) highly inaccurate praise. Then he sits down and everyone forgets it all. I think I will decline future offers. At least I should.[2]

Yesterday we started back for Delhi with a long intervening stopover in Rome. With any wisdom, one would never make the trip without such a break. Last night, we drove out Via Appia Antica and drank wine and ate pasta among the vineyards. It was very nice. We also stopped by the Embassy for a cultural party. The Ambassador is in the hospital with an ulcer. In Rome that shouldn't be necessary.

This morning we strolled around St. Peter's. The Swiss Guards

[2] I didn't.

were ushering in the Cardinals for a ceremony in connection with the selection of the new Pope. They are not, I regret to say, very healthy-looking. The Church should insist on more vigorous exercise or, at a minimum, a more rigorous diet. St. Peter's was filled with people and seemed even more immense than usual.

July 1 — New Delhi

The last two weeks have been hot, stuffy and given over to an incredible round of protocol. I have dispensed with the farewell calls to the other ambassadors and have sent them a letter instead. But I must be more considerate of Indian officialdom. So each day I call on two or three and spend ten minutes. Then each evening there is a farewell dinner and more to come. In response to a touching speech, I say that I am deeply touched. In moments of unnatural generosity, I mention Bowles favorably as my successor.

Coupled with all of this, there has been quite a bit more work than usual. I finally extracted from Washington a military program for the next fiscal year. It isn't large enough, but it will do. I conveyed the details to various officials and got a promise in return to be conciliatory on Kashmir, to support us in South Asia and to keep us advised on their military planning.

After some consideration, I decided to make my principal farewell speech in Bombay. The papers there are good and I am more of a novelty than in Delhi. That was last Friday, today being Monday, and we took the Convair down, had lunch and a press conference. The speech was at the University of Bombay. I used the occasion to twit the local left-wingers on military aid. I noted that they accuse us on military matters of doing both too little and too much. This is almost the first time that I have taken on the local Communists directly. This is partly because it is a mistake to take them seriously and partly because the best strategy for the United States is to stand above the scene. Debate puts you on the level of those with whom you are debating and gives excuse and encouragement to the opposition.

The monsoon has begun in Bombay and it was a pleasant relief after the heat and dust of Delhi. However, it also had a highly adverse effect on my sinus which is worse again. Airplane travel also added to my problems. The pain was practically blinding and could be relieved only by enough aspirin and codeine to put one in a condition of stupor. I had, in the end, to have some kind of minor operation.[3]

There is no hope of a settlement of the Kashmir issue in the foreseeable future, but it is very important for Congressional relations in the United States and thus the aid program to keep the effort alive. The Indians' proposal of mediation did help. Since once something is started by the State Department it can never be stopped, McConaughy in Karachi has been trying for the last several weeks to sell the idea to Pakistan. Initially, as I have noted, they attached a vast number of conditions — veto on military aid to India, a rigid time limit on the mediation, a panel rather than a single mediator, and several other impossible requirements. Gradually McConaughy managed to get most of their objections removed. Meanwhile, M. J. Desai has gone off to Japan for a holiday and Nehru has been up in Kashmir. In their absence, I was officially informed that the mediation was off. I had had some hint that this was coming and it developed that those who were conveying the bad news were unaware of promises I had just received of a conciliatory stance. So what looked like a vigorous initiative became a disastrous bungle. When it was all over, we were about back where we started.

As I get ready to take leave, I find myself very sorry for the Prime Minister. He has been in very poor health the last year and has suffered a series of political reverses. In these last months, he has had to dismiss Krishna Menon by popular demand and also K. D. Malaviya, a lesser minister. These were the two leading members of the left in the Cabinet. In consequence, he is more deter-

[3] They wheeled in a hospital table at the Consulate and it took place between courses at an official luncheon.

mined than ever to stand up to the Americans and the British and also on Pakistan.

This afternoon, I attended my third celebration of the Ghana National Day. We also looked in on a private party of the Canadians. The press gave me a luncheon which was more agreeable than most such occasions and this afternoon at a press conference I was able to announce the completion of an $80 million loan for the Tarapur Atomic Energy Plant. This represents two years of work and agitation; on completion, it will be one of the two largest atomic energy plants in the world.

July 6 — New Delhi

The farewell parties continue. Today we had lunch at the Rashtrapati Bhavan with the President. It was vegetarian but otherwise agreeable. The President seemed pleased with his visit to both the United States and the U.K. He noted that he was in competition with race problems at the University of Alabama in the U.S. and with Miss Christine Keeler in England. This subtracted from his press attention which he felt was not excessive. He gave Kitty a very attractive scarf and sari. I received his portrait.

Most of the gifts that are exchanged these days I have discovered are related to vanity. They anticipate long days ahead when the individual in question will have nothing to do but look at the mementos of his past. Framed and inscribed portraits are by all odds the best for this purpose. They last well and can easily be displayed.

On the Fourth of July, the day before yesterday, we broke with the regular routine of farewell appearances and got up at half-past five to go to Leh in Ladakh. There was the usual painstaking procedure of checking instruments, engines, doors and all the rest on the C-130 before we took off. I was impressed again with how meticulous and uncasual these operations are. The Ganges Plain was covered with a thick haze of dust but we broke out of it after 6,000 feet and crossed the Himalayas at about 25,000 feet. As compared with six months ago, there was much less snow but it is still one of the grandest sights in all the world and in the distance one could see the even greater heights of the Karakorums.

Leh itself was bathed in bright sunshine and with patches of green where potatoes and pulses are growing with some irrigation water from the Indus. A new airfield is under construction, the supply dumps have been tidied up, and all in all, it looked much more organized and workmanlike than when we saw it before Christmas. I inspected the new airfield and then we climbed up to the monastery where we were given tea. It is an ancient building made of stone and mud mortar with a complement of about a hundred monks and a spectacular outlook over the valley. Then we went to the town of Leh where we saw some weaving and had a pleasant lunch at the Officers' Mess. The latter, a sizable house with a pleasant garden, is in the good British tradition of making the best of any available circumstances. I presented the Mess with some books and a case of whisky and we took off at about half-past three for Delhi.

Back in Delhi, we found a horse-drawn Victoria awaiting us which some friends have loaned us for our last days. We took it over to the opening of the new Swiss Embassy and made a certain impression. I then gave my third Fourth of July speech in India. I am able to talk on most subjects but the art of a Fourth of July speech escapes me. The audience expects something serious and even a trifle pompous. It is uneasy if you are otherwise; I am uneasy if I am.

Last night, we had a vast farewell reception at the Residence — somewhere between five hundred and a thousand. The house is so big that they were swallowed up with no appearance of crowding and despite the fact that it was much too hot to go out in the garden. The Prime Minister came and remained about an hour. Those visibly most saddened by my departure were the art dealers. As they shook hands, one could sense emotion reinforced by the prospect of grave financial deprivation.

Quite a few of the guests were uninvited. People who do not get an invitation for such events are forgiving, write it off as a minor oversight and come anyway. A minor Maharajah not only came but brought his heir. And while he may have been well down in the salute list, he was a rather impressive sight as he took up a position in front of the bar and went to work with both hands.

When it was over, we still had to go to an Open House of the Marines who have just moved into new quarters.

I am very uncertain as to the purpose of a reception. People arrive, stand around for a while, talk and depart. Many make little effort at conversation. Some of the women are obviously there to see and be seen. But more come shyly and with obvious reluctance. Since whisky is very scarce, some guests do have, as a legitimate objective, the alcohol. But this is a small minority; most drink pineapple juice. I have a feeling that receptions are something that got started and no one has ever thought to stop.

Today was Saturday and much easier. We are on the verge of considerable decisions on the matter of air defense and another move on mediation. For the first time in nearly two-and-a-half years, I am not anxious for the State Department to move with excessive rapidity on a subject. I want to leave further negotiation on the Kashmir mediator for Bowles. I want him to have all the glory.

July 15 — New Delhi–Madras

This is the last communiqué from India. It concerns the problem of detaching oneself from a country and that is a formidable matter. I can perhaps indicate what is involved by appending my appointment schedule for my last day in Delhi. This, however, seems not to be the whole thing for it carries only until four-forty in the afternoon. There was another page.

AMBASSADOR'S SCHEDULE
Thursday — July 11

8:30 A.M.	Physical examination — Holy Family Hospital
10:00 A.M.	Pictures with houseguests — Residence
11:00 A.M.	Farewell call at USIS
11:30 A.M.	Farewell call at USAID
12:00 noon	Staff Meeting — Embassy
12:30 P.M.	Receive Dr. Allan Kline (Head of CARE in India) — Embassy
12:45 P.M.	Receive Mr. D. N. Saraf, Handicrafts and Handloom Director — Embassy
1:15 P.M.	Lunch with Prime Minister — P.M.'s house
2:50 P.M.	Presentation of $1,000 check to Military Relief
3:00 P.M.	BBC (Ivor Jones) taped interview — Embassy
3:15 P.M.	AIR (All-India Radio) taped interview — Embassy
4:00 P.M.	Call on Mr. Morarji Desai
4:30 P.M.	Call on Mr. Rajeshwar Dayal — M.E.A.
4:40 P.M.	Call on Mr. S. K. Banerji — M.E.A.

Today is Monday. Last Thursday, as the above schedule shows, I made calls on the outlying parts of the mission — USIS and AID. I had met with the military at Dharbanga House the day before. Then at noon, we had a family dinner with the Prime Minister at which he was very silent. I had also had a long discussion with him the evening before at which I stressed the need for a conciliatory policy toward Pakistan and my hope that the air defense arrangements would go smoothly. Also on Thursday, I had a variety of newspaper interviews including a series of parties with the press at one of which the American correspondents presented me with a couple of handsome books on Indian art. And in the evening we had the last of our farewell parties, this one again at the Ashoka given by M. J. Desai. I observed that our policy on China was to strengthen India's hand in a quiet way and then entrust to M.J. the making of whatever bargain he deemed sensible and wise. At the end of the mutual encomiums, I asked Desai what was his guess on the air defense arrangements. He told me the answer would be yes, and he thought we would have it in the next three or four days. I sent off a Top Secret to Washington on this. They will be relieved, as indeed am I. The long and unforgivable delay by Washington gave every opportunity to the opposition here.

Friday morning a little before ten, we went out to the airport and there was a sizable crowd to see us off. The day before, it had seemed we might not depart. The Convair had developed acute propeller trouble; to fly to Colombo in the Navy C-47 through (as distinct from over) the monsoon would be tedious, uncomfortable and of questionable wisdom. There was a suggestion that we take a C-130 down but I vetoed that. In the end, we borrowed Karachi's Convair again. The servants garlanded us to the extent of several pounds gross weight before we left the house and we acquired several pounds more at the airport from Indian officials, professional friends of the U.S. and quite a few personal friends who were there to say goodbye. I had slept badly the night before and the whole thing is a rather hazy mosaic in my mind. After we had shaken hands, waved, *namasted* and got on board, the crowd lined up by the plane and one of the engines failed to start. Hands were becoming a little limp in the warm, humid atmosphere by the time we got away.

We stopped at Madras where I had my second farewell press conference and we refueled, and then we went on to Colombo for two days of press conferences, receptions and a lecture before the Ceylon Council of World Affairs. I urged efficiency which is foreign to all Ceylonese philosophy. Nevertheless, it went well, such being the difference between theory and practice.

Now we are again in Madras on the way to Calcutta where early tomorrow morning I catch a plane to Majorca for a fortnight's rest. Kitty, whose taste for travel is still unsatisfied, is going back by way of Kabul, Tehran, Athens and Yugoslavia.

THE FELINE SIDE OF DIPLOMACY

In the spring of 1962, during an official visit to Governor Jung of the State of Gujarat our two sons were presented with Siamese kittens of some slight personality. The name of one can be lost to history. The other our offspring called Ahmedabad in honor of its birthplace.

Later in the same year, my wife was showing reporters over the newly opened Roosevelt House. They asked her if it presented any peculiar housekeeping problems. She replied that the kittens could pass with ease through the concrete screens that are an Edward Durell Stone specialty and which served as interior walls in the house. And she added that one of them greatly preferred the bed then being occupied by Ambassador Averell Harriman, a guest in the house. Harriman, who was allergic to cats, she added, did not at all care for the intruder. The notion that Averell Harriman could be harassed by anyone or anything, man or beast, was a story. The reporters asked for this kitten's name. By now, it had been shortened to Ahmed.

Eventually, the story appeared in the international edition of *Time*. It was at a moment of tension in Pakistan resulting from our aid to India in the recent border war with China. The effect was, to say the least, electric. The windows of our Consulate in Lahore were broken. A jeep loaded with either our soldiers or our bureaucrats was overturned. *Mullahs* inveighed against us and, in their prayers, arranged for me an especially ghastly posthumous reception. A student strike was called. For Ahmed, alas, is one of the several hundred names of the Prophet. I do not think the Pakistanis were particularly sensitive. In the darker reaches of our Bible Belt, there would have been criticism of a Pakistan ambassador who, at a moment of friction between our two nations, had, however innocently, named his dog Jesus.

I sensed the scale of the impending trouble within seconds after seeing a cable from Karachi reporting on the first demonstrations. I assembled a press conference to explain that my children had acted in all innocence, that the name of the kitten was nonetheless now Gujarat.

Gujarat né Ahmedabad and the negotiable screen

I then sought out the Pakistan High Commissioner, told him of my trouble and heard with relief that his government would do everything possible to dampen the indignation. It did. In all of this, I was alarmed by the damage that might be done to our relations with Pakistan. And I was almost equally distressed by the knowledge that even the friendliest Foreign Service Officers would point with honest joy to this further example of the awful risks which a great nation runs when it entrusts its diplomacy to amateurs. Amateurs will never understand how much can turn on the name of a kitten.

As the result of my prompt action, the crisis, international and personal, was averted. But for months the Indian newsmen continued to ask me to account for my mistake. It became rather wearying. Finally, on an incredibly hot and humid night in the spring of 1963, I gave a lecture at the University of Patna in the city of the same name on the lower Ganges Plain. It was followed by a press conference. The questions droned on into the night; my pressman dozed off leaving me with no one to bring the ordeal to an end. Finally came the inevitable question. A reporter rose: "Mr. Ambassador, would you tell us about the name of your cat?"

With an effort, I got hold of my patience. I replied:

"I will answer once more but you must write the story very carefully, very systematically for it is the last time. Here are the facts:

"First: It was not a cat but a kitten.

"Second: It was not my kitten but my children's kitten.

"Third: My children did not name the kitten Ahmed for the Prophet but Ahmedabad for its birthplace.

"Fourth: Ahmedabad was not named for the Prophet but for Sultan Ahmed Shah, its founder, in A.D. 1411. (I had looked this up.)

"Fifth: So that no one's feelings could possibly be hurt, my children have renamed the kitten Gujarat."

There was a moment's silence while everyone scribbled. Then a tall dark man rose at the back of the room, waited a second for silence and then in a strongly formidable voice, said:

"Mr. Ambassador. My name is Ahmed. I am a Mussulman. I find your explanation satisfactory."

I was never asked about the kitten again. It was a complete exoneration.

XXVII

It Was All Over

November 26, 1963

This journal was to have ended with the last entry in Madras. Now a last, sad chapter must be added.

In August, at the President's request, I returned to Washington to spend five or six weeks, first negotiating a settlement of an ancient airline dispute with the Canadians. After Kashmir, it was pleasant to find an issue where only naked financial self-interest was involved.[1] Then, a more interesting task, I made a new survey of the balance-of-payments problem. I wrote a stiff paper on the subject which was taken up at a couple of meetings in the White House, but it led to no real action. We ended with an agreement to limit capital exports which had been already accomplished pro tem by the interest equalization tax the Treasury had proposed to levy retroactively earlier in the summer.

Between these tasks, I worked on the book on the Scotch,[2] corrected the final proofs on Dr. McLandress[3] and began a series of articles for *Look* for which they are paying me $5,000 each for three.[4] And of course when autumn came, I resumed teaching here

---

[1] The problem, that of allowing Canadian airlines to fly to destinations deep in the United States in return for similar rights in Canada (complicated by the fact that all Canadian cities are close to the border), was eventually resolved to the reasonable satisfaction of all concerned.

[2] *The Scotch* (Boston: Houghton Mifflin, 1964).

[3] See page 382.

[4] None ever appeared in *Look*. One, "The American Ambassador," was published in the *Foreign Service Journal* of June 1969.

at Harvard. My classes were sizable with a fair number of tourists looking in at least briefly to see one of the local sights.

Last Friday, November 22, I went to New York to have lunch with Kay Graham, now the directing head of the *Washington Post* and *Newsweek*.[5] Arthur Schlesinger was to join us and also some *Newsweek* editors. Arthur and Kay were flying up from Washington together. They arrived late, and I drank tomato juice in Kay's office while the *Newsweek* editors had Old-Fashioneds. Arthur and Kay arrived and ordered drinks and they had just picked them up when a staff man of the magazine opened the door rather tentatively, almost apologetically, and said, "I think I should interrupt. President Kennedy has just been shot in Dallas." There was a moment of horrified silence; someone said, "It couldn't be." Kay's face suddenly looked haggard. We went out to the newsroom and to the tickers where everyone was gathered around a radio. The further word was that he had been shot in the head. It all sounded much too real to be a mistake, and I confess at this juncture that I gave up hope. Imagining what it means to be shot in the head, mentally destroyed, I wished momentarily that the news might have been that he was dead. Then the radio reported that a Secret Service man traveling with Mrs. Kennedy by the name of Clint Hill had said, "The President is dead." Clint Hill was the advance man on Mrs. Kennedy's trip to India. He is a well-organized and thoughtful man who would never in any emergency be wrong. His reaction, if accurately reported, was bound to be right.

For half an hour, we alternated between Kay's office, the radio and the television. Now I found myself hoping it was just a wound, even a bad wound. Word came that two priests had gone into the hospital. Further word came that blood was being sent in. Finally, these details were interrupted with the announcement that the President of the United States was dead.

Kay had come up in the *Washington Post* plane. We went down to the car, over to the Century Club to pick up my bags and

[5] Philip Graham having died a few weeks earlier.

out to the Marine Terminal at LaGuardia and flew back to Washington. My strongest thought was that we were paying the price for the poisonous hatred stirred up so casually by the extreme right. Somehow or other, national indignation should have intervened to shut them up and thus to have excluded the incitement to violence for those whose mental discrimination is too slight. We all three took for granted that it was done by right-wing extremists. Stevenson had been roughed up in Dallas only a few weeks before. Lyndon Johnson and his wife had been pummeled there during the 1960 campaign. For a brief moment, there was word that Johnson had been wounded also.

At Washington, we went to the White House and Ralph Dungan's office where preliminary efforts were being made to organize life. There is in the United States a great latent capacity for self-organization. Some people take charge; some take orders. This was already beginning to make itself felt. Dungan was organizing the arrangements for the return of the President's body and the new President and J.B.K. to Andrews Field. Most of the members of the Cabinet were over the Pacific on their way to a meeting in Japan; sub-Cabinet members were gathering at the White House. In the early evening — I did not make any note of exact times — we got into helicopters and White House cars and made our way to Andrews Field. Bob Roosa, Undersecretary of the Treasury, and Clarence Martin,[6] one of the Undersecretaries of Commerce, were my companions in one of the cars. We had a motorcycle escort through the home-going traffic and we had only a few moments to wait at Andrews Field before Air Force-I came in. There was already a considerable crowd of onlookers on the way and near the airfield, and quite a number of Congressmen and Senators had arrived. A lift arrangement of the kind that is used to put food aboard a commercial plane was wheeled up to the jet as it came abreast of the ramp, and after a little time the coffin

6 Until we were nearly at the field, I thought Martin was Franklin D. Roosevelt, Jr. My mind simply had not registered.

was maneuvered out, brought down and put into a gray Navy hearse. The lift arrangement, truck and all, was not overwhelming in its dignity.

Then Robert Kennedy brought Jackie off the plane followed by President Johnson and the rest of the party. J.B.K. was pale but otherwise in control. Evidently it had been intended that she should go to the White House by helicopter. Instead she went in the hearse to the Bethesda Naval Hospital. We went back to the White House. Arthur and I had our first meal of the day in the White House Mess, and I went on to Averell Harriman's. George Backer[7] was there and one or two others. I can rarely remember an evening when a deadlier or drearier pall fell over a group. No one had anything to say or indeed seemed to wish to talk. Presently Arthur Schlesinger, who had come with me, disappeared and soon I had a call from him, asking me to come down to the White House. Two problems were being resolved: one, the arrangement for the stationing of the coffin in the East Room which was Bill Walton's[8] responsibility; and the other, the preparation of the lists of people to be invited to view the coffin the next day at various times which Sarge Shriver was handling. These were the two natural leaders of the evening.

On the first, there were plans available to the White House, updated as recently as 1958 (evidently at the time of one of Ike's illnesses) for the funeral of a President while in office. Walton got out books and pictures showing how the East Room had been decorated for Lincoln's funeral but decided that the taste in crepe of that era was too extravagant. He contented himself with some simple black drapes. Word was sent out to arrest the inflow of flowers, and he set himself to standing off the undertakers and the Catholics. The undertakers had numerous artifacts and rich satin backgrounds to display; some churchmen felt that this was a time

[7] Friend, journalist and fellow amateur novelist. A longtime leader in New York Democratic politics.
[8] See page 137.

for a considerable ceremonial and liturgical exercise. The Kennedy family supported a control of both of these extravagances and, in the end, everything was simple, in good proportion and in good taste.

The problem of deciding who would visit the White House at various times was more difficult. One had the conflicting claims of politics, officialdom and friendship and the possibility that some individuals would fall between all stools. In a way, politics and officialdom fell into fairly straightforward categories. One invited all governors and officials above a certain rank as a matter of course. The friends and faithful supporters were more difficult, but this problem was partly resolved when we got a list of people who had been invited to Kennedy dinners.

It was midnight or one o'clock when I got home to Kay Graham's. Others waited for the coffin to come from the Bethesda Hospital. The work of the evening was therapeutic.

During the afternoon, Al Friendly of the *Washington Post*, in response to a not fully considered suggestion that I would be willing, asked me to write an appreciation of Kennedy. On second thought, I declined, but next morning, though I woke up under the drugged effect of too many sleeping pills, I changed my mind again. I wrote most of it in bed before breakfast and then reworked it the rest of the morning. I gave it no title and the *Post* called it merely "A Communication." I avoided the mistake of other writers who tried to assess Kennedy in his whole person and in his relation to history. I confined myself to a single facet of his personality — his intelligence, wit and information.[9]

At noon, I went down with Kitty, who had meanwhile arrived, to Blair House and the White House to visit the bier. This was the first of several times when my emotions were severely taxed. We were, however, almost alone at the time. The article had kept me until after most of the friends of the family had disappeared. From the East Room of the White House, we went to Arthur Schlesin-

[9] The article is at the end of this Journal.

ger's office and then on to the Occidental for lunch. The Sam
Beers,[10] Seymour Harris,[11] Paul Samuelson,[12] Bill Walton and
one or two others were present for lunch. Arthur (naturally
enough) was in a rather poor mood. But like most people interested in politics, he was reacting too much to the chemistry of the
moment.

Walter Heller, who was at the lunch, left early for Johnson's
first Cabinet meeting and the rest of us made our more leisurely
way back to the White House. I went over to the West Basement
to say a word to Ted Sorensen who was badly broken up. In some
ways, he had invested more in John F. Kennedy than anyone else.
His personal life, everything else had been subordinated to the
Kennedy career.

From there, I went on to the Executive Office Building to see
Robert Komer and look at the India cables. I was waiting meanwhile for the galley proofs to come back from the *Post* for correction. However, I decided halfway to Komer's office that I had no
heart to talk about India and returned to get a White House car to
go to the Grahams'. As I turned, I encountered President Johnson
who told me he had just sent for me. He asked me to come to his
office. When we got there, he threw out a waiting Texas judge and
made a strong plea for support.[13] He also asked me to work with
Sorensen on the message for a joint session of Congress to be given
on Wednesday. He asked how I worked with Sorensen and I answered that I got along with him very well. Johnson then said he
wanted to continue the Kennedy policies, reminded me he was a
Roosevelt liberal, and said that he was going to affirm his support

[10] Past National Chairman of A.D.A. and Professor of Government at Harvard.
[11] See page 254.
[12] See page 381.
[13] He also asked me what problems I thought he faced. I told him by far the
most serious was in foreign policy. And this would be the tendency of the foreign
policy establishment, which had gone along reluctantly with Kennedy, to relapse
into Cold War adventures. The point evidently seemed sufficiently commonplace,
even banal at the time, so that I did not bother to mention it in these notes. In
the light of later history, it is more interesting. However, I do not want to exaggerate its importance. Neither President Johnson nor any other man could have
registered mentally all of the advice being given in those days.

for the Kennedy programs. I asked specifically about civil rights. He said he was for civil rights, not out of loyalty to the President but out of loyalty to the idea. I told him that I was a Democrat as well as a friend and would, of course, give him any help I could.

The incident had an interesting relation to the problem of the change in power. Like the other members of the Kennedy group, I had become accustomed to wandering through the White House and through the press without anyone paying the slightest attention. Johnson had been seen taking me into his office so when I came out, I was overwhelmed by newspapermen and photographers. I brushed them off.

I tried my hand at the speech that afternoon and showed it to Arthur. He was appalled by it. His judgment was in fact clearer than mine. I had drafted out a liberal program; it was pretty bad. He correctly said that this was not what the occasion called for.

Kitty and I had dinner at the Grahams' with the Graham children who were down from Radcliffe and Harvard for the occasion, and then went briefly to the Harrimans'. Arthur divided the community in Washington into two categories, the realists and the loyalists. The loyalists would resign and try to find an alternative to Johnson. The realists, a group to which, alas, I was assigned, took the Democratic Party in earnest and would continue to give their best to it, however little that might be.

I went home early and went to bed.

Sunday morning, I concluded that the speech was in fact very bad and wrote a new and better version. It was balanced and liberal and set about the right tone. I finished it just in time to go to the White House to join the White House staff to go to the Capitol. We drove down by a circuitous route, went up the Capitol steps and into the Rotunda where a catafalque had been prepared in the center. After a little, in came Congressmen, Senators, members of the Supreme Court and various officials. The Congressmen who were immediately adjacent to us seemed principally concerned in their conversation with whether or not they were to be invited to the funeral the next day. They obviously couldn't be since the Cathedral holds only some fifteen hundred people, and by this time it was evident that most of the chiefs of state of the world were flying in for the occasion. Otherwise, the conversation was on the weather, the identity of various people in the crowd and funerals in general. News was just beginning to circulate in this weekend of Texas violence that Lee Oswald, the President's presumed assassin, had also been shot. This, I must say, struck me in some ways as the most unforgivable thing of all. Perhaps it is impossible to prevent a madman from getting a rifle and striking down the President but surely peace officers should be able to protect a prisoner in their own custody.

Then an honor guard came in, followed by six soldiers — actually, Navy, Marine, Air and Army enlisted men — carrying the coffin. Their approach was quiet and impressive. Speeches followed. Mike Mansfield had a poem; the symbolism had to do with a ring on a finger, gaiety, wit, stillness, and it was good. John McCormack, now (as Speaker) next in line for the Presidency, left much to be desired. The Chief Justice gave a magnificent talk and he said the one thing that needed to be said, namely that while few will advocate assassination, many will contribute to the climate which causes men to contemplate it.

J.B.K. had come in with the coffin and with the two youngsters. However, John, Jr., had become restless and a Marine guard took him away. At the conclusion of the speeches, she came forward with Caroline and with silent eloquence knelt and kissed the coffin. Then President Johnson came forward a bit haltingly and put a large wreath of roses before the coffin. We then went back to the White House. It was almost midafternoon.

At the White House, I encountered Lee Radziwill who asked me if I had seen J.B.K., and she said she thought she wanted to see me. I went upstairs to one end of the central hall where she was resting and still in perfect control. She asked me if I wouldn't have a drink; I broke down for the first time in a long while to have one.

We talked a little bit about the events of the morning and more about the funeral the next day. She was holding firm to her determination that J.F.K.'s sense of pageantry would be respected. All sorts of suggestions that people ride in cars for security reasons were being made. She was determined that the coffin would be drawn on a caisson, that people would follow on foot, and that bands and soldiers would add as much stately solemnity to the occasion as might be possible. The Ormsby Gores were there and she recalled how much J.F.K. had enjoyed the visit of the Black Watch a few days before. He offered to get them back to Washington for the occasion.

In moments of this sort, what seem to be simple matters assume enormously difficult proportions. J.B.K., it developed, had no place to go on leaving the White House. Her parents had no accommodations large enough for her substantial household. It was necessary for her to have a place to which members of the Kennedy political entourage would have reasonably easy access. It had to be in Washington. And, money apart, you cannot buy a house on the spur of the moment and move in. I took this on. It occurred to me that Averell Harriman, who has more real estate than he knows what to do with, could offer her his house. At this time of year, Marie Harriman usually goes to New York or Hobe Sound. It is a large, comfortable house in the most agreeable part of Georgetown and has the particular advantage of some of the best impressionist paintings in the world.

After seeing J.B.K. and a session with Sorensen, some more work on the speech took me until early evening. I then went back to the Grahams' for dinner — I had had no lunch. After dining, I went over to Harriman's to brace him on the real estate question. This proved to be no problem, and he straightaway called Jackie to make the offer. She, however, had gone to bed and so he made it through Lee. I then talked the matter over with Bob Kennedy who was delighted with this resolution.

In the general resolution of the funeral arrangements, Kitty's name and mine had been on no list. This was not remarkable in fact because my only qualification was in the category of friends — or possibly as a sometime member of the White House staff. Except possibly for Roswell Gilpatric,[14] not even those of the rank of Undersecretary were invited. There must have been a considerable number of damaged feelings. When Bob learned of the oversight, he had it corrected with great speed and not without some expressions of anger. Arthur, meanwhile, took on the problem of Averell Harriman who had similarly been excluded, the offer of the house to J.B.K. notwithstanding.

Yesterday, which was the day of the funeral, I did a final version of the speech. My piece appeared in the *Washington Post*. I think on the whole it was quite good, and this, I believe, was the common view. I got some satisfaction from having done it.

We gathered in the lobby of the White House at 10:30 A.M. where the great from all countries were now arriving. Lord Home, Prince Philip, Mikoyan, Pearson,[15] all lined up to sign the book as though waiting for their hats and coats. The caisson with the coffin came from the Capitol, and as it passed through the White House grounds, we fell in behind. My companions for the march up Connecticut Avenue were Lem Billings[16] and Nathan Pusey.[17] Kitty and Marian Schlesinger had gone ahead to the Cathedral. The weather was beautiful. Soldiers and airmen lined the route. The crowds were huge and utterly somber. Far ahead, we heard occasionally the piping of the Black Watch. I had little impression of the pageantry in fact. Anyone watching from the sidelines saw much more.

The church when we arrived was full, and I squeezed into a seat with the Harrimans, Marian and Kitty. The funeral service itself, my first experience with a full Catholic mass, was long and very formal. The only secular part was a reading from the Inaugural

[14] His rank was, in fact, that of Deputy Secretary of Defense.
[15] Leaders from England, Russia and Canada.
[16] See page 245.
[17] See page 13.

Address. At the end, the coffin was wheeled out; J.B.K. followed with Bob. Then the other members of the family and then the heads of state. I imagine no one ever looked down a narrow aisle and saw quite so many before: de Gaulle, Home, Pearson, U Thant, Erhard, the Japanese Foreign Minister, Belgians, Dutch, on and on. Eventually we made our way out, on down the steps to our cars and began the long ride out to Arlington. The caisson by this time was well on its way, and we gradually closed up with it. We came to the gates just as the flypast was marking the beginning of the graveside ceremony.

The ceremony at Arlington was the most heartrending time of all. The sky was blue and bright, and one had the impression of a day that had very little to do with death. People were massed on the hillside with flowers scattered everywhere. There was a prayer by Cardinal Cushing,[18] not eloquent but full of emotion. The twenty-one gun salute sounded and the muskets fired from the brilliantly polished ranks of soldiers, sailors and Marines. The music from the band was impressive and the playing of Last Post almost unbearably so. At the end, the flag was folded and given to J.B.K. It was over.

The rest was anticlimax. We went back and had a bite to eat at the Harrimans' and then I went to the White House to deliver the final version of the speech to the President and to Sorensen. I forgot to say that sometime during Sunday afternoon, I also had gone over the draft with Udall,[19] Wirtz,[20] and Freeman, the liberal wing of the Administration. Then I went to the State Department for a diplomatic reception for the heads of state. This was on the top floor in the vast room for such receptions and included a buffet supper. There were not enough high-ranking Americans available for all of the important people present. As the result, one saw Em-

18 See page 17.
19 See page 47.
20 See page 51.

peror Haile Selassie seated all by himself at a table with no one to talk to. Harriman introduced me to Dobrynin[21] who took me to Mikoyan who greeted me as the prophet of affluence and the man who had marked out the competition which the Soviet Union was to meet. He asked me what the effect of Kennedy's death would be on American-Soviet relations. I told him that I was sure that both countries remained in the hands of men of reason. He seemed to agree. He then asked me when I was coming to Russia. I told him that I had had some hope of going there next January as President Kennedy's representative, not as an expert on the Soviet Union but as an expert on the United States economy and to get some feeling of the economic prospect as between our two countries. He seconded the invitation.[22]

At this juncture, Hervé Alphand, the French Ambassador, asked me if I would like to meet de Gaulle. He was only a few feet away, and I had a ten- or fifteen-minute conversation with him. De Gaulle began by pointing to Mr. Mikoyan and asking why I had been conversing with such a short man. I said he obviously agreed with me that the world belongs to the tall men. They are more visible, therefore their behavior is better and accordingly they are to be trusted. He said that he agreed and added, "It is important that we be merciless with those who are too small." We then admired each other's books and he asked me the usual question. I told him I thought there was a real resilience in our political system; that we could survive the death of John F. Kennedy; that we needed to reflect less on the consequences of this action and more on the wickedness of the violence which struck down a man who so thoroughly loved life. De Gaulle said he agreed, that we had come to be far too casual about death. France and the United States both had a core of violent people still at large. Alphand joined the conversation to agree.

After a while, I felt that I had done my duty and made my way

[21] The Russian Ambassador.
[22] The journey did not materialize.

out. A very large crowd was assembled outside the State Department and I received an ovation. I was too surprised to respond.

I went back to the Grahams' and to bed.

I should say that at the reception, I had another brief chat with Johnson and told him that I had handed in the draft. I also told him that I would happily stay in town should he want me but otherwise would return to my classes.

This morning, Kitty called on various friends as did I — Elizabeth Condon,[23] Florence Mahoney[24] — and then at noon, I had a long talk with J.B.K. She seemed rather more distraught than when I saw her on Sunday. The barrenness of life seemed to be staring her in the face. We talked of how women used their time, what she might write about, friends and a great many other things.

She also contrasted the events of the last few days with the death of the baby.[25] The newspaper and TV men had managed to make the first into a theatrical production. This time they were somber. "It is the first time I have been out of the White House without people shouting, 'There's Jackie.'"

Then I had lunch with Arthur who was much more composed and, I think, partly reconciled to the thought of coming back to Cambridge. But not completely reconciled. Then we caught the two-thirty plane home.

[23] Then on Mrs. Kennedy's staff.
[24] See page 32.
[25] Patrick Bouvier Kennedy was born prematurely in August and lived less than two days.

Appendices

"Mother Doesn't Do Much"[1]

BY CATHERINE A. GALBRAITH

THE CHILDREN of the fourth grade at the American International School of New Delhi were required to write an essay on what their parents did. Our youngest son, James, said the following: "My father is Ambassador to India, or the chief United States official here. He does many different types of work. He writes reports for the United States Government on Indian conditions. He has conferences with the Indian Government to improve diplomatic relations. And also Dad makes speeches to make a little better the understanding between the U.S. and India and he represents the President on official occasions. Mother doesn't do much except arrange entertainment and administer the household."

He has a point. I don't rush about doing housework and errands. From 1951 until November 1962, when we moved, the official Residence of the United States Ambassador to India was a one-story white bungalow set in a bright green garden in a pleasant residential section of New Delhi. On the staff at this residence were three bearers, two cooks, a sweeper, a laundryman, a driver, three gardeners and three watchmen — fourteen regular servants for a six-room house. The new house, being much larger, requires more. In addition I have a Darzi to sew for us, and our housekeeper from the United States looks after the boys.

In running my household I give the instructions, then check up and recheck. Sometimes we have too much help. One day my

---

[1] This article first appeared in *The Atlantic Monthly* in May 1963. Copyright © 1963 by the Atlantic Monthly Company.

husband wanted a badminton net in the garden. Our three gardeners summoned six more helpers to put up two light bamboo poles.
Another day, to hang three small photographs our bearer called
the carpenter, who came with two assistants; one brought a tape
measure, one a hammer, and one nails.

In an Indian household the mistress of the house not only supervises the servants she employs, but she looks after their families as
well. As our cook said one day, "Madam is the mother of us all" —
that meant fifty children at last count. We must care for them
when they are sick, settle an odd quarrel and keep a strict watch on
their work. A gentle hand doesn't pay — now and then I have to
lay down the law. On the whole, though, they do well; also, they
can organize extra help to handle our heavy schedule. We must
be impartial in our favors; whatever is done for one must be done
for all. We give a glass of milk and cookies to the children every
day, tea to the servants, new saris to the wives at Diwali, small gifts
and money at Christmas. All of these things, plus medical bills, run
into quite an expense. I have wanted to set up a cooperative medical
health insurance plan for the domestic employees of the American
community, but the initial costs for this are high.

My day, in the hot weather (which is most of the time), begins
about six o'clock. It is the only possible hour for exercise, so I go
horseback riding. After a Hindi class at the Embassy I consult with
our secretaries and then return to the Residence to check the day's
arrangements with the head bearer and cook, make out our accounts, and decide any other matters that arise. The brass name-
plate on the gate is tarnished; must the sweeper or the watchman
polish it? Should bougainvillaea be planted instead of the old cedars
in the garden? Which gray should be selected for slipcovers for
the official car? What books are we to present to the children's
ward at Safdarjang Hospital? May the second bearer have a chit
to order his new shoes at a special store since his feet are so big?
Should the ladies wear gloves, hats and stockings to our Newcomers' Teas? In a six-room house, where do you hang thirty-one

paintings on loan to us from the Museum of Modern Art? On that I had lots of advice, all different; these paintings have attracted lively comment, much favorable.

The rest of the day there are calls and callers, meetings, interviews, receptions, dinners. We either go out or have guests, often both noon and night, almost every day in the week. Arranging the entertainment is a constant occupation. I have heard of one career ambassador's wife who, on her husband's retirement, gave away all her clothes except slacks.

We have given parties for a remarkable variety of American visitors and Indian guests. We had been in Delhi six weeks when Vice-President and Mrs. Johnson, Stephen and Jean Kennedy Smith dropped in for three days. The temperature was just under 120 degrees, but they bore up nobly. Since then we have had the Harvard Glee Club, the Davis Cup players, the Joey Adams troupe, the World Council of Churches, the World Medical Conference, the Bairds and their marionettes, Mark Robson and José Ferrer, who were here to make a film on the death of Gandhi, the American polo team, Henry Luce, Winthrop Aldrich, museum directors, zoo directors, Nobel Prize winners, several senators, the presidents of Harvard and Princeton, two young girl graduates hitchhiking their way around the world for two years on $500 each, the Peace Corps, the crews of our C-130's, who came to fly Indian troops and supplies to NEFA and Ladakh, James Farley, Yehudi Menuhin, Louis Untermeyer, Angie Dickinson, Averell Harriman, Luther Hodges, Arthur Schlesinger, Jr., Orville Freeman, Lowell Thomas, Norman Rockwell, Barbara Ward and, of course, Mrs. Kennedy.

Her visit was a major event of the spring, eagerly awaited, much enjoyed and not without problems. One was the number of people with an ironclad claim to meet her. She could see only a few thousand, and I was afraid we would not have a friend left in India. Yet in the end almost everyone was happy. Another problem was where she could stay in Delhi, since our house was too small; we rented a secluded little bungalow across the road. Word came that when alone she liked toasted cheese sandwiches for lunch. A selection of cheese was sent from Beirut, and the Indian cook practiced until the result was judged to be exactly like a drugstore sandwich at home. We held our farewell dinner for her at the new Edward Stone Chancery. Since this is strictly an office building and had never before been used as a dining hall, we held a dress rehearsal with the same menu two weeks ahead.

In arranging guest lists, I have help. Indeed, I often do not know until a few minutes beforehand just who is coming for lunch or dinner, and the seating plan and place cards are sent over by our social secretary. It is quite a different principle from arranging a dinner in Cambridge, Massachusetts. There the seating is largely determined by who should talk to whom to make a pleasant evening. And the guests are people we know well or hope to know better. In Delhi there is protocol. Usually this is not my headache, since it is all worked out at the office. But not everything goes according to plan.

One noon we were having a luncheon for some generals. The number of acceptances had risen during the last hour before lunch from fourteen to sixteen. Fourteen was all our regular dining-room table would hold, and so at that point we had to shift to two round tables each seating eight. The guests began arriving at one-fifteen; at one-twenty I found myself meeting a general and his wife who were not on the guest list, and the total number was obviously now eighteen. What to do? There was no time to change from two tables of eight to three of six, so I told the bearer to remove the butter plates; this way we could fit in nine at each table. I thought we had concealed the error, but I heard later that our unexpected guests had noticed that the handwriting on their place cards was different from that on the rest.

Another day our eager staff set up a luncheon for a visitor to Delhi described as "the Civilian Assistant to the Secretary of the Navy" (I slightly disguise matters here). Suitable admirals and other top-ranking officials were invited. Our guests of honor seemed a bit overwhelmed by all the brass, and they thanked us effusively for our kindness to them. During the course of luncheon I discovered they were an elderly couple on a world tour and that their son had once been in charge of some sea scouts.

Many of our housekeeping difficulties have been due to the size of the Residence. Now we have moved to a beautiful new mansion next door to the Chancery, also designed by Mr. Stone. In April 1961, when we arrived, construction had already begun, and since the United States Government was in charge and the experts had long ago made the plans, I did not expect to be involved. However, I soon found out that, like Blandings, I was building a house.

The servants' quarters lacked windows and bathrooms; we redesigned them to provide both. I was asked to suggest what to put in the garden and set about learning the names and characteristics of the flowering trees and shrubs that make New Delhi so lovely. The local press noted that full-grown trees were being hauled in by bullock cart. Transplanting at this stage is not usual in India, possibly with good reason; though now everywhere else the landscape is lush and green, our new trees look like November in Vermont.

The new Residence was built by hand. Stonecutters chipped away at rocks; plasterers and painters hung from apparently precarious scaffolding made of bamboo tied with rope; and beautiful straight-backed Rajasthani women in red swirling skirts and silver anklets carried away countless baskets of earth from foundations, swimming pool and sunken garden, and lifted trays of cement into the house and up the spiral staircase on their heads. And they patiently planted thousands of tufts of grass to make our lawn, with their children squatting beside them.

Our first party at the new house was for those five hundred workers who toiled night and day for a year and a half to get it completed only a few months behind schedule. It was a gay afternoon of song and dance, and we joined them in a strenuous Punjabi number called the Bhangra. There were Coca-Colas and sweets, toys for the children, and speeches. Mine, in Hindi, brought a warm response, since it was brief and the only one they could understand.

Our new house gives us space. We can once more live under the same roof with our children, and it is easy to entertain in.

My callers usually come for some purpose. An Indian student may want to know how to apply to an American college. I am asked to visit a welfare center, a clinic, or to help with a fair. The Americans in Delhi have many projects in which we take an interest, including the construction of the new American International School. That, too, is taking longer and costing more than expected, but the architect, Joseph Allen Stein, an American who has been working in India for more than ten years, has created a most imaginative building, one which may well become a model for future school design.

I am often invited to go to the theater, to concerts, dance programs and art exhibits. A troupe hopes to tour in the United States; I must find out how they should go about it or give an opinion as to how an American audience would react. This can be delicate. Once in a while I get in over my depth. I was told I should hear a famous South Indian singer, so I went. She sang devotional songs I could not understand, for more than four hours without a break. The Indian audience was ecstatic.

A small part of the day is devoted to mail. I am wary of the letters that begin "Gracious Lady Galbraith" or "Beloved Mother." One young man wanted me to treat him as a son and send him ten lakhs of rupees (over $200,000) for a purpose he would tell me about later. A man from Kerala merely wanted me to build him a house. Another asked for books for a children's library; we discovered that the library was his own. A Bible Society heard that an embassy car was for sale and hoped I would buy it for them to use to distribute Bibles, instead of their 1932 jalopy. The mother of a little girl who cannot speak would like to send her to the United States because there is no speech therapist in all of India; I could tell her that our medical program includes plans to bring a speech therapist to the All India Medical Institute in Delhi and to send Indians to the United States for this training.

We have attended impressive state functions — banquets for heads of state held under the regal portraits of former viceroys, receptions in the Moghul Gardens of the Rashtrapati Bhavan, national festivities such as those for Republic Day or the inauguration of the new President. These ceremonies are conducted with great dignity and style, for the Indians have carried over the pageantry of their past into their new national life. The ceremonies are also conducted with great sobriety; because there is semiprohibition the toasts are drunk with fruit juice.

It is exciting to be in India now, for one can see the old beside the new. India's history goes back thousands of years. At the time the Pilgrims were building log cabins in Salem, Shah Jahan was building the Taj Mahal. But India became an independent nation a decade and a half ago. The contrasts are striking. In Delhi, buses, scooter taxis, and bicycles weave in among the tongas and oxcarts. New housing developments spring up around old tombs and ancient forts; those monuments are so familiar and numerous that no one can tell you for whom or when they were built. You go to a village, even on the outskirts of a city, and you see how life has gone on in the same way for centuries. There are the same wooden plows and plodding bullocks, the same cow-dung fires and Persian waterwheels, the same bright saris bending over the rice fields — though the ubiquitous black umbrellas used for sunshades must have come in with the British. You think there has been no change, and then you discover that the village now has a small dispensary, very simple by our standards; a handful of nurses and a doctor serve thousands of patients. Or there is an eye clinic, set up in tents so that it can be moved from district to district; two hundred thin old men and women lie on charpoys waiting for operations for glaucoma. Each operation takes about ten minutes, and the doctors are busy all day. Or a farmer comes proudly to show off his new crop of peas; they are much fatter and sweeter than before, because of improved varieties, irrigation and fertilizer.

But it has become a time of peril for India. Its problems are very great. With half the area of the United States, it has nearly three times the population. People are everywhere — in the lonely jungle, clinging to the steep Himalayas, sleeping on the city streets, and clustered all over the plains. Most of these people are poor, customs are diverse, and many tensions have threatened to disunite the nation. India so far has kept a full parliamentary system of government, its heritage from the British, but the Chinese have already marched. In its plans for development India counted on peace. Will the cost of war to a poor country be disaster, or will the need for preparation hasten progress? Right now people are donating their gold bangles, their life savings, their blood; women are forming knitting parties, and girls in saris are training on the rifle range. In the villages the people are asking what they can do. There is a sense of urgency and national purpose, and also, initially, bewilderment. The Chinese action was a great jolt.

Since Independence progress has been made, though the answers to India's problems are not simple. For instance, DDT has checked malaria, but the decline in disease has raised the birthrate. The solution to poverty can start with small things — a new well, better seeds, an outside market for village handwork, a teacher and a little school. It can also start with big things — dams and power plants and factories. The United States has helped with both.

One of our great privileges has been the opportunity to travel and to see what is going on. Usually we fly in one of our Embassy planes — a Convair if the airfields are 4,500 feet long, otherwise a DC-3, which can land even on the meadow in the narrow Kulu Valley. The Convair is comfortable for long distances. In addition to seats for sixteen passengers, it has a rear section for the Ambassador, with two couches, a large leather lounge chair, a table and desk.

When we arrive at the airport on official visits we are garlanded, photographed and driven off to the governor's mansion or the state guesthouse. Usually a police inspector rides in the front seat. (Once, outside Calcutta, our protector jammed his finger in the car door and fainted; my husband picked up his bodyguard and laid him gently on the nearest table.) We call on the governor, the chief minister, the mayor; attend receptions, cultural programs, and dinners at which we forgather in good academic fashion, men on one side, wives on the other. We shop hurriedly for handicrafts at the government emporium, and, if we are lucky, have a little time for sightseeing. I may have a special schedule arranged by worthy women's organizations. There are press conferences, and my husband often speaks. By now he has lectured at most of the leading universities in India.

At major functions my husband makes the speeches while I sit quietly on the platform and share the garlands. But if he is not around to talk, then I must. This can happen without warning. The first time was at a girls' school in Cochin, where, having been invited to pay an informal call, I was led to the platform in front of the entire student body, seated on a red plush chair between the principal and the archbishop, and handed a printed program which read "Speech by Mrs. Galbraith."

Twice I have presented mobile kitchens (jeeps with trailers) from Wheat Associates to be used to teach the village women how to cook the wheat we give them when the rice crop fails. I have judged floats in parades, distributed sweets to children, awarded prizes. In one village, after inspecting a neat little hospital, I was handed a baby spotted deer which promptly began to munch the flowers around my neck.

I have even undertaken trips on my own, to celebrate, as a state guest, the harvest festival in Kerala, when they have the wonderful snake-boat processions and the noisiest fireworks, and to visit the first Peace Corps group in the Punjab. That was in August, and it was hot. But despite the wearing heat, minor discouragements and a few amoebas, they were hard at work raising chickens, designing housing for villages, teaching, studying and demonstrating methods of farming. Every one of them was enthusiastic about being in India, and no one complained of the simple living conditions. They were a good group, glad for what they were learning and eager to be of more service. They have already won the regard of their Indian neighbors.

Our travels have covered most of India, from the lush coconut groves of Kerala to the cool valleys of Kashmir, and from the monumental Gateway of India in Bombay to the small Naga villages beyond Assam. Our two weeks in April 1962 near the North East Frontier now seem to have been planned with special prescience.

On this trip we stayed at a cinchona plantation near Kalimpong and feasted on roast sheep and beer made by pouring hot water over millet in bamboo mugs; it ferments while you wait. Next we visited the Maharajah of Sikkim in the tiny mountain capital of Gangtok, where we were protected by five-foot palace guards in uniforms which make Hollywood seem real. In Shillong, the capital of Assam, we stayed with the Governor in a large Tudor-style mansion, and then we crossed the Brahmaputra River to go to a game preserve just over the border in Bhutan. This little frontier country is so remote that it did not then even have a postal system; the first Bhutanese stamps were issued last October. We thought we would be roughing it, but we found that three hundred people had worked fourteen days to build us a camp on a bluff above the rushing Manas River. Out of split bamboo they had created a village of basket-weave houses which they had furnished with real beds, new sheets, full-length-mirror dressing tables, all brought in by dugout for our two-night stay. We, too, were poled up the river in dugouts and were met on the opposite shore by six large elephants which carried us the rest of the way along a path lined with bright prayer flags. The riverbank on which we stayed is now one of the danger routes into India. It all seemed very peaceful then.

Our final stop was Manipur, in the green hills by the Burmese border. It was here that we saw polo played by men on little ponies, and danced with the Naga tribes, my husband wearing a

headband with peacock feathers and I a golden cardboard crown.
women do all the work, but they also control the purse strings and,
The valley people are a different lot, easygoing and gentle. Their
The Naga tribes, not long ago headhunters, are mostly in the hills.
being independent, are free to change or discard a husband when
convenient. They were a happy, graceful people, fond of bright
clothes and dancing. Now they are close to the fighting.

We travel in order to get acquainted with regional problems and
politics, and also to highlight American aid. Of course, this help is
not new; Americans have been contributing for years to agricultural and industrial development, to medicine and to education,
through our government, our foundations and other agencies. We
do not believe, however, that such work should be done in secret.
In Kerala, the most literate and the most unsettled politically of all
the Indian states, my husband not long ago announced a loan for
two vast dams which will more than double the present supply of
electricity. In Calcutta, too, a loan was announced for a thermal
power plant. On this occasion everything went wrong with the
ceremony. It began with a cloudburst. The two speakers, my
husband and the late Dr. B. C. Roy, got there by jeep, but the audience bogged down in the mud, so the speeches were not made. The
teacups blew away, and when my husband planted the symbolic
gulmohar tree he dug with such enthusiasm that the silver trowel
broke in half. He symbolically watered the tree while it rained an
inch an hour. However, all these disasters served to make a better
story.

Some of the most heartwarming work is what we have done for
children. This is largely accomplished through CARE. In Mus-
soorie, in the mountains north of Delhi, I visited a Tibetan refugee
camp; the triple-decker cots, as many as seventy in a room, and
much of the kitchen supplies had come from CARE. In Madras we
met a ship which was unloading four million pounds of powdered
milk from the United States Government for CARE. One of our

most beautiful mornings was spent at a school just outside Trivandrum in Kerala which was inaugurating a school-lunch program for several hundred children, with food also provided by the United States Government through CARE. Girls in bright blue skirts and white blouses greeted us with coconut lamps, flower petals and garlands, and under the *shamiana* (colorful awning) which had been set up for the ceremony were chandeliers made of fragrant white tuberoses. Meanwhile, outside, little boys and girls sat patiently in rows, their leaf plates and brass cups in front of them, waiting for the end of the speeches so that they could eat. We were told that the school lunches do away with the truant officer; sometimes this is the only meal these children get in twenty-four hours. The program starts with the first grade, and poor parents have been advancing the ages of their four-year-olds to get them into school early so they will be fed. We have recently also opened another school-lunch program for 500,000 children in Rajasthan.

In early October we went by special train through central India on a ten-day U.S. AID tour. Our party of fifty included twenty-eight Indian and American journalists, for by showing them our projects at first hand, we thought they would become aware of the contribution of the United States to Indian development. Our train had nine cars — three of air-conditioned bedroom compartments, two dining cars, two baggage cars, a car for the officials of the railway accompanying us, and the Ambassador's special coach, belonging to the president of the railway. Divisional superintendents were instructed to ensure "stabling" at quiet sidings, to keep platforms and surroundings scrupulously clean and the staff on duty tidy, to supply chilled boiled water and ice, and hot water for baths, good food, laundry facilities and a doctor "equipped to meet any emergency" throughout the journey.

To go across India in this way, just after the monsoon, protected from the hubbub of the highways, is in itself a delightful experience. As the sun rises in the rain-clear sky you see the farmer already out in the bright green rice fields driving his white bullocks and the women in blue or red or green saris coming from the well with shining brass water jugs on their heads, and in the remote stretches where only the railway tracks pass, the villages with their red-tiled roofs look very well kept.

We were busy. We visited power plants, a coal washery, the docks at Bombay where American wheat was being unloaded, training centers for teaching the use and maintenance of heavy equipment, a district experimenting in raising food production by putting into practice modern agricultural techniques and the new Indian Institute of Technology, now being started with the help of some of our leading professors, that aspires to equal M.I.T. South of Hyderabad we inspected a huge dam which, except for two tall U.S. cranes, is being built like the pyramids of old, by thousands of workmen, some of them children (though that is illegal), carrying concrete on their heads up zigzag bamboo ramps. For buildings up to the height of 120 feet we were told that human labor is cheaper than machines. It must always be remembered that this is a country of many poor people, and many people need jobs.

We also paid a visit to Literacy Village in Lucknow, the dream come true of a remarkable American, Mrs. Welthy Fisher, now over eighty. Here young women are trained to go out into the villages to teach reading, books are written, and ways of communicating new ideas to illiterates are devised. A favorite method is through puppets. We were treated to a skit on family planning, the romance of Birju and Chanda, whose happy marriage turns to despair when in five years they have five children. The bride has become an old woman, the children fight and one who is ill vomits yellow liquid over the edge of the stage. When Chanda whispers to Birju that she is expecting yet another baby, he rushes out to hang himself, but is rescued by the village-level worker, who sends him to the doctor at the block headquarters for much-needed advice.

The trip accomplished its purpose. Many articles were written about our work in India. A week later the Chinese marched into the North East Frontier. After that, there was hardly any need to emphasize American aid. When my husband went to the Lok Sabha one day, even his car was garlanded, and strangers rushed up to thank him as though he were providing the assistance from his own pocket. But the appreciation of U.S. generosity and compassion is no sudden thing. It has existed for a long time, even in out-of-the-way places. On our way to Bhutan across the hot dusty roads of Assam, where we had not met another car for miles, my husband was dozing in the back seat of the car with his shoes off when I noticed ahead of us crowds of people gathering as though for a fair. But they came to see us. In this poor little village they had heard we were passing through; they stopped the car to give us a letter, written in longhand and framed, expressing their warm friendship for the United States.

In spite of differences of opinion that arise, our relations with India rest on respect. The Indians know that we help them not because we are richer and want power but because we care and because we believe, as they do, in the value of human life and in the freedom and dignity of the individual. It is to our mutual advantage and interest to stand by one another since we hold the same faith.

Art, Diplomacy and Vice Versa[1]

AT A BIG farewell reception at the Embassy Residence in New Delhi just prior to my departure in 1963, my Deputy Chief of Mission observed that the only real manifestation of grief he could detect was that of the art dealers. "I think you see in *their* faces," he said, "the deeper emotion of men who are facing financial loss." I looked closely at one of my special friends. There was, indeed, a suggestion of a tear in his deeply dishonest eyes.

For going on three years these men had been my most frequent and, on the whole, my most welcome visitors. But it was not so much my occupationally cautious purchases they would miss. It was my advertising value — the chance to say impressively to other customers, "Sahib, I happen to know that the American Ambassador likes *this* piece. I showed it to him only last night." I would guess that a considerable fraction of the paintings changing hands in New Delhi and Jaipur during these years, including some terrible frauds, had my strong and often wholly imaginary endorsement.

This was unfortunate for the purchasers, although the price was modest as compared with Berenson's authentications, and most of them could afford it. The advantage for me was overwhelming. Nothing serves an ambassador like a reputation, deserved or otherwise, as an expert on the arts. One can not only admire the local wonders, which is the oldest strategy of ingratiation, but give an

[1] This article first appeared in the March 1967 issue of *Esquire Magazine*. Copyright © 1967 by Esquire, Inc.

impromptu lecture on them as well. Once when I apologized to Nehru, a man of meticulous promptness, for being a few minutes late for an appointment, he said, "I always imagine that you have something more important to do, such as looking at paintings." Not long before we left, he came over to our new Residence to inspect some interesting items I had found. On an earlier visit to India, he told me that he had just finished reading *The Affluent Society*. It was my impression — it didn't seem tactful to come out and ask — that he thought both the writing and reading pretty much a waste of time. But no one associated with the arts can be so accused; art by its nature is indifferent to time. And, unlike economics, engineering or astronomy, an interest therein is not assumed to reflect some new and uniquely crafty manifestation of American imperialism.

Besides, the Indian subcontinent is an artistic and architectural treasure-house of simply endless fascination. That was partly the reason I was there. During an earlier stay in India, I went one day with my wife to lunch with John Sherman Cooper, then President Eisenhower's Ambassador and the American for whom, next perhaps only to Mrs. Kennedy, Prime Minister Nehru entertained the greatest affection. It occurred to me during lunch that the Embassy would be an admirable base for anyone who wanted to get his back into Indian problems in general and Indian art in particular. By the end of the 1960 campaign, I had managed to convey some hints of this revelation to the successful candidate, although with rather greater emphasis on economics than art. It was not certain how far the President-elect would go in indulging what he seemed likely to consider the lighter fancies of his friends and supporters. On my earlier trips to India, I had made a start on architecture, temple sculpture and the Buddhist painting — that of Ajanta in particular — to which almost all later work is indebted. After the first few months, for the rest of my tour of duty, I managed to find an hour or two a day for these matters. This was not so difficult as the legend holds. The job of an ambassador is much like that of an airline pilot — there are hours of boredom and minutes of panic.

Art is a reliable antidote to boredom and by far the best relaxation in times of stress. The last is a very practical matter, for the alternative is a heavy dose of sleeping pills. You are then in poor shape for an emergency which, dependably, will strike an hour later. This, I gather, explains what happened in Santo Domingo.

Eventually I found myself concentrating on Indian paintings of the sixteenth, seventeenth and eighteenth centuries, especially the latter part of this period, one of the most fascinating epochs in the history of art.

The interest lies less in the artists than the patrons. In addition to the Buddhist painting which I have mentioned, there is an ancient tradition of artistic patronage in India. But neither there nor elsewhere were there ever any patrons like the Moghuls. This dynasty established itself in India from central Asia in 1526 and ruled, or anyhow endured, for the next three hundred and twenty-five years. After Akbar the Great (1556–1605), the administrative skills of the dynasty were not visible; perhaps the greatest military accomplishment of the rulers was in getting the great Rajput princes to do their fighting. (The Rajputs, who are Hindus and who until 1948 held great feudatory states in western India, are the descendants, it is generally believed, of yet earlier invaders from Asia. In those days they were endemically belligerent.) Nor were the Moghuls especially diligent or ambitious. A description survives of the daily rountine of Jahangir, son of Akbar, written by an English companion, one William Hawkins. In the morning, after prayers, the Emperor showed himself to the people at an oriel window in the palace. Having provided this reassurance, he went to the women's apartments with such effect that he then rested until three in the afternoon. Then he witnessed elephant fights or other sports and heard grievances and held court. Thereafter he went to his evening meal, for which he liked five kinds of meat, and then retired to his private apartments where he had five cups of wine, topped off with opium. This was in his active years; later on he drank and smoked more and turned practical matters over to Nurjahan, the most talented of his wives.

But Jahangir, like his father and Shah Jahan who followed him, was a man of impeccable taste. His court, like that of his father and his son, supported a great atelier of artists. (Akbar had more than a hundred.) Court personalities, court activities, sports and careful scientific studies of flora and fauna were all subjects. Even more important were the great pictorial histories of Courts and Rulers — the *Timur-namah*, *Babur-namah* and *Akbar-namah*. The Moghuls were Moslems and the orthodox of that faith believe that on the Day of Judgment, God will call upon all painters to put life in their pictures, a challenging prospect for Rubens and the abstract expressionists. Those who fail will be sent to hell, and, in consequence, Islam has generally been hostile to painting. The Moghuls rejected this doctrine, quite frankly, as foolish and bigoted.

After Jahangir came Shah Jahan who, with Lorenzo, must be counted one of the two greatest art patrons of all time. Architecture was his supreme achievement. Everything he did is marked by a magic which involves almost instant recognition. Had he not built the Taj Mahal, he would be remembered for the Red Fort in Delhi; and had he not built this majestic structure, the walls of which soar before your eyes and fade into the distance, the Pearl Mosque in Agra and half a dozen other buildings would secure his fame. His delight in his creations is attested by the exuberant verse he had inscribed in the Delhi Fort: *If there is heaven on the face of the earth,/It is this! It is this! It is this!*

The Moghuls did not recognize primogeniture; accordingly, when the emperor died, the sons fought democratically for the succession, and the survivor succeeded to the throne. With the passage of time, the fighting tended to break out whenever the emperor seemed infirm, and later still there was a strong tendency to anticipate infirmity with assassinations. Shah Jahan was a prodigious womanizer; each year there was an eight-day fair at his court at which the most attractive specimens from his dominions were displayed (under cover of selling ordinary merchandise) for his inspection and choice. He was allowed to take goods on approval. In his late sixties he fell ill, one gathers from the carefully guarded comments of Bernier, a French physician then at the Court, from an overdose of an aphrodisiac. His sons promptly began fighting, and, when he showed signs of getting well, he was deposed and locked up in the Agra fort with a distant view of the Taj Mahal. Presently one finds him writing his son not to demand his liberty but to protest against a protective barbican which was being placed over the gates of the Red Fort and which, the old Emperor said, would spoil the face of his lovely mistress. Though he reduced somewhat the number of painters maintained by the Court, Shah Jahan's taste was even more exacting than that of his father and grandfather.

In the time of Akbar, Persia was the recognized artistic and literary center of Islam and the Near East. Akbar's father, Humayun, lost his throne for a time and took his son to Persia. He persuaded two master artists, Abdus Samad and Mir Sayyid Ali, to return with them to India. Early Moghul painting shows, even to the casual eye, its Persian antecedents. The figures are small and beautifully executed; bright reds and brilliant blues flash from the picture in the manner of a Persian miniature and almost that of a stained-glass window. Before long, however, the painting began to reflect Hindu traditions and its own style. The figures became larger, and the portraiture developed a deep and luminous quality which unquestionably improved on the subjects. The painting was almost always on paper, of which the Moghuls soon provided a local supply, and the size was set by the comparatively small sheets. All Indian painting, early and late, is meant to be looked at in portfolios. It was never hung on walls.

A hundred artists, working diligently from dawn to dusk and perhaps with an apprentice to do the donkey-work of sky or vegetation, can turn out a great many paintings in a year. With the passage of time, moreover, artists who could not attach themselves to the royal atelier set up in town and sold their work to the nobles of the court or in the bazaars. Some of these men were talented copyists, and, since the original work at the palace was mostly unsigned, not even the most erudite critic can now distinguish with certainty between the first treatment of a subject or theme and that of a really talented copyist who came later. This is another source of fascination. A considerable amount of this work survives, and anyone can have an opinion as to what is original and is entitled to believe that what he owns or likes most certainly is.

The provincial governors and nabobs imitated the great courts at Delhi and Agra and had also their artists. They probably had even more faithful copyists. One of the most popular of all Indian themes is the love of an early Moslem ruler, Baz Bahadur, for his Hindu queen, Rupmati, a romance which seems to have been conducted entirely on horseback.

Invasion, fire, pillage, white ants and farseeing Englishmen have accounted for most of the painting of the great Moghul courts. But the artists who worked there were the source of a yet greater tradition of painting, and this work is still coming to light.

To the west and south of Delhi are the Rajput Kingdoms, great and small. Some of these had long been the custodians of the older Hindu tradition in painting, and in all of them the Moghuls stimulated a great artistic revival. To be reputable, a prince had to have a school of painters, and, recurrently, one imagines, what began as an appurtenance of courtly life became an obsession. To some of the courts, such as the great desert kingdom of Bikaner, the Moghuls sent artists as a form of cultural extension.

The Rajput painting was stronger in its use of colors than that of the Moghuls and generally less precise — or inhibited — in its drawing. The Hindu Epics were, for the Rajput painters, what the New Testament was to the Renaissance artists. Instead of Mary and the Christ Child, Krishna, a playful incarnation of the Hindu god Vishnu — for unknown reasons always painted in blue — appears in picture after picture. He is either surrounded by milk-maids, called Gopis, in highly lecherous pursuit of them, or the subject of their equally amorous search. The *Kama Sutra* had the same fascination for the Rajput artists as for the modern pornographer and conceivably for the same reasons. In consequence, the act of love was portrayed in precise and exquisite detail and with an inventiveness that my generation always attributed to modern Paris. The Rajput husbands were usually away fighting, and the painters reassured them with innumerable paintings showing how their women suffered in their absence. Much of this work is frankly lesbian, and it gave me, a year or two ago, a marvelous insight into the American sexual response, at least at the higher academic levels. With Mr. Cary Welch, the noted Harvard authority on Indian paintings, I helped assemble a collection of Rajput paintings for exhibition at the Fogg Museum at Harvard, then at the Asia House Gallery and later in Baltimore and Utica. Paintings of wholesome, face-to-face heterosexual encounter of superb quality were virtuously excluded as indecent. An aggressively lesbian painting went unremarked through the entire exhibition. Women, if they want to be respectable, will keep to themselves in this country.

Although the Rajput painting had common themes and a common commitment to strong colors, each court had its own styles and idioms. These also changed over time, and it is the pride of the accomplished student of the subject that he can tell at which court — Amber (now Jaipur), Mewar (now Udaipur), Kotah, Bundi, Jodhpur, or Bikaner — and within a few years, where and when a painting was done. It is equally his pride, sometimes rather fierce, that anyone who disagrees is wrong. The Jaipur rulers got along well with the Moghuls, whom they served both as generals and governors, and, indeed, were considered by some houses to have carried collaboration to extremes. Their painting, appropriately enough, reflects the strongest Moghul influence of any of the Rajput courts.

After Shah Jahan was imprisoned in 1658, the Delhi empire fell into artistic and, soon thereafter, into acute administrative disrepair. The later rulers were lushes or sloths; from coronation to the routine assassination was sometimes only a year or two. More and more artists sought the patronage, as well as the comparative secu-

rity, of the Rajput courts. There were brief periods of revival —
one from 1707 to 1739 — but, in general, the movement was away.
Then, in 1738, Nadir Shah, the Persian marauder, invaded India,
and in the following year he seized Delhi, conducted a notable mas-
sacre of the citizens and departed with numerous works of art, including the Peacock Throne. The result was one of the most remarkable episodes in all the history of art, for numerous artists took
refuge in the remote valleys of the Himalayas and did marvelous
work which remained unknown to the world at large for a hundred
and fifty years.

One other great school was lost for a similar time. In 1943, Eric
Dickinson, a Professor of History at Government College in Lahore, visited Kishangarh, a small Rajput state on the plains something under a hundred miles south of Jaipur. After looking at some
commonplace work in the collection of the Maharajah, he was
shown, apparently with some reluctance, a portfolio of rather
larger paintings. As he later said, "Before our astonished gaze was
revealed a decor and a milieu that to match so rare a content might
have taxed the Abyssinian maid singing on Mount Abora." It was
an occasion for hyperbole and even slightly irregular syntax. The
painting done in the mid-years of the eighteenth century at this
lovely little court has a magic grace and refinement, a subtle exaggeration of face and feature and an enchanting aura of mystery.
The patron was a poet prince called Sawant Singh, who, eventually, gave up his throne to become a religious recluse. His mistress,
a poetess known as Bani Thani, was beautiful in the manner of the
Mona Lisa and is thought to be the model for many of the Kishangarh pictures. Somewhat exceptionally among Indian painting, the
name of the greatest of the Kishangarh artists is known. His work
is unsigned. But aware without doubt of its quality, he painted himself into a beautiful court scene and duly identified himself in the
legend as Nihal Chand, Master Artist. Although the best Kishangarhs have been published, few people to this day have seen the
originals. They remain with the Maharajah and are rarely shown.

But the even more spectacular episode of the lost art was in the hills. North and west of Delhi, on the top left-hand face of the Indian diamond, valleys from the Punjab plain extend into the Himalayas. Some of these, like the Kangra and Kulu Valleys, are some fifty miles in length and several wide; others are only tiny rifts in the mountains. All are cool, green and beautiful and flanked by the world's highest peaks. For hundreds of years, until the beginning of the nineteenth century, they were the domain of a score or more of minor rajahs. Some of these rulers had fiefs of only a few square miles, but many had palaces and castles of considerable pretense or even grandeur. It was here that the artist, in flight from Delhi, found refuge. At least one tiny principality, that of Basohli, already had a tradition of painting. It featured bold reds and yellows and vigorous line and it may well have been a source of some envy by the other rajahs. The newly arrived artists, and those they taught, now made it possible for any mountain prince to be a patron. So when they were not fighting each other, they compared and exchanged the work of their ateliers, and, when their daughters went off to marry, they took portfolios of paintings along with them as a reminder of home.

The painting varied in idiom and also in quality from court to court. The best, rivaling the best of Indian painting, was (subject to some scholarly dispute) done at Guler. This small state stood at the entrance to the Kangra Valley from the plains and owed its existence to one of the more remarkable accidents of nation-making. In 1405, the ruler of the neighboring and much larger state of Kangra was out hunting, got separated from his companions, and, after nightfall, fell into a well, presumably an irrigation well, in a field. He was rescued some days later by a passing merchant, but by then his wives had committed *sati*, i.e., had immolated themselves on a fire as custom obliged, and his brother had ascended the throne. An inordinately thoughtful man, the prince reflected on the enormous inconvenience he would cause if he returned home. So he proceeded to the present site of Haripur, built a fortress and

626   AMBASSADOR'S JOURNAL

founded a new kingdom. In the eighteenth century, it harbored
two talented Kashmiri Brahmin brothers, Manak and Nain Sukh,
one of whom, Manak, remained. He founded a school of incom-
parable grace and delicacy of line at this tiny court. In the paintings
from Guler the color is much more closely controlled and delicate
than the painting of the plains. The women of the mountain valleys
are tall, with firm, high breasts, striking black hair, clear skin and
pure strong faces. They may be as lovely as any women on earth,
and they grace all of the paintings of these valleys. It cannot be
said that it does them more than justice.

The Guler school set a style and a standard for the other courts.
The most important of these was Kangra, and in 1776 another of
the notable patrons to whom Indian painting owes so much made
his appearance there. This was Sansar Chand, who, in 1776, at the
age of ten, came to the throne in Tira Sajanpur, a magic little capital on a glade and hill overlooking the Beas River in the Kangra
Valley. Ten years later, he took possession of the towering fortress
at Kangra, which for centuries had dominated the valley and neighboring states, and which is still one of the great sights of the valley.
Artists flocked to Sansar Chand's courts; there was a great outpour-
ing of work, depicting the Hindu Epics, court scenes, the seasons
and a fabulous amount of love and lovemaking. Not all of this
work is good, and the provenance of some of the best is disputed.
But with that in Guler and, in lesser quality and amount, at neighboring courts, it represented a remarkable burst of artistic creativ-
ity. The Kangra court gave its name to much of the other painting
in the hills. To the outside world it remained unknown.

Sansar Chand, like Shah Jahan, had an unhappy end. The Gurkhas, whose belligerent tendencies had not yet been harnessed
for pay by the British, were then a great nuisance. They came
down from Nepal and threatened his kingdom. He called on the
Sikhs in the plains below for help, and they rescued him and made
him *their* vassal. Discouraged, he locked himself up in his palace.
Courtiers and others who came to pay respects were required to

give them to a kamal tree at the entrance to the palace. In New Delhi, dozens of people — Indian politicians, American business-men, tourists from all lands, other diplomats, the educated unem-ployed and the elegantly underemployed — come to pay their re-spects to the American Ambassador. I thought constantly of call-ing up a nursery and getting a kamal tree. But I concluded that the State Department probably had some regulation or other against it.

Some fifty or sixty years ago, people with a feeling for such mat-ters began to notice that some remarkable paintings were turning up in the bazaars of Amritsar in the Punjab, and elsewhere on the plains, and were being sold — one supposes — for a few cents. The work was traced back into the valleys and mountains, and in the years of World War I they became the subject of a great pioneer-ing study by the Sinhalese art authority, Ananda K. Coomara-swamy. (He assembled the great collection of this painting in the Boston Museum of Fine Arts.) Interest again lagged, but in the last two decades painting in the valleys has been the subject of intense search and study. Magnificent collections have come to light, some of them in the hands of descendants of the rajahs and some pos-sessed by people who were quite unaware of their treasure. A few are still being found. Some collections have been dispersed, but the best, fortunately, are in the Indian museums and private Indian col-lections. The best-known, most diligent and scholarly of the new generation of scholars is an Indian Civil Servant, naturalist, soil-conservation expert, museum buyer and (at this writing, 1967) administrator of the Corbusier city of Chandigarh, named M. S. Randhawa.

By the 1830's and 1840's, British power and influence was para-mount in the upper Ganges and extending into the domains of the Rajputs and the mountain rajahs. This higher civilization of Vic-toria brought inexpensive lithography and, a little later, that yet greater invention, the camera. It also brought inexpensive pig-ments to replace the earth colors — the ground-up rock — which the Indian painters had laboriously prepared and mixed with vegetable oils. The patrons soon came to measure their artistic prestige not by their paintings but by their reproductions, snapshots and photographs. And the new dyes, splashed on the old burnished papers, were hideous. Within a decade or two, so compelling was the higher culture, all worthwhile painting came to an end.

Now in Udaipur, Jaipur and one or two other places — such is the remarkable capacity of Indian craftsmanship to accommodate itself to a market — there is a slight revival. It consists in copying the ancient masterworks for Western tourists, to whom they are sold as originals. These were among the paintings to which vendors imaginatively accorded my authentication. Once in the spring of 1963 in Udaipur, where I was the guest for the opening of a new hotel in the middle of Pichola Lake, an American lady brought me a Kishangarh which she had just purchased. The dealer had told her I thought well of it; I guessed conservatively it might be three weeks old. The originals of the *genre* are still mostly with the Maharajah; good ones come up for sale only at rare intervals. But I gave the forgery my endorsement. The lady liked it. It was far less expensive than the original, and her purchase encouraged the revival.

APPENDIX III

A Communication[1]

IN THESE LAST FEW HOURS, hundreds, thousands of men have tried to write about John F. Kennedy. This is not wholly a ritual of the modern newspaper, one of the final rites of the great. Millions of people on this dark and somber weekend want to read about, and then to reflect on this man who was so profoundly a part of their lives. This wish the papers are seeking to serve.

My justification for this brief word is not that of a friend but of a writer who knew the President a trifle better than most of those who must tell of him in these days.

No one knew the President well. In a sense no one could for it is part of the character of a leader that he cannot be known. The rest of us can indulge our moments when we open the shutters to our soul. We are granted our moments of despair — the despair, indeed, that we felt on Friday when that incredible flash came in from Dallas. But a Kennedy or a Roosevelt can never turn the palms of his hands outward to the world and say: "Oh God. What do we do now?" That armor which ensures confidence in power and certainty in command may never be removed even for a moment. No one ever knew John F. Kennedy as other men are known.

But he carried his armor lightly and with grace and, one sometimes thought, with the knowledge that having it without escape, at least it need not be a barrier before his friends and associates. He surprised even friends with the easy candor with which he spoke

---

[1] This article first appeared in *The Washington Post*, November 25, 1963. Copyright © 1963 by The Washington Post Co.

of touchy problems, half-formed plans, or personal political dangers. Without malice or pettiness, he contemplated the strengths and weaknesses of high officials and influential politicians. He was constantly and richly amused by the vanities of men in high places. He freely discussed ideas the mention of which would make most men shudder. Last summer during the visit of President Sarvepalli Radhakrishnan of India, in a social moment before a formal dinner, mention was made of some woman politician. He turned and asked me why there had been so few women politicians of importance — whether women were poorly adapted to the political art. Here surely was a politically ticklish subject; women are half the voting population and might not react well to wonder at their political shortcomings. I struggled to come up with examples — the first Elizabeth, Mrs. F.D.R., one or two others. The President admitted of the exceptions but good-humoredly returned to the rule. He knew he could discuss an interesting point without anyone supposing that he was against the Nineteenth Amendment.

"The political campaign won't tire me," he said in the spring of 1960, "for I have an advantage. I can be myself." He had learned one of the hardest lessons of life which is that we all have far more liberty than we use. And he knew beyond this, that others because they admired it would respect the informality with which he passed through life. No President ever said so much to so many friends and acquaintances and so rarely had to disavow or explain.

John F. Kennedy was much interested in writing. This, I think, provides one small clue to understanding. Good writing requires a sense of economy and of style and that absence of vanity which allows a man to divorce his writing at least a little from himself. A writer can be interesting when he is speaking to others; he is rarely if ever interesting when he is speaking to himself except to himself.

Mr. Kennedy hated verbosity. Though he rejoiced in politics, he hated the wordiness of the political craft. He never, at least in his adult life, opened his mouth without having something to say.

Never even in conversation did he speak for the pleasure of hearing his own words and phrases. Many of us have a diminished interest in the words of others. Mr. Kennedy was impatient with wordy men. But he was the rare case of the man who applied the rules with equal rigor against himself.

The Kennedy style, though it involved detachment from self, involved no self-deprecation. In the early years when he was enlisting followers, he did not offer a program for universal salvation. He was suspicious of resonant formulae from whatever source — he rightly regarded some of the liturgy of American liberalism as corrupt. It is trundled out at election time as once were the candidate's trains, urged in a torrent of words and then put away for four years. His case again had the merit of candor. He said essentially, I am a man worth following, you can count on me to be honestly better at the art of government than any other possible contender, and, an important detail, I know how to get elected.

That he was qualified in the art of government there will never be any question. His style called for unremitting good taste and good manners. It called also for a profound commitment to information and reason. He did not think that man had been civilized as an afterthought; he believed it was for a purpose. Perhaps there are natural men, those who have the original gift of art and insight. Mr. Kennedy without being so rude as to say so would believe such pretension an excuse for laziness. His reliance was on what men had learned and had come to know.

What Mr. Kennedy had come to know about the art and substance of American Government was prodigious. I first knew Jack Kennedy twenty-five years ago when I was a comparatively young tutor and he was an undergraduate in Winthrop House at Harvard. He was gay, charming, irreverent, good-looking and far from diligent. What no one knew at the time was that he had the priceless notion that education never stops. Some of us who later worked with him on economic issues — farm policy, interest rates, Federal Reserve policy, the control of inflation, other arcane or technical matters — used to say that we had observed three stages in his career in the House and more particularly in the Senate: The first was when he called up to ask how we thought he should vote; the second was when he telephoned to ask fifteen or twenty quick questions as to what lay behind the particular action or measure; the third was when he did not call at all or inquired as to why, as he had gleaned from an article or a letter to the *Times*, we seemed to be acting on some misinformation. My Harvard colleague Professor Carl Kaysen, who has worked in the White House these last years, has said that when asked who is the most knowledgeable of the President's advisers he always felt obliged to remind his questioner that none was half so well-informed as the President himself.

Departments and individuals, in approaching the President, invariably emphasized the matters which impress them most. Mr. Kennedy knew how to make the appropriate discounts without anyone quite realizing they were being made. He had a natural sense for all of the variables in a problem; he would not be carried away by anyone.

Like all men of deep intelligence, he respected the intelligence of others. That was why he did not talk down to the American people; it was why he was contemptuous of the arm-waving circus posturing of the American politician which so many American newspapermen so much admire right up to the moment of final defeat.

The President faced a speaker with his wide gray-blue eyes and total concentration. So also a paper or an article. And, so far as one could tell, once it was his it was his forever. This, of course, was not all.

Knowledge is power. But knowledge without character and wisdom is nothing, or worse. These the President also had in rich measure. But I come back to the grasp of issues, the breadth of information and the power of concentration. Perhaps these come naturally. I suspect, in fact, that few men in history have ever combined natural ability with such powers of mental self-discipline.

Index

Index